D1271355

Enterprise Network Testing

Andy Sholomon

Tom Kunath

Cisco Press

800 East 96th Street

Indianapolis, IN 46240

Enterprise Network Testing

Andy Sholomon, Tom Kunath

Copyright© 2011 Cisco Systems, Inc.

Published by:
Cisco Press
800 East 96th Street
Indianapolis, IN 46240 USA

Printed in the United States of America 1 2 3 4 5 6 7 8 9 0

First Printing April 2011

Library of Congress Cataloging-in-Publication number is on file.

ISBN-13: 978-1-58714-127-0

ISBN-10: 1-58714-127-2

Warning and Disclaimer

This book is designed to provide information about enterprise network testing. Every effort has been made to make this book as complete and as accurate as possible, but no warranty or fitness is implied.

The information is provided on an "as is" basis. The authors, Cisco Press, and Cisco Systems, Inc. shall have neither liability nor responsibility to any person or entity with respect to any loss or damages arising from the information contained in this book or from the use of the discs or programs that may accompany it.

The opinions expressed in this book belong to the author and are not necessarily those of Cisco Systems, Inc.

Trademark Acknowledgments

All terms mentioned in this book that are known to be trademarks or service marks have been appropriately capitalized. Cisco Press or Cisco Systems, Inc. cannot attest to the accuracy of this information. Use of a term in this book should not be regarded as affecting the validity of any trademark or service mark.

Feedback Information

At Cisco Press, our goal is to create in-depth technical books of the highest quality and value. Each book is crafted with care and precision, undergoing rigorous development that involves the unique expertise of members from the professional technical community.

Readers' feedback is a natural continuation of this process. If you have any comments regarding how we could improve the quality of this book, or otherwise alter it to better suit your needs, you can contact us through e-mail at feedback@ciscopress.com. Please make sure to include the book title and ISBN in your message.

We greatly appreciate your assistance.

Publisher: Paul Boger

Associate Publisher: Dave Dusthimer

Executive Editor: Mary Beth Ray

Managing Editor: Sandra Schroeder

Senior Project Editor: Tonya Simpson

Editorial Assistant: Vanessa Evans

Book Designer: Louisa Adair

Cover Designer: Sandra Schroeder

Composition: Mark Shirar

Manager, Global Certification: Erik Ullanderson

Business Operation Manager, Cisco Press: Anand Sundaram

Development Editor: Kimberley Debus

Copy Editor: Bill McManus

Technical Editors: Tyler Pomerhn and Don Sautter

Indexer: Tim Wright

Proofreader: Sheri Cain

Americas Headquarters
Cisco Systems, Inc.
San Jose, CA

Asia Pacific Headquarters
Cisco Systems (USA) Pte. Ltd.
Singapore

Europe Headquarters
Cisco Systems International BV
Amsterdam, The Netherlands

Cisco has more than 200 offices worldwide. Addresses, phone numbers, and fax numbers are listed on the Cisco Website at www.cisco.com/go/offices.

CCDE, CCENT, Cisco Eos, Cisco HealthPresence, the Cisco logo, Cisco Lumin, Cisco Nexus, Cisco StadiumVision, Cisco TelePresence, Cisco WebEx, DCE, and Welcome to the Human Network are trademarks; Changing the Way We Work, Live, Play, and Learn and Cisco Store are service marks; and Access Registrar, Aironet, AsyncOS, Bringing the Meeting To You, Catalyst, CCDA, CCDP, CCIE, CCIP, CCNA, CCNP, CCSP, CCVP, Cisco, the Cisco Certified Internetwork Expert logo, Cisco IOS, Cisco Press, Cisco Systems, Cisco Systems Capital, the Cisco Systems logo, Cisco Unity, Collaboration Without Limitation, EtherFast, EtherSwitch, Event Center, Fast Step, Follow Me Browsing, FormShare, GigaDrive, HomeLink, Internet Quotient, IOS, iPhone, iQuick Study, IronPort, the IronPort logo, LightStream, Linksys, MediaTone, MeetingPlace, MeetingPlace Chime Sound, MGX, Networkers, Networking Academy, Network Registrar, PCNow, PIX, PowerPanels, ProConnect, ScriptShare, SenderBase, SMARTnet, Spectrum Expert, StackWise, The Fastest Way to Increase Your Internet Quotient, TransPath, WebEx, and the WebEx logo are registered trademarks of Cisco Systems, Inc. and/or its affiliates in the United States and certain other countries.

All other trademarks mentioned in this document or website are the property of their respective owners. The use of the word partner does not imply a partnership relationship between Cisco and any other company. (0812R)

About the Authors

Andy Sholomon, CCIE No. 15179, works as a Network Consulting Engineer (NCE) in Cisco's Central Engineering Performance and Validation Testing team. He routinely plans and performs network testing for some of Cisco's largest Enterprise customers. In his six years at Cisco, Andy has been involved in both planning and deploying some of the largest enterprise data centers in the United States. He has also worked with some of Cisco's large service provider customers. Before joining Cisco, Andy worked as a Network Engineer in the global financial industry, spending 5 years at UBS in multiple roles, including security engineering, and worked as a Systems Engineer at Spear, Leeds & Kellogg (now a part of Goldman Sachs Group). Andy has been a speaker at the Cisco Live Networkers Conference. Besides the CCIE, Andy holds multiple industry certifications, including the CISSP and MCSE. Andy lives with his wife, daughter, and Great Dane in Chapel Hill, North Carolina.

Tom Kunath, CCIE No. 1679, is a Solutions Architect in Cisco's Advanced Services Central Engineering team, where he works as a design and test consulting engineer. With nearly 20 years in the networking industry, Tom has helped design, deploy, and operate many of Cisco's largest Enterprise and Financial customer networks. Before joining Cisco, Tom worked at Juniper Networks' Professional Services Group as a Resident Engineer supporting several service provider IP and MPLS backbones, and prior to that as a Principal Consultant at International Network Services (INS). In addition to his CCIE, Tom holds several industry certifications, including a Juniper JNCIS and Nortel Networks Router Expert. Tom lives in Raleigh, North Carolina, with his wife and two children.

About the Technical Reviewers

Tyler Pomerhn, CCIE No. 6676 (Routing/Switching, SNA/IP, Security, Service Provider), is an engineer with Cisco Systems within the Central Engineering Performance and Validation Testing Services (PVTS) group based in Research Triangle Park, North Carolina. He has worked in PVTS and the Customer Proof of Concept (CPOC) testing organizations for six years within Cisco, testing all manner of topologies and technologies for Fortune 100 companies to ensure their deployments were a success. Prior to working with testing groups inside Cisco, he worked with the Inside Sales team within Cisco in RTP, providing in-depth engineering resources to sales teams in the Federal Channels organization. Tyler holds a bachelor's degree in electrical engineering from SUNY Buffalo, as well as a bachelor's degree in physics from SUNY Fredonia, and has a total of 13 years of experience with computer networking.

Don Sautter, CCIE No. 13190 (Routing and Switching), is a Network Engineer at Cisco Systems within the Central Engineering Performance and Validation Testing Services (PVTS) group based in Research Triangle Park, North Carolina. He has worked for Cisco Systems for 10 years, the last 4 within PVTS performing systems solution testing and design validation. Don has 30 years of networking experience, during which he has performed a wide variety of engineering functions and held various positions within the industry.

Dedications

This book is dedicated to our loving families and our Cisco customers—the network engineers and managers who challenge us to provide them with the truth and offer them the simplest solution to meet their most complex problems.

"All fixed set patterns are incapable of adaptability or pliability. The truth is outside of all fixed patterns."

—*Bruce Lee*

Acknowledgments

We'd like to give special recognition to all of the Cisco engineers who contributed valuable content to this book: Gery Czirjak, for helping to write Chapter 3, "Testing and Lab Strategy Development;" Yenu Gobena, for helping to write Chapter 15, "IPv6 Functionality Test Plan;" Connie Varner, for sharing her insight on working in a large test organization and using the right test tools to get the job done; Tejas Suthar, who, as a network architect, understands first hand the role and value of structured testing in validating design; Varghese Thomas, for providing a case study on network readiness testing for VoIP; and our technical editors, Don Sautter and Tyler Pomerhn, who are also seasoned network test engineers in their day jobs, for keeping us honest and on track.

We'd also like to recognize our test tool vendors, in particular Ixia Networks and Spirent Communications, for their outstanding products and technical support; and Thomas Maufer, for an excellent contribution on application simulation, and the Mu Dynamics automated approach of creating test cases with live packet captures.

A quadruple "thumbs up" goes out to the production team for their help with this book. All of them have been incredibly professional and a pleasure to work with. Thank you for giving us the flexibility to finish this book while attending to the needs and timeframes of our own customer testing projects.

Finally, to our wives, for their support and encouragement with this project. Thank you both for picking up the "parenting slack" that we left during all the nights and weekends that we spent hunkered around our computers to get this done.

Contents at a Glance

Contents

Icons Used in This Book

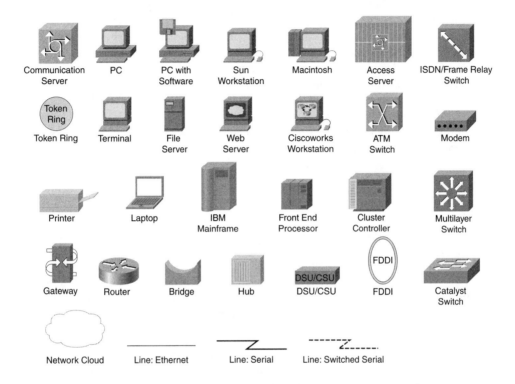

Command Syntax Conventions

The conventions used to present command syntax in this book are the same conventions used in the *Cisco IOS Command Reference*, which describes these conventions as follows:

- **Boldface** indicates commands and keywords that are entered literally as shown. In actual configuration examples and output (not general command syntax), boldface indicates commands that are manually input by the user (such as a **show** command).

- *Italics* indicate arguments for which you supply actual values.

- Vertical bars (|) separate alternative, mutually exclusive elements.

- Square brackets [ ] indicate optional elements.

- Braces { } indicate a required choice.

- Braces within brackets [{ }] indicate a required choice within an optional element.

Introduction

As many as 17 billion devices are projected to be connected to the Internet by 2014, fueled by more and more computing tasks now being handled online, from phone calls to personalized searches to downloading entertainment. In an effort to enhance the value of user transactions, corporations are increasingly transforming their network infrastructures from "packet plumbing" into "business platforms," converging ever more application and network functions along the way. This transformation has placed unprecedented pressures on network managers, now charged with meeting application service-level agreements for uptime and performance dictated to them by leaders of the business. Once considered an optional activity, network testing has become mandatory in many organizations and is a critical step toward meeting the expectations of near-zero downtime.

Goals and Methods

There is currently a void in publications that address test methodologies as they relate to the enterprise network lifecycle, particularly in the area of advanced technologies. Existing test publications, such as IETF RFCs and vendor test tool documentation, focus on test procedures for particular products and technologies, as opposed to complete network systems. While these are well known and used throughout the industry, they do not offer a complete blueprint to an organization that wants to know when, what, and exactly how to test products, solutions, and advanced technologies to keep its business up and running.

The primary goal of this book is to help you understand how you can develop effective test methods to discover in your network designs flaws or weaknesses that could potentially bring down your network. The intent is that this will be accomplished through the following methods:

- Establishing the importance of structured systems testing as a fundamental component of an enterprise architecture strategy

- Explaining the different types of testing that complement decision making during the various phases of a network's lifecycle

- Outlining a business and technical blueprint for developing a testing organization and lab facility

- Providing a series of customer case studies that reinforces the benefits of testing in the various phases of the networks lifecycle

- Providing test plan templates for various technical solutions that can be customized and used by readers in their own testing

Who Should Read This Book?

This book is intended to be read by network professionals who want to understand what structured system testing is, and how to effectively test complex network systems and technologies. The sample test plans included in this book are intended to be used as a reference, and can be customized for individual use.

How This Book Is Organized

Although this book could be read cover to cover, it is designed to be flexible and to allow you to easily move between chapters and sections of chapters to cover just the material that you need more work with. Part I, "Introduction to Enterprise Network Testing" (Chapters 1 through 5), is an introduction to systems testing, covering fundamental concepts with a focus on the relationship of testing to an enterprise architecture and design process. These chapters are mainly nontechnical, setting the stage for the case studies (Part II) and test plans (Part III) that follow in Chapters 6 through 18, which are the core chapters and can be covered in any order. If you intend to read them all, the order in the book is an excellent sequence to use.

Chapters 1 through 18 cover the following topics:

- **Chapter 1, "A Business Case for Enterprise Network Testing"**—This chapter introduces fundamental concepts of network testing and its critical role in validating design and making sound deployment decisions. The chapter begins with a discussion of why IT dollars should be spent on testing, and the evolution of the network as a platform for business. This is followed by a discourse on the cost of network downtime to the business, and how testing can be used to improve availability by validating design and reducing human error. The chapter concludes with an introduction to the different types of testing and a discussion about a structured approach to testing.

- **Chapter 2, "Testing Throughout the Network Lifecycle"**—This chapter builds upon the concepts introduced in Chapter 1 by explaining how a structured testing program complements the architecture and design process of the enterprise. An introduction to the Cisco Lifecycle Services approach of Plan, Prepare, Design, Implement, Operate, and Optimize (PPDIOO) follows, with examples of the different kinds of test activities that would commonly occur in each phase.

- **Chapter 3, "Testing and Lab Strategy Development"**—This chapter examines many of the business and technical considerations when developing an organizational testing strategy. The chapter includes a business cost analysis of building, staffing, and operating a lab, presenting the reader with various possible funding models. Best practices for test lab facility design and an estimate of the resources (equipment, tools, and people) that are necessary to sustain it are presented in depth, so that the reader can make an intelligent decision about whether it makes sense to build a lab or outsource testing.

- **Chapter 4, "Crafting the Test Approach"**—This chapter walks through the details of a structured approach to handling, scoping, and planning for different types of test requests. It begins with a suggested approach for assessing and scoping a test project, and offers guidance on how to identify the test scenarios, design and build a lab topology, select appropriate test tools, and write a detailed and concise test plan.

- **Chapter 5, "Executing the Test Plan"**—This chapter delves into many of the low-level details associated with system-level testing. Best practices for building a functional prototype of a network design are discussed, including methodologies for accommodating scale testing with the minimal amount of equipment. An introduction to several commercial, free, and Cisco IOS test tools is included, with tips on how to best leverage them for different types of testing.

- **Chapter 6, "Proof of Concept Testing Case Study"**—This chapter walks through a case study of how a financial customer leveraged proof of concept (POC) testing to gain confidence in a new network architecture that was proposed as part of a data center centralization/consolidation strategy.

- **Chapter 7, "Network Readiness Testing Case Study"**—This chapter walks through a case study of how a software development company leveraged network readiness testing on its production network to identify gaps and gauge readiness for a planned Unified Communications deployment.

- **Chapter 8, "Design Verification Testing Case Study"**—This chapter walks through a case study of how a university leveraged design verification testing to validate and refine a low-level design (LLD) for a new MPLS backbone infrastructure.

- **Chapter 9, "Migration Plan Testing Case Study"**—This chapter walks through a case study of how a university leveraged testing to validate the low-level steps and device configurations necessary to incrementally migrate its legacy IP network to a new MPLS/VPN network.

- **Chapter 10, "New Platform and Code Certification Case Study"**—This chapter walks through a case study of how a financial organization leveraged predeployment acceptance testing to certify new hardware, operating systems, and software features as part of a corporate change management compliance policy.

- **Chapter 11, "Network Ready for Use Testing Case Study"**—This chapter walks through a case study of how network ready for use (NRFU) testing was used as a final check to certify that a newly opened sports and entertainment complex was functional and ready to offer IP services to the staff and public on opening day.

- **Chapter 12, "Inter-Organization Secure Data Center Interconnect: Firewall Test Plan"**—This chapter introduces a technical solution for securely interconnecting the data centers of two separate enterprise networks, and then presents a detailed test plan for validating its performance and scalability.

- **Chapter 13, "Site-to-Site IPsec Virtual Private Networking: DMVPN and GET VPN Test Plans"**—This chapter discusses the motivation and details of two different site-to-site VPN designs based on IPsec technologies, and then presents detailed test plans to validate the functionality and scale of each.

- **Chapter 14, "Data Center 3.0 Architecture: Nexus Platform Feature and Performance Test Plan"**—This chapter discusses the low-level details of a next-generation data center solution built upon on the Nexus family of switches. A test plan is provided to validate the platform and system functionality of the solution components, which include: Nexus 5000 End-of-Row (EoR) Switches, Nexus 2000 Top-of-Rack (ToR) Fabric Extenders, Nexus 7000 core switches, and MDS 9500 Director-class SAN switches.

- **Chapter 15, "IPv6 Functionality Test Plan"**—This chapter includes an IPv6 technology primer and functionality test plan for some of its basic features.

- **Chapter 16, "MPLS/VPN: Scalability and Convergence Test Plan"**—This chapter discusses the low-level details of a hierarchical MPLS/VPN design that securely segments a global enterprise network. A systems test plan is provided to validate the solution, focusing on fast convergence, scalability, and high availability features.

- **Chapter 17, "WAN and Application Optimization: Performance Routing and Wide Area Application Services Test Plan"**—This chapter discusses a solution that includes PfR and WAAS features to optimize application performance across a WAN. A test plan is provided to validate the feature functionality and scalability, and to quantify the performance gains of deploying PfR and WAAS on the WAN.

- **Chapter 18, "Using the Lab for Hands-on Technology Training: Data Center 3.0 Configuration Lab Guide"**—This chapter illustrates how an enterprise lab can be used as a field enablement resource for hands-on training. A sample lab guide showing step-by-step Nexus 7000, MDS, and Unified Computing System provisioning tasks is provided as an example of how training materials should be structured to facilitate self-study using a custom-built lab topology.

Introduction to Enterprise Network Testing

Part I takes an in-depth look at why testing has become so critical for enterprise organizations striving to increase network uptime, and how it can be leveraged during various points in a network's lifecycle to validate designs and changes to the IT infrastructure. An entire chapter is devoted to building an effective test organization, including examples of the types of personnel, gear, and facilities you may need; the chapter also discusses whether you should conduct testing in-house or outsource it.

The focus of Part I then shifts to a pragmatic discussion on how to write an effective test plan, detailing the essential elements of the plan itself, and calling out the types of tools that can be leveraged to effectively and thoroughly test a solution. It explores several "tricks of the trade" that are commonly used at Cisco labs during systems testing, including an exploration of several free tools built into Cisco IOS Software. Finally, it gives you tips on how to execute the test plan and capture results effectively.

The chapters in Part I are as follows:

Chapter 1   A Business Case for Enterprise Network Testing

Chapter 2   Testing Throughout the Network Lifecycle

Chapter 3   Testing and Lab Strategy Development

Chapter 4   Crafting the Test Approach

Chapter 5   Executing the Test Plan

A Business Case for Enterprise Network Testing

This chapter covers the following topics:

- Why Testing Is Important

- The Network as a Business Platform

- The Cost of Network Downtime

- Network Changes and Downtime

- Testing in Support of Change Control

- Testing and the Pursuit of "Five Nines"

- A Structured Approach to Systems Testing

Network testing has a critical role in validating design and making sound deployment decisions. In this chapter, we examine why IT dollars should be spent on testing; the evolution of the network as a platform for business; the cost of network downtime to the business; and how testing can be used to improve availability by validating design and reducing human error. We also introduce the different types of testing, as well as a structured approach to testing that defines a phased process for planning, setup, execution, and results preparation.

Why Testing Is Important

Chances are that you understand the importance of testing as it relates to validating network design and change control, given the fact that you are reading this book. It would also be a safe assumption that not everyone in your company shares the knowledge of how critical network testing is for a sound architectural and deployment process. Chances are also high that when approached for a testing budget, your senior executive will likely ask some of the following questions:

- "Why should I spend time and money testing my network? Isn't testing the job of our vendors?"

- "How much testing is really needed before we put the new system into production?"

- "We tested our WAN two years ago! Why do we need to test it again?"

The answers might be obvious to the experienced IT professional:

- "A stable, high-performance, multiservice network is the result of careful planning, design, testing, implementation, and operations. Although vendors often perform exhaustive systems testing, they cannot reproduce every customer's environment."

- "Effective testing is the best indicator of production readiness. On the other hand, ineffective testing may lead to a false sense of confidence, causing downtime or other support issues. A structured approach to testing is the best way to discover and fix the highest number of defects in the least amount of time, at the lowest possible cost."

- "It is as important to test the readiness of existing production networks prior to the launch of new services as it is to test "green field" networks, built entirely from scratch."

Your CxO (CEO, CFO, COO, and so on) might not find these answers to be so obvious, particularly if he or she does not come from a technical background. Perhaps some reinforcement in the form of an analogy may help:

- "Would you consider a graduate from a university with no formal testing policies to be suitably qualified as a member of your staff?"

- "Think of network testing as 'practicing' for the big game. Remember your football/baseball/soccer coach saying that you will play only as well as you practice?"

The Network as a Business Platform

Most corporations today maintain some form of web presence that serves as a critical element of their business. In the world of e-commerce, financial transactions are conducted almost exclusively by consumers that connect over the Internet to company servers in the data center, making the network a platform for profitability. From the consumer perspective, website availability is often the only indicator of the company's existence, and its unavailability can generate misconceptions about a company's competence. As more consumers become comfortable doing their banking, shopping, trading, and communicating online, the network has become a vital artery feeding the heart of e-commerce business.

Social networking and web collaboration tools within an enterprise have emerged seemingly overnight, and their widespread adoption has transformed traditional business processes in many large corporations. These software tools are all the rage today, claiming to increase productivity within workgroups, while at the same time saving both time and travel costs for the company. It is not unusual to see project teams creating and using a wiki to disseminate information and work in parallel, where in the past this was done by distributing and updating documents in serial fashion. People have become comfortable using web conferencing for meetings, presentations, and training to the point where travel for such routine activities has diminished significantly. Overshadowing the savings, many companies report that they feel their employees are more productive and display higher morale when they have the latest technological gadgets available to do their jobs. Some journalists and industry insiders are starting to talk about "Web 3.0," where all of the new media will come together, IT phenomena such as blogs and Twitter will become ubiquitous in the workplace, and we will have more and more information at our fingertips. More than ever before, as the network evolves into the enterprise platform for productivity, higher expectations for availability and performance will be placed upon it.

To further illustrate the concept of the network evolving into a platform for business, consider the case of the Cisco TelePresence meeting solution. With this high-definition videoconferencing solution, users can experience real-time, face-to-face communication and collaboration with colleagues, prospects, and partners from across the globe. This reduces not only travel expenses but also the time lost by employees during transit. While popular and powerful, TelePresence imposes unprecedented demands on the network, as it must deliver and synchronize ultrahigh-definition video and high-quality audio according to stringent customer service-level agreements (SLA). Although companies are eager to reap the benefits of TelePresence, they are not willing to deploy dedicated, separately managed infrastructures to handle them. On the contrary, companies are demanding that their existing converged networks be capable of handling the demands of TelePresence and other next-generation applications to come. This is forcing companies to upgrade or augment their network infrastructure so that it can provide sufficient bandwidth, nonstop communications, quality of service (QoS), integrated security, and operational simplicity. To create a network platform for global virtual face-to-face communications, companies are re-architecting and augmenting their existing core networks in record numbers. As more critical business functions depend on the network as a platform, having it available and behaving in a predictable manner becomes essential to your business's success. Network testing as part of a well-defined architectural process is absolutely necessary to make a network infrastructure more predictable and robust—it will serve as a readiness benchmark for how and when new features and services can be deployed without jeopardizing production and impacting revenue.

The Cost of Network Downtime

Many organizations do not fully understand the impact of downtime on their business. Calculating the cost of this impact can be difficult because it requires an understanding of both tangible and intangible losses. Tangible losses are quantifiable, hard costs; they include lost revenue, cost to recover lost information, disaster recovery, and business continuity costs. Intangible costs include damage to your company's reputation, lost customers, and employee productivity costs. In many ways, the damage associated with intangible costs can have a greater long-term impact on an organization than that of tangible costs.

According to Gartner Research, the losses associated with network downtime include

■   Productivity losses

■   Revenue losses

■   Damaged reputation

■   Impaired financial performance

According to a July 2009 whitepaper titled "Navigating Network Infrastructure Expenditures During Business Transformations," written by Lippis Consulting, the cost of network downtime for a financial firm's brokerage services was calculated to be $7.8 million per hour. A one-hour outage for a financial firm's credit card operations can cost upwards of $3.1 million. A media firm could lose money on pay-per-view revenues, an airline company on ticket sales, and a retail company on catalog sales. Table 1-1 gives a few more examples of losses by industry sector.

This data paints a fairly dismal picture of monetary losses that your business could incur during network downtime. But where monetary losses can arguably be recovered, can the same be said about customer confidence? Every time a customer tries to reach your website or execute a transaction that fails, you risk losing that customer's business to one of your competitors.

Employee productivity also suffers during network downtime. Consider an example using the data from Table 1-1. A major U.S. insurance company has a campus with 9000 users; it experienced several systemic failures lasting one to four hours each. An insurance sector employee's time is valued at $370 per hour. Assuming the network unavailability provided only a cost of $25 per hour per employee in lost productivity, this would still value the downtime at $3750 per minute.

Table 1-1   *Loss of Revenue for Network Downtime Broken Down by Several Industries*

Industry Sector	Revenue/Hour	Revenue Employee-Hour
Energy	$2,817,846	$569
Telecommunications	$2,066,245	$186
Manufacturing	$1,610,654	$134
Financial Institution	$1,495,134	$1,079
Insurance	$1,202,444	$370
Retail	$1,107,274	$244
Transportation	$668,586	$107
Average	$1,010,536	$205

Source: Gartner Group

Network Changes and Downtime

Industry experts estimate that roughly 60 to 70 percent of network failures are caused by human error. Conventional wisdom within the IT world is that improving tools and processes can reduce the occurrences and impact of human error. Better training for the operations staff, strict change control procedures, better documentation, automated provisioning tools, and better network management are among the initiatives that are discussed following a critical outage. But with most of today's networks currently in growth phase, resources are scarce for such initiatives.

Today's large enterprises are generally very risk-averse due to the tremendous potential for loss associated with network downtime. It has been observed that the larger the enterprise, the more conservative it tends to be about network change—or anything else that can potentially produce any downtime. The unfortunate result is that network engineers have very few windows of opportunity to make changes and improvements on their networks. Some companies have one change window per month, and sometimes even that can get moved or cancelled. This often leads to several changes having to be made in a very short period of time, placing extreme pressure on network operators who are often undertrained, overworked, and in many cases, due to the nature of the business, operating on lack of sleep.

The more changes you make, the more likely you are to run into unforeseen side effects. For example, you bring up a new circuit between two data centers and find that application traffic is now following an asymmetrical routing path. Your traffic goes out from Data Center A to Data Center B on the old circuit, but comes back on the new one. This is a fairly common scenario that can be fixed in a few minutes. Now you have a decision to make: Do you try to fix the issue, or will you back out your change and wait until next month to bring the new circuit into production? What does the change control procedure say? Is there a change control procedure? Will this asymmetrical routing situation even pose a problem? This is a lot of information to quickly process for an operator who most likely does not have a full view of the big picture, and who is running on pizza, Cokes, day-old coffee, and minimal sleep! It is not rare to have an engineer make a small change to fix a routing issue only to cause a major core meltdown or application failure. The Cisco Technical Assistance Center (TAC) is very busy on weekend nights, the time when most enterprises execute network changes.

Testing in Support of Change Control

The asymmetrical routing scenario described in the previous section likely could have been avoided with minimal testing effort. Analyzing the impact of a change on the IP routing environment normally could be accomplished with a minimal number of routers, or even with a network simulator. When considering the scope and scale of network testing, you must take into account the complexity of your network and how many systems are affected by its availability. Today's network is a very complicated environment; you are not just touching your routing and switching systems, which are complex enough on their own. You need to take into account the high availability, fast failover, redundancy, and dozens of protocols working in conjunction to keep your traditional network components working smoothly. In addition, a small network change can potentially affect your packet voice, IP video, and network storage (if you are using Fibre Channel over Ethernet [FCoE], Fibre Channel over IP [FCIP], or Internet Small Computer System Interface [iSCSI]). In some more advanced systems, even virtualized servers in your cloud environment, sharing memory and CPU cycles over Layer 2 connections, are affected. After a major change, it is important to test not only your network plumbing, but your entire enterprise IT system. For instance, a minor network change once brought down badge access for an entire company with hundreds of offices across the United States. No one bothered to test it.

On top of all the complexity discussed thus far, you also need to layer on advanced features running in your enterprise network—such as security features, including firewalls, intrusion detection/prevention systems (IDS/IPS), and your encryption environment. The asymmetrical routing condition previously discussed becomes a real problem if you have these security features enabled, that typically expect traffic symmetry. You should also take into account network management features, such as Cisco IOS NetFlow, which are critical in many enterprise networks. They are used for troubleshooting, security, and even billing. How does a router handle double the usual traffic load during a failover? Many network engineers have not thought through that scenario. How much will CPU utilization spike when flow records from tens, or even hundreds of thousands of flows are collected and exported by core routers? Will this affect routing protocol stability? Are new platforms manageable with existing NMS platforms and applications? Will the SNMP MIBs work the same way they did before? Are the syslog messages still formatted the way your NMSs expect them to be? Will your authentication, authorization, and accounting (AAA) work as expected during heavy utilization? How about when your TACACS or RADIUS systems are down or unreachable? A good system test will take into account and answer all of these questions and require you to back out changes far less often.

Larger or more complex network changes should always trigger a test effort. If you can call a test a Proof of Concept Test, a Feature Test, a Network Ready for Use Test, a Migration Test, or a Security Test, you should definitely consider the five-step testing process described at the end of this chapter. It may sound like a lot of work, but it will definitely improve your network's availability, and also have side benefits. First, it will help in educating the network engineers involved in the testing about the feature or network they are going to be deploying and soon supporting. Second, it will help you document the part of the network you are testing. Your test plan should have network diagrams and expectations of features' behaviors, failover times, capacity, and other critical aspects. When you record your test results and file your test plan, you create a wealth of information for the rest of the network engineers and support personnel in your enterprise.

Testing and the Pursuit of "Five Nines"

Today's enterprises with business-critical applications are deploying next-generation networks that are beginning to closely resemble those of network service providers, in terms of both equipment and protocols. And like their service provider counterparts, these enterprises are beginning to strive for five nines of availability when developing their network designs. "Five nines" is a phrase that industry insiders use to express excellence. It refers to 99.999 percent network uptime, and is often defined as the target for expected availability in network SLAs. A typical SLA quantifies network performance in terms of availability, packet loss, latency, and jitter. In many situations, enterprises and service providers are responsible to pay financial penalties if the guaranteed SLA is not met.

Five nines usually applies to the availability of the network; the other parts of the SLA typically specify other units of measure, such as that latency will not exceed 80 milliseconds in any part of the North American Network, or that jitter will be less than 300 microseconds. It is important to consider the five nines concept as it relates to a network design and potential failure scenarios. The network design must be rigorously tested for validation to ensure that recovery during those failure scenarios occurs with the least impact possible.

What does five nines really mean to you, and how can testing help you achieve it? First, you need to decide how you are going to measure your network availability. Is downtime during change windows counted? Will you measure availability or uptime? A router can be up and your network management software can still reach it via ping or SNMP poll, but it may not be passing packets; technically the router is up, but it is not available. The router being up but unavailable is often the hardest thing to troubleshoot and needs to be taken into account when creating test plans.

Once your company has decided how it will measure availability, you can begin to craft your network designs and test plans to achieve your goal. It is very important to understand what you are getting yourself into when you shoot for five nines availability. Take a look at Table 1-2 to see what five nines availability means in terms of downtime.

Table 1-2 illustrates that to achieve five nines availability, you need to design and test a network that has only 25.9 seconds of measurable downtime per month. The real key here is that the downtime must be measurable. If a router crashes but your critical network traffic reconverges in two seconds, you might have had only two seconds of measurable downtime, not the time it takes to bring the router back up. It is not a revelation to any network engineer that a design that includes redundant equipment and circuits is the only way to achieve five nines. It is also important to plan for and test the events caused by your equipment coming back online. Sometimes during testing, you find that you have a perfect failover when you bring a piece of equipment down; however, when it comes back up, it causes 45 seconds of instability. It is critical to measure recoveries from outages in your testing.

Table 1-2   *Amount of Downtime Allowed by Percentage of Network Availability*

Availability %	Downtime per Year	Downtime per Month*	Downtime per Week
90%	36.5 days	72 hrs	16.8 hrs
95%	18.25 days	36 hrs	8.4 hrs
98%	7.3 days	14.4 hrs	3.36 hrs
99%	3.65 days	7.20 hrs	1.68 hrs
99.5%	1.83 days	3.6 hrs	50.4 min
99.8%	17.52 hrs	86.23 min	20.16 min
99.9% (three nines)	8.76 hrs	43.2 min	10.1 min
99.95%	4.38 hrs	21.56 min	5.04 min
99.99% (four nines)	52.6 min	4.32 min	1.01 min
99.999% (five nines)	5.26 min	25.9 sec	6.05 sec
99.9999% (six nines)	31.5 sec	2.59 sec	0.605 sec

*For monthly calculations, a 30-day month is used.

Proper testing will help you achieve your availability needs. Planning should take into account the main causes of network outages, which include the following:

- Hardware failures
- Software failures
- Interconnecting equipment failures (your cabling)
- Transmission media failures (your circuits)
- Lack of capacity
- Human error
- Facilities problems

These causes are easy to test and prepare for, with the exception of human error. In later parts of this book, we will discuss several scenarios for testing how the network will react to hardware, software, cabling, circuit, and capacity issues. There is no easy way to test for human error. You can add to your test plan common human errors seen in your network, if it makes sense. However, for the purposes of this book, the best way to minimize human error (you can never avoid it altogether) is to have strong operational procedures. It was mentioned before how onerous change management procedures can be in a large enterprise. These procedures are meant, in great part, to prevent any measurable downtime caused by human error.

Some failures caused by facilities problems such as power failures or water damage are covered by redundancy testing, so long as they are planned for in your network design. Redundant equipment should not be located next to each other, to avoid many common facilities issues such as water damage, HVAC failure, and certain electrical issues. If your equipment is placed far enough apart to make a difference in testing, you should take the distance, hardware differences due to special optics, and delay into account in your test plan. Even if the equipment is sitting next to each other in your lab, you can still create a realistic testing environment.

Once you know how your network will be measured for availability, you can create the appropriate test plans. Your testing parameters will differ depending on whether you measure based on "human perceived" availability or on "machine perceived" availability. To help clarify this point, imagine your coworker is going to check her web mail. She clicks her browser and 15 seconds pass; she gets impatient and clicks the Refresh button in her browser, at which point her web mail becomes available to read. From her perspective, she just did something she does every day, refresh her browser, and everything is fine. From a system's perspective, hundreds of things might have gone wrong during those 15 seconds. She might have just been redirected to an entirely different data center across the globe when she refreshed the browser window. If you are testing for human perception, you may allow a 15-second outage and not count it toward a lack of availability; this is actually how a lot of enterprises measure availability. On the other hand, a network management system would likely consider 15 seconds to be a major outage.

It is imperative to understand how an entire application system will behave during network instability. Will application servers "lock up" if they lose communications with their backend database server for ten seconds, or failover to the backup server with minimal impact to their users? Will the servers flip back and forth between primary and backup database servers if the network is unstable? Will these conditions trigger a "human-perceived" outage despite the fact that the absolute threshold of 15 seconds defined in the SLA has not been crossed?

When defining test plan objectives and their success criteria, it is important to consider all of the critical enterprise IT applications. For example, that same 15-second network event, which might not be perceived as an outage on a web server, is going to be a big problem for viewers of a videoconference. The point to be made here is that there often are different expectations with respect to availability depending on a particular application's tolerance for loss. In the absence of a defined SLA, test plans should be written to meet objectives of the most stringent applications, as opposed to the most tolerant. The suggestion to be made here is that application requirements should be used to define the success criteria of network test plans. If 1 second of downtime in your core is considered an outage, then obviously a failover time of less than 1 second should be one of the requirements to pass each convergence test for that part of the network. As you test your network with an eye toward reaching five nines availability, you should run the tests multiple times and record all the results. Having accurate results, recorded in the right format, will allow you to rerun the tests later with new hardware or features enabled, and compare them to make sure they will help you in your quest to improve your network.

Take into consideration that you likely will not be able to achieve a five nines network if you have

- Single points of failure
- High probability of redundancy failure (failure not detected or redundancy not implemented)
- High probability of double failures
- Long convergence times for rerouting traffic
- Outages required for hardware and software upgrades
- Long recovery times for reboot or switchover
- No tested hardware spares available on site
- Long repair times due to a lack of troubleshooting guides and process
- Inappropriate environmental conditions
- Large fault domains
- Reactive support model
- No IT service management framework

If you design your network with the right types of redundancy and relevant features, and test it to make sure they will work as expected, you will be well on your way to five nines availability. The right kinds of tests can be complex because you will be checking your network for high-availability features, fast convergence, hierarchy, hardware, circuit and cabling redundancy, scalability, path diversity, manageability, and so forth. Having the right testing procedures, writing a good plan, and having the right test facilities, equipment, and personnel will be an essential part of getting you there.

Obviously, because of the complexity of today's networks, downtimes can take longer to troubleshoot and resolve. If you have an effective testing strategy, you will certainly minimize network downtime and losses incurred due to changes. You will have a more available network, be able to troubleshoot more effectively, and have to back out far fewer changes. You will be able to roll out new features and hardware with more confidence, and help make your company more profitable. While testing is not the only thing you can do to avoid losses associated with long downtimes, it definitely offers a great return on your investment in both time and money.

A Structured Approach to Systems Testing

Although the benefits of proactive testing are well known, most network planning and support organizations do not actively and methodically stress their network components in the ways that their applications will. Testing is too commonly an infrequent and poorly planned exercise, and returns significantly less value than the time and money spent. Lack of experience and guidance, limited resources, and poor productivity from previous test efforts are the reasons that many existing corporate testing facilities are underfunded and eventually shut down. That said, the need for testing remains.

System testing is a proven approach for validating the existing network infrastructure and planning for its future. This section outlines a structured five-step approach for effective systems testing.

Step 1: Assessment

In this step, you engage directly with your customer or stakeholder to determine the overall testing objectives. Once the motive and objectives for testing are clearly understood, you can select and customize a test methodology to match. This is the first point of your test customization where important decisions are made regarding risk assessments, priorities, and timelines. By defining what needs to be achieved at the start of the engagement, you can ensure that expectations are clearly established for the remainder of the test cycle. Some examples of "test triggers" include the following:

- **New application or service launch:** Can the network handle the increased load?

- **Network integration between two companies that merged:** Can you validate the routing, NAT, and data center consolidation strategies?

- **Proof of concept for a new technology:** Can you show that the new technology works as expected?

- **New network platform or code certification:** Will it perform as expected when subjected to a customized suite of tests applicable to your enterprise?

- **Network ready for use:** Has the network been deployed as designed and is it ready to carry production traffic?

- **Large network outage:** Can the problem be reproduced and eliminated?

Step 2: Test Planning

In this step, you must collaborate with the stakeholders to determine specifics regarding the test execution, expected behaviors, and what constitutes success. You must discuss and agree upon the lab topology, software version and configuration, test cases, data to collect, and results format. This is an important step in the process, because it requires many decisions and significant teamwork. As with every step in the process, risk assessments, priorities, topology, and timelines will be revisited to ensure on-time completion. Most system tests fit into one of the following four categories:

- **Baseline testing:** During this phase, you must identify the overall network design, hardware, software, and specific feature requirements, as well as expectations with respect to performance, resiliency, and stability. All features will be configured in the presence of each other so that potential interoperability issues can be uncovered.

- **Feature testing:** Once all features have been configured in the test bed, they should be individually tested and validated. This is the portion of the test that is useful for design refinement, where you can test several "what if" scenarios.

- **Negative or failover testing:** During this phase, you force your test bed to recover or reconverge after a number of "simulated" failures. You measure the impact on the applications, test traffic, and network devices in order to characterize the behavior under failure and recovery.

- **Performance or scalability testing:** The primary goal behind this effort is to determine the point where network resources will need to be increased to support additional demand before a significant degradation of the services provided by the network occurs. This is often the most difficult suite of tests, as it requires a large number of network nodes or test equipment capable of simulating them.

Step 3: Setup

During this step, you physically set up and cable your lab. You load software configurations and take the system to its initial state prior to test execution. At this point, you can make decisions regarding aspects of the topology and software configurations, as the practical experience of setting up the lab refines your initial test plan. The learning that happens during this step is often the most important part of the entire test.

Step 4: Execution

The execution phase often proves to be the most intense and active phase of the test. You must execute the test plan methodically and gather the results accurately. You then must decide whether to adjust priorities and refine the test cases as you gather results and find unexpected outcomes. This last part is where most of the teamwork must happen. Often, unexpected results will cause a redesign or a test reassessment.

Step 5: Results

This is where you compile the raw test results into a final document. The document should include both a summary of the test results and all the test details. Most importantly, the document should include conclusions and findings regarding the test objectives outlined in the assessment phase.

This five-step test cycle ensures that the testing objectives and test plan are understood and agreed upon prior to test execution. Each of the steps will be covered in depth later in this book.

Summary

This chapter covered the importance of testing in minimizing network downtime. The chapter introduced the concepts of five nines availability and how testing can help you reach your SLA goals. Finally, this chapter introduced a structured approach to systems testing. It is essential to understand that in a modern and complex enterprise network, achieving a high level of availability is almost impossible without some form of formalized testing.

Chapter 2

Testing Throughout the Network Lifecycle

This chapter covers the following topics:

- Enterprise and Network Architecture Primer

- How the Enterprise Architecture Comes Together

- Following a Convergence Vision

- The Cisco Lifecycle Services Approach (PPDIOO)

- Testing and the Network Lifecycle

Chapter 1, "A Business Case for Enterprise Network Testing," presented a business case for why an enterprise should adopt network testing as a practice and introduced the structured systems testing approach. This chapter builds upon these concepts by explaining how a testing program complements the architecture and design process of an enterprise, giving examples of the types of tests that support design activities during different phases of a network's lifecycle.

Enterprise and Network Architecture Primer

To appreciate the role of network testing in your enterprise, you must first understand the fundamentals and significance of enterprise architecture. Enterprise architecture can be defined in terms of both a structure and a strategy. As a structure, enterprise architecture refers to a company's computer applications and IT systems, and their relationship to its business goals. As a strategy, it refers to the development of a "master plan" for continuous alignment of a company's IT services and business goals. When exercised effectively, the enterprise architecture enables a corporation's business goals and strategies, helping it gain a competitive advantage through IT. There are several ways to approach enterprise architecture. The Open Group Architecture Framework (TOGAF) outlines a comprehensive approach to the design, planning, implementation, and governance of enterprise information architecture. TOGAF is developed by The Open Group (www.opengroup.org/), an industry consortium established to set vendor- and technology-neutral open standards for computing infrastructure. In line with this framework, network architecture may be described as the elements that form an enterprise communications network. The architecture includes

- Specification of a network's physical components
- The network components' functional organization
- The network components' configuration
- Operational principles and procedures
- Data formats used in operation

The processes used for network architecture involve the continual evolution and adaptation of the enterprise's infrastructure to ensure that it has the capacity, intelligence, and flexibility to meet the requirements for the ever-changing applications that support the business. Testing, as will be discussed later in this chapter, is a fundamental and necessary component of this evolution and adaptation process.

How the Enterprise Architecture Comes Together

Technical services exist to support the business processes that enable revenue growth. These services must be well planned and implemented so that they help the company grow market share in a cost-effective manner. Corporate users and consumers take advantage of technical services to do their jobs or process transactions by interfacing with applications. From a user perspective, an application should appear to be a simple computer program that allows instructions to be input from a keyboard or mouse, while displaying output on a screen or to a printer as a hard copy. Software developers work hard to create an illusion of simplicity with their applications, hiding the details of the complex systems, software, and database architectures that they are built upon. A solid network foundation is critical to the entire enterprise architecture structure, as all of the individual architectures depend on it for interprocess communications. This relationship is represented in Figure 2-1.

As with any underlying foundation that supports a complex structure, the network architecture must be well designed, solidly built, and continuously tested throughout its lifecycle.

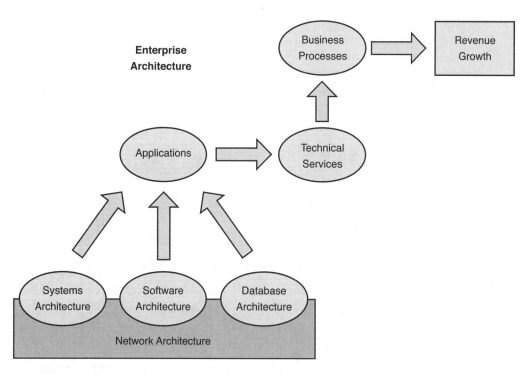

Figure 2-1   *Components of Enterprise Architecture*

Following a Convergence Vision

An industry trend toward technological convergence has been one of the drivers of new enterprise architecture efforts over the past decade. While the context of "convergence" as it relates to multiple technologies coexisting on a single platform has changed over this time, it has historically involved the introduction of smarter, highly versatile equipment into the IT infrastructure. New and advanced technologies enable equipment vendors to support more features, functions, or services on less hardware and software than before. Convergence is highly desirable to the enterprise architect from a cost, manageability, and simplicity standpoint. From a network perspective, Cisco has been the focal point of many convergence trends over the years. Many programs were specifically developed to enable convergence in the network, including the following:

- **Cisco Fusion:** A plan for the convergence of Layer 2 and Layer 3 inside switches and routers

- **Cisco Blue:** A plan for the convergence of IBM SNA protocols into IP

- **End-to-End:** A plan for the consolidation of the enterprise network across LAN and WAN, small branch, and large campus

- **Architecture for Voice, Video, and Integrated Data (AVVID):** A plan for the convergence of voice and video, with data, onto IP

Enterprise networks are currently focusing on the convergence of communications services architectures. Voice communication services architectures, security services architectures, mobility services architectures, and application services architectures are all being collapsed in a single converged network. This current trend is what Cisco refers to as Service-Oriented Network Architecture, or SONA. To understand how the SONA architecture fits into the enterprise architecture described earlier take a look at Figure 2-2.

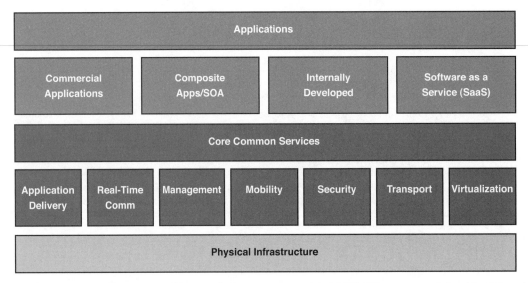

Figure 2-2   *Applications and Network Convergence with SONA (Figure copyrighted by Cisco.)*

Figure 2-2 illustrates how the network applications and the common core services that support them are converging onto a unified physical infrastructure. Although attractive from a business perspective, this converged architecture is much more complex than the networks of just a few years ago, when application and network architectures were typically designed and operated in silos. Recognizing this increased complexity, most enterprise architects are now taking on multidisciplinary roles when developing the convergence strategy, providing guidance on facilities, security, applications, and network architectural issues. When trying to understand how, where, and when network testing fits into an overall convergence vision, it is helpful to understand the steps, listed next, that an enterprise architect would take when engaging in a business transformation project:

Step 1.   Interview the business leaders and key stakeholders across the organization to understand and document the short- and long-term business strategy.

Step 2.   Review the currently deployed technology and identify any gaps that need to be addressed to meet the business requirements.

Step 3.   Suggest to the business leaders technology ideas that help execute this business strategy.

Step 4.   Prepare a financial analysis to help select from various available options. A thorough understanding of the organizational structure and corporate dynamics is required so that the enterprise architect can help provide an analysis of the total cost of ownership for each option.

Step 5.   Produce a high-level architectural specification that would serve as a "technology roadmap," helping to guide the network architects, telecommunications planners, and software developers as they prepare the low-level designs in each of their functional areas.

The actions described in these four steps would be considered appropriate during the Prepare Phase of a network's lifecycle, which represents a particular time in a network's period of existence. The Cisco Lifecycle Approach is a methodology used by many businesses to successfully plan, design, deploy, and operate complex systems. The next section discusses this approach in detail, to help you understand how a testing program should be included in a network's lifecycle.

The Cisco Lifecycle Services Approach (PPDIOO)

The Cisco Lifecycle Services approach is a design methodology that consists of six phases: Plan, Prepare, Design, Implement, Operate, and Optimize (PPDIOO). Most enterprises typically have different places in the network existing in different phases of the lifecycle. For example, a recently deployed branch WAN would be considered to be in the Operate Phase while architects are in the Prepare or Plan Phase for the next-generation data center. The Cisco Lifecycle Services approach defines a set of activities and deliverables to help customers successfully deploy and operate technologies and optimize their performance throughout the lifecycle of the network. The following sections briefly explain the six phases associated with the PPDIOO approach to Cisco Lifecycle Services.

PPDIOO Phase 1: Prepare

The goal of the Prepare Phase is to ensure that sound financial decisions are made when considering new networking or technology projects. This involves planning and strategy sessions so that the business needs, high-level requirements, and the challenges and shortcomings of the current network infrastructure can be identified. This effort includes a series of interviews with key stakeholders to develop and propose a viable solution, balance competing needs, and understand the business and technical environment.

PPDIOO Phase 2: Plan

The goals of the Plan Phase are to assess the readiness of the current architecture and operational environment and to begin the high-level design (HLD) process. The business requirements and preliminary strategy developed during the Prepare Phase are refined so that a HLD can be defined during a set of design workshops. A project plan helps manage the tasks, responsibilities, critical milestones, and resources required to implement the changes to the network. The project plan should align with the scope, cost, and resource parameters established in the original business requirements.

PPDIOO Phase 3: Design

The requirements and HLD developed in the Plan Phase drive the network design team's activities during the Design Phase. The goal of the Design Phase is to develop the low-level design (LLD) that will ultimately be used to implement the solution. The technical details of the LLD are assembled during design workshops with a team that typically includes network engineers, telecommunications planners, application architects, operations specialists, and key business stakeholders. In many cases, service providers, equipment vendors, and consultants are included in the design workshops so that industry best practices can be exchanged and incorporated into the LLD.

PPDIOO Phase 4: Implement

In the Implement Phase, a company works to integrate devices and new capabilities into the existing architecture, or roll out a new architecture in accordance with the design. Implementation and verification normally begins after the design has been approved and fully tested. The network, and any additional components, is built according to the design specifications, with the goal of integrating devices without disrupting the existing network or creating points of vulnerability.

PPDIOO Phase 5: Operate

In the Operate Phase, the project starts the transition to an operational function, which is the final test of the design's readiness and capability to meet the needs of the business. The Operate Phase involves maintaining network health through day-to-day operations, which provide a set of conditions and stresses that can rarely be completely simulated in a test lab environment. This is true because it is very difficult to simulate the combination of data flows, rates, and errors typically associated with operational computing environments, or the behavior of network users and operators on a day-to-day basis. The fault detection and performance monitoring that occur in daily operations provide the initial performance baseline for the network lifecycle's Optimize Phase.

PPDIOO Phase 6: Optimize

The design team likely will fade into the background during the Optimize Phase, which is where opportunities for improvements are discovered by the operations teams based on proactive network management and feedback from users of the network. The goal of the Optimize Phase is to identify and resolve issues before chronic problems arise and the business is affected. In the PPDIOO process, the Optimize Phase might lead to a network redesign if too many network problems or errors arise, if performance does not meet expectations, or if new applications are identified to support organizational and technical requirements. The design team may be consulted to reassess the network design during the Optimize Phase if reactive fault detection and troubleshooting become commonplace, and proactive management cannot predict and mitigate failures. As enterprises move through this phase, the enterprise architect may be consulted to reassess the HLD periodically, particularly if business goals or technical requirements have changed significantly. As an organization looks to optimize its network and prepares to adapt to changing needs, the lifecycle begins anew—continually evolving the network and improving results. Figure 2-3 is a graphical representation of the six phases of the PPDIOO model. It shows some of the key deliverables of each phase and makes it clearer that this is a process that never really ends.

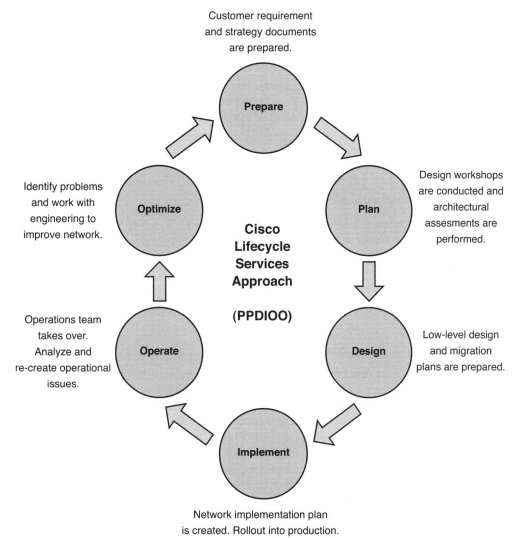

Figure 2-3   *Cisco Lifecycle Services Approach (PPDIOO)*

The following sections discuss several of the planning, design, and test activities commonly associated with each phase of the PPDIOO network lifecycle.

Testing and the Network Lifecycle

As discussed in Chapter 1, there are some common questions to be expected from executives when testing budgets are discussed. Network managers also ask questions about testing. Some of the most frequent ones are

- "What types of tests will be needed to validate our new design?"
- "How long will testing take before we can make a deployment decision?"

The answers are not as straightforward as they would seem to be. They will vary depending on the scope of the projects and, more importantly, the type of test that will be necessary to provide input into a design or deployment deliverable. This section explores several different types of tests, using the PPDIOO model to help categorize them, and discusses the common design deliverables appropriate in each phase of the Cisco Lifecycle Services approach.

Prepare Phase: Design and Test Activities

The Prepare Phase is important to obtain a forward-looking view of the new proposed architecture or service, to determine project feasibility and alignment with business goals. Although actual testing rarely occurs during the Prepare Phase, it is often the ideal time to begin budgeting for test resources or strategizing on the development of an internal test organization. The following sections describe some deliverables associated with the Prepare Phase.

Customer Requirements Document

Designing a network without understanding customer requirements is a recipe for disaster. Understanding the project scope is the first step in deploying a network that meets the technical needs of a business without the risk of under- or overengineering a solution. Developing a written Customer Requirements Document (CRD) is an essential starting point during the network lifecycle. The CRD begins with a summary of the current network deployment, applications, and features being used. It then covers the proposed changes, business drivers, risks, technical requirements, performance requirements, and service-level agreement (SLA) associated with the new project. The CRD becomes a living document for the engineering and project management teams, who will be engaged throughout the process.

Network Architectural Strategy Development

Executive interest in new networking projects will become piqued as the CRD is circulated among the stakeholders for approval. At this point in the process, the executive team needs to clearly understand the business justification and costs associated with the initiative. To assess total costs of ownership, there should be a thorough examination of vendors for all requirements, such as hardware, software, and service providers. Factors such as scaling and operational simplicity are carefully evaluated. The overall network architecture strategy is then used for the business case development. The vendor selection process is typically handled by a Request for Information (RFI) or Request for Proposal (RFP) process. Following this process can help organizations negotiate a better overall solution package and pricing, as opposed to having to do so on individual components. Determining a strategy for single or multiple vendors is also essential during this process. The RFP process can be open for internal teams or outsourcing. In some cases, where the risk of carrying out a large and complex project is elevated due to lack of in-house expertise, a system integrator (SI) plays a vital role in technology and operations outsourcing. The discussion about outsourcing to an SI is a topic in itself, but it's important to ensure that if an outsourcer is selected, they follow a strict lab testing and solution certification process.

Business Case Document

A business case document requires some degree of pricing from the equipment, software, and service provider vendors, in addition to consulting or contracting costs from the professional services or contracting firms needed for outsourced assistance. A business case document typically covers multiple models and approaches that could possibly meet the key requirements set in the CRD, each having unique capital expenditure (CAPEX) and operational expenditure (OPEX) requirements.

Note   CAPEX and OPEX are covered in more detail in Chapter 3, "Testing and Lab Strategy Development."

The business case often attempts to provide a return on investment (ROI) estimate. An ROI study is important to assess the immediate and long-term CAPEX and monthly recurring costs. In addition to the monthly recurring costs, it is also important to assess the consulting and service provider contract obligations, and things like change fees, upgrade costs, and flexibility for possible changes.

Network Testing and Lab Strategy Development

Architects from various IT functional areas are often called upon to provide input to the business case development of any large project. This is particularly true when it comes time to forecast and justify expenses for a new project. This exercise typically includes an assessment of both the short- and long-term CAPEX and OPEX associated with the project. As discussed in Chapter 1, one of the key factors for the success of any large networking project is thorough testing based on realistic scenarios. Because realistic scenarios require a test environment that closely simulates the production environment, the architects should strongly consider the CAPEX and OPEX costs associated with testing. Having a well-developed test lab strategy, with measurable benefits and showing a good ROI, is crucial in gaining acceptance and funding. A test lab development strategy document should define the business reasons for testing. It should discuss the different types of testing, along with testing environments, resources, and intellectual capital required for startup. An insourced test strategy would include an estimate of costs associated with the facilities, equipment, and test tools, as well as the staff resources required to operate the lab and run the tests. In situations where it makes business sense to outsource testing, the strategy would include an estimation of costs associated with contracting an outside test organization to develop and execute tests. In addition, the costs of governance resources of an outsourced model should also be considered. Chapter 3 details the planning, costs, and decisions associated with the startup of a test organization.

Facilities Readiness Assessments

This type of assessment has become much more common recently. The transformation to high-density, virtualized computing environments in the data center has been a source of considerable excitement and innovation throughout the IT industry. Solutions such as Cisco's Unified Computing System (UCS) offer great processing power and flexibility, in a small form factor. This enables enterprises to scale up their compute resources without having to expand the size of a data center. Although extremely popular, these solutions have posed many challenges to facilities planners, as most require many times the power and cooling of existing systems. This might sound like a bad thing at first, but consider that the new machines are at least four times more efficient when it comes to power and cooling than ones from just five years ago. The issue is that while you have 20 times the compute power, per square foot of data center, you also need five times the amount of power for each square foot. Careful planning and site preparation for power, cooling, cabling, and equipment rack layouts must be done; otherwise, environmental conditions could cause the blade servers or fabric interconnects to shut down to protect their components. One of the first decisions that enterprise architects and their business clients need to make when planning a data center consolidation is whether to retrofit existing data centers to meet these challenges, or to build new "greenfield" data centers from the ground up.

> **Note** Greenfield data centers generally refer to brand new data center facilities, while existing data centers that are expanded or redesigned are often referred to as "brownfield data centers."

To meet this challenge, many equipment vendors and consulting companies offer "environmental readiness assessments," in which they evaluate all aspects of facilities preparation for potential deployments. These assessments typically involve a combination of visual inspections and measurements of power output, grounding systems, cooling capacity, humidity, and airflow, in addition to an analysis of the existing cable plant infrastructure. A company that wants to take an insourced approach to this effort may turn to its test team for leadership. Often, test teams are the first to certify new products. This gives them a better perspective on the environmental requirements of any gear to be used in the data center of the future, as well as any challenges caused by things such as the size and weight of the equipment. Upon completion of the site inspection, the test team will prepare a report with recommendations about tile and rack positions, row configurations, server and storage system placement, venting strategies, and any other things that may affect the cooling and power capabilities of the data center. This data would be used by a project team as input when trying to estimate the costs associated with retrofitting an existing data center versus building a new greenfield one.

Plan Phase: Design and Test Activities

A networking project transitions from concept to reality during the Plan Phase. This is the time in the network lifecycle when budgets are allocated, project plans are drafted, and the design process is set in motion. An opportunity for test execution presents itself in the Plan Phase, as proof of concept and network readiness tests are conducted to investigate possible solutions and to assess the current operational environment's capability to meet the new requirements. A few of the deliverables associated with the Plan Phase are described next.

Architecture Design Workshops

The Business Case and Customer Requirements Documents developed in the Prepare Phase should clearly articulate the connection between business and technical requirements of a project. When crafting a design to meet these requirements, further technical discussions will be required because various solution approaches will have different technical pros and cons. Architectural design workshops offer a forum for these discussions, giving the architects and key stakeholders the opportunity to propose and collaborate on the various different technical options that exist. For complex projects with multiple options, it is sometimes necessary to prepare a detailed *SWOT analysis* (Strengths, Weaknesses, Opportunities, and Threats), so that all stakeholders have a thorough understanding of the risks associated with each proposal.

Current Architectural Assessment

Concurrent or subsequent to the architectural design workshops, a detailed assessment of the current network architecture is conducted. This helps to identify any issues or limitations in the current network design. Also, before a new architecture is proposed, it is important to understand how much impact the new design will have on the operations teams that have to support it. An excellent forward-looking architecture that is cost-efficient from a CAPEX standpoint but has a significant amount of rework on the current network can become less attractive. Therefore, the current architectural design also plays a significant role in the new design.

High-Level Design

A high-level design (HLD) is crafted after all of the decisions and options are taken into account from the customer requirements, architectural workshops, and architectural assessments. The HLD specifies the products and technologies that will be chosen to meet the enterprise's technical and business goals. It will include the overall topology, network diagrams depicting major equipment layout and major physical layer connections, the types of equipment to be used, and overall software feature recommendations. High-level recommendations, such as "QOS will be used," are also part of the HLD.

Proof of Concept Testing

Proof of concept (POC) testing is generally conducted during the Plan Phase of a network lifecycle to validate the concepts and assumptions made in the HLD. A POC test also helps engineers and operators gain hands-on experience with a proposed design or technology that they may not be familiar with, helping to reduce risk and time to implementation. A POC test is often facilitated and hosted by an equipment vendor or service provider during a pre-sales effort, with the goal of inspiring customer confidence in the particular design or solution being sold. While a POC test should not be a substitute for a documented network design, the outcome often generates implementation guidelines and a bill of materials that are used as input into the HLD and LLD deliverables. POC tests are most effective when conducted in a structured manner, using the HLD as a starting point for test plan development. The test plan is the "script" for the POC test, and contains the set of test cases to be executed—each documented with objectives and expected and observed results. See Chapter 6, "Proof of Concept Testing Case Study of a Cisco Data Center 3.0 Architecture," for a case study example of a POC test.

Network Readiness Testing

Network readiness testing is often performed prior to the launch of a new service or application to help determine whether an existing network can handle an increased traffic load or deliver against an application SLA. The difference between a POC and a network readiness test is that the latter is typically conducted on the live production network rather than in a test lab. A network readiness test often starts with a detailed inventory of network devices to determine their operational hardware, software, and provisioning details. This helps to determine whether upgrades or changes to the logical configurations will be necessary to meet the new standards. An audit of the operational performance of each device (CPU, memory, interface statistics) is often included as part of a network readiness test, particularly when this information is not routinely collected and reported as part of a network management program. In some cases, a network readiness test involves the injection of test traffic closely resembling that of the new application so that it can be systematically measured across various test points on the network. This data is then analyzed to predict how the application will behave, and whether existing services such as QoS are configured and performing as expected. Cisco IP SLA is a feature, included in Cisco IOS Software, that uses a type of active probe technology to inject relevant traffic into the network for the purposes of monitoring and measuring overhead network performance. See Chapter 9 for a case study example of a network readiness test.

Network Capacity Planning and Testing

Capacity planning is commonly srecognized as a network management discipline. It involves data collection and reporting on information such as the available circuit band-width, disk storage, or memory usage of operational network devices for the purposes of forecasting when upgrades will be needed. This is an important business function, because upgrades to capacity can be executed more smoothly if there is a common Forward Schedule of Changes (FSC). What makes capacity planning a complicated science is the nonlinear nature of network traffic during unforeseen conditions. What happens to the traffic load on circuit X of device A if circuit Y on device B fails? Will we have enough storage in our data center disk array during the holiday retail spike? What happens to core bandwidth after the company merger occurs? Although it might be feasible to answer some of these questions by analyzing the network topology, routing protocols, and baseline traffic statistics, incorporating a testing approach to analyze this problem provides more reliable and predictable results. Most business operational models do not permit such failover testing to be conducted during production hours, so network capacity testing is normally conducted in a lab or with a network simulator.

Design Phase: Design and Test Activities

In the same way as there is overlap that occurs between the Prepare and Plan Phases in the PPDIOO approach, there is some overlap between the Plan and Design Phases as well. As some deliverables in the Plan Phase are being finished, others in the Design Phase are being started. The Design Phase includes several deliverables, described next.

Low-Level Design

A low-level design (LLD) is typically developed after the HLD is accepted and validated through testing. The LLD includes more detailed network topology diagrams, including specifications on hardware and circuit physical and logical connectivity, routing protocol design, and custom policies. The LLD also includes details of the features and topologies that offer network resiliency and high availability. Configuration templates are part of this document, as well as proposals for network management tools used for operational readiness. The Bill of Material is listed with the new hardware and software that has been ordered. The equipment ordering often takes place concurrent to the LLD development to save time. From a project management standpoint, it is important to use this phase to develop parallel activities. The budget and project management schedule, however, needs be flexible to account for any incremental change in equipment requirements based on the testing outcome. Generating an accurate LLD often requires access to lab equipment for the development of the configuration templates. If real equipment is not available to validate the configurations, it is almost impossible to get this part accomplished.

Migration Plan

With the exception of entirely new greenfield networks built from the ground up, a migration from the old network design to the new network design will need to occur. For very simple design changes or small networks, the entire migration could be implemented during a single maintenance window as part of a "flash cut." This reduces the exposure of a network that is "half-migrated" but introduces some risk, as all elements must be successfully changed at once—otherwise, the migration would need to be aborted. More commonly, a network implementation is done over a period of time, where certain portions of the network are operating on the old network design while others are operating on the new. In both scenarios, a detailed migration plan is required, explaining the high- and low-level steps that detail the change, success indicators, and backout procedure if the change fails.

Design Verification Testing

Verification testing is an extremely critical step in certifying a new design, or refining a plan for new technology introduction into an existing network. Design verification testing, sometimes referred to as predeployment testing, represents the most common test trigger for an enterprise because of the high level of visibility and risk associated with major network infrastructure changes. Following a structured systems test approach, enterprises can reduce this risk and speed network deployments by exposing weaknesses or defects early in the design process. A structured systems test approach that has proven to be successful includes the following five phases:

- **Phase 1: Baseline testing:** In baseline testing, you configure a miniaturized replica of the new design and perform a set of test cases that ensures basic functionality when all of the devices, features, protocols, and services are enabled simultaneously. The baseline test topology should represent the network architect's vision of what the design will ultimately look like when all features are enabled.

- **Phase 2: Feature testing:** In feature testing, you configure, validate, and analyze the impact of specific features in greater depth. This is the phase where "what if" scenarios can be investigated to help refine the design. An example of this would be changing the values of timers in your routing protocol.

- **Phase 3: Negative testing:** Also referred to as failure testing, in negative testing, you create simulated failures on specific devices and components to measure network convergence and to record collateral damage.

- **Phase 4: Performance and scalability testing:** You conduct performance testing to obtain a baseline of the speed at which individual components and the overall network system can process traffic or offer a specific network service. This is the phase of testing where throughput testing or VPN tunnel setup rate testing might be conducted to obtain a "best case" benchmark. With scalability testing, the performance boundaries of components and the network system are determined by increasing design variables such as test traffic load, number of routes, and number of routing adjacencies. Performance tests are often rerun with the network system under the stress of induced load so that a "worst-case" benchmark of performance during peak usage conditions can be determined.

■ **Phase 5: Duty cycle testing:** The objective of duty cycle testing is to verify that the test topology will be able to endure the likely stresses that will occur during normal network operations. The primary intent is to illustrate how the topology, as a whole, will react to various "stress" events, collectively, over a specific period of time. Common network stresses include provisioning changes, network management functions, power failures, code upgrades, reloads, and traffic spikes.

See Chapter 8, "Design Verification Testing Case Study," for several examples of design verification testing.

Migration Plan Testing

Migration plan testing is a crucial step in preventing service disruptions as certain portions of the network are moved to the new infrastructure during the Implement Phase. All too often, network architects focus solely on the new design, without considering how the network will operate in a partially migrated state. Will there be routing loops when new routing protocols are introduced in an existing environment? How will the applications perform when clients and servers are on different portions of the network? Will performance suffer for users on the old design as a result of increased latency during the transition period? A detailed migration plan test will attempt to answer these questions by executing a "dry run" of the migration, using the migration plan as the script. In many cases, the migration plan is developed directly from output from this testing.

Implement Phase: Deliverables and Test Activities

In this phase, the network engineers move away from working on paper and in labs to rolling out the new features into a production environment. Some of the deliverables in the Implement Phase are described next.

Network Implementation Plan

A network implementation plan (NIP) is a site-specific guide that details all the steps necessary to deploy the new design. The NIP includes details like upgrades required to the existing hardware and software, new hardware deployments, and new physical and logical connectivity between the existing network and the new devices. It has configuration templates for enabling any new features or modifying existing ones. This plan should have a step-by-step guide to get the existing network from where it is to where it needs to be. It should contain checkpoints to make sure everything is working as expected. Finally, it should have a step-by-step backout plan in case there is a reason for the change to be aborted.

Network Ready for Use Test

A network ready for use (NRFU) test typically is executed on a new network infrastructure as a last step in certifying that it is ready to carry production traffic. During an NRFU test, network devices are methodically checked to ensure that they have been implemented according to the design specifications and that no errors are occurring. If available, test traffic generators are injected into the network at particular points so that performance can be verified against network SLA metrics for throughput, loss, delay, and jitter. Convergence testing also is conducted by failing over portions of the network and measuring the failover times. The new network is then brought under control of the network management systems (NMS) so that fault, capacity, application performance, and security features can be verified. The final step of an NRFU test is often a test of live sites as part of a limited production pilot. Upon certification that applications behaved as expected, the network is considered to be ready for customer provisioning.

Operate Phase: Deliverables and Test Activities

In this phase of the PPDIOO approach, the network transitions to the operations team. In this phase, the deliverables described next are common.

Hands-On Lab Training

One of the most overlooked but valuable aspects of maintaining an inventory of lab equipment is the ability to conduct formal or informal hands-on training when the lab is not in use for testing. As most network engineers will attest, any training is good training, but there is no substitute for hands-on experience. Investing in this experience pays huge dividends in the form of higher morale and better technical employee retention, in addition to a more efficient technical staff that is less apt to create service outages due to human error.

Re-creation of Network Problems

One of the most difficult decisions that an engineer is faced with during a network outage is whether to continue troubleshooting a complex problem in search of the root cause or to restore service using any means possible. More often than not, a manager at some level will ultimately make the call for service restoration, whether that requires rerouting network traffic down a redundant path, reseating a line card, or rebooting a network device. Unfortunately, these measures rarely help determine the root cause of the outages, which are likely to happen again if they are tied to a software or hardware defect. One of the most efficient and reliable methods of detecting and resolving such defects is to attempt a re-create of the problem discovered on the network. The following process is used by Cisco Technical Assistance Center (TAC) engineers to solve the most difficult problems seen in customer networks:

Step 1.   Re-create the problem.

Step 2.   Analyze the root cause.

Step 3.   Work with development engineers to code a potential fix.

Step 4.   Test the fix in the lab topology where the problem was originally re-created.

Unfortunately, not all vendor TACs are created equal, and many do not have the facilities or skilled personnel to attempt a network re-create, particularly if the problem is intermittent and not being reported by multiple customers. Having an in-house lab where a mock-up of the environment can be quickly built is the fastest route to problem resolution. This is particularly true if the enterprise can allow vendors to have remote access through a VPN connection to analyze the root cause once the problem is re-created. The other side of the coin can be just as important. If you or your peers and management are convinced that a particular feature or command caused an outage on your network, it is helpful to be able to prove or disprove it. Many times, you can show that a problem is very unlikely to reoccur, or you can figure out what the trigger for the outage was. You can then take steps to keep it from happening again.

Optimize Phase: Deliverables and Test Activities

In this phase, the network engineers work with the operations team to establish and identify system improvements. Some deliverables for this phase are described next.

Predeployment Testing for Minor Design Changes

Many large enterprise IT organizations have "Sustaining Engineering" groups. These groups handle functions such as provisioning, small design changes, and change control. The members of such groups are often responsible for developing complete "mini-design" solutions, which may include specifying, or certifying, new hardware or software. These solutions often require them to generate device configurations, and develop small-scale implementation plans, which are used by network operators to effect the required changes. They must certify that these new designs are in line with the LLD and the architectural specifications laid out for the network. Having an onsite lab to verify the changes prior to deployment is an invaluable resource for these functions.

Software Acceptance Testing

Enterprise IT organizations must continuously upgrade network and server operating system code to protect against security vulnerabilities, resolve defects, and support new hardware or software features. Although software developers bear the most responsibility with respect to the code quality, support engineers and customers also play a major role. A large majority of software defects are detected and remediated during the product vendor's software development process. All of the leading network equipment vendors maintain rigorous software quality assurance programs, leveraging dedicated development and systems test groups that focus solely on acceptance and defect testing of their code. Still, testing can never completely identify all the defects within software. It cannot establish that a product functions properly under all possible conditions. Knowledge of how their product is generally deployed by their customer base guides vendors in their testing efforts. However, it would be naive to assume that a vendor's test team should or could have full awareness of every possible use case. Most network service providers and many sophisticated enterprise organizations understand the reality of vendor test limitations and thus maintain their own complementary acceptance and regression test programs. In these programs, they create a test lab that looks as similar to their production environment as possible. Acceptance testing is normally done to certify new hardware or software, where the testing team runs a predefined set of tests with an expected output based on the existing production environment. Upon completion, suspected software defects are reported to the vendor for analysis and remediation. The test environment and scenarios under which these defects were discovered are recorded so that the test team can repeat them again using new versions of software or hardware as part of a regression test program. See Chapter 10, "New Platform and Code Certification Testing Case Study," for an example of a bug fix testing plan.

Summary

This chapter explored the enterprise architecture and design process as well as its role in the Cisco Lifecycle Services approach. The chapter explained and provided examples of several types of network testing, which not only complement the lifecycle but also enable it to be successful. It is also important to understand that without a good testing strategy and a well-managed test lab, it would be extremely hard to execute the Prepare, Plan, Design, Implement, Operate, and Optimize (PPDIOO) network lifecycle approach effectively.

Chapter 3

Testing and Lab Strategy Development

This chapter covers the following topics:

- Cost Analysis and Resource Planning

- Test Organization Financing Models

- Outsourced Testing

- Test Lab Facilities Design

- Test Lab Operations

Chapter 1, "A Business Case for Enterprise Network Testing," examined the significant role that an IT infrastructure plays in enabling revenue growth and driving cost efficiencies in a business. In the process of considering this role, we examined the monetary costs of IT service outages to a business, and found that they are often the result of network problems caused by unverified changes or unpredictable behavior during equipment or software failure. Chapter 2, "Testing Throughout the Network Lifecycle," went on to explain how adopting a structured test program can help to minimize these outages, and how testing fits into the overall Enterprise Architectural strategy of an organization.

All of this theory is useful, but applying it to a real business with a closely scrutinized budget for IT spending can be challenging. You need to know the costs associated with building, staffing, and operating a lab, understand best practices when building a lab facility, and know when it make sense to outsource certain test functions.

This chapter explores all of these issues. The chapter opens with a business cost analysis of test organization startup, followed by a discussion of various funding models. Best practices for test lab facility design are then presented, and the chapter concludes with a section on test lab operations.

Cost Analysis and Resource Planning

As with any business venture, the decision to undertake a test exercise has costs associated with its adoption and risks associated with its rejection as a course of action. Assuming that the risks of whether or not testing should be done in the first place are well understood, as discussed in previous chapters, this section provides some guidance with respect to the cost analysis of a proposed test environment.

Generally, business costs are examined in terms of capital expenditures (CAPEX) and operational expenditures (OPEX). CAPEX is typically defined as expenditures necessary to acquire assets with a useful life extending beyond the current tax year (hence the need to capitalize or depreciate the costs over a period of time). OPEX, on the other hand, can be defined simply as the ongoing costs of running a system or product.

A business entity's desire to use capital versus operational funds can be influenced by the current business and economic climate. These considerations may override other drivers pushing the business decision in a direction that is not otherwise indicated by the technical analysis.

Note that an initial "build versus buy" decision could also be made with respect to network testing. That is, the test effort can be either executed in-house or outsourced to a test services provider. This decision has a clear business impact: An outsourced approach would have minimal, if any, CAPEX costs and would be primarily accounted as an operating expense. The initial establishment of a test facility can be very costly, and careful assessment of the return on investment (ROI) needs to be made to determine the appropriate approach for any given venture.

Estimating CAPEX Necessary to Create a New Test Lab

The initial establishment of a medium- to large-sized test lab can be very costly and usually has significant CAPEX impact. Space needs to be established, and fixed assets need to be procured to support the test efforts. These components factor into the initial capital outlay to establish the lab, as well as ongoing capital expenditures to enhance the facility. The following sections examine these considerations in greater detail.

Environmental Considerations

The environmental requirements for test labs can vary significantly, ranging from a small amount of network gear located in a separated area to multithousand-square-foot facilities with electric consumption in the megawatt dimension.

In either case, a test lab should be given sufficient dedicated space to allow staff to perform their duties and provide the results needed, as dictated by the business requirements. Failure to provide sufficient lab resources to perform the expected level of work is simply wasteful and should not be attempted, although frequently the cost analysis provides an inclination to cut corners.

The following environmental factors should be taken into consideration when evaluating the startup of a new test facility:

- Physical space

- Power

- Climate control

- Access

- Other infrastructure

Physical Space

The test facility needs to be a distinct, separated area that is not subject to the vagaries of staff needs or production network issues. Dedicating the space (and other resources) is critical to establishing a properly run lab. The space considerations need to include

- Network equipment

- Equipment racks

- Test gear

- Supporting servers

- Tools storage

- Lab infrastructure space (for items such as cable plant and power distribution systems)

- Infrastructure storage (cables, screws, consumables)

- Human space for staff movement and physical work aspects (for example, card extraction, installation activities)

The actual lab space may simply be a closed room reserved for this purpose, a controlled area in a data center environment, or even dedicated test-specific building spaces. It is important that the lab space be a controlled-access area to prevent "unauthorized reallocation" of the gear contained therein. You do not want the lab gear to be cannibalized for production projects or to become a "spares depot." The lab may or may not have raised flooring, depending on the approach taken for cooling and cabling. Applying antistatic measures to the lab area is highly recommended. This may include static-free flooring, antistatic treatments, static-free workbenches, static grounding straps for staff, and so forth. Compliance with the antistatic measures from both a staff and physical environment perspective should be verified at regular intervals. In all likelihood, these policies are already defined for the production environment and need to be applied to the lab as well.

Tip   Make sure to verify that you meet safety requirements for your new lab location. Many locations across the world have stringent environmental, health, and human safety regulations. Also, it is a good idea to verify that your company's insurance will cover your lab as it built.

Power

The power consumption of a test lab needs to be examined and carefully laid out. This exercise begins with an understanding of the gear to be deployed within the lab and its power requirements. For example, power needs may vary from simple 110-V/15-A AC feeds, to 3-phase 13-kW AC or even 48-V/60-A DC plants. You need to determine the amount of power needed for initial lab establishment, and apply further analysis to estimated future needs. Installing power upfront typically is easier than adding it later.

When planning for growth, consider locating the power source as close to the lab as possible. If it is not run through the lab itself, at least establish breaker panel space and central feed capacity in the lab. Also, consider conduit limitations in this planning exercise, as the cost of adding conduit capacity to the testing facility may eclipse the cost of the additional circuits, depending on how the conduit is run. It is better to include larger conduit diameters early on than to rerun them later.

Grounding also needs to be addressed—not only from an antistatic perspective, as discussed previously, but also with respect to power and signal grounding. Sources of noisy ground loops can be very difficult to pinpoint and can result in highly erratic behavior of electronic equipment. The criticality of the lab operation may also drive the need for an uninterruptible power supply (UPS) system capable of supporting the needs of the environment. These systems are usually specified in terms of the amount of power that can be drawn over a given period of time. An analysis of the critical lab components and expected outage tolerances will lead to a determination of the level of UPS required (if any). Very expensive and sophisticated electronic gear will be housed in this lab space, some of which does not take well to simply being powered off mid-operation.

The power distribution grid also needs to be considered. It may be sufficient in some smaller facilities to simply use power strips with sufficient capacity. Other situations may call for busbar-based power distribution systems, typically mounted overhead. Some environments may use a combination of both. Note that power strips are now available that can be programmatically controlled, resulting in benefits of reduced power consumption as well as the capability to remotely power cycle the test equipment.

Any power distribution proposal should be vetted by and installed by professionals to ensure that installation is to specification, complies with all local codes, and is safe to operate.

Climate Control

As with other considerations, the need for a controlled-climate space will be dictated by the amount and type of equipment in the lab as well as human needs. Most of today's small network gear, such as 1-rack-unit (1RU) appliances or other equipment that is not typically rack-mounted, has been designed to operate within the confines of an office space or equipment closet and can tolerate considerable temperature swings. Larger equipment usually has more stringent environmental demands, and these should be observed in consideration of the greater cost of this hardware as well. Most manufacturers provide heat output and temperature operating tolerance information in their specification sheets. It is typically sufficient to simply total the heat dissipation numbers for all the gear in the lab to arrive at an expected thermal footprint (include network gear, test tools, and so forth). If heat output numbers are not available for some equipment, simply use a worst-case estimate that all of the energy consumed by the unit is converted to heat. Buildings personnel will be able to assist with interpreting this thermal output in terms of the required cooling for the area.

In the calculation of a total thermal energy number, factor in human involvement. For instance, if the lab is to be manned by several people, and a significant amount of their daily time will be spent in the space, then cooling for their own heat generation should be considered. Also, to support a comfortable work environment, lab staff should be able to change the temperature as long as it's within the equipment's acceptable heat tolerance range.

Also consider the actual airflow produced by individual pieces of equipment with respect to other pieces of equipment. Simply calculating a total heat number in a large space will not be sufficient if, for instance, one device's exhaust heat blows directly into the intake of another device. You also must consider how the airflow will occur, rack to rack and device to device, and how cold air enters the facility and how excess heat might be vented.

Tip   Consider redundant climate control and power management systems for large labs. Losing power may impact several testing projects at once, and having cooling problems could damage millions of dollars worth of equipment.

Heating and cooling are not the only considerations for climate control: Appropriate humidity levels also help to mitigate static issues. Other considerations are airborne particles and pollutants; electronic equipment should not be run in "dusty" areas.

You also need to examine lighting from a lab operations perspective, because this will be a lab environment, not a heads-down office space. Staff needs sufficient lighting to perform their tasks in the lab, and this may include both general overhead lighting and task-oriented lights such as flashlights. However, if the staff is not normally present in the lab itself, lighting may be controlled so that it is in use only when needed.

Access

As indicated previously, physical access to the lab space must be controlled. An operational lab is totally dependent on the availability of the equipment within it, and the repurposing of such gear is a frequent failure point for many labs. Additionally, there is typically a considerable equipment investment in the test lab, including test gear and small consumables such as transceivers, pluggable optics, memory, and so on. The availability of this equipment is critical to a test lab and needs to be controlled. The lab staff should be cognizant that multiple activities may be ongoing at any given time, and limiting access to the lab also reduces the likelihood of interruptions to a test exercise because, for example, someone tripped over a cable.

Access to the test facility needs to accommodate bringing equipment in and out of the environment. Consider the need for accessibility, from loading docks to elevators to lab entryways, doors, and ramps, when planning the lab facility. Depending on the size and weight of the equipment in the lab, you might need to consider weight distribution, especially in areas where raised flooring is used or in labs located in older structures whose subflooring may not be able to hold the weight of some larger equipment. Some gear weighs thousands of pounds, and having a lab on the second floor of a building will require some thought. There are several stories about companies reinforcing the floor on the second floor lab in their building to support the extra-heavy gear, only to be foiled by an elevator that isn't capable of bringing the gear up. This lack of forethought has forced more than one facilities manager to remove windows and hire a crane to lift pallets of equipment into an office building.

An additional access perspective relates to how the lab staff accesses the equipment locally or remotely. Frequently, console port access, through the use of IP terminal servers, is used to configure and manage the device in the test bed. Such access is relatively slow, however, and if possible, there should be an out-of-band (OOB) IP management network in place to facilitate the use of protocols such as Simple Network Management Protocol (SNMP), Telnet, and Secure Shell (SSH). Other tools may also be accessible via Remote Desktop Connect (for Windows appliances), Virtual Network Connect (for virtual hosting services), XWindows (for UNIX/Linux environments), or even HTTP/HTTPS connections for web-based management.

As previously noted, programmatically controlled power strips are also available. This accessibility allows staff members to access the equipment and perform their tasks remotely from locations outside the lab. In most corporations, many of the lab users are not physically near to the equipment, and they may possibly not even be direct members of the test organization with administrative rights to gain physical access. Such power control units allow for a wider range of staff to participate in the testing.

Remote, or out-of-band, access can help to make the testing more meaningful to a larger community of interest and potentially increase the use of the gear (with a correlating improvement in ROI). To provide the infrastructure to support this operation, you need to establish network connectivity into the lab environment. This connectivity needs to be carefully provisioned so as to prevent violations of corporate security policies, and also to avoid inadvertent lab traffic leaking into the production network. It is recommended that the lab network space be isolated as much as possible from the production network space, preferably through the use of firewalls, to prevent lab tests from injecting instabilities into the production environment.

Other Infrastructure

The infrastructure aspects relevant to a test facility are often underestimated. The following should be considered in your test lab design.

Cabling   Test labs have a voracious appetite for cables, and typically most estimates of cable needs are far too low to meet demand. Imagine how embarrassing it would be to explain to your VP that a critical test could not be completed because of a cabling shortage. At a minimum, sufficient cable should be on hand to accommodate all the available ports of the equipment in the facility. This should include unshielded twisted-pair (UTP), fiber optic, and serial cabling as appropriate. Because of repeated reuse and general abuse, cabling in a lab does not last anywhere as long as it does in your production environment. Cables do break and fray with use, and consequently will appear as an ongoing cost; as such, cabling should be accounted for in the OPEX budget for the lab.

Cabinetry   Virtually all lab facilities can benefit from the use of racks or cabinets to house the test equipment. Even a small test bed of six or so devices will quickly devolve into a "rat's nest" of cables and have gear subject to sliding and even falling during use. A cabinet can be acquired, complete with shelving, power strips, and cable management hardware, for approximately $1000 and is well worth the cost.

Network Connectivity   As previously discussed, a "lab network" can support IP connectivity for staff members who are not physically in the lab facility itself. A well-planned lab infrastructure will have considerations for remote user connectivity in addition to local connectivity to "shared services" on which test operations rely, such as NTP, DNS, TFTP, and FTP. Lab devices (routers, switches, appliances, and servers) often have a separate "management port" that is dedicated to these purposes, and it is common practice to design an out-of-band "lab network" with a singular purpose of connecting the management ports.

Structured Cabling   If the lab is large enough to warrant a structured cabling plant, investment in one might be appropriate. In such a system, the equipment racks have prewired patch-panel "cans" available, which are run directly to a central patching area similar to a telco main distribution frame (MDF), where patches, manual or automated, are used to interconnect equipment which sits in rack distribution frames (RDF). Figure 3-1 provides a simple example of a structured wiring system. In this example, the router port in cabinet 10.07 can be interconnected to the Ethernet switch in cabinet 11.08 without running a "temporary" cable overhead or on the floor.

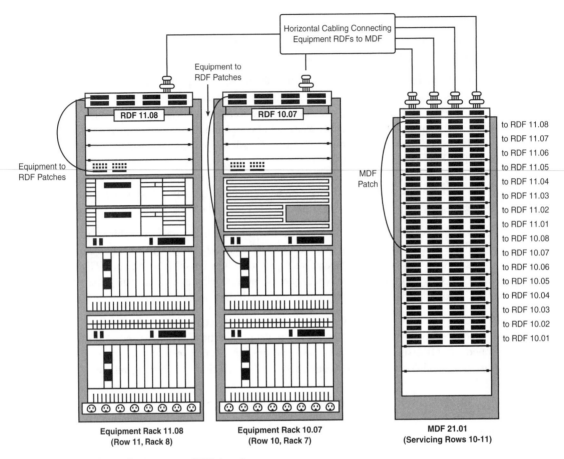

Figure 3-1   *Example Structured Wiring System*

Unit Under Test (UUT) Network Devices   Any testing focused on network verification requires some level of simulated network infrastructure. To accomplish this, some amount of network gear is required to provide an environment representative of the production network. You should carefully review the production network environment and include the results as input to the test bed design exercise. Note that the test bed design effort is analogous to any design exercise in that it needs to consider all of the components used to provide the services supported in production. This necessitates the acquisition of sufficient equipment to be used as unit under test (UUT) network devices to conduct reasonable testing. Pricing for this equipment will vary greatly, depending upon the production network topology and the level of discounting your organization receives.

Test Tools   Third-party tools are available specifically for testing needs. From an OSI model perspective, these include Layer 1 tools such as line simulators, line impairment insertion tools, and delay simulators. Layer 2 tools include repeaters, switches, and devices that can provide control and impairment mechanisms.

At Layer 3, there may be a requirement for tools that can drive traffic, emulate routers and networks, and offer "canned" test scripts (such as those described in RFC 2544). These tools may also provide Layer 4–7 simulation, or more specialized tools may be needed to address those requirements. This test gear is notoriously expensive and can easily run in excess of $250,000 for a modestly equipped system.

In certain cases, custom (often internally developed) tools that are not directly available from the tool vendors (perhaps due to market or copyright constraints) might be needed to support operations. These custom tools may include internally developed scripts coded in Tool Command Language (TCL), SNMP control scripts, and so forth. Note that, typically, internally developed tools do not impact CAPEX costs other than for the acquisition of the processing platforms upon which they reside. However, they may incur long-term OPEX costs if the engineering staff needs to perform ongoing maintenance, bug fixes, and new feature enhancements.

Antivirus Protection   The use of antivirus software should not be neglected in the lab environment. While typically demanded in production user environments, the need for such protection is equally applicable to the lab with its stable of servers, test tools, and even general-use computers at risk. In some testing venues, there may even be intentional impairments being driven to cripple systems, and if a mistake causes the impairment to travel outside of the test area, the other devices should be protected as well as possible.

Monitoring Tools   Ideally, the lab monitoring toolset should closely mimic your production environment. A wide variety of monitoring mechanisms are deployed in modern IP-network environments. Many are UNIX- or Linux-based tools, although Windows-based tools are becoming more commonplace. The decision to select a particular operating system platform depends on the availability of hardware to run the platform within the testing organization, internal support capabilities of staff, and the product availability itself. Most monitoring tools in IP-centric networks use the SNMP mechanisms (typically version 2c). Additionally, management tools may use Internet Control Message Protocol (ICMP), Extensible Markup Language (XML) scripts, and even CLI-based scripts using languages such as TCL, Expect, or Perl. Other approaches also exist, based upon ITU standards, but these have primarily been relegated to management of telco backbone facilities.

Tip   For reference, the Stanford Linear Accelerator Center website has a large listing of both for-fee and freeware tools for network monitoring at www.slac.stanford.edu/xorg/nmtf/nmtf-tools.html.

Clearly, the costs of providing network monitoring platforms for the test facility can be very wide-ranging. A small lab environment may find that open source and simple CLI tools are sufficient to meet their needs. A larger facility may find that use of for-fee third-party tools is necessary to provide the information data points needed in a scalable manner.

Estimated OPEX to Operate a Test Lab

As previously described, OPEX costs are recurring expenses related to some business function. A test lab will also incur ongoing expenses in several areas, described next, as part of its operation.

Staffing

Staffing is generally the largest operational expense of a test lab. Staff costs include salaries and benefits, training costs, and ancillary costs associated with providing the tools and environment that enable personnel to perform their duties (such as leased computers). Staff costs for a lab may be somewhat mitigated by establishing a hierarchy of individuals based upon skill sets.

It can be beneficial for a test facility to incorporate a staffing structure that has some high-level, senior staff to lead the operation of the lab. These staff members would be involved in test planning and scoping, planning for lab growth, and providing support and a development path for junior staff. Frequently, test labs can gain valuable and cost-effective staff augmentation by bringing in college student interns during their co-op program phases at school. This approach benefits both the test facility, in that the staffing costs can be somewhat controlled, and the interns, providing an opportunity for them to learn from a real-world business environment. Many schools actively support such programs.

As the test facilities become larger, additional staffing may be necessary to accommodate internal tools development. This staff overhead usually applies only to the largest facilities, where such costs can be absorbed and having employees of several different skill levels can be productive. In large test facilities, a staffing structure as reflected in Table 3-1 would be appropriate.

There are more in-depth explanations of the job roles described in Table 3-1 in the "Test Lab Operations" section, later in this chapter.

Power

Power consumption for your lab's operations will be driven by the equipment in use and the environmental equipment needed to control the climate and lighting for the area. Minimizing these costs can be beneficial when lobbying for funds on an annual basis. As previously discussed, using automated tools for controlling power availability and even "lights-out" operation can help mitigate power consumption and, hence, associated costs. Keeping gear powered off when it is not being used is a great way to cut costs, and being able to power it on and off remotely, if you just need to check out a configuration or a command, makes it more likely that you will get great return on your investment.

Table 3-1 *An Example of a Test Lab Staffing Structure*

Title	Responsibility
Test Lab Manager	Overall responsibility for work efforts, lab operations, and staff
Project Manager	Manages the overall timelines and resources associated with all of the test projects
Lab Administrator	Oversees lab operations and ensures availability of equipment
Senior Test Engineer	Oversees project scoping and sizing, test plan development, execution of complex projects, staff guidance
Test Engineer	Executes majority of test activities
Part-Time Staffing	Provides staff augmentation, including test bed setup, inventory management, test execution assistance

Physical Facility

Depending on corporate policy, the costs of the actual lab space may be a chargeable item. If the facility is leased, the costs are clearly contracted, but many companies have also implemented cost-center approaches that implement departmental chargebacks based upon the space used. Fortunately, lab equipment usually can be highly compressed from a space consumption perspective, and if the lab itself is unmanned, those costs can be minimized.

Maintenance Obligations

Additional ongoing costs for the lab are the maintenance contracts relating to the equipment being used. Depending upon the criticality of the lab work, these agreements may be customized to control costs. With respect to larger test facilities, do not overlook the need for management tools to aid in the management of the lab and its ancillary components. You need to consider systems to manage tasks undertaken, scheduling of equipment, builds and teardowns, and inventory management. These systems will have some impact on OPEX, and these costs will appear as the overhead of keeping the databases' content current, customization of the environments, internal support needs, and ongoing software costs.

Other OPEX

You should also make budget allowances for small consumables associated with the lab operation, as previously discussed. Items such as small tools like screwdrivers, fasteners (screws, tie-wraps), and the like are needed in day-to-day operation. Budget should always be allocated on a recurring basis for replacement cables, as they tend to degenerate or get lost over time.

As the test environments become larger, the need for additional overhead management tools becomes apparent. A large facility needs an inventory system of some type to track the purchased gear for both operational and audit purposes. It can be difficult for the lab management to request funding for additional equipment without a clear, documentable understanding of the current lab inventory. In addition, the inventory system provides support data for any depreciation exercises that need to be executed.

A large lab with multiple staff members and several concurrent tests will also likely require an equipment management "checkout" tool. This will likely tie back into the inventory system and provide control over the use and availability of the lab gear. This can aid greatly in management of lab resources and prevent use conflicts by different projects. In addition, the utilization statistics from such a system can aid with determining which lab elements are under- or overprovisioned, providing a basis for lab growth planning and the support of funding requests. This type of system can also allow you to plan for and buy different maintenance levels for gear that is in high demand, as compared to gear that has low demand or for which spares usually are available. As gear stops being used, it may become worthwhile to take it off of maintenance altogether or trade some part of it in. Remember that some amount of "legacy" gear is always required for interoperability tests. However, once the legacy gear is no longer in use in your production environment, you are very unlikely to need it in your lab.

Test Organization Financing Models

There are some variations on funding approaches for a test lab. The choices presented in this section are generally applicable based upon the size and the related financial commitment of the facility in question. Funding is considered primarily from a cost perspective, with some perspective provided on ROI models.

Cost of Business

In a small network environment, it may be sufficient to absorb the costs of testing as simply the "cost of doing business." A minimalist test area may simply be a small amount of gear acquired concurrent with a network rollout, enabling network operations staff to reproduce problems, test various proposals, and augment training through experimentation in the test space. Generally, this approach is satisfactory only for the smallest organizations in which minimal funding is available.

Project-Based Funding

A widely used model for test facilities is the approach of funding as part of the costs of a specific project. For example, the rollout of a new Voice over IP (VoIP) suite of products may have a test lab cost built into the overall project costs. This model provides an easy justification path for equipment needed for the specific project. However, the total funding cost may become unclear over time, as follow-on projects are encountered and their costs become only incremental over the existing test environment. This may lead to audit questions as existing equipment becomes depreciated (against some other accounting line item) and skews project cost analysis.

Departmental Chargeback

Another approach to testing is to have a chargeback mechanism where the measured or perceived costs of test exercises can be charged back to the department benefiting from the work. As an example, finance traders might need higher-speed access to their data, necessitating some network change to accommodate this increased need. The testing of this enhancement can then be charged back to that department, because the traders are the primary beneficiaries of the change. This model also tends to suffer from the previously described issue wherein the costs of the needs of one department may be shouldered by another organization. In the preceding example, perhaps a management application also requires a higher speed of access to use a bandwidth-intensive application such as video conferencing, and it benefits from the finance traders' investment without having to pay for the testing at all.

Testing as a Business Function

Larger-scale test facilities may be able to demonstrate that there is sufficient scope of work to have a permanent, self-supporting test environment. An extreme example would be a professional services business that sells test services to third parties, where the test lab is an actual revenue generation tool. Without reaching that extreme, arguments can still be made for the definition of internal test services as an essential component of the operating costs of the business, in the same manner as with the operation of the production network. With this approach, a clear funding mechanism is established in which the testing efforts are forecasted (based upon business needs). They are then budgeted through an annual budget cycle or, minimally, on a per-project basis. Resources are then scheduled to meet those needs and results, and costs are tracked and reported as with any business effort.

Return on Investment

Return on investment (ROI), sometimes called rate of return (ROR), in its most simplistic sense, is the measure of the profitability of an investment. ROI is usually expressed as a percentage, given by the division of the revenue (or perceived revenue/cost avoidance) minus the actual costs of the item in question, by its actual costs, as shown in the following formula:

ROI = (revenue − cost)/cost

For example, if your lab brings in $800,000 in revenue, and your costs for the lab were $500,000, then your ROI is 60%, as shown in the following example:

ROI = ($800,000 − $500,000) / $500,000 = 60%

As a different example, we can calculate the ROI for a lab by assuming that it can save your enterprise one hour of downtime each year. Let's use $1,107,274 (the cost of one hour of downtime for a retail company taken from Table 1-1 in Chapter 1) as the savings/revenue for avoiding the downtime. Now assume we have spent $1,000,000 in lab costs. The ROI for the lab would be

ROI = (1,107,274 − 1,000,000) / 1,000,000 = 10.73%

In the case of a revenue-generating lab supporting a business of testing services, the processes to determine revenues/expenses and hence profitability (ROI) are reasonably clear and would follow general accounting principles. Where the test lab is not a direct revenue generator, the ROI for the facility can be difficult to quantify. In this case, it is necessary to consider both the hard and soft benefits of a testing facility. Some of these benefits were discussed in Chapter 1 and are summarized in Table 3-2.

Table 3-2   *Test Lab Return on Investment Considerations*

Test Lab Hard Benefits	Test Lab Soft Benefits
Network downtime avoidance	Personnel training
New technology and solution proof of concept	Industry certification preparation
Predeployment design verification	Engineer morale/retention
Accelerated application development	Showcase new technology

Outsourced Testing

An option for enterprises that want to avoid the costs associated with establishing a significant test facility is to use the services of a test services vendor. Many for-fee service organizations exist in the marketplace and may present a solution for the enterprise that does not have the expertise, tools, or time to execute on a test requirement.

The clear advantage to the enterprise, from a cost perspective, is that it will incur limited (if any) CAPEX costs—almost all costs associated with this type of approach will be accounted as OPEX. In addition, there will be a considerable reduction in staff workload, because the vendor will execute most of the test tasks. The enterprise will still need to provide test objectives and requirements, review results, and monitor the work efforts of the vendor. As well, the vendor presumably possesses the technical expertise to undertake the task in question, relieving the enterprise from the burden of developing the same. This includes not just the technical solution under evaluation, but also the tools and approach required to execute the testing.

Outside of cost, the primary consideration in using any external test vendor is the matter of trust. The enterprise must be certain that the service supplier can be trusted to perform the tasks on time, within budget, and in confidence. Note that outsourcing a test exercise does not totally devolve the burden of this work from the enterprise. The enterprise using the contracted services must ensure that the vendor is meeting its needs, that these requirements are well understood, and that the results are in line with expectations. This approach should be viewed as a partnership with the contractor, where the benefits and responsibilities are mutually recognized.

Selecting the right organization to outsource testing activities to for a particular project can often be challenging. Evaluation of potential candidates requires the same process as would be used to select a managed service provider or professional services firm to provide design functions. A request for references of similar test engagements, skill levels, and certifications of test engineers, and representative samples of project plans, test plans, and test results documentation, is required to make an informed decision. Remember that the enterprise engineer that coordinates the contract, rather than the test vendor, will ultimately be held responsible for the failure of a networking project that was improperly tested or inadequately documented.

Test Lab Facilities Design

The exercise of designing a lab facility is very similar to the efforts involved in designing the production network. The primary objective in the lab design, from a topological perspective, is to enable the test area to mimic the production network environment to the largest extent possible, within given budgetary constraints. Over and above that, the physical aspects of the lab facility, explored in the previous cost discussions, also need attention from a design perspective.

Functional Lab Design: Selecting the Hardware and Software

The corporate test lab should mirror the standard computing and networking environment in use within the enterprise. Ideally, a lab designer should be familiar with not only the architectural and operational aspects of this environment, but also the scope and charter of the test organization that will operate the lab. For example, a lab designer should not invest excessively in server or storage equipment if the test organization's charter is limited to testing the network infrastructure. When possible, the lab designer should enlist the support of the executive lab sponsors, in addition to the production design architects and operations engineers, who can provide invaluable input to the test facility's development. Most enterprises will not be engaged in abstract "black box" performance or feature testing. An enterprise's interest in testing is to assess the operation of the item for use in the production environment. As such, the results of any lab testing will be relevant only if the environment is tailored to replicate the production network as much as possible. The lab designer should consider the following when selecting hardware and software for the lab:

- Type and quantity of network nodes needed (actual equipment as well as those that can be simulated with test tools)

- Simulation tools (capabilities and availability)

- WAN and LAN physical specifications

- End systems (hosts and servers) needed to verify operations

- IT software applications (commercial and custom)

Physical Design

The amount of funding receivedfor a lab project will determine the level of sophistication that a team will be able to add into the physical design. Whereas the right level of funding will allow an organization to build an impressive showcase for emerging technology, inadequate funding will result in a lab that more closely resembles an equipment storage room—hot, cramped, dimly lit, with haphazardly strewn cabling that completely obscures the presence of equipment.

The implications of a poor lab design extend beyond that of aesthetics. Operation of the lab facility will be greatly impacted by the physical aspects of the environment. Good physical design will improve productivity and enhance the work environment. The following considerations should be addressed when gathering requirements for a lab's physical design:

- **Square footage:** Be sure to consider rack space, workbenches, intrarack shelving, cable management systems, and storage within the work area and outside of it. Many of the larger lab facilities are constructed as separate "computer rooms" inside a data center so that they can benefit from the power distribution, HVAC, and corporate network access. At a minimum, a lab facility should be controlled in terms of physical access and HVAC capabilities. A smaller lab's requirements could be met with a 15- by 15-foot space with a 10-foot ceiling to accommodate the equipment racks and cable management system. Space-saving measures such as master Keyboard, Video and Mouse (KVM) switches that use one monitor, mouse, and keyboard to control several machines can be used to minimize clutter in these smaller facilities.

- **Power availability and layout:** Consider total power, differing modalities (AC/DC/voltage/connector types), the total number of connection points, your power strip requirements, and the distribution method (overhead or under the floors are most popular). The size and amount of equipment will drive much of your power requirement. Do not forget to take into account cooling, lighting, and UPS when planning. UPS may also require special physical space considerations.

■ **Air conditioning and airflow:** Assess the total cooling load, determine the distribution (under floor, open room/rack-specific methods), review the placement of hot/cold aisles, and ensure that interequipment airflows are minimized (in other words, try to minimize the amount of hot air you are blowing from one piece of gear onto another).

■ **Cabling:** Examine cabling solutions for intrarack and interrack connectivity, as well as interconnects to servers, test tools, and external feeds (such as Internet, production, or video feeds). A large facility may choose to use a structured cabling approach, with racks prewired to rack distribution frames (RDF) and RDFs prewired back to a centralized patching area commonly called a main distribution frame (MDF), as previously shown in Figure 3-1. Also assess the need for appropriate cable troughs and conduits.

■ **Special and free-standing gear:** Determine whether there is a need to support large hardware platforms, such as a Cisco CRS-1 or storage and mainframe systems, which can require their own floor space and special power connections. Ascertain the need for test tools (such as third-party test equipment) and various infrastructure services platforms (such as FTP, TFTP, NTP, DNS, and certificate servers) and address the relevant power and accessibility requirements for them. You must factor these special items into the physical and topological planning previously discussed.

■ **Equipment storage:** Establish a separated, lockable area for storage of valuable unused gear. Assess the need for non-ESD card racks and their relevant sizes, cable storage, shelving, and drawers for consumables (such as SFPs, attenuators, splitters, and connectors). Ensure that the working lab space has sufficient storage to meet the immediate needs of your staff, including cable hangers, small hand tools, power tools, and cable construction tools.

Figure 3-2 shows an example layout of a large lab facility. This example follows the recommendations made for computer room design in ANSI/TIA-942, "Telecommunications Infrastructure Standard for Data Centers."

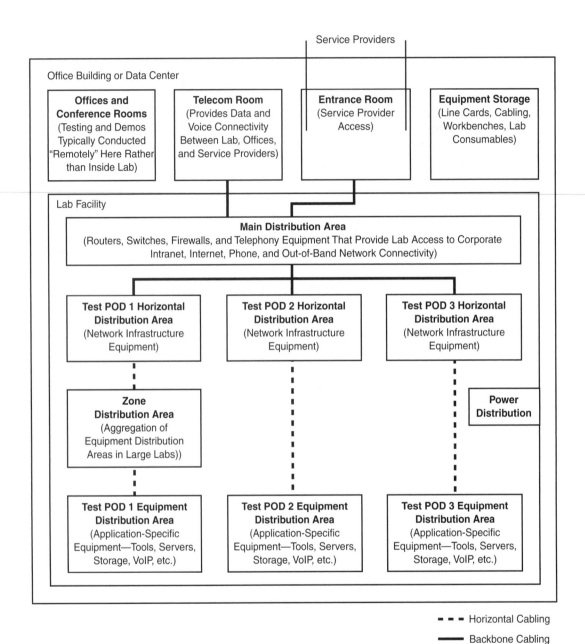

Figure 3-2 *Example Large Test Lab Layout Based on Standard Computer Room Design*

Note This standard specifies the minimum requirements for telecommunications infra-structure of data centers and computer rooms, including single-tenant enterprise data centers and multitenant Internet hosting data centers. The topology proposed in this document is intended to be applicable to any size data center.

Equipment Cabinet Floor Plan Layout

The physical space that the equipment cabinets will occupy will depend on several factors:

- Type of equipment

- Amount of equipment (initial and future growth)

- Cabinet size

- Aisle spacing

- Amount and location of freestanding equipment

- Room dimensions and obstructions

Estimating the type and amount of equipment needed in a test lab can sometimes be a challenge, particularly when you are trying to forecast future needs. The types of equipment needed vary from lab to lab, based on the particular network architecture and focus of the design elements to be tested. In many cases, the CAPEX budget will determine what is available for initial installation, leaving the staff with the task of estimating what will be needed in the future. This future estimation should ideally be based on a 5- to 10-year expected growth forecast, unless there are other considerations that will cause the facility to be used for a shorter duration (such as the project-based funding model, covered earlier).

Calculating the number of cabinets needed for the facility is a fairly simple exercise, once the type and quantity of equipment is known. Most vendors follow standard rack unit (RU) height design with their products. While an organization might be tempted to fully populate its cabinets with equipment when developing the provisioning plan, this should be avoided if possible. It is common practice in many labs not to populate the upper third, or sometimes even the upper half, of lab cabinets (depending on the devices installed in the cabinet), due to the inability to efficiently cool the upper half of a rack. In some cases, there is also a structural component, which means that if all racks are completely filled, the subfloor may not be able to handle the weight. In considering the cooling implications for the cabinets, take a conservative approach when planning how many cabinets will be necessary to house the equipment; we recommend no more than 75 percent cabinet subscription.

After the number of required cabinets is known, determine the physical footprint of the equipment cabinets themselves. Taking into consideration the exceptional depth of today's equipment (for example, the Cisco Carrier Routing System or many blade server implementations), and the cable management and power delivery systems that will occupy the rear of the cabinet, a deeper cabinet will serve better than a shallower one. A conservative approach would entail planning for cabinets up to 48 inches deep and 32 inches wide. Planning for such extrawide cabinets will help facilitate cable management within the enclosure, particularly if you plan to employ a closed cabinet design with front and rear doors for physical security or environmental purposes. Having plenty of space inside your cabinets for effective cable management also facilitates the effective cooling of your gear and the testing work you will be performing. Having cables hanging in front or behind your test gear can make pulling out or replacing line cards, power supplies, and servers (something you do fairly often during testing) an onerous task.

The final decision to be made before developing an equipment cabinet floor plan regards aisle spacing around the perimeter and in between cabinet rows. In many cases, site-specific safety codes ultimately dictate this, but in general, allocate at least four feet of aisle space around the perimeter of the cabinet rows. This should be adequate for people to pass unobstructed, even with equipment pallets in tow. Interrow aisle spacing will depend on the cabinet orientations, in particular whether a hot-aisle/cold-aisle strategy is employed.

Note   In its simplest form, the hot-aisle/cold-aisle design involves lining up server and other equipment racks in alternating rows with cold air intakes facing one way and hot air exhausts facing the other. The rows composed of rack fronts are called cold aisles. Typically, cold aisles face air conditioner output ducts. The rows the heated exhausts pour into are called hot aisles. Typically, hot aisles face air conditioner return ducts.

Because all cooling architectures (except for fully enclosed rack-based cooling, as required by some blade server implementations) benefit dramatically from hot-aisle/cold-aisle layout, this method is a recommended design strategy for any floor layout.

Note   The use of the hot-aisle/cold-aisle rack layout method is well known and the principles are described in other books and whitepapers, such as *Thermal Guidelines for Data Processing Environments, Second Edition* (2009), published by the American Society of Heating, Refrigerating and Air-Conditioning Engineers (ASHRAE), and the 2002 whitepaper from the Uptime Institute titled "Alternating Cold and Hot Aisles Provides More Reliable Cooling for Server Farms."

Aisle spacing between cabinet rows is determined when you establish the aisle pitch for the cabinet locations. Aisle pitch is the distance from the center of one cold aisle to the center of the next cold aisle, either to the left or right, and is based on floor tile size. Data centers often use a seven-tile aisle pitch. This measurement allows two 2- by 2-foot floor tiles in the cold aisle, 3 feet in the hot aisle, and a 42-inch allowance for the depth of the cabinet or rack. For larger cabinets or cabinets with high-power servers, there may be a need to use an eight-tile pitch to facilitate airflow.

The sample floor plan in Figure 3-3 is an example of the number of large equipment cabinets one could expect to fit into a relatively small (600 square foot) test lab.

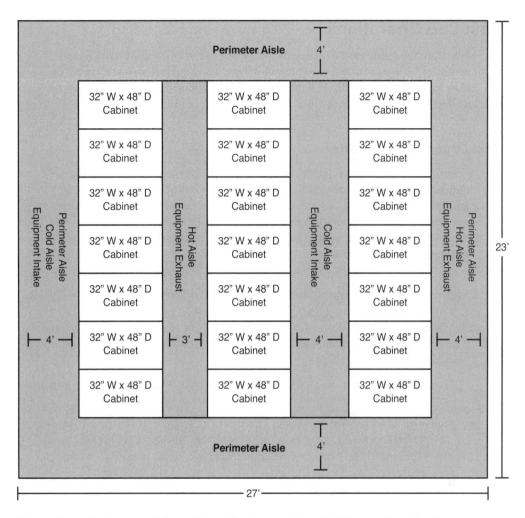

Figure 3-3 *Equipment Cabinet Floor Plan Layout for a 600-Square-Foot Facility*

Armed with these design considerations, you are now ready to design your lab facility. This exercise may be as simple as a meeting over coffee and drawing some diagrams on paper, or complex enough to require several weeks and multiple individuals' focused efforts. In either case, taking the time to understand the objectives and requirements of the test lab, and the commitment that the enterprise is willing to make to it, will help to clarify expectations and drive the building of a superior testing facility to a successful conclusion.

Test Lab Operations

Many differing operational models exist for running a test lab, and are usually outgrowths of the culture of the enterprise itself. The following provides an example of a model for operating a test lab and may be applicable to a medium-sized to large corporate structure.

Test Organization Charter

A formal test organization typically has a documented charter, which defines the operational guidelines for the group. Such a document helps others to understand the lab's capabilities and business focus, aids in organizing the relationships and engagement approach with other corporate entities, and guides the lab staff in their direction and operation. Having a formal charter helps alleviate the requests for your team to test the latest desktop image if you are a team focused on network testing; and more importantly, it should minimize the times you will hear "I did not know your team did that."

Examples of the types of statements that may appear in the charter include the following:

- **Mission statement:** A formal, short, written statement of the purpose of a company or organization. A mission statement for a test lab group may look something like the following:

  "To provide testing services relative to corporate initiatives, with a focus on improvements to network stability, and easing of integration of new services."

- **Statement of focus:** A short, written statement of the types of testing activities that the organization would primarily address. Some test organizations, for example, would focus solely on network infrastructure testing, while others may expand this focus to network services (telephony, video, servers) as well. A statement of focus for a test lab group may look something like the following:

  "To address any and all production-related testing as it may pertain to new product introduction, protocol enhancements, services improvements/changes, and scalability in the network, voice, and video infrastructure."

- **Responsibility directive:** A short, written statement that describes the purpose of the test lab, as it relates to the architectural process. A responsibility directive for a test lab group may look something like the following:

  "All network change plans must include test verification by the test facility team prior to adoption in production."

- **Engagement statement:** A short, written statement that describes how the test lab organization should be engaged. An engagement statement for a test lab group may look something like this:

  "Engage the test team at the earliest opportunity in project planning. Contact us via testteam.ourcompany.com or e-mail testgurus@ourcompany.com."

The test team should establish a website or something similar (wikis have become very popular) to describe its charter, capabilities, and engagement process in greater detail for use by the rest of the organization.

Team Roles and Responsibilities

When building a testing organization, you will likely be required to define the roles and responsibilities, as well as create job descriptions for the staff you will be employing. As mentioned earlier in this chapter, most test teams of any significant size have the following:

- **Test lab manager:** This individual provides a leadership presence to guide the team's direction, productize its services, control budgets, manage staff, and address other management issues as they may surface.

- **Project manager:** If appropriate, the team may also include a project manager who manages individual project flows, tracks schedules, and acts as an engagement "controller" to ensure that the team is not overloaded with concurrent work to the point that it becomes unsuccessful.

- **Lab administrator:** A lab of significant size will also benefit from the establishment of a lab administrator who focuses on lab operational requirements, ensures availability of equipment and sundries, helps manage resource allocations and budget, and generally ensures smooth operation of the test facility. In all likelihood, the lab administrator will manage the maintenance arrangements and undertake the repair and replacement of defective gear as needed.

- **Senior test engineers:** The technical members of the group will likely include one or more senior members who guide the group technologically, scope initial work efforts, and undertake highly complex test efforts. Senior test engineers are an escalation point for the rest of the testing staff in all of their efforts. They often are the liaisons between senior network architecture staff, operations engineers, and other project stakeholders, and the rest of the engineers on the testing team.

- **Test engineers:** These engineers conduct the bulk of the testing work and write most of the test result documents. These team members work with the senior test engineers in executing any work as appropriate. The test team can also be an excellent training ground for operations staff, who may be rotated through the testing facility, and for design engineers and architects, to sharpen their understanding of specific technologies as needed.

- **Part-time staff:** As previously discussed, the test team may also include some members who are university co-op students. These staff members gain the opportunity to learn technology and become exposed to business operations and may end up becoming excellent pretrained recruits for the company upon their graduation. They are often responsible for maintaining the lab inventory, setting up the test beds, and providing assistance with any test execution as needed.

Management Systems

As a testing facility comes online and gear starts arriving, you will find that keeping track of everything can be challenging. Because it is easier to get your management systems online at the same time (or before) your lab infrastructure gear and equipment arrives, you should consider investing in some of the following systems as part of your startup costs.

Equipment Inventory System

As discussed in the "Estimated OPEX to Operate a Test Lab" section earlier in this chapter, in consideration of the significant costs of operating a test lab, an inventory management system is a clear requirement. All gear should be inventoried upon receipt prior to being placed into operation in the lab. The system should be detailed enough to manage product identification (part number, name, serial number, and internal asset tag). As the lab grows, such a system can become invaluable in many of the aspects of the facility's operation, including equipment availability and scheduling, defect management (repair and return), and data for budget and purchasing decisions.

Equipment Scheduling/Lab Checkout Tool

A lab checkout tool can greatly aid in the operation of a lab with multiple users and multiple concurrent tests. Such a system can help prevent overscheduling of equipment for tests and aid the test engineer in finding the equipment needed for a particular work effort. It should provide for both short- and long-term (indefinite) checkout scheduling. A well-designed checkout system closely integrates with the inventory management system to tie the gear in use with appropriate asset management information. The close operation of these tools also greatly aids in budget planning cycles for both equipment and staffing, because they can be employed to report on utilization of the lab resources.

A larger test facility may wish to introduce another layer of management to help keep track of resources from a project management perspective. This tool can support management of project acceptance, costing (if chargebacks are applicable or simply to demonstrate value), and scheduling of equipment and staff, help management of the individual projects in detail, and provide a closure and reporting mechanism.

Team Website

As discussed earlier, the test team should deploy a website or wiki to present a visible focal point to the rest of the organization and to showcase team efforts. This site should also provide a tool that allows users to request a test engagement from the testing team. Such an instrument should have an easy-to-use interface that provides sufficient information to begin the engagement exercise without being so onerous as to hamper client usage.

At a minimum, the GUI should present fields for the following:

- Requestor name

- Organization and contact information

- Requested engagement dates

- A brief description of test needs and business drivers

- An option for inclusion of more detailed information such as "bill of materials" data and topology descriptions or diagrams if available

The system should automatically notify appropriate team members of the request (at least the manager and project manager) and provide an expected response interval to the user.

There should also be a secured area where documentation such as test plans, network information, test logs, and test reports can be maintained for the consumption of the test team only. As the test team works various exercises, the methodologies, scripts developed, and ancillary information that is learned should be captured and saved in this repository. This data can prove invaluable in efforts to streamline new engagements and help train future staff in lab operations.

Other Operational Considerations

The need for security in the lab facility cannot be overstated. All lab facilities need to be established in a secure manner, with access limited to authorized staff members. The physical security requirement exists both to protect the valuable equipment and to avoid the cost of test cycle interruptions. In this same context, fire prevention and control considerations should lead to the provisioning of smoke detection equipment, manual fire control devices, and, possibly, automated systems. The requirements for these safety devices are likely already addressed by corporate building policies. In addition, the ready availability of first-aid kits is highly recommended along with staff training with respect to its usage.

Summary

This chapter focused on the business and organizational requirements involved in building and running a successful testing organization. The chapter covered the costs and planning associated with starting the test facility, and the physical considerations that should go into it. You also learned about the staffing requirements and other OPEX costs of a typical testing organization. In addition, the chapter explored outsourcing your organization's testing, and some of the pros and cons that come with that approach. Also, you learned what designing a typical network test lab infrastructure would include. Finally, the chapter covered test lab operations and a testing group charter. The next chapter explains how to craft the test approach and how to get ready to conduct your enterprise network testing.

Chapter 4

Crafting the Test Approach

This chapter covers the following topics:

- Motivations for Different Types of Testing
- Test Scoping
- Test Planning
- Choosing the Right Test Tools
- Writing the Test Plan

Chapter 1, "A Business Case for Enterprise Network Testing," stressed the importance of assessing the business reasons for testing as your first step in crafting an effective test approach. In the same way that a network designer would be foolish to specify equipment or make technical recommendations without prior knowledge of customer requirements, a test engineer would be misguided to attempt writing a test plan without first understanding the triggers, scope, motives, and expectations for the test initiative. By rushing ahead and skipping this critical step, you risk missing the mark in your testing, focusing on the wrong types of tests, or capturing erroneous results. This will waste precious time and resources as you continuously redefine your test plan; add, remove, or modify equipment to your lab topology; rerun your test cases; and generate reports. Taking time to identify the objectives and outline an assessment is critical before you ever step foot into the lab. Only after the following questions are answered should you begin to write a detailed test plan or build a lab topology:

- What are the test triggers?
- Who is requesting the test and what are their motives?
- How much testing is necessary and what constitutes success?

- What is the impact of test failure and what are the known risks?

- What are the resources (people, lab equipment, and test tools) required to execute the test?

As discussed in Chapter 2, "Testing Throughout the Network Lifecycle," a complimentary relationship between network testing and design functions exists in organizations that execute enterprise architecture effectively. We explained how structured testing complements and validates design deliverables, by providing examples of the different types of test requests that you can expect throughout the network's lifecycle.

This chapter will begin to fill in the practical details of what is necessary to build an effective approach toward different types of test requests. It begins with a suggested approach for assessing and scoping a test project, and offers guidance and best practices for the following considerations:

- How to identify test case scenarios

- How to develop a lab prototype

- How to choose the proper test tools necessary to execute the different types of tests

- How to write a detailed test plan

As with most technical undertakings, there is no absolute right way to approach systems testing. We do not promote ours as the only way to conduct successful testing. However, this is a proven method that will improve your chances of getting it right the first time.

Motivations for Different Types of Testing

The first step in assessing the objective and scope of a test effort is to understand the reasons for why it was requested, and the motives of the people or organization that requested it. In some instances, your client may be able to clearly tell you why they want testing and what they expect from testing, while others may only be able to tell you that their proposed deployment "is critical to the business and must be tested." In cases of the latter, you will need to rely on knowledge of your client, personal experience, and industry best practices to determine the objective and scope of the test effort. Following are some of the most common triggers and motivations associated with the different types of testing.

Proof of Concept Testing

Proof of concept (POC) testing is normally conducted during the Plan Phase of a new network design, or prior to the introduction of a new technology or service into an operational network. A network architect will often request that a POC test be completed to ensure that a new product or technology will work as expected in the context of their design. Successful POC testing is often the criteria for purchasing or moving into the low-level design (LLD) phase of a project, and in some cases POC testing is a mandatory milestone to be completed before purchasing approval will be granted. In general, POC testing should be conducted systematically but persist only as long as necessary to prove that a proposed solution will work as expected. An exception to this general rule is when POC testing is used as a means to differentiate between similar products as part of a "bake-off" test. These types of tests often require extensive scale and feature testing in order to provide the necessary data to differentiate between competing products.

Network Readiness Testing

Network readiness testing is often included as part of a network assessment to determine whether a production network can meet the needs of a new application or service, and to identify any gaps that may hinder it. This type of testing is commonly conducted prior to deploying a Cisco Unified Communications (UC) solution, to help an enterprise determine whether its network will be able to meet the stringent requirements associated with real-time applications. Network readiness testing for UC often involves test tool injection and measurement of synthetic application traffic across a live network to predict how the actual application will perform when network elements are running in steady-state conditions, during day-to-day operations. Success criteria for this type of testing is easy to define because the SLA requirements with respect to delay, jitter, and loss are well understood for UC applications. Careful planning and coordination is often necessary when this type of network readiness testing is conducted so that production service disruption can be avoided.

Design Verification Testing

As the name suggests, this type of testing occurs during the Design Phase of a network's lifecycle. Design verification testing is similar to POC testing in that both are performed in order to gain confidence in a proposed design or solution prior to deployment. Design verification testing is typically more extensive than POC testing, however, as it often represents the last opportunity before implementation to fully examine whether all aspects of a design will function as expected when subjected to various stress conditions. Design verification testing is focused on performance, scalability, failover, operations, and manageability elements of a design. The output from this type of testing often feeds into the software recommendations, hardware specifications, and device configuration templates of an LLD document.

Hardware Certification Testing

Hardware certification testing often occurs during the Optimize Phase of a network's lifecycle as new platforms are introduced into existing operational networks to provide enhanced capabilities, better performance, or to replace equipment that is reaching end-of-life (EOL) status from a vendor supportability standpoint. Engineering and operations groups of an enterprise often require that hardware certification testing be completed before a product can be deployed in the production network. While it is generally accepted that equipment vendors will subject new platforms to a variety of tests during the product development cycle, there is no substitute for customized, enterprise-specific testing to uncover defects or feature limitations that would not be found otherwise. It is nearly impossible for an equipment manufacturer to predict how a customer might deploy every feature, or the level of stress that a platform might be subjected to in an operational network with unique requirements. Likewise, it would be impractical for an equipment vendor to perform interoperability testing with every other vendor's equipment that might be deployed on a customer network. Hardware certification tests generally are simple in nature and shorter in duration as compared to other tests because they focus mainly on "unit level" test cases that can be conducted on relatively small lab topologies.

Network Operating System Testing

This type of testing is often required by the operations teams responsible for OS upgrades and is similar in scope to hardware certification testing. Network OS testing is often performed during the Optimize Phase of a network's lifecycle, as operating software reaches its end of life, or when new features or bug fixes are needed. Overall, there are many different levels of network OS testing that can be undertaken, some of which are only appropriate during the product development phase by the equipment vendor test groups. The most common types of tests conducted by clients are software acceptance tests, which are a customized suite of tests executed to verify general feature functionality. Regression tests are a variant of software acceptance tests, in which critical features that worked in the past are retested to ensure that they are still functioning properly in the new OS. The scope of network OS testing ranges from small, short-duration tests (such as bug fix verifications), to longer-duration, multithreaded tests that involve multiple features to be verified in parallel.

Migration Plan Testing

One of the most challenging and critical aspects of a networking project is the migration of users and services to a new network infrastructure. Even the best network designs are destined for failure if they cannot be implemented without causing extended service outages. Yet despite the risks, many network architects spend a disproportionate amount of time focused on the "end state" of their network designs, developing migration plans as an afterthought, if at all. A good migration plan should address how routing protocols and applications will interact when the network is partially migrated, providing success indicators and a backout plan when unexpected behavior is encountered during a migration. Testing of a migration plan is an essential part of the design process for networking projects of any scale. It is sometimes a requirement of the implementation or operations groups responsible for making changes to the network. In some instances, a migration plan can be developed during a design verification lab test effort by repeating the baseline and performance test scripts on the interim topology consisting of the old and new networks.

A high-level migration test plan approach for a new network backbone might look something like this:

Step 1.   Build a prototype of the old and new network backbone topologies.

Step 2.   Run a baseline test using known traffic patterns from the existing and new networks.

Step 3.   Physically and logically interconnect the old and new network backbone topologies, as they will be connected during the migration. If this will take multiple steps, each interim topology should be tested.

Step 4.   Run the same set of baseline tests on the interim network that you ran on the old network.

Step 5.   Simulate device and circuit failure scenarios in each interim step of the migration in order to understand the impact on test traffic and whether any collateral damage occurs.

Step 6.   Disconnect the old portion of the network or reprovision it on the new backbone. This should be done the same way as the migration plan will be done. If this will be done in multiple steps in your plan, you should test each one of them.

Step 7.   Repeat the set of baseline tests.

Step 8.   Run a set of new tests that exercise any new features or services to be offered by the new network.

A migration test would be considered successful when the baseline test results meet or exceed the performance of the old network and the features offered by the new network are verified.

Network Ready for Use Testing

A network ready for use (NRFU) test typically is executed on a new greenfield network infrastructure as a last step in certifying that it is ready to carry production traffic. During an NRFU test, network devices are methodically checked to ensure that they have been implemented according to the design specifications and are running in an error-free state.

Some of the tests commonly associated with NRFU testing include the following:

- Device tests (hardware/software inventory, power, syslog error checking)

- Circuit tests (throughput, delay, jitter, errors)

- Routing tests (adjacencies, routing table consistency)

- Traffic tests (end-to-end traffic testing)

- Network service tests (multicast, QoS, WAN acceleration)

■   Application tests

■   Management/NMS/security tests

In some cases, the NRFU testing extends to a limited production pilot where a low-risk site or portion of the network is cut over to the new network and monitored closely for a "probationary" period of time.

Test Scoping

Two questions you can expect from your clients when discussing potential test engagements are

■   "How long will this testing take?"

■   "How much will it cost?"

You would be wise to refrain from giving an answer to either question until you have a good understanding of the scope of what you will be testing. Defining the test scope will help you estimate the extensiveness of the test process and help you forecast costs. For example, a bug fix verification test is a test with a narrow scope and would not normally require a complicated lab topology to be built or an extended set of test cases to complete. The test scope would broaden as more devices, features, and test cases are added to the requirements.

It is sometimes difficult to define the scope of a test when you do not have a technical understanding of the solution or design you are being asked to verify. For this reason, consider involving your most senior technical people during the scoping exercise, despite their protestations to avoid it. Whenever possible, you should spend time with the network architects to review the proposed network design prior to scoping a test so that you can accurately estimate the necessary tools, people, and equipment.

The sections that follow describe some considerations when scoping a test engagement, the steps for which are as follows:

Step 1.   Categorize the type of test to be completed.

Step 2.   Identify project stakeholders.

Step 3.   Identify indicators of test success.

Step 4.   Estimate the resources required to complete the test.

Step 5.   Identify risks.

Step 6.   Identify the timeline for completion.

Step 1: Categorize the Type of Test to Be Completed

Identify the reasons for testing and try to determine whether the type of test fits into one of the categories described earlier in the chapter. Try to clearly articulate the trigger and objectives in one sentence, such as:

- *"Proof of concept test*, with the goal of gaining confidence and experience with the new voice gateway platform."

- *"Network ready for use test* to certify the new data center in Syracuse is operationally ready to be cut over into production and carry live customer data."

- *"Design verification test* to ensure that the next-generation WAN design will work and support company business needs for the next 3 to 5 years."

Categorizing a test as shown in the previous examples will allow you to consider and compare a potential test with similar engagements you may have completed in the past.

Step 2: Identify Project Stakeholders

Stakeholders are people or groups who have a vested interest in the outcome of the test initiative. They may include the company leadership, representatives from the business units, application developers, network architects, network operations staff, and contracted professional services firms. Early in the project, work with your project sponsor to create a list of all possible stakeholders so that you can develop an effective communications plan. The goal is to gain and sustain commitment to the test initiative, and to avoid negative behaviors such as stalling or undermining from people who demand to be "in the loop." It is a good idea to solicit input to the test plan from a wide variety of stakeholders so that a comprehensive approach can be taken.

For very large test efforts requiring input from multiple stakeholders, it may be helpful to assign and designate them using a well-known method from organizational design known as RACI (Responsible, Accountable, Consulted, Informed):

- **Responsible:** This person is responsible for completing a task.

- **Accountable:** This person will be called to account if the task is not completed and may manage the person who is responsible for completing the task. Project managers often have this role.

- **Consulted:** Though not accountable or responsible for completion, this person is consulted about aspects of the task.

- **Informed:** The holder of this passive role is kept informed but isn't accountable or responsible for tasks.

Step 3: Identify Indicators of Test Success

It is critical to get agreement from the stakeholders on what constitutes testing success; otherwise, exiting the test may become difficult. You don't need to identify success criteria for each and every test case during the Scoping Phase—that will come later during test planning. What you need to understand at this point is what constitutes overall test success, so that you have a good idea of which elements are important to build test cases around. Here are some examples of success criteria for various types of tests.

Network Design Verification Test

- Test Pass Criteria:

    - 100 percent of test cases have been executed.

    - Network design meets customer requirements with respect to feature functionality, performance, and convergence around failures.

    - No Severity 1 or 2 defects encountered.

    - All Severity 3 defects (if any) have been documented/filed and workarounds have been provided.

- Test Fail Criteria:

    - Severity 1 defects are found with no workaround in an area critical to the solution.

    - Severity 2 defects are found that can put in jeopardy the on-time deployments of the solution.

    - One or more "key" features are missing, are not operational, or don't meet customer-specific requirements.

Network Ready for Use Test

- Test Pass Criteria:

    - 100 percent of test cases have been executed.

    - All device hardware and line cards power up properly and successfully pass self-test diagnostics.

    - All devices configured with the hardware and Cisco IOS Software specified in the LLD document.

    - No device crashes observed during testing.

    - All circuits passing traffic in an error-free state.

    - Test traffic reroutes around failures within the constraints of the SLA specified in the LLD.

- All devices can be monitored and managed by the NMS platforms in the NOC.

- Test Fail Criteria:

    - Device crashes observed during testing that cannot be correlated to faulty hardware.

    - Circuit errors incrementing.

    - Excessive errors seen in device logs that cannot be explained.

    - Test traffic does not converge around failures within the constraints of the SLA specified in the LLD.

    - Devices unreachable by the NMS platforms in the NOC.

Step 4: Estimate the Resources Required to Complete the Test

An estimation of the people, lab equipment, and test tools needed to complete the testing activities will be necessary to develop a reasonably accurate project timeline, and to provide pricing for the test if procurement is necessary. When estimating the people required, be sure to account for the skill level and number of people required for each of the necessary tasks; for example:

- Test plan development (high skill level)

- Equipment cabling and lab assembly (low skill level)

- Test plan execution (medium to high skill level, depending on technology and scale of test)

- Test results development (medium to high skill level, depending on technology and scale of the test)

It will be difficult to accurately estimate equipment resources needed for testing unless fairly complete design documentation is available for review. At a minimum, you should request a high-level network topology diagram so that you can identify any major components lacking in your lab inventory that will need to be procured. This will have an impact on the price and timeline for test execution. Be sure to consider that special software licenses may be needed if you are conducting applications testing. If new equipment will need to be installed, consider the space, power, and cooling impact to existing facilities. When scoping test engagements where unfamiliar platforms or new technology is involved, it may be necessary to allocate additional time for staff training or even account for assistance from outside consultants.

Test tools are also lab assets and need to be considered when estimating resources. Choosing the proper tool for a particular test is an art in itself, as explained in a later section, aptly titled "Choosing the Right Test Tools." Work with your test tool vendors to help you understand whether their products have the capabilities to perform the types of tests you will be executing. They are an invaluable resource, and many of the larger vendors often lease test tools for the duration of a test engagement if necessary.

Step 5: Identify Risks

A risk is an event or condition that, if it occurs, could negatively impact your test project. Sometimes risks are outside your control, such as when an equipment or software manufacturer cannot ship critical hardware or tools on time. This type of risk can be mapped to external dependencies. In other cases, risks can be mapped to internal dependencies, as in the case of having to hire staff with the appropriate skill set to complete a test. Tests that do not have clear objectives or well-documented designs present a risk of going over budget as the test team wastes time testing the wrong features or design scenarios. A few of the most common risk factors to consider when planning test schedules include the following:

- Shipping issues with equipment

- Third-party equipment requiring special skills from an outside vendor

- Lack of responsiveness from customer technical leaders or decision makers

- Contention for equipment due to a critical outage in another test bed or production area of the company

- Personnel without appropriate skills

- Personnel leaving the group/company

Step 6: Identify the Timeline for Completion

Large testing projects often require contributions from multiple people across different departments and even companies. Good teamwork, clear communications, and dedication to the project are necessary so that testing of a particular design or solution does not last forever. Because network testing is commonly triggered by a proposed network deployment, deadlines are often readily available and documented in an overall project plan. A challenge you will often face is developing a realistic test timeline that allows you to execute your testing thoroughly, while at the same time meeting the deadlines of the project. It is often helpful to allocate time to each of the various test phases when constructing your timeline; for example:

- Assessment of Objectives: 1 week

- Test Case Planning: 2 weeks

- Test Lab Setup: 2 weeks

- Test Execution: 2 weeks

- Test Documentation and Analysis: 1 week

Understand that there are dependencies that may affect your timeline, causing it to slip past the eight calendar weeks given in the preceding example. For example, you will not be able to move into the test execution phase if you are waiting for critical equipment or test tools to be procured, as identified in the assessment phase. Also, it is extremely important to obtain stakeholder feedback and signoff on your test plan prior to moving into your lab setup. Otherwise, you risk the chance of last-minute test changes or additions being requested by the stakeholders. A clear and continuous communications plan during this process is necessary to maintain an accurate test timeline.

Once the goals, objectives, and test scenarios are clearly stated and acknowledged by the stakeholders, you should be able to define success criteria, execute the tests, deliver the results, and exit the engagement.

Test Planning

Now that you and your client clearly understand and agree on the test scope, objectives, and criteria for success, it is finally time to roll up your sleeves and start working on the test plan. As always, it is important to collaborate with the stakeholders on the test plan to determine specifics regarding the application characteristics, behaviors, and new features that are expected of the new system. The prototype network system, equipment specifications, test cases, test tools, data to be collected, and results format must also be discussed and agreed upon. This is an important step in the process because it requires many decisions and significant teamwork.

Design the Functional Prototype Network System

For most types of tests, a working prototype network system of the intended design will serve as the platform upon which functionality, operation, and performance of the new system will be evaluated. A prototype network system is commonly illustrated in a set of network topology diagrams that represent a miniaturized version of the end-state network.

Note   NRFU and network readiness tests typically do not require working prototypes to be built because testing and evaluation are conducted on the preproduction or operational network.

Designing the working prototype for the lab requires experience, creativity, ingenuity, and a deep understanding of the network design, solutions, and technologies to be evaluated. An awareness of the test triggers and motivations of the clients requesting the test is also necessary so that the right aspects of the design are represented and modeled. The first challenge you will face when designing the prototype is how much of the network system will need to be implemented to convince your client that the design meets business and technical requirements. The working prototype must be functional and able to demonstrate performance under stress and scale conditions, but it rarely needs to be a full-scale implementation of the new system. The design and scale of a prototype will vary, depending on the type of test you are conducting and what features or components of the design must be showcased for your clients. How little or much of the network is represented in the prototype will be bounded by the people, money, equipment, and time you have to complete the test.

Use the information you collected during the Scoping Phase to help you determine the size and design of the network prototype, particularly the input and requirements from the key stakeholders. Whereas the design architect may be primarily focused on technical issues, such as validating a routing design or gaining performance benchmarks, network operations may be concerned only with the manageability and usability benefits of the new design. Pay attention to corporate politics and organizational structure with the client. For example, the primary stakeholder funding the project may be someone from the business side of an organization, possibly having rejected designs that the stakeholder considered overbuilt and expensive. The stakeholder's motivation might be to evaluate a "bronze standard" version of the design, composed of less costly components.

Constructing a High-Level Lab Topology Diagram

Early in the Plan Phase, you need to process all the input gathered from the Scoping Phase and develop a high-level topology diagram to start the test plan dialog with your clients. The high-level topology diagram is your initial draft of what the final lab network topology will look like, and it should be one of the first documents you share with your customer when discussing your approach. This diagram should include the major devices, including routers, switches, firewalls, servers, workstations, telephony, video, WAN simulators, test equipment, and so forth, that will be necessary to conduct the tests. Connections between the various devices should be shown, using "clouds" where appropriate to represent elements that will provide connectivity to the system, but not necessarily be under evaluation, such as a provider Multiprotocol Label Switching (MPLS) backbone or the Internet.

Figure 4-1 illustrates an example of a high-level lab topology diagram.

Note the relative lack of detail as compared to a typical network topology diagram. There are no IP addresses, equipment hardware configuration details, circuit speed indicators, or port numbering information. This is completely acceptable for a high-level test diagram considering that its purpose at this point is simply to gain consensus on the topology that you are proposing, and to serve as a reference to the test cases you will be developing. You will add details to this diagram to facilitate the lab build, and you most likely will be adding test-specific diagrams that illustrate particular test cases when it comes time to finalize the test plan.

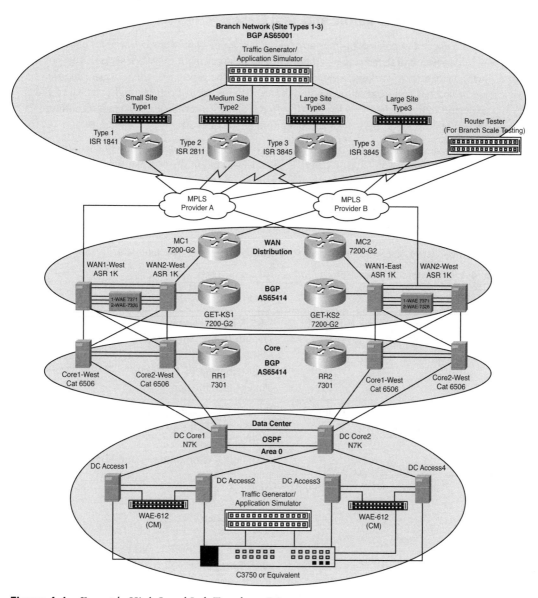

Figure 4-1 *Example High-Level Lab Topology Diagram*

Identifying the Test Suites and Test Cases

A test case in the context of internetworking is a set of conditions or variables under which a tester will determine whether or not a design element (network service, component, or feature) is working correctly. Test cases are the essence of the test plan, and they are sometimes collected or aggregated into test suites. Identifying the right test cases and expected output is an art form in itself, often requiring a series of conversations with the project stakeholders, architects, and operators of the network.

A simple description of the test cases you expect to run, and accompany the network topology diagram you have prepared, is sufficient to begin the test plan dialog. Your client may already have some ideas of the kinds of tests they want to see, so you should request their input right away. However, some clients have no idea on how testing is conducted; in these situations, you need to rely on your own testing experience and an understanding of the design goals, test triggers, and motivations for the testing.

A sample list of test suites and cases would look something like Table 4-1.

Table 4-1 *Example Test Suites and High-Level Test Cases*

Test Suite #	Test Suite	Test Case
1	Open Shortest Path First (OSPF) Routing	ABR Summarization Default Route Announce OSPF NSSA Redistribution BGP to OSPF Timer Optimizations
2	Border Gateway Protocol (BGP) Routing	Data Center iBGP Optimizations CE-PE eBGP Optimizations BGP Aggregation BGP Policy (Communities and Local-Pref)
3	Quality of Service (QoS)	Marking Queuing Traffic Shaping Policing Remarking at CE-PE to MPLS QoS Transparency Across MPLS CoPP
4	Cisco Wide Area Application Services (WAAS)	WCCP Redirects CIFS/FTP Acceleration
5	LAN	Campus Switching Branch Switching HSRP
6	Multicast	PIM Sparse Mode AnyCast RP with MSDP MVPN–MPLS

Table 4-1 *Example Test Suites and High-Level Test Cases*

Test Suite #	Test Suite	Test Case
7	Cisco Performance Routing (PfR)	Fast Reroute Load Balancing Interop with WAAS
8	Cisco Group Encrypted Transport VPN (GET VPN)	Group Member at Branch and WAN Distribution Cooperative Key Servers
9	Network Management	SNMP SSH AAA NTP Logging NetFlow
10	Performance/Scalability	Branch Router Performance (RFC 2544) WAN Route Saturation WAAS Scale
11	Negative Testing	Circuit Path Failover Line Card Failover Route Processor Failover Power Failures MPLS Cloud Hard Failures MPLS Cloud Soft Failures BGP Flapping

Choosing the Right Test Tools

"Take these three items—some WD-40, a vise grip, and a roll of duct tape. Any man worth his salt can fix almost any problem with this stuff alone."
—Clint Eastwood as Walt Kowalski in the movie *Gran Torino*

In contrast to simple home repair, system testing can be very complicated. In most cases, completing system testing without the assistance of sophisticated test tools is not practical or even feasible. Choosing the right tools and knowing how to use them is extremely important to effectively guide and streamline test execution and reporting of results. There are myriad test tools to choose from, and, as with anything else in networking, no single tool is right for every test or for every tester. While it would not be practical to mention every product or type of test tool in this book, the following sections describe some of the common categories of tools and which type of tests they would commonly be used for.

Stateless Packet Generators (Bit Blasters)

Packet generators are one of the simplest, but most important, types of test tool. Many different vendors sell packet generators, and the products differ from each other by many criteria such as the type of interface or interfaces supported, packets per second (pps) capacity, packet and traffic manipulation capability, results reporting, and automation.

Interfaces

Test tool vendors have historically differentiated themselves competitively by producing multiple interface cards for their products. When the world of low-speed WANs included multiple physical interface specifications (such as RS-232, V.35, and X.21), vendors were at the ready with interfaces, adaptor cables, and the like, to allow direct connection to the WAN circuit. With the growing popularity of Ethernet, including Gigabit Ethernet (GE) and 10-Gigabit Ethernet (10GE) offerings from service providers, many vendors now focus their product offerings on these interfaces, with the assumption that if the network under test includes a WAN link, the packets needed for testing can be forwarded to it via a router or switch over a Gigabit or 10-Gigabit Ethernet interface. Thus, the days of specialized interfaces on packet generators are essentially over, and test tool vendors are focused more specifically on the port density (feeds) and capacity (speeds) of their products.

A packet generator with Gigabit Ethernet interfaces generally has an RJ-45 (Category 5-style) interface, and you need to pay attention to the physical media settings of Gigabit or 100-Mbps operation and half-duplex, full-duplex, or duplex autonegotiation. When using a packet generator with a 10-Gigabit Ethernet interface, you are faced with choices about media adapters (XFPs, SFPs, etc.) and single- or multimode fiber cables.

Tool Power/Capacity

Protocol analyzers, such as Wireshark, which can be installed on a laptop computer, are capable of generating a low-speed stream of packets, which may be adequate for a basic feature test. An example of this usage would be to verify that a packet actually traverses a device or network under test, or that it is blocked, for instance, by an access list. Analyzer-based generators may also have the capability to replay a captured stream of packets back into the network. Analyzer-based generators are especially useful for field technicians, who are dispatched to network trouble sites and who are usually troubleshooting either Layer 1/physical-type problems or device misconfigurations.

For lab-based testing, more powerful devices are generally needed; depending on the vendor, you'll find generators of varying capacity. Packet generators at this level are usually chassis based, and you purchase different types of cards (GE or 10GE, etc.) for the chassis. The cards have varying numbers of generating ports (for instance, ten 1-GE ports or four 10GE ports) and you should pay attention to any caveats regarding capacity that the vendor lists in its documentation. For example, a four-port card may be capable of generating at full line rate on only two ports simultaneously, or a port may be able to support full line rate but is limited as to the number of unique streams it can send; you need to know this as you plan your tool use in the test bed. Generally, these types of generators are also capable of packet capture and inspection (protocol analysis) when they are not being used for generation. Again, check the documentation to assess the product capabilities, preferably before you commit to the purchase!

Packet/Traffic Manipulation

There are many ways in which manipulation of the packets being generated is important to network testing. The address fields (both MAC and IP addresses) need to be easily modifiable so that the packets traverse the network as expected. The Layer 4 header can also be modified to specify a certain TCP or UDP port in order to simulate a certain type of network traffic, or test access lists. The packet payload can also be populated with specific content.

Most packet generators have the capability to send errored packets—for instance, packets that are too long, too short, or have bad checksums. This can be important if the purpose of a test is to verify that the device under test (DUT) does not forward an errored packet and, perhaps more importantly, that it does not experience operational stress, such as a lockup, high CPU, and so on, if it receives a steady stream of errored packets. In addition, the generator may allow the engineer to set the packet size within the range of valid sizes, either as fixed or incremental, or variable in accordance with some particular algorithm.

Other popular packet manipulations include the capability to set QoS bits within a packet, such as those used for Type of Service (ToS) or Differentiated Services Code Point (DSCP). These capabilities make it straightforward to test classification or queuing features in a switch or router.

For manipulating the traffic itself, most packet generators provide the capability to send traffic continuously or to send only a specified number of packets, which can be useful if the focus of the test is to determine if there is any packet loss. Other traffic rate possibilities include

- Sending by percentage of line rate

- Send rate in pps

- Send rate in bps

- Send rate determined by interpacket gap

Almost all packet generators on the market today have these packet- and traffic-manipulation capabilities, although the look and feel of the user interface makes some easier to learn and use than others.

Results

In some test scenarios, test results are collected exclusively from the device or network under test. However, the packet generator provides useful information regarding what it is doing, displaying the traffic being generated in metrics such as

- Transmit rate in bps
- Transmit rate in pps
- Number of packets, in total, transmitted
- Number of bytes, in total, transmitted

Most test tools have the further capability to coordinate information such as packets sent and received, and to use timestamps applied to the traffic being generated, across two or more ports in the same chassis, giving the tester important data such as packets lost, flow latency, and, for convergence tests, packet loss duration.

Traffic generators also generally have the capability to save and/or export these statistics in various formats, the most basic of which is a comma-separated values (CSV) file. The more sophisticated test tools are capable of generating graphs or pie charts within their own software, which can be very useful for producing result reports on the fly as tests are completed.

Automation

Some testing is conducted manually, with single-threaded test cases being executed and observed by the test engineer, and with data collected and conclusions drawn as the tool is in use. Other types of testing, such as regression testing, require a longer duration of tool use, with the expectation that test cases are run sequentially, and device and tool configurations are changed automatically as individual tests within a greater test suite are completed. For automated testing, the test tool must have some type of scripting interface. The most popular scripting language in the world of test engineers is Tool Command Language (TCL). Almost all packet generators available today have the necessary support for scripted operation via TCL. Further, most test tools have their own proprietary automation interface. An advantage to the use of TCL for automation is that it is a global application—for instance, with TCL, you could kick off a router configuration change, and then change the test tool configuration and restart the traffic flows. With the test tool's proprietary automation application, it's not likely that you could reconfigure a router.

When to Use Stateless Packet Generators

Packet generators are useful for many different types of tests. They can be used to create a certain level of background traffic as other application-specific tests are run. They can be used for stress testing, where the desired result is something like a performance chart for a DUT—for instance, pps compared with processor CPU. They are also useful for

QoS testing, because the tool allows you to set the ToS or DSCP bits, in addition to manipulating the packets sent in the other ways previously discussed.

Packet Generator Vendors

At press time, the North American market for packet generators is essentially shared by two major corporations—Spirent Communications and Ixia—although there are other "niche market" players:

- **Spirent:** The "classic" Spirent tool is called SmartBits; as additional software capabilities such as stateful traffic generation (see the next section) were added to the basic packet generator, new product names were rolled out. These new names are used to differentiate the SmartBits tool from the one with the new features, even though all products run on the same physical chassis. Spirent's present flagship test platform is TestCenter.

- **Ixia:** Like Spirent, the "first generation" Ixia product and the subsequent "feature-enhanced" software packages for IP traffic run on the same underlying chassis. The packet generator engine is called IxExplorer. Subsequent software packages such as stateful traffic generation are, as of this writing, called IxNetwork and IxLoad. Ixia currently supports another popular packet generator, the Agilent N2X, as Ixia acquired Agilent in 2009. Ixia has renamed the N2X product line IxN2X.

Stateful Packet Generators (Application Simulators)

For many years, packet generators verged on the capability of doing stateful traffic. Examples of what might be deemed "semistateful" capabilities include

- Capability to form a routing protocol (BGP, OSPF, etc.) neighbor relationship with a router and inject routes or other routing information such as OSPF link-state advertisements (LSA) into the network

- Capability to inject a multicast stream at one point in the network, and have a different test port send a "Join" for that stream, thus allowing multicast to be tested without a real multicast source in the test bed

What was lacking in these early tools was the capability to respond to network conditions, as a real TCP-enabled network node does. If a "real" network device running an application over TCP experiences packet loss, the normal behavior is to request a resend of the packets that were not received and then "window" the packet rate down, to avoid future packet loss. A stateless packet generator simply cannot do this, which is a reason why it is sometimes referred to as a "packet blaster."

Another benefit of most stateful tools is their capability to interact with devices in the network, as opposed to simply interacting with other test tool ports. Examples of this capability include tools that can send traffic through firewalls, and those that can work with external servers or server load balancers.

Stateful Generation Tool Vendors

The first commercial stateful packet generator was a product called Chariot, and it consisted of endpoint software, installed on Microsoft Windows or UNIX/Linux computers, and console software, installed on a separate machine. The console computer controlled the endpoints (directing them to send application test traffic) and collected results. The Chariot endpoint software was acquired by Ixia, which integrated the endpoint software into the Ixia chassis line cards, with the display console running on a GUI called IxChariot. The current version of this stateful traffic generator is called IxLoad.

Spirent's Avalanche 3100 appliance solution is similar to Ixia's IxLoad product, with the capability to generate stateful traffic at high speeds for application and performance testing. The Avalanche 3100 is a line-rate, 1-Gbps and 10-Gbps Layer 4–7 multiprotocol stateful traffic performance solution with multi-10-Gbps capacity for stateful application traffic generation.

Results Reporting

To be useful for most types of testing, stateful tools must also provide the same basic types of results as packet generators, such as packets sent/received, packet rate sent/received, loss, and latency. However, stateful tools generally have a more sophisticated format for test results. Because stateful tools generally seek to mimic various types of applications, such as a DNS lookup or an HTTP Get, they need to provide measurements that are reflective of the "user experience" for an application. Examples of such metrics include the following:

- Response time (for instance, on an HTTP Get)
- Throughput (for instance, for an FTP Put)
- Transactions per second (for highly interactive applications with small-packet payloads)
- Voice quality (simulations of Voice over IP, with Mean Opinion Scores being derived from delay, jitter, and loss measurements)
- Connection setup rate or maximum concurrent connections for firewall

As with stateless tools, the product must offer some capability to export results data from the tool, and the GUI for transferring these results should not be overly complex.

When to Use Stateful Packet Generators

Stateful generators are required when testing devices or technologies that do not respond correctly to stateless packets, and they add value to many other kinds of tests. They can be used for many of the same types of tests as packet generators—to provide a level of background traffic, or to stress test a device such as a stateful firewall. More information on choosing stateful or stateless traffic is available in the "Understanding the Different Types of Test Traffic" section of Chapter 5.

When used as a routing protocol generator, injecting routes and traffic that follows them, a stateful tool is well suited to testing the scalability and resilience of a particular network design. A stateful generator can also be used for determining the capacity of a given design, particularly if it includes a low-speed link (such as a WAN link), by drawing on user experience results such as response time, or Mean Opinion Score for VoIP. There are many newer technologies, such as Cisco Performance Routing (PfR), that are best tested with stateful flows; for example, with PfR, the PfR Master Controller makes decisions about managing traffic based on delay and throughput metrics that it can collect from real TCP-based transactions. A stateful generator is also useful for QoS testing, where the test is expected to produce user experience results—for instance, where low-priority TCP flows are expected to back off in the face of congestion, allowing preferred service to other types of traffic.

Network Delay and Impairment Tools

Another important tool in the tester's toolkit is a device, sometimes referred to as a "black box," that allows the injection of delay or impairment into a network under test. When it is crucial to understand how a technology, an application, a device, or a design copes with impairment or delay, this kind of tool is invaluable.

Delay

There are many sources for delay in a network, including serialization delay, propagation or transit delay, and queuing delay with network devices. Delay is especially troublesome if a network includes low-speed links, and if a user application is delay-sensitive. Far too often, applications are tested on a single LAN, with no thought given to how they may perform with a client device located miles away from a server. To properly assess the user experience in the face of delay, a test lab should include the capability to simulate network delay. This is commonly achieved using appliance-based impairment tools, or in some cases extremely (several kilometers) long spools of fiber.

Impairment

As with delay, impairment at the physical layer of the network is another stress that should be considered when rolling out a new design, technology, or application. When bit-level losses cause packet corruption, TCP-based applications detect packet loss and require acknowledged retransmission, which slows down application throughput and user response time. In the face of packet loss, UDP-based applications simply lose integrity; the most obvious instance of this being VoIP traffic, where packet loss is noted by the end users in the form of poor voice quality (for instance, "choppiness" or a sense of the voice dropping in and out). An imprecise way to introduce errors at the physical layer is to wiggle connectors or use cables that are known to have bad conductors or internal shorts. However, it is very difficult to do this scientifically; a cable that is simply a little bit bad one day may be completely "shot" the next, making it impossible to produce the same error condition. It is far better to use a tool that introduces a programmable and predictable amount of impairment.

> **Note**   Fortunately, most devices that function as delay generators also function as impairment generators.

Network Modeling and Emulation Tools

In some instances, it is simply not practical or feasible to send test traffic into a prototype network system built with actual network equipment. Network architects are often asked to evaluate one or more alternatives to a proposed network design, comparing the functionality and estimated performance of various topologies or routing protocol configurations. In these situations, it is often preferable to leverage a modeling tool, which uses software and mathematical models to analyze the behavior of a network, or an emulation tool, which duplicates the functions of a network device by implementing its operating software on another computer.

Network Modeling Tools

Network modeling tools offer the capability to create visual simulations of network topologies by using actual production device configurations as the "seed" files. These tools rely on network device libraries that model the behavior of major networking devices (routers, switches, firewalls) and simulate the interconnection speeds and performance of circuits so that network capacity, resiliency, and application performance can be estimated in a variety of conditions. Network modeling tools are more easily set up than real test topologies and can allow alternatives to be more quickly compared and easily evaluated. Typical applications of network modeling tools include simple tasks such as device configuration audits, to complex sophisticated functions such as capacity planning and application performance analysis. Modeling tools should be used for early decision making on a design. They may point out obvious issues before you build out your test bed, and thus save you valuable time.

Network Modeling Tool Vendors

Cisco Advanced Services teams use several different network modeling tools. They can be invaluable for getting a quick evaluation of the effects a change will have on a large network topology. Three of them are discussed in the following sections.

OPNET Technologies

One of today's market leaders of network modeling tools is OPNET Technologies (www.opnet.com), which provides several products that enable enterprise and service provider planners to analyze how network devices, protocols, applications, and servers operate. OPNET's products model Cisco's and other vendors' device configurations, and they include tools for taking captured data and analyzing which components are the bottlenecks.

Shunra Software

Another one of today's market leaders of modeling tools is Shunra Software (http://www.shunra.com), which offers a suite of products known as Virtual Enterprise Solutions. Like the others, Shunra provides tools that have the capability to simulate network topologies and conditions, allowing users to predict application performance and play "what-if" scenarios prior to deployment. In addition to its software tools, Shunra also offers a hardware-based appliance that offers the capability to plug actual multimedia devices into it so that voice and video can be evaluated subjectively by users, rather than relying solely on numerical presentation. This enables performance to be evaluated against real applications as delay, packet loss, jitter, or reduced bandwidth is introduced.

Analytical Engines

NetRule 7.1, from Analytical Engines (www.analyticalengines.com), is another software modeling tool that allows users to simulate networks and predict application performance. According to the Analytical Engine website, NetRule costs far less than other predictive network applications on the market.

Application Simulation Tools

In the early days of networks, the network infrastructure was managed as its own entity, and the applications were managed separately. Typical IT organizations were often broken into three groups: Network Engineering/Support, Desktop Support, and Application Development/Support. However, the network has evolved to be more application-aware, and the applications have evolved to be more network-aware, creating organizational gray areas on one level, and requiring much more application intelligence in the testing of the network.

As a reflection of the trends toward the blending of applications and infrastructure, testing has evolved from simple single-protocol bit blasting at Layer 2 and Layer 3, to full-fledged stateful multiprotocol, multihost application simulation. Similarly, application testing has evolved from UI-oriented testing, such as that offered by Mercury Interactive and others, to approaches that are much more network-aware.

Application simulation is distinguished from protocol testing because it recognizes that protocols don't exist in a vacuum. Applications are increasingly IP based, complex, and changing at ever-faster rates. Real applications involve vendor proprietary extensions, multiple protocols, and multiple cooperating systems. Testing based on actual network traffic, which includes many not-quite-standard protocol extensions, is much more "real world" than testing based on whatever the standards bodies say should be on the network.

Real application traffic is much different from what is in those standards (after all, standards bodies focus on protocols; very few applications are standardized), so it's essential that application simulation start from reality, not from the ivory tower. Even if there were a standard for applications, the configuration fingerprint of an application in one particular enterprise environment would be unique, and moreover, these configurations change frequently (as components are upgraded, new components are added, new code is rolled out, new users are defined, etc.).

Mu Dynamics (www.mudynamics.com) has taken an approach that is based on actual application traffic, which isolates the application from the transport. The key thing that differentiates application simulation from bit blasting, or from packet replay, is that Mu's approach involves re-creating the same stateful application flow over a dynamically created transport. Application state is maintained by tracking important session variables (cookies, tokens, initial values, sequence numbers, call IDs, etc.) throughout the session, so it is indistinguishable from a session created by a real client device (or server device). In fact, many applications depend on concurrent usage of multiple protocols, involving multiple cooperating systems.

Application simulation testing in these dynamic environments must capture and represent this unique configuration so that the test harness is as close as possible to the behavior of real clients talking to real servers. This is the core reason why Mu Dynamics' Test Suite turns packets into test cases, within an automation framework that magnifies the productivity of test teams by at least an order of magnitude. Application simulation depends on accurately reproducing application flows so that the test traffic is indistinguishable from real application traffic.

Security Testing Tools

Security and penetration test cases are often required components of hardware and software certification test plans. There are several security and penetration test tools available, some of which are marketed commercially, others developed and distributed as freeware by "hackers" on the Internet. In either case, your company's information security team and your code of business conduct should be consulted before any security tool is used on your network.

The best known and most commonly used security tools are referred to as port scanners. Port scanners, such as the open source and free Nmap utility, operate by exploring an address range for active hosts using ping (ICMP ECHO and REPLY) packets. Once active hosts have been identified, they are scanned for open TCP and UDP ports, which can provide indication of the network services operating on that host. A number of these tools support different scanning methods and have different strengths and weaknesses; these are usually explained in the scanner documentation. For example, some are better suited for scans through firewalls, and others are better suited for scans that are internal to the firewall. Some port scanners are capable of gathering additional information, such as the target operating system, using a method known as system fingerprinting. For example, if a host has TCP ports 135 and 139 open, it is most likely a Windows host. Other items such as the TCP packet sequence number generation and responses to ICMP packets (for example, the Time To Live, or TTL, field) also provide a clue to identifying the operating system. Operating system fingerprinting is not foolproof; firewalls can be configured to filter certain ports and types of traffic, and system administrators can configure their systems to respond in nonstandard ways to camouflage the true operating system.

In addition to discovering a target operating system, some scanners are also capable of discovering whether host applications that leverage well-known TCP ports are running. For example, if a scanner identifies that TCP port 80 is open on a host, it can be assumed that the host is running a web service. Even more sophisticated scanners are capable of identifying which vendor's web server product is installed, which can be critical for identifying vulnerabilities that can be exploited. For example, the vulnerabilities associated with Microsoft's IIS server are very different from those associated with Apache web server. This level of application identity can be accomplished by "listening" on the remote port to intercept the "banner" information transmitted by the remote host when a client (a web browser in this example) connects. Banner information is generally not visible to the end user; however, when it is transmitted, it can provide a wealth of information, including the application type, application version, and even operating system type and version. Again, this is not foolproof, because a security-conscious administrator can alter the transmitted banners. The process of capturing banner information is sometimes called banner grabbing.

Many rudimentary security tests on network gear consist of conducting a port scan to check that only the expected ports—those that have services active such as Telnet or SSH—are open. For these basic requirements, a freeware tool such as Nmap should be adequate. When doing more complete or specific security and vulnerability testing, there are several good freeware and commercially available tools on the market. These tend to be much more complex and can require some security and scripting expertise to operate.

Packet-crafting tools such as HPING can be used to assemble and send custom packets to hosts, with the goal of obtaining information from the received replies. These kinds of tools are often used when trying to probe hosts behind a firewall by spoofing a well-known application's TCP port. A tool such as HPING can also be used to create malformed protocol packets in an attempt to launch a denial-of-service (DoS) attack. One common example of such an attack would be to send fragmented BGP packets to a router with the intention of creating a software crash.

Yersinia (www.yersinia.net) is a network tool designed to take advantage of some weaknesses in different network protocols. Attacks for the following network protocols are implemented:

- Spanning Tree Protocol (STP)

- Cisco Discovery Protocol (CDP)

- Dynamic Trunking Protocol (DTP)

- Dynamic Host Configuration Protocol (DHCP)

- Hot Standby Router Protocol (HSRP)

- IEEE 802.1Q

- IEEE 802.1X

- Inter-Switch Link (ISL) Protocol

- VLAN Trunking Protocol (VTP)

You can use a tool like Yersinia to harden your Layer 2 design and implementation.

Other security tools that can be used during testing are common password crackers, wireless scanners, and DoS tools, just to name a few.

Network Protocol Analysis Tools

These tools are often referred to as "sniffers." The best-known one is a free tool called Wireshark (formerly known as Ethereal, found at www.wireshark.org/), which can decode hundreds of protocols, including OSPF, BGP, SNMP, Telnet, and just about any other protocol your production network may have running. Sniffers used with a spanned port on a Cisco switch are invaluable tools for troubleshooting.

Writing the Test Plan

After you and your client have agreed upon the scope of the prototype and the test suites to be carried out, it is time to write a plan that describes exactly how you will test them. A test plan should address the following topics, which will be described in detail in the next few sections of this chapter:

- Overall project scope and objectives

- Test objectives and success criteria

- Test resources required (people, hardware, software, test tools)

- Test schedule

- Developing detailed test cases

Overall Project Scope and Objectives

A brief description of the overall project scope serves as a primer for stakeholders who are unfamiliar with the triggers and motivations for the testing project, in addition to guiding the testers' efforts as they create meaningful test cases. The following are some examples of specific project objectives that were written for particular customers:

- First Integrity Financial plans to build two new data centers in 2010 and is in the process of selecting a networking vendor with the best possible solution. Based on the customer's requirements for the new data centers, the account team has proposed a design that will be proof of concept tested in the Independent Network Services testing facility. Results of the tests will be presented to First Integrity as input into the vendor selection process.

- Spacely Sprockets is in the process of building a next-generation WAN to meet an increased, intergalactic demand for its superior bicycle components. A low-level design developed by Spacely Sprockets' network architects will be verified in the Independent Network Services testing facility to ensure that any weaknesses or limitations are found prior to deployment. Findings during the test effort will be documented and sent to the architects for LLD refinement.

Test Objectives and Success Criteria

Test objectives and s uccess criteria should be developed based on a client's business and technical goals for the network design, and they should include any known SLAs associated with applications or services. The test objectives should simply be to measure the outcome of the test case, and they should be based, as much as possible, on industry standards for all relevant technologies and services. For example, VoIP quality can be measured quantitatively using a Mean Opinion Score.

A MOS score is a subjective test of a call quality that was originally designed by the Bell Companies to quantify the quality of a voice call, with 1 being unacceptable and 5 being superlative.

This information will help the test plan developer define relevant test cases with clearly identifiable success or failure metrics that can be agreed upon by the tester and client. The following are examples of test objectives and success criteria that were written for a particular customer:

- Measure the response time for the Trading application Delta when the network path is 45 percent loaded, which is the average estimated load during trading hours. The acceptance criteria, per the SLA, for Trading application Delta is that the response time must be 300 ms or less.

- Measure the throughput for the Trading application Delta when the network is 90 percent loaded, which is the peak estimated load during a failure scenario in the primary path. The acceptance criteria, per the SLA for Trading application Delta, is that the throughput must be at least 1 Mbps

- Measure the impact to test traffic when various components in the WAN path are failed over. The availability SLA for Trading application Delta specifies that less than .1 percent loss be encountered on a flow running at 1000 pps during a failover event.

Test Resources Required

The people, hardware, software, and test tools necessary to complete the test should be included in the test plan for resource estimation, test build guidance, and historical recording purposes. It is very important to accurately document the exact hardware and software versions of the components that will be tested, as even small variations in hardware or software versions can produce different results with certain test scenarios. This information will provide a valuable baseline should operational issues occur further down the road.

Table 4-2 is an example of how equipment details can be captured in the test plan.

Table 4-2 *Example Hardware Equipment to Be Tested*

PE Router—Generic Configuration

Product	Description	Qty
XR-12000/10	Cisco XR 12000 Series Original Router	4
12410	Cisco XR 12000 Series 10-Slot Router	1
12416	Cisco XR 12000 Series 16-Slot Router	1
12816	Cisco XR 12000 Series 16-Slot Router	1
12406	Cisco XR 12000 Series 6-Slot Router	1
XR-PRP-2	Cisco XR 12000 Series Performance Router Processor 2	5
12000-SIP-601	Cisco XR 12000 and 12000 Series SPA Interface Processor-601	11
SPA-1X10GE-L-V2	Cisco 1-Port 10GE LAN-PHY Shared Port Adapter	2
XFP-10GLR-OC192SR	Multirate XFP module for 10GBASE-LR and OC192 SR-1	2
SPA-2X1GE-V2	Cisco 2-Port Gigabit Ethernet Shared Port Adapter	5
SPA-8X1GE-V2	Cisco 8-Port Gigabit Ethernet Shared Port Adapter	1
SPA-8X1FE-TX-V2	Cisco 8-Port Fast Ethernet (TX) Shared Port Adapter	3
SPA-4XOC3-POS-V2	Cisco 4-Port OC-3 POS Shared Port Adapter	4
SFP-GE-S	1000BASE-SX SFP (DOM)	4
GLC-T	1000BASE-T SFP	16
SFP-OC3-IR1	OC-3/STM-1 pluggable intermediate-reach 15 km trans	4
SPA-10X1GE-V2	Cisco 10-Port Gigabit Ethernet Shared Port Adapter	3

If applicable, it is also a good idea to provide per-node details of how the line cards are to be installed in modular node chassis. This will assist with the test build and remove any ambiguity regarding the exact hardware that was tested if questions arise during test results analysis. Figure 4-2 shows an example of an equipment slot configuration diagram that can be added to the test plan.

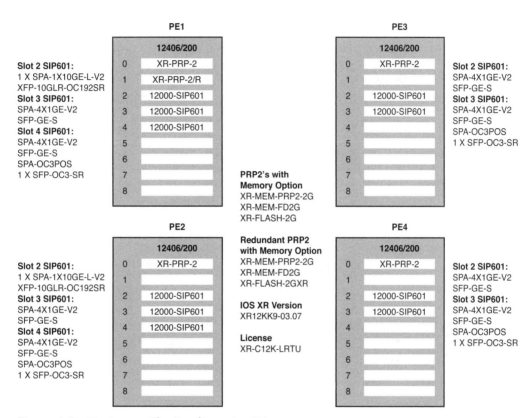

Figure 4-2   *Equipment Slot Configuration Diagram*

The exact software feature set and version should be recorded for each device type and role in the network, as shown in Table 4-3.

Table 4-3   *Example Software Versions to Be Tested*

Platform	Role	Cisco IOS Software Version	Image/Feature Set
2811	CE Router	12.3(14)T7	c2800nm-adventerprisek9-mz.123-14.T7.bin
2821	CE Router	12.3(14)T7	c2800nm-adventerprisek9-mz.123-14.T7.bin
4500/Sup III	L3 Switch	12.2(25)	cat4000-i5k91s-mz.122-25.EWA14.bin
4500/Sup 6E	L3 Switch	12.2(46)	cat4500e-entservicesk9-mz.122-46.SG.bin
C3750	L2 Switch	122-25.SEB4	c3750-ipbase-mz.122-25.SEB4.bin

Large test organizations often tackle several projects simultaneously, some of which are long term, requiring a team approach. An estimate of the resources allocated to a particular test should be included in the test plan, as shown in Table 4-4.

Table 4-4   *People, Roles, and Time Allocation*

Role	Name	Resource Allocation
Program Manager	Cosmo Spacely	As required
Test Manager	George Jetson	25%
Test Lead	Joseph Barbara	100%
Test and Documentation	Henri Orbit	100%
	George O'Hanlon	50%

Test Schedule

A test schedule designates work to be done and specifies deadlines for completing milestones and deliverables. Test entrance and exit criteria should be clearly defined so that everyone understands what tasks must be completed prior to the start of testing, and when testing is considered to be complete. An example of test entrance criteria may be that a client must approve the test plan, at which point no more changes will be allowed without a redefinition of the test scope. Test exit criteria may include running all of the planned tests, identifying or filing bugs for any defects found, and/or reviewing test results with the customer.

Table 4-5 shows a sample test schedule.

Table 4-5   *Sample Test Schedule*

Date	Milestones	Deliverables/Comments
10/1/2009	Test Plan Start	High-level test case review with customer and account team
10/5/2009	Test Plan—Review & Approval	Test Plan document review with customer and account team
10/6/2009	Entrance Criteria (EC) Approval	Project Execution Commit with sponsors
10/6/2009	Test Start	Dependent on test entrance criteria documented in EC
10/13/2009	Test Complete	Completion of all test cases
10/20/2009	Test Result Report Complete	Final test results report complete
10/23/2009	Internal Test Document Review	Review test document with internal team prior to customer review
10/26/2009	Test Document Review with Customer	Customer review of test document
11/2/2009	Lab Topology Teardown	Test Project complete

Developing the Detailed Test Cases

As explained earlier, test cases are the essence of the test plan, as they ultimately will be followed to produce results that will determine whether the device, feature, or system under test has passed or failed. As the test plan writer, you must be very concise when specifying the set of preconditions, steps, expected output, and method of data collection that should be followed. This is particularly important when the people executing the tests have not been involved in the development of the test plan, or are working on several different tests concurrently. When the time comes for test execution, engineers need to understand

■   What they are testing

■   Why they are testing it

■   How they are going to test it

■   What information they need to capture

■   The format in which they need to record results

Test cases are often classified as being either formal or informal.

Formal test cases can be directly mapped to test requirements with success criteria that are measurable through quantifiable metrics. Formal test cases have a known input and an expected output, which are worked out before the test is executed. For example, a formal test case could be developed to verify a vendor's claim that a particular firewall product can support 64,000 concurrent connections. The expected output might be that the platform should be able to forward traffic at a particular pps rate with the specified preconditions that it must be performing stateful inspection and filtering on 1 to 64,000 sessions. This type of formal case would be considered a "positive" test. A "negative" test could similarly be defined where the number of concurrent sessions was gradually increased above 64,000 at a rate of 1000 per second so that the effect on packet forwarding rate, CPU, memory, and general device health could be observed and measured. Formal test cases such as this should be linked to test requirements using a traceability matrix.

For features or network services without formal requirements or quantifiable success criteria, test cases can be written based on the accepted normal operation of features or services of a similar class. For example, an informal test case could be written to demonstrate the capability of a WAN acceleration appliance (such as Cisco WAAS WAE) to improve performance on a particular TCP application. As there are no industry standards that quantify "WAN acceleration," the informal test case could simply measure the time it takes to transfer a file via FTP from a remote server with, and then without, WAN acceleration enabled. The expected output could simply be that the time to retrieve the file should be "less" when WAN acceleration is enabled, which would then be recorded as a benchmark.

Understanding System Test Execution Methodologies

Chapter 1 introduced a four-phased approach to systems testing that has proven to be effective in replicating a customer's network design and in modeling application traffic characteristics. This approach includes developing a comprehensive set of test cases categorized as baseline, feature, negative, or scalability.

This section introduces a few common test methodologies that can be used to help develop test cases for each phase. These include conformance tests, functional and interoperability tests, and performance and scalability tests.

Conformance Testing

Conformance testing is used to verify compliance with standards and is often a key component of network hardware and software certification test plans. These types of tests are often challenging to develop because many network protocols are difficult to implement consistently between different vendors. Despite the existence of RFCs and IETF standards, implementations often have subtle differences because the specifications are typically informal and inevitably contain ambiguities. Sometimes there are even changes in implementation between different code levels within the same vendor's products.

Conformance tests are usually made up of both positive and negative test cases to verify how network devices comply with specific protocol standards. Conformance testing tools perform their tests as a dialog by sending protocol-specific packets to the device under test, receiving the packets sent in response, and then analyzing the response to determine the next action to take. This methodology allows conformance test tools to test complicated scenarios much more intelligently and flexibly than what is achievable by simple packet generation and capture devices.

When conducting conformance tests, keep in mind that even the test tool makers must interpret an RFC, and, as mentioned earlier, there may be differences in implementation between the test tool and the network equipment under test. If you see discrepancies, record them and work with the vendors to find a feasible workaround. Often times, these differences have been seen before.

A BGP conformance test plan is provided in Chapter 6, "Proof of Concept Testing Case Study of a Cisco Data Center 3.0 Architecture," as an example.

Functional and Interoperability Testing

Functional and interoperability tests are geared toward evaluating specific device features as they would be implemented in a "realistic" setup, and as such these tests are commonly seen in POC and design verification testing. Interoperability testing is a critical aspect of testing IP services that determines if elements within the architecture interact with each other as expected, to deliver the desired service capability. In contrast with conformance testing, which provides proof of RFC-defined protocols working between a few devices, generally two tests—functional and interoperability—allow engineers to expand the test coverage from a simple, small lab setup, to a more realistic, real-world configuration.

Functional and interoperability testing is the determination through a larger systems test of whether the behavior of a network architecture, in specific scenarios, conforms to the test requirements. For example, when you enable that QoS feature on your WAN edge network, will it reduce jitter for your voice traffic, or will it cause CPU spikes, fill your interface queues, and cause your routing protocol to drop? In this type of test, you will have multiple features enabled and competing for resources.

Functional and interoperability testing is often conducted as part of baseline testing, where all of the network features are enabled together. Only when all the features that will be working in conjunction in your network are combined with all of the types of hardware and software you will be using, will you be able to have a real view of how they will all interact together. Using the preceding QoS example, the routing protocol may work perfectly by itself, and the QoS policy may be doing exactly what you expect; but when you combine them together with the correct Cisco IOS Software and hardware, as well as some SNMP polling, you may see an issue. This combination of complex features, hardware, and software is what functional and interoperability tests are all about.

While the functional and interoperability tests do not specifically test for conformance, they sometimes help you identify conformance issues. For example, if you connect a new router to an existing lab network, you may find that the OSPF neighbors end up stuck in the Exstart/Exchange State. This problem occurs frequently when attempting to run OSPF between a Cisco router and another vendor's router. The problem occurs when the maximum transmission unit (MTU) settings for neighboring router interfaces don't match.

Performance and Scalability Testing

Performance and stress tests take the architecture to the next level. Assuming that everything is working as expected in your test environment under various test scenarios, including negative or failure tests, the next question is how well the network will work under different scenarios with an increased traffic load. There are many performance metrics you should collect, as well as stress scenarios that you should try out, before the network is deployed into production and required to support revenue-generating traffic.

Performance and stress tests are actually two different things. In performance testing, you are trying to create a baseline for how the network will behave during typical and increased loads, as well as during failover scenarios. The goal of performance testing is to find and eliminate bottlenecks and establish a roadmap for future regression testing. To conduct performance testing is to engage in a carefully controlled process of measurement and analysis, until you hit a predetermined threshold, be it CPU, memory, interface utilization, or something else.

Stress testing, on the other hand, tries to break the system under test by overwhelming its resources or by taking resources away from it, in which case it is sometimes called *negative testing*. The main purpose behind this is to make sure that the system fails and recovers gracefully, as well as to find the point at which the system will become inoperable.

When conducting a performance test, you would want to see, for example, how long it takes a router to bring up 15 OSPF neighbors each advertising 1000 routes. In a stress test, you would check how many OSPF neighbors advertising 1000 routes would cause the router to start behaving incorrectly. Both of these types of testing tend to require very expensive and extensive test gear.

Format for Written Test Case

There are several articles written, and even commercial software products available, to help you develop written test cases. While there is no absolute right way to write a test case, experience and best practices suggest that it should be written clearly, simply, with good grammar. It is recommended that the following information should be included at a minimum:

- **Test ID:** The test case ID must be unique and can also be associated with the test logs and other collected data.

- **Node List:** The list of the actual hardware being tested in this test case.

- **Test Description:** The test case description should be very brief.

- **Test Phase:** Baseline, Feature, Negative, or Scalability.

- **Test Suite:** If applicable, include the feature or service that this test case will be used to verify. Examples may include OSPF, QoS, High Availability, or VoIP.

- **Test Setup:** The test setup clearly describes the topology, hardware, logical configurations, test tools, applications, or other prerequisites that must be in place before the test can be executed. For complex tests, it is often helpful to include a diagram to help illustrate exactly how the test should be set up.

- **Test Steps:** The test steps are the step-by-step instructions on how to carry out the test. These should be very detailed so that testers with minimum experience can execute the tests.

- **Expected Results:** The expected results are those that describe what the system must give as output or how the system must react based on the test steps.

- **Observed Results:** The observed results are those outputs of the action for the given inputs or how the system reacts for the given inputs.

- **Pass/Fail:** If the expected and observed results are the same, then the test result is Pass; otherwise, it is Fail.

Summary

This chapter covered the motivations for different types of testing and the best way to scope and plan a well-thought-out test. The chapter also went over some of the most often used test tools and where they should be used in your testing. Finally, this chapter explained how to write an effective test plan. The next chapter provides examples of written test cases and gives you tips to help you be successful in your testing.

Chapter 5

Executing the Test Plan

This chapter covers the following topics:

- Building and Operating the Functional Network Prototype System

- The Test Engineer's Toolkit

- Test Execution

- Running the Test Cases

- Capturing and Saving Results

Once the test plan has been written and approved by the project stakeholders, it is time to get busy setting up the network equipment and test tools that will make up the functional prototype network system. Building the network prototype and running the test cases are activities that engineers usually enjoy the most because they finally get the chance to step into the lab and work with the equipment. When the right amount of attention has been put into the assessment and planning for a test, execution of test cases can often progress relatively quickly. This is not to imply that this step of system testing is trivial, or that it can be performed by a low-skilled intern. On the contrary, test engineers must possess strong technical acumen and deductive reasoning skills to determine when unexpected results are caused by actual bugs or limitations, as well as problems with the lab topology setup, test method, or test tools. When valid discrepancies are uncovered during test cases, they must be documented, verified, and reproduced consistently by the test engineer.

To execute system testing effectively, an engineer needs to understand precisely what to do before, during, and after the test cases are run. This includes understanding how to build and manage the prototype network system, how to configure and operate the test tools, and how to capture and record results that will ultimately determine success. This chapter focuses on several of these important aspects of test execution. It begins with tips on how to document, set up, and manage equipment and tools that will comprise the network prototype system. It discusses how to make the most of test tools, giving advice on how to avoid common pitfalls and how scripts and automated, industry-standard tests can be used to economize your efforts. The chapter continues with examples of how to simulate a large environment to conduct scalability testing, and finishes with best practices for effective test execution and results gathering.

Building and Operating the Functional Network Prototype System

Building and operating a complex network prototype can be a cumbersome chore for test engineers with little or no experience with network design or operations. This section offers some best practices for lab processes and procedures that, when put in place, simplify and streamline this task.

Equipment Allocation and Connectivity

All test organizations need to have some sort of documented process in place to check out and reserve physical and virtual lab assets for tests. There is nothing more frustrating than to find components missing or cable connections disconnected from your equipment while you are in the middle of testing. The size and breadth of coverage that a facility provides often dictates the level of process necessary for managing test resources such as equipment, tools, servers, and software licenses. Many large test organizations deploy sophisticated automated systems for this purpose, using barcodes or even RFID systems to inventory and reserve equipment as it moves in and around the lab for various tests. Smaller test facilities, on the other hand, often get by with simpler systems to manage requests, reservations, and schedules. Even something like a simple spreadsheet maintained on a shared network drive is better than no system at all. In any case, test engineers should be required to submit equipment reservation requests prior to building their lab topology, scheduling plenty of time to complete the testing and follow up on any discrepancies or defects found. Returning the equipment into the "available pool" as soon as a test is concluded is critical. This allows other engineers to conduct their testing and often prevents having to buy or rent extra gear.

After the equipment is secured for your tests, you should create a detailed lab topology diagram to illustrate how it should be cabled and configured from a physical and logical standpoint. This is especially important if you plan to enlist others to help with the build, but it will also serve as a great reference for ongoing troubleshooting and analysis as the test cases are run. A detailed lab topology diagram is similar to what a design engineer would include in a low-level design (LLD) document. It should contain everything that someone with little or no knowledge of the test project would need to assemble the lab topology unassisted. Details such as equipment model numbers, lab rack locations, software versions, cabling type and physical port connectivity, IP addressing, VLAN numbering, and routing protocol details are all good information to include in this diagram. If you developed a high-level lab topology diagram during the Plan Phase (as discussed in

Chapter 4, "Crafting the Test Approach"), you can often simply add the additional details to create this diagram. An example of a detailed lab topology diagram is shown in Figure 5-1.

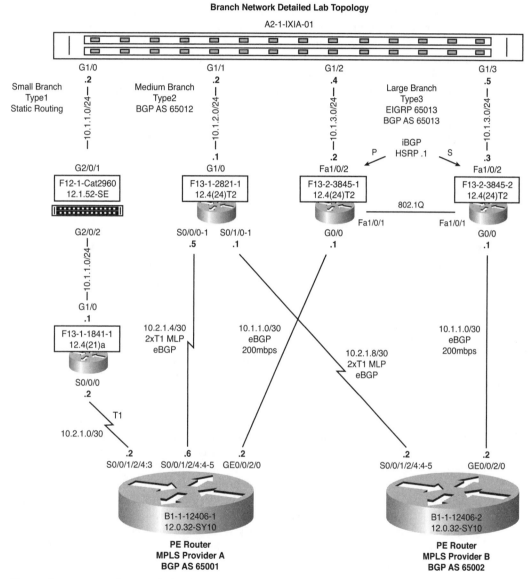

Figure 5-1   *Example Detailed Lab Topology Diagram*

Test Lab Telemetry

Today's enterprise organizations are beginning to perceive their lab facilities less as "manned uncontrolled facilities" and more as "mini data centers," accessed and managed remotely. Remote work is encouraged, as reduced physical access results in fewer accidents, better energy conservation, and tighter access control. Automated systems to monitor and control cooling and power distribution down to the cabinet level have become more popular, given their capability to activate fans as needed or remotely shut down equipment when it is not in use. This allows for a "greener" lab as well as significant savings in power and cooling. Equipment can be managed and configured remotely, using IP or through terminal server connectivity to console ports. A test lab's telemetry system functions as its central nervous system, carrying the instructions necessary to configure, manage, and monitor network devices, test tools, physical servers, and virtual machines. As such, the telemetry system must be flexible, multifaceted, and highly available.

There are many different methods that test engineers can use to configure, manage, and operate network equipment and test tools:

- Console port access is almost always used for the initial configuration of the network devices and can be accessed remotely via Telnet- or SSH-capable terminal servers.

- Terminal servers offer a flexible method of remote access and should be included in a lab infrastructure design that includes fixed rack configurations.

- File servers and test tool controllers with limited console support often require traditional keyboard and video monitors for initial configuration and operations. They can also be configured remotely by the use of IP-connected *KVM* (keyboard, video, mouse) gear.

- In the case of many servers, applications such as Windows "remote desktop connection" or "virtual network computing" (VNC) can be used for graphical remote control, using the lab's IP network.

In contrast to production environments, where systems administrators often manage servers and network devices using the production IP network, lab engineers typically cannot rely on the IP infrastructure of a test topology to provide continuous in-band management to their tools, servers, and devices. Network instabilities are expected in lab topologies, as test traffic is often "blasted" at high rates, and components are stress tested or failed over during negative testing scenarios. Out-of-band (OOB) management addresses this challenge by employing a management channel that is physically and logically isolated from the data channel where the test traffic is running. Designing an OOB network for a lab normally involves deploying a dedicated Ethernet network, upon which all of management traffic (SSH, Telnet, SNMP, TACACS, SYSLOG, VNC, and so on) will be forwarded.

In addition to providing connectivity between the test tools, network management systems, and the test topology, the OOB network should also provide access to necessary resources on the corporate intranet or the Internet as the company security policy dictates. At a minimum, the OOB network should be able to access an FTP server on a DMZ with Internet capabilities, so engineers can download network and operating code and server patches. Access to antivirus updates, web-filtering updates, and Internet software activations is a typical requirement when testing security products.

Tip   The OOB network should not run any routing protocol, because routing updates received on the management interface might invalidate certain tests, even if they are ignored. Instead, static routing should be employed to forward management traffic onto the OOB network. Be aware of any static route redistribution that may force traffic through your topology, particularly if you are configuring a default route toward a management interface. A default route pointing to a management interface should be avoided when possible, as it can result in test traffic saturating the entire OOB network when improperly addressed. Some lab administrators deploy traffic rate limiting within the OOB infrastructure to reduce the impact of such mistakes. This kind of rate limiting can be painful when you are uploading and downloading large files, but it will save you a lot of grief in the long run.

Console connectivity to network device "supervisor" cards (both active and standby) and servers in your test topology is an absolute necessity if you plan to conduct remote testing. Console access often is the only method to configure or monitor your devices during initial setup, or when a failure occurs in the IP network topology. Also, a fair number of startup messages that may contain important information to be captured for your test are sent only to the console during a reload of a device. For example, messages about configuration parser errors and ignored or unsupported parameters will be visible only in console messages. Certain operations, such as In Service Software Upgrades (ISSU), either recommend or require the use of console ports. Last but not least, the console connection can be used remotely as a way to clear vty lines in your devices when too many OOB IP sessions have been left open and you can't reach an open line. Take a look at Figure 5-2 for a high-level diagram of a lab OOB network.

It helps to maintain a single database or spreadsheet with all the OOB IP addresses, console addresses, usernames, and passwords for the gear in your test topology.

Tip   If at all possible, set up the username and password to be the same for all the devices in your test bed, as this will simplify any scripting you may need to do. Having to use different username and password combinations adds to the complexity of the scripts and forces you to reference and update a separate database.

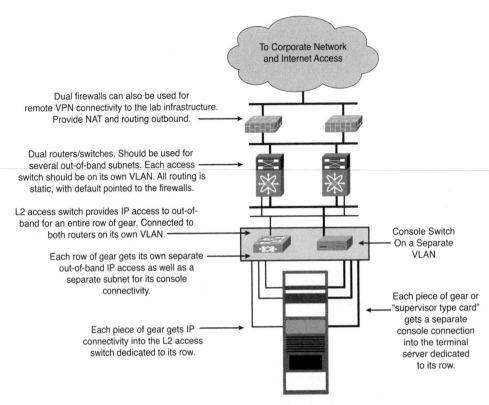

Figure 5-2 *Sample Diagram of a Lab Out-of-Band Network*

Table 5-1 is an example of the type of information you should document for the smooth operations of a test bed.

Table 5-1 *Example of Login Information for a Test Bed*

Device Name	OOB Mgmt. IP	Username	Password	Console URL	Device Type
4948-1	10.1.82.20	admin	test123	telnet://10.1.80.20:2032	Catalyst 4948
4948-2	10.1.82.21	admin	test123	telnet://10.1.80.20:2033	Catalyst 4948
Server-Win1	10.1.82.22	admin	test123	telnet://10.1.80.20:2034	UCS Blade
Server-Linux1	10.1.82.23	admin	test123	telnet://10.1.80.20:2035	UCS Blade
NetApp-NY	10.1.82.24	admin	test123	telnet://10.1.80.20:2036	NetApp Filer
NetApp-Phi	10.1.82.25	admin	test123	telnet://10.1.80.20:2037	NetApp Filer
NEX-5020-NY-1	10.1.82.26	admin	test123	telnet://10.1.80.20:2038	Nexus 5020
NEX-5010-NY-2	10.1.82.27	admin	test123	telnet://10.1.80.20:2039	Nexus 5010

Table 5-1   *Example of Login Information for a Test Bed*

Device Name	OOB Mgmt. IP	Username	Password	Console URL	Device Type
NEX-5020-PH-1	10.1.82.28	admin	test123	telnet://10.1.80.20:2040	Nexus 5020
NEX-5010-PH-2	10.1.82.29	admin	test123	telnet://10.1.80.20:2041	Nexus 5010
MDS-9506-NY-1	10.1.82.30	admin	test123	telnet://10.1.80.20:2042	MDS 9506
MDS-9506-NY-2	10.1.82.31	admin	test123	telnet://10.1.80.20:2043	MDS 9506
MDS-9506-PH-1	10.1.82.32	admin	test123	telnet://10.1.80.20:2044	MDS 9506
MDS-9506-PH-2	10.1.82.33	admin	test123	telnet://10.1.80.20:2045	MDS 9506
NEX-7010-NY-1	10.1.82.34	admin	test123	telnet://10.1.80.20:2046	Nexus 7010
NEX-7010-NY-2	10.1.82.35	admin	test123	telnet://10.1.80.20:2047	Nexus 7010
NEX-7010-PH-1	10.1.82.36	admin	test123	telnet://10.1.80.20:2048	Nexus 7010
NEX-7010-PH-2	10.1.82.37	admin	test123	telnet://10.1.80.20:2049	Nexus 7010

Tip   Set up your OOB connectivity using the same types of protocols you will use in production. If your production network only allows SSHv2 for CLI management of your routers, then that is all you should allow in your test bed.

The Test Engineer's Toolkit

If you could go back 25 years and land a job as a data communications technician, your toolkit would likely be limited to a punch-down tool, cable crimper, breakout box, and a pair of wire cutters. These items, along with the equipment manuals, an oscilloscope, bit error rate tester, and, if you were really lucky, a packet analyzer, would be the extent of the toolkit available to troubleshoot your company's Token Ring, Ethernet, serial, and packet-switched networks. As history proved, even that limited toolkit was enough to get the job done, with much of the credit going to the technicians and engineers who mastered and made the most of it.

The performance and complexity of network technologies increased dramatically in the 25 years that followed, to keep pace with evolving software applications and increased processing speed and storage capacity of computing platforms, which were observed to double roughly every two years (Moore's Law). As engineers and network operators struggled to manage these complex systems with their limited toolsets, network vendors responded by creating an abundance of sophisticated test tools that are a necessary part of the engineer's toolkit today.

Some of these tools are explored in the following sections, with advice and leading practices given on how to make the most of them to execute your testing.

Understanding Your Test Tools: Quirks and Limitations

In Chapter 4, we introduced several categories of free and commercial test tools available to test engineers, and explained briefly how they are applied to specific types of tests. When leveraging these test tools to automate testing, simulate applications, or emulate network impairments, it is important to understand exactly how they work. This extends not only to their features and capabilities, but also to their quirks and limitations. Today's test tools can be quite complex, and when operated incorrectly may produce false positives, leading you to believe a certain test has failed when in fact it has not. Before reporting a test case discrepancy, a test engineer must eliminate the possibility of a test tool deficiency or improper configuration as the root cause. The following are a few examples where issues or problems with test tools have led engineers astray during testing:

■ Certain packet generators have been observed to reset their network interface cards (NIC) prior to initiating traffic in order to clear statistics and error counters. This reset causes a brief "flap" of the interface on the connected network device, which may cause excessive packet loss if the connected device happens to be a Layer 2 switch running spanning tree. This packet loss is the expected behavior for a switch port that has flapped, as it will not begin forwarding traffic until the required spanning tree states (blocking, listening, learning, forwarding) have been completed. During this time, all ingress and egress traffic for the test port would be dropped, skewing the results, and possibly leading you to believe a problem exists in the network or device under test.

Note   The partial workaround for this situation would be to enable the "PortFast" feature on the L2 switch port to avoid forwarding delay associated with spanning tree startup.

■ Many test tools do not implement full TCP/IP protocol stacks, which can cause unpredictable behavior when interacting with network equipment and actual IP hosts. For example, there have been situations where the lack of gratuitous arp support in test tool TCP/IP stacks have caused false positives when testing router first-hop redundancy protocols such as HSRP and VRRP. There have also been instances where poor TCP stack implementations did not allow dynamic tuning of receive windows, preventing test traffic generation tools from filling "network pipes" with TCP/IP traffic.

■ Do not assume your test tool will be capable of generating traffic at line rate, especially when you are sending synthetic traffic patterns such as HTTP, FTP, POP, or SMTP through your system under test. Even simple bit blasters have been known to record errors when sending stateless traffic at line rate between directly connected ports. Many engineers routinely run quick back-to-back throughput tests between test ports to obtain performance benchmarks from their tools prior to initiating a test.

■ Be aware of test tool protocol conformance issues. During a recent multicast scalability test, an engineer reported a 75 percent loss between two test ports. One port was sourcing traffic to 1000 different multicast groups and the second port was expected to receive all of the traffic. The receiving (second) port was configured as an IGMP host and was supposed to "join" (issue host membership reports) each of the 1000 groups. After checking for interface drops, access-list blocking, and quality of service (QoS) issues, the engineer finally realized that the last-hop router had only processed 250 of the 1000 IGMP host membership reports, sent by the second host. Upon further examination, the engineer found that while the test tool was indeed generating reports for all 1000 groups, it was generating them in too short of a window for the last-hop router to process. The router would only process 250 IGMP joins per time interval, per interface, which was the expected and documented behavior.

An extract from RFC 1054, "Host Extensions for IP Multicasting," explains the proper behavior for an IGMP host:

> When a host receives a Query, rather than sending Reports immediately, it starts a report delay timer for each of its group memberships on the network interface of the incoming Query. Each timer is set to a different, randomly-chosen value between zero and D seconds. When a timer expires, a report is generated for the corresponding host group. Thus, Reports are spread out over a D second interval instead of all occurring at once.

After discovering the unexpected behavior, the engineer contacted the test tool vendor, who pointed out a configuration parameter that would control the number of joins per time interval. Once configured to an acceptable level, all of the traffic was received.

These are just a few of the examples where tool limitations resulted in confusion and unexpected results during testing. Be mindful of similar quirks that may exist with your test tools when determining whether a test has actually failed.

Understanding the Different Types of Test Traffic

Most commercial packet generators are capable of creating and analyzing various types of data traffic for general-purpose data testing, meeting the majority of systems testing needs. For many tests, it does not matter what type of traffic is generated, as long as valid IP packets are being sent, received, and correlated between test-set pairs. There are certain types of tests, however, that require specialized tools capable of sending simulated application traffic or even creating and transmitting malformed, illegal packets. Test plans that are executed to validate application performance across a system under test, for example, may call for stateful traffic that simulates the IP characteristics of the application under analysis. Network throughput and convergence test plans often specify traffic profiles with a particular size distribution and quantity per second. There are several RFCs that cover traffic distribution for these types of throughput tests, some of which will be covered in the next section.

The basic traffic choices to be made are IP, UDP or TCP, and stateless or stateful traffic generation. This choice becomes extremely relevant when application or security testing is involved, as security devices such as firewalls and IDS appliances will expect to examine stateful application traffic. This is very complex when dealing with TCP traffic and stateful firewalls (or any other stateful device). Stateful firewalls will expect a TCP three-way handshake, with the correct SYN, SYN ACK, and ACK packets being sent between two endpoints before establishing a flow and allowing data to traverse the device, assuming the traffic is permitted. The firewall will check packets in the established flow to make sure that they are using valid sequence numbers and are acknowledged correctly. The firewall will also expect correct FIN and FIN ACK packets to tear down an existing flow. Most firewalls will also delete a flow after a predetermined amount of idle time. Stateful firewalls are also able to track the state of flows in connectionless protocols such as UDP. Such sessions are usually placed into the ESTABLISHED state by the firewall immediately after the first packet is detected, and removed after a fixed period of time where no further traffic is received—this is commonly referred to as *aging*.

Stateless test traffic is a lot simpler to generate than stateful, as there is no two-way session establishment required between test port pairs. For stateless traffic, a packet generator simply sends TCP or UDP packets (or, indeed, any type of IP packet) right away, sometimes never even changing the sequence numbers. In some cases, the packet generator will be able to generate only one type of packet per port; for example, all of it will be UDP packets with a source address of 10.10.10.1, a source port of 2895, a destination address of 10.100.100.2, and a destination port of 5400, and all of the packets will be 256 bytes. In other cases, the packet generator can send different combinations of

■ Packet type (UDP or TCP usually)

■ Source IP address

■ Source port

■ Destination IP address

■ Destination port

■ Packet size

■ Packet rate

■ If TCP, stateless or stateful

There is a lot to consider when taking into account all of these choices. Every flow may even be sending traffic from multiple sources to multiple destinations (usually in the same subnet) with random port numbers and packet sizes. You must understand the capabilities of your test tool to make the appropriate decision for traffic generation.

The correct packet sizes and rates to be used in your testing are usually considered carefully by the test author and written into the plan. The rate typically is expressed in packets per second (pps) or data rate, where data rate is described as something like 4.5 Mbps, and packets per second is described as something like 2500 pps of 64-byte packets. When choosing and setting up packet sizes for your test, take into account the maximum transmission unit (MTU) of all the interfaces the traffic will traverse, and all the encapsulations that will be added to your traffic. Encapsulations such as IPsec, GRE, dot1q, and others can add several bytes to your generated packets. Consider whether this will force the packets to be fragmented or dropped. Is this the intent of the test? If your test is meant to use jumbo frames, make sure all of your hardware, software, and test tools support them.

Test engineers often suggest using IMIX traffic to validate network features or for performance benchmarking. The concept of IMIX (or Internet Mix) refers to the typical size and distribution of the Internet traffic passing through network equipment such as routers, switches, or firewalls. IMIX profiles are defined based on statistical samples gathered from Internet routers so that they can be re-created by test tools and leveraged to validate different types of test cases. Different IMIX profiles exist for IP, TCP, IPsec, and IPv6 traffic. Distributions are similar but frame sizes vary given the differences in packet overhead and upper layer 2 limitations.

One of the best-known mixes is called Simple IMIX, shown in Table 5-2.

Table 5-2 *Simple IMIX Traffic*

Parts	Packet Size
7	64 bytes
4	570 bytes
1	1518 bytes

There are several other mixes, and the most important point to take from this is to use the same mix when doing comparison testing. The type and distribution of IMIX traffic used in your testing should be carefully recorded in order to allow a rerun of the test at a later date or using different test tools, which may define the mix of traffic differently.

There are some types of traffic that need to be examined by every router or even every host in a network. Broadcast, multicast, and packets with option flags set can have unexpected effects on your systems, so use them only if the test plan calls for them, and be aware of any rate limiters enabled on your systems that may drop them. Also, be aware of special reserved addresses such as the 224.0.0.0/24 multicast subnet. A packet generator will happily send traffic to that network, potentially causing all sorts of mayhem in your network.

A test plan should specify the amount and type of traffic to be sent during a particular test. This can be a simple "point-to-point" test stream, such as "Run 20 mbps of 1400-byte packet UDP traffic between interface Gig5/1 of router DELTA6500-1 and interface Gig6/3 of router DELTA6500-3."

Or it may be a more "fully meshed," complex set of test streams, as described in Table 5-3.

Understanding the capabilities of advanced test tools will allow you to set up composite traffic patterns suitable to most network and capacity tests. Test tools can be used for a multitude of testing and validation, from application, security, and protocol compliance testing to several types of throughput testing, and anything in between. Some test tools can even run automated IETF RFC test methodologies.

Table 5-3 *Example of a Complex Traffic Flow Matrix*

Background Unicast Data Flows Use UDP Src Port 100 D

Test Port (Connected Device)	Simulated Data Flow	Destination	Packet Size	Data Rate (Bidirectional)
1A (DELTA6500-1)	Site-NY1 to Site-CT1	2A (DELTA7600-1)	Variable	10 Mbps
	Site-NY1 to Site-FL1	3A (DELTA3800-1)	Variable	100 Mbps
	Site-NY1 to Site-FL1	3C (DELTA4500-2)	Variable	40 Mbps
	Site-NY1 to External Customers-A	4A (DELTA3750-1)	Variable	10 Mbps
1B (DELTA6500-2)	Site-NY2 to Site-CT2	2B (DELTA7600-2)	Variable	10 Mbps
	Site-NY2 to Site-CT2	3B (DELTA3800-2)	Variable	100 Mbps
	Site-NY2 to External Customers-B	4B (Delta3750-2)	Variable	10 Mbps
2A (DELTA7500-1)	Site-NY1-SAT to Site-CT-1-SAT	2C (DELTA7304-1)	Variable	80 Mbps
	Site-NY1-SAT to Site-FL1	3A (DELTA3800-1)	Variable	100 Mbps
	Site-NY1-SAT to External Customers-A	4A (Delta3750-1)	Variable	40 Mbps
2B (DELTA7500-2)	Site-NY2-SAT to Site-CT2	3B (DELTA3800-2)	Variable	40 Mbps
	Site-NY2-SAT to External Customers-A	4B (Delta3750-2)	Variable	40 Mbps
5A (DELTA6500-3)	10G Capacity Test	5B (DELTA6500-4)	Variable	10 Gbps

RFCs Pertaining to Test Execution

A number of RFCs have been written exclusively to address network and application testing. It is important for test engineers to be aware of these RFCs, as test plans often reference them by name. For example, a test plan to measure latency through a system under test may simply direct you to "execute RFC 2544 Latency Testing." Also, many of these RFCs provide excellent, industry-accepted examples of methodologies that can be included when developing your test plans. The following RFCs are some of the most often used and mentioned in test plans.

RFC 2544: Benchmarking Methodology for Network Interconnect Devices

RFC 2544 discusses and defines a number of tests that may be used to describe the performance characteristics of a network-interconnecting device. In addition to defining the tests, this RFC also describes specific formats for reporting the results of the tests. RFC 2544 describes six different tests designed to capture a wide range of operating statistics, including throughput and latency. It describes very specifically the frame sizes, rates, and ways to calculate several performance characteristics of network devices. It also sets up the test procedure to be used for each type of test. Take a look at the latency test (section 26.2 of RFC 2544), reproduced here, as an example of the procedures and reporting format this RFC defines:

26.2 Latency

Objective: To determine the latency as defined in RFC 1242.

Procedure: First determine the throughput for DUT at each of the listed frame sizes. Send a stream of frames at a particular frame size through the DUT at the determined throughput rate to a specific destination. The stream SHOULD be at least 120 seconds in duration. An identifying tag SHOULD be included in one frame after 60 seconds with the type of tag being implementation dependent. The time at which this frame is fully transmitted is recorded (timestamp A). The receiver logic in the test equipment MUST recognize the tag information in the frame stream and record the time at which the tagged frame was received (timestamp B).

The latency is timestamp B minus timestamp A as per the relevant definition from RFC 1242, namely latency as defined for store and forward devices or latency as defined for bit forwarding devices.

The test MUST be repeated at least 20 times with the reported value being the average of the recorded value.

This test SHOULD be performed with the test frame addressed to the same destination as the rest of the data stream and also with each of the test frames addressed to a new destination network.

Reporting format: The report MUST state which definition of latency (from RFC 1242) was used for this test. The latency results SHOULD be reported in the format of a table with a row for each of the tested frame sizes. There SHOULD be columns for the frame size, the rate at which the latency test was run for that frame size, for the media types tested, and for the resultant latency values for each type of data stream tested.

A few testing equipment vendors sell RFC 2544 test tools that run full suites of RFC 2544 tests procedures and reports. These tests are meant to give you well-understood apples-to-apples benchmark comparisons.

Note You can view the full text of any of these RFCs by going to http://tools.ietf.org and using the Search tool to search for the RFC by number.

RFC 2889: Benchmarking Methodology for LAN Switching Devices

The Introduction to RFC 2889 explains its purpose as follows:

> This document is intended to provide methodology for the benchmarking of local area network (LAN) switching devices. It extends the methodology already defined for benchmarking network interconnecting devices in RFC 2544 to switching devices.
>
> This RFC primarily deals with devices which switch frames at the Medium Access Control (MAC) layer. It provides a methodology for benchmarking switching devices, forwarding performance, congestion control, latency, address handling and filtering. In addition to defining the tests, this document also describes specific formats for reporting the results of the tests.

As with RFC 2544, some test tool vendors provide RFC 2889 tests suites to test your Layer 2 switch capabilities.

RFC 3511: Benchmarking Methodology for Firewall Performance

This RFC defines a number of tests that may be used to describe the performance characteristics of firewalls. It covers benchmark tests for IP throughput, concurrent TCP connection capacity, maximum TCP connection establishment rate, maximum TCP connection teardown rate, denial-of-service handling, HTTP transfer rate, maximum HTTP transaction rate, illegal traffic handling, IP fragmentation handling, and latency. As with the two preceding RFCs, you can get more information about RFC 3511 at http://tools.ietf.org.

Tools to Execute Complex Testing

As noted earlier, there are a multitude of test tools available to fill your test toolkit. How you use the tools available to you in a complex test ultimately determines how successful you are. There are many clever techniques and tricks of the trade that can make complex testing easier. Being able to use a couple of routers and a packet generator to simulate a 500-router network is just one of them.

Scale Testing: Simulating Large Networks with Limited Devices

As discussed in Chapter 4, a functional prototype network system will be built in the lab to test the performance of the proposed design. With the exception of very small networks, this prototype would rarely be built to full scale. Consider a case where you have been asked to certify a router's capability to provide secure aggregation services for a WAN consisting of 500 remote sites. The primary goal of such a test would be to certify that the device under test (DUT), in this case the router, will be able to perform adequately in a "fully loaded" state, when all 500 remote site routers are sending protocol messages and application traffic at various rates. Because it would not be practical to install 500 routers in a lab for this purpose, you need to come up with a method to simulate the control plane and forwarding plane load of this number of sites sending traffic to the DUT. Two different approaches to simulating large networks with a limited amount of hardware are discussed next.

Using Test Tools to Simulate Large Routing Topologies

One approach to scale testing is to leverage a commercial test tool like one of the router testers discussed in Chapter 4 that has routing, IPsec VPN, and traffic generation capabilities. These tools are well suited for scale testing, as they can typically emulate very complex topologies with hundreds or even thousands of routers, providing control plane load and forwarding plane load by sending test traffic to the DUT. Lab setup is often as simple as connecting the tool directly to a DUT with a pair of Ethernet connections, as shown in Figure 5-3.

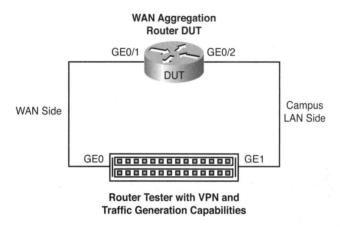

Figure 5-3 *Simple Connectivity for Scale Testing with a Traffic Generator*

The router tester would then be configured to emulate the WAN topology, in this case by provisioning 500 emulated customer premises equipment (CPE) routers behind an emulated service provider router, as shown in Figure 5-4.

The resulting topology would allow a test engineer to generate the load of 500 IPsec-encrypted GRE tunnels connecting to a DUT, each appearing as a separate EIGRP neighbor. Traffic flows could be created to appear as being sourced from the LAN connections behind each remote site CPE router to stress the forwarding plane capabilities of the DUT.

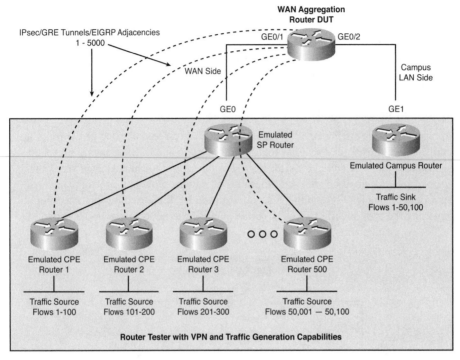

Figure 5-4   *Simulated Router Tester Topology*

This approach, while simple, does have its drawbacks. For one, sophisticated tools like router testers are not cheap, particularly when you require modular chassis with a variety of interface types. Also, some of these tools only support Ethernet media, which can also be limiting if you are trying to certify a device with Serial or SONET connections. But perhaps the biggest drawback of using test tools for network-scale simulation is the relative lack of features as compared to a Cisco router. For example, while many test tools claim IPsec capabilities, will they interoperate with your public key infrastructure (PKI)? Will your tool support Cisco VPN solutions such as Dynamic Multipoint VPN (DMVPN) or Group Encrypted Transport VPN (GET VPN)? Does it support EIGRP routing? If so, will it also have support for advanced features such as EIGRP stub, MD5 authentication, filter lists, route maps, or timer tuning? How about other advanced WAN features such as Performance Routing (PfR) or application optimization? Chances are that even the most sophisticated and expensive tools will not support many of the features you need to certify the capabilities of today's next-generation WAN products.

Using Virtualized Routers to Simulate Large Routing Topologies

An alternate approach to simulating a large routing topology can be taken by connecting high-performance "loading" routers into your topology and configuring them to appear as many different routers to the DUT. This is accomplished by taking advantage of a Cisco IOS virtualization feature known as *VRF-lite*, which allows you to partition a router into multiple routing and forwarding instances, running in parallel. Using VRF-lite allows you to create the large number of routing adjacencies needed to simulate the necessary load on the control and forwarding planes of the DUT. The advantage of using a Cisco router in place of a commercial router tester is that any Cisco IOS feature supported in the context of a virtual routing and forwarding (VRF) instance would be able to be included in the test, resulting in a more realistic prototype network system.

Note   Not all Cisco IOS features are supported in VRF-lite mode. Refer to Cisco IOS–specific release notes on Cisco.com for a list of the features that are not supported.

A traffic generator would be connected to the loading routers over an 802.1q trunk, so that individual test flows could be mapped to particular VRF instances to make them appear to come from different neighbors from the DUT's perspective.

Figure 5-5 offers an example of how you might use five "loading" routers to emulate 500 remote routers, each running IPsec, DMVPN, and EIGRP services.

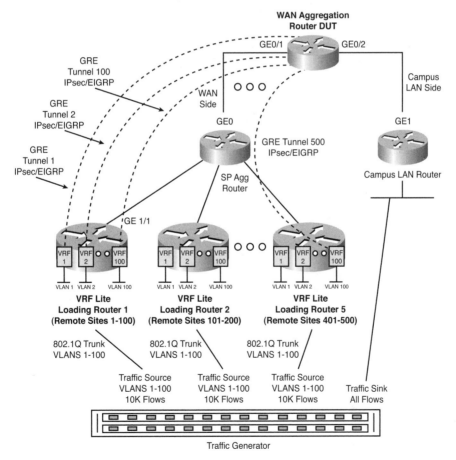

Figure 5-5   *Example of Using Five Routers to Emulate 500 Neighbors*

When using this approach, it is important to deploy the right number and type of loading routers to ensure they do not become the weak link in the lab topology. Provisioning too many GRE tunnels, IPsec security associations (SA), and EIGRP adjacencies onto a software-based router will drive CPU usage up and eventually start to cause instabilities. Symptoms of high CPU instability may include slow response from router console, SYS-3-CPUHOG error messages, and intermittent routing adjacency and tunnel flaps. Refer to hardware-specific documentation when deciding how far to provision the loading routers, and even then be conservative. The last thing you want is a false positive because of a weak link in the loading router infrastructure.

Steps to Build a Large Configuration File for a Loading Router

Follow these steps to build a large configuration file for a loading router:

Step 1. Obtain a remote site router configuration file from a production device or design document so that you can test it on a standalone router in your lab, before you attempt to replicate it across hundreds or thousands of VRF-lite instances. As an example, consider the case of a simple remote site that is configured for IPsec, DMVPN, and EIGRP, as shown in Example 5-1.

Example 5-1 *Sample Remote Router Site Configuration File*

```
hostname branch_1
!
ip cef
!
! -------------Crypto Parameters --------
crypto isakmp policy 1
 authentication pre-share
crypto keyring REMOTES pre-shared-key address 0.0.0.0 key cisco1
!
crypto ipsec transform-set trans2 esp-des esp-md5-hmac
!
crypto ipsec profile vpnprof
 set transform-set trans2
!
! -------------DMVPN GRE Tunnel
interface Tunnel1
 description to WANAGG Router 1
 bandwidth 1000
 ip address 10.0.0.1 255.255.255.0
 no ip redirects
 ip mtu 1416
 ip nhrp map 10.0.0.254 172.17.0.1
 ip nhrp map multicast 172.17.0.1
 ip nhrp network-id 99
 ip nhrp holdtime 300
```

```
 ip nhrp nhs 10.0.0.254
 load-interval 30
 tunnel source Ethernet0/0
 tunnel mode gre multipoint
 tunnel key 100000
 tunnel protection ipsec profile vpnprof
!
! -------------Loopback interface
interface Loopback0
 ip address 10.0.254.1 255.255.255.255
!
! -------------WAN facing interface
interface Ethernet0/0
 description WAN link to MPLS Service Provider
 ip address 172.17.1.1 255.255.255.252
!
! -------------LAN facing interface
interface Ethernet1/0
 description local LAN link
 ip address 10.4.1.1 255.255.255.0
!
! -------------EIGRP Process
router eigrp 64512
 network 10.0.0.0 0.0.255.255
 no auto-summary
 passive-interface Ethernet0/0
eigrp stub connected
!
! -------------Static default route needed for GRE tunnel / nhrp nhs
ip route 0.0.0.0 0.0.0.0 172.17.1.2
```

Step 2.   Once the configuration is successfully tested on a standalone router, convert it into a VRF configuration as shown in Example 5-2. Test on a loading router to ensure that all features are supported within a VRF context in the version of Cisco IOS Software that you will be testing with.

Example 5-2   *Sample "Virtualized" Remote Router Site Configuration File*

```
hostname branch_1_vrf_lite <----------- Hostname modified to reflect vrf lite
!
ip cef
!
ip vrf 1 <----------- VRF 1 defined and assigned unique route-distinguisher
 rd 1:1
```

```
!
! --------------Crypto Parameters remain unchanged---------
crypto isakmp policy 1
 authentication pre-share
crypto keyring REMOTES vrf vrf1 <------------ Provides VRF awareness to ISAKMP
 Phase 1 pre-shared-key address 0.0.0.0 key cisco1
!
crypto ipsec transform-set trans2 esp-des esp-md5-hmac
!
crypto ipsec profile vpnprof
 set transform-set trans2
!
! --------------DMVPN GRE Tunnels to be replicated on loading routers
interface Tunnel1
 description simulates tunnel from remote site 1
 bandwidth 1000
 ip vrf forwarding 1 <------------ interface mapped to VRF1
 ip address 10.0.0.1 255.255.255.0
 no ip redirects
 ip mtu 1416
 ip nhrp map 10.0.0.254 172.17.0.1
 ip nhrp map multicast 172.17.0.1
 ip nhrp network-id 99
 ip nhrp holdtime 300
 ip nhrp nhs 10.0.0.254
 load-interval 30
 tunnel source Ethernet0/0.100 <------------ tunnel source must be in VRF1
 tunnel mode gre multipoint
 tunnel vrf vrf1 <----------------- Provides VRF awareness to GRE Tunnel
 tunnel key 100000
 tunnel protection ipsec profile vpnprof
! --------------Loopback interface to be replicated on loading routers
interface Loopback0
ip vrf forwarding 1 <------------ interface mapped to VRF1
ip address 10.0.254.1 255.255.255.255
!
! --------------WAN facing interface converted to 802.1Q Sub and mapped to VRF1
interface Ethernet0/0
 description link to MPLS SP1
 no ip address
!
interface Ethernet0/0.100
 description ce-pe connection for site 1
 encapsulation dot1Q 100
 ip vrf forwarding 1 <------------ interface mapped to VRF1
```

```
 ip address 172.17.1.1 255.255.255.252
! ------------LAN facing interface converted to 802.1Q Sub and mapped to VRF1
interface Ethernet1/0
 description local LAN link
 no ip address
!
interface Ethernet1/0.100
 description local LAN link for site 1
 encapsulation dot1Q 100
 ip vrf forwarding 1 <----------- interface mapped to VRF1
 ip address 10.4.1.1 255.255.255.0
!
! ------------EIGRP Process virtualized
router eigrp 64512
 passive-interface default
 no passive-interface Ethernet0/0.100
 no auto-summary
 !
 address-family ipv4 vrf 1
 network 10.0.0.0
 no auto-summary
 autonomous-system 1
 eigrp stub connected
 exit-address-family
! ------------Static default route in VRF needed for GRE tunnel / nhrp nhs
ip route vrf 1 0.0.0.0 0.0.0.0 172.17.1.2
```

Step 3.   Once the virtualized remote site router has been successfully tested, replicate it as many times as is needed per loading router. See Example 5-3 for a description of what parameters would need to be replicated for 100 sites.

Example 5-3   *Sample "Virtualized" Configuration File for 100 Remote Sites*

```
hostname branch-1-100-vrflite
!
! Define 100 VRF's per loading router
ip vrf 1 <----------- VRF 1 already defined
 rd 1:1
!
ip vrf 2 <----------- VRF 2 added
 rd 2:2
!
ip vrf 3 <----------- VRF 2 added
 rd 3:3
```

```
.....
ip vrf 100 <------------  VRF 100 added
 rd 100:100
!
! ------------- Define 100 DMVPN GRE Tunnels per loading router
interface Tunnel2
 description simulates tunnel from remote site 2
 bandwidth 1000
 ip vrf forwarding 2
 ip address 10.0.0.2 255.255.255.0
 no ip redirects
 ip mtu 1416
 ip nhrp map 10.0.0.254 172.17.0.1
 ip nhrp map multicast 172.17.0.1
 ip nhrp network-id 99
 ip nhrp holdtime 300
 ip nhrp nhs 10.0.0.254
 load-interval 30
 tunnel source Ethernet0/0.200
 tunnel mode gre multipoint
 tunnel key 100000
 tunnel protection ipsec profile vpnprof
!
interface Tunnel3
 description simulates tunnel from remote site 3
 bandwidth 1000
 ip vrf forwarding 3
 ip address 10.0.0.3 255.255.255.0
 no ip redirects
 ip mtu 1416
 ip nhrp map 10.0.0.254 172.17.0.1
 ip nhrp map multicast 172.17.0.1
 ip nhrp network-id 99
 ip nhrp holdtime 300
 ip nhrp nhs 10.0.0.254
 load-interval 30
 tunnel source Ethernet0/0.300
 tunnel mode gre multipoint
 tunnel key 100000
 tunnel protection ipsec profile vpnprof
....
interface Tunnel100
 description simulates tunnel from remote site 100
 bandwidth 1000
```

```
 ip vrf forwarding 100
 ip address 10.0.0.100 255.255.255.0
 no ip redirects
 ip mtu 1416
 ip nhrp map 10.0.0.1 172.17.0.1
 ip nhrp map multicast 172.17.0.1
 ip nhrp network-id 99
 ip nhrp holdtime 300
 ip nhrp nhs 10.0.0.1
 load-interval 30
 tunnel source Ethernet0/0.1000
 tunnel mode gre multipoint
 tunnel key 100000
 tunnel protection ipsec profile vpnprof
!
! -------------- Additional Loopback interfaces
interface Loopback2
ip vrf forwarding 2
ip address 10.0.254.2 255.255.255.255
!
interface Loopback3
ip vrf forwarding 3
ip address 10.0.254.3 255.255.255.255
...
interface Loopback100
ip vrf forwarding 100
ip address 10.0.254.100 255.255.255.255
! ------------- Additional WAN facing interface 802.1Q Subinterfaces
interface Ethernet0/0.102
 description ce-pe connection for site 2
 encapsulation dot1Q 102
 ip vrf forwarding 2
 ip address 172.17.1.5 255.255.255.252
!
interface Ethernet0/0.103
 description ce-pe connection for site 3
 encapsulation dot1Q 103
 ip vrf forwarding 3
 ip address 172.17.1.9 255.255.255.252
!
interface Ethernet0/0.1000
 description ce-pe connection for site 1000
 encapsulation dot1Q 1000
 ip vrf forwarding 1000
```

```
 ip address 172.17.4.5 255.255.255.252
 !
 ! ------------ Additional LAN facing interface 802.1Q Subinterfaces
interface Ethernet1/0.102
 description Site 2 LAN link
 encapsulation dot1Q 102
 ip vrf forwarding 2
 ip address 10.4.1.2 255.255.255.0
 !
interface Ethernet1/0.103
 description Site 3 LAN link
 encapsulation dot1Q 103
 ip vrf forwarding 3
 ip address 10.4.1.3 255.255.255.0
 !
...
interface Ethernet1/0.1000
 description Site 100 LAN link
 encapsulation dot1Q 1000
 ip vrf forwarding 100
 ip address 10.4.1.100 255.255.255.0
 !
 ! ------------- EIGRP Process virtualized
router eigrp 64512
 passive-interface default
 no passive-interface Ethernet0/0.100
 no auto-summary
 !
 address-family ipv4 vrf 2
 network 10.0.0.0
 no auto-summary
 autonomous-system 2
 eigrp stub connected
 exit-address-family
 !
address-family ipv4 vrf 3
 network 10.0.0.0
 no auto-summary
 autonomous-system 3
 eigrp stub connected
 exit-address-family
 !
...
address-family ipv4 vrf 100
```

```
network 10.0.0.0
no auto-summary
autonomous-system 100
eigrp stub connected
exit-address-family

! ------------- Additional Static default routes in VRF
ip route vrf 2 0.0.0.0 0.0.0.0 172.17.1.6
ip route vrf 3 0.0.0.0 0.0.0.0 172.17.1.10
....
ip route vrf 1 0.0.0.0 0.0.0.0 172.17.4.6
```

Step 4.   Repeat this configuration on as many additional dummy routers as necessary to reach the desired number of protocol adjacencies and tunnels on the DUT. As you can imagine, a good knowledge of scripting tools that can replicate configurations from a template and spreadsheet with addressing variables will be a big time saver.

High-Availability Testing: How to Measure Convergence Times

Measuring convergence times around node and circuit failures in your test network is a key aspect of high-availability testing. There are several ways that this can be accomplished; one of the easiest is by sending and receiving "marker flows" between test ports at constant rates. Consider Figure 5-6.

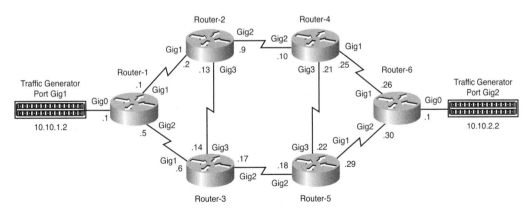

Figure 5-6   *Typical Network with Multiple Forwarding Paths*

In this example, a marker flow is transmitted at 1000 pps, from Traffic Generator Port Gig1 to Traffic Generator Port Gig2. In this case, a simple routing design has been implemented, with all traffic being forwarded over Router-1 Interface Gig1 during steady state due to a preferred metric to the destination. (The path over Router-1 Interface Gig2 has a higher cost and will only be used during a failure.) Once you have the traffic running steadily from Traffic Generator Port Gig1 to Traffic Generator Port Gig2, you should clear all the counters in your traffic generator, or at least the "dropped traffic" counters. If you fail Router-1 Interface Gig1, and you see 2500 packets have been dropped before traffic starts running, without any drops, over the Router-1 Interface Gig2, you can assume that it took 2.5 seconds for the path to fail over.

On the other hand (still using the network in Figure 5-6), if routing has two equal cost paths that it can take from Router-1 to reach the 10.10.2.0 network, a single flow may not go over the path that you want to fail. If you choose the right set of source and destination address pairs, and assuming your gear is doing load balancing on source/destination IP addressing, you can watch the failover and its effects on traffic going over the failed path, as well as the traffic going over the path that should not be affected.

You should use two marker flows from Traffic Generator Port Gig1 to Traffic Generator Port Gig2.

In a Cisco router running Cisco IOS Software, you can find the correct source and destination IP pairs by issuing the command

show ip cef [**vrf** *vrf-name*] **exact-route** *source-address destination-address*

In the following example for Marker Flow 1, the command would be (assuming no VRF)

```
Router-1#show ip cef exact-route 10.10.1.2 10.10.2.2
10.10.1.2 -> 10.10.2.2 :GigabitEthernet1 (next hop 10.1.0.2)
```

Using the preceding command, we found

Marker Flow 1 is 10.10.1.2 fi 10.10.2.2 goes to Gig1 on Router-1

Marker Flow 2 is 10.10.1.3 fi 10.10.2.3 goes to Gig2 on Router-1

Using these two marker flows, each running 1000 pps, you should be able to pull out the cable in Router-1 Interface Gig2 and never affect Marker Flow 1, which is running over Interface Gig1. Marker Flow 2 should then fail over, while still not affecting Marker Flow 1 (we are assuming that Interface Gig1 can pass the 2000 pps at the packet sizes we are sending). In this case, after seeing 500 packets dropped in Marker Flow 2, we would know that failover occurred in half a second. Also, no packets (or very few) should be dropped for Marker Flow 1 in this type of test.

The same can be done with return traffic from Traffic Generator Port Gig2 to Traffic Generator Port Gig1. Depending on your router's load-balancing algorithms, you may need to use TCP ports as part of the load-balancing decision.

Tip   The number of packets per second should be easy to use for failover calculations. Something like 100 pps or 1000 pps is ideal. With 1000 pps, you can assume that every packet dropped is equal to 1 ms of failover time. In other words, if you are running a marker flow at 1000 pps that fails over after 40 packets have been dropped, you can say that the failover time was around 40 ms.

Caution   When choosing sizes and packets per second for marker flows, make sure that when all the flows are failed over onto a single link, you are not going to overrun the capacity of that link.

Convergence Testing: How to Trigger a Failover

There are several methods that you can use to simulate a circuit or node failure in your test bed. It would seem that issuing an administrative shutdown, route processor switchover, or reboot command would have the same effect as removing a cable, removing a route processor, or shutting off the power to a device. However, this is not the case. Triggering a forced failover using a software command may give you a particular failover behavior, while a failover caused by disconnecting hardware or media very often results in a different outcome. Upon receiving a software instruction, many routers will send a "warning" message to neighbors before they bring down an interface, or switch supervisors, allowing their neighbors to gracefully react. Removing a cable, pulling a line card or supervisor card, or shutting off power to the gear does not allow the trigger packet, if it exists, to go out, and it forces the routers to use a different mechanism, such as link failure or timer expiry, to force a switchover. It is important to test both types of events to make sure all forms of failovers will work as expected.

Also, do not forget to test the recovery events. Having a router come up and enter a busy network can often cause more problems than having it go down and stay down. This mechanism of failover triggers and recovery is also true for server and application testing, and can be used accordingly.

Sometimes when a line card is pulled out or inserted, it can cause a bus stall, which can prevent any traffic from being transmitted out the device. Even if your company policy does not allow online insertion and removal (OIR) during production hours, you should at least understand the behavior of the feature in the lab. An emergency OIR may help you restore service in some instances, while in others it may create a bigger problem than it is solving. The lab is the place to find out and document this behavior. s

Testing Using Delay, Jitter, and Errors

As discussed in the "Choosing the Right Test Tools" section in Chapter 4, the availability of network delay and impairment tools now allows for lab testing that is much more representative of your WAN or MAN infrastructure than ever before. Testing that includes an infrastructure capable of delay and jitter simulation has become critical as certain applications are becoming more and more intolerant of even the slightest delays. For example, where a 50-ms delay may be acceptable for real-time applications such as voice and video, it may completely break a synchronous storage replication application, where a 2-ms round-trip time can be the requirement. These types of delay-sensitive applications and their requirements for high availability frequently trigger the need for data center high-availability testing. One of the most important but more difficult things to accurately accomplish in these types of tests is to predict how the delay-sensitive applications, in two separate data centers, will respond to a failover event or QoS on data center interconnect links that travel dozens or hundreds of miles. A delay generator is one of the only practical ways to conduct this kind of testing.

Jitter, delay, and circuit errors can also cause issues when subsecond timers are used in Hot Standby Router Protocol (HSRP) or other routing protocols. If your organization is planning to deploy subsecond timers between two remote sites, it would be very useful to use one of these error generator tools to understand any issues that may occur if you have circuit problems between your sites.

Some labs actually buy long spools of test fiber, sometimes hundreds of miles long, as an alternative to electronic delay generators. These spools are amazingly compact, and you can store 100 miles' worth of fiber in a small cabinet. You need to consider having the optics and equipment to drive an optical signal across this distance when you're choosing this alternative for delay generation.

Tip   Remember that when you are doing delay testing, you should factor in not only the delay for the packet traveling the distance between the two data centers, but also the delay generated by every device that packet crosses.

Using Cisco IOS Test Tools

Several free tools available in Cisco IOS Software can be leveraged for testing; following are a few examples of the most easily and widely used.

Chargen Service

The chargen service is based on the Character Generator Protocol defined in RFC 864. Chargen, as the name implies, can be used to generate characters that can be transmitted between clients and servers that support the protocol. According to RFC 864, a host may connect to a server (or in this case, a router) that supports the chargen protocol on either TCP or UDP port 19. Upon opening a TCP connection, the router begins sending arbitrary characters to the connecting host and continues until the host closes the connection. The service requires you to turn on **service tcp-small-servers.** When you telnet to the chargen port (TCP port 19) of the Cisco IOS devices with **tcp-small-servers** enabled, it will generate a continuous stream of ASCII character data back to the source, where it will be displayed as text in the Telnet window.

Example 5-4 shows output of a Telnet session to the chargen service.

Example 5-4 *Chargen Service Output*

```
$ telnet 10.0.96.46 chargen
Trying 10.0.96.46...
Connected to 10.0.96.46.
Escape character is '^]'.
 !"#$%&'()*+,-./0123456789:;<=>?@ABCDEFGHIJKLMNOPQRSTUVWXYZ[\]^_`abcdefg
!"#$%&'()*+,-./0123456789:;<=>?@ABCDEFGHIJKLMNOPQRSTUVWXYZ[\]^_`abcdefgh
"#$%&'()*+,-./0123456789:;<=>?@ABCDEFGHIJKLMNOPQRSTUVWXYZ[\]^_`abcdefghi
#$%&'()*+,-./0123456789:;<=>?@ABCDEFGHIJKLMNOPQRSTUVWXYZ[\]^_`abcdefghij
$%&'()*+,-./0123456789:;<=>?@ABCDEFGHIJKLMNOPQRSTUVWXYZ[\]^_`abcdefghijk
%&'()*+,-./0123456789:;<=>?@ABCDEFGHIJKLMNOPQRSTUVWXYZ[\]^_`abcdefghijkl
&'()*+,-./0123456789:;<=>?@ABCDEFGHIJKLMNOPQRSTUVWXYZ[\]^_`abcdefghijklm
'()*+,-./0123456789:;<=>?@ABCDEFGHIJKLMNOPQRSTUVWXYZ[\]^_`abcdefghijklmn
()*+,-./0123456789:;<=>?@ABCDEFGHIJKLMNOPQRSTUVWXYZ[\]^_`abcdefghijklmno
)*+,-./0123456789:;<=>?@ABCDEFGHIJKLMNOPQRSTUVWXYZ[\]^_`abcdefghijklmnop
*+,-./0123456789:;<=>?@ABCDEFGHIJKLMNOPQRSTUVWXYZ[\]^_`abcdefghijklmnopq
+,-./0123456789:;<=>?@ABCDEFGHIJKLMNOPQRSTUVWXYZ[\]^_`abcdefghijklmnopqr
```

This ASCII traffic will continue to be generated indefinitely until it is stopped by an operator; it can be used as a type of "poor man's" traffic generator. While it does not create a significant load on your network and will be interrupted when your Telnet session closes, it can be useful for situations where you need a constant traffic stream generated from a router. For example, it could be used to generate the "interesting traffic" necessary to initiate dial-backup, an IPsec session, or used as a simple monitor to observe while conducting failover testing. During a failover, the screen will freeze and should recover if the traffic finds a path to reestablish the session before the TCP timers terminate it.

Tip The UDP implementation of CHARGEN service is supported in the **service udp-small-servers** Cisco IOS command, but it is less useful for testing. It discards the datagram you send and responds with a 72-character string of ASCII characters terminated with a CR+LF (carriage return and line feed).

Because all of the minor services enabled by TCP and UDP Small Servers can be misused, they should only be used for testing purposes and should never be left enabled on production systems.

Cisco IOS IP Service-Level Agreements

Cisco IOS IP SLAs is another test tool embedded in Cisco IOS Software as a feature, but it is much more powerful than the relatively simple CHARGEN service.

Cisco IOS IP SLAs allows customers to analyze IP service levels for IP applications and services by using active traffic monitoring. It allows the generation of traffic in a continuous, reliable, and predictable manner to measure network performance. Cisco IOS IP

SLAs can perform network assessments, verify QoS, ease the deployment of new services, and assist with network troubleshooting. It simulates network data and IP services and collects network performance information in real time. Cisco IOS IP SLAs generates and analyzes traffic either between Cisco IOS devices or from a Cisco IOS device to a remote IP device such as a network application server. Measurements provided by the various Cisco IOS IP SLAs operations can be used for troubleshooting, for problem analysis, or for designing network topologies.

Depending on the specific Cisco IOS IP SLAs operation, various network performance statistics are monitored within the Cisco device and stored in both command-line interface (CLI) and Simple Network Management Protocol (SNMP) MIBs. Cisco IOS IP SLAs packets have configurable IP and application layer options such as source and destination IP addresses, UDP/TCP port numbers, a Type of Service (ToS) byte (including Differentiated Services Code Point [DSCP] and IP Prefix bits), virtual routing and forwarding (VRF) instance, and URL web address.

Because Cisco IOS IP SLAs is Layer 2 transport independent, you can configure end-to-end operations over disparate networks to best reflect the metrics that your systems are likely to experience. Cisco IP SLAs collects a unique subset of the following performance metrics:

■ Delay (both round-trip and one-way)

■ Jitter (directional)

■ Packet loss (directional)

■ Packet sequencing (packet ordering)

■ Path (per hop)

■ Connectivity (directional)

■ Server or website download time

Because Cisco IOS IP SLAs is SNMP-accessible, it can also be used by performance-monitoring applications like CiscoWorks Internetwork Performance Monitor (IPM) and other third-party performance management products.

Note The information in this section was obtained from Cisco.com, "Configuring IP SLA," https://www.cisco.com/en/US/docs/switches/lan/catalyst4500/12.2/44sg/configuration/guide/swipsla.html. To learn more about configuring Cisco IOS IP SLA, read the rest of the article.

Cisco IOS IP SLAs is a very simple feature to configure and an extremely powerful test tool. Take a look at Example 5-5 to see how to configure a simple jitter test.

Example 5-5   *Configuring a Simple Cisco IOS IP SLAs Jitter Test*

```
Router1(config)#ip sla monitor 10
Router1(config-sla-monitor)#type jitter dest-ipaddr 10.10.10.134 dest-port 5000
Router1(config-sla-monitor-jitter)#frequency 30
Router1(config-sla-monitor-jitter)#exit
Router1(config)#ip sla monitor schedule 10 life forever start-time after 00:00:10


!!! TO CONFIGURE A RESPONDER ON THE TARGET ROUTER !!!


Router2(config)#ip sla responder udp-echo 10.10.10.134 5000
```

Tip   The one trick to take away from the configuration in Example 5-5 is the fact that we set the IP SLAs monitor to start after 10 seconds. There is a good reason for this: when a router reloads, it parses its configuration in the order it is saved. If you have several IP SLAs operations configured (let's say 50, for example), all of them will kick off just about at the same time. If you add an element of randomness to the start times—that is, you set them all to start after a different amount of time has elapsed—the CPU impact of all 50 operations will be diminished. You can use the IP SLAs entry number as the wait time (for example, for entry 5, wait 5 seconds, and for entry 20, wait 20 seconds) before you start the operation.

When measuring delay, Cisco IOS IP SLAs can take advantage of the IP SLAs responder, enabled on the target device. When the responder is enabled, it allows the target device to take two timestamps: when the packet arrives on the interface at interrupt level and again just as it leaves. This eliminates processing time. This timestamping is made with a granularity of sub-millisecond (ms). The responder timestamping is very important because all routers and switches in the industry will prioritize switching traffic destined for other locations over packets destined for its local IP address (this includes Cisco IOS IP SLAs and ping test packets). Therefore, at times of high network activity, ping tests can reveal an inaccurately large response time; conversely, timestamping on the responder allows a Cisco IOS IP SLAs test to accurately represent the response time due.

Note   This information was taken from Cisco.com; "Cisco IOS IP Service Level Agreement Data Sheet." www.cisco.com/en/US/technologies/tk648/tk362/tk920/technologies_white_paper0900aecd8017531d.html.

Many of Cisco's enterprise and ISP customers use IP SLA probes in their production environments. Table 5-4 shows all of the operations available within the IP SLA framework.

This is a very powerful testing, reporting, and troubleshooting tool. Using Cisco IOS IP SLAs, an engineer can conduct tests on a running production network without causing outages or having to introduce other test tools. Best of all, it is included in most Cisco IOS versions for free.

Table 5-4   *Cisco IOS IP SLAs Operations and Applications*

Operation	Measurement Capability	Key Applications
UDP Jitter	Round-trip delay, one-way delay, one-way jitter, one-way packet loss One-way delay requires time synchronization between the Cisco IOS IP SLAs source and target routers	Most common operations for networks that carry voice or video traffic, such as IP backbones
UDP Echo	Round-trip delay	Accurate measurement of response time of UDP traffic
UDP Jitter for VoIP	Round-trip delay, one-way delay, one-way jitter, one-way packet loss VoIP codec simulation G.711 ulaw, G.711 alaw, and G.729a MOS and ICPIF voice quality scoring capability One-way delay requires time synchronization between the Cisco IOS IP SLAs source and target routers	Useful for VoIP network monitoring
TCP Connect	Connection time	Server and application performance monitoring
Domain Name System (DNS)	DNS lookup time	DNS performance monitoring, troubleshooting
Dynamic Host Configuration Protocol (DHCP)	Round-trip time to get an IP address	Response time to a DHCP server
FTP	Round-trip time to transfer a file	FTP get performance monitoring
HTTP	Round-trip time to get a Web page	Web site performance monitoring
Internet Control Message Protocol (ICMP) Echo	Round-trip delay	Troubleshooting and availability measurement using ICMP ping
ICMP Path Echo	Round-trip delay for the full path	Troubleshooting

Table 5-4   *Cisco IOS IP SLAs Operations and Applications*

Operation	Measurement Capability	Key Applications
ICMP Path Jitter	Round-trip delay, jitter, and packet loss for the full path	Troubleshooting
Data Link Switching Plus (DLSw+)	Peer tunnel performance	DLSw peer tunnel performance monitoring

Tip   Entire chapters in books dealing with network management and QoS have been written on the topic of using Cisco IOS IP SLAs. If you want more detailed information on this feature, you can find white papers and configuration guides on Cisco.com. For the purposes of this book, our high-level explanation of the feature should show its usefulness in testing.

Embedded Event Manager Scripting

Cisco IOS Embedded Event Manager (EEM) is another powerful tool embedded into Cisco IOS Software as a feature for system management that can be very useful during router and switch testing. EEM offers the ability to monitor events and take informational, corrective, and other actions when the monitored events occur or when a particular threshold is reached.

Note   This information was taken from Cisco.com; "EEM Configuration for Cisco Integrated Services Router Platforms," www.cisco.com/en/US/prod/collateral/iosswrel/ps6537/ps6555/ps6815/config_guide_eem_configuration_for_cisco_integrated_services_router_platforms.html.

Following is a simple example of steps taken by an EEM script that could be useful during a router test scenario:

Step 1.   Monitor route processor CPU utilization.

Step 2.   Measure traffic rate on interface gig5 if CPU utilization reaches 75 percent.

Step 3.   Shut down interface gig5 once CPU utilization reaches 85 percent.

Step 4.   Send out a syslog message to a network management station.

EEM Monitored Events

There are a multitude of events a router can monitor when EEM is enabled. Table 5-5 has a partial list of event detectors that can be used with EEM. It is reproduced from the whitepaper "Cisco IOS Software Embedded Event Manager, Harnesses Network Intelligence to Increase Availability": www.cisco.com/en/US/prod/collateral/iosswrel/ps6537/ps6550/prod_white_paper0900aecd803a4dad_ps6815_Products_White_Paper.html.

Table 5-5 *Partial List of EEM Event Detectors*

Event Detector Name	Description
Cisco IOS Command Line Interface (CLI) Event Detector	Triggers policies based on commands entered via the CLI. Uses a regular expression match.
Cisco IOS Counter Event Detector	Policies can be triggered based on a change of the designated counter. The counter event detector is used to manipulate counters named by the policy writer and internal to EEM.
Cisco IOS Redundancy Facility (RF) Event Detector	The Cisco IOS RF provides for detection of hardware and software failures related to the stateful switchover service. This event detector will trigger policies based on the RF state change. It is also used to initiate switchovers as a result of a policy action.
Cisco IOS Resource Threshold Event Detector	Triggers policies based on global platform values and thresholds. Includes resources such as CPU utilization and remaining buffer capacity.
Cisco IOS Timer Services Event Detector	Policies can be scheduled to occur at the designated time or interval. This event detector provides an option to create time-based triggers similar to the UNIX CRON facility.
Cisco IOS Watchdog/System Monitor Event Detector	Triggers policies based on certain conditions relative to a certain Cisco IOS Software process or subsystem's activity.
EEM Application Specific Event Detector	Application specific events can be detected or set by a Cisco IOS Software subsystem or a policy script. This provides the ability for one policy to trigger another policy.
Interface Counter Event Detector	Policies can be triggered based on the specific interface counter. Includes thresholds.
Online Insertion and Removal (OIR) Event Detector	Triggers policies based on hardware installation and removal activity.

Table 5-5   *Partial List of EEM Event Detectors*

Event Detector Name	Description
Routing Event Detector	Triggers policies based on routing protocol events.
Simple Network Management Protocol (SNMP) Event Detector	Triggers policies based on the associated SNMP MIB variable. Includes MIB variable thresholds.
Syslog Event Detector	Triggers policies based on the regular expression match of a local Syslog message.
System Manager Event Detector	Triggers policies based on conditions relative to a certain Cisco IOS Software process or subsystem's activity. This event detector is unique to Cisco IOS Software Modularity for the Cisco Catalyst 6500 Series Switch.

EEM Actions

There are several actions the router can take once a monitored event has been triggered. These actions include the following:

- Executing a Cisco IOS CLI command

- Generating a Cisco Networking Services (CNS) event for upstream processing by Cisco CNS devices

- Setting or modifying a named counter

- Requesting system information when an event occurs

- Sending a short e-mail

- Manually running an EEM policy

- Publishing an application-specific event

- Reloading the Cisco IOS Software

- Generating an SNMP trap

- Generating prioritized syslog messages

- Reading the state of a tracked object

- Setting the state of a tracked object

- Running a specific TCL script

The preceding list was taken from "EEM Configuration for Cisco Integrated Services Router Platforms": www.cisco.com/en/US/prod/collateral/iosswrel/ps6537/ps6555/ps6815/config_guide_eem_configuration_for_cisco_integrated_services_router_platforms.html. If you wish to learn more about EEM please read the document on Cisco.com.

Another simple application of EEM in a test environment would be to monitor for an OSPF-neighbor-down syslog message; if it occurs, execute the commands **show processes cpu sorted** and **show ip ospf neighbor**, save the output in flash memory, and then send out a specially crafted syslog message. The EEM script configuration would look something like Example 5-6.

Example 5-6 *Configuring an EEM Applet*

```
event manager applet OSPF
event syslog pattern "Neighbor Down: Dead timer expired"
action 1.0 cli command "enable"
action 1.1 cli command "sh proc cpu sorted | append flash:cpu_info"
action 1.2 cli command "show ip ospf neighbor | append flash:ospf-nei_info"
action 1.3 syslog msg "ROUTER GREEN OSPF NEIGHBOR DOWN"
```

More complex EEM testing policies can also be written in TCL. As with Cisco IOS IP SLAs, EEM is not only useful for testing, but also can be used for everyday operations in your production network.

Tip   As of the writing of this book, there is a place on Cisco.com for customers to share and download scripts for EEM. It is located at www.cisco.com/go/ciscobeyond.

Using Customized Scripts

In computer programming, a script is a program or a sequence of instructions that is carried out by another program. When applied to Cisco IOS testing, scripts can be used to retrieve information or provide automated instructions to a network device, or set of devices. Many terminal-emulation applications embed into their products scripting capabilities that allow you to automate basic functions such as configuration backups, code upgrades, device health monitoring, and wholesale configuration changes. Using scripts is an excellent way to do repetitive tasks during your testing and will reduce the chances of inconsistent results due to human errors associated with manual input.

Note   This is not a scripting book. There are several great books that have been written on the subject, along with thousands of websites providing scripting guidance and examples.

You do not have to be a programming expert to write and take advantage of simple scripts in your testing. Many test engineers take advantage of very basic scripts that can be customized with very little effort to get the job done. Be sure to give some thought about how you set up access to your devices if you plan to use scripting. Whenever possible, you should set your usernames and passwords to be the same in every device, and set them all up to run the same terminal protocol, such as SSHv2 or Telnet. This will keep the number of scripts necessary to a minimum.

For the sake of simplicity, many test engineers maintain "vanilla" scripts that contain instructions for every possible type of network device in their lab. This allows them to reuse the same set of commands for all devices, despite the fact that some instructions may not be relevant. If your script telnets into an ISR router and does a **show module** command, it will obviously receive an error, but that same command should get a valid response in a Nexus 7010. With a very simple script, you may get some invalid command responses, but your script will get all of the information you need nonetheless. Take a look at the simple script in Example 5-7. It is a VBScript script that takes advantage of a terminal-emulation program called Secure CRT (from VanDyke Software, www.vandyke.com/) to run and capture several commands.

Example 5-7 *Script to Run Several Commands and Capture Their Output to a File*

```
# $language = "VBScript"
# $interface = "1.0"
'GENERAL VARIABLES TO RUN THE SCRIPT
Dim FSO, Shell, Windir, Runservice, oFile, oFile1
Const ForReading = 1
Const ForWriting = 2
Const ForAppending = 8
Set FSO = CreateObject("scripting.filesystemobject")
Set Shell = CreateObject("WScript.Shell")
Set objDictionary = CreateObject("Scripting.Dictionary")
Set objScriptTab = crt.GetScriptTab
g_nNewTabIndex = 0
Sub Main()
'GET THE IPA FROM A FILE LOCATED AT "C:\Captures\IPs.txt"
      SwitchIPFile = "C:\Captures\IPs.txt"
      Set SwitchIP = FSO.opentextfile(SwitchIPFile, ForReading, False)
'SET THE PATH FOR LOG FILES TO "C:\Captures"
      Logfiles = "C:\Captures"
'START LOOPING THRU IPA FILE
      While Not SwitchIP.atEndOfStream
      IP = SwitchIP.Readline()
'CONNECT TO HOST AND LOGIN ON PORT 23
 Dim objNewTab
 If ConnectInTab("/TELNET " & IP & " 23", objNewTab) Then
'BEGIN LOGIN TO A FILE WITH NAME = IP + TIMESTAMP
```

```
    If objNewTab.session.logging then objNewTab.Session.Log False
    objNewTab.session.logfilename = Logfiles & "\" & IP & "_Date%Y%M%D_Time%h%m.Log"
    objNewTab.screen.Synchronous = True
    objNewTab.session.Log True
'SEND A CARRIAGE RETURN IF YOU DON'T GET A REPLY OF "admin"
    if objNewTab.screen.WaitForString("Username:",2) = false then
    objNewTab.screen.send vbcr
    objNewTab.screen.WaitForString "Username:"
    End if
'LOGIN PARAMETERS
    objNewTab.screen.send "admin" & vbCr
    objNewTab.screen.WaitForString "Password:"
    objNewTab.screen.send "Cisco.123" & vbCr
'GET INTO ENABLE MODE
        objNewTab.screen.WaitForString ">"
        objNewTab.screen.send "enable" & vbCr
        objNewTab.screen.WaitForString "Password:"
        objNewTab.screen.send "Cisco.123" & vbCr
'SET THE TERMINAL LENGHT TO ZERO
        objNewTab.screen.WaitForString "#"
        objNewTab.screen.Send "terminal length 0" & vbCr
        objNewTab.screen.WaitForString "#"
'BEGIN RUNNING COMMANDS
        objNewTab.screen.Send "show clock" & vbCr
        objNewTab.screen.WaitForString "#"
        objNewTab.screen.Send "show version" & vbCr
        objNewTab.screen.WaitForString "#"
        objNewTab.screen.Send "show module" & vbCr
        objNewTab.screen.WaitForString "#"
        objNewTab.screen.Send "show proc cpu sorted" & vbCr
        objNewTab.screen.WaitForString "#"
        objNewTab.screen.Send "show interface counters" & vbCr
        objNewTab.screen.WaitForString "#"
        objNewTab.screen.Send "show ip interface brief" & vbCr
        objNewTab.screen.WaitForString "#"
'SET THE TERMINAL LENGHT BACK TO 24, STOP LOGGING AND DISCONNECT
        objNewTab.screen.Send "terminal length 24" & vbCr
        objNewTab.screen.WaitForString "#"
    objNewTab.Session.Log False
        objNewTab.session.Disconnect
        If objNewTab.index > 1 then objNewTab.Close
    Else
'WRITE A FAILURE TO CONNECT TO A FILE
    Set Tempfile = FSO.OpenTextFile(Logfiles & "\NoConnect.txt", ForAppending, True)
```

```
  TempFile.writeline Now & ": Could Not Connect to " & IP
  TempFile.Close()
  End If


  Wend
End Sub


'~~~~~~~~~~~~~~~~~~~~~~~~~~~~~~~~~~~~~~~~~~~
Function ConnectInTab(szConnectInfo, ByRef objTab)
  On Error Resume Next
  Set objTab = crt.session.ConnectInTab(szConnectInfo)
  If Err.Number = 0 then
  objTab.screen.Synchronous = True
  ConnectInTab = true
  If g_nNewTabIndex = 0 Then g_nNewTabIndex = objTab.Index
  Else
  If objScriptTab.session.Connected and g_nNewTabIndex = 0 then g_nNewTabIndex =
crt.GetTabCount
  ConnectInTab = false
  End if
  On error goto 0
End Function
```

The script in Example 5-7 uses the terminal-emulation program and telnets into the first of the routers listed in a text file called IPs.txt (saved in the folder C:\Captures\); it will then begin logging, and then log in and send the following commands one at a time:

1. terminal length 0

2. show clock

3. show version

4. show module

5. show proc cpu sorted

6. show interface counters

7. show ip interface brief

8. terminal length 24

After it runs the commands, the script will stop logging and disconnect. It will then go to the next router in the IPs.txt file and repeat the process until it reaches the end of the file. The capture files will be saved as <router name from the IPs.txt file> + <a timestamp>.

It would be easy to add or change commands in this simple script by simply adding two lines to it at the appropriate place. You could have the script look for a text file with all of the commands you want to have run. You could even change the name format it uses to save the capture files to match·your test plan requirements.

This is certainly a very simplified example; there are several more-complex considerations, such as what happens if you connect to a router that returns a "Login" prompt instead of "Username," or a command returns the "#" character as part of its output, but the logic is sound. This is the kind of thing you can easily find on a website. You don't need to be a programming expert to customize it a little to fit your testing needs.

Some of the most often used scripting languages for testing are Perl, Visual Basic, TCL, and Expect. Using any of these scripting tools and a little know-how will allow you to create very complex and complete scripts that you can use for creating large configurations, grabbing more complex captures, loading code onto devices, creating VMs, or just about anything else you can imagine.

Another way to capture many forms of information during testing is to use one of the various network management tools to poll your devices using SNMP or even the CLI. Some network management tools can also be used to load code, change configurations, monitor device health and utilization, grab configuration snapshots, receive syslog and NetFlow messages, and perform many other useful tasks. Depending on the tools your enterprise uses, all of these capabilities should be a part of your test plan. If your network management tools are not part of your test environment, you can use some of the tools discussed in Chapter 3, "Testing and Lab Strategy Development," to help you in your testing.

> **Note**   Some commands can be very CPU intensive or even disruptive. You should take into account the effect running your script can have on your test results.

Test Execution

As mentioned earlier in the chapter, test execution tends to be the favorite part of the entire testing process for most engineers. This is often the part where the engineers get to "play" with the new gear and features, and to see how well it all works. Even though it is "play" time, it does not mean that careful consideration does not need to go into carrying out the test cases and capturing all the relevant results. There are a few things you can do to make this phase go as smoothly as possible.

Before You Begin

At this point, all of your gear is cabled and the out-of-band console and IP connectivity is established. It is time to configure the devices in your test bed. The configuration for all of the devices should include the following, unless the test plan says otherwise:

1.   All of the devices should point to the same Network Time Protocol (NTP) server and should be set to UTC/GMT time. Some devices or servers may have different patch levels and set daylight savings times at different times. Setting all devices to use

UTC/GMT time will keep this from being an issue. Having the time synchronized in your test bed will help with troubleshooting and log collection, and allow features like IPsec, which requires close time synchronization, to work correctly. If a device does not use NTP, then you should manually set its time as close as possible to the time in the rest of the devices in the test bed.

2. In routers, you should set the load interval of all your interfaces to the minimum value. This changes the length of time for which data is used to compute load statistics on the interfaces. In other words, you will see the average traffic load for the last 30 seconds (the minimum) instead of for 5 minutes (the default). This will give you real interface usage statistics much more quickly and accurately when checking them using the CLI during the test.

3. Logging levels should be set to debugging (or whatever will give you the most information), time stamped, and sent to at least as many syslog servers as you use in your production environment. The OOB network should be used to send all of the syslog messages if at all possible. Using the OOB network will help you to both avoid affecting traffic patterns and allow logs to reach the syslog servers during network outages caused by the testing. The logging will affect the CPU utilization for your gear; however, this should be part of any test plan.

4. Set SNMP traps and SNMP read and write communities in the same way they are set up in your production environment. If you have four trap receivers in your production environment, set up the same number in your test bed. As with syslog, use the OOB network and be aware of effects on CPU and memory utilization. Also, make sure you SNMP poll the devices in the same way they will be polled in production, and make this a part of your test plan.

5. Save all of your configurations to a separate server before you begin your testing. This is easy for network gear, but a bit harder for servers. It is strongly recommended that you save a clone image of your servers before you begin testing. It is often faster to reimage a server, or a piece on network gear, back to a known good point than to troubleshoot a configuration problem for hours. It is also going to allow you to quickly rerun a test if necessary.

Taking the time to do the steps in this list before a complex test begins will often save you time and effort during troubleshooting. It will also help you gather valid results for your testing.

Order of Testing: Getting Organized

Many times, the engineer who actually executes the test plan is not the person who wrote it. In these cases, it is important that the test engineer understand the reasons the testing is happening. If the test is a software certification, for example, are you testing the functionality of new features or hardware, or to verify that a critical software defect has been resolved in the current version? When the test engineer understands the reason a test is happening, the engineer can make intelligent and informed decisions regarding the order of test execution. If a particular defect is causing production issues, and this is the main reason you are testing, then it does not matter that the new feature is working perfectly. In that case, you want to run the defect verification testing first. Because that is the critical piece of the test, failing it makes the entire code unusable in your production network, and the rest of the testing may not be necessary. Before any test execution begins, the entire test plan should be read and understood. If it becomes obvious that the order of test execution does not makes sense, it should be resolved, sometimes by having all of the stakeholders weigh in.

A chronological list of tasks done in a typical test execution may look something like the following. Note that this example is provided as one possible illustration of how a structured test would be ordered. Your test plan may require tasks to be accomplished in a different order.

1. Bring the network into a steady-state condition before any testing is conducted. All device interfaces should be passing traffic in an error-free state, protocol adjacencies should be stable, and no software or hardware crashes should be observed.

2. Leave the network in a steady state, with traffic flowing for a period of time to make sure you do not have any obvious hardware or software issues. Pay special attention to CPU and memory utilization trends during this period. Some organizations prefer to keep the network in steady state for several hours, days, or even up to a week in an attempt to monitor for issues such as memory leaks that are typically not immediately apparent.

3. Take snapshots of the baseline configuration files and protocol states. You may spend hours troubleshooting the reasons why a BGP neighbor did not recover after a negative test, when in fact it was never up in the first place during the baseline testing.

4. Always run your test cases more than once, and check whether you get consistent results after each iteration. If results are inconsistent, be sure you can explain why.

5. Document all of your results and save your captures in appropriately named files. It is often useful to name these capture files with a method that can be later mapped to the test case. Some examples of appropriate names are discussed later in this chapter.

6. Bring your network back into a steady state between "failure" test cases, unless required otherwise by the test plan. Bringing the network back up can sometimes be more disruptive than failing it. Document the restoration of services, just as you would a failure.

It is critical that you understand the exit criteria for any test plan. In most cases, exit criteria require that you complete 100 percent of the test cases, unless you run into a critical defect with no viable workaround. If you observe unexpected results during your tests, you need to understand, without a shadow of a doubt, whether they are valid problems, as opposed to problems with your test tools, method, or procedures.

If and when a bug or defect is suspected during testing, follow these steps to perform root cause analysis and obtain resolution:

Step 1. Attempt to consistently reproduce any problems found during testing. This will help you validate the problem and understand the possible triggers. Clearly document the baseline environment and set of conditions that preceded the unexpected results.

Step 2. Open a trouble ticket with your equipment or software vendor if the problem is reproducible and a bug is suspected. If you have not found a workaround, check with your vendor to find out if one exists.

Step 3. Verify with your vendor that the unexpected result is indeed a software or hardware defect and not expected behavior.

Step 4. Find out from your vendor when a fixed version of the software or hardware will be available, if it is known.

Step 5. If you run into a critical defect during your testing and cannot find a valid workaround, discuss the issue with the stakeholders and decide if it is worthwhile to continue with the testing. Take into account the availability of fixed software or hardware.

Step 6. Be ready to test the workaround or the fixed software or hardware as soon as the vendor makes it available.

Tip   Knowing when a defect is critical enough to stop testing is usually a question of common sense and understanding your test project's objectives and requirements. Keeping the project stakeholders informed is critical during these situations, as they may be able to offer guidance. Be sure that you understand and can articulate the impact, triggers, and workarounds if they exist.

Running the Test Cases

A well-written test case should contain everything that an engineer needs to perform a test, including a concise description of the setup, steps, and format to be used for recording the results. If they are known, the test case will also provide the engineer with what would be considered the expected results. The test case shown in Table 5-6 is an example of a simple, yet effective, format that an engineer could literally rip out from the rest of the document and follow as a "recipe" as the test is conducted.

Note   "Figure 1" and "Section 5-2" are used in Tables 5-6 and 5-7 as examples. In a well-written test plan, you would have a diagram depicting how the test topology is to be built and clear instructions on how to save results and captures.

Table 5-6 *Example of a Test Case for OSPF*

Test ID:	DELTA-BASE-01
Node List:	Backbone routers: DELTA6500-Core1, DELTA6500-Core2, DELTA6500-Core3, DELTA6500-Core4
Test Phase:	Baseline
Test Description:	OSPF Baseline Test
Test Setup:	Backbone routers interconnected in full mesh with Gigabit Ethernet and OC-48 SONET links as shown in the detailed lab topology diagram in Figure 1.
	Test ports Gig1/0–Gig1/4 on traffic generator IXIA1 connected to the backbone router ports Gig2/0–G2/4 as shown in Figure 1.
Test Steps:	**Step 1.** Enable screen logging in terminal window.
	Step 2. Start full mesh of Ixia loading traffic, 1000 pps with packet size of 64 bytes.
	Step 3. Verify the traffic is received on each test port and there are no packet drops (received rate from each stream is 1000 pps).
	Step 4. Capture OSPF status on each core router with the following commands: **show ip ospf interface** **show ip ospf neighbor**
	Step 5. Record as baseline by saving log file in the standard format described in Section 5-2.
Expected Results:	All interfaces configured in OSPF Area 0, with OSPF network type "point to point." Each backbone router will have three OSPF neighbors in FULL state.
Observed Results:	
Pass/Fail:	

Notice the level of detail in the test steps. While this may seem like overkill for such a simple scenario, it will guarantee that no ambiguity exists, allowing the engineer to repeat the test at a later time if needed, using the exact conditions in which it was originally conducted.

In some instances, it may be convenient to reference a different portion of the test plan to describe the test setup or set of preconditions. In Table 5-7, a complex traffic mesh is used for several sets of tests.

Table 5-7   *Example Test Case for QoS*

Test ID:	DELTA-QOS-02
Node List:	All Delta backbone routers (DELTA6500-Core1, DELTA6500-Core2, DELTA6500-Core3, DELTA6500-Core4)
Test Phase:	Feature
Test Description:	Quality of Service (QoS) Feature Test
Test Setup:	Backbone routers interconnected in full mesh with Gigabit Ethernet and OC-48 SONET links as shown in the detailed lab topology diagram in Figure 1.
	Test ports Gig1/0–Gig1/4 on traffic generator IXIA1 connected to the backbone router ports Gig2/0–G2/4 as shown in Figure 1.
Test Steps:	**Step 1.** Enable screen logging in terminal window.
	Step 2. Start full mesh of Ixia traffic as shown in the traffic mesh in Table 3-1 of this test plan.
	Step 3. Verify that each class of traffic is received on the test ports at the expected rate described in Table 3-1 of this test plan.
	Step 4. Capture QoS statistics on each router with the following command: **show policy-map interface** *core interface*
	Step 5. Record as baseline by saving log file in the standard format described in Section 5-2.
Expected Results:	Traffic statistics for each of the eight service classes will be displayed in the CLI capture and on the receiving IXIA port at the rates described in Table 3-1.
Observed Results:	
Pass/Fail:	

The integrity of any test depends on meticulous, accurate data gathering. In general, most people reading a test report will only look at the outcome of the test case, often skimming to the Pass/Fail results. However, having all the relevant data to back up the Pass/Fail result is required.

Capturing and Saving Results

The representation of test case results should include the following elements:

Step 1.   Indication of whether the test resulted in a "Pass" or "Fail." In cases without defined success criteria (such as scale testing), a result of "Other" should be recorded with supplemental information provided. For example:

■   The router had 55 BGP neighbors in the ESTABLISHED state before the CPU utilization reached 95 percent.

■   The system under test was able to forward 8 Gbps of bidirectional (IMIX) traffic without any drops or errors occurring.

Step 2.   A set of raw data files containing all of the data that was captured via the CLI during the testing. A suggested format for the names of the raw files is as follows:

<Test ID>_<Device>_TR<Test Run><Test Iteration>.doc

where

■   <Test ID> = Test ID identified in the Test Case section of the test plan

■   <Device> = Device Name

■   <Test Run> = Test Run Number

■   <Iteration> = Letter to represent the iteration, A=First, B=Second, etc.

Here are more examples for further clarity:

DELTA-BASE-01_DELTA6500-1_TR1A.txt = initial baseline of DELTA6500-1 switch

DELTA-BASE-01_DELTA7600-2_TR1A.txt = initial baseline of DELTA7600-2 router

DELTA-BASE-01_DELTA6500-1_TR2B.txt = second test run and the second iteration of the baseline for this switch

Step 3.   A set of files containing SNMP trap information generated by each test, which would use a similar format, as follows:

<Test ID>_SNMP-<Test Run><Test Iteration>.doc

where

- <Test ID> = Test ID identified in the Test Case section of the test plan

- <Test Run> = Test Run Number

- <Iteration> = Letter to represent the iteration, A=First, B=Second, etc.

An examples for further clarity is shown here:

DELTA-BASE-01_SNMP_TR1A.txt = SNMP traps generated as a result of the first iteration of Test Run 1 of Baseline Test #1

Step 4.   A set of files containing screen captures taken during the test, which would use a format as follows:

<Test ID>_CAP<Capture Number>_<Test Run><Test Iteration>.gif

where

- <Test ID> = Test ID identified in the Test Case section of the test plan

- <Capture Number> = The order of the capture, 1 = First screen capture, 2 = Second screen capture, and so on.

- <Test Run> = Test Run Number

- <Iteration> = Letter to represent the iteration, A = First, B = Second, and so on.

The following is an example for further clarity:

DELTA-BASE-01_CAP3_TR1A.gif = The third screen capture generated as a result of the first iteration of Test Run 1 of Baseline Test #1

The format for results capturing should be clearly defined in the test plan. This will allow any relevant captures to be easily found at a later date.

Organizing the Capture Files

Creating separate folders on a shared drive will help keep results documentation organized and archived. A folder named DELTA-BASE-01, for example, would contain all of the capture files associated with that particular test case:

Folder DELTA-BASE-01 contains capture files:

DELTA-BASE-01_DELTA6500-1_TR1A.txt

DELTA-BASE-01_DELTA6500-2_TR1A.txt

DELTA-BASE-01_DELTA6500-3_TR1A.txt

DELTA-BASE-01_DELTA6500-4_TR1A.txt

Router Configuration Files

The router configuration files used during each test should be saved and included with the test. This applies to the initial configuration file, and any files that are changed during the test procedure. The extent of the changes should be detailed using the following three types of files:

- **Start-of-test router configuration files:** This would include any changes to the original starting configuration files made before testing begins.

- **Interim test configuration files:** This would include any change to the configuration not specified by the test plan. This includes configuration changes made as a result of a workaround, correction of a configuration error, or a configuration change to validate an item not specified by the test plan.

- **End-of-test router configuration files:** This would include the configuration files loaded at the end of the testing.

All of these naming conventions may seem overcomplicated as you read this for the first time. Only after you run a test with 80 different test cases, each of which needs to be run three times on 20 different devices, will all of this organization prove its worth. While painstakingly slow and tedious at first, this system will eventually become second nature, and ultimately spare you from having to repeat testing in the future.

Data Archival

Test results and all of the supporting data should be saved on a shared network folder that is regularly backed up. It is not a bad idea to have the folder password-protected if the configurations used in your testing contain sensitive company information, such as security ACLs, preshared keys, or any other information you wish to remain confidential. Storing the capture files on a shared folder will also allow you to distribute a fairly "lean" results document to all interested parties, with the supplemental data listed as a reference. You may find that most people want to know only whether a test case passed or failed and are not interested in looking through hundreds of pages of captures. Those that need to access the raw data for a closer analysis can simply follow the links to the shared network folder that contains the raw data.

Summary

This chapter covered some of the leading practices for effectively organizing and executing network testing. The chapter provided example processes and test methods to help you conduct complex testing using a variety of test tools and Cisco IOS features. The importance of accurate results gathering and data archival was stressed in an effort to help you get your testing done correctly the first time.

In the next part of this book, we will present a case study that will walk through a new deployment of a next-generation data center network. Real-world examples of tests that would occur during each phase of the deployment will be provided to help you absorb many of the concepts discussed in the first five chapters of the book.

Part II

Case Studies

Part II consists of case studies on several enterprise network testing projects. Each case study examines a test initiative conducted during a different time in the network lifecycle. Part II serves to further illustrate how network testing should be continuously leveraged to mitigate risks associated with a new architecture, technology introduction, or changes to the network infrastructure. The companies depicted in each study in the list that follows are fictional, but the designs and test plans are based on actual customer deployments. Individual chapters have been dedicated to each case study, as follows:

Chapter 6

Proof of Concept Testing Case Study

This chapter covers the following topics:

- Background for the Proof of Concept Testing Case Study
- Proof of Concept Test Strategy

Proof of concept (POC) testing is often conducted to assist architects and network managers in qualifying a new design or to obtain confidence when introducing new technology into the enterprise. As explained in Chapter 2, "Testing Throughout the Network Lifecycle," a POC test helps engineers and operators "test drive" a proposed network design or technology solution prior to deployment, helping reduce risks and time to implementation.

The following case study demonstrates how ATC Federated Bank conducted a POC test to gain confidence in a new network architecture that was proposed as part of a data center centralization/consolidation strategy.

Background for the Proof of Concept Testing Case Study

ATC Federated Bank is a regional financial services company with a portfolio of diversified services, including full-service commercial and retail banking, wealth management, and asset management. In contrast to most of the competition, ATC Federated Bank continued to operate in growth mode during the near meltdown of the financial markets in 2008, increasing its branches from 30 to over 200 in the Southeastern Region. This unprecedented growth was largely attributed to modern financial IT systems that enable a self-service model, and an aggressive strategy of mergers and acquisitions.

The explosive growth of ATC Federated has created serious challenges for the IT leadership of the company. In particular, the rash of acquisitions left the company with ten data centers to manage, each operating autonomously with its own staff, procedures, and unique computing, storage, and network infrastructures. IT operating costs skyrocketed for ATC Federated with the acquisitions, and the integration of disparate systems was painfully slow. The different procedures, hardware and software components, and service contracts also created an impossible disaster recovery and data retention dilemma. With different backup and restore methods and hardware, there was no way to create a cohesive plan for the entire enterprise.

As part of a new vision to reduce operating costs, accelerate integration of newly acquired companies, and establish a reliable disaster recovery strategy, ATC Federated's executives launched "Project Legion," which involved the consolidation of the ten existing data centers into four "super centers" based on Cisco Data Center 3.0 architectural principles and equipment.

High-level requirements for the new data center architecture include the following:

■ Provide inherent disaster recovery and business continuity by grouping data center pairs into "shared grids," where servers appear to be connected to a common "cloud"

■ Capability to offer virtualized resources (servers, storage, applications, and networking) on demand to accelerate the integration of newly acquired companies

■ Capable of horizontal scaling (scaling out) in which nodes or servers can be added quickly to increase the capacity of the application environment

■ Low-latency, lossless 10-Gigabit Ethernet network fabric with Fibre Channel over Ethernet (FCoE) capability

■ Fault-tolerant site infrastructure with redundant electrical, cooling, and distribution facilities guaranteeing 99.995 percent availability

■ Capability to support moving resources between the two shared-grid data centers on demand and automatically according to a predefined policy, replacing the need for equivalent manual tasks

Proposed Data Center Architecture

In response to a Request for Proposal (RFP), a Cisco Gold Certified Partner and the ATC Federated Cisco Account team developed a high-level design for the new data center. A "cloud computing" environment was proposed that included a multitier design with distinct access, aggregation, and core layers, with the Cisco Unified Computing System (UCS) and service provider connectivity, as shown in Figure 6-1.

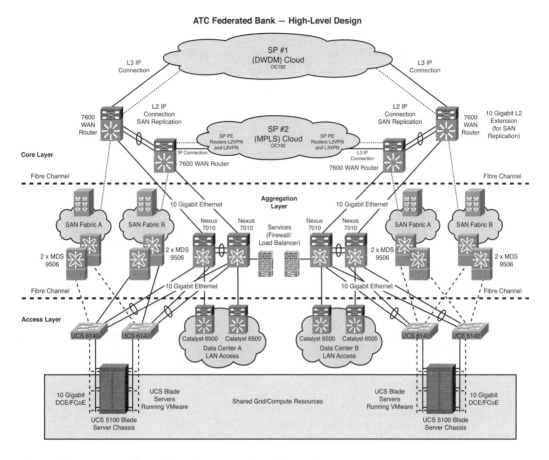

Figure 6-1   *ATC Federated Bank Proposed High-Level Design*

Compute Infrastructure

The new compute infrastructure was built upon the Cisco UCS, a next-generation data center platform that unites server, network, storage access, and virtualization functionality into a cohesive system. The Cisco UCS consists of the following components:

■ **Cisco UCS 6100 Series Fabric Interconnect Switches:** A family of line-rate, low-latency, lossless, 10-Gigabit Ethernet interconnect switches that consolidate I/O within the system and accommodate expansion modules that provide Fibre Channel and 10-Gigabit Ethernet connectivity to the Server Blade Chassis.

■ **Cisco UCS 5100 Series Blade Server Chassis:** Supports up to eight blade servers and up to two fabric extenders in a 6-RU enclosure without the need for additional management modules.

■ **Cisco UCS 2100 Series Fabric Extenders:** Bring the unified fabric into the blade-server chassis, providing up to four 10-Gigabit connections each between blade servers and the fabric interconnect, simplifying diagnostics, cabling, and management.

- **Cisco UCS B-Series Blade Servers:** Based on Intel Xeon 5500 Series processors, adapt to application demands, intelligently scale energy use, and offer best-in-class virtualization. Each blade server uses network adapters for access to the unified fabric. Cisco's unique memory-expansion technology substantially increases the memory footprint, improving performance and capacity for demanding virtualization and large-data-set workloads. In addition, the technology offers a cost-effective memory footprint for less-demanding workloads.

- **Cisco UCS network adapters:** Offered in a mezzanine-card form factor. Three types of adapters offer a range of options to meet application requirements, including adapters optimized for virtualization, compatibility with existing driver stacks, or efficient, high-performance Ethernet.

- **Cisco UCS C-Series Rack-Mount Servers:** Can be deployed as an integrated element of the Cisco UCS or standalone. They extend the standards-based innovation, TCO reductions, and increased business agility that the UCS offers to customers who require rack-mount servers as well as blade servers, addressing the vast majority of data center computing requirements.

Storage Infrastructure

A redundant dual-fabric storage-area network (SAN) was designed for each data center pair, leveraging the FCoE capabilities of the Cisco UCS, and redundant pairs of Cisco MDS 9506 Multilayer Directors serving as the front-end switches to the EMC VMAX storage arrays.

The redundant SAN fabrics at each location allow replication to occur between the data center pairs by leveraging Fibre Channel over IP (FCIP) connectivity running over the IP service provider networks that form the redundant WAN transport. Each SAN will be configured as "read/write" for the local site, and "read only" in its replicated site across the WAN. Each SAN fabric will have redundant Cisco MDS 9509 Multilayer Director switches with virtual SAN (VSAN) capabilities.

LAN Infrastructure

The multitiered LAN infrastructure at each data center is composed of Cisco Catalyst 6500 Series Switches at the access layer and Cisco Nexus 7010 Series Switches at the distribution layer. The Catalyst 6500 switches connect the legacy network to shared network services and applications residing on the Cisco UCS by way of the Nexus 7010 aggregation-layer switches.

The Cisco UCS is connected to the aggregation layer with multiple 10-Gigabit Ethernet links that are bundled into port channels and split across the pair of Nexus 7010 switches. The Nexus 7010 switches are deployed with virtual PortChannel (vPC) technology, a feature that allows a port channel to be aggregated across two Nexus chassis. The use of multichassis vPCs eliminates the need for blocking in spanning tree and its failover constraints, allowing all of the 10-Gigabit Ethernet links to carry traffic, and at the same time providing redundancy and resiliency during single chassis failures.

WAN Infrastructure

A redundant WAN infrastructure between the data centers is proposed using circuits and backbone networks leased from the service provider. This WAN infrastructure will transport the IP application and FCIP (SAN replication) traffic between data center pairs. A pair of Cisco 7604 WAN routers at each data center will terminate the service provider 10-Gigabit Ethernet handoffs and facilitate inter–data center forwarding.

The Cisco 7604 WAN routers will be configured with Layer 2 Data Center Interconnects (DCI), based on Ethernet over MPLS (EoMPLS) technology in order to facilitate the Layer 2 network requirements of VMware VMotion and Distributed Resource Scheduler (DRS). The 10-Gigabit Ethernet core-facing interfaces of the DCI will connect to a service provider Layer 2 service such as L2VPN or dense wavelength-division multiplexing (DWDM) lambda service. For inter–data center LAN traffic, the WAN routers will connect to a Layer 3 (MPLS/VPN) service or directly to a Layer 2 (DWDM) service with routed/BGP connections.

Virtualization Software

Because ATC Federated Bank is already using VMware for a pilot program, the POC is leveraging VMware ESX 4.0 Update 2 software for virtualization services. VMware tools and scripts such as VMotion and DRS are used for moving workloads and for disaster recovery. The requirements of some of these tools drive the need of Layer 2 extensions across the two "partner" data centers.

Summary of New Data Center Architectural Elements

Nexus 7010 Data Center Core LAN Switches with virtual Port Channel to provide simplified redundancy and bandwidth aggregation

Cisco Unified Computing System (UCS) to replace legacy servers and blade chassis solutions

Storage-area network (SAN) solution to replace existing local and legacy storage, as well as tape-based backup systems

Data Center Interconnect (DCI) Layer 2 extensions between "partner" data centers

Risks of Deploying the Proposed Solution

The executives at ATC Federated Bank are extremely anxious about deploying any new technology solution that has the potential to cause an outage and disrupt the business. Although ATC Federated has been a longtime Cisco customer, the Nexus 7010 and UCS platforms have not yet been deployed in the network, and the executives are concerned that the solution may not perform or interoperate as expected. The RFP that was generated mandates that any proposed solution must pass a proof of concept test as part of the evaluation and selection criteria.

Proof of Concept Test Strategy

Due to the amount of equipment and new technology involved in the test, it was decided that the best location to conduct the POC testing would be in one of the Cisco Enterprise testing facilities. Working with the Cisco Gold Certified Partner and the Account team, the architects of ATC Federated developed a high-level test plan that would be jointly executed with Cisco test engineers.

POC Test Objectives

Four primary objectives were identified for the POC testing:

- **Obtain confidence with the end-to-end solution:** Ensure that all of the architectural elements (LAN, SAN, compute) perform as expected during steady-state and failure conditions.

- **Gain experience with the UCS platform:** By participating in the POC tests, ATC Federated engineers and operators were able to get a firsthand look at the UCS platform, and hands-on experience in provisioning compute resources using the UCS Manager (UCSM).

- **Gain experience with Nexus/NX-OS hardware and software platforms:** The Nexus platform and NX-OS software are new to ATC Federated, and this was their first chance to get experience with configuring, troubleshooting, and managing the platform.

- **Identify the bill of materials for the new solution:** At the conclusion of POC testing, ATC Federated wanted to be able to identify a bill of materials for the exact equipment (chassis, line cards, software, and licensing) that needed to be ordered to implement this architecture.

POC Test Topology

The topology in Figure 6-2 was built in the Cisco Enterprise test lab for the purposes of this POC test.

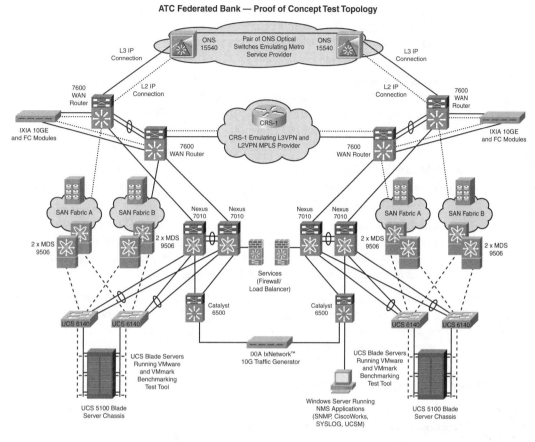

Figure 6-2 *ATC Federated Data Center Proof of Concept Test Topology*

The test topology built in the Cisco test lab included all of the functional elements of the proposed architecture, in addition to simulated service provider networks for WAN connectivity, network management systems (NMS), and Ixia Traffic Generators with 10-Gigabit Ethernet and Fibre Channel capabilities. A summary of this equipment is as follows:

■ **Cisco Systems test gear:** Nexus 7010s, MDS 9506s, Catalyst 6506, Cisco 7604s, ONS 15454, CRS-1, Cisco UCS (6140 Fabric Interconnects, 5100 Blade Server Chassis, 2104 in chassis fabric extenders, B-Series Blade Servers with CNAs).

■ **EMC:** EMC VMAX SE Storage Systems with Symmetrix Remote Data Facility (SRDF) and PowerPath/VE licensing. PowerPath/VE software for the UCS blades.

■ **Ixia IxNetwork:** The Ixia IxNetwork testing application suite was used to generate traffic, measure latency, perform route injection, and determine route convergence times during the failure scenarios.

- **Ixia IxSAN:** The Ixia IxSAN testing application is used as a SAN test solution for real-world, large-scale emulation of Fibre Channel Protocol (FCP) targets and initiators over Ethernet, which allows the characterization of I/O performance of converged network systems.

- **Network management software (UCSM, CiscoWorks, syslog, SNMP):** A Windows server was connected into the topology with all of the necessary NMS tools to manage the devices, and with a browser to access the Cisco UCSM application, which resides on the UCS 6140 Fabric Interconnect and is used to provision the UCS system.

- **VMware Virtualization Software:** ESX 4.0 Update 2 software was used with VMware vSphere Enterprise Plus licenses. The system was run with dual vCenter servers running as virtual machines (VM).

- **VMware VMmark benchmarking tool:** VMmark is a free tool by VMware that measures the performance and scalability of hardware running applications in virtualized VMware environments. This tool was used to drive and measure the compute resources running across both partner data centers.

- **Iometer storage testing tool:** Iometer is an I/O subsystem measurement and characterization tool for single and clustered systems. This tool is often used to create load on the storage arrays and was used to measure maximum input/output operations per second (IOPS) on the storage arrays.

Proof of Concept Test Scope

Proof of concept testing was divided into specific tests that focus on the components or functional areas described in the sections that follow.

Network Baseline Test

The network baseline test consisted of capturing the state of the network during normal operations with typical traffic flows. The network baseline test included basic information for the simulation. This consisted of validating that the routing emulation and data and storage flows were as expected. Data flows were monitored for content (source, destination, load rate) and path information through the infrastructure, by the use of marker flows generated by Ixia IxNetwork. For each (Layer 2, Layer 3, and FCIP storage) flow, the simulation baseline information required identifying the path and rate information for a specific marker flow. The remaining simulated flows were measured for aggregate rate only.

Application Baseline Test

The application baseline test consisted of capturing the state of the applications during a normal operating condition with typical traffic flows. The application baseline test included a typical simulation to see how well a host runs a set of well-known applications as VMs under a steady state. VMware's VMmark tools were used for parts of this test.

Network and Application Integrity Test

The network and application integrity test consisted of validating that the network and applications were working as expected following the execution of a test. Additionally, it was used to validate that the network and applications remained stable over an extended-run test. It consisted of obtaining and comparing information with the network baseline information. The data flows were measured for packet loss during this interval; the application was tested, and the results were compared to the ones obtained during the application baseline test. The network integrity test was performed using one data load condition. The test was performed to validate network and application integrity after various tests.

Failure/Recovery Test

The failure/recovery test consisted of performing various selective failures within the infrastructure. A network and application integrity test was performed after the failure or recovery was conducted. The levels of network and application integrity tests performed were identified in the test procedure document and were meant to show normal behavior during "expected" and "likely" failures.

Feature Validation Tests

The feature validation test consisted of performing various actions to verify that critical features identified by the customer worked as expected within the data center architecture as it was built in the lab.

Automation Validation Test

The automation validation test was performed to show that several of the VMware automation processes and tools planned to be used by ATC Federated Bank in its disaster recovery and disaster avoidance procedures, which relied on Layer 2 being extended across the two partner data centers, worked as expected. It also measured the time required to perform the automated migrations between data centers.

Performance/Scalability/Capacity Test

The first part of the capacity test consisted of generating data up to the 10-Gigabit line rate at various packet sizes across the LAN and WAN infrastructures. The test was built to assess the saturation and breaking point for the data center architecture. It also tested the behavior of the application and storage replication once the LAN and WAN began to be overwhelmed. It showed how QoS, control plane policing (CoPP), and several network management features work within the proposed architecture. The second part of the test consisted of putting a high load on the compute/memory/storage resources to see how far they could be pushed for the particular applications running on the cloud. The third part tested the disk IOPS for the storage arrays. The final part consisted of stressing the network and compute/memory/storage resources at the same time to see how the entire cloud responded.

Summary of POC Test Cases

Table 6-1 provides a list of test cases that were performed during the POC.

Table 6-1 *POC Test Case Summary*

Test Case	Test Name	Short Test Description
Network Baseline Tests		
1.1	Base Topology Physical Configuration and Connectivity Verification	Step-by-step configuration procedures explained and logged for future reference. Capture **show** commands from device consoles (where available) to demonstrate connectivity.
1.2	Aggregation Layer Routing Protocol Configuration and Verification	Enable OSPF on the Nexus 7010 and Catalyst 6500 in each data center.
1.3	WAN Layer 3 Routing Configuration and Verification	Configure eBGP between 7604 WAN router and MPLS/VPN PE router. Configure eBGP between 7604 routers connected to Layer 2 service provider in each data center.
1.4	WAN Data Center Interconnect (DCI) Configuration and Verification	Configure EoMPLS pseudowire between Cisco 7604 routers in partner data centers to support Layer 2 extensions for VMware requirements.
1.5	End-to-End Routing Verification	Verify routing between data centers. Pings and traceroutes to validate forwarding plane.
1.6	SAN Configuration	Configure two separate VSAN fabrics on the MDSs and add zoning information. Configure LUNs and masking on the EMC VMAX arrays. Configure SRDF synchronous and asynchronous replication between the arrays. Configure FCIP connectivity between the MDSs in the partner data centers to enable SRDF replication.
1.7	UCS Configuration	Configure UCS interfaces, MAC address pools, WWNN and WWPN pools, vNIC and vHBA templates, UUID pools, server pools, boot policies, firmware policies, service profile templates, service profiles, and other necessary features. Configure the PowerPath/VE software for storage load balancing. Boot blade servers from SAN in their local data center.

Table 6-1   *POC Test Case Summary*

Test Case	Test Name	Short Test Description
1.8	IXIA Traffic Verification	Send test traffic between data centers and measure latency and any associated loss at various rates.

Application Baseline Tests

2.1	Load the VMmark Tiles onto the ESX Hosts	All six VMmark VMs (tile) must be loaded onto each host. The tiles consist of an Exchange server, a Java server, a file server, a standby server, a database server, and a web server.
2.2	VMmark Steady State Test	Run a full VMmark test on an ESX host running eight full tiles (48 VMs) during steady-state operation. The clients should be in the same DC as the VMs. Record the scores for future reference.
2.3	VMmark Steady State Test Across Partner DCs	Run the full VMmark test on the ESX host when the clients are in the partner data center. Record the scores for future reference.

Network and Application Integrity Tests

3.1	Short VMmark Test	Run a 15-minute VMmark test using only one tile out of the eight running on the host. (Run this test three times and use the average for the baseline.) This will be the baseline for all future verification testing. Once failures and migrations are run, this baseline test should be rerun for validation.
3.2	Long Term VMmark and Network Tests	Run the VMmark test for a 24-hour period on both data centers while running the WAN at a 50% load rate. This should be run with all required features, such as QoS, NetFlow, logging, CoPP, VMware FT, SRDF, etc., enabled.
3.3	Long Term SAN/SRDF Replication Test	This test is run in conjunction with the preceding Long Term VMmark and Network Tests. It should show that sync and async replication work as expected during the entire 24 hours.

Failure/Recovery Test

4.1	Network Failure and Test Traffic Convergence Testing (Links)	Perform failures/recoveries on active and passive links on the Nexus 6100s, Nexus 7010s, Catalyst 6500s, and 7600s. These tests should be run with 40% traffic on the network and the VMmark testing running. Measure convergence events using Ixia IxNetwork and make sure the VMmark test and SRDF do not fail.

Table 6-1   *POC Test Case Summary*

Test Case	Test Name	Short Test Description
4.2	Network Failure and Test Traffic Convergence Testing (Chassis)	Perform failures/recoveries on active and passive chassis including a Nexus 6100, Nexus 7010, Catalyst 6500, and 7600. These tests should be run with 40% traffic on the network and the VMmark testing running. Measure convergence events using Ixia IxNetwork and make sure the VMmark test and SRDF do not fail.
4.3	SAN Failure and Traffic Convergence Testing (Links)	Perform failures/recoveries on active and passive links between the MDS and the EMC VMAX, the MDS and the Nexus 6100, and finally the MDS and the LAN. Make sure the VMmark test and SRDF do not fail.
4.4	SAN Failure and Traffic Convergence Testing (Chassis)	Perform failures/recoveries on an MDS 9506 Chassis MDS and the LAN. Make sure the VMmark test and SRDF do not fail.
4.5	VMware FT Failover	Fail the host of a VM that is running fault tolerance and make sure the backup takes over. Make sure the VMmark test does not fail.
4.6	Short VMmark Test Verification	Run a 15-minute VMmark test using only one tile out of the eight running on the host. Check the results against the baseline in Test 3.1.
Feature Validation Tests		
5.1	QoS Testing	Validate QoS on Nexus 7010, Catalyst 6500, and Cisco 7604 WAN QoS.
5.2	SAN Feature Testing	Make sure that FC, FCoE, and FCIP connectivity works as expected. Check vHBA load balancing on the ESX host.
5.3	Data Center Interconnect (DCI)	Perform EoMPLS, VPLS tests.
5.4	Virtual Port Channel (vPC)	Nexus 7010 vPC testing. This is in addition to the link failure scenarios.
5.5	BFD Tests	Nexus 7010, Catalyst 6500, and Cisco 7604 BFD testing at various timers.
5.6	Security Test	Validate that CoPP, iACL, AD, and AAA work as expected.

Table 6-1 *POC Test Case Summary*

Test Case	Test Name	Short Test Description
5.7	Network Management Test	Test SNMP, NetFlow v9, and syslog on all the hardware. Deploy the correct logging and management using an out-of-band network.
5.8	Duty Cycle Test	Use UCSM and CiscoWorks to load and upgrade firmware/code on devices. Test backup and restore operations using UCSM and CiscoWorks.
Automation Validation Tests		
6.1	Validate VMotion	VMotion a server from its original location to a host in the partner DC, while running VMmark and 50% network traffic.
6.2	Validate Storage VMotion Within Same DC	Perform a Storage VMotion within the same DC from one datastore to another while running VMmark and 50% network traffic.
6.3	Validate Storage VMotion Between Two Partner DCs	Perform a Storage VMotion from a "local" datastore to a datastore that resides in the partner DC while running VMmark and 50% network traffic.
6.4	Validate DRS Scripts	Use the customer's DRS scripts to migrate from one DC to its partner DC to simulate a DR scenario.
Performance/Scalability/Capacity Tests		
7.1	Network Saturation Test	In this test, Ixia IxNetwork is used to generate ever-more-increasing network traffic loads on the architecture until we see that compute and/or replication operations stop working. The amount of traffic generated to start should be 90% of the available bandwidth on the WAN. It should increase in 50-Mbps iterations. This should be run with all required features such as QoS, NetFlow, logging, CoPP, VMware FT, SRDF, etc. enabled.
7.2	Compute Performance Test	VMmark testing should begin with eight tiles on the compute resource. One tile should be added with each iteration of this test until it fails or the tile usability score is unacceptable. This should be run with 50% traffic on the network and all compute features such as VMware FT enabled.

Table 6-1 *POC Test Case Summary*

Test Case	Test Name	Short Test Description
7.3	Storage Performance Test	Several VMs running Iometer software should be deployed to test the IOPS performance of the storage arrays. This test should be run will all storage features such as replication enabled.
7.4	System Performance Test	Run a 24-hour test with the network, compute, and storage systems running at 85% of the maximum values found in tests 7.1, 7.2, and 7.3. If the test fails, back off 2% for each component until a maximum steady state can be found.

Summary

After spending several weeks modeling and evaluating the new architecture in the Cisco enterprise labs, ATC Federated Bank had a much better understanding of the capabilities of a Cisco Data Center 3.0 architecture. They realized that their design would need to be changed slightly to take into account the requirements for storage replication and disaster recovery. They discovered that they need to minimize latency in their WAN connectivity, and that their server consolidation ratios from real servers to virtual machines were too aggressive. They found that replication, both synchronous and asynchronous over FCIP, worked better than they expected, even in times of WAN congestion, and that the UCS system running SAN multipathing software worked very well. ATC Federated network engineers were very impressed with the vPC feature on the Nexus 7010 and have decided to test it along with Fabric Extenders for a new top-of-rack switching project. Management has decided to go ahead and roll out a pilot Data Center 3.0 architecture between two of their existing data centers. If the pilot works as designed, ATC Federated Bank will adopt this architecture for all of the data centers in "Project Legion." ATC Federated Bank will be working with Cisco Advanced Services, their Cisco, EMC, and VMware account teams, and the Cisco Gold Certified Partner to roll out the pilot.

Chapter 7

Network Readiness Testing Case Study

This chapter covers the following topics:

- Background for the Network Readiness Testing Case Study

- Network Readiness Assessment Approach and Findings

Network readiness testing can be an extremely worthwhile exercise when you are attempting to gauge how well a new application or solution will perform on an existing network infrastructure. This type of testing often occurs during the planning phase of a new project, either as a prequalification for a proposed solution, or as part of a network audit to identify gaps in the infrastructure that will need to be remediated prior to deployment. Because the performance requirements for VoIP are well defined in terms of loss, delay, and jitter, organizations planning to deploy IP Telephony or Unified Communications (UC) solutions often conduct testing on their live network to help gauge its readiness. Industry experts agree that assessing the network prior to deployment makes VoIP rollouts faster, more successful, and less costly by reducing post-implementation troubleshooting.

The following case study shares the details of how a software development company was able to successfully leverage network readiness testing as part of the overall certification of a Unified Communications design.

Background for the Network Readiness Testing Case Study

MilSpec Software Solutions is a U.S.-based software development company with major campus offices in Boston, Massachusetts, and Research Triangle Park (RTP), North Carolina. The company develops smartphone applications with a focus on enterprise feature integration. In line with the success of an industry that has boomed in recent times, MilSpec Software Solutions has grown at a rate of 15 percent year over year. The company has a 19 percent market share of the U.S. mobile enterprise application solutions segment, and is in the process of taking over another startup company located in San Francisco, California. The management is keen to acquire additional companies as part of a strategy to generate new business growth by opening up new markets. Around 30 percent of the company's workforce is composed of teleworkers, based out of home offices when not traveling to customers' and partners' sites. Teleworkers connect to the office using a software VPN solution.

Legacy Network Infrastructure Overview

MilSpec Software Solutions has been a Cisco Systems customer since its inception in 2001. Following the best practices guidelines for a hierarchical network design, its network has been deployed with clearly defined core, distribution, and access layers. The company operates two major data centers in its campus locations; one in the Headquarters site in Boston, and the other in a recently acquired company's main site located in RTP, North Carolina. The two locations are interconnected with a pair of OC12 circuits, forming the backbone of the network core. In addition to the Boston and RTP campus sites, MilSpec has 20 remote locations, where a distributed sales force, development group, and support teams maintain offices. These remote locations gain access to the corporate IT (data only) systems over a WAN built on a service provider Layer 3 MPLS service. Remote locations typically connect to the MPLS WAN by means of fractional T1 links, ranging from 512 Kbps to 768 Kbps depending on individual needs. The enterprise voice environment includes legacy PBXs at the campus sites and key telephone systems (KTS) obtained from various manufacturers at the remote locations. As part of the RTP campus site acquisition, the company inherited a legacy PBX from a different manufacturer than the one that was in place at its parent site in Boston, limiting the voice features that could be offered between the two major campuses. Figure 7-1 shows a high-level view of the MilSpec Software Solutions campus and remote office WAN connectivity.

Cisco Unified Communications Proposed Solution

MilSpec Software Solutions decided to invest in a Cisco Unified Communications infrastructure to improve workforce productivity, reduce operational costs, and ease the integration associated with company acquisitions. The first phase of UC deployment included a complete retrofit of legacy phone systems to Cisco VoIP, followed by the introduction of Cisco Contact Center Enterprise for streamlined call center operations. The primary drivers to justify this investment included the following:

■   Reduced OPEX due to centralized management and control.

■   Reduced time to offer unified voice capabilities to new companies that are acquired and integrated.

■   Mobile workforces can have Single Number Reach (SNR) feature functionality.

■   Reduced travel expenses as the UC solutions provide easier and more direct collaboration between coworkers, suppliers, and clients at different sites.

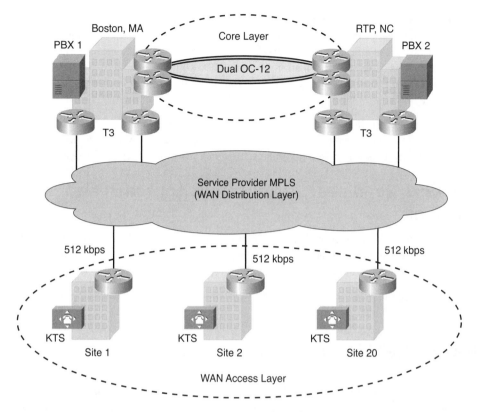

Figure 7-1   *Existing MilSpec Software Solutions Network Design*

Risks Associated with Implementing the Proposed Solution

Although the CIO was eager to realize the benefits of Unified Communications, he recognized that rushing the deployment could risk failure of the UC project and potentially impact data network stability. A primary concern for the CIO and his engineering team was whether the existing data network was capable of handling the unique demands of real-time VoIP traffic, and whether the performance of business data applications would be degraded under the additional strain. It was determined that a formal analysis would need to be completed to determine what gaps, if any, needed to be remediated prior to deploying the solution. To seek guidance with this analysis, the CIO hired a Cisco Advanced Services consultant specializing in VoIP and UC deployments. Having dealt with several clients with similar projects and concerns, the consultant recommended that a thorough assessment be carried out, involving the following activities:

■ **Network Readiness Assessment (NRA):** Involves an audit of the network devices to determine operational health and compliance with standards and best practices for VoIP deployments. Information gained during the network audit would be used as a baseline to identify gaps in the device hardware, software, provisioning, and configuration standards that would need to be remediated.

- **Network Path Analysis (NPA):** Involves injection of synthetic VoIP traffic between various endpoints on the live production network. Results from the NPA would provide a good indicator of the voice quality that could be expected once the UC solution was deployed. Information from the NPA would be used to help guide decisions on whether circuit upgrades, QoS, or routing changes might be needed prior to deployment.

- **Summary of Recommendations:** Includes any predeployment actions that would need to be resolved prior to deployment (for example, hardware upgrades, enabling QoS features) and post-deployment processes and procedures for day-2 operations.

Network Readiness Assessment Approach and Findings

The following sections provide details on how the Network Readiness Assessment (NRA) and testing was accomplished, and how the associated findings were used to help MilSpec Software Solutions to prepare, deploy, and operate the new UC infrastructure.

The audit reports and recommendations delivered by the Cisco Advanced Services consultant are included after each section.

Network Readiness Assessment

The goal of the NRA is to identify the gaps, if any, that must be remediated on the network to support the additional requirements of real-time applications. An audit of design documentation, physical topology, running configurations, and operational performance statistics from network management system (NMS) reports is conducted during this exercise.

The NRA report is organized into several subsections that address different aspects of the core design.

Hierarchy and Modularity

This assessment evaluates whether an existing network infrastructure follows the Cisco best practice of hierarchical and modular design. This model offers many advantages over an unstructured, organically grown design, as it has proven to be easier to troubleshoot, upgrade, operate, and maintain. Network modularity helps to scale the design and simplify implementation and management because it is constructed from uniform building blocks and template configurations.

A manual review of the network topology and device hardware and software features and functionality is conducted.

Audit Report

- The network topology has been deployed in a hierarchical and modular fashion. Network routers and switches have been deployed in core, distribution, and access roles, each optimized for the specific functions that they entail. MilSpec has deployed standardized equipment models, Cisco IOS versions, and configurations across the network elements in each level of the hierarchy. The equipment models are all currently supported under a Cisco SMARTnet contract and their Cisco IOS versions will support the required QoS features needed for converged traffic.

- New Catalyst 6500 access layer switch lines cards are recommended for both campus sites to support power requirements and Ethernet connectivity of the Cisco IP Phones. The existing line cards do not support 802.1af (Power over Ethernet [PoE]) or the conditional endpoint QoS trust model.

- The remote office switches are Catalyst 3760s, which are PoE capable. It is recommended that a UPS be installed in each of the wiring closets to provide continuous service to the IP Phones in the event of a power outage.

Utilization and Redundancy

This assessment evaluates critical network resource utilization of production devices and circuits during peak usage hours. This includes short- and long-term sampling of link, CPU, and memory utilization of relevant routers and switches. A review of the circuit provisioning ratios throughout each layer of the hierarchy is also conducted to determine the oversubscription ratios that have been put in place. These ratios are compared against Cisco campus provisioning best practices to determine the likely congestion points that may cause problems when additional VoIP traffic is added to the network.

Note   Current best practices suggest distribution to access oversubscription ratio of 1:20, and core to distribution oversubscription ratio of 1:4.

The redundancy aspect of the verification includes checking for any single points of failure (SPOF) in the network. This includes a check for redundant supervisors, line cards, power supplies, and links at the critical paths of the infrastructure. The right level of network redundancy allows faster network convergence, which is an important consideration for real-time traffic like voice.

Audit Report

- The existing network has been provisioned within the guidelines of Cisco best practices for bandwidth oversubscription ratios. No more than ten access switches have been connected via 1-Gbps uplinks to any distribution level switch, reflecting a 1:10 distribution to access ratio, and the core to distribution ratio is less than 1:2.

- The peak utilization on all access layer uplinks is less than 20 percent. The OC-12 links between the data centers are underutilized (less than 25 percent) during office hours, but rise to 60 percent utilization during off-hours due to extensive backups and server mirroring. The WAN links to remote offices have been measured at relatively high utilization (above 60 percent) during office hours, spiking to over 80 percent in some cases. This is an area of concern for the planned IP telephony deployment because these circuits will require additional bandwidth for "on-net" interoffice calls. It is recommended that the WAN bandwidth at all remote locations be increased to at least a full T1.

■   The NMS historical report does not indicate any device crash or resource depletion (CPU or memory high utilization) for the past 12 months. A 12-month review was conducted to take into account any seasonal peak utilization variation (for example, MilSpec has a new software release cycle every 6 months, and hence there is a heavier workload expected during that time).

■   MilSpec has implemented an Active/Active redundancy methodology on its production IT/IS systems and servers. A high degree of device redundancy (node, route processor, line card, circuit, power supply) has been enforced accordingly in critical places in the network. No SPOFs have been noted outside of user PCs that are single-homed to access switches.

Access Layer Links

This assessment examines the connectivity between the access and distribution layers of the network infrastructure for conformance with Cisco best practices and recommendations. Some of the most important include the following:

■   Redundant, Layer 3 connections between access and distribution switches.

■   When Layer 3 is not possible, Layer 2 devices and links should be enabled with Rapid Spanning Tree Protocol (RSTP) to provide convergence times consistent with a typical Layer 3 topology.

■   Other Layer 2 optimizations should be enabled to improve convergence, including port-fast, manual duplex and trunk negotiations settings, lowered Hot Standby Router Protocol (HSRP) timers, BPDU Guard, Root Guard, and UniDirectional Link Detection (UDLD) configurations.

■   The number of hosts in a broadcast domain should be limited to 512 or fewer.

Audit Report

■   MilSpec has Layer 2 links from access to distribution switches and relies on default STP timers for network convergence. It is recommended that MilSpec reconfigure the Layer 2 links between access and distribution to Layer 3 links if possible so that convergence can be optimized.

■   If a conversion to Layer 3 links is not possible, it is recommended that access to distribution links be enabled with RSTP to provide faster convergence. HSRP timers should also be reduced to 250 ms on the distribution layer switches to improve first hop redundancy convergence.

■   A few of the access VLANs have grown exceptionally large, in some cases reaching nearly 1000 hosts. These VLANs should be repartitioned to limit the impact of the broadcast domains. A recommendation is made to change the current /21 VLAN allocation to /23, so that the site administrators will be less tempted to exceed the recommended number of 512 hosts/VLAN.

- New voice VLANs should be defined at each site for the purposes of infrastructure (gateway and server) connectivity. These VLANs should not span multiple switches.

- MilSpec has Cat5E cabling in place for Ethernet connectivity to all hosts and existing digital phones. No hubs or splitters were found in any of the offices that were randomly selected for inspection.

- Access LAN switches are enabled with recommended configurations to avoid broadcast storms associated with Layer 2 loops.

IP Routing

This assessment evaluates how the routing protocols have been deployed by manually inspecting the configurations and operational output from routers. It is important that routing convergence be as fast as possible throughout the data network (5 sec end to end) to avoid dropped calls or brownouts during failure scenarios. The size and stability of the routing database is checked from device logs, and features enabled to increase stability or improve convergence are recorded.

Audit Report

- MilSpec's network team deployed the OSPF routing protocol within the enterprise and uses the BGP routing protocol to connect with the ISP.

- Route summarization and area summarization are in place and the NMS report shows that the network has been stable, without much flapping, over the last 6 months.

- On Layer 3 connections, all the redundant links are load-balanced using Cisco Express Forwarding (CEF). Core network elements are capable of Nonstop Forwarding (NSF) functionality and currently have the feature active.

- It is recommended that Bidirectional Forwarding Detection (BFD) be configured on all of the routed uplinks and that OSPF shortest path first (SPF) timers be lowered to improve convergence during link failures.

QoS

This assessment evaluates the existing QoS configurations to determine whether changes are needed to support a converged network. The enterprise QoS policy is verified for Cisco best practices and checked for any deviations from the standard recommendations. This includes verifying both LAN and WAN QoS configurations, as well as the service provider's QoS policy to have QoS available from end to end via the service provider's network.

Audit Report

- In an effort to align with its MPLS service provider's QoS offering, MilSpec is in the process of revising its enterprise QoS design. The current enterprise QoS policy has provisions for 12 classes of service, but MilSpec is collapsing it down to six because its service provider offers a total of six QoS classes.

- It is recommended that three classes be reserved for UC requirements: Platinum for VoIP bearer traffic, Gold for call signaling, and Silver for inter-cluster traffic.

- The network latency between the Boston and RTP data centers is around 40 ms, which is an acceptable value for the UC cluster servers that are planned to be deployed "split" between these two data centers.

- No QoS features have currently been deployed in the access layer. It is recommended that MilSpec investigate and test the QoS features that will be necessary to support UC (for example, thresholds for CoS, congestion avoidance, DSCP to CoS mapping, and hardware queuing).

- LAN interface statistics indicate intermittent packet drops from the default queue. The new QoS strategy should include provisions for segregating different types of traffic to different hardware queues rather than sending all traffic to one default hardware queue.

- Current WAN routers have traffic shaping in place, but more work is needed to map the MilSpec QoS model to match the service provider's capabilities.

- From the voice traffic engineering study, at least 30 percent of the bandwidth (30 percent of a T1) is needed for voice media, and hence the necessary class-maps and policy-maps need to be modified in the WAN routers.

Network Path Analysis

While a network audit can be useful in ascertaining device level compliance and resource availability in general, it does little to predict how efficiently packets will be forwarded across an end-to-end path consisting of various devices and links under different load conditions. An audit essentially provides a snapshot of individual network device status at a particular point in time, making it difficult to detect variable conditions such as traffic "micro-bursts" that result in hardware queue overflows, or transient routing loops that cause packet drops or delay variations affecting VoIP call quality. Due to this variable nature of data traffic and networks, it is often necessary to send "simulated VoIP" test traffic on the live network, so it can be collected, measured, and used to estimate end-to-end network path quality.

As discussed in Chapter 4, "Crafting the Test Approach," there are many test tools available that use "probing" technologies to actively measure network performance, such as Cisco IOS IP SLA. The network operations team at MilSpec Software Solutions has experience with IP SLA, as they have previously deployed the feature on their WAN routers to actively measure the service quality of the MPLS network. While they considered the IP SLA feature to be very useful in measuring WAN network quality, they did not see how it could be used to probe effectively all the various LAN and WAN segments that the call signaling and bearer traffic would traverse in a UC deployment.

After rejecting several options they deemed to be too costly, intrusive, or inconclusive, MilSpec sought assistance from Cisco Advanced Services UC consultants to conduct an NPA. The NPA exercise uses active probing software that can very accurately simulate

VoIP traffic between various UC endpoints and subsequently measure, grade, and use the results to predict voice quality. The Cisco Media Traffic Analysis Agent (MTAA) software is used to conduct an NPA. It is loaded from a bootable USB flash drive and launched from user endpoint workstations to conduct a complete network analysis for voice quality measurement. At least two MTAA agents are needed to send, receive, and measure the synthetic VoIP traffic between endpoints. After the probes have successfully booted and are running the NPA utility, a centralized collector tool (UCAT collector) is used to communicate, control, measure, and record the test results, as shown in Figure 7-2.

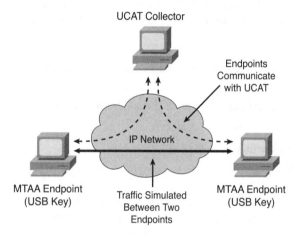

Figure 7-2   *Network Path Analysis with MTAA Probes*

Details of Network Path Analysis Testing

The objectives of the NPA are to measure the voice quality between endpoints, and to quantify the expected load on the network at the expected call volume and during peak usage times. The goal of the NPA is to certify that a network can meet the service-level agreement (SLA) for "toll quality voice" as follows:

- **Jitter:** Less than 30 ms
- **Packet loss:** Less than 1 percent
- **Delay:** 300 ms round-trip time (RTT) between endpoints (IP Phones); a 200-ms RTT between any endpoint and the UC server
- **MOS values:** 3.6 to 4.2

It is important to understand the nature of UC traffic patterns in order to configure and place the NPA probes at appropriate locations to provide a meaningful analysis. The expected call flow details of the MilSpec UC solution are as follows:

- Interoffice calls are carried out via the converged IP network.
- All calls that get established over a WAN link will use the G.729 codec, which consumes less bandwidth.

- All calls that get established within a site will use the G.722 codec, which provides very high quality voice performance.

- All voice mail messages are saved only in the Boston data center, and all users will be checking their voice mail from their respective offices. This results in additional voice traffic to the Boston office.

The NPA tool is capable of sending probes that resemble Real-time Transport Protocol (RTP) bearer traffic of various codec types as well as call control messages using the Skinny Call Control Protocol (SCCP). Probes were configured between the following locations to create a test sample consistent with all the MilSpec locations to be deployed:

- Media probes between two remote sites that were geographically the farthest, with the most interoffice delay

- Media probes between one remote site and both data centers

- Media probes between data centers

- Media probes within a single site (LAN only)

- Call signaling probes (SCCP) from one remote site to both data centers

The UCAT collector produces a report that can be used to correlate results with NMS performance reports, which provides a holistic view of network performance. Both NMSs and the UCAT collector are time-synced with NTP servers to provide a consistent analysis.

Tip   The NPA should be run after NRA audit recommendations have been implemented.

Table 7-1 shows an example of the NPA report.

Table 7-1   *Example of Results for an NPA Report*

Local Site	Remote Site	Traffic Type	MOS	Pkt Loss %	Latency ms	Jitter ms
Site 1	Boston	SCCP	—	0	40	10
Site 1	Boston	Media	3.8	0	40	10
Site 1	RTP	SCCP	—	0	45	10
Site 1	RTP	Media	3.8	0	45	10
Site 1	Site 2	Media	3.8	0	120	15
Site 1	Site 1	Media	4.2	0	4	1

The MilSpec NMSs were monitored while the NPA probes were running; there were no network faults or performance issues reported during the time the test was carried out.

Summary of Recommendations

The following recommendations were made based on the findings of the Network Readiness Assessment and the Network Path Analysis testing.

UC Deployment QoS Considerations and Recommendations

The MilSpec Enterprise QoS design should be modified to meet best practices for UC deployments:

■ UC servers use CS3 as the default DSCP marking for both call signaling and mission-critical traffic between cluster member servers. Because MilSpec currently has a QoS "Gold" class of service in place that matches packets marked as AF31, it is recommended that changes be made to the UC default DSCP marking behavior so that packets are marked as AF31 instead of CS3 to minimize network device reconfigurations.

■ All UC servers should be considered as "trusted" from the perspective of the Catalyst switch QoS "trust boundary."

■ Voice gateways should be connected into voice VLANs that would similarly be trusted from the perspective of a Catalyst switch QoS trust boundary.

■ All voice gateways should be configured to mark DSCP values appropriately. This includes marking voice media traffic as EF and call signaling traffic as AF31.

■ All trusted endpoints (Cisco IP Phones) should be sending call signaling with AF31 marking and media traffic with EF marking.

■ All workstations behind Cisco IP Phones should be considered "untrusted" so that classification and marking can be based on ACLs defined in the QoS design.

■ 802.1Q/802.1p should be enabled on all Catalyst switch access ports that connect to IP Phones and workstations.

Recommendations for Proactive Monitoring for Day-2 Operations

Proactive monitoring of the UC solution must be done as part of operational best practices. The following recommendations are made to help forecast additional bandwidth requirements, identify device upgrades, and aid with troubleshooting efforts:

■ Enable Call Management Record (CMR) in Cisco Unified Communications Manager to generate voice quality metrics after call completions.

■ Utilize the Cisco Unified Service Monitor solution that uses the CMR records to generate detailed voice quality reports that include MOS scores.

■ Because MilSpec's executives are sitting in their campus sites, it is of utmost importance to monitor voice quality on a real-time basis. To capture and measure voice quality in real time, Cisco 1040 sensors should be used in both campuses in conjunction with the Unified Service Monitor solution.

- NMS historical reports should be used to understand traffic and utilization pattern deltas (variations from the baseline) to identify whether network utilization is consistently going up due to extra traffic or due to any network abnormalities. If utilization is increasing consistently, then a network or link upgrade may be necessary to guarantee good VoIP quality.

- Amend existing IP SLA WAN monitoring to include the RTP VoIP Operation. This new functionality, which is available in the current router codes deployed at MilSpec, calculates voice quality scores using the onboard voice gateway Digital Signal Processors (DSP), and measures performance characteristics for VoIP calls using RTP.

Summary

MilSpec Software Solutions diligently followed the recommendations in the NRA audit report. They particularly recognized the importance of completing the QoS auditing and validation exercise before the VoIP project rollout. This exercise allowed them to tightly align the UC, enterprise, and service provider QoS standards. They were able to make all of the required changes to their network over two maintenance windows without any issues. The subsequent NPA analysis went well, and the results provided MilSpec executives with confidence that the end-to-end network paths would be capable of providing sufficient call quality.

Following the operational best practices recommendations in the analysis, MilSpec was able to develop tools and procedures for conducting ongoing, routine monitoring tests for day-2 support. This provided invaluable input into capacity planning activities, and prevented many "reactionary" user incidents from occurring after the UC rollout was complete.

The Network Readiness Assessment testing and recommendations helped MilSpec to complete the UC rollout project on time, and without issues. Addressing existing issues prior to the UC deployment allowed them to avoid costly last minute changes that could have delayed the project launch. MilSpec management has called the project the "Gold Standard" to be followed in all future technology deployments.

Chapter 8

Design Verification Testing Case Study

This chapter covers the following topics:

- Background for the Design Verification Testing Case Study

- High-Level Design for Blue Ridge University MPLS Backbone

- Low-Level Design for Blue Ridge University MPLS Backbone

- Low-Level Design Verification Test Strategy

Design verification testing is an integral part of the enterprise architectural process, and is often the last chance for designers and architects to "get it right" before a network roll-out begins. Testing is crucial when device configuration templates are developed as part of the low-level design (LLD) and given to implementation engineers for provisioning network devices. With complex or large-scale deployments, there is often zero tolerance for configuration errors, and even subtle syntax mistakes can result in outages or unpredictable behavior when they are undetected and loaded onto the network devices. Design verification testing is often a hard requirement with network designs that include service level-guarantees (SLG) to customers, as testing presents the opportunity to verify that features and services will perform appropriately in both normal and worst-case scenarios. By taking a test-to-failure approach, a test team can help architects develop sensible provisioning guidelines based on actual test data, rather than speculation or marketing data sheets. A test-to-failure approach is also critical in verifying service-level agreements (SLA), which commonly specify the maximum amount of packet loss, jitter, or latency that can be tolerated during device or circuit failures. By injecting errors or simulating failures in the topology, test engineers can verify that the routing and high-availability features of the design are working as expected.

The following case study illustrates how Blue Ridge University executed a design verification test to validate and refine a low-level design for a new MPLS backbone infrastructure that was being deployed to increase capacity and enhance network security through logical traffic segmentation.

Background for the Design Verification Testing Case Study

Founded in 1995 and situated in the foothills of the North Carolina mountains, Blue Ridge University (BRU) serves an integral role in the academic and economic health of the region. One of the nation's top research universities, BRU has more than 30,000 undergraduate and 5000 graduate students enrolled on two main campuses. With an academic focus on liberal arts, information technology, and medicine, BRU attracts a diverse student population from within and outside the United States. The Blue Ridge University Medical Center offers state-of-the-art care in more than 100 specialty areas and serves as the region's main Level 1 Trauma Center.

Considered by many to be the most innovative institution in the region, BRU relies on the latest technologies to support its pursuits. State-of-the-art computer systems located at data centers on each campus enable the research, development, and day-to-day operations of the administration and student population. BRU owns a large private fiber infrastructure, leveraging right-of-way access gained from the old R&R railroad, one of the university's major benefactors. It uses this dark fiber to create a multi-Gigabit Ethernet backbone built upon Cisco Catalyst 6500 Layer 3 switches, interconnecting the student housing, classrooms, administrative offices, data center, and medical center facilities.

By 2010, BRU found that it needed to increase its backbone network capacity as it began to strain under the growing student population's IT needs and the increased bandwidth demands of medical-imaging file transfers. The emergence of integrated data, voice, and video applications supporting distance-learning programs exposed the need for an end-to-end QoS redesign. Discussions on implementing a Cisco HealthPresence solution forced the Medical Center administration to take a hard look at the various infrastructure improvements that would be needed to meet a high-availability SLA.

Note The Cisco HealthPresence solution helps connect patients with medical providers conveniently and efficiently, regardless of distance. Using the network as a platform for telemedicine, it creates an environment similar to what patients experience when they visit their medical provider. It combines high-definition video, advanced audio, and network-transmitted medical data. More information may be found at www.cisco.com/web/strategy/healthcare/cisco_healthpresence_solution.html.

Security deficiencies within the university network infrastructure provided a final justification to completely overhaul the backbone, after an internal security audit cited HIPAA regulatory violations related to how patient data was being transmitted across the network.

Note The Health Insurance Portability and Accountability Act of 1996 (HIPAA) dictates that medical data traversing public networks must be safeguarded for privacy. The BRU approach toward safeguarding medical data involved the implementation of IP access lists configured on the Catalyst 6500s, restricting access to specific source/destination IP pairs. This was an operational challenge, prone to error, and complicated by fact that medical staff, nurses, and residents maintained office space throughout the campus, and could be assigned IP address space from the same blocks allocated to students or administrative staff.

The CIO of BRU cited these issues and limitations in a business case that was presented to the University General Administration for a complete backbone network overhaul. The business case was unanimously accepted, and in 2010 the BRU IT department obtained funding for the project.

High-Level Design for Blue Ridge University MPLS Backbone

Working with a Cisco Gold Certified Partner, the architects at BRU developed a network design featuring carrier-class routers, 10-Gigabit Ethernet, and MPLS virtual private networking (MPLS/VPN) technologies. With MPLS/VPNs, BRU could build a foundation layer of network security by placing patient, student, and faculty routing information into their own Virtual Routing and Forwarding (VRF) tables at the network edge. The high-level design (HLD) called for the installation of a completely new network backbone, onto which existing services would be migrated. The core of the backbone included four new Cisco CRS-1 routers interconnected in a redundant 10-Gigabit ring topology using BRU's existing dark fiber infrastructure. The CRS-1 routers were deployed as MPLS "P" routers, and as such would switch MPLS-encapsulated data between Provider Edge (PE) routers at the network edge. Separation of traffic between the various campus entities was accomplished through the use of VRF tables on the PE routers.

The design included new Cisco ASR 1006 routers for the critical sites (data and medical centers), and existing Catalyst 6500s with upgraded Cisco Supervisor 720 modules in the campus buildings. Three VRFs would be initially provisioned, one each for the medical center, students, and administrative communities. A fourth Internet VRF would separate Internet traffic through the Internet edge firewall architecture to the respective users in the other VRFs. Finally, a Catalyst 6506 "fusion router" would be deployed to provide inter-VRF forwarding of traffic to accommodate shared services and applications common to all user communities. The fusion router would be outfitted with a pair of Firewall Services Modules (FWSM) to accommodate an additional layer of security. Figure 8-1 illustrates the new logical topology.

To gain acceptance, the new backbone design needed to seamlessly support existing campus services and access methods. Provisions were made for both wired and wireless connections on campus, and IPsec VPN access to the network was extended to users in remote locations and home offices. Incorporating the university Internet and Web 2.0 services required development of a detailed routing plan to integrate the new design with an extensive "Internet edge" infrastructure hosted at the medical and data Centers. Multicast VPN (MVPN) was enabled to optimize the support for real-time sporting event broadcasts, digital signage, streaming media, and an extensive campus video surveillance system. A QoS methodology was integrated into the new design so that critical applications would experience consistent performance during times of peak usage. Network support for a new server and storage virtualization service was enabled by provisioning a Layer 2 extension Ethernet over MPLS (EoMPLS) connection between the data and medical centers. When deployed, this virtualization service would allow BRU to reduce its dependence on a costly but crucial data center disaster recovery service.

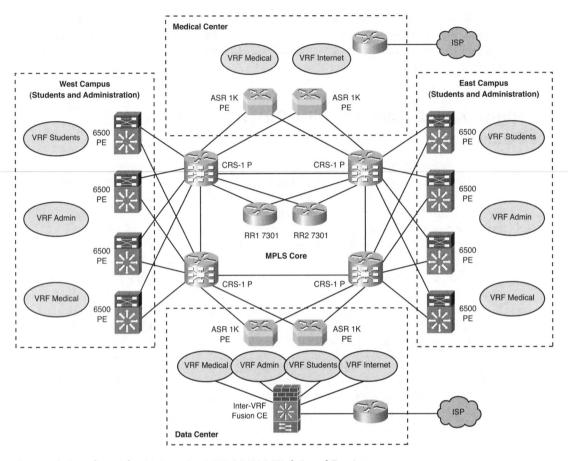

Figure 8-1   *Blue Ridge University MPLS/VPN High-Level Design*

Several of these HLD concepts and services were demonstrated during a three-day proof of concept (POC) test in a Cisco lab. This gave the BRU architecture team a first look at feature functionality and the new hardware required for the project. Upon completion of the POC test, the architecture team accepted the HLD and the project moved into the LLD phase.

Low-Level Design for Blue Ridge University MPLS Backbone

With the help from their Cisco Gold Certified Partner and the Cisco Account team, BRU architects began work on an LLD that precisely specified how the new infrastructure would be implemented. During the process of writing the LLD, it became apparent to the team that detailed testing would be necessary to complete many of the technical sections. Table 8-1 provides a summary of the LLD contents.

Table 8-1 *Blue Ridge University Low-Level Design*

LLD Section	LLD Subsection	Description	Comments
Network Services	Layer 3 VPN (Intranet)	Intranet VRF topology details (RD/RT assignments, full-mesh or hub-and-spoke topologies)	Testing Required
	Layer 3 VPN (Extranet)	Inter-VRF routing via services POD, nonsecured and/or NAT	Testing Required
	Internet Access	Internet access through Internet VRF (eBGP to ISP, iBGP/OSPF default routing, NAT, firewall)	Testing Required
	IPsec Access to VPN (CE to PE)	IPsec tunnel in access layer terminating in a VRF on the PE	Testing Required
	Remote Access to VPN	VPDN L2TP termination on PE from RAS	Testing Required
	Wireless Access to VPN	Existing access points create Lightweight Access Point Protocol (LWAPP) tunnels to wireless LAN controller (WLC) in 6500 PE routers	Testing Required
	Multicast VPN	Intranet and extranet MVPN design	Testing Required
	Quality of Service	Classification, marking, policing, queuing, and drop profiles	Testing Required
	L2VPN Data Center Interconnect (DCI)	EoMPLS tunnels for VMware VMotion and stretched clusters between data center and medical center server farms	Testing Required

Table 8-1   *Blue Ridge University Low-Level Design*

LLD Section	LLD Subsection	Description	Comments
Physical Network Design	Detailed Network Topology Diagram	Device-specific port assignments, hardware details, circuit speeds, dark fiber physical assignments	
	Hardware Specifications	Bill of materials. Device diagrams with chassis slot configurations and hardware details (Cisco CRS-1, ASR 1K)	
	Software Versions	CRS-1, ASR 1K IOS versions, feature sets, SMU, memory requirements	Testing Required
	Rack Layouts	Rack face elevations, power, cabling standards	
Logical Addressing Design	IPv4 Addressing	MPLS core (P-P, PE-P, PE-PE), CE to PE addressing, wireless	
	VRF Addressing	IPv4 address space allocated to VRF, VPNv4 addresses, RD/RT assignments	
	Multicast	MDT addressing per VRF (default and data)	
	NAT to Internet	Dynamic and static NAT pools	
Network Protocol Design	OSPF Core Design	Area assignment, interface network types, BFD, timers, convergence tuning, authentication	Testing Required
	iBGP Design	Route reflector (RR) placement and optimizations, timers, BFD, authentication, iBGP multipath, convergence tuning	Testing Required
	LDP Design	Authentication, session protection, advertise tags ACL, core MTU size	Testing Required
	CE to PE Routing Design	BGP and OSPF details from CE to PE	Testing Required
	Internet Routing	Default route, community and local preference policies, NAT, eBGP peering to ISP	Testing Required

Table 8-1 *Blue Ridge University Low-Level Design*

LLD Section	LLD Subsection	Description	Comments
Security Design	Wireless	WPA2 wireless authentication and AES encryption	
	Inter-VRF	Routing through fusion router, firewall rules	Testing Required
	Internet	Firewall rules, DMZ topology	Testing Required
	VPN Service Security	IACL, black hole filtering, black hole routers, sinkholes, IP ACL against virus/worms, uRPF, IP Options Selective Drop, CPP, disable traceroute across MPLS core	Testing Required
High-Availability Features	Network Hardware Resiliency	Power supplies, RP, line cards Software features: NSR, ISSU, NSF, NSF/SSO	Testing Required
	Network Services Resiliency	Redundant RR	Testing Required
	Dark Fiber Connectivity Redundancy	Dual-homed devices (CE, PE, P)	
Scalability Definitions	PE to CE	Maximum routes/VRF Maximum BGP peers/PE	Testing Required
	P and PE	Maximum labels/P and PE	
Policy Definitions and Configurations	BGP Policy (route maps, use of communities/localpreference)		Testing Required
	Firewall Policies		Testing Required
	Access Lists		
Management Definitions	SNMP and SYSLOG Requirements for MPLS Features	New management requirements due to new feature (MPLS) and hardware rollout	Testing Required

Table 8-1   *Blue Ridge University Low-Level Design*

LLD Section	LLD Subsection	Description	Comments
Device Configuration Templates	Network Devices		Testing Required
	Security Devices		Testing Required
	Wireless Devices		Testing Required

Risks of Deploying the Proposed Solution

Administrative leaders of BRU were understandably concerned with the major infrastructure changes planned. The backbone network functions as a central conduit, interconnecting the academic, research, and medical center IT systems and users, and the impact of an outage would be widespread. None of the university's network engineers have had experience or training on the new platforms or operating systems being deployed, and a big question was how application traffic patterns would change when the network is partitioned into Layer 3 VPNs. Because the risks of incurring an extended outage with an untested solution were considered extremely high, the question was not *whether* testing was necessary, but rather *how* and *where* it would be accomplished.

Low-Level Design Verification Test Strategy

Working with the Cisco Gold Certified Partner and the Account team, the architects of BRU developed a low-level design verification test plan that would be jointly executed with Cisco test engineers in one of Cisco's major enterprise testing facilities.

Test Objectives

The following primary objectives were identified for this testing:

■   Identify features necessary to provide network services, along with the versions of code that would be deployed.

■   Analyze traffic patterns and performance after network devices are virtualized into VRFs.

■   Develop configuration templates needed to provision network devices during the implementation phase.

■   Develop provisioning guidelines based on scale testing.

■   Capture a baseline of the network performance in steady-state and failover conditions.

Test Topology

The topology in Figure 8-2 was built in a Cisco Enterprise test lab for the purposes of verifying the MPLS/VPN design.

The test topology included all of the functional elements of the new design. In an effort to minimize equipment requirements and accelerate testing, certain portions of the network were built with less redundancy than what was called for in the new greenfield network backbone topology. This was deemed to be acceptable because redundancy would be tested at other points in the topology.

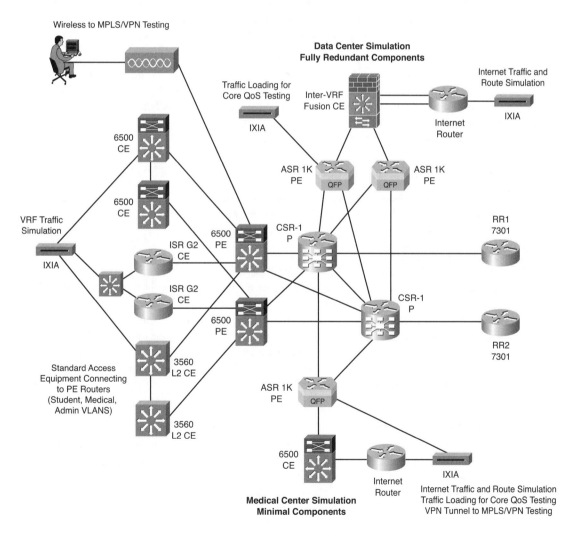

Figure 8-2 *Blue Ridge University Low-Level Design Test Topology*

Legacy access layer devices were included in the topology for the functionality/interoperability tests. These included ISR G2 routers, 6506 Layer 3 switches, 3560 workgroup switches, wireless access points, and an ASA firewall acting as the VPN concentrator. Network management systems (NMS) and Ixia Traffic Generators with stateless and application simulation capabilities were also included in the topology. A summary of this equipment is as follows:

- **Cisco Systems test gear:** CRS-1 (4-slot chassis), Catalyst 6506, ASR 1K, Catalyst 3560, ISR G2, Cisco 7301 Routers, ASA 5580 and Cisco Aironet 1260 Series wireless access points.

- **Ixia IxNetwork:** The Ixia IxNetwork testing application suite was used to generate traffic, measure latency, perform route injection, and determine route convergence times during the failure scenarios.

- **Network management systems:** BRU uses the Ionix IT Operations Intelligence family from EMC for its NMS needs. Formerly EMC Smarts, this product family leverages automated real-time, cross-domain root-cause and impact analysis of physical and virtualized environments (http://www.emc.com/products/family/smarts-family.htm). The system was used during the testing to validate interoperability with the new hardware and software under test.

Design Verification Test Scope

The design validation testing was divided into specific tests that focused on the components and functional areas described in the sections that follow.

Network Baseline Test

Network baseline testing does not typically assume any pass or fail conditions. It is used to verify feature functionality and operation of the network under the configured traffic load conditions. During this phase, test traffic representative of BRU's typical applications and load profile is sent over a fully functional lab topology, configured with all the services and features to be used in the greenfield network backbone topology. The lab network is then monitored for operationally impacting issues, which, if found, are researched and resolved. Device configurations are logged and test traffic performance statistics (delay, loss, jitter) are recorded.

Feature/Functionality Tests

Two types of feature/functionality testing are included in this phase, feature combination and feature interaction. Feature combination testing focuses on testing a feature when various combinations of other features are enabled or disabled. Feature interaction testing is conducted to verify dependencies between features.

Negative/Destructive Tests

Negative/destructive testing specifically tests the fault tolerance of the network environment. These test cases are designed to stress the network to identify any potential issues that may occur during future operation within the production network, and to test traffic convergence during failures.

Performance/Scalability Tests

This phase of testing is used to determine performance boundaries of the proposed network design. The goal of this phase is to determine the point at which the network will require additional resources to support future demands, before the degradation of the existing services. To achieve this, a new load model is designed, to find the breaking point for a specific device and/or the entire design.

Operations/Duty Cycle Tests

These tests are designed to validate that everyday tasks performed by the operations teams will work as expected. General maintenance tasks, such as making configuration changes and upgrading software, are tested to verify that they will not cause unexpected outages.

Summary of Design Verification Test Cases

Table 8-2 outlines the test cases that were performed during the design verification testing conducted at the Cisco enterprise test lab facility.

Table 8-2 *Design Verification Tests*

Test Case	Test Name	Short Test Description
Network Baseline Tests		
1.1	Backbone Network Physical and Logical Configuration and Connectivity Verification	All network devices configured for basic IP connectivity, routing protocols enabled and verified. MPLS forwarding and L3VPN features enabled on backbone P and PE routers. Step-by-step configuration procedures explained and logged for future reference.
		IP connectivity and MPLS/VPN control plane verified and logged from device command-line interface.
1.2	CE to PE Logical Configuration and Connectivity Verification	PE routers configured to support connections to the different types of access layer/CE devices. This includes direct PE connections (Ethernet, VLAN, and PortChannel), wireless via the WLC, and IPsec/GRE access via Catalyst 6500.
		Configurations logged so that templates can be generated for CE and PE devices.

Table 8-2 *Design Verification Tests*

Test Case	Test Name	Short Test Description
1.3	IXIA Traffic Verification	IPv4 unicast and multicast flows sent between Ixia ports to identify traffic paths, and to identify performance baseline during steady state. Packet sizes of test traffic range from 64 to 9216 bytes. End-to-end delay, jitter, and loss (if any) logged for each iteration.
1.4	Long Traffic Test	IPv4 unicast and multicast traffic is run at 20% of the line rate for all test ports available. This test runs for 72 hours to ensure network stability and that no traffic loss occurs.

Feature/Functionality Tests

Test Case	Test Name	Short Test Description
2.1	OSPF Feature Testing	Core OSPF: MD5 authentication enabled and verified between P and PE routers. BFD enabled and verified on core links for fast detection and reporting to OSPF of link or neighbor failure. OSPF optimizations (SPF and LSA throttle timers) enabled and verified. **Auto-Cost Reference-bandwidth** enabled to support 10-Gigabit Ethernet standard.
		CE to PE: OSPF MD5 authentication between CE and PE routers. BFD enabled on access devices with Cisco IOS support. OSPF lowered hello/dead timers tested when BFD not supported.
		MPLS/VPN specific: Domain-ID feature verified. Sham-link configured between remote PE to support backbone OSPF link.
2.2	BGP Feature Testing	MP-iBGP: Dual-homed RRs connected to P routers in different locations, peering to all PE routers in separate clusters. BGP tables examined on PE routers to verify VPNv4 prefix exchanges. TCP optimizations enabled on RR (PMTUD, Selective Packet Discard [SPD]), input queues increased. MD5 authentication enabled to (PE router) peers. iBGP multipath configured on RR and PE routers to support load balancing across the backbone. PE routers configured to import multiple paths to protect against RR failures. Selective Next-Hop Tracking (NHT) enabled to ensure fast BGP convergence during remote PE failures. Redistribution between OSPF and MP-BGP verified and logged.
		eBGP: BGP enabled to CE routers not configured for OSPF (fusion routers, wireless gateways, IPsec/VPN gateway). Internet routing design verifications (default-route generation, route-maps/policy testing on PE and CE).

Table 8-2 *Design Verification Tests*

Test Case	Test Name	Short Test Description
2.3	Layer 3 VPN Feature Testing	Full mesh and hub-and-spoke intranet VPNs provisioned and forwarding planes verified by sending Ixia traffic. Maximum-prefixes feature to limit imported routes from CE tested by injecting a large number of routes from Ixia into the VRF routing table of a PE.
		Import route-map feature configured in a VRF to test that filtering of specific prefixes into the VRF works as expected. VRF export map feature configured on a PE to dynamically set the route target when sending BGP update to RR (based on a particular attribute of the originating update).
2.3	LDP Feature Testing	MD5 authentication between LDP peers configured and tested. LDP session protection enabled to avoid convergence during single link failures. Label advertisement constrained to core prefixes by configuring ACL to advertise only specific tags. Core MTU size on all links increased to support label stacking (jumbo frames enabled). LDP autoconfiguration feature tested on CRS-1.
2.4	MPLS-TE Feature Testing	MPLS-TE tunnel support enabled on all PE and P routers (global and OSPF). RSVP configured on core interfaces and verified. Dynamic and explicit MPLS-TE path setup tested. Bandwidth reservation, tunnel priorities, Fast Reroute (link and node) protection configured and tested.
		Link attributes enabled to support constraint-based (affinity) tunnel path selection. Class-Based Tunnel Selection tested to send high-priority (DSCP EF/EXP5) traffic over specific links. Per-VRF traffic engineering configured to send traffic to particular destinations to specific PE routers across TE tunnels.
2.5	Layer 2 VPN Feature Testing	Possible Data Center Interconnect solutions tested and evaluated. EoMPLS VLAN and Port modes tested. Virtual Private LAN Service (VPLS) tested.
		MPLS-TE traffic engineering of ATOM/VPLS pseudowires tested.
2.5	CE-PE Multicast Testing	PIM-SM with static RP tested with Anycast RP configured on PE routers in appropriate VRF. PIM timer optimizations enabled for faster convergence.

Table 8-2   *Design Verification Tests*

Test Case	Test Name	Short Test Description
2.6	MVPN Testing	Intranet MVPN with Default MDT discovery enabled through PIM-SM and PIM-BIDIR tested. Data MDT discovery enabled with PIM-SSM.
2.7	QoS Testing	Uniform mode and short pipe mode MPLS QoS modes tested and evaluated. Classification, marking, policing, queuing, and drop profiles defined and tested on CE and PE routers. Class-Based Tunnel Selection configured between a pair of PE routers to demonstrate how voice and data traffic can dynamically take different TE paths.
2.8	Network Management Tests	Extranet VRF enabled on all PE routers, to support connections to NMS stations and shared services. Management loopback interfaces added to this VRF on PE routers. Global table route leakage configured to support NMS management of P routers.
		VRF support for various NMS applications (syslog, SNMP traps, Telnet, TFTP, SFTP, SCP, SSH, NTP) verified on all devices.
2.9	Security Feature Tests	IACL, black hole filtering, black hole routers, sinkholes, IP ACL against virus/worms, uRPF, IP Options Selective Drop, CPP, disable traceroute across MPLS core.
Negative/Destructive Tests		
3.1	Network Convergence Testing (unicast traffic)	Full mesh of unicast IPv4 test traffic sent between Ixia ports. Various failure scenarios induced and traffic loss measured and graphed: • P router failure • PE router failure • Dark fiber failures • Route processor failure (NSF/SSO/NSR tests) • Rapid SNMP polling • Induced software-forced crash • Line card failures • CE router failures • Power supply failure

Table 8-2 *Design Verification Tests*

Test Case	Test Name	Short Test Description
3.2	Network Convergence Testing (multicast traffic)	Tests in 3.1 repeated with multicast traffic enabled, with additional tests: • PIM-RP failure (Anycast IP test) • Core RP failure (BIDIR case) • Video source failure (priority cast test)

Performance/Scalability Tests

Test Case	Test Name	Short Test Description
4.1	P and PE Router Maximum Forwarding Rates	RFC 2544 test suite to determine the maximum no-drop forwarding rates of new PE and P router platforms.
4.2	Maximum Peers Supported by PE	Test to determine the maximum number of BGP and OSPF peers supported by each PE router.
4.3	Maximum Routes (unicast and multicast)	Test to determine the maximum number of IPv4 unicast routes and multicast state that can be simultaneously maintained by PE routers.

Operations/Duty Cycle Tests

Test Case	Test Name	Short Test Description
5.1	In Service Software Upgrade (ISSU) Test	This test is performed on both the CRS-1 and ASR 1006. A chassis of each type is upgraded at a time while all traffic types are running, to ensure test traffic is not interrupted.
5.2	Hardware OIR Test	This test is performed on the CRS-1, ASR 1006, and Catalyst 6500. Various line cards are removed and replaced while the system is forwarding traffic, to ensure traffic is not interrupted and no crashes occur.
5.3	Provisioning Test	This test is performed to ensure traffic is not interrupted while routine maintenance activities are performed on the network. It includes the following: • Adding a new VRF to a PE router • Adding a new CE to an existing PE router • Modifying QoS parameters on an existing PE to CE connection • Removing a VRF from a PE router • Modifying BGP route-map

Summary

The design verification test experience gave Blue Ridge University a much more realistic idea of how their new MPLS backbone would need to be deployed. They discovered flaws in their design that may not have been caught in production until peak usage occurred; these were corrected and the solutions were retested. Most significant of these flaws was the plan to deploy a centralized "fusion" router as the single inter-VRF and Internet routing point. This strategy was revisited after traffic was polarized onto a single firewall, presenting a bottleneck that caused test traffic to experience significant jitter and loss during moderate to high rates. The problem was avoided after testing a more distributed solution, with additional fusion routers deployed in pairs as Virtual Switching Systems (VSS) at each campus and at the medical center. This change in design extended the testing effort by two days, as it was necessary to deploy additional equipment, upgrade Catalyst and FWSM operating code to support VSS integration, and modify routing policies.

The concept of using MPLS-TE tunnels to steer VRF traffic around network hot spots, while sound in principle, was deemed to be unmanageable from an operational standpoint after operators were exposed to all of the complex configurations necessary to implement per-VRF traffic engineering. Instead, the more elegant solution of Class-Based Tunnel Selection (CBTS) was chosen after it was tested, and it proved to be successful in redirecting traffic marked as *high priority* down an explicit path that diverged from the more heavily used "shortest path" chosen by OSPF.

Engineers of the BRU network architecture team also commented on how the test effort helped preserve their technical reputation after they discovered minor errors in the configuration files that would have been published in the LLD. For example, they found it necessary to update their configuration templates with the command **mpls traffic-eng multicast-intact** to avoid routers improperly selecting MPLS-TE tunnels as outgoing interfaces for multicast, causing Reverse Path Forwarding (RPF) checks to fail.

Finally, the operators were very grateful to have gained the hands-on experience with the new CRS-1 and ASR 1K platforms and their associated operating systems (Cisco IOS-XR and Cisco IOS-XE). They felt that the configuration and troubleshooting knowledge they gained was invaluable, helping them to develop detailed and accurate operating and maintenance procedures.

Chapter 9

Migration Plan Testing Case Study

This chapter covers the following topics:

- Background for the Migration Plan Testing Case Study

- Legacy and New Network Design Overview

- New Backbone Design

- End-State Network Design

- High-Level Network Migration Plan

- Migration Test Plan

In the planning leading up to the migration to a new network infrastructure, network designers often face the realization that they have spent a disproportionate amount of time and effort designing and testing an end solution, and not enough time considering how they will migrate an existing network from its current state. It is inevitable that at some point during a large networking project, you will be asked to craft, or sign off on, a migration plan, one that will quite possibly need to be executed during a four-hour maintenance window on a Sunday morning at 3 a.m. "Oh, and by the way," a superior will tell you, "you need to guarantee that service X and application Y will be continuously available during the migration!"

Developing a migration plan with the right amount of detail and precision to be executed without error can be an art all unto itself. The unfortunate reality is that organizational politics and power struggles often prevent design engineers and architects (the people most familiar with the new design) from making changes on the actual network devices. Instead, they are given the daunting task of developing migration scripts, which are the exact set of steps and commands that will be followed precisely by potentially less experienced operations or implementation teams. Faced with even the slightest issue during the migration, these teams are often *required* to back out their changes, pushing the migration back to the next available change window, which may be weeks away.

This challenge provides yet another business justification to incorporate structured testing into your architectural process. Without a rehearsal, how will you discover flaws in the migration plan? Rely on your *past experience*? Probably not, because no two operational networks or designs are ever truly the same. Ask your vendor to *certify* your plan? Possibly, but without having the time and motivation to test your plan in a lab topology representative of your environment, the risk of human error still exists. The only way you can confidently guarantee success for a complex migration is to dry run the steps in a test topology that includes a prototype of the existing and new design.

In Chapter 8, "Design Verification Testing Case Study," you followed a case study of how Blue Ridge University (BRU) leveraged systems testing to validate a new MPLS/VPN backbone design. In this chapter, we come back to BRU as it prepares for the migration from its existing routed IP network to the new MPLS/VPN network that was validated in the Cisco lab.

Background for the Migration Plan Testing Case Study

After certifying its new MPLS/VPN design in the Cisco enterprise test lab, BRU was given the approval to start planning the implementation. New equipment orders were processed, additional fiber capacity was provisioned, and facilities were prepared for installation of the new network devices. At the first planning meeting for the deployment, a university project manager told the network architects that the operations team required that a detailed migration plan be prepared, specifying all the steps necessary to complete the cutovers. In addition to the steps, the migration plan would need to specify exact configuration scripts, success and failure criteria, contact numbers for escalations, and a detailed set of backout instructions should problems be encountered during the migration.

After much consternation and debate, the architecture team decided that the only way to provide this level of accuracy was to conduct detailed testing of the migration plan. The team decided to build a test topology using the actual equipment that was ordered for the MPLS backbone, in addition to onsite spares and equipment loaned from the Cisco Account team to simulate the legacy network.

Legacy and New Network Design Overview

The physical topology of the legacy network design loosely adheres to a two-tier hierarchy, with Catalyst 6506, Layer 3 switches with Supervisor 2 engines forming a collapsed core/distribution layer, and a mixture of Catalyst (2924, 2960, 3560) LAN switches and ISR (2911, 2921, 3925) routers forming an access layer to connect hosts and servers. A Gigabit Ethernet backbone is maintained by a partial mesh of the Catalyst 6500s, interconnecting over dark fiber that is owned and managed by the university. The access layer switches and routers are dual-homed to different core/distribution devices whenever practical to provide fault tolerance. Over time, this strict hierarchy has been relaxed, and administrators have allowed hosts and servers to be directly connected into LAN ports on the Catalyst 6500 as access switch capacity has become exhausted. This has increased the operational complexity of the network as administrators have implemented complex access control lists (ACL) to isolate student VLAN traffic from that of medical staff and faculty.

Administrators have allocated all IP addresses from the private RFC 1918 space, with user VLANs receiving /24 blocks from the 10.0.0.0/8 space, and infrastructure allocations coming out of the 172.16.0.0/16 space. EIGRP has been deployed as the routing protocol, with all of the Catalyst 6500 L3 switches and routers participating in a single EIGRP autonomous system (AS). Address aggregation is performed on all of the core/distribution devices so that /21 aggregates are announced toward the core.

BRU file and application servers are distributed around the campus, generally located in close proximity to the user groups that they serve. E-mail and Web 2.0 applications are hosted out of BRU's primary data center, located in the south campus, and all hospital systems (research, clinical, and patient records) are hosted from a small computer room in the hospital. Offsite disaster recovery (data storage and online backups) for BRU is provided by a third-party organization.

BRU maintains network connectivity in over 40 buildings, supporting the academic, administrative, and medical communities. Access switches and wireless access points are installed on each floor to support fixed and roaming users. The access and collapsed distribution/core devices are interconnected with vertical fiber connections in each building, as illustrated in Figure 9-1.

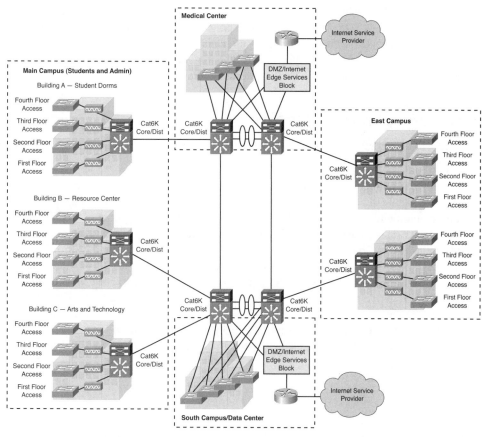

Figure 9-1   *Blue Ridge University Legacy LAN Design*

New Backbone Design

A new core backbone was proposed to fulfill a much-needed bandwidth upgrade and service enhancement to the legacy network. As discussed in Chapter 8, the new core backbone design was validated and refined during a predeployment testing exercise in a Cisco enterprise lab facility. The new backbone design leverages high-end routers and 10-Gigabit Ethernet backbone connectivity to offer increased bandwidth, faster convergence, and a strict three-tier hierarchy with better fault isolation and resiliency. MPLS technologies are used to provide Layer 3 VPN separation between the various user communities, in addition to a Layer 2 Data Center Interconnect (DCI) service to support server clustering and virtualization.

The new core design consists of four CRS-1 (4-slot) routers functioning as the MPLS provider (P) routers. These routers interconnect all of the campus locations, data center, and medical center at 10 Gbps. Four ASR 1006 routers function as new provider edge (PE) routers, with two deployed at each of the data center and medical center "critical sites." These ASR routers offer WAN aggregation services for remote locations and SOHO users, in addition to functioning as the PE routers for hosts and servers at the critical sites. Two pairs of Catalyst 6500s with redundant Firewall Services Modules (FWSM) are additionally installed at these sites to provide secure inter-VRF services for BRU. Each pair of Catalyst 6500s has been configured as a separate Virtual Switching System (VSS) to simplify routing policies and traffic symmetry through the firewalls. Finally, two Cisco 7301 routers function as BGP route reflectors (RR) to provide control plane services for the new MPLS/VPN core, as shown in Figure 9-2.

End-State Network Design

Figure 9-3 illustrates the end-state vision of the network topology after the migration to the new MPLS/VPN backbone.

As shown in Figure 9-3, much of the equipment in the legacy design was repurposed for the new MPLS/VPN backbone. All of the Catalyst 6500 core/distribution L3 switches in the campus buildings were upgraded with a pair of redundant Supervisor 720 (VS-S720-10G-3C) engines so that they could be deployed as MPLS PE routers and interconnect via uplinks at 10 Gbps to the CRS-1 P routers. As PE routers, they would provide VRF segmentation for the various user communities on the campus, and send MPLS labeled traffic to the core. The Catalyst 6500s in the data center and medical center were similarly upgraded with the VS-S720-10G-3C, and also outfitted with FWSMs, so that they could function as secure fusion CE routers. In this capacity, they would function as secure inter-VRF transit points for unicast IPv4 application traffic on the network that could not be completely decoupled along the strictly defined VRF boundaries.

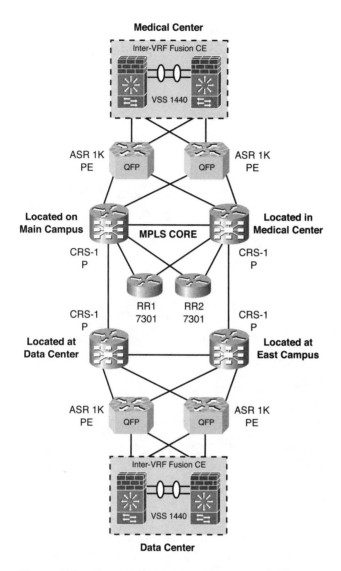

Figure 9-2 *New MPLS/VPN Backbone Topology*

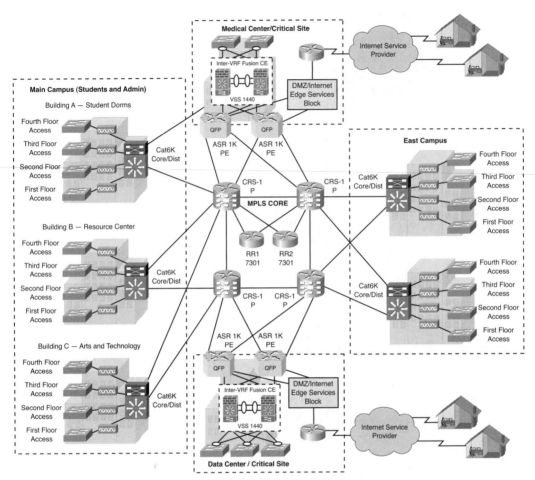

Figure 9-3   *End-State Design After Migration*

Note   The Virtual Switching System (VSS) is a feature on Cisco Catalyst 6500 Series Switches that effectively allows clustering of two physical chassis together into a single logical entity. The integration and deployment of FWSMs in a VSS environment is done transparently and does not require special configuration. There are only minor changes on the Cisco Catalyst 6500 Series side that need to be considered, and these are very much contained within the changes that are inherent to the VSS model of Cisco IOS Software. The main change involves a slight change to the CLI for the VLAN groups assigned to the FWSM. The new configuration is shown here:

```
firewall switch 1 module 5 vlan-group 2
firewall switch 2 module 5 vlan-group 2
```

This configuration and more VSS information may be found at www.cisco.com/en/US/prod/collateral/switches/ps5718/ps9336/white_paper_c11_513360.html.

High-Level Network Migration Plan

Architects and engineers proposed the following high-level plan to transition BRU to the new MPLS/VPN network:

1. Perform a configuration backup of all devices in the legacy network.

2. Install and interconnect the new MPLS backbone equipment in parallel to the legacy network (see Figure 9-2 for details).

3. Perform network ready for use (NRFU) testing on the new MPLS backbone network to certify that it is ready to carry live traffic.

> **Note**   NRFU testing is introduced in Chapter 2, "Testing Throughout the Network Lifecycle." Chapter 11 provides a detailed case study on NRFU testing.

4. Interconnect the fusion CE routers (Catalyst 6500 VSS pairs with FWSM) with the legacy CE (core/distribution Catalyst 6500 at the critical sites) with back-to-back 10-Gigabit Ethernet connections.

5. Configure eBGP peering sessions between the fusion CE routers and legacy CE (Catalyst 6500 core/distribution) routers:

   a. Legacy CE routers will announce only two aggregate routes (10/8 and 172.16/16) into BGP.

   b. Fusion CE routers will advertise default route toward legacy CE routers in addition to specific subnets.

   c. Legacy CE routers at both locations will originate the default route into OSPF toward legacy network.

6. Upgrade each of the campuses' Catalyst 6500 core/distribution routers with Supervisor 720 (and supported Cisco IOS Software) to prepare them for their role as MPLS PE routers in the new architecture.

7. Interconnect legacy Catalyst 6500 to a pair of diverse CRS-1 (P) routers with 10-Gigabit Ethernet connections. Enable OSPF and LDP on the new interfaces connecting to the P routers.

8. Configure each Catalyst 6500 with MP-iBGP peering sessions to the 7301 BGP RRs.

9. Enable MPLS QoS configurations on the Catalyst 6500 core interfaces.

10. Provision Multicast VPN (MVPN) services on the MPLS network devices.

11. Migrate (wired and wireless) VLANs in each building into the new VRFs provisioned on the Catalyst 6500 PE.

12. Test inter-VRF routing through fusion CE routers. Verify routing and NAT policies ensure symmetry for each session.

13. Provision Layer 2 EoMPLS circuit between the data center and medical center to extend VLANs that will support server clustering and virtualization.

14. Discover all devices with network management systems.

15. Test backout plan.

Migration Test Plan

The topology in Figure 9-4 was built in BRU's data center for the purposes of this test. The test topology was assembled from the new equipment ordered for the project, loaned equipment, and legacy equipment procured from test and spares inventory. Although the primary goal of this test was to validate the migration plan, a side benefit was that BRU was able to "burn in" the new equipment prior to installation in the field.

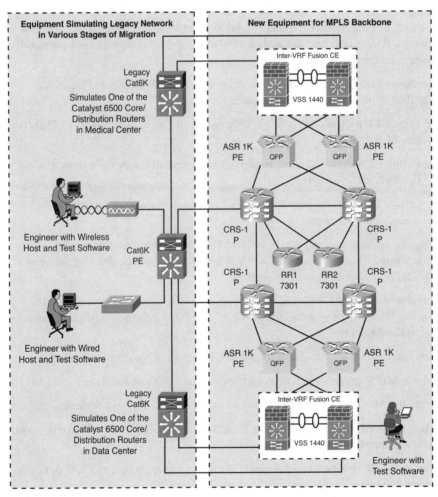

Figure 9-4 *Blue Ridge University Migration Plan Test Topology*

Summary of Migration Plan Testing

Table 9-1 outlines the test cases that were performed on the test topology.

Table 9-1   *BRU Migration Test Cases*

Migration Step	Description of Migration Step	How Validated During Testing
1	Perform backup of all devices in legacy network.	Configuration files sent via TFTP to backup server in test lab and saved to onboard disks.
2	Install and interconnect the new MPLS backbone equipment in parallel to the legacy network.	Equipment installed in data center racks and configured per design standards. Line cards installed, devices powered up, and appropriate code and configurations applied. Devices interconnected in back-to-back configurations to verify connectivity and routing protocols.
3	Perform NRFU testing on the new MPLS backbone network to certify that it is ready to carry live traffic.	Equipment configured with MPLS and routing protocols, verified through CLI and traceroutes. Fusion CE Catalyst 6500 VSS systems configured and verified. L3VPN test VRF provisioned, test traffic sent end to end within backbone. CLI and syslog monitored for hardware errors or software crashes.
4	Interconnect the fusion CE (Catalyst 6500 VSS pairs with FWSM) with the legacy CE (core/distribution Catalyst 6500 at the critical sites) with back-to-back 10-Gigabit Ethernet connections.	Fusion CE interconnected with legacy CE devices with dual 10-Gigabit Ethernet connections. IP addressing is configured and checked.
5	Configure eBGP peering sessions between the fusion CE and legacy CE devices. Legacy CE routers will announce only two aggregate routes (10/8 and 172.16/16) into BGP. Fusion-CE routers will advertise default route toward legacy CE routers in addition to specific subnets. Legacy CE routers at both locations will originate the default route into OSPF toward legacy network.	eBGP configured, OSPF default route originated, and routing verified between legacy and MPLS networks. Redundancy tested by disconnecting each of the interconnects and verifying that an eBGP default route is still available on the legacy CE devices.

Table 9-1　*BRU Migration Test Cases*

Migration Step	Description of Migration Step	How Validated During Testing
6	Upgrade each of the campus Catalyst 6500 core/distribution routers with Supervisor 720 (and supported Cisco IOS Software) to prepare them for their role as MPLS PE routers in the new architecture.	Upgrade procedure tested and documented on one of the legacy Catalyst 6500s. Legacy code is still kept on local disk in case of backout.
7	Interconnect legacy Catalyst 6500 to a pair of diverse CRS-1 (P) routers with 10-Gigabit Ethernet connections. Enable OSPF and LDP on the new interfaces connecting to the P routers.	Legacy Catalyst 6500 interconnected to pair of CRS-1 routers using the 10GE uplinks on the Supervisor. OSPF and LDP enabled and verified.
8	Configure each Catalyst 6500 PE router with MP-iBGP peering sessions to the 7301 BGP RRs.	iBGP brought up between Cat6K PE router and pair of 7301 RRs.
9	Enable MPLS QoS configurations on the Catalyst 6500 PE routers.	QoS enabled and verified by sending test traffic to/from legacy network with various markings.
10	Provision MVPN services on the MPLS network devices.	MVPN provisioned on all PE and P routers in test topology. VLC used to source multicast video file from legacy to new backbone network.
11	Migrate (wired and wireless) VLANs in each building into the new VRFs provisioned on the Catalyst 6500 PE.	Connect access switch to Catalyst 6500 PE router in test topology, and provision into test VRF. Send traffic end to end from wired host in legacy network to host in MPLS network. Connect access point to WLC in Catalyst 6500 PE router. Test appropriately with wireless host.
12	Test inter-VRF routing through fusion CE routers. Verify routing and NAT policies ensure symmetry for each session.	Send test traffic from source in VRF test from legacy portion of the network to destination in VRF test2 in new portion of the network. Ensure bidirectional traffic passes through the same fusion router and FWSM.

Table 9-1 *BRU Migration Test Cases*

Migration Step	Description of Migration Step	How Validated During Testing
13	Provision Layer 2 EoMPLS circuit between the data center and medical center to extend VLANs that will support server clustering and virtualization.	Configure pair of EoMPLS L2 VLAN connections by provisioning a pseudowire between ASR PE routers. Configure fusion CE router VLAN to be in same subnet, verify with ping and traceroute.
14	Back out migration (if necessary) by applying necessary change scripts.	Backout strategy tested by applying change files to each device. Cisco IOS Software brought back to original levels as required.

Summary

The network architects of Blue Ridge University had much better confidence in the accuracy of their migration plan after conducting a dry run in their lab topology. Minor syntax errors were caught and corrected in the change files, which may have caused the migration to be backed out during a change window. A flaw in the inter-VRF routing strategy was discovered that resulted in asymmetrical traffic to flow between different fusion CE routers. This asymmetrical routing situation caused traffic to fail stateful inspection checks in the FWSMs, triggering session drops for application traffic when source and destination IP hosts terminated in different VRFs. Modifying the BGP route policy and deploying unique NAT pools on each of the fusion CE/FWSM devices corrected this asymmetrical routing problem.

The network operations team was grateful to have had a chance to gain additional hands-on experience with the new equipment and operating systems. They were able to refine many of their operational procedures, including hardware installation standards, code upgrade guides, and migration backout procedures.

After the migration test was concluded, the actual migration was scheduled to be conducted in the university's next global change window.

Chapter 10

New Platform and Code Certification Case Study

This chapter covers the following topics:

- Background for the New Platform and Code Certification Case Study

- Proposed Top-of-Rack Architecture

- Hardware for the New Infrastructure

- Platform and Code Certification Test Plan

Chapter 2, "Testing Throughout the Network Lifecycle," described enterprise architecture in terms of an organization's computer applications and IT infrastructure, and the processes put in place to align IT with corporate strategy and business goals. Change management addresses how upgrades or maintenance to the network are managed to minimize the chance of service outages or degraded application performance. In effective change management, all infrastructure changes must be justified, assessed, and documented prior to implementation. With major projects such as a new platform introduction or operating system upgrade, change management often dictates that a certification process be completed prior to implementation. This process typically involves an evaluation of any known bugs or caveats associated with the new platform or operating software, along with a set of common test criteria that must be met to qualify it for deployment on the enterprise network.

This case study examines how a financial organization leveraged predeployment acceptance testing to certify a new feature, new hardware, and operating software upgrade, as part of compliance with corporate change management policy. Testing was conducted in the financial organization's onsite lab facility using demonstration equipment provided by its Cisco Account team.

Background for the New Platform and Code Certification Case Study

ATC Federated Bank is the regional financial services company that was introduced in the case study in Chapter 6, "Proof of Concept Testing Case Study of a Cisco Data Center 3.0 Architecture." In an effort to reduce costs and streamline operations, ATC Federated launched an initiative known as "Project Legion," which took advantage of network, storage, and server virtualization concepts to consolidate ten of its legacy data centers down to four facilities based on a new Cisco Data Center 3.0 architecture. During the planning phase of this project, ATC Federated engineers visited a Cisco Proof of Concept (CPOC) test lab to witness firsthand how the new products and technologies would function, scale, and operate in an environment that simulated ATC Federated's proposed design. After completing a week of focused testing with Cisco Nexus 7010 Series Switches, MDS 9506 Multilayer Directors and the Cisco Unified Computing System (UCS) comprising the new architecture, ATC Federated engineers were able to refine their design and obtain approval for deployment as part of a pilot in two data centers.

During the pilot, ATC Federated discovered that some of its legacy applications were not compatible with the new Cisco UCS deployment model. Specifically, many of these applications could not be installed on virtual machines running VMware, the enterprise-wide solution being deployed on all the blade servers. In an effort to accommodate these legacy applications with the least amount of operational complexity, a decision was made to add a number of "classic" (nonvirtualized) rack-mounted servers into the architecture, supplementing the UCS blade servers. This would introduce additional costs and infrastructure, but would keep the consolidation project moving forward and on schedule.

To accommodate the classic rack-mounted server requirements, the network engineering team decided to incorporate a top-of-rack (ToR) design component into the data center architecture. This type of solution was desirable to ATC Federated as it would help it rapidly turn up racks of compute resources as demand required.

Note   ToR switching is a great choice for dense 1-rack unit (RU) server environments, as a standard rack can often hold up to 45 1-RU servers, making logical sense to put a 48-port ToR switch into each rack to offer network connectivity. This approach saves money in cabling costs because all the servers in a rack can use shorter cables to connect directly into the infrastructure, instead of having to use a patch-panel approach. The ToR solution also complements a rack-at-a-time deployment scenario by placing switching resources in each rack so that server connectivity can be aggregated and interconnected with the rest of the data center through a small number of cables connected to the end-of-row (EoR) aggregation-layer switches.

ATC Federated engineers decided on a physical topology that included dual 10-Gigabit connections into a pair of redundant aggregation switches. This topology was put into place to increase resiliency during failures; however, it would not increase the total ToR system throughput, as the Spanning Tree Protocol (STP) would allow only one link to forward traffic at any given time. With traditional STP operations, only a single uplink is usable for forwarding traffic, as the other must remain in "blocking mode" to prevent forwarding loops. This approach reduces the usable bandwidth by 50 percent, and can also decrease service availability during link failures while the STP converges.

While considering the single 10-Gigabit link/spanning tree limitation, the ATC Federated engineering team recalled a feature known as virtual PortChannel (vPC) that had impressed them during the POC test. This feature allows a port channel to be aggregated across two separate Nexus chassis, giving access switches the capability to bundle both (or multiple) 10-Gigabit uplinks into port channels that have the appearance of connecting to a single aggregation switch. With this feature, all of the 10-Gigabit Ethernet links are able to carry traffic, and redundancy and resiliency is preserved in the case of single aggregation chassis failures. ATC Federated decided to investigate the use vPCs with its ToR switches for its new data centers.

Note   The Cisco Nexus family of data center switches is designed to meet the requirements of the next-generation data center. All these switches use NX-OS Software, an operating system designed specifically for high availability, scalability, and flexibility.

For more details about NX-OS Software, go to

www.cisco.com/en/US/products/ps9372/index.html

www.cisco.com/en/US/products/ps9441/Products_Sub_Category_Home.html

As the design team explored the vPC feature and how it would fit into their ToR design, the Cisco Account team proposed a design using Nexus 2000 Series Fabric Extenders (FEX) in place of regular ToR switches. To give the ATC Federated engineering team more comfort with the architecture, the Cisco Account team arranged for a loan of several Nexus 2000 FEXs and a couple of Nexus 5020 Series Switches for lab certification.

Proposed Top-of-Rack Architecture

As the ATC Federated Engineering team worked through all of their requirements, they decided to propose two different ToR designs:

- ToR design variant 1 would accommodate redundant connectivity to high-value and high-performance compute nodes (or servers). These nodes would connect to the network using a pair of redundant, 10-Gbps Converged Network Adapters (CNA). For this solution, they would deploy the Cisco Nexus 2232PP 10G Fabric Extender.

- ToR design variant 2 would present a more classic ToR approach using the Cisco Nexus 2148T, which provides 48 ports of 1-Gbps Ethernet for servers. This variant would be deployed for servers using local storage, and lower-value assets such as quality assurance (QA) boxes. It will still provide redundant ToR connectivity by allowing servers to connect to two separate 2148Ts in two adjacent racks if required.

> **Note** CNAs combine data networking (Ethernet) and storage networking (Fibre Channel) onto a single physical adapter. A CNA can do the work of a discrete FC Host Bus Adapter (HBA) and an Ethernet NIC. This convergence means fewer cables, fewer switches, less power consumption, reduced cooling, and easier LAN and SAN management.

Figure 10-1 illustrates the ATC Federated ToR design.

ATC Federated Bank - Top-of-Rack Design

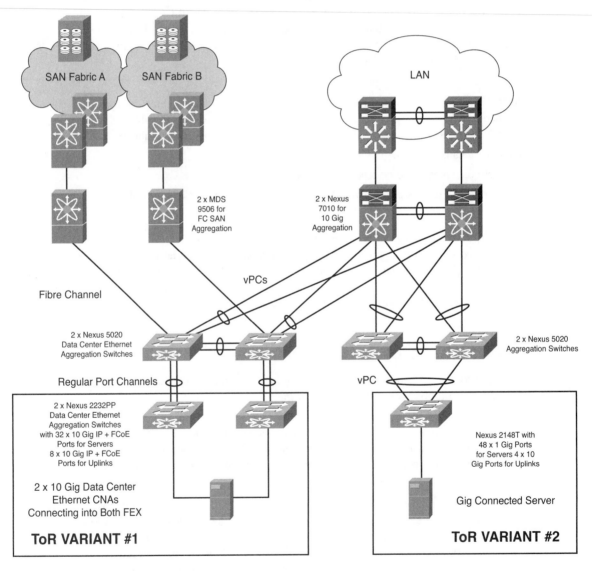

Figure 10-1 *ATC Federated Bank Proposed Top-of-Rack Design Variants*

This design provides several improvements over the existing server connectivity standard:

- Higher throughput due to having all 10-Gbps uplinks between the Nexus 5000s and Nexus 7000s in forwarding mode

- Faster convergence in case of link and aggregation-layer failures

- Lower costs due to the Nexus 2322PP's capability to replace ToR storage switches

- Simplified and more centralized management because each FEX appears logically and acts as a "line card" inside the Nexus 5000 Series chassis

Leveraging the vPC feature support on the Cisco Nexus 5020 and Nexus 7000 switches in this design, a server can be dual connected to a pair of FEXs. Each redundant FEX is connected to at least one Nexus 5020 Series Switch, thus giving ATC Federated server, FEX, IP, and SAN connectivity redundancy. Network interface card (NIC) teaming increases the resilience of this design, providing active-standby or active-active connectivity for the servers that support it.

Because all device configurations are managed on the Cisco Nexus 5020 switches, configuration information is downloaded directly to the Nexus 2000 Fabric Extender using in-band communication. There is no configuration required (or indeed even possible) for any of the ToR switches. Software maintenance and compatibility problems are eliminated because the FEX software is embedded in the Nexus 5020 switch software. The FEX automatically downloads the software image from the Nexus 5020 in the same way that a line card would download from the Cisco Supervisor Engine in a modular chassis. The number of management points is significantly fewer than when discrete switches are used at the top of the rack. A traditional 10-rack design using a discrete, redundant pair of Gigabit Ethernet switches at the top of each rack has 20 management points. The equivalent architecture using the Cisco Nexus 2000 Series has only two. This offers an obvious reduction in management complexity.

In Service Software Upgrade (ISSU) on the FEXs provides the capability to perform transparent software upgrades, reducing downtime and allowing ATC Federated to integrate the newest features and functions with little or no effect on network operation for Ethernet, storage, and converged network environments.

Hardware for the New Infrastructure

The ATC Federated Bank architecture team chose to deploy the Cisco Nexus 5020 Series Switch for it aggregation layer, and Nexus 2148T and 2232PP Fabric Extenders as ToR switches:

- **Cisco Nexus 5020 Series Switch:** The Cisco Nexus 5020 is a 2-RU, 10-Gigabit Ethernet, Fibre Channel over Ethernet (FCoE), and Fibre Channel switch built to provide 1.04 terabits per second (Tbps) throughput with very low latency. It has 40 fixed 10-Gigabit Ethernet and FCoE Small Form-Factor Pluggable Plus (SFP+) ports. The first 16 fixed ports support both 10-Gigabit Ethernet and Gigabit Ethernet in hardware, providing a smooth migration path to 10-Gigabit Ethernet. Two expansion module slots can be configured to support up to 12 additional 10-Gigabit Ethernet and FCoE SFP+ ports, up to 16 Fibre Channel switch ports, or a combination of both.[1] The Nexus 5020 can support up to 12 FEXs over vPCs.

- **Cisco Nexus 2148T:** The Cisco Nexus 2148T provides 48 Gigabit Ethernet server ports and four 10-Gigabit Ethernet uplink ports in a compact 1-RU form factor.[2] The Nexus 2148T will be used as a replacement for the "typical" IP-only 1-Gbps ToR switch.

- **Cisco Nexus 2232PP:** The Cisco Nexus 2232PP 10G provides 32 10-Gbps Ethernet and FCoE SFP+ server ports and eight 10-Gbps Ethernet and FCoE SFP+ uplink ports in a compact 1-RU form factor.[3] The Nexus 2232PP Fabric Extender will be used to provide high-performance and -value servers with 10-Gbps connectivity as well as replace ToR storage switches. All high-value servers will be rolled out with CNAs to take advantage of these features.

Tip   You can also connect some FEXs directly into a Nexus 7000.

Each pair of Nexus 5020s will support three pairs (six total) of Nexus 2232PP FEX and six Nexus 2148Ts. Each 2232PP will connect using eight 10-Gbps uplinks into the Nexus 5020 pair, for a total of 48 total ports (in six separate port channels). The 2148Ts will use all four uplinks for a total of 24 10-Gbps ports (in six vPCs). This will use 52 out of the total 80 combined ports available in the fixed modules for both Nexus 5020s. It will allow ATC Federated to support up to 96 dual 10-Gbps Data Center Ethernet–connected servers, plus 288 1-Gbps single connected servers per pair of Nexus 5020s.

Note   As of the writing of this book, Cisco does not recommend that you place FCoE traffic on an Ethernet topology that spans two fabrics. As such, if you want to use FCoE on the CNAs connected to your 2232PP FEX, they should not be connected to the upstream Nexus 5000 using a vPC. In addition, any Nexus 5000 carrying FCoE traffic and running vPCs should not forward the FCoE VLANs across its vPC peer links. This will ensure that all FCoE traffic is kept in two separate fabrics, as per best practices.

The Nexus 5020s also connect into both SAN fabrics in the data center. Nexus 5020-1 will connect into SAN Fabric A using four 8-Gbps Fibre Channel interfaces on a 6-port native 8/4/2/1-Gbps Fibre Channel expansion module. These four SAN uplinks will be configured as a 32-Gbps port channel running an ISL trunk to allow multiple VSAN connectivity, higher throughput, and faster reconvergence during outages. Nexus 5020-2 will be similarly connected in SAN Fabric B.

All Layer 3 forwarding and switching will occur on a pair of Nexus 7010 switches. These switches will aggregate several pairs of Nexus 5020s, which in turn have up to another 12

Nexus 2000 Series FEXs connected to them. All of the Nexus 5020s will connect to the Nexus 7010s using 80-Gbps vPCs (until the Nexus 7010s run out of 10-Gigabit ports to allocate, at which time a second pair would need to be installed). These vPCs will also be configured as Layer 2 trunks, which will allow several different VLANs to be presented to the servers attached to each Nexus 2000 ToR FEX. If it is desirable, each server can have a trunk with several VLANs connected to its NIC using 802.1Q encapsulation.

To get a better understanding of how the Nexus 2000 FEX will connect into the Nexus 5020s, and from there into the LAN and SAN cores, look at Figure 10-2, which shows the physical connectivity for a pair of Nexus 2232PPs.

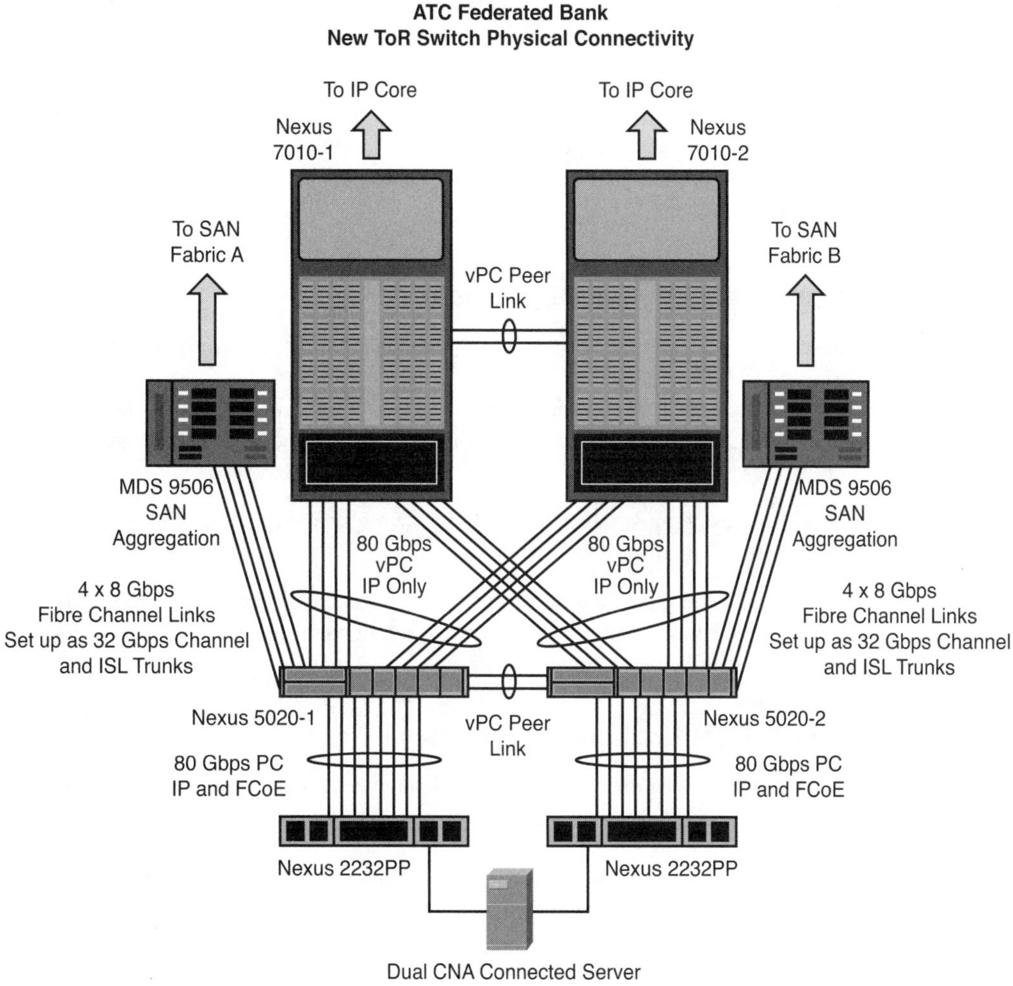

Figure 10-2 *Physical Connectivity for New Top-of-Rack Design for Nexus 2232PP FEX*

Platform and Code Certification Test Plan

ATC Federated maintains an architectural governance board composed of representatives from the business units, engineering, and operational groups, and is responsible for reviewing all changes for standards compliance and potential impacts to the business. Upon reviewing the new ToR design, the governance board decided that testing would be necessary to certify the new design, as it would require introduction of a new hardware platform *and* upgrade to a new major software release. ATC Federated had not previously deployed the Nexus 2000 Fabric Extender platform on its network; its only exposure with the hardware was with the Nexus 2104 FEX inside the Cisco UCS Blade Chassis. The code version required to support the dual connected FEX running over vPCs was one major release newer than the code ATC Federated was running in its existing Nexus 5020s.

ATC Federated maintains an onsite test facility that it often uses to certify new hardware and software. Any new hardware or software that is proposed for use in its environment must meet the minimum requirements specified in a standards template maintained by ATC Federated.

New Platform Certification Objectives

Three main requirements must be met before a new hardware platform is certified:

- ATC Federated must be confident that the new hardware will fit in with the rest of the architecture as expected in the existing design. This requires an interoperability and features test.

- The new hardware must meet the performance requirements set by the architecture and engineering teams. This requires a performance test.

- The new hardware must be understood and manageable by the operations group. This requires some hands-on experience for the operations group as well as interoperability testing with the management systems.

New Software Certification Objectives

To be approved for deployment in the ATC Federated Bank network, all new software must pass the following requirements:

- A review of known software defects must be performed to ensure that no known bugs exist in the operating software that could be considered potentially business impacting.

- The software must be tested and meet the minimum management interoperability requirements set forth by the architecture, engineering, and operations teams. This includes "manageability" features, such as SSHv2, syslog, and SNMP.

■   The new software must support all the features that are required to provide a specified service, and interoperate correctly with existing platforms and software.

New Platform and Code Certification Test Topology

The topology in Figure 10-3 was built in the ATC Federated test lab for the purposes of this new platform and code certification test.

ATC Federated Bank - Top-of-Rack Design Test Topology

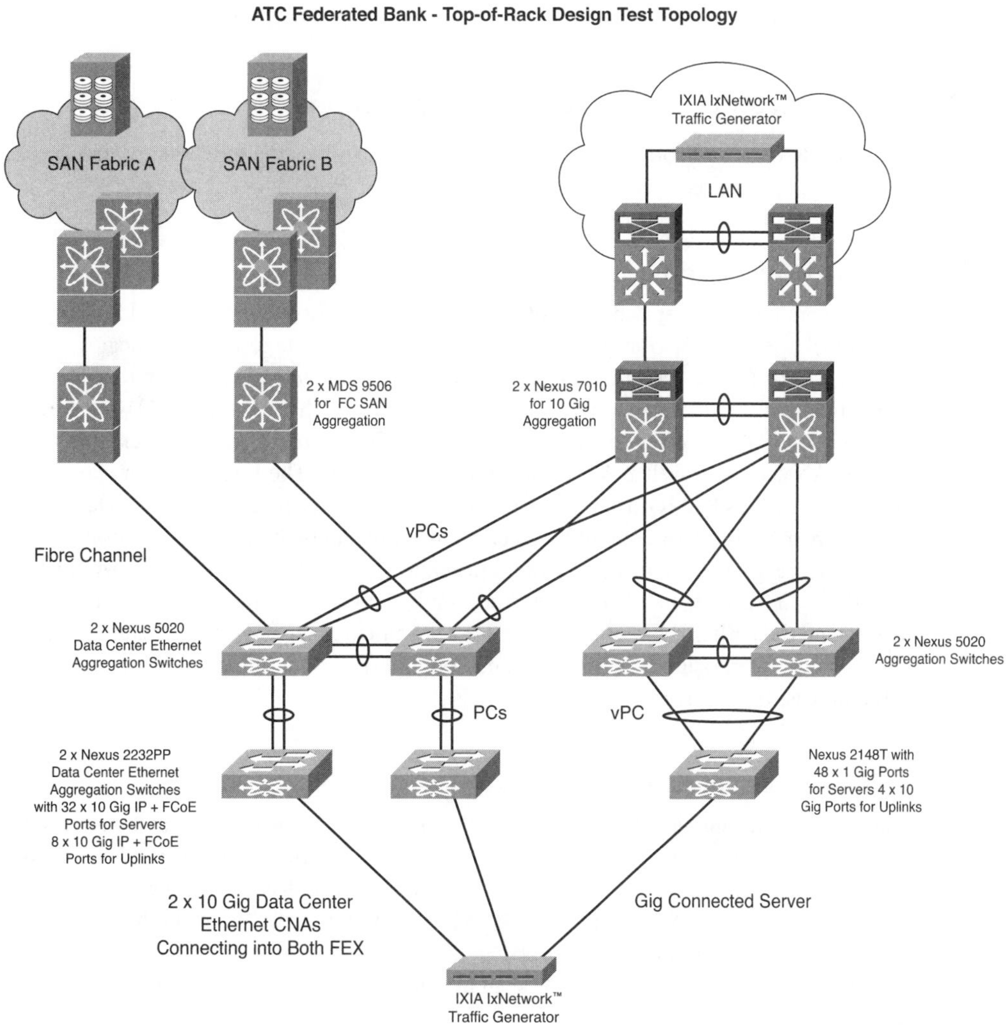

Figure 10-3   *Test Topology for New Platform and Code Certification Test*

This test topology was built to emulate both ToR design variants proposed by the architecture team. One part of the topology had the dual Nexus 2232PPs connected into the Nexus 5020s, and the second part used the Nexus 2148T dual connected into the second pair of Nexus 5020s using a vPC. Ixia IxNetwork and IxSAN test tools were used to test both the unified I/O capabilities of the 2232PP FEX and the IP capabilities of both the 2148T and the 2232PPs.

The Nexus 5020s were in turn connected to both the SAN and LAN to prove interoperability with the MDS 9506s, as shown in Figure 10-3 and Nexus 7010s.

New Platform and Code Certification Test Scope

The new platform and code certification test was divided into the following specific tests that focused on the required components or functional areas for certification.

Network and SAN Baseline Tests

The network baseline test consisted of capturing the state of the network and SAN during normal operations with typical flows. The network baseline test used typical observed loads for the server infrastructure. This also consisted of validating that the new ToR infrastructure did indeed offer VLAN separation, and that the Nexus 7010 aggregation layer routed and switched packets as expected. FCoE operation was checked to ensure SAN access, as well as VSAN separation and zoning. The Ixia ports were connected into the FEX as 802.1Q trunk ports to simulate similarly connected servers. Data flows were monitored for content (source, destination) and path information through the infrastructure, by the use of marker flows generated by Ixia IxNetwork and IxSAN. For each (Layer 2, Layer 3, and FCoE) flow, the simulation baseline information required identifying the path and rate information for a specific marker flow. The remaining simulated flows were measured for aggregate rate only. Tests were conducted for both unicast and multicast IPv4 traffic.

Management Functionality Test

The management functionality test consisted of running a suite of tests that are required to certify any new hardware and software. These tests were performed using the existing management infrastructure in the test lab. This infrastructure has everything from Cisco Secure Access Control Servers (ACS) to SNMP and syslog servers used by the operations team for network monitoring and reporting. Certain functionality, such as a banner message (which is required by security or legal mandates), was also evaluated in this phase of testing.

Failure/Recovery Test

The failure/recovery test consisted of performing various selective failures within the infrastructure. Particular attention was paid to recovery times to ensure that the availability SLA for data center infrastructure could be met by the new infrastructure. The test cases were designed to show behavior during "expected" and "likely" failures.

Feature Validation Test

The feature validation test consisted of performing various actions to verify that critical features identified by the architecture team worked as expected within the ToR infrastructure as it was built in the lab. In particular, ISSUs were tested extensively.

Performance/Scalability/Capacity Tests

The ATC Federated Bank engineers did not have enough test ports to do a full capacity test on the new hardware. That would have required 48 1-Gbps test ports for the Nexus 2148T and 32 10-Gbps ports for the Nexus 2232PP. They asked the Cisco enterprise test team to conduct this test. They were able to observe the test remotely and verify the full capacity of the FEX. They did, however, run performance and capacity tests on several ports to check for line rate capability as well as delay and jitter.

Summary of New Platform and Code Certification Test Cases

Table 10-1 outlines the test cases that were performed during the new platform and code certification test.

Table 10-1 *New Platform and Code Certification Test Cases*

Test Case	Test Name	Short Test Description
Network and SAN Baseline Tests		
1.1	L2 Configuration Baseline Test	All vPCs are configured on the Nexus 7010 and Nexus 5020 platforms, all port channels are verified, and the FEXs are brought up.
1.2	L2/L3 VLAN Configuration	All the VLANs are configured and the switch virtual interfaces (SVI) are brought up.
		Trunking is enabled down to the FEX ports.
		IXIA ports are brought up as trunks and ping their default gateway.
1.3	Baseline Traffic Test (Unicast)	Unicast marker flows are started. These flows should hash across all of the physical interfaces in the vPCs.
		Traffic is originated from the FEX to the core and from the core to the FEX ports.

Table 10-1   *New Platform and Code Certification Test Cases*

Test Case	Test Name	Short Test Description
1.4	Baseline Traffic Test (Multicast)	Multicast marker flows are started. The sources should be at each FEX. The destinations should be the core as well as "clients subscribed" at the FEX.
1.5	Baseline SAN Configuration	The SAN port channels are brought up between the Nexus 5020s and the MDSs they are connected to in this test.
1.6	VSAN Configuration	VSANs are configured on the Nexus 5020 and MDSs.
1.7	VSAN Trunking Test	All the VSANs in each fabric are trunked across the port channels between the Nexus 5020s and MDSs.
1.8	SAN/VSAN Zone Merge Test	Zonesets are activated in the MDSs to see how they merge with active zones on the Nexus 5020s.
1.9	FCoE Configuration Test	FCoE is enabled and configured on the Nexus 5020s and 2232PP FEX. The HBA is brought up and tested using IxSAN.
1.10	SAN Traffic Test	IxSAN is used to generate traffic between the FCoE ports on the FEX and the storage arrays connected to the two fabrics of the SAN.
1.11	Long Traffic Test	Unicast, multicast, and FCoE traffic is run at 20% of the line rate for all test ports available. This test runs for 72 hours.
Management Functionality Tests		
2.1	SSHv2 and SFTP Test	SSHv2 and SFTP are tested. SFTP is used to back up configs as well as load new code.
2.2	AAA Functionality	Authentication is tested using an ACS server (TACACS+). Authorization is tested for a "read-only" group as well as an "admin" group. Accounting is tested for failed authentications and command authorization.
2.3	Banner Test	A message-of-the-day (MOTD) banner with legal information is tested.
2.4	SNMP Test	SNMP MIB and trap functionality is tested using the production management tools used by the operations teams. Particular attention is paid to make sure used functionality works as expected. New MIBs are tested. SNMP read and write functionality is tested.

Table 10-1 *New Platform and Code Certification Test Cases*

Test Case	Test Name	Short Test Description
2.4	SNMP Security Test	SNMP ACL security is tested to ensure that only allowed systems using the correct authentication are able to access the machine.
2.5	NTP and NTP Security Test	NTP and NTP Security are tested. Timezone and summertime are tested.
2.6	SYSLOG Test	Syslog and logging-level functionality are verified.
2.7	SPAN Test	Port and VLAN spanning is tested. Encapsulated Remote SPAN (ERSPAN) is tested if supported.
Failure/Recovery Tests		
3.1	vPC Link Failure Test	vPC links are brought down and back up while traffic runs across them. Recovery times are recorded for all traffic types affected.
3.2	vPC Peer Link Failure Test	vPC peer links are brought down and back up while traffic runs across the vPCs. First one then both peer links are brought down to check that the keepalive link works as expected.
3.3	vPC Keepalive Link Failure Test	The vPC keepalive link is brought down and back up while traffic is running over the vPCs.
3.4	Chassis Failure Test	Nexus 7010s, 5020s, and 2000s, as well as the MDS 9500, are each brought down and back up while traffic is running. Recovery times for all traffic types affected, multicast, unicast, and FCoE, are recorded (only if there is a redundant path).
3.5	Fibre Channel Link Failure Test	Links between one of the Nexus 5020s and the MDS are brought down and back up. FCoE traffic convergence is measured.
Feature Validation Tests		
4.1	SAN Operations Feature Test	Features used by the ATC Federated SAN operations team are verified, such as distributed device alias services, host-to-switch and switch-to-switch FC-SP authentication, fabric binding for FC, FC port security, domain functionality, Enhanced zoning, Cisco Fabric Analyzer, FC traceroute, FC ping, FC debugging, and Cisco Fabric Manager support.

Table 10-1 *New Platform and Code Certification Test Cases*

Test Case	Test Name	Short Test Description
4.2	Multicast Feature Test	Multicast functionality, such as IGMP snooping and replication, is tested.
4.3	L2 Feature Test	STP features such as PortFast and BPDU Guard are tested on the FEX. UDLD is tested on all of the platforms that support it.
4.4	In Service Software Upgrade (ISSU) Test	This test is performed on both the Nexus 7010s and the 5020s. A chassis of each type is upgraded at a time while all traffic types are running. The ISSU upgrade of the FEX is tested for both the Nexus 2148T and the 2232PP to ensure nonstop forwarding of all traffic types during a code upgrade.
4.5	NIC Teaming Test	Verify that the Ixia chassis can bundle two interfaces connected to the FEX.
4.6	Jumbo Frame Test	Test the jumbo frame support for all three platforms, Nexus 7010, 5020, and FEX, running the latest code.
4.7	QoS Feature Test	Validate that the QoS trust is extended to the FEX. Verify that IEEE 802.1Qbb PFC (per-priority pause frame support) is working between the Nexus and the Ixia/server. This test may require the port to be spanned.
4.8	Security Feature Test	ACLs, port ACLs, and VLAN ACLs are tested for the Nexus 5020s and both types of FEX.
Performance/Scalability/Capacity Tests		
5.1	Unicast Line Rate Performance Test	Unicast throughput, jitter, and delay are tested between two ports on the same FEX, two ports on two separate FEXs on the same set of Nexus 5020s, and two ports on separate Nexus 5020s.
5.2	Multicast Line Rate Performance Test	Multicast throughput, jitter, and delay are tested between two ports on the same FEX, two ports on two separate FEXs on the same set of Nexus 5020s, and two ports on separate Nexus 5020s.
5.3	End to End Performance Test	Using Ixia ports connected to the core and access layers, end-to-end testing is performed for latency and jitter.
5.4	End to End SAN Performance Test	Using IxSAN, throughput and jitter for FCoE to FC storage is tested between the 2232PP FEX and the EMC arrays.

Summary

Upon completing the new platform and code certification testing, ATC Federated Bank approved the Nexus 2148T and Nexus 2232PP Fabric Extenders for use in conjunction with Nexus 5020s as their new top-of-rack switches. It was demonstrated that the new FEX infrastructure would work as expected in their design, and the code required to support the new hardware was proven to be stable. Some issues were found, particularly the lack of certain SNMP MIBs, used by the ATC Federated operations team to create utilization reports, on the Nexus 2148T and 2322PP. The operations team approved an exception to certify these platforms without this visibility until the next major release of NXOS, in which these MIBs are expected to be available. That new major release will lead ATC Federated Bank into a new code certification test.

End Notes

1 www.cisco.com/en/US/partner/prod/collateral/switches/ps9441/ps9670/data_sheet_c78-461802.html

2 www.cisco.com/en/US/products/ps10118/index.html

3 www.cisco.com/en/US/products/ps10784/index.html

Chapter 11

Network Ready for Use Testing Case Study

This chapter covers the following topics:

- Background for the NRFU Testing Case Study

- Sports and Entertainment Stadium Architecture Overview

- Network Topology

- Network Ready for Use Test Strategy

Most of the case studies that we have presented to this point involved system testing on a "prototype network system," which frequently is a miniaturized representation of a proposed network topology, built and operated in a lab facility. This is the most common scenario for system testing, because test engineers are able to execute test plans in a controlled environment, where variables can be kept to a minimum. In this chapter, we present a case study of a completely different type of activity known as network ready for use (NRFU) testing, one where tests are carried out not in a lab, but on the newly installed infrastructure, just prior to "cutting it over" onto the live enterprise network.

NRFU testing is often a mandatory, final step in certifying that a new network infrastructure has been implemented correctly and is ready to carry production traffic. During NRFU testing, every device is methodically checked to ensure that its has been implemented according to the design specifications and is operating error-free. Network services are verified, devices are added as elements into NMS and Operational Support Systems (OSS) systems, and a baseline of application performance is recorded.

The following case study describes how the Carolina Cats, a new National Basketball Association (NBA) expansion team, hired Cisco Systems Advanced Services engineers to conduct an NRFU test in a new sports and entertainment complex that was preparing to open its doors to the public for the first time. The case study goes into detail about how the NRFU test was conducted, giving tips on how to perform an effective final check of a network infrastructure to certify it is "ready to go live."

Background for the NRFU Case Study

The Carolina Cats are a new NBA expansion team located in Charleston, South Carolina, home of parent company Cochise Industries. As part of its winning bid for an expansion franchise, Cochise Industries included plans for a new state-of-the-art sports and entertainment complex in Charleston, to be called Cochise Stadium. The new complex will showcase high-end technological innovations geared toward enhancing the fan experience, helping Cochise Industries to create new revenue streams by enticing people to attend other events in the venue.

Cochise Industries hopes to bring a National Hockey League (NHL) franchise team to South Carolina in the near future, and having a multiuse, high-tech complex is a big part of its strategy. Cochise realizes that today's sports fan has high expectations when attending live sporting events, and it has committed to offering a vast array of technical services to enhance the stadium experience, beginning with free wireless LAN (WiFi) access throughout the venue. This WiFi access will lay the foundation for an unprecedented fan interaction experience, providing spectators access to scores, statistics, and instant replays on their handheld devices, allowing them to share this information with other participants, or with anyone on the Internet using social networking applications. Cochise Industries has even developed a smart phone application that gives season ticket holders the ability to preorder and pay for food from their phones and pick it up from special kiosks with much shorter lines.

Digital signage technology is critical to Cochise Industries' vision to build a multiuse facility. With digital signage, the stadium can present an identity as the Carolina Cats' home today, and the South Carolina Frogs' home tomorrow. It will be used for safety and security announcements, menu displays at food concessions, and to direct traffic in and out of the stadium before and after events.

The new stadium has 2000 high-definition (HD) TV displays in the concourse, club, and concession areas featuring customized game footage and real-time information. The Cats can customize displays with pre-event, event, and post-event content, such as out-of-town games and scores, team trivia, weather, traffic and news, in addition to the actual game or event footage. Fans in the 100 luxury suites are able to choose video options and order food and concessions from a touch-screen IP phone.

The stadium uses Cisco IP–enabled video surveillance both inside and outside the arena to create a secure, flexible, and efficient environment for employees, partners, and guests. The gate control system and office badge readers work in conjunction with the video surveillance equipment, offering enhanced access capabilities and centralized security management.

A high-speed Cisco network infrastructure functions as a conduit for all the technical services in the stadium. Continuous availability of this infrastructure is crucial, as without network services, the stadium's staff and vendors cannot do their jobs, and the fans' experience becomes greatly diminished. Because of this critical importance, it is imperative that the network infrastructure be installed properly and be able to offer continuous service prior to the opening day of the stadium. Understanding the risks and criticality of the network infrastructure in providing this access, Cochise Industries has chartered Cisco Advanced Services to develop and execute an NRFU test to ensure that there are no last-minute surprises. The NRFU test will verify several components of the physical and logical design, including the following:

- All device chassis and modules are powered up and running without errors.

- The correct operating system/Cisco IOS Software is running on all network devices, servers, and appliances.

- In-house cabling between all devices is correct.

- External circuits are up and running in error-free conditions.

- IP routing design (unicast and multicast) is working properly.

- Security features are enabled and operating correctly.

- High-availability features are working as designed.

- All devices are manageable by the NMS/OSS systems.

- Network services, such as wireless, video, and VPN, are available and functioning properly.

Sports and Entertainment Stadium Network Architecture

It is critical to have a deep understanding of a network architecture and how it will deliver services when you are developing an NRFU test plan. For example, a traffic test procedure that is generic in nature or that only specifies the generation of unicast IP flows may not demonstrate a network's readiness to carry video traffic that is intended to be encoded and sent as multicast IP traffic. In this same light, if video is planned to be sent as unicast IP only, then including a suite of multicast routing test cases would be a waste of time.

After several meetings with the network architects of the new stadium, the Cisco Systems Advanced Services engineers responsible for developing the NRFU test plan were able to obtain a thorough understanding of the network architecture. Several key areas of the architecture were highlighted to help frame out the test plan.

The network infrastructure designed for the Cochise Stadium complex follows a well-known three-tier hierarchical design model. The design offers a highly scalable and redundant architecture based on the stadium's requirements, including provisioning for video distribution, IP telephony, video surveillance, ticketing, and point-of-sale VPN access, as well as fan, media, and luxury suite guest access, all via one common IP infrastructure.

The design permits Cochise Stadium to have a segregation of user groups, as well as supporting 10-Gigabit Ethernet technologies to interconnect the entire topology. From a high-level perspective, the design comprises the following three tiers:

■   A high-speed core layer made up of two Nexus 7010s

■   An intelligent distribution layer made up of five pairs of Nexus 7010s

■   An access layer made up of Catalyst 6509s and wireless access points (AP)

Figure 11-1 shows an illustration of the network architecture for Cochise Stadium.

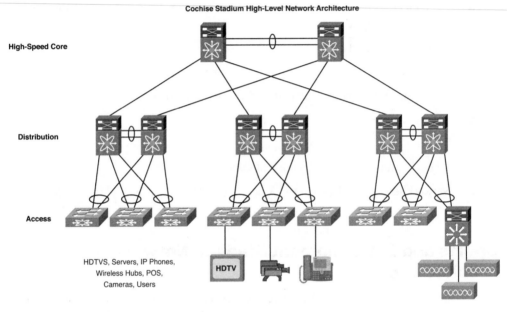

Figure 11-1   *Cochise Stadium High-Level Network Architecture*

The network infrastructure in Cochise Stadium was required to support the following capabilities for fans, media, staff, and vendors within the stadium environment on day one:

■   Eighty video channels and camera angles streamed to HD screens distributed throughout the stadium for fan, media, and staff viewing convenience

■   Wireless access for fans to enhanced in-stadium shopping experience and premium Internet access

■   High-speed wired network access for the media

■   A secure ticketing and point-of-sale infrastructure

■   State-of-the-art voice and contact center network

■   A high-speed, resilient network infrastructure for the entire stadium

■   Integrated video surveillance network solution

■   Digital signage capabilities for all HD TV screens in the stadium

The design leverages a converged common infrastructure with virtualized capabilities and modular building block solutions to provide a reliable, secure, high-speed set of services. The infrastructure is logically segmented into four separate virtual networks across a common core to isolate the distinct functions. The virtual network partitions are made up of the following networks:

■   Public and Media Network

■   Point-of-Sale (POS) Network

■   Staff Network

■   Common Infrastructure Network, offering shared services such as Internet access

Architects chose to deploy a traffic segmentation technology based on Virtual Routing and Forwarding (VRF) features to create secure routing and forwarding environments for each of the four logical partitions. While VRF technology is commonly deployed in conjunction with an MPLS-enabled backbone to achieve end-to-end separation, architects of Cochise Stadium chose to leverage GRE tunneling as an alternative to MPLS in an effort to reduce operational complexity. Shared services such as voice, video, and Internet are delivered as an extranet service to each of the separate (Public, POS, and Staff) VRFs using a similar set of GRE tunnels. The logical network segmentation is depicted in Figure 11-2.

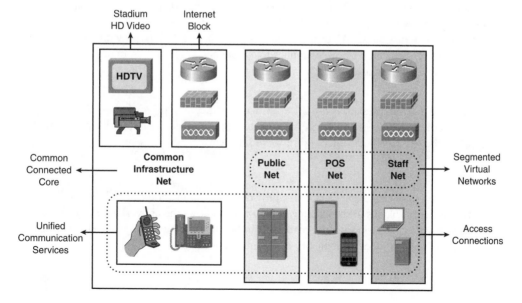

Figure 11-2 *Cochise Stadium Logical Virtual Network Separation Diagram*

Network Topology

The network is built upon a three-tier hierarchical design made up of core, distribution, and access layers.

The core layer comprises high-speed and redundant components, capable of forwarding packets between network devices at 80 Gbps. It serves as the backbone for the network, and as such, a "less is more" approach is taken with this layer. A minimal configuration in the core reduces configuration complexity, limiting the possibility for operational errors that can affect the entire infrastructure.

The distribution layer divides the network to allow isolation of failures and provide dedicated bandwidth and paths for specific traffic from and to the core. The distribution layer aggregates nodes from the access layer, protecting the core from high-density peering and reducing complexity. High availability in the distribution layer is provided through dual equal cost paths from the distribution layer to the core and from the access layer to the distribution layer. This results in fast, deterministic convergence if a link or node fails. With the redundant paths that are present, failover depends primarily on hardware link failure detection instead of timer-based software failure detection. This layer also provides a centralized point of control for multicast traffic, global security ACLs, and route aggregation.

The access layer is the first point of entry into the network for wireless devices, wired end stations, IP-enabled HD TV screens, and IP phones. The switches in the access layer are connected to two separate distribution layer devices for redundancy. The user areas are segregated using virtual LANs (VLANs) to contain traffic within confined work areas and avoid broadcast or L2 network issues from affecting other areas. VLANs are also used to separate traffic between different types of devices such as wireless APs and IP phones in luxury suites. All of the 6500 host ports are capable of providing PoE, thus eliminating the need for power supplies for IP phones, wireless APs, or any other devices that can take advantage of 802.3af technology.

Note   The 802.3af standard is the IEEE-ratified specification for Power over Ethernet (PoE). It covers the capability for the LAN switching infrastructure to provide power over a copper Ethernet cable to an endpoint (powered device).

The three-tier hierarchical design also provides a way to methodically add extra distribution or access blocks to the existing network. This allows the network to easily increase its size and capacity modularly, enabling it to handle future growth, while eliminating the need for any additional complexity or a complete redesign.

Physical Network Topology

Understanding how the network is interconnected is critical when developing an NRFU test plan, as several test cases focus on verifying the Bill of Materials (BoM) and physical connectivity. Physical diagrams depicting connectivity must exist before the NRFU test can begin, so that test engineers can methodically check each and every connection. If an external circuit was not provisioned, or a cable connection was overlooked, a physical check against an accurate final connectivity diagram is the only reliable method to detect it. Otherwise, the network may reroute traffic around a redundant path and hide the issue, creating a single point of failure in the process. The physical documentation should also contain device hardware details for inventory purposes. If a switch was supposed to have six line cards and it only has five, the NRFU test is the last chance to find this out.

The components comprising the Cochise Stadium physical network are described next.

Core Layer Components

The two core Nexus 7010 switches are interconnected via an 80-Gbps connection (8×10-Gbps Ethernet), with fiber connections distributed across four line cards, to form a resilient high-speed core for the entire network. The links are configured individually to provide seamless L3 native interfaces, which are used by OSPF as equal cost paths. Each core switch is equipped with two Supervisor modules, allowing failover and redundancy if a single Supervisor fails, and In Service Software Upgrade (ISSU) capabilities. The switches have five redundant fabrics, and all four 32-port 10-Gbps interface modules are capable of doing distributed forwarding. Each switch has three separate power supplies with two separate inputs each. Each input in an individual power supply is connected to a different 220-V power source. Two individual power sources backed up by an Uninterruptible Power Supply (UPS) and generators are available for each switch in the entire infrastructure.

Distribution Layer Components

The distribution layer is similarly made up of Nexus 7010 switches. These devices also run OSPF to exchange routing information and are interconnected with each other by means of eight 10-Gbps Ethernet interfaces. They connect to each core switch via four 10-Gbps Ethernet individual L3 links to provide both link and core switch redundancy for transit traffic. Future scaling of the network would involve building further pairs of distribution switches with their subtended access layer switches. In the initial design, three pairs of distribution switches make up the aggregation layer of the network.

As with the core, each distribution layer switch is equipped with two Supervisor modules, five fabric modules, four 32-port 10-Gbps interface modules, and three dual connected power supplies; these allow failover and redundancy in the event of a single Supervisor, fabric, line card, or power supply failure.

Access Layer Components

The access layer is made up of Catalyst 6509 switches provisioned with redundant Supervisor modules, each equipped with two 10-Gbps Ethernet uplink interfaces for connectivity to the Nexus 7010 switches in the distribution layer. The access to distribution layer connections is made with direct fiber connections, alternating the Supervisor uplink ports for redundancy purposes. The remaining open slots in each 6509 chassis are populated with 802.3af (POE)–capable line cards, to support user connections. To support the line card power requirements, each Catalyst 6500 is outfitted with dual 6000-W power supplies with two separate inputs each. Each input in an individual power supply is connected to a different 220-V power source.

The server farm and video encoder access switches will not have PoE requirements, as they will be dedicated to server and video encoder "hardwired" connections. These devices will be outfitted with the higher-performing WS-X6748-GE-TX line cards, which allow near line rate 1-Gbps server connectivity.

Multicast Architecture

Multicast testing was identified as one of the most important activities in the NRFU testing, as so many video services depend on multicast infrastructure availability to function. Cochise Stadium has four distinct types of multicast video feeds:

- **Stadium HD video feed:** 80 video channels and camera angles are streamed to HD screens distributed throughout the stadium for fan viewing convenience.

- **Multimedia conferencing feed:** Conference rooms require the use of IP multicast to support business application viewing on wall-mounted screens. These rooms are used for video conference calls between stadium staff and corporate employees at other Cochise Industries offices.

- **Cochise Stadium private video feed:** These are secure, Cochise-only video channels for bench area camera angles and practice films.

- **Security video feed:** This services the integrated video surveillance network solution running over its own multicast feed.

The four video feeds all have different requirements for the sources and receivers, but can be serviced by two distinct IP multicast deployment scenarios. These scenarios are classified as Stadium HD Video and General IP multicast.

Stadium HD Video

The Stadium HD Video topology services the HD video feed for all of the 80 HD channels available to the fans and concession stands. Special encoders turn the satellite feeds from the cable company and the NBA into multicast traffic available throughout the entire stadium. Stadium HD video must be continuously available and thus requires redundant server and network devices for each channel in the event of a failure of the primary video feed.

Each HD video channel has an active and a standby server implemented in an Active-Active configuration. The two servers for each channel are connected to separate access switches. While both servers in a channel are actively sending video streams of the same content, the secondary server's traffic is used in the network only if the primary video stream fails. The network automatically fails over the primary video feed to redundant hardware or links in case of any failures in its path. If the primary server's directly connected router/port fails, the network converges to the secondary video feed.

To accomplish the Stadium HD Video IP multicast delivery, PIM sparse-mode is implemented. The implementation requirements are as follows:

- All configuration traffic is in the Common Infrastructure VRF's routing table.

- PIM sparse mode (PIM-SM) is enabled on all interfaces in the path.

- PIM hellos are set to 1-second timers for quicker failover.

- The first-hop router (FHR) and rendezvous point (RP) are the same physical router.

- An anycast source video design, where multiple servers sharing the same IP address send the same video content, providing a high degree of resiliency.

- Two separate RPs are configured using two different prefix network masks, a less specific subnet mask for the "secondary" and a more specific subnet mask for the "primary" to allow for an active/backup topology based on routing.

- Two video sources, for the same channel, are connected to the two video distribution switches using L3 point-to-point interfaces.

- The primary servers and RP are on the same video distribution router using the more specific network mask.

- A separate static RP configuration is used for the multicast groups supporting the Stadium HD video multicast topology.

- Multicast Source Discovery Protocol (MSDP) is not required or configured for this topology.

Figure 11-3 depicts the Stadium HD multicast topology.

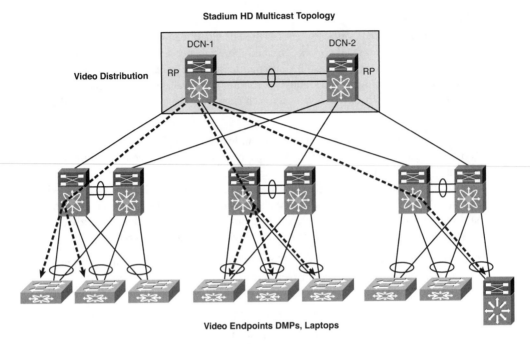

Figure 11-3 *Stadium HD Multicast Topology*

General IP Multicast Topology

The General IP multicast topology is used for the Multimedia Conferencing, Cochise Stadium Private Video and the Security Video feeds. To accomplish this, the General IP Multicast topology in the stadium uses an Anycast-RP with PIM-SM design. The use of PIM-SM is consistent with the Stadium HD Video scenario. The implementation points are

- All configuration/traffic is in the Common Infrastructure VRF's routing table.

- PIM-SM is enabled on all interfaces in the path.

- PIM hellos are set to 1 second.

- FHR and RP may not be the same router.

- An Anycast-RP design is used.

- Three RPs are configured on the distribution routers, each with the same loopback IP address using a /32 subnet mask.

- A separate static RP configuration is used for the multicast groups supporting the General IP multicast topology.

- MSDP is required in this design and is used to share source information between the three RPs.

Multicast Source Discovery Protocol (MSDP) is used to support the Anycast-RP technique deployed in the General IP multicast topology. The purpose of MSDP is to share Source information between RPs. It accomplishes this by sending a Source Advertisement (SA) containing the Source, Group, and RP (S,G,RP) information, from the router that received the Register, to all the configured MSDP peers. With this information, all three RPs in the topology have the same multicast routing information. Because all three RPs advertize the same /32 loopback address, configured as the static RP for all the routers in the network, all three are used as "primary" RPs depending on "closest" routing distance. This allows for high availability in the case of an RP failure as well as load balancing for the topology.

Figure 11-4 depicts the Cochise Stadium General IP Multicast topology.

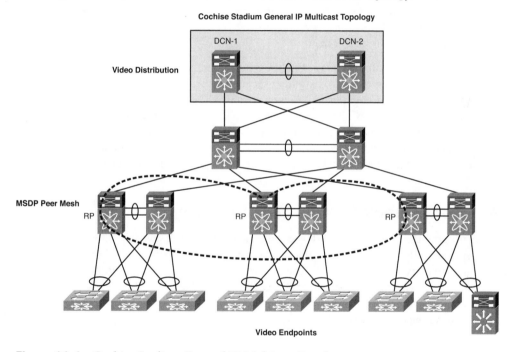

Figure 11-4 *Cochise Stadium General IP Multicast Topology*

Having both of these multicast stream options allows for flexibility in the delivery of video and audio throughout the entire stadium complex. If a particular event requires high-quality video delivered to the HD TV or giant screens, it is just a question of addressing the content with the correct multicast group. Also, new screens can be added, or existing ones moved, and the only requirement to get high-quality video to them is an Ethernet connection.

Because each of these multicast delivery topologies is slightly different, the NRFU test had two separate test sections to account for them.

Additional Infrastructure Considerations

Because so much of the information traveling across the network is real-time in nature, quality of service (QoS) is implemented to guarantee assured and "on time" delivery during periods of peak usage. Voice and video quality are directly affected by all three QoS quality factors: loss, latency, and jitter. Because of this, all the VoIP, HD video, and signaling data has to be treated as priority traffic. Video conferencing is another key real-time application that needs special QoS consideration, and as such it was granted its own QoS queue with guaranteed bandwidth. Other unique classes with bandwidth allocations were created for vital applications, such as POS and ticketing. Once the critical applications are identified and classified, the traffic is then marked with the appropriate DSCP values within its IP header. This traffic is then placed into queues that will guarantee appropriate on-time delivery. In general, user-generated traffic is marked for best-effort delivery. The NRFU took QoS configuration into consideration and confirmed that it was implemented and working correctly.

Because users attending events at Cochise Stadium will have access to the network and the Internet, it is imperative to have tight security controls in place. Authentication, authorization, and accounting (AAA) is enabled on all of the network devices, along with infrastructure ACLs (iACL) and control plane policing (CoPP). Users will be kept in the "Public Net" as much as possible, with very restrictive firewall rules to allow them access to concessions, stadium video, and the Internet. Because of their importance, correct security configurations should always be checked as part of the NRFU test strategy.

Network Ready for Use Test Strategy

Soon after the proposed network was built and configured, it was to be subjected to a series of NRFU tests to confirm that the infrastructure was deployed as designed, and ready to carry production traffic. The primary aim of the tests was to show the reliability and resilience of the network under normal operating conditions. The tests were conducted on site and performed by the Cochise Stadium network team in conjunction with the Cisco Advanced Services team.

Success Criteria

This test was not a feature or capacity test; those were conducted well before this network was built, during design verification testing. It was meant to be a final check of all the network components before they were scheduled to go live. All of the test cases were written with Pass/Fail criteria. Any software issues discovered during testing were to be addressed as production problems and handled appropriately by the network operations team. Any hardware or circuit issues found would be addressed via replacement or repair as soon as possible and then retested.

Test Prerequisites

Before the NRFU test could begin, the following prerequisites needed to be met:

- All work detailed in the Network Staging Plan was complete.

- All work detailed in the Network Implementation Plan was complete.

- All Cisco-supplied equipment was online and in service.

- All circuits were in place and provisioned correctly by the provider.

- All equipment was powered from permanent power supplies.

- All software was at agreed go-live levels.

- All configurations were finalized.

- All physical connectivity was "dressed" and would not be moved unless necessary.

Test Phases

The testing was broken into four separate phases:

- **Phase I:** During this phase, device-level verification was done. This phase included activities such as serial number verification, line card checks, Cisco IOS level confirmation, and power checks.

- **Phase II:** This phase included logical configuration and connectivity verification. In this phase, actions such as circuit connectivity verifications, routing protocol checks, and traceroutes were performed. Multicast and QoS configurations were checked.

- **Phase III:** This included service verification and traffic testing. Service verification included features such as IP telephony, video, wireless, and common IP services (DHCP, DNS, NTP).

- **Phase IV:** This was the application testing phase. Production applications and network and security management were tested during this phase.

The tests performed in each phase were further broken into three different types:

- Tests that were performed on all Cisco routers and switches installed
- Platform/role-specific tests:
    - Access layer switches
    - Core layer switches
    - Distribution layer switches
    - Video distribution switches
    - Server farm switches
- Service-specific tests

Test Tools

Because the Cochise Stadium NRFU test was conducted with the entire IT infrastructure already built, very few test tools were needed to verify functionality and performance. A pair of portable Ixia Traffic Generators were used to ensure there were no packet drops during the short and long traffic tests. Actual services and applications were also demonstrated during the test to verify the server and video infrastructure functioned as expected on the new network. Finally, a laptop with Wireshark Network Analyzer software was used to verify certain security features.

Summary of NRFU Test Cases

Table 11-1 outlines the test cases that were performed for the Cochise Stadium NRFU.

Table 11-1   *Cochise Stadium NRFU Test Cases*

Test Case	Test Name	Short Test Description
Device-Level Verification Tests		
1.1	Physical Check	Physically check every network device: 1. Check that all physical hardware is installed per the BoM. 2. Check that all power supply inputs are connected per plan. 3. Check that all modules and ports are showing "green." 4. Check that all cables are "dressed" correctly. 5. Check that all module screws are tightened. 6. Check that all devices are labeled correctly. 7. Check that all console and out-of-band (OOB) ports are connected for both Supervisors (as needed). 8. Make sure the room's AC is working. 9. Verify wireless APs are mounted where they are supposed to be and their antennas are pointed correctly. 10. Verify that the IP cameras are mounted correctly.
	Out of Band Check	During test 1.1, connect to the console ports of each device directly to check whether the hostname is correct, and then remotely to make sure the OOB console and IP connectivity are working and connected as planned. Check that the username and password for OOB access are set correctly.
1.2	Serial Number Verification	Connect into every device and capture the serial numbers of all chassis, cards, power supplies, wireless APs, cameras, etc. Save this into a database for later reference.

Table 11-1   *Cochise Stadium NRFU Test Cases*

Test Case	Test Name	Short Test Description
1.3	Device Software Verification	Connect into every device and verify: 1. It is running the correct OS level. 2. It is set to boot the correct OS in case of a reload or crash. 3. The OS is present on the device primary and backup Supervisors.
1.4	Device Card Verification	Connect into every device and verify that all the cards/fabrics are running and their status is OK.
1.5	Device Uptime Verification	Connect into every device and verify how long it has been up, that it is the expected amount of time, and that it is running on its "primary" Supervisor if appropriate.
1.6	Device Environmental Verification	Connect into every device and verify: 1. Power capacity and output for each power supply are as expected. 2. Temperature is as expected for all power, supplies, cards, and fabrics. 3. Fans are all powered up and running as expected.

Connectivity and Configuration Verification Tests

Test Case	Test Name	Short Test Description
2.1	Logical Connectivity Verification	Connect into every network device and do the following: 1. Using the final connectivity diagram, use the **show cdp neighbors** command to verify the physical connectivity is correct. 2. Verify that each connected interface has the correct description configured (device name + physical interface of neighbor). 3. If the interface is L3, ping the neighbor interface and make sure the subnet mask is set up correctly.
2.2	Uplink Interface Configuration Verification	Connect into every device and verify that all uplink interfaces are configured to support the correct MTU size.

Table 11-1 *Cochise Stadium NRFU Test Cases*

Test Case	Test Name	Short Test Description
2.3	User Interface Configuration Verification	Connect to all access switches and verify that all user interfaces are configured correctly by verifying: 1. The correct VLAN is configured. 2. Correct PoE state is configured. 3. Correct Speed/Duplex/Auto Negotiation is configured. 4. PortFast is configured where appropriate. 5. Security features such as port security or VACLs are configured as required. 6. VoIP features are configured correctly. 7. QoS features such as marking are configured as expected. 8. Helper addresses for DHCP are configured on the L3 interfaces correctly.
2.3	Server Farm Interface Configuration Verification	Connect into all the server farm access switches and run all of the verifications in test 2.2.
2.4	Internet Circuit Connectivity Verification	1. Connect into the Internet edge devices and verify that the Internet circuits are up and running error free. 2. Verify that the BGP session is up with the service providers and that the routers are receiving the default route as expected 3. Verify that the correct circuit number is configured per the description.
2.5	Loopback Interface Verification	Connect into every L3 device and make sure its loopback0 interfaces are configured correctly.
2.5	OSPF Neighbor Verification	1. Connect into every device running OSPF and verify that the OSPF neighbors are up across all of the interfaces that should be enabled for the feature. 2. Verify that authentication is configured correctly. 3. Verify that the neighborships are in the correct VRFs. 4. Verify that the loopback0 interfaces are being advertised as expected.
2.6	GRE Interface Verification	Connect into every distribution switch and verify that the GRE tunnels between VRFs are up and that OSPF routing is working across them as expected.

Table 11-1 *Cochise Stadium NRFU Test Cases*

Test Case	Test Name	Short Test Description
2.7	OSPF Routing Verification	1. Verify that routes are being learned as expected, and that all equal cost paths are being utilized. 2. Verify that correct routes are seen in the appropriate VRFs. Make sure that the default route is being learned as expected. 3. Verify that "paired devices" have the same number of routes in each VRF as appropriate.
2.8	Traceroute Verification	Run appropriate traceroutes from access layer switches to see how routing is working for relevant services such as POS devices, Internet access, VoIP call managers, video farms, etc. Run these from all of the VRFs.
2.9	Global Multicast Configuration Verification	Connect into every L3 device and verify: 1. Multicast is enabled. 2. All of the required interfaces have "ip pim sparse-mode" configured, and the correct PIM timers are set. 3. The PIM-enabled interfaces "see" their PIM neighbors. 4. The correct static RPs are configured for each multicast topology (Stadium HD and General) using the correct ACLs/groups. 5. GRE tunnel interfaces are configured as expected to pass video between VRFs as required.
2.10	Stadium HD Topology Specific Multicast Verification	Along with the test in 2.9, check the following specific configurations: 1. Verify that the correct routers are configured as the RPs using their loopback10 interfaces with the correct subnet mask to designate primary/secondary RPs. Verify the loopback10 interfaces are configured for multicast. 2. Verify that the loopback10 addresses are being seen in the network as expected. 3. Verify that the server farm switches with the video feeds are configured as expected for the L3 interfaces connected to the video feed servers.

Table 11-1   *Cochise Stadium NRFU Test Cases*

Test Case	Test Name	Short Test Description
2.11	General Multicast Topology Specific Verification	Along with the test in 2.9, check the following specific configurations: 1. Verify that each Anycast-RP (one in each distribution pair router) is configured correctly and set to advertize its loopback10 IP address with the same subnet mask. Verify the loopback10 interfaces are configured for multicast. 2. Verify that the loopback10 addresses are being seen in the network as expected. 3. Verify that the three RP have MSDP enabled and configured correctly in a full mesh.
2.12	QoS Configuration Verification	1. Verify that the correct global QoS configuration is applied to every device. 2. Verify the correct queues are configured. 3. Verify the correct shaping policy is configured.
2.13	Network Management Configuration Verification	Connect into every network device and verify that 1. The correct SNMP configuration is applied, including traps, communities, and security filtering ACLs. 2. The correct syslog server and facilities are configured. 3. The correct NetFlow configuration, including export destination, is applied.
2.14	Security Feature Configuration Verification	Connect into every device and verify that all of the appropriate security features are enabled. Features such as AAA, iACL, sinkholes, IP ACL against virus/worms, uRPF, IP Options Selective Drop, and CPP should be verified.
2.15	Firewall Configuration Verification	Check that all the required routes are configured. Make sure the configuration is correct, including features such as HA, DoS prevention, and NAT. Verify with the security group to make sure all the rules are applied as expected.
2.16	Wireless AP Verification	1. Verify that all of the APs have powered and registered as expected. 2. Verify that the wireless configuration and VLANs are set up correctly. 3. Run the radio diagnostics tests.

Table 11-1 *Cochise Stadium NRFU Test Cases*

Test Case	Test Name	Short Test Description
Service Verification and Traffic Tests		
3.1	DHCP Service Verification	1. Connect a laptop or other wired host into every VLAN/VRF to make sure the helper addresses on the L3 interfaces of the access switches are working correctly. 2. Use a wireless host in all the separate wireless zone of the stadium, including fan, media, and office spaces, to make sure DHCP is handing out IP addresses correctly. 3. Test POS and ticketing wireless devices for DHCP leases in the appropriate VRFs.
3.2	IP Telephony Phone Verification	1. Visually check each IP Phone for power, the correct phone line number, and dial tone. 2. Verify each phone for the correct template (soft buttons, etc.). 3. Test phones in each area by making an internal and external phone call. 4. Check phones in each area for OS load. 5. Verify services for phones in each area, such as food menus. 6. Verify voice services such as conference calling and call forwarding for the stadium staff phones. 7. Verify voice mail services for staff phones. 8. Verify E911 service.
3.3	IP Telephony Network Verification	1. Check VoIP VLANs to see if they are working correctly in the access switches. 2. Verify QoS settings to make sure that voice and signaling data are hitting the correct queues. 3. Check PoE to make sure it is applying the correct amount of inline power to the IP phones.
3.4	Wireless Verification	1. Verify that you can move between access points and maintain network connectivity. 2. Verify that the correct QoS parameters are getting set for wireless traffic. 3. Verify that the APs are getting the correct amount of PoE. 4. Verify that the "secure" wireless reserved for POS, ticketing, and other stadium-only devices cannot be "reached" by regular fan devices. 5. Verify that the POS and ticketing devices can reach their internal servers as required. 6. Verify that handheld WiFi devices can use their Cochise Stadium apps for concessions and special video.

Table 11-1 *Cochise Stadium NRFU Test Cases*

Test Case	Test Name	Short Test Description
3.5	IP Camera and Security Systems Verification	1. Verify video reception from every security camera. 2. Verify badge security systems. 3. Verify that correct QoS marking is happening for security video traffic.
3.6	Short Unicast Traffic Test	1. Clear all counters and logs in every device. 2. Connect Ixia ports in each VRF (Public, POS, Staff, and Common Infrastructure). Ixia ports should be connected to each of the six distribution switches, five user access switches, and one data center access switch. 3. Create a "traffic mesh" between the Common Infrastructure VRF and the other three VRF using the IPAs available on the switches. 4. Run traffic using random packet sizes to a total of 20% of line rate for 3 hours. 5. Check interface counters and logs for any errors. 6. Record results.
3.7	Short Multicast Traffic Test	1. Using the same connectivity as test 3.6, create multicast traffic sourced at the data center access switch for multicast groups in both the Stadium HD Video and General Multicast topologies. 2. Subscribe to all the groups from all the rest of the Ixia ports. 3. Clear all counters and logs. 4. Run multicast traffic using 64-byte packet sizes to a total of 20% of line rate for 3 hours. 5. Check mroutes and RPs. 6. Check interface counters and logs for any errors. 7. Record all of the results.
3.8	Long Term Traffic Test	1. Clear all counters and logs. 2. Run the traffic patterns in tests 3.6 and 3.7 together for 48 hours. 3. Check interface counters and logs for any errors. 4. Record all of the results.

Table 11-1   *Cochise Stadium NRFU Test Cases*

Test Case	Test Name	Short Test Description
Application Tests		
4.1	Stadium Application Checkout Test	Running the traffic from test 3.8 as background traffic, run the following verification tests all at once: 1. Turn on the HD TVs in every luxury suite and tune them to a random channel and use the IP Phones to order concessions. 2. Turn on all the concession HD TVs and make them display video, menus, and ads as appropriate. 3. Turn on all the stadium boards and "big screens" and display regular ads, video, and audio. 4. Check as many of the concession applications, such as POS and ticketing, as possible. 5. Place phone calls from all the different places (VRFs) in the network. 6. Surf the Internet, watch video, and use the Cochise Stadium app over several WiFi devices. 7. Operate the security cameras and badge readers. 8. Test regular office applications such as email and video conferencing.
4.2	Network Management Application Checkout Test	While running test 4.1: 1. Verify that all of the network management tools are working as expected. 2. Verify that interface usage and NetFlow visibility exists. 3. Verify the memory and CPU usage of all the devices under management is "normal." 4. Record "normal" usage statistics.

Summary

At the conclusion of the NRFU testing for Cochise Stadium, the entire IT staff felt excited and confident that their infrastructure was deployed in accordance with the design documentation. They took comfort in the knowledge that all of their main applications worked and that the network infrastructure was installed and configured correctly. During the test, it was found that an uplink connection between a distribution switch and the core had never been run, and that one of the existing connections between an access switch and the distribution was run using a badly bent fiber, thus causing interface errors; both issues were fixed immediately. One of the security cameras failed to come online and was replaced. Having all HD TVs and digital signage up and running at the same time was the culmination of two years of work for most of the staff and was greeted with cheers and hugs. The Cochise Stadium management team has decided to sign a contract with the Cisco Advance Services team who conducted the NRFU to come on site for the first four events in the stadium and help ensure the smooth operation of the network.

Test Plans

Part III is made up of representative sample test plans to help you validate the functionality and performance of new designs in various places in the network. These example test plans are intended to be used as starting points for developing your own customized documentation; they should not be considered completed "test scripts." Many low-level details have been intentionally left out of these examples, such as device configuration and command-line interface input/output samples, which are customarily found in detailed test plans. These details will vary widely by design, platform, and operating system, and it would be impossible to capture every possible variation. The goal of Part III is to help you understand which design aspects should be analyzed for different technologies and places in the network, and how to structure a successful test plan.

Part III concludes with a detailed hands-on lab guide developed as the supporting documentation to an in-house training curriculum that leverages resources in the test lab. This guide could also be customized for different technologies or platforms, and is provided as a template.

The test plans are broken down by technologies into the following chapters:

Manageability Cases

Each chapter in Part III contains detailed test cases to help evaluate a specific technology, feature, solution, or network design. With few exceptions, each focuses on a different place in the network, and consequently the features and protocols tested vary widely by chapter. As it is equally important to evaluate the ability to manage the network devices that comprise a design, a set of "manageability" tests would normally be included in each test plan to satisfy operational requirements. These minimum requirements should be part of any test plan you write and execute, including the ones in the following chapters. Enterprise minimum requirements usually include features such as

- Telnet, SSHv2, and console access

- SNMP access and security

- Syslog

- NTP

- AAA and TACACS+

- Banners

As with everything in this part of the book, these features are just an example of requirements that should be tested. Your enterprise should have a checklist of features that are absolute necessities for certifying any piece of hardware or software. These requirements should be a part of any test plan you write and execute.

The Test Case Format

All the detailed test cases in this part of the book are presented in the form of tables. Tables are one of the most often used formats for test plans, as they provide concise fields for capturing and archiving methods and results. The colors and captions often vary, but the content is more or less the same for all of them. Table P3-1 shows an example and explanation of the format used throughout this part of the book for detailed test cases.

Table P3-1 *Example of the Format for a Detailed Test Case*

Test ID:	The unique name for this test.
Node List:	The list of the actual hardware being tested in this test case.
Test Phase:	Baseline, Performance, Feature, or Duty Cycle, for example.
Test Description:	Short description of the test.

Table P3-1 *Example of the Format for a Detailed Test Case*

Test Setup:	Setup steps to be taken before this test case is begun.
Test Steps:	Actual steps taken for this test case.
Expected Results:	Expected results before the test is conducted.
Observed Results:	Actual observed results during the test. Captures or pointers to files can be inserted here.
Pass/Fail:	Pass or fail criteria are dependent on expected results. This can be interpreted differently in the case of performance testing.

Note When you write a test plan, each test case should stand on its own. Oftentimes, more than one engineer conducts tests, and having a test case that is incomplete or references another case may cause confusion. Sometimes, only particular parts of a test plan need to be rerun, and having each case stand on its own will save you time. If you are writing a test plan that may be executed by someone else, having complete information in each test case, even if it is repetitive, is very useful.

Detailed Minimum Requirement Test Cases

This section gives you some samples of detailed test cases created to verify the minimum feature requirements for any hardware or software certification test. As mentioned before, the following examples, or something similar to them, should be used with every test you conduct.

Table P3-2 *SSH and Console Access Baseline Test*

Test ID:	MIN-BASE-1
Node List:	All devices under test
Test Phase:	Baseline
Test Description:	SSHv2 and Console Access
Test Setup:	Load all devices with the appropriate code versions. Connect and configure all of the devices as per the test design.

Table P3-2 *SSH and Console Access Baseline Test*

Test Steps:		
	Step 1.	Configure all devices under test (DUT) for only SSHv2 remote access.
	Step 2.	Configure a login banner in all DUTs.
	Step 3.	Configure the device hostname.
	Step 4.	Configure the device prompt (if required).
	Step 5.	Configure an exec idle timeout of 5 minutes.
	Step 6.	Configure a username and password with full read/write privileges (if applicable).
	Step 7.	Configure a username and password with read-only privileges (if applicable).
	Step 8.	SSH into the DUTs using SSHv2 and log in using the username/password with full read/write privileges. Verify that the banner is displayed. Show the device's configuration. Check whether changes can be made to the device's configuration. Log out.
	Step 9.	SSH into the DUTs using SSHv2 and login using the username/password with read-only privileges. Show the device's configuration. Check whether changes can be made to the device's configuration. Logout.
	Step 10.	Attempt to login into the DUTs using TELNET and SSHv1.
	Step 11.	Console into the DUTs and login using the username/password with full read/write privileges. Verify that the banner is displayed. Show the device's configuration. Check whether changes can be made to the device's configuration. Logout.
	Step 12.	Console into the DUTs using the username/password with read-only privileges. Show the device's configuration. Check whether changes can be made to the device's configuration. Logout.
	Step 13.	SSH into the DUTs and leave the window idle for 5 minutes. Verify whether the session is terminated.
	Step 14.	Console into the DUTs and leave the window idle for 5 minutes. Verify whether the session is logged off.
Expected Results:		The configuration will work as expected, and the banner, device name, and prompt will be displayed correctly. SSHv1 and Telnet will not work for device access. The idle timeout will cause sessions to disconnect after 5 minutes of inactivity.

Table P3-2 *SSH and Console Access Baseline Test*

Observed Results:

Pass/Fail:

Table P3-3 *NTP Operation Baseline Test*

Test ID:	MIN-BASE-2
Node List:	All devices under test
Test Phase:	Baseline
Test Description:	NTP Operation
Test Setup:	Load all devices with the appropriate code versions. Connect and configure all of the devices as per the test design.
Test Steps:	**Step 1.** Configure all DUTs to use NTP. Verify that the devices have synched their times with the NTP server.
	Step 2. Configure the correct time zone in the DUTs. Verify that the time zone works as expected.
Expected Results:	The time will sync and the time zone will work correctly.

Observed Results:

Pass/Fail:

Table P3-4 *TACACS+ and AAA Operation Baseline Test*

Test ID:	MIN-BASE-3
Node List:	All devices under test
Test Phase:	Baseline
Test Description:	TACACS+ and AAA Operation
Test Setup:	Load all devices with the appropriate code versions. Connect and configure all of the devices as per the test design.

Test Steps:	**Step 1.**	Configure all devices to use AAA and point them at the lab ACS (TACACS+) server for authentication, authorization, and accounting. Create and configure a local username and password to be used in case the ACS server is unavailable.
	Step 2.	In the ACS server, configure a user with full read/write access and a second user who is only allowed to execute the **show version** command.
	Step 3.	SSH into the DUTs and log in using the read/write user account configured in the ACS server. Verify that this account can show the configuration and make changes. Check the ACS server to make sure all commands entered are being logged (accounting is working correctly).
	Step 4.	SSH into the DUTs and log in using the second user account (the one only allowed to use the **show version** command) configured in the ACS server. Verify whether this account can show the configuration or make changes. Issue the **show version** command and validate that it does work. Check the ACS server to make sure all commands entered are being logged (accounting is working correctly).
	Step 5.	Disconnect the ACS server from the network. Verify that the local username can be used to log in and make changes in all devices.
	Step 6.	Repeat Steps 3 through 5 using console access.

Expected Results:	TACACS+ and AAA will work for all devices as expected.
Observed Results:	

Table P3-4   *TACACS+ and AAA Operation Baseline Test*

Pass/Fail:

Table P3-5   *SNMP and Syslog Operation Baseline Test*

Test ID:	MIN-BASE-4
Node List:	All devices under test
Test Phase:	Baseline
Test Description:	SNMP and Syslog Operation
Test Setup:	Load all devices with the appropriate code versions. Connect and configure all of the devices as per the test design.
Test Steps:	**Step 1.** Configure all devices to use SNMP and syslog as per the company configuration standards. Configure the SNMP read and write communities. Create and apply an ACL to the SNMP configuration to only allow a single SNMP server to "communicate" with the devices (where applicable).
	Step 2. Create a change to the configuration that will cause an SNMP trap and a syslog message to be sent to the lab SNMP/syslog server. Verify that the logs and traps are sent correctly.
	Step 3. Poll the interface MIBs of the DUTs, using the correct SNMP community, from the "allowed" server.
	Step 4. Poll the interface MIBs of the DUTs, using an *incorrect* SNMP community, from the allowed server.
	Step 5. Poll the interface MIBs of the DUTs, using the correct SNMP community, from a server that is *not* allowed by the ACL applied to the SNMP configuration.
	Step 6. Attempt to change the hostname of the DUTs via SNMP, using the correct SNMP write community, from the "allowed" server.
	Step 7. Attempt to change the hostname of the DUTs via SNMP, using an *incorrect* SNMP write community, from the "allowed" server.
	Step 8. Attempt to change the hostname of the devices via SNMP, using the correct SNMP write community, from a server that is *not* allowed by the ACL applied to the SNMP configuration.

Table P3-5 *SNMP and Syslog Operation Baseline Test*

Expected Results:	SNMP and syslog will work as expected. The correct SNMP communities and server IP address will be required to poll or make changes on all DUTs.

Observed Results:

Pass/Fail:

Chapter 12

Inter-Organization Secure Data Center Interconnect: Firewall Test Plan

This test plan assists you in validating a solution to securely interconnect the data centers of two completely separate enterprise networks. This scenario is common during a network merger or acquisition, when a requirement exists to begin routing email and replicating data over private network connections as soon as an acquisition is completed. The network topology presented in this chapter is considered a "day-1" solution that most organizations would consider temporary until the full network integration between the merging companies would be completed.

Background

During the planning meetings leading up to the network merger of two companies, it was discovered that both had allocated IP addresses from the RFC 1918 space, and that two data centers had some overlapping subnets in the 10.0.0.0/8 range. Because it was not feasible to reassign IP addresses in either data center prior to day 1, architects agreed to deploy Network Address Translation (NAT) on Catalyst 6500 Firewall Services Modules (FWSM) at the data center edge to translate the overlapping subnets into unique addresses. Another discovery was that while each company had deployed OSPF as the routing protocol, neither had extended the backbone (Area 0) into the data centers. Instead, both chose to deploy regular (nonbackbone) areas, leaving the migration planners with a routing challenge on how to interconnect. To avoid a major OSPF redesign, a decision was made to deploy BGP to exchange only the necessary data center server farm prefixes. Implementation of this solution was scheduled immediately after the merger was official, which raised network security concerns in both organizations because each viewed the other as "unknown" and, as such, "untrusted." Because of this, both companies agreed to implement Cisco ASA 5500 Series Adaptive Security Appliances ("ASA firewalls") to filter traffic at the interconnection points.

In an effort to effectively manage and troubleshoot during day-2 operations, Cisco Security Manager (CSM) was deployed at the parent company's data center to manage firewall rules and NAT configurations at both locations. Cisco Catalyst Series Network Analysis Modules (NAM) were installed in each of the Catalyst 6500 WAN routers to help diagnose any possible application problems that might crop up after the migration.

Physical and Logical Test Topology

Figure 12-1 illustrates the test topology.

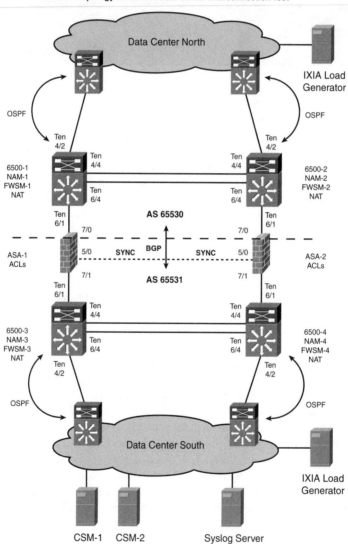

Network Topology for Secure Data Center Interconnection Test

Figure 12-1 *Network Topology for Secure Data Center Interconnection Test*

Technical details of the test setup are as follows:

- Catalyst 6500 (6500-1, 6500-2, 6500-3, 6500-4) switches are deployed in pairs at each data center edge to provide 10-Gigabit Ethernet connectivity, NAT, and BGP peering between organizations. Each Catalyst 6500 is equipped with 10-Gigabit Ethernet line cards, FWSMs, and NAMs.

- FWSM-1 and FWSM-2, as a high availability (HA) pair, do the NAT for overlapping IP traffic originating from Data Center North.

- FWSM-3 and FWSM-4, as an HA pair, do the NAT for overlapping IP traffic originating from Data Center South.

- A pair of ASA 5580 firewalls are installed between the Catalyst 6500 WAN routers of each organization, configured as an active/standby HA pair. All security access rules on these firewalls are administered using the CSM application.

- External BGP (eBGP) multihop routing is configured between Catalyst 6500s in Data Center North (AS 65530) and Data Center South (AS 65531) for the purposes of exchanging the corporate and unique IP addressing associated with NAT pools at each company. Overlapping routes between the two organizations are not advertised.

- Internal BGP (iBGP) routing is enabled between 6500-1 and 6500-2 - in AS 65530, and 6500-3 and 6500-4 in AS 65531.

- BGP-learned routes are redistributed into OSPF inside each data center.

Test Objectives

The primary objectives for this test are as follows:

1. Validate that the proposed routing and NAT designs will work to connect the two data centers together.

2. Discover what the real scalability will be for the *entire* firewall infrastructure, because the firewalls are the gating factor in this inter-organization secure Data Center Interconnect (DCI).

3. Ensure the CSM application can effectively manage this firewall solution.

Test Case Summary

Table 12-1 briefly summarizes the tests to be conducted to certify the inter-organization secure DCI previously described.

Table 12-1   *Test Cases Summary Table*

Test ID	Brief Test Description
FW-BASE-1	Network Baseline Test
FW-PERF-1	Maximum Throughput Test
FW-PERF-2	Maximum TCP Connection Establishment Rate Test
FW-PERF-3	Firewall Logging Test
FW-PERF-4	Firewall Latency Test
FW-FEAT-1	CSM Configuration Update Under High CPU Test
FW-FEAT-2	CLI Configuration Update Under High CPU Test
FW-FEAT-3	CSM Backup and Restore Test
FW-FEAT-4	6500 VACL and SPAN Redirect to NAM Test
FW-DUTY-1	Chassis Failure and Recovery Test
FW-DUTY-2	Line Card Failure and Recovery Test
FW-DUTY-3	Interface Failure and Recovery Test
FW-DUTY-4	Software Forced Failover Test

Detailed Test Cases

The following tables contain detailed test cases to be conducted to certify the topology described earlier. These cases provide you with guidance on testing inter-organization secure DCI and should be modified to fit your specific needs.

Table 12-2   *Network Baseline Test*

Test ID:	FW-BASE-1
Node List:	Routers: 6500-1, 6500-2, 6500-3, 6500-4
	FWs: FWSM-1, FWSM-2, FWSM-3, FWSM-4, ASA-1, ASA-2
	NAMs: NAM-1, NAM-2, NAM-3, NAM-4
Test Phase:	Baseline
Test Description:	Network Baseline Test

Table 12-2 *Network Baseline Test*

Test Setup:	• Build the network, as shown in Figure 12-1. • Configure all of the routing protocols. • Push the production firewall rule set onto the ASAs and the NATs onto the FWSMs using the CSM application. • Configure the Switched Port Analyzer (SPAN) feature on each Catalyst 6500 so that traffic is sent to the NAM blades for analysis.
Test Steps:	This test is run for 24 hours.
	Step 1. Verify that BGP is up between 6500-1, 6500-2, 6500-3, and 6500-3 routers.
	Step 2. Start 1000 bidirectional flows from the Ixia toolset running at a total of 2 Gbps. 10% of the traffic flows should be sourced from IP addresses that will hit the NAT rule in FWSM-1/FWSM-2. These flows will become translated and be permitted through the ACLs in ASA-1/ASA-2. 10% of the traffic flows should be sourced from IP addresses that will hit the NAT rule in FWSM-3/FWSM-4. These flows will become translated and be permitted through the ACLs in ASA-1/ASA-2. 80% of the traffic flows should be sourced from IP addresses that will bypass the NAT rules. These flows will be permitted through the ACLs in ASA-1/ASA-2.
	Step 3. Start 100 bidirectional flows from the Ixia toolset running at a total of 200 Mbps. 100% of this traffic should bypass the NAT rules and be denied by the ACLs in ASA-1/ASA-2. Verify that the traffic that should be making it through the NATs and ACLs is passing and that the traffic that should be dropped is indeed failing to make it through the firewalls.
	Step 4. Verify the logs on all devices are being updated as expected.
	Step 5. Verify that the NAM blades are receiving the traffic that has been SPANed to them as expected. Using the NAM blades, verify that the traffic from the Ixia is indeed correctly created.
	Step 6. Verify the CPU and memory utilization on all of the devices in the Node List every 30 minutes.

Table 12-2 *Network Baseline Test*

Expected Results:	All NAT and permitted traffic will pass thorough the entire network.
	All denied traffic will be dropped and logged.
	All DUTs in the Node List will remain stable throughout the 24 hours.
Observed Results:	
Pass/Fail:	

Table 12-3 *Maximum Throughput Test*

Test ID:	FW-PERF-1
Node List:	Routers: 6500-1, 6500-2, 6500-3, 6500-4
	FWs: FWSM-1, FWSM-2, FWSM-3, FWSM-4, ASA-1, ASA-2
Test Phase:	Performance
Test Description:	Maximum Throughput Test
Test Setup:	• Build the network, as shown in Figure 12-1. • Configure all of the routing protocols. • Push the production firewall rule set onto the ASAs and the NATs onto the FWSMs using the CSM, and make sure there is a "permit any" in the rule set to allow the throughput test traffic. • Disable firewall logging.
Test Steps:	**Step 1.** Run the Ixia IxAutomate RFC3511 IP Throughput test using test flows with IP addresses that will bypass the NAT rules. Verify the CPU and memory utilization on all of the devices in the Node List during each iteration of this test. Run this test to completion three times and record the results.
	Step 2. Run the RFC3511 IP Throughput test using test flows with IP addresses that will hit the NAT rules in FWSM-1/FWSM-2 only. Verify the CPU and memory utilization in all of the devices in the Node List during each iteration of this test. Run this test to completion three times and record the results.

Table 12-3 *Maximum Throughput Test*

Expected Results:	This is a scalability test for the entire firewall architecture (not for a single firewall). The results of the test will be reported in the Observed Results section.
Observed Results:	
Pass/Fail:	

Table 12-4 *Maximum TCP Connection Establishment Rate Test*

Test ID:	FW-PERF-2
Node List:	Routers: 6500-1, 6500-2, 6500-3, 6500-4 FWs: FWSM-1, FWSM-2, FWSM-3, FWSM-4, ASA-1, ASA-2
Test Phase:	Performance
Test Description:	Maximum TCP Connection Establishment Rate Test
Test Setup:	• Build the network, as shown in Figure 12-1. • Configure all of the routing protocols. • Push the production firewall rule set onto the ASAs and the NATs onto the FWSMs using the CSM, and make sure there is a "permit any" in the rule set to allow the "connection" test traffic. • Disable firewall logging.
Test Steps:	**Step 1.** Run the Ixia RFC3511 TCP Maximum Connections Rate test using test flows with IP addresses that will bypass the NAT rules. Verify the CPU and memory utilization on all of the devices in the Node List during each iteration of this test. Run this test to completion three times and record the results.
	Step 2. Run the RFC3511 TCP Maximum Connections Rate test using test flows with IP addresses that will hit the NAT rules in FWSM-1/FWSM-2 only. Verify the CPU and memory utilization in all of the devices in the Node List during each iteration of this test. Run this test to completion three times and record the results.

Table 12-4   *Maximum TCP Connection Establishment Rate Test*

Expected Results:	This is a scalability test for the entire firewall architecture (not for a single firewall). The results of the test will be reported in the Observed Results section.
Observed Results:	
Pass/Fail:	

Table 12-5   *Firewall Logging Test*

Test ID:	FW-PERF-3
Node List:	Routers: 6500-1, 6500-2, 6500-3, 6500-4 FWs: FWSM-1, FWSM-2, FWSM-3, FWSM-4, ASA-1, ASA-2
Test Phase:	Performance
Test Description:	Firewall Logging Test
Test Setup:	• Build the network, as shown in Figure 12-1. • Configure all of the routing protocols. • Push the production firewall rule set onto the ASAs and the NATs onto the FWSMs using the CSM, and make sure there is a "permit any" in the rule set to allow the "connection" test traffic. • Enable firewall logging for permitted and denied traffic on all firewalls.
Test Steps:	**Step 1.** With logging enabled, run the Ixia RFC3511 TCP Maximum Connections Rate test using test flows with IP addresses that will bypass the NAT rules. Verify the CPU and memory utilization on all of the devices in the Node List during each iteration of this test. Run this test to completion three times and record the results. Verify that the firewall is logging all sessions that are created.
	Step 2. With logging enabled, run the RFC3511 TCP Maximum Connections Rate test using test flows with IP addresses that will hit the NAT rules in FWSM-1/FWSM-2 only. Verify the CPU and memory utilization in all of the devices in the Node List during each iteration of this test. Run this test to completion three times and record the results. Verify that the firewall is logging all sessions that are created.

Table 12-5 *Firewall Logging Test*

Expected Results:	This is a scalability test for the entire firewall architecture (not for a single firewall). The results of the test will be reported in the Observed Results section.
Observed Results:	
Pass/Fail:	

Table 12-6 *Firewall Latency Test*

Test ID:	FW-PERF-4
Node List:	Routers: 6500-1, 6500-2, 6500-3, 6500-4
	FWs: FWSM-1, FWSM-2, FWSM-3, FWSM-4, ASA-1, ASA-2
Test Phase:	Performance
Test Description:	Firewall Latency Test
Test Setup:	• Build the network, as shown in Figure 12-1.
	• Configure all of the routing protocols.
	• Push the production firewall rule set onto the ASAs and the NATs onto the FWSMs using the CSM, and make sure there is a "permit any" in the rule set to allow the "latency" test traffic.
Test Steps:	**Step 1.** Run the Ixia RFC3511 Latency test using test flows with IP addresses that will bypass the NAT rules. Run this test to completion three times and record the results.
	Step 2. Run the RFC3511 Latency test using test flows with IP addresses that will hit the NAT rules in FWSM-1/FWSM-2 only. Run this test to completion three times and record the results.
Expected Results:	This is a latency test for the entire firewall architecture (not for a single firewall). The results of the test will be reported in the Observed Results section.

Table 12-6   *Firewall Latency Test*

Observed Results:

Pass/Fail:

Table 12-7   *CSM Configuration Update Under High CPU Test*

Test ID:	FW-FEAT-1
Node List:	FWs: FWSM-1, FWSM-2, FWSM-3, FWSM-4, ASA-1, ASA-2 CSM-1
Test Phase:	Feature
Test Description:	CSM Configuration Update Under High CPU Test
Test Setup:	• Build the network, as shown in Figure 12-1. • Configure all of the routing protocols. • Push the production firewall rule set onto the ASAs and the NATs onto the FWSMs using the CSM, and make sure there is a "permit any" in the rule set to allow the "connection and throughput" test traffic. • Enable firewall logging. • Make sure all of the firewalls in the Node List are managed by CSM-1. • Use the Ixia ports to run bidirectional background traffic at 90% of the maximum connection rate seen in the FW-PERF-3 test. • Set up one Ixia marker flow running at 1 Mbps using an IP address and TCP port combination that will be permitted by the ASA rule set. • Set up a second Ixia marker flow running at 1 Mbps with an IP address that will be translated by the NAT rules in the FWSM-1/FWSM-2 pair.
Test Steps:	Wait for 5 minutes after the Ixia traffic is started to allow it to build to a steady rate. Measure the CPU and memory utilization of all the firewalls in the Node List, and record the results as a baseline. Check that the two marker flows are passing through the firewall architecture.

Table 12-7 *CSM Configuration Update Under High CPU Test*

Step 1.	With the traffic running, push a new syslog server to all of the firewall devices managed by the CSM. Measure the CPU and memory utilization of the firewalls during this change.
Step 2.	Reverse the change in Step 1 using the CSM. Measure the CPU and memory utilization of the firewalls during this change.
Step 3.	With the traffic running, push a new ACL to block the first marker flow created for this test, using the CSM. Measure the CPU and memory utilization of the ASAs during this change. Verify that the marker flow traffic is being dropped after the change.
Step 4.	Reverse the change in Step 3 using the CSM. Measure the CPU and memory utilization of the ASA firewalls during this change. Verify that the marker flow traffic is being permitted after the change.
Step 5.	With the traffic running, push a new NAT rule that will stop translating the second marker flow created for this test. Verify the CPU and memory utilization of the FWSM-1/FWSM-2 firewalls during this change. Verify that the marker flow traffic is no longer being translated after the change.
Step 6.	Reverse the change in Step 5 using the CSM. Measure the CPU and memory utilization of the FWSM firewalls during this change. Verify that the marker flow traffic is being translated after the change.
Step 7.	With the traffic running, use the CSM to push a new ASA rule set modifying an existing object group. Measure the CPU and memory utilization of the ASAs during this change. Verify that the object group was changed.
Step 8.	Reverse the change in Step 7 using the rollback feature in the CSM. Measure the CPU and memory utilization of the ASA firewalls during this change. Verify that the object has indeed been changed back.
Expected Results:	The changes will be applied correctly by the CSM.

Table 12-7   *CSM Configuration Update Under High CPU Test*

Observed Results:

Pass/Fail:

Table 12-8   *CLI Configuration Update Under High CPU Test*

Test ID:	FW-FEAT-2
Node List:	FWs: FWSM-1, FWSM-2, FWSM-3, FWSM-4, ASA-1, ASA-2
Test Phase:	Feature
Test Description:	CLI Configuration Update Under High CPU Test
Test Setup:	• Build the network, as shown in Figure 12-1. • Configure all of the routing protocols. • Push the production firewall rule set onto the ASAs and the NATs onto the FWSMs using the CSM, and make sure there is a "permit any" in the rule set to allow the "connection and throughput" test traffic. • Enable firewall logging. • Use the Ixia ports to run bidirectional background traffic at 90% of the maximum connection rate seen in the FW-PERF-3 test. • Set up one marker flow running at 1 Mbps using an IP address and TCP port combination that will be permitted by the ASA rule set. • Set up a second marker flow running at 1 Mbps with an IP address that will be translated by the NAT rules in the FWSM-1/FWSM-2 pair.
Test Steps:	Wait for 5 minutes after the Ixia traffic has started, to allow it to build to a steady rate. Measure the CPU and memory utilization of all the firewalls in the Node List and record the results as a baseline. Check that the two marker flows are passing through the firewall architecture.
	Step 1. With the traffic running, add a new syslog server to all the firewalls using the CLI. Measure the CPU and memory utilization of the firewalls during this change.

Table 12-8 *CLI Configuration Update Under High CPU Test*

Step 2.	Reverse the change made in Step 1 using the CLI. Measure the CPU and memory utilization of the firewalls during this change.
Step 3.	With the traffic running, create a new ACL to block the first marker flow created for this test. Measure the CPU and memory utilization of the ASAs during this change. Verify that the marker flow traffic is being dropped after the change.
Step 4.	Reverse the change in Step 3 using the CLI. Measure the CPU and memory utilization of the ASA firewalls during this change. Verify that the marker flow traffic is being permitted after the change.
Step 5.	With the traffic running, create a new NAT rule that will stop translating the second marker flow created for this test. Verify the CPU and memory utilization of the FWSM-1/FWSM-2 firewalls during this change. Verify that the marker flow traffic is no longer being translated after the change.
Step 6.	Reverse the change in Step 5 using the CLI. Measure the CPU and memory utilization of the FWSM firewalls during this change. Verify that the marker flow traffic is being translated after the change.
Step 7.	With the traffic running, use the CLI to modify an existing object group in the ASA. Measure the CPU and memory utilization of the ASAs during this change. Verify that the object group has been changed correctly.
Step 8.	Reverse the change made in Step 7 using the CLI. Measure CPU and memory utilization on the ASA firewalls during this change. Verify that the object group has been changed back correctly.

Expected Results:	The changes will be applied correctly.

Observed Results:

Pass/Fail:

Table 12-9   *CSM Backup and Restore Test*

Test ID:	FW-FEAT-3
Node List:	CSM
Test Phase:	Feature
Test Description:	CSM Backup and Restore Test
Test Setup:	This test will use the CSM-1 configuration created in the FW-FEAT-1 test.
Test Steps:	**Step 1.** Create a backup file of the CSM-1 database using **Tools > Backup.**
	Step 2. Export the backup to the CSM-2 server using FTP.
	Step 3. Restore the backed-up configuration from CSM-1 onto CSM-2: <ul><li>Stop all services on CSM-2 using **net stop crmdmgtd.**</li><li>Restore the database by using **C:\Progra~1\CSCOpx\bin\perl C:\Progra~1\CSCOpx\bin\restorebackup.pl -d C:\var\backup** or the appropriate filenames/directories.</li><li>Restart the services by using **net start crmdmgtd.**</li></ul>
	Step 4. Verify that all the devices, their configurations, and rules have been imported into CSM-2 correctly.
	Step 5. Verify that the configurations match the firewalls by adding a syslog server for all of them and checking the "delta" of the configuration before pushing the change.
	Step 6. If the "delta" configuration in Step 5 looks correct, push the change to all of the firewalls to verify that the CSM can manage them as expected.
Expected Results:	The CSM configuration will be exported and restored properly. CSM-2 will be able to manage all of the firewalls.
Observed Results:	
Pass/Fail:	

Table 12-10 *6500 VACL and SPAN Redirect to NAM Test*

Test ID:	FW-FEAT-4
Node List:	Routers: 6500-1, 6500-2, 6500-3, 6500-4 NAMs: NAM-1, NAM-2, NAM-3, NAM-4
Test Phase:	Feature
Test Description:	6500 VACL and SPAN Redirect to NAM Test
Test Setup:	• Build the network, as shown in Figure 12-1. • Configure all of the routing protocols. • Push the production firewall rule set onto the ASAs and the NATs onto the FWSMs using the CSM, and make sure there is a "permit any" in the rule set to allow the "marker flow" test traffic below. • Enable firewall logging. • Use the Ixia ports to create and run bidirectional background traffic at 40% of the maximum throughput rate seen in the FW-PERF-1 test. • Set up 10 Ixia marker flows running at 1 Mbps each, with IP address and TCP port combinations that will be permitted by the ASA's ACLs. These flows should originate in Data Center North and use IP address combinations that will "hash/send" traffic to both 6500-1 and 6500-2 WAN routers, and bypass the NAT rules in FWSM-1/FWSM-2. • Set up a second set of 10 Ixia marker flows running at 1 Mbps each, with IP address and TCP port combinations that will be permitted by the ASA's ACLs. These flows should originate in Data Center North and use IP address combinations that will "hash/send" traffic to both 6500-1 and 6500-2 WAN routers, and be translated by the NAT rules in FWSM-1/FWSM-2.
Test Steps:	**Step 1.** Set up a SPAN in 6500-1 that will send all incoming traffic to NAM-1. Verify that the traffic is received by NAM-1 and that it is still getting across the firewall infrastructure. Verify the CPU and memory utilization of both 6500-1 and NAM-1.
	Step 2. Create a filter in NAM-1 such that only the marker flows created in the Test Setup section (and reaching 6500-1) will be displayed. Verify that the filter works correctly. Verify the CPU and memory utilization of both 6500-1 and NAM-1.

Table 12-10 *6500 VACL and SPAN Redirect to NAM Test*

Step 3.	Set up a VACL in 6500-2 to redirect a copy of the second set of marker flows created in the Test Setup section to NAM-2. Verify that NAM-2 receives only the traffic being redirected by the VACL. Confirm that the traffic being copied and redirected by the VACL is also making it through the firewall infrastructure. Check the CPU and memory utilization of both 6500-2 and NAM-2.
Step 4.	Set up a VACL to redirect all already translated marker traffic entering 6500-3 to NAM-3. Configure a filter on NAM-3 to display only one of the marker flows being redirected. Verify that NAM-3 displays only the filtered translated traffic. Check the CPU and memory utilization of both 6500-3 and NAM-3.
Expected Results:	Both SPAN and VACL redirected traffic will be received by the NAMs. The NAMs will be able to filter traffic as required.
Observed Results:	
Pass/Fail:	

Table 12-11 *Chassis Failure and Recovery Test*

Test ID:	FW-DUTY-1
Node List:	Routers: 6500-1, 6500-2, 6500-3, 6500-4 FWs: FWSM-1, FWSM-2, FWSM-3, FWSM-4, ASA-1, ASA-2 NAMs: NAM-1, NAM-2, NAM-3, NAM-4
Test Phase:	Duty Cycle
Test Description:	Chassis Failure and Recovery Test

Table 12-11 *Chassis Failure and Recovery Test*

Test Setup:	
	• Build the network, as shown in Figure 12-1.
	• Configure all of the routing protocols.
	• Push the production firewall rule set onto the ASAs and the NATs onto the FWSMs using the CSM, and make sure there is a "permit any" in the rule set to allow the "marker flow" test traffic below.
	• Enable firewall logging.
	• Use the Ixia ports to create and run bidirectional background traffic at 40% of the maximum throughput rate seen in the FW-PERF-1 test.
	• Set up ten Ixia marker flows running at 1 Mbps each, with IP address and TCP port combinations that will be permitted by the ASA's ACLs. These flows should originate in Data Center North and use IP address combinations that will "hash/send" traffic to both 6500-1 and 6500-2 WAN routers, and bypass the NAT rules in FWSM-1/FWSM-2.
	• Set up a second set of ten Ixia marker flows running at 1 Mbps each, with IP address and TCP port combinations that will be permitted by the ASA's ACLs. These flows should originate in Data Center North and use IP address combinations that will "hash/send" traffic to both 6500-1 and 6500-2 WAN routers, and be translated by the NAT rules in FWSM-1/FWSM-2.
	• Set up a third set of ten Ixia marker flows running at 1 Mbps each, with IP address and TCP port combinations that will be permitted by the ASA's ACLs. These flows should originate in Data Center South and use IP address combinations that will "hash/send" traffic to both 6500-3 and 6500-4 WAN routers, and bypass the NAT rules in FWSM-3/FWSM-4.
	• Set up a fourth set of ten Ixia marker flows running at 1 Mbps each, with IP address and TCP port combinations that will be permitted by the ASA's ACLs. These flows should originate in Data Center South and use IP address combinations that will "hash/send" traffic to both 6500-3 and 6500-4 WAN routers, and be translated by the NAT rules in FWSM-3/FWSM-4.
	• Set up SPANs and VACLs in each 6500 sending marker traffic to the NAMs.

	• Make sure the following firewalls are in active state:
	  • FWSM-1
	  • ASA-1
	  • FWSM-3

Table 12-11   *Chassis Failure and Recovery Test*

Test Steps:	Monitor the four sets of marker flows created in the Test Setup section for drops and failover times during every iteration of this test.
	Monitor all syslog messages generated by these tests.
	Step 1. Power down 6500-1.
	Step 2. Wait until the network is stable after Step 1 and power 6500-1 back up.
	Step 3. Power down ASA-1.
	Step 4. Wait until the network is stable after Step 3 and power ASA-1 back up.
	Step 5. Power down 6500-3.
	Step 6. Wait until the network is stable after Step 5 and power 6500-3 back up.
	Step 7. Make the "standby" firewalls (in this case they should be FWSM-1, ASA-1, and FWSM-3 after the preceding steps) "active."
Expected Results:	All the traffic should fail over successfully.
Observed Results:	
Pass/Fail:	

Table 12-12   *Line Card Failure and Recovery Test*

Test ID:	FW-DUTY-2
Node List:	Routers: 6500-1, 6500-2, 6500-3, 6500-4
	FWs: FWSM-1, FWSM-2, FWSM-3, FWSM-4, ASA-1, ASA-2
	NAMs: NAM-1, NAM-2, NAM-3, NAM-4
Test Phase:	Duty Cycle
Test Description:	Line Card Failure and Recovery Test

Table 12-12   *Line Card Failure and Recovery Test*

Test Setup:	• Build the network, as shown in Figure 12-1.
	• Configure all of the routing protocols.
	• Push the production firewall rule set onto the ASAs and the NATs onto the FWSMs using the CSM, and make sure there is a "permit any" in the rule set to allow the "marker flow" test traffic below.
	• Enable firewall logging.
	• Use the Ixia ports to create and run bidirectional background traffic at 40% of the maximum throughput rate seen in the FW-PERF-1 test.
	• Set up ten Ixia marker flows running at 1 Mbps each, with IP address and TCP port combinations that will be permitted by the ASA's ACLs. These flows should originate in Data Center North and use IP address combinations that will "hash/send" traffic to both 6500-1 and 6500-2 WAN routers, and bypass the NAT rules in FWSM-1/FWSM-2.
	• Set up a second set of ten Ixia marker flows running at 1 Mbps each, with IP address and TCP port combinations that will be permitted by the ASA's ACLs. These flows should originate in Data Center North and use IP address combinations that will "hash/send" traffic to both 6500-1 and 6500-2 WAN routers, and be translated by the NAT rules in FWSM-1/FWSM-2.
	• Set up a third set of ten Ixia marker flows running at 1 Mbps each, with IP address and TCP port combinations that will be permitted by the ASA's ACLs. These flows should originate in Data Center South and use IP address combinations that will "hash/send" traffic to both 6500-3 and 6500-4 WAN routers, and bypass the NAT rules in FWSM-3/FWSM-4.
	• Set up a fourth set of ten Ixia marker flows running at 1 Mbps each, with IP address and TCP port combinations that will be permitted by the ASA's ACLs. These flows should originate in Data Center South and use IP address combinations that will "hash/send" traffic to both 6500-3 and 6500-4 WAN routers, and be translated by the NAT rules in FWSM-3/FWSM-4.
	• Set up SPANs and VACLs in each 6500 sending marker traffic to the NAMs.
	• Make sure the following firewalls are in active state:
	• FWSM-1
	• ASA-1
	• FWSM-3
Test Steps:	Monitor the four sets of marker flows created in the Test Setup section for drops and failover times during every iteration of this test.
	Monitor all syslog messages generated by these tests.
	Step 1. Remove Line Card 4 from 6500-1.

Table 12-12 *Line Card Failure and Recovery Test*

	Step 2. Wait until the network is stable after Step 1, and reinsert Line Card 4 into 6500-1.
	Step 3. Remove FWSM-1 from 6500-1.
	Step 4. Wait until the network is stable after Step 3, and reinsert FWSM-1 back into 6500-1.
	Step 5. Remove NAM-1 from 6500-1.
	Step 6. Wait until the network is stable after Step 5, and reinsert NAM-1 into 6500-1.
	Step 7. Remove the active Supervisor from 6500-1.
	Step 8. Wait until the network is stable after Step 7, and reinsert the supervisor into 6500-1.
	Step 9. Make the secondary supervisor in 6500-1 active.
	Step 10. Repeat Steps 1 through 9 for 6500-3.
Expected Results:	All the traffic should fail over successfully.
Observed Results:	
Pass/Fail:	

Table 12-13 *Interface Failure and Recovery Test*

Test ID:	FW-DUTY-3
Node List:	Routers: 6500-1, 6500-2, 6500-3, 6500-4
	FWs: FWSM-1, FWSM-2, FWSM-3, FWSM-4, ASA-1, ASA-2
	NAMs: NAM-1, NAM-2, NAM-3, NAM-4
Test Phase:	Duty Cycle
Test Description:	Interface Failure and Recovery Test

Table 12-13 *Interface Failure and Recovery Test*

Test Setup:	<ul><li>Build the network, as shown in Figure 12-1.</li><li>Configure all of the routing protocols.</li><li>Push the production firewall rule set onto the ASAs and the NATs onto the FWSMs using the CSM, and make sure there is a "permit any" in the rule set to allow the "marker flow" test traffic below.</li><li>Enable firewall logging.</li><li>Use the Ixia ports to create and run bidirectional background traffic at 40% of the maximum throughput rate seen in the FW-PERF-1 test.</li><li>Set up ten Ixia marker flows running at 1 Mbps each, with IP address and TCP port combinations that will be permitted by the ASA's ACLs. These flows should originate in Data Center North and use IP address combinations that will "hash/send" traffic to both 6500-1 and 6500-2 WAN routers, and bypass the NAT rules in FWSM-1/FWSM-2.</li><li>Set up a second set of ten Ixia marker flows running at 1 Mbps each, with IP address and TCP port combinations that will be permitted by the ASA's ACLs. These flows should originate in Data Center North and use IP address combinations that will "hash/send" traffic to both 6500-1 and 6500-2 WAN routers, and be translated by the NAT rules in FWSM-1/FWSM-2.</li><li>Set up a third set of 10 Ixia marker flows running at 1 Mbps each, with IP address and TCP port combinations that will be permitted by the ASA's ACLs. These flows should originate in Data Center South and use IP address combinations that will "hash/send" traffic to both 6500-3 and 6500-4 WAN routers, and bypass the NAT rules in FWSM-3/FWSM-4.</li><li>Set up a fourth set of ten Ixia marker flows running at 1 Mbps each, with IP address and TCP port combinations that will be permitted by the ASA's ACLs. These flows should originate in Data Center South and use IP address combinations that will "hash/send" traffic to both 6500-3 and 6500-4 WAN routers, and be translated by the NAT rules in FWSM-3/FWSM-4.</li><li>Set up SPANs and VACLs in each 6500 sending marker traffic to the NAMs.</li><li>Make sure the following firewalls are in active state:<ul><li>FWSM-1</li><li>ASA-1</li><li>FWSM-3</li></ul></li></ul>

Table 12-13 *Interface Failure and Recovery Test*

Test Steps:	Monitor the four sets of marker flows created in the Test Setup section for drops and failover times during every iteration of this test.
	Monitor all syslog messages generated by these tests.
	Step 1. Remove the cable from the interface between 6500-1 and the data center router.
	Step 2. Wait until the network is stable after Step 1, and reinsert the cable.
	Step 3. Remove the cable from the interface between 6500-1 and ASA-1.
	Step 4. Wait until the network is stable after Step 3, and reinsert the cable. Make ASA-1 the "active" firewall again.
	Step 5. Remove the cable from one of the interfaces between 6500-1 and 6500-2.
	Step 6. Wait until the network is stable after Step 5, and reinsert the cable.
	Step 7. Remove the cable from the interface between 6500-3 and the data center router.
	Step 8. Wait until the network is stable after Step 7, and reinsert the cable.
	Step 9. Remove the cable from the interface between 6500-3 and ASA-1.
	Step 10. Wait until the network is stable after Step 9, and reinsert the cable.
	Step 11. Remove the cable from one of the interfaces between 6500-3 and 6500-4.
	Step 12. Wait until the network is stable after Step 11, and reinsert the cable.
Expected Results:	All the traffic should fail over successfully for each test.
Observed Results:	
Pass/Fail:	

Table 12-14 *Software Forced Failover Test*

Test ID:	FW-DUTY-4
Node List:	Routers: 6500-1, 6500-2, 6500-3, 6500-4 FWs: FWSM-1, FWSM-2, FWSM-3, FWSM-4, ASA-1, ASA-2 NAMs: NAM-1, NAM-2, NAM-3, NAM-4
Test Phase:	Duty Cycle
Test Description:	Software Forced Failover Test

Test Setup:	• Build the network, as shown in Figure 12-1.
	• Configure all of the routing protocols.
	• Push the production firewall rule set onto the ASAs and the NATs onto the FWSMs using the CSM, and make sure there is a "permit any" in the rule set to allow the "marker flow" test traffic below
	• Enable firewall logging.
	• Use the Ixia ports to create and run bidirectional background traffic at 40% of the maximum throughput rate seen in the FW-PERF-1 test.
	• Set up ten Ixia marker flows running at 1 Mbps each, with IP address and TCP port combinations that will be permitted by the ASA's ACLs. These flows should originate in Data Center North and use IP address combinations that will "hash/send" traffic to both 6500-1 and 6500-2 WAN routers, and bypass the NAT rules in FWSM-1/FWSM-2.
	• Set up a second set of ten Ixia marker flows running at 1 Mbps each, with IP address and TCP port combinations that will be permitted by the ASA's ACLs. These flows should originate in Data Center North and use IP address combinations that will "hash/send" traffic to both 6500-1 and 6500-2 WAN routers, and be translated by the NAT rules in FWSM-1/FWSM-2.
	• Set up a third set of ten Ixia marker flows running at 1 Mbps each, with IP address and TCP port combinations that will be permitted by the ASA's ACLs. These flows should originate in Data Center South and use IP address combinations that will "hash/send" traffic to both 6500-3 and 6500-4 WAN routers, and bypass the NAT rules in FWSM-3/FWSM-4.
	• Set up a fourth set of ten Ixia marker flows running at 1 Mbps each, with IP address and TCP port combinations that will be permitted by the ASA's ACLs. These flows should originate in Data Center South and use IP address combinations that will "hash/send" traffic to both 6500-3 and 6500-4 WAN routers, and be translated by the NAT rules in FWSM-3/FWSM-4.
	• Set up SPANs and VACLs in each 6500 sending marker traffic to the NAMs.
	• Make sure the following firewalls are in active state:
	  • FWSM-1
	  • ASA-1
	  • FWSM-3

Table 12-14 *Software Forced Failover Test*

Test Steps:	Monitor the four sets of marker flows created in the Test Setup section for drops and failover times during every iteration of this test. Monitor all syslog messages generated by these tests.
	Step 1. Rerun all of the tests in FW-DUTY-1, FW-DUTY-2, and FW-DUTY-3 using Cisco IOS commands to cause the "failures." Reload the 6500s, reset or soft power down the line cards, and shut down the interfaces as appropriate.
	Step 2. Cause a failover by resetting the OSPF process in 6500-1.
	Step 3. Cause a failover by resetting the BGP process in 6500-1.
Expected Results:	All the traffic should fail over successfully for each test.
Observed Results:	
Pass/Fail:	

Chapter 13

Site-to-Site IPsec Virtual Private Networking: DMVPN and GET VPN Test Plans

Site-to-site Virtual Private Networks (VPN) provide a flexible and economical method to extend network resources to branch offices, home offices, and business partner sites. In a traditional solution, each branch ("spoke") and corporate ("hub") site would be connected to the Internet with a dedicated circuit. This circuit could be an Ethernet, T-carrier, or a less expensive business-level broadband connection such as DSL or cable. A tunneling protocol such as GRE, L2TP, or IPsec would then be used to create a "virtual circuit" between each spoke and the hub location, over which data would be sent in either clear (GRE) or encrypted (L2TP or IPsec) format.

The major drawback of traditional IPsec VPN solutions is that they present tunnel management and scalability challenges as the number of sites and features increases in the WAN. This problem has been exasperated as newer peer-to-peer applications require direct "spoke-to-spoke" tunnels to reduce the latency associated with backhauling through a hub site. Cisco has addressed these challenges with the development of two newer IPsec VPN solutions known as Dynamic Multipoint VPN (DMVPN) and Group Encrypted Transport VPN (GET VPN).

DMVPN is a Cisco solution for building IPsec + GRE VPNs in an easy, dynamic, and scalable manner. DMVPN relies on two proven technologies:

- **Next Hop Resolution Protocol (NHRP):** Creates a distributed (NHRP) mapping database of all the spoke tunnels to real (public interface) addresses.

- **Multipoint GRE (mGRE) tunnel interface:** A single GRE interface to support multiple GRE and IPsec tunnels; it simplifies the size and complexity of the configuration.

Cisco's Group Encrypted Transport VPN (GET VPN) introduces the concept of a trusted group to eliminate point-to-point tunnels and their associated overlay routing. All group members (GMs) share a common security association (SA), also known as a group SA.

This enables GMs to decrypt traffic that was encrypted by any other GM. In GET VPN networks, there is no need to negotiate point-to-point IPsec tunnels between the members of a group, because GET VPN is tunnel-less. GET VPN had the following advantages over other IPsec solutions:

- Provides instantaneous large-scale any-to-any IP connectivity using a group IPsec security paradigm.

- Takes advantage of underlying IP VPN routing infrastructure and does not require an overlay routing control plane.

- Seamlessly integrates with multicast infrastructures without the multicast replication issues typically seen in traditional tunnel-based IPsec solutions.

- Preserves the IP source and destination addresses during the IPsec encryption and encapsulation process. Therefore, GET VPN integrates very well with other WAN features such as QoS, Cisco Wide Area Application Services (WAAS), and Cisco Performance Routing (PfR).

The following test plans will assist you in validating a site-to-site IPsec VPN WAN design based on either solution.

Background

A global enterprise has decided to redesign its site-to-site VPN WAN as part of a branch refresh project to replace end-of-life equipment. The existing design predominately uses Cisco 2600XM and 3745 routers at the branches that connect into Cisco VPN 3000 Concentrators at regional hub sites by means of IPsec-encrypted GRE tunnels. Certain theatres use the Internet exclusively for transport, while others use commercial MPLS/VPN service offerings or Layer 2 solutions such as Frame Relay and ATM, over which the overlay of encrypted tunnels are built.

Architects responsible for the redesign chose to exploit the advantages of both DMVPN and GET VPN where the transport method would permit. DMVPN was chosen for regions where Internet transport is predominant, as tunnels are necessary to "hide" internal private addressing from the ISP. GET VPN was chosen for regions with exclusive private WAN transport mechanisms such as MPLS/VPN, Frame Relay, and ATM so that the benefits of the tunnel-less GET VPN solution can be realized.

Physical and Logical Test Topology

Figure 13-1 illustrates the topology to be tested.

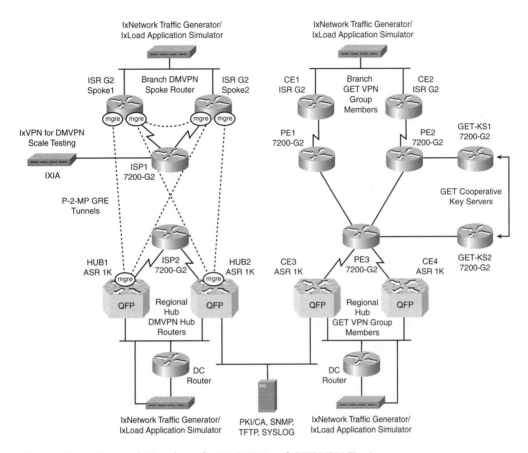

Figure 13-1   *Network Topology for DMVPN and GET VPN Testing*

Technical details of the test setup are as follows:

- ISR G2 routers (Cisco 2900, Cisco 3900) are used for branch router testing. The decision to deploy either model in production will depend on the throughput and features deployed; therefore, both solutions (DMVPN and GET VPN) will be qualified for each platform.

- Branches deploying DMVPN will be tested in the following configurations:

    - Class A Branch: single CE to dual hub

    - Class B Branch: dual CE to dual hub

    - WAN access options from N×T1 up to Gigabit Ethernet.

- Branches deploying GET VPN will be tested in the following configurations:

    - Class A Branch: single CE to single PE

    - Class B Branch: dual CE to dual PE

- WAN access options from N×T1 up to Gigabit Ethernet

- Hub routers for both solutions are Cisco ASR 1006 outfitted with dual route processors (ASR100-RP2) and embedded services processors (ASR1000-ESP20) providing up to 8 Gigabit hardware encryption capability. Hub router WAN access options from DS3 up to 5-Gigabit Ethernet.

- DMVPN logical details:

  - Dual DMVPN cloud topology spoke-to-spoke deployment model

  - Hub1 is primary hub router and Hub2 is secondary

  - IKE CAC enabled on hub routers

  - IPsec transport mode enabled (necessary for NAT interoperability)

  - AES 256 encryption

  - IP MTU set to 1300 on the tunnel interface (to accommodate GRE/IPsec overhead)

  - EIGRP routing across the tunnels

  - Digital certificates and Public Key Infrastructure (PKI)

  - QoS enabled on hub and spoke routers

- GET VPN logical details:

  - Router at spokes and at hub sites are GET VPN group members (GM)

  - Multicast registration/rekey is preferred method when MPLS/VPN offers multicast (MVPN) as a service

  - Regional key servers configured as cooperative key servers in HA cluster

  - Digital certificates from PKI used for GM to key server registration

  - AES 256 encryption

  - Traffic selector ACLs to exclude control plane traffic from being encrypted

  - Time-based antireplay

  - IKE CAC enabled on key servers

  - BGP routing from CE to PE

  - QoS enabled on all GMs

Figure 13-2 illustrates the topology used for the DMVPN performance testing carried out on the ASR 1000 hub router. This testing is performed using a test suite called IxVPN running on an Ixia test chassis.

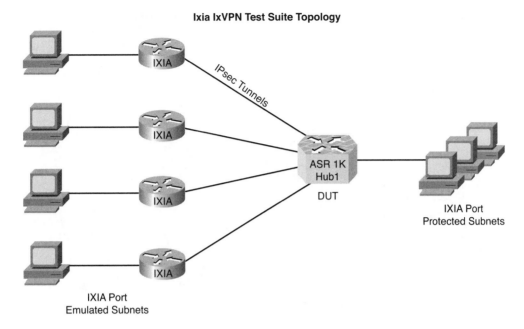

Figure 13-2 *Test Topology for Hub DMVPN Performance Testing Using IxVPN*

Figure 13-3 illustrates the topology used for the GET VPN performance testing carried out on the ASR 1006 CE routers, as well as the 7200 G2 cooperative key servers. This testing is performed using two 7200 G2 routers running 150 "simulated routers" each. The 7200 load routers take advantage of VRFs, as described in the "Using Virtualized Routers to Simulate Large Routing Topologies" section in Chapter 5, "Executing the Test Plan." The 7200s map each "virtual router" VRF to a separate subinterface on the WAN and LAN sides. This allows each simulated router to have unique IP addressing for its WAN and LAN subnets. The network traffic generators are connected to the 7200s using Dot1Q trunking, enabling each LAN subinterface to generate separate traffic flows. This separate-LAN-subinterface-per-VRF model allows for staggered start times for the traffic, creating a more-realistic load-testing scenario.

Each 7200 G2 load router will use a single certificate for ISAKMP authentication for all of its simulated routers. All 150 simulated routers (GMs) in 7200-G2-Load-1 will use GET-KS1 as their preferred "registration" key server, while the 150 simulated GMs in 7200-G2-Load-2 will use GET-KS2 as their "registration" key server.

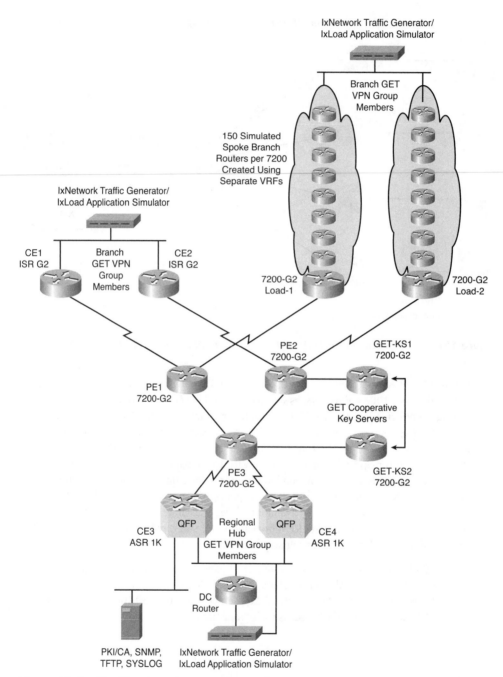

Figure 13-3   *Test Topology for GET VPN Performance Testing Using Simulated Routers*

Test Objectives

The primary objectives for this test are as follows:

1. To validate that the proposed DMVPN functionality and routing works in the branch environments, leveraging the Internet for WAN transport.

2. To validate that the proposed GET VPN functionality and routing works in the branch environments, leveraging MPLS/VPN for WAN transport.

3. To determine control plane and forwarding plane scalability of the ASR 1006 routers functioning as DMVPN hub routers and GET VPN GMs.

4. To validate the resiliency of the system during failure conditions.

DMVPN Test Cases Summary

Table 13-1 contains a brief summary of the tests to be conducted to certify the DMVPN functionality previously described.

Table 13-1   *Test Cases Summary Table*

Test ID	Test Description
DMVPN-BASE-1	DMVPN Baseline Functionality Test
DMVPN-BASE-2	DMVPN Baseline Traffic Test
DMVPN-PERF-1	DMVPN Spoke Performance Test
DMVPN-PERF-2	DMVPN Large MTU Performance Test
DMVPN-PERF-3	DMVPN Hub Performance Test
DMVPN-FEAT-1	DMVPN PKI/CA Feature Test
DMVPN-FEAT-2	Per-Tunnel QoS for DMVPN Test
DMVPN-FEAT-3	Security ACL Test
DMVPN-FEAT-4	In Service Software Upgrade (ISSU) Test
DMVPN-DUTY-1	Chassis Failure and Recovery Test
DMVPN-DUTY-2	Line Card Operational Insertion and Removal (OIR) Test
DMVPN-DUTY-3	Interface Failure and Recovery Test
DMVPN-DUTY-4	Software Forced Failover Test
DMVPN-DUTY-5	Spoke to Spoke Failover Test

Detailed DMVPN Test Cases

The following tables contain detailed test cases to be conducted to certify the DMVPN functionality described earlier. These cases provide you with guidance on testing DMVPN and should be modified to fit your specific needs.

Table 13-2   *DMVPN Baseline Functionality Test*

Test ID:	DMVPN-BASE-1
Node List:	Spoke1, Spoke2, ISP1, ISP2, Hub1, Hub2
Test Phase:	Baseline
Test Description:	DMVPN Baseline Functionality Test
Test Setup:	Build the network, as shown in Figure 13-1. Configure branch and hub routers per the design documentation: • DMVPN dual hub/single cloud configurations • PKI/digital certificates • EIGRP routing • QoS features Both spokes connected at 10 Mbps.
Test Steps:	**Step 1.** Start a number of bidirectional flows from the Ixia traffic generator at a total of 4 Mbps. Flows should run between Spoke1 and the DC, Spoke2 and the DC, and Spoke1 and Spoke2.

	Step 2. Verify DMVPN operation (tunnels, NHRP, EIGRP, IPsec) between the branch routers (Spoke1 and Spoke2) and the hub routers (Hub1 and Hub2) by using the following commands:
	
	 `show interface tunnel <number>`
	 `show ip nhrp dynamic`
	 `show ip nhrp traffic interface tunnel<number>`
	
	 `show dmvpn`
	 `show dmvpn detail`
	 `show ip eigrp neighbor`
	 `show crypto engine configuration`
	 `show dmvpn`
	 `show crypto isakmp sa`
	 `show crypto ipsec sa`

	Step 3. Verify the CPU and memory utilization on all of the devices in the Node List by issuing the appropriate CLI commands or through SNMP polling.

Table 13-2 *DMVPN Baseline Functionality Test*

Expected Results:	All tunnels and routing protocol adjacencies will come up and features will works as expected.
Observed Results:	
Pass/Fail:	

Table 13-3 *DMVPN Baseline Traffic Test*

Test ID:	DMVPN-BASE-2
Node List:	Spoke1, Spoke2, ISP1, ISP2, Hub1, Hub2
Test Phase:	Baseline
Test Description:	DMVPN Baseline Traffic Test
Test Setup:	Build the network, as shown in Figure 13-1.
	Configure branch and hub routers per the design documentation:
	• DMVPN dual hub/single cloud configurations
	• PKI/digital certificates
	• EIGRP routing
	• QoS features
	Both spokes connected at 10 Mbps.
Test Steps:	This test is run for 24 hours.
	Step 1. Start a number of bidirectional flows from the Ixia traffic generator at a total of 4 Mbps. Flows should run between Spoke1 and the DC, Spoke2 and the DC, and Spoke1 and Spoke2. This will be used as background traffic.
	Step 2. Create and send a single flow for each QoS service class to be supported on the network (e.g., voice, video, bulk) between the branch and hub routers.
	Step 3. Enable logging to a syslog server on all devices. Logs should be checked for errors periodically for the entire duration of the test.
	Step 4. Verify the CPU and memory utilization on all of the devices in the Node List every 30 minutes by issuing the appropriate CLI commands or through SNMP polling.

Table 13-3   *DMVPN Baseline Traffic Test*

Expected Results:	All bidirectional test flows will be delivered without unexpected drops or delays.
	All devices under test (DUT) in the Node List will remain stable throughout the 24 hours.
Observed Results:	
Pass/Fail:	

Table 13-4   *DMVPN Spoke Performance Test*

Test ID:	DMVPN-PERF-1
Node List:	Spoke1, Spoke2, Hub1, Hub2
Test Phase:	Performance
Test Description:	DMVPN Spoke Performance Test
Test Setup:	Build the network, as shown in Figure 13-1.
	Configure branch and hub routers per the design documentation:
	• DMVPN dual hub/single cloud configurations • PKI/digital certificates • EIGRP routing • QoS features
	Both spoke routers configured as Class A Branches (single CE).
	Both spokes connected at 1 Gigabit.
Test Steps:	**Step 1.** Run the Ixia RFC2544 Throughput test between Spoke1 and Hub1 (sourced at Spoke1 LAN and destined to the DC LAN). The frame sizes for this test should not exceed the MTU of 1300. Verify the CPU and memory utilization on all of the devices in the Node List. Run this test to completion three times and record the results.
	Step 2. Run the Ixia RFC2544 Throughput test between Spoke1 and Spoke2 (sourced at Spoke1 LAN and destined to the Spoke2 LAN). The frame sizes for this test should not exceed the MTU of 1300. Verify the CPU and memory utilization on all of the devices in the Node List. Run this test to completion three times and record the results.

Table 13-4 *DMVPN Spoke Performance Test*

Expected Results:	This is a scalability test for the DMVPN spoke routers. The results of the test will be reported in the Observed Results section.

Observed Results:

Pass/Fail:

Table 13-5 *DMVPN Large MTU Performance Test*

Test ID:	DMVPN-PERF-2
Node List:	Spoke1, Spoke2, Hub1, Hub2
Test Phase:	Performance
Test Description:	DMVPN Large MTU Performance Test
Test Setup:	Build the network, as shown in Figure 13-1. Configure branch and hub routers per the design documentation: • DMVPN dual hub/single cloud configurations • PKI/digital certificates • EIGRP routing • QoS features Both spoke routers configured as Class A Branches (single CE). Both spokes connected at 1 Gigabit.
Test Steps:	**Step 1.** Start a throughput test with TCP traffic flows originating from Spoke2 destined for Hub1 (sourced at Spoke2 LAN and destined to the DC LAN). Use a mix of frame sizes using MTUs between 1301 and 1500. Make sure a *DF bit is not set* for all of the frames. Verify the CPU and memory utilization on all of the devices in the Node List. Run this test to completion three times and record the results.
	Step 2. Start a throughput test with TCP traffic flows originating from Spoke2 destined for Hub1. Use a mix of frame sizes using MTUs between 1301 and 1500. Make sure a *DF bit is set* for all of the frames. Verify the CPU and memory utilization on all of the devices in the Node List. Run this test to completion three times and record the results.

Table 13-5 *DMVPN Large MTU Performance Test*

Step 3.	Start a throughput test with TCP traffic flows originating from Hub1 destined for Spoke2 (sourced at DC LAN and destined to the Spoke2 LAN). Use a mix of frame sizes using MTUs between 1301 and 1500. Make sure a *DF bit is not set* for all of the frames. Verify the CPU and memory utilization on all of the devices in the Node List. Run this test to completion three times and record the results.
Step 4.	Start a throughput test with TCP traffic flows originating from Hub1 destined for Spoke2. Use a mix of frame sizes using MTUs between 1301 and 1500. Make sure a *DF bit is set* for all of the frames. Verify the CPU and memory utilization on all of the devices in the Node List. Run this test to completion three times and record the results.
Step 5.	Start a throughput test using bidirectional TCP and UDP traffic flows between Hub1 and the two spoke routers (sourced at the DC LAN and destined to the Spoke1 and Spoke2 LANs). Use a mix of frame sizes using MTUs between 1301 and 1500. Make sure a *DF bit is not set* for all of the frames. Verify the CPU and memory utilization on all of the devices in the Node List. Run this test to completion three times and record the results.
Step 6.	Start a throughput test using bidirectional TCP and UDP traffic flows between Hub1 and the 2 spoke routers. Use a mix of frame sizes using MTUs between 1301 and 1500. Make sure a *DF bit is set* for all of the frames. Verify the CPU and memory utilization on all of the devices in the Node List. Run this test to completion three times and record the results.
Step 7.	Start a throughput test using bidirectional TCP and UDP traffic flows between Spoke1 and Spoke2 (sourced at Spoke1 LAN and destined to Spoke2 LAN). Use a mix of frame sizes using MTUs between 1301 and 1500. Make sure a *DF bit is not set* for all of the frames. Verify the CPU and memory utilization on all of the devices in the Node List. Run this test to completion three times and record the results.
Step 8.	Start a throughput test using bidirectional TCP and UDP traffic flows between Spoke1 and Spoke2. Use a mix of frame sizes using MTUs between 1301 and 1500. Make sure a *DF bit is set* for all of the frames. Verify the CPU and memory utilization on all of the devices in the Node List. Run this test to completion three times and record the results.

Table 13-5 *DMVPN Large MTU Performance Test*

Expected Results:	This is a scalability test for router fragmentation. The results of the test will be reported in the Observed Results section.
Observed Results:	
Pass/Fail:	

Table 13-6 *DMVPN Hub Performance Testing*

Test ID:	DMVPN-PERF-3
Node List:	Hub1
Test Phase:	Performance
Test Description:	DMVPN Hub Performance Testing
Test Setup:	Build the network, as shown in Figure 13-2.
	Configure the hub router per the design documentation:
	• DMVPN dual hub/single cloud configurations
	• PKI/digital certificates
	• EIGRP routing
	• QoS features
	Configure the IxVPN test tool to emulate the branch routers using
	• PKI/digital certificates
	• IPsec set to DMVPN with GRE
	• EIGRP routing
Test Steps:	This is a DUT test performed using the IxVPN test suite from Ixia. **Note** For more information, refer to www.ixiacom.com/products/ixvpn/ixvpn_datasheet/index.php.
	Perform the following tests three times each:
	Step 1. Tunnel Capacity
	• Measures the maximum number of concurrent tunnels that can be sustained by the DUT.

Table 13-6 *DMVPN Hub Performance Testing*

Step 2. Tunnel Setup Rate
This test should be performed with IKE CAC enabled and disabled.
• Measures the rate at which tunnels are set up by the DUT.
• Reports setup rate as a function of the number of tunnels established on the DUT.
Step 3. Tunnel Rate Validation Test
This test should be performed with IKE CAC enabled.
• Validates that a DUT can sustain a user-specified tunnel initiation rate.
• Includes provisions for decreasing the rate as the DUT slow down.
Step 4. Rekeying
• Measures rekey rate and failures.
• Designed to test long-term stability of IPsec VPNs.
Step 5. Soak Test
• Measures long-term stability and performance.
• Varying packet sizes and IMIX.
Step 6. RFC2544 test over IPsec tunnels
• Measures encryption and decryption throughput, latency, and frame loss per RFC 2544.
• Varying packet sizes and IMIX.
Step 7. IxChariot Traffic over VPN Tunnels
• Send a variety of application traffic over the IPsec tunnels to assess the impact on application performance.
• Real-time graphs showing end-to-end throughput and latency per tunnel.
Expected Results: This is a scalability test for the DMVPN hub router. The results of the tests will be reported in the Observed Results section.
Observed Results:
Pass/Fail:

Table 13-7 *DMVPN PKI/CA Feature Test*

Test ID:	DMVPN-FEAT-1
Node List:	Spoke1, Spoke2, ISP1, ISP2, Hub1, Hub2
Test Phase:	Feature
Test Description:	DMVPN PKI/CA Feature Test
Test Setup:	Build the network, as shown in Figure 13-1. Configure branch and hub routers per the design documentation: • DMVPN dual hub/single cloud configurations • PKI/digital certificates • EIGRP routing • QoS features Both spoke routers configured as Class A Branches (Single CE). Run bidirectional traffic flows between Hub1 and the spoke routers running IMIX frame sizes at 5 Mbps. Also, run bidirectional traffic between the Spoke1 and Spoke2 running IMIX frame sizes at 1 Mbps.
Test Steps:	**Step 1.** Set the Certificate Revocation List (CRL) cache time to expire after 2 minutes on Hub1 using the **crl-cache delete-after 2** command. On the Certificate Authority (CA), revoke the certificate for Spoke1. Wait 5 minutes to make sure a new CRL is loaded on Hub1, and clear the ISAKMP and IPsec SAs for Spoke1 on the Hub1 router. Verify whether a new ISAKMP SA is negotiated between the routers. Load a valid certificate on Spoke1 and check to see if new ISAKMP and IPsec SAs are negotiated between the routers.
	Step 2. Disable the auto-rollover feature on Spoke1. Create and load a new certificate on Spoke1 with a 10-minute lifetime (or whatever the minimum is for the CA). Wait for 15 minutes (the time for the certificate to expire plus 5 minutes for Hub1 to load a new CRL). Clear the ISAKMP and IPsec SAs for Spoke1 on the Hub1 router. Verify whether a new ISAKMP SA is negotiated between the routers. Check the logs in both routers.
	Step 3. Enable the auto-rollover feature on Spoke1. Create and load a new certificate on Spoke1 with a 10-minute lifetime (or whatever the minimum is for the CA). Wait for 10 minutes (the time for the certificate to expire). Clear the ISAKMP and IPsec SAs for Spoke1 on the Hub1 router. Verify whether a new ISAKMP SA is negotiated between the routers. Check the log files to verify a new certificate was obtained by Spoke1.

Table 13-7   *DMVPN PKI/CA Feature Test*

Step 4.	Enable the auto-rollover feature on Spoke1. Create and load a new certificate on Spoke1 with a 10-minute lifetime (or whatever the minimum is for the CA). Disconnect the CA from the network. Wait for 10 minutes (the time for the certificate to expire). Clear the ISAKMP and IPsec SAs for Spoke1 on the Hub1 router. Verify whether a new ISAKMP SA is negotiated between the routers. Check the log files to verify if a new certificate was obtained by Spoke1. Verify the logs in Hub1 to check if a new CRL was able to be loaded.
Step 5.	Reconnect the CA to the network after Step 4 is finished. Verify whether Spoke1 automatically re-enrolls. Check whether Hub1 will load a new CRL automatically once the CA is available (this may take some time). Check if traffic can be delivered by Spoke1 once a new certificate has been enrolled.
Step 6.	Set the CRL cache time to expire after 2 minutes on Spoke1 using the **crl-cache delete-after 2** command. On the CA, revoke the certificate for Hub1. Wait 5 minutes, to make sure a new CRL is loaded on Spoke1, and clear the ISAKMP and IPsec SAs for Hub1 on the Spoke1 router. Verify whether a new ISAKMP SA is negotiated between the routers.
Step 7.	Disable the auto-rollover feature on Hub1. Create and load a new certificate on Hub1 with a 10-minute lifetime (or whatever the minimum is for the CA). Wait for 10 minutes (the time for the certificate to expire). Clear the ISAKMP and IPsec SAs for Hub1 on the Spoke1 router. Verify whether a new ISAKMP SA is negotiated between the routers. Check the logs in both routers.
Step 8.	Enable the auto-rollover feature on Hub1. Create and load a new certificate on Hub1 with a 10-minute lifetime (or whatever the minimum is for the CA). Wait for 10 minutes (the time for the certificate to expire). Clear the ISAKMP and IPsec SAs for Hub1 on the Spoke1 router. Verify whether a new ISAKMP SA is negotiated between the routers. Check the log files to verify a new certificate was obtained by Hub1.

Table 13-7   *DMVPN PKI/CA Feature Test*

	Step 9. Enable the auto-rollover feature on Hub1. Create and load a new certificate on Hub1 with a 10-minute lifetime (or whatever the minimum is for the CA). Disconnect the CA from the network. Wait for 10 minutes (the time for the certificate to expire). Clear the ISAKMP and IPsec SAs for Hub1 on the Spoke1 router. Verify whether a new ISAKMP SA is negotiated between the routers. Check the log files to verify if a new certificate was obtained by Hub1. Verify the logs in Spoke1 to check if a new CRL was able to be loaded.
	Step 10. Reconnect the CA to the network after Step 9 is finished. Verify whether Hub1 automatically re-enrolls. Check whether Spoke1 loads a new CRL automatically once the CA is available. Check the logs in both routers. Verify that traffic is being encrypted between the routers.
Expected Results:	The certificates will be used for authentication. Certificates that have been revoked will cause authentication to fail. Auto-enrollment and the CRLs will work as expected.
Observed Results:	
Pass/Fail:	

Table 13-8   *Per-Tunnel QoS for DMVPN Test*

Test ID:	DMVPN-FEAT-2
Node List:	Spoke1, Spoke2, ISP1, ISP2, Hub1, Hub2
Test Phase:	Feature
Test Description:	Per-Tunnel QoS for DMVPN Test
Test Setup:	Build the network, as shown in Figure 13-1. Configure branch and hub routers per the design documentation: • MVPN dual hub/single cloud configurations • PKI/digital certificates • EIGRP routing Both spoke routers configured as Class A Branches (single CE). Set a QoS policy on ISP1 that will allow 1-Mbps outbound traffic to Spoke1 and 5-Mbps outbound traffic to Spoke2.

Table 13-8 *Per-Tunnel QoS for DMVPN Test*

Test Steps:	**Step 1.** Enable the Per-Tunnel QoS feature:

Step 1. Enable the Per-Tunnel QoS feature:

- Configure Spoke1 to use NHRP group SMALL and Spoke2 to use group LARGE, by using the command
  ip nhrp group *group-name*

- Configure NHRP-group-to-QoS-policy mapping on a Hub1, by mapping
  - NHRP group SMALL to QoS Policy QOS-SMALL
  - NHRP group LARGE to QoS policy QOS-LARGE
    using the following command:

    ip nhrp map group *group-name* **service-policy output** *qos-policy-map-name*

- Create the QoS policies (QOS-SMALL and QOS-LARGE) to shape outgoing traffic for a 1-Mbps pipe for QOS-SMALL and a 5-Mbps pipe for QOS-LARGE with the following queues:
  - **Realtime:** Low-latency queue with 10% bandwidth reservation for VoIP and routing traffic.
  - **Video:** Class-Based Weighted Fair Queue with 10% bandwidth reservation for UDP video traffic.
  - **Bulk:** Class-Based Weighted Fair Queue with 30% bandwidth reservation for TCP bulk traffic.
  - **Default:** The remaining (unclassified) traffic falls into a default queue that receives the remainder of the interface bandwidth after shaping occurs.

- Bring up the DMVPN tunnels by sending bidirectional traffic between Hub1 and the two spoke routers.

Step 2. Verify that the Per-Tunnel QoS feature is working correctly by issuing the following commands:

```
show dmvpn detail
show ip nhrp
show ip nhrp group-map [group-name]
show policy-map multipoint [tunnel tunnel-interface-number]
show tunnel endpoints
```

Table 13-8   *Per-Tunnel QoS for DMVPN Test*

	Step 3. Create four IXIA traffic flows from Hub1 to Spoke1 with the following characteristics: • **Emulated Voice:** UDP traffic marked with IP Precedence 6, packet size 64 bytes, constant rate of 90Kbps. • **Emulated Video:** UDP traffic configured with source ports 1000–1100, variable packet size ranging from 64–1300 bytes, constant rate of 90 Kbps. • **Emulated Bulk:** TCP traffic configured with destination port 9900, variable packet size ranging from 64–1300 bytes, constant rate of 300 Kbps. • **Emulated HTTP:** TCP traffic configured with destination port 80, variable packet size ranging from 64–1300 bytes, constant rate of 700 Kbps.
	Step 4. Create a group of flows from Hub1 to Spoke2 with the following characteristics: • **Emulated Voice:** UDP traffic marked with IP Precedence 6, packet size 64 bytes, constant rate of 450 Kbps. • **Emulated Video:** UDP traffic configured with source ports 1000–1100, variable packet size ranging from 64–1300 bytes, constant rate of 450 Kbps. • **Emulated Bulk:** TCP traffic configured with destination port 9900, variable packet size ranging from 64–1300 bytes, constant rate of 1.5 Mbps. • **Emulated HTTP:** TCP traffic configured with destination port 80, variable packet size ranging from 64–1300 bytes, constant rate of 3 Mbps.
	Step 5. Run the traffic from Steps 4 and 5 for 15 minutes and verify that the emulated voice, emulated video, and emulated bulk traffic is forwarded to the spoke routers without any drops and that the TCP port 80 traffic is experiencing drops as expected. Measure the jitter on the emulated voice traffic.
	Step 6. Disable the Per-Tunnel QoS feature. Run the traffic from Steps 4 and 5 for 15 minutes and check the loss on each of the flows. Measure the jitter on the emulated voice traffic.
Expected Results:	The Per-Tunnel QoS feature will work as expected. Critical traffic will be dropped without QoS enabled.

Table 13-8 *Per-Tunnel QoS for DMVPN Test*

Observed Results:

Pass/Fail:

Table 13-9 *Security ACL Test*

Test ID:	DMVPN-FEAT-3
Node List:	Spoke1, Spoke2, ISP1, ISP2, Hub1, Hub2
Test Phase:	Feature
Test Description:	Security ACL Test
Test Setup:	Build the network, as shown in Figure 13-1.
	Configure branch and hub routers per the design documentation:
	• DMVPN dual hub/single cloud configurations
	• PKI/digital certificates
	• EIGRP routing
	Both spoke routers configured as Class A Branches (single CE).
Test Steps:	**Step 1.** Create an access control list (ACL) with only the required protocols and ports for DMVPN allowed. Generally, you will need to permit the following:
	• UDP port 500—ISAKMP as source and destination
	• UDP port 4500—NAT-T as a destination
	• IP protocol 50—ESP
	• IP protocol 51—AH (if AH is implemented)
	• IP protocol 47—GRE
	Apply this incoming ACL to the ISP-facing interfaces of Spoke1, Spoke2, Hub1, and Hub2. Note that any other required services such as routing protocols, ICMP, etc. must be added to this ACL in production environments.
	Step 2. Start running UDP bidirectional traffic between Spoke1 and Hub1, Spoke2 and Hub1, and Spoke1 and Spoke2 at 500 Kbps for each flow. Verify that all the tunnels come up and traffic is being delivered as expected. Check the CPU and memory utilization on all of the devices in the Node List.

Table 13-9 *Security ACL Test*

Step 3.	While the traffic from Step 2 is still running, add a line to the end of the ACL on Spoke2 denying all ICMP (assuming there is no line permitting ICMP earlier in the ACL). Verify that all the tunnels stay up and traffic is being delivered as expected. Ping the ISP-facing interface of Spoke2 from Hub1 (Hub1 should permit the ICMP traffic; otherwise, any replies will be dropped). Check the CPU and memory utilization on all of the devices in the Node List.
Step 4.	While the traffic from Step 2 is still running, remove the line added in Step 3 from the ACL and add one permitting all ICMP. Verify that all the tunnels stay up and traffic is being delivered as expected. Ping the ISP-facing interface of Spoke2 from Hub1 (Hub1 should permit the ICMP traffic; otherwise, any replies will be dropped). Check the CPU and memory utilization on all of the devices in the Node List.
Step 5.	While the traffic from Step 2 is still running, add a line to the end of the ACL on Hub1 denying all ICMP (assuming there is no line permitting ICMP earlier in the ACL). Verify that all the tunnels stay up and traffic is being delivered as expected. Ping the ISP-facing interface of Hub1 from Spoke1 (Spoke1 should permit the ICMP traffic; otherwise, any replies will be dropped). Check the CPU and memory utilization on all of the devices in the Node List.
Step 6.	While the traffic from Step 2 is still running, remove the line added in Step 5 from the ACL and add one permitting all ICMP traffic. Verify that all the tunnels stay up and traffic is being delivered as expected. Ping the ISP-facing interface of Hub1 from Spoke1 (Spoke1 should permit the ICMP traffic; otherwise, any replies will be dropped). Check the CPU and memory utilization on all of the devices in the Node List.
Expected Results:	The ACLs will work as expected, allowing the DMVPN tunnels to come up, while denying all traffic that is not permitted. Valid changes to the ACLs, even while traffic is running, should not cause drops for permitted traffic.
Observed Results:	
Pass/Fail:	

Table 13-10 *In Service Software Upgrade (ISSU) Test*

Test ID:	DMVPN-FEAT-4
Node List:	Spoke1, Spoke2, ISP1, ISP2, Hub1, Hub2, DC-Router
Test Phase:	Feature
Test Description:	In Service Software Upgrade (ISSU) Test
Test Setup:	Build the network, as shown in Figure 13-1. Configure branch and hub routers per the design documentation: • DMVPN dual hub/single cloud configurations • PKI/digital certificates • EIGRP routing Both spoke routers configured as Class A Branches (single CE). Run bidirectional traffic flows between Hub1 and the spoke routers running IMIX frame sizes at 5 Mbps, with a maximum MTU of 1300. Also, run bidirectional traffic between the Spoke1 and Spoke2 running IMIX frame sizes at 1 Mbps.
Test Steps:	Start the bidirectional traffic and wait until it is running stable. Clear all counters and logs in the routers in the Node List.
	Step 1. Perform an ISSU on Hub2.
	Step 2. Once Hub2 is upgraded, perform an ISSU on Hub2.
Expected Results:	The In Service Software Upgrade should cause no impact to any traffic forwarding.
Observed Results:	
Pass/Fail:	

Table 13-11 *Chassis Failure and Recovery Test*

Test ID:	DMVPN-DUTY-1
Node List:	Spoke1, Spoke2, ISP1, ISP2, Hub1, Hub2, DC-Router
Test Phase:	Duty Cycle
Test Description:	Chassis Failure and Recovery Test
Test Setup:	Build the network, as shown in Figure 13-1. Configure branch and hub routers per the design documentation: • DMVPN dual hub/single cloud configurations. • PKI/digital certificates. • EIGRP routing. • Class B Branch (dual CE). • Enable HSRP spoke router LAN interfaces so a virtual IP address functions as the default gateway for the packet generator. Configure HSRP priorities such that Spoke1 is the HSRP active router and Spoke 2 is the standby. Configure Spoke1 for HSRP preempt so that it will take over as primary in the event of LAN interface outage and recovery. • Enable EIGRP neighborship between the DC-Router and the Hub1 and Hub2 routers. The hub routers should advertise the branch subnets to the DC-Router to allow for failover. The DC-Router should be the default gateway for the packet generator on the data center side. • Branch WAN circuits set to 5 Mbps. • DMVPN Per-Tunnel QoS enabled. Create bidirectional traffic flows between the hub and branch networks. The flows should use IMIX frame sizes up to 1300-byte MTU running at 3 Mbps total.
Test Steps:	Start the bidirectional traffic and wait until it is running without drops. Clear all counters and logs in the routers in the Node List. Record the failover times for each of the steps in this test. Check the log files and CPU and memory utilization for all of the routers in the Node List throughout this test.
	Step 1. Power down Hub2.
	Step 2. Wait until the network is stable after Step 1 and power Hub2 back on.
	Step 3. Power down Hub1.
	Step 4. Wait until the network is stable after Step 3 and power Hub1 back on.
	Step 5. Power down Spoke2.
	Step 6. Wait until the network is stable after Step 5 and power Spoke2 back on.

Table 13-11 *Chassis Failure and Recovery Test*

	Step 7. Power down Spoke1.
	Step 8. Wait until the network is stable after Step 7 and power Spoke1 back on.
Expected Results:	All the traffic should fail over successfully.
Observed Results:	
Pass/Fail:	

Table 13-12 *Line Card Failure and Recovery (OIR) Test*

Test ID:	DMVPN-DUTY-2
Node List:	Spoke1, Spoke2, ISP1, ISP2, Hub1, Hub2, DC-Router
Test Phase:	Duty Cycle
Test Description:	Line Card Online Removal and Insertion (OIR) Test
Test Setup:	Build the network, as shown in Figure 13-1.

Configure branch and hub routers per the design documentation:

- DMVPN dual hub/single cloud configurations.
- PKI/digital certificates.
- EIGRP routing.
- Class B Branch (dual CE).
- Enable HSRP spoke router LAN interfaces so a virtual IP address functions as the default gateway for the packet generator. Configure HSRP priorities such that Spoke1 is the HSRP active router and Spoke 2 is the standby. Configure Spoke1 for HSRP preempt, so that it will take over as primary in the event of LAN interface outage and recovery.
- Enable EIGRP neighborship between the DC-Router and the Hub1 and Hub2 routers. The hub routers should advertise the branch subnets to the DC-Router to allow for failover. The DC-Router should be the default gateway for the packet generator on the data center side.
- Branch WAN circuits set to 5 Mbps.
- DMVPN Per-Tunnel QoS enabled.

Configure the ASR 1000s for Route Processor Redundancy (RPR) and enable the Non Stop Forwarding and Stateful Switchover features on all the data center routers.

Create bidirectional traffic flows between the hub and branch networks. The flows should use IMIX frame sizes up to 1300-byte MTU running at 3 Mbps total.

Table 13-12   *Line Card Failure and Recovery (OIR) Test*

Test Steps:	Start the bidirectional traffic and wait until it is running without any drops. Clear all counters and logs in the routers in the Node List. Record the failover times and log messages for each of the steps in this test. Check the log CPU and memory utilization for ASR routers during the OIR tests.
	Step 1. Remove the SPA connected to the ISP router from Hub1.
	Step 2. Wait until the network is stable after Step 1 and reinsert the SPA.
	Step 3. Remove the SIP connected to the ISP router from Hub1.
	Step 4. Wait until the network is stable after Step 3 and reinsert the SIP.
	Step 5. Remove the active Route Processor from Hub1.
	Step 6. Wait until the network is stable after Step 5 and reinsert the Route Processor. Verify whether the Route Processor properly initializes after it is reinserted.
Expected Results:	All the traffic should fail over successfully. The ASR router should stay stable through the OIR operations.
Observed Results:	
Pass/Fail:	

Table 13-13   *Interface Failure and Recovery Test*

Test ID:	DMVPN-DUTY-3
Node List:	Spoke1, Spoke2, ISP1, ISP2, Hub1, Hub2, DC-Router
Test Phase:	Duty Cycle
Test Description:	Interface Failure and Recovery Test

Table 13-13   *Interface Failure and Recovery Test*

Test Setup:	Build the network, as shown in Figure 13-1.
	Configure branch and hub routers per the design documentation.
	• DMVPN dual hub/single cloud configurations.
	• PKI/digital certificates.
	• EIGRP routing.
	• Class B Branch (dual CE).
	• Enable HSRP on the LAN side of the branch network as the default gateway for the packet generator. Spoke1 should be HSRP active router and preempt should be configured.
	• Enable EIGRP neighborship between the DC-Router and the Hub1 and Hub2 routers. The hub routers should advertise the branch subnets to the DC-Router to allow for failover. The DC-Router should be the default gateway for the packet generator on the data center side.
	• Branch WAN circuits set to 5 Mbps.
	• DMVPN Per-Tunnel QoS enabled.
	Create bidirectional traffic flows between the hub and branch networks. The flows should use IMIX frame sizes up to 1300-byte MTU running at 3 Mbps total.
Test Steps:	Start the bidirectional traffic and wait until it is running without drops. Clear all counters and logs in the routers in the Node List. Record the failover times for each of the steps in this test. Check the log files and CPU and memory utilization for all of the routers in the Node List throughout this test.
	Step 1. Remove the cable between the ISP router and Hub2.
	Step 2. Wait until the network is stable after Step 1 and reconnect the cable.
	Step 3. Remove the cable between the ISP router and Hub1.
	Step 4. Wait until the network is stable after Step 3 and reconnect the cable.
	Step 5. Remove the cable between the ISP router and Spoke2.
	Step 6. Wait until the network is stable after Step 5 and reconnect the cable.
	Step 7. Remove the cable between the ISP router and Hub1.
	Step 8. Wait until the network is stable after Step 7 and reconnect the cable.
	Step 9. Remove the cable between the DC-Router and Hub1.
	Step 10. Wait until the network is stable after Step 9 and reconnect the cable.

Table 13-13 *Interface Failure and Recovery Test*

	Step 11. Remove the LAN cable from the Spoke1 router.
	Step 12. Wait until the network is stable after Step 11 and reconnect the cable.
Expected Results:	All the traffic should fail over.
Observed Results:	
Pass/Fail:	

Table 13-14 *Software Forced Failover Test*

Test ID:	DMVPN-DUTY-4
Node List:	Spoke1, Spoke2, ISP1, ISP2, Hub1, Hub2, DC-Router
Test Phase:	Duty Cycle
Test Description:	Software Forced Failover Test
Test Setup:	Build the network, as shown in Figure 13-1. Configure branch and hub routers per the design documentation: • DMVPN dual hub/single cloud configurations. • PKI/digital certificates. • EIGRP routing. • Class B Branch (dual CE). • Enable HSRP on the LAN side of the branch network as the default gateway for the packet generator. Spoke1 should be HSRP active router and preempt should be configured. • Enable EIGRP neighborship between the DC-Router and the Hub1 and Hub2 routers. The hub routers should advertise the branch subnets to the DC-Router to allow for failover. The DC-Router should be the default gateway for the packet generator on the data center side. • Branch WAN circuits set to 5 Mbps. • DMVPN Per-Tunnel QoS enabled. Configure the ASR 1000s for RPR and enable the Non Stop Forwarding and Stateful Switchover features on all the data center routers. Create bidirectional traffic flows between the hub and branch networks. The flows should use IMIX frame sizes up to 1300-byte MTU running at 3 Mbps total.

Table 13-14   *Software Forced Failover Test*

Test Steps:	Start the test traffic and verify that it is running without drops. Clear all counters and logs in the routers in the Node List. Record the failover times for each of the steps in this test. Check the log files and CPU and memory utilization for all of the routers in the Node List throughout this test.
	Step 1. Cause a failover by clearing the crypto ISAKMP and IPsec SAs in Hub1.
	Step 2. Cause a failover by clearing the EIGRP process in Hub1.
	Step 3. Cause a failover by switching over the active supervisor in Hub1 by using the **redundancy force-switchover command**, and then entering the **hw-module slot** *slot* **reload** command.
	Step 4. Wait until the "new" secondary supervisor comes online and reset it again by issuing the entering **hw-module slot** *slot* **reload** command. Once it comes online again, make it the primary supervisor.
	Step 5. Cause a failover by resetting the Hub1 SIP connected to the ISP router.
	Step 6. Cause a failover by resetting the Hub1 SPA connected to the ISP router.
	Step 7. Cause a failover by shutting down the interface between Hub1 and the ISP router. Once the network is stable, bring the interface back up.
	Step 8. Cause a failover by shutting down the interface between Hub1 and the DC-Router. Once the network is stable, bring the interface back up.
	Step 9. Cause a failover by rebooting Hub1.
	Step 10. Cause a failover by clearing the crypto ISAKMP and IPsec SAs in Spoke1.
	Step 11. Cause a failover by clearing the EIGRP process in Spoke1.
	Step 12. Cause a failover by doing an OIR on the WAN interface of Spoke1. To do this, issue the command `hw-module sm {slot} oir-stop` and remove the appropriate WAN card.
	Step 13. Wait until the network is stable after Step 12, reinsert the card, and enable it by issuing the following command: `hw-module sm {slot} oir-start`

Table 13-14 *Software Forced Failover Test*

	Step 14. Verify that the card comes up and traffic resumes to flow.
	Step 15. Cause a failover by shutting down the LAN interface on Spoke1. Wait until the network is stable, and bring the interface back up.
	Step 16. Cause a failover by reloading the Spoke1 router.
Expected Results:	All the traffic should fail over.
Observed Results:	
Pass/Fail:	

Table 13-15 *Spoke to Spoke Failover Test*

Test ID:	DMVPN-DUTY-5
Node List:	Spoke1, Spoke2, ISP1, ISP2, Hub1, Hub2, DC-Router
Test Phase:	Duty Cycle
Test Description:	Spoke to Spoke Failover Test
Test Setup:	Build the network, as shown in Figure 13-1. Configure branch and hub routers per the design documentation: • DMVPN dual hub/single cloud configurations • PKI/digital certificates • EIGRP routing Both spoke routers configured as Class A Branches (single CE). Run bidirectional traffic flows between Hub1 and the spoke routers running IMIX frame sizes at 5 Mbps. Also, run bidirectional traffic between the Spoke1 and Spoke2 running IMIX frame sizes at 1 Mbps.
Test Steps:	Start the bidirectional traffic and wait until it is running without drops. Clear all counters and logs in the routers in the Node List. Record the failover times for each of the steps in this test. Check the log files and CPU and memory utilization for all of the routers in the Node List throughout this test.
	Step 1. Cause a failover by clearing the crypto ISAKMP and IPsec SAs in Hub1.
	Step 2. Cause a failover by clearing the EIGRP process in Hub1.

Table 13-15 *Spoke to Spoke Failover Test*

	Step 3. Cause a failover by reloading Hub1.
	Step 4. Cause a failover by clearing the crypto ISAKMP and IPsec SAs in Spoke1.
Expected Results:	All the traffic should fail over.
Observed Results:	
Pass/Fail:	

GET VPN Test Cases Summary

Table 13-16 contains a brief summary of the tests to be conducted to certify the GET VPN functionality described earlier.

Table 13-16 *Test Cases Summary Table*

Test ID	Test Description
GETVPN-BASE-1	GET VPN Baseline Functionality Test
GETVPN-BASE-2	GET VPN Baseline Traffic Test
GETVPN-PERF-1	GET VPN Spoke Performance Test
GETVPN-PERF-2	GET VPN Fragmentation Performance Test
GETVPN-PERF-3	GET VPN Key Server Multicast Performance Test
GETVPN-FEAT-1	GET VPN Fail Close Mode Feature Test
GETVPN-FEAT-2	GET VPN Concatenated Policy Test
GETVPN-FEAT-3	GET VPN Cooperative Key Server Test
GETVPN-FEAT-4	GET VPN PKI/CA Feature Test
GETVPN-DUTY-1	Chassis Failure and Recovery Test

Detailed GET VPN Test Cases

The following tables contain detailed test cases to be conducted to certify the GET VPN functionality described earlier. These cases provide you with guidance on testing GET VPN and should be modified to fit your specific needs.

Table 13-17   *GET VPN Baseline Functionality Test*

Test ID:	GETVPN-BASE-1
Node List:	CE1, CE2, CE3, CE4, GET-KS1, GET-KS2, PE1, PE2, PE3
Test Phase:	Baseline
Test Description:	GET VPN Baseline Functionality Test
Test Setup:	Build the network, as shown in Figure 13-1. Configure branch and hub routers per the design documentation: • GET VPN group members (GM) • Cooperative key servers • PKI/digital certificates • Multicast configured on PE routers; multicast registration and rekey • BGP routing from CE to PE • EIGRP routing between hub GMs and DC-Router • QoS features Both spoke CEs configured as Class A Branches connected at 10 Mbps (use outgoing QoS on PE1 and PE2 to accomplish this).
Test Steps:	**Step 1.** Start 20 bidirectional flows between the branches and the hubs using the Ixia traffic generator at 2 Mbps per spoke, using IMIX frame sizes.
	Step 2. Start a bidirectional traffic flow between CE1 and CE2 running at 1 Mbps.

	Step 3. Verify GET VPN operation (IPsec tunnels, routing, key exchange) by using the following commands:
	
	`show crypto gdoi`
	`show crypto gdoi ipsec sa`
	`show crypto gdoi gm <options>`
	`show crypto gdoi gm acl`
	`show crypto gdoi gm rekey`
	`show crypto gdoi gm replay`
	`show crypto gdoi group <group name> <options>`
	`show crypto ipsec sa`
	`show crypto isakmp sa`

	Step 4. Verify the CPU and memory utilization on all of the devices in the Node List by issuing the appropriate CLI commands or through SNMP polling.

Table 13-17   *GET VPN Baseline Functionality Test*

Expected Results:	All tunnels and routing protocol adjacencies will come up, and traffic will be delivered as expected. Keys will be obtained for the key server (KS) using multicast.
Observed Results:	
Pass/Fail:	

Table 13-18   *GET VPN Baseline Traffic Test*

Test ID:	GETVPN-BASE-2
Node List:	CE1, CE2, CE3, CE4, GET-KS1, GET-KS2, PE1, PE2, PE3
Test Phase:	Baseline
Test Description:	GET VPN Baseline Traffic Test
Test Setup:	Build the network, as shown in Figure 13-1. Configure branch and hub routers per the design documentation: • GET VPN GMs • Cooperative key servers • PKI/digital certificates • Multicast configured on PE routers; multicast registration and rekey • BGP routing from CE to PE • EIGRP routing between hub GMs and DC-Router • QoS features Both spoke CEs configured as Class A Branches connected at 10 Mbps (use outgoing QoS on PE1 and PE2 to accomplish this).
Test Steps:	This test is run for 24 hours.
	Step 1. Start 20 bidirectional flows between the branches and the hubs using the Ixia traffic generator at 2 Mbps per spoke, using IMIX frame sizes.
	Step 2. Start a bidirectional traffic flow between CE1 and CE2 running at 1 Mbps.
	Step 3. Using the traffic generator, create a multicast group sourcing traffic at 500 Kbps originating from the data center subnet. Subscribe to the multicast group using IGMP from both branch LANs.

Table 13-18 *GET VPN Baseline Traffic Test*

	Step 4. Enable logging to a syslog server on all devices. Logs should be checked for errors periodically for the entire duration of the test.
	Step 5. Verify the CPU and memory utilization on all of the devices in the Node List every 30 minutes by issuing the appropriate CLI commands or through SNMP polling.
Expected Results:	All test flows will be delivered without unexpected drops or delays.
	All DUTs in the Node List will remain stable throughout the 24 hours.
Observed Results:	
Pass/Fail:	

Table 13-19 *GET VPN Spoke Performance Test*

Test ID:	GETVPN-PERF-1
Node List:	CE1, CE2, CE3, CE4, GET-KS1, GET-KS2, PE1, PE2, PE3
Test Phase:	Performance
Test Description:	GET VPN Spoke Performance Test
Test Setup:	Build the network, as shown in Figure 13-1.
	Configure branch and hub routers per the design documentation:
	• GET VPN GMs
	• Cooperative key servers
	• PKI/digital certificates
	• Multicast configured on PE routers; multicast registration and rekey
	• BGP routing from CE to PE
	• EIGRP routing between hub GMs and DC-Router
	• QoS features
	Both spoke CEs configured as Class A Branches connected at 1 Gigabit.
Test Steps:	**Step 1.** Run the Ixia RFC2544 Throughput test between CE1 and CE3. The frame sizes for this test should not exceed 1400 bytes. Verify the CPU and memory utilization on all of the devices in the Node List. Run this test to completion three times, and record the results.

Table 13-19 *GET VPN Spoke Performance Test*

	Step 2. Run the Ixia RFC2544 Throughput test between CE1 and CE2. The frame sizes for this test should not exceed 1400 bytes. Verify the CPU and memory utilization on all of the devices in the Node List. Run this test to completion three times, and record the results.
Expected Results:	This is a scalability test for the GET VPN spoke routers. The results of the test will be reported in the Observed Results section.
Observed Results:	
Pass/Fail:	

Table 13-20 *GET VPN Large MTU Performance Test*

Test ID:	GETVPN-PERF-2
Node List:	CE1, CE2, CE3, CE4, GET-KS1, GET-KS2, PE1, PE2, PE3
Test Phase:	Performance
Test Description:	GET VPN Fragmentation Performance Test
Test Setup:	Build the network, as shown in Figure 13-1. Configure branch and hub routers per the design documentation: • GET VPN GMs • Cooperative key servers • PKI/digital certificates • Multicast configured on PE routers; multicast registration and rekey • BGP routing from CE to PE • EIGRP routing between hub GMs and DC-Router • QoS features Both spoke CEs configured as Class A Branches connected at 1 Gigabit.

Table 13-20 *GET VPN Large MTU Performance Test*

Test Steps:	**Step 1.** Start a throughput test with TCP traffic flows originating from CE2 destined for CE3. Use a mix of frame sizes ranging from 1450 to 1500 bytes. Make sure a *DF bit is not set* for all of the frames. Verify the CPU and memory utilization on all of the devices in the Node List. Run this test to completion three times, and record the results.
	Step 2. Start a throughput test with TCP traffic flows originating from CE2 destined for CE3. Use a mix of frame sizes ranging from 1450 to 1500 bytes. Make sure a *DF bit is set* for all of the frames. Verify the CPU and memory utilization on all of the devices in the Node List. Run this test to completion three times, and record the results.
	Step 3. Start a throughput test with TCP traffic flows originating from CE3 destined for CE2. Use a mix of frame sizes ranging from 1450 to 1500 bytes. Make sure a *DF bit is not set* for all of the frames. Verify the CPU and memory utilization on all of the devices in the Node List. Run this test to completion three times, and record the results.
	Step 4. Start a throughput test with TCP traffic flows originating from CE3 destined for CE2. Use a mix of frame sizes ranging from 1450 to 1500 bytes. Make sure a *DF bit is set* for all of the frames. Verify the CPU and memory utilization on all of the devices in the Node List. Run this test to completion three times, and record the results.
	Step 5. Start a throughput test using bidirectional TCP and UDP traffic flows between CE3 and the two spoke routers. Use a mix of frame sizes ranging from 1450 to 1500 bytes. Make sure a *DF bit is not set* for all of the frames. Verify the CPU and memory utilization on all of the devices in the Node List. Run this test to completion three times, and record the results.
	Step 6. Start a throughput test using bidirectional TCP and UDP traffic flows between CE3 and the two spoke routers. Use a mix of frame sizes ranging from 1450 to 1500 bytes. Make sure a *DF bit is set* for all of the frames. Verify the CPU and memory utilization on all of the devices in the Node List. Run this test to completion three times, and record the results.

Table 13-20   *GET VPN Large MTU Performance Test*

	Step 7. Start a throughput test using bidirectional TCP and UDP traffic flows between CE1 and CE2. Use a mix of frame sizes ranging from 1450 to 1500 bytes. Make sure a *DF bit is not set* for all of the frames. Verify the CPU and memory utilization on all of the devices in the Node List. Run this test to completion three times, and record the results.
	Step 8. Start a throughput test using bidirectional TCP and UDP traffic flows between CE1 and CE2. Use a mix of frame sizes ranging from 1450 to 1500 bytes. Make sure a *DF bit is set* for all of the frames. Verify the CPU and memory utilization on all of the devices in the Node List. Run this test to completion three times, and record the results.
Expected Results:	This is a scalability test for router fragmentation and packet drops. The results of the test will be reported in the Observed Results section.
Observed Results:	
Pass/Fail:	

Tip   The GETVPN-PERF-3 Test could also be repeated using unicast registration and rekey.

Tip   Crypto throughput testing for the ASR "standalone" router is performed in the DMVPN-PERF-3 test. If the DMVPN testing is not being performed, ASR crypto throughput testing would be appropriate at this point.

Table 13-21 *GET VPN Key Server Multicast Performance Test*

Test ID:	GETVPN-PERF-3
Node List:	CE3, CE4, GET-KS1, GET-KS2, 7200-G2-Load-1, 7200-G2-Load-2
Test Phase:	Performance
Test Description:	GET VPN Key Server Multicast Performance Test
Test Setup:	Build the network, as shown in Figure 13-3.
	Configure branch and hub routers per the design documentation:
	• GET VPN GMs
	• Cooperative key servers
	• PKI/digital certificates
	• Multicast configured on PE routers
	• Multicast registration and rekey
	• BGP routing from CE to PE
	• EIGRP routing between hub GMs and DC-Router
	• QoS features
	• CAC enabled
	Both spoke CEs configured as Class A Branches connected at 1 Gigabit.
	7200-G2-Load-1 is set to use GET-KS1 as its registration server and 7200-G2-Load-2 is set to use GET-KS2 as its registration server.
Test Steps:	Verify the CPU and memory utilization on all of the devices in the Node List throughout this test.
	Step 1. Stop all traffic. Clear all GET VPN information from all routers by issuing the following commands in all of the routers in the Node List:

```
clear crypto isakmp
clear crypto sa
clear crypto gdoi replay
clear crypto gdoi ks coop counter (KSs only)
clear crypto gdoi ks coop role (KSs only)
clear crypto gdoi
```

Verify that all crypto/GET VPN information is cleared.

Step 2. For each 7200 load router, start traffic flows from 50 simulated routers' LAN interfaces destined to the data center. These flows should be running at 50 Kbps. Record how long it takes for all the traffic flows to begin reaching the data center.

Table 13-21　*GET VPN Key Server Multicast Performance Test*

Step 3.	Repeat Step 1 to clear all crypto/GET VPN information. For each 7200 load router, start traffic flows from 50 simulated routers' LAN interfaces destined to the data center. These flows should be running at 50 Kbps. Wait 10 seconds and start another 50 simulated router flows. Record how long it takes for all the traffic flows to begin reaching the data center.
Step 4.	Repeat Step 1. For each 7200 load router, start traffic flows from 50 simulated routers' LAN interfaces destined to the data center. These flows should be running at 50 Kbps. Wait 10 seconds, and start another 50 simulated router flows. Wait another 10 seconds, and start the last 50 simulated router flows. Record how long it takes for all the traffic flows to begin reaching the data center.
Step 5.	Wait until the network is stable after Step 4. Verify that the key servers have synchronized their states and change the crypto ACL in GET-KS1 (primary server) to force a rekey of all GMs. Check the CPU and memory utilization in the GET-KS1 router while all the rekeys happen.
Step 6.	Configure 7200-G2-Load-2 to use GET-KS1 as its registration server. Repeat Step 1. For each 7200 load router, start traffic flows from 50 simulated routers' LAN interfaces destined to the data center. These flows should be running at 50 Kbps. Wait 10 seconds and start another 50 simulated router flows. Wait another 10 seconds and start the last 50 simulated router flows. Record how long it takes for all the traffic flows to begin reaching the data center.
Step 7.	Disable CAC and repeat Steps 1 to 6.
Expected Results:	This is a scalability test for the key server routers. The results of the test will be reported in the Observed Results section.
Observed Results:	
Pass/Fail:	

Table 13-22 *GET VPN Fail Close Mode Feature Test*

Test ID:	GETVPN-FEAT-1
Node List:	CE1, CE2, CE3, CE4, GET-KS1, GET-KS2, PE1, PE2, PE3
Test Phase:	Feature
Test Description:	GET VPN Fail Close Mode Feature Test
Test Setup:	Build the network, as shown in Figure 13-1. Configure branch and hub routers per the design documentation: <ul><li>GET VPN GMs</li><li>Cooperative key servers</li><li>PKI/digital certificates</li><li>Multicast configured on PE routers; multicast registration and rekey</li><li>BGP routing from CE to PE</li><li>EIGRP routing between hub GMs and DC-Router</li><li>QoS features</li></ul> Both spoke CEs configured as class A branches connected at 10 Mbps. Configure all GMs with fail close mode enabled by specifying the appropriate ACLs on the CE routers. The data center LAN routes should be seen in CE1's routing table, and the CE1 LAN route should be seen in CE3, CE4, and DC-Router's routing table even without the GET VPN being enabled.
Test Steps:	**Step 1.** Create a 400-Kbps bidirectional traffic flow between CE1's LAN and the data center LAN. Verify that the traffic is being delivered as expected using an IPsec SA created using GET VPN.
	Step 2. Disconnect both KSs from the network. Issue **clear crypto gdoi**, **clear crypto isakmp**, and **clear crypto sa** commands on CE1, CE2, and CE3. Verify whether the test traffic is now being dropped.
	Step 3. Reconnect the KSs into the network and verify that traffic starts being delivered once the CE routers obtain the new keys.
	Step 4. Disable fail close mode on all GET VPN GM. Clear all the crypto information from all GM and let them rekey. Verify all the test traffic is being delivered.
	Step 5. Disconnect both KSs from the network. Issue a **clear crypto gdoi**, **clear crypto isakmp** and **clear crypto sa** command on CE1, CE2 and CE3. Verify whether the test traffic is still being delivered.

Table 13-22 *GET VPN Fail Close Mode Feature Test*

	Step 6. Reconnect the KSs into the network, and verify that traffic starts being delivered over IPSec SAs once the routers rekey.
Expected Results:	Traffic should be dropped between the CE routers if the fail close mode feature is enabled while there are no valid IPsec SAs and the KSs are unavailable. Traffic should be forwarded unencrypted if KSs are not available and default mode of fail open is enabled.
Observed Results:	
Pass/Fail:	

Table 13-23 *GET VPN Concatenated Policy Test*

Test ID:	GETVPN-FEAT-2
Node List:	CE1, CE2, CE3, CE4, GET-KS1, GET-KS2
Test Phase:	Feature
Test Description:	GET VPN Concatenated Policy Test
Test Setup:	Build the network, as shown in Figure 13-1. Configure branch and hub routers per the design documentation: • GET VPN GMs • Cooperative key servers • PKI/digital certificates • Multicast configured on PE routers; multicast registration and rekey • BGP routing from CE to PE • EIGRP routing between hub GMs and DC-Router • QoS features Both spoke CEs configured as Class A Branches connected at 10 Mbps. Enable syslog/local logging on all CE routers.
Test Steps:	**Step 1.** Because BGP between CEs and PEs should be unencrypted as per the design, create an ACL in each CE denying BGP traffic: `deny tcp any eq bgp any` This ACL will be used to keep the traffic unencrypted when concatenated with the ACL downloaded from the KS. Apply this ACL to the GDOI crypto map on the CE routers.

Table 13-23 *GET VPN Concatenated Policy Test*

Step 2.	On the key servers, create a new ACL that encrypts all traffic: `permit ip any any` Apply this ACL to the crypto GDOI group used for this specific GET VPN.
Step 3.	Clear all the GET VPN tunnels by issuing the **clear crypto gdoi**, **clear crypto isakmp**, and **clear crypto sa** commands in all of the CE routers.
Step 4.	Start a 400-Kbps bidirectional traffic flow between CE-1's LAN and the data center LAN. Verify that the traffic is being delivered as expected using an IPsec SA created using GET VPN.
Step 5.	Verify that the ACLs in the CE routers and the KSs have combined by issuing the following command: `show crypto gdoi <gm> acl <local or download>` Check syslog/local logs to verify that a GM_ACL_MERGE operation has indeed occurred. Make sure that the BGP sessions between the CEs and PEs are still up.
Step 6.	Ping the locally connected PEs from the CE routers, and record the results.
Step 7.	Stop all test traffic flows.
Step 8.	Change the local ACL in the CEs to only deny ICMP traffic (remove the **deny** statement for BGP): `deny icmp any any` Apply this ACL to the GDOI crypto map on the CE routers.
Step 9.	Clear all the GET VPN tunnels by issuing the **clear crypto gdoi**, **clear crypto isakmp**, and **clear crypto sa** commands in all of the CE routers.
Step 10.	Restart the test traffic. Check whether the CEs have rekeyed with the KS. Verify that the ACLs in the CE routers and the KSs have combined by issuing the following command: `show crypto gdoi <gm> acl <local or download>` Check syslog/local logs to verify that a GM_ACL_MERGE has indeed occurred. Check whether the BGP sessions between the CEs and PEs are still up.

Table 13-23 *GET VPN Concatenated Policy Test*

	Step 11. Ping the locally connected PEs from the CE routers, and record the results. The local CE and KS crypto ACLs will be combined to form the encryption policy.
Observed Results:	
Pass/Fail:	

Table 13-24 *GET VPN Cooperative Key Server Test*

Test ID:	GETVPN-FEAT-3
Node List:	CE1, CE2, CE3, CE4, GET-KS1, GET-KS2
Test Phase:	Feature
Test Description:	GET VPN Cooperative Key Server Test
Test Setup:	Build the network, as shown in Figure 13-1. Configure branch and hub routers per the design documentation: • GET VPN GMs • Cooperative key servers • PKI/digital certificates • Multicast configured on PE routers • Multicast registration and rekey • BGP routing from CE to PE • EIGRP routing between hub GMs and DC-Router • QoS features • Fail-Closed feature enabled Both spoke CEs connected as Class A Branches connected at 10 Mbps. Enable syslog/local logging on all CE and KS routers. CE1 and CE3 should be configured to register with GET-KS1 first and GET-KS2 as a backup. CE2 and CE4 should be configured to register with GET-KS2 first and GET-KS1 as a backup.

Table 13-24 *GET VPN Cooperative Key Server Test*

Test Steps:	**Step 1.** Configure GET-KS1 as the primary key server via a higher-priority command for the GDOI group. Clear the KS state and trigger an election by executing the following commands on both key servers:
	
	`clear crypto gdoi ks coop role`
	`clear crypto gdoi`
	
	Verify that GET-KS1 is now the primary key server and that GET-KS2 is secondary by executing the following command on both key servers:
	
	`show crypto gdoi ks`

	Step 2. Start a 400-Kbps bidirectional traffic flow between CE1 and CE2's LAN and the data center LAN. Verify that the traffic is being delivered as expected using an IPsec SA created using GET VPN. Check GET-KS1 to verify that the key server and GM info are in sync.
	Step 3. Make a change to the crypto ACL used in GET VPN on the secondary KS (GET-KS2) by adding a **permit icmp any any.** Verify whether this change was sent to any of the CE routers, particularly CE2 and CE4, which registered using GET-KS2.
	Step 4. Make a change to the crypto ACL used in GET VPN on the primary KS (GET-KS1) by adding a **permit icmp any any.** Verify whether this change was sent to the CE routers, particularly CE2 and CE4, which registered using GET-KS2. Check the log messages in the GMs (CE routers) looking for rekey and ACL change messages.
	Step 5. Reload GET-KS2. Check the coop KS state in GET-KS1 every 10 seconds until GET-KS2 is back to secondary state. Verify that no traffic was dropped during this transition.
	Step 6. Reload GET-KS1. Check the coop KS state in GET-KS2 every 10 seconds until GET-KS1 is back up, and verify that it is in secondary state. Check the priorities of both KSs. Verify that no traffic was dropped during this transition. Check the logs in the GMs (CE routers) for KS transition and rekey messages.

Table 13-24 *GET VPN Cooperative Key Server Test*

	Step 7. With the traffic still running, wait until the key-encryption keys (KEK) in all CE routers expire. Check that all GMs (CE routers) have rekeyed their KEKs using the GET-KS2 as the primary KS.
	Step 8. Force a re-election between the KSs by issuing the following command on both KS routers: `clear crypto gdoi ks coop role` Check whether GET-KS1 is now the primary KS.
	Step 9. Force a rekey/reregistration of all the GMs (CE routers) by issuing the following command on the KS routers: `clear crypto gdoi` Verify that all of the CE routers have rekeyed and re-registered with the "new" primary KS. Check the logs in the GMs (CE routers) for KS transition and rekey messages.
	Step 10. With the traffic still running, wait until the KEKs in all CE routers expire. Check that all GMs (CE routers) have rekeyed their KEKs using the GET-KS1 as the primary KS.
Expected Results:	The key servers will run in cooperative mode. The secondary KS will back up the primary one. Changes made to the secondary KS will not be pushed to the GMs. Changes made to the primary KS will be pushed to all the GMs. A reloaded KS will come back as secondary KS, irrespective of its priority, as long as there already is an active KS. All of the rekeys are handled only by the primary KS.
Observed Results:	
Pass/Fail:	

Table 13-25 *GET VPN PKI/CA Feature Test*

Test ID:	GETVPN-FEAT-4
Node List:	CE1, CE2, CE3, CE4, GET-KS1, GET-KS2
Test Phase:	Feature
Test Description:	GET VPN PKI/CA Feature Test
Test Setup:	Build the network, as shown in Figure 13-1. Configure branch and hub routers per the design documentation: • GET VPN GMs • Cooperative key servers with GET-KS1 as primary • PKI/digital certificates • Multicast configured on PE routers; multicast registration and rekey • BGP routing from CE to PE • EIGRP routing between hub GMs and DC-Router • QoS features • All CEs configured with the FAIL-CLOSED feature enabled Both spoke CEs configured as Class A Branches connected at 1 Gigabit. All CE routers register and rekey with GET-KS1. Run bidirectional traffic flows between CE1's LAN and the data center running IMIX frame sizes at 5 Mbps. Also, run bidirectional traffic between CE1's and CE2's LANs running IMIX frame sizes at 1 Mbps.
Test Steps:	**Step 1.** Set the CRL cache time to expire after 2 minutes on all routers in the Node List by using the **crl-cache delete-after 2** command. On the CA, revoke the certificate for CE1. Wait 5 minutes, to make sure a new CRL is loaded on GET-KS1, and clear the ISAKMP SAs for CE1 on the GET-KS1 router. Force a rekey on all CEs by issuing a **clear crypto gdoi** on the KS. Verify whether a new ISAKMP SA is negotiated between CE1 and the GET-KS1 router. Check whether traffic is being delivered between CE1 and the data center, and also CE1 and CE2.
	Step 2. Disable the auto-rollover feature on the CE1 router. Create and load a new certificate on CE1 with a 10-minute lifetime (or whatever the minimum is for the CA). Wait for 10 minutes (the time for the certificate to expire). Clear the ISAKMP SAs for CE1 on the GET-KS1 router. Force a rekey on all CEs by issuing a **clear crypto gdoi** on the KS. Verify whether a new ISAKMP SA is negotiated between CE1 and the GET-KS1 routers. Check whether traffic is being delivered between CE1 and the data center, and also CE1 and CE2.

Table 13-25 *GET VPN PKI/CA Feature Test*

Step 3.	Enable the auto-rollover feature on CE1. Create and load a new certificate on CE1 with a 10-minute lifetime (or whatever the minimum is for the CA). Wait for 10 minutes (the time for the certificate to expire). Clear the ISAKMP SAs for CE1 on the GET-KS1 router. Force a rekey on all CEs by issuing a **clear crypto gdoi** on the KS. Verify whether a new ISAKMP SA is negotiated between CE1 and the GET-KS1 routers. Check whether traffic is being delivered between CE1 and the data center, and also CE1 and CE2. Check the log files to verify a new certificate was obtained by CE1.
Step 4.	Enable the auto-rollover feature on CE1. Create and load a new certificate on CE1 with a 10-minute lifetime (or whatever the minimum is for the CA). Disconnect the CA from the network. Wait for 10 minutes (the time for the certificate to expire). Clear the ISAKMP SAs for CE1 on the GET-KS1 router. Force a rekey on all CEs by issuing a **clear crypto gdoi** on the KS. Verify whether a new ISAKMP SA is negotiated between CE-1 and the GET-KS1 routers. Check whether traffic is being delivered between CE1 and the data center, and also CE1 and CE2. Check the log files to verify whether a new certificate was obtained by CE1.
Step 5.	Reconnect the CA to the network after Step 4 is completed. Verify whether CE1 automatically re-enrolls. Check whether GET-KS1 will load a new CRL automatically once the CA is available (this may take some time). Check if traffic can be delivered by CE1 once a new certificate has been enrolled.
Step 6.	Disable the auto-rollover feature on GET-KS1 and GET-KS2. Create and load a new certificate on GET-KS1 and GET-KS2 with a 10-minute lifetime (or whatever the minimum is for the CA). Wait for 10 minutes (the time for the certificate to expire). Clear the ISAKMP SAs for GET-KS1 on all CE routers. Wait for a rekey for all CEs (or force one). Verify whether a new ISAKMP SA is negotiated between the routers. Record all log messages regarding rekey and the KSs. Check all traffic to verify whether it is being encrypted and delivered.

Table 13-25   *GET VPN PKI/CA Feature Test*

Step 7. Enable the auto-rollover feature on GET-KS1 and GET-KS2. Create and load a new certificate on GET-KS1 and GET-KS2 with a 10-minute lifetime (or whatever the minimum is for the CA). Wait for 10 minutes (the time for the certificate to expire). Clear the ISAKMP SAs for GET-KS1 on all CE routers. Wait for a rekey for all CEs (or force one). Verify whether a new ISAKMP SA is negotiated between the routers. Record all log messages regarding rekey and the KSs and verify that the KSs received a new certificate. Check all traffic to verify whether it is being encrypted and delivered.

Step 8. Enable the auto-rollover feature on GET-KS1 and GET-KS2. Create and load a new certificate on GET-KS1 and GET-KS2 with a 10-minute lifetime (or whatever the minimum is for the CA). Disconnect the CA from the network. Wait for 10 minutes (the time for the certificate to expire). Clear the ISAKMP SAs for GET-KS1 on all CE routers. Wait for a rekey for all CEs (or force one). Verify whether a new ISAKMP SA is negotiated between the routers. Record all log messages regarding rekey and the KSs and verify whether the KS received a new certificate. Check all traffic to verify whether it is being encrypted and delivered.

Step 9. Reconnect the CA to the network after Step 8 is finished. Verify whether GET-KS1 and GET-KS2 automatically re-enroll. Check whether all the CE routers will load a new CRL automatically once the CA is available (this may take some time). Verify whether a new ISAKMP SA is negotiated between the routers. Record all log messages regarding rekey and the KSs. Check all traffic to verify whether it is being encrypted and delivered.

Step 10. On the CA, revoke the certificate for GET-KS1. Wait 5 minutes, to make sure a new CRL is loaded on the CE routers, and clear the ISAKMP SAs on all CEs. Wait for a rekey for all CEs (or force one). Verify whether a new ISAKMP SA is negotiated between the routers. Record all log messages regarding rekey and the KSs. Check all traffic to verify if it is being encrypted and delivered.

Table 13-25 *GET VPN PKI/CA Feature Test*

	Step 11. Load a valid certificate on both GET-KS1 and GET-KS2. Verify whether all the CE routers will reregister and rekey with the KSs. Make sure traffic begins being delivered between the CEs.
Expected Results:	The certificates will be used for authentication. Certificates that have been revoked will cause authentications to fail. Auto-enrollment will work as expected, particularly for the KSs.
Observed Results:	
Pass/Fail:	

Tip In Service Software Upgrade (ISSU) testing for the ASR is performed in DMVP-FEAT-4. If the DMVPN testing is not being performed, ISSU testing for the ASRs would be appropriate at this point.

Table 13-26 *Chassis Failure and Recovery Test*

Test ID:	GETVPN-DUTY-1
Node List:	CE1, CE2, CE3, CE4, GET-KS1, GET-KS2, 7200-G2-Load-1, 7200-G2-Load-2
Test Phase:	Duty Cycle
Test Description:	Chassis Failure and Recovery Test

Table 13-26 *Chassis Failure and Recovery Test*

Test Setup:	Build the network, as shown in Figure 13-3.

Configure branch and hub routers per the design documentation:

- GET VPN GMs.
- Cooperative key servers (GET-KS1 as primary).
- PKI/digital certificates.
- PE routers with multicast enabled.
- Multicast registration and rekey.
- BGP routing from CE to PE.
- EIGRP routing between hub GMs and DC-Router. Both hub GMs redistribute/advertise a single branch prefix to the DC-Router for load balancing.
- CA and QoS features.
- CAC Enabled.
- Data center subnets should be advertised with the same metrics from both CE3 and CE4 for load balancing of incoming traffic.

Both spoke CEs connected as a class B branch connected at 1 Gigabit. CE1 is HSRP active for the branch LAN.

7200-G2-Load-1 is set to use GET-KS1 as its registration server with GET-KS2 as backup, and 7200-G2-Load-2 is set to use GET-KS2 as its registration server with GET-KS1 as backup.

To create the background traffic for this test, in each 7200 load router, start bidirectional traffic flows for 150 simulated routers' LAN interfaces destined to/from the data center. These flows should be running at 50 Kbps. The 300 flows (150 for each router) should have staggered start times until all are running without drops.

To create the marker flows for this test, create

- Four bidirectional flows at 1 Mbps each running between the spoke routers' branch LAN and the data center LAN.
- A multicast group sourcing traffic at 500 Kbps originating from the data center subnet. Subscribers to the multicast group at the branch LANs using IGMP.
- A single bidirectional flow at 50 Kbps running between a simulated router's LAN on 7200-G2-Load-1 and another simulated router's LAN on 7200-G2-Load-2 (to provide a spoke-to-spoke marker flow).

Table 13-26 *Chassis Failure and Recovery Test*

Test Steps:	Clear all counters and logs in the routers in the Node List. Throughout this test, measure convergence using the marker flows. Also follow the background flows for any unusual activity/failures. Record the failover times for each of the steps in this test. Check the log files and CPU and memory utilization for all of the routers in the Node List throughout this test.
	Step 1. Power down CE3.
	Step 2. Wait until the network is stable after Step 1 and power CE3 back on.
	Step 3. Power down CE4.
	Step 4. Wait until the network is stable after Step 3 and power CE4 back on.
	Step 5. Power down CE2.
	Step 6. Wait until the network is stable after Step 5 and power CE2 back on.
	Step 7. Power down CE1.
	Step 8. Wait until the network is stable after Step 7 and power CE1 back on. KS failures have been tested in GETVPN-FEAT-3.
Expected Results:	Minimal traffic loss expected during the loss of any single Group Member.
Observed Results:	
Pass/Fail:	

Tip   Duty Cycle Tests for OIR, interface, and software forced failures were performed in DMVPN-DUTY-2, DMVPN-DUTY-3, and DMVPN-DUTY-4. Similar tests should be performed for GET VPN using the Test Setup used in the GETVPN-DUTY-3 test.

Chapter 14

Data Center 3.0 Architecture: Nexus Platform Feature and Performance Test Plan

Today's enterprise architects are finding it necessary to take on new schools of thought to meet current expectations for growth, availability, operational efficiency, and security in their data centers. Stringent demands for uptime and serviceability, coupled with rapidly evolving technology and new products, present new challenges for the network architecture. Organizations in virtually every market are increasingly dependent on highly available business applications, fueling the installation of more and more servers in the data center, and even the activation of secondary data centers to ensure business continuity during disasters.[1] Power, cooling, and cabling are primary considerations for nearly every data center transformation project, forcing architects to take a second look at existing "siloed" hosting solutions that are often associated with low utilization of CPU, memory, and storage capacity of the servers that consume the majority of these valuable data center resources.

The Cisco Data Center 3.0 strategy presents IT architects with a phased approach to migrating from customized, siloed hosting environments, to standardized "cloud" environments that address many of today's business challenges and environmental considerations. This strategy includes a series of steps, starting with standardization and consolidation of server, storage, and network resources for improved operational efficiency, greater utilization, and enhanced resilience. Many enterprise organizations following a Data Center 3.0 roadmap begin their transformation projects with the creation of a "unified network fabric" to consolidate the I/O of both LAN and storage-area network (SAN) traffic onto a single physical infrastructure. This step alone drastically reduces the equipment footprint and the associated power and cooling resources.

The Data Center 3.0 architecture encourages the deployment of modular data centers, where fully populated racks of servers are brought online at the same time. These new rack systems are often purchased in a partially installed state, with power, network, and storage cabling preinstalled so that complete racks can be commissioned quickly after they arrive. Top-of-rack (ToR) designs complement rack-at-a-time deployment by simplifying and shortening cable runs and facilitating the replication of rack configurations. This rack-deployment model offers a solution by placing switching resources in each rack so that server connectivity can be aggregated and interconnected with the rest of the data center through a small number of cables connected to end-of-row (EoR) access or aggregation layer switches.

Cisco offers a compelling ToR solution that is supported by Cisco Nexus products. Using the Cisco Nexus 2000 Fabric Extender (N2K FEX) and Cisco Nexus 5000 (N5K) Series Switches at the access layer, data centers can build self-contained racks of servers with Gigabit Ethernet connectivity using a small number of 10-Gigabit Ethernet fibre or CX-1 connections to an EoR or middle-of-row (MoR) switch.

This test plan assists you in validating a unified I/O solution built upon on Nexus 5000 EoR Switches, Nexus 2000 ToR Fabric Extenders, Nexus 7000 core switches, and MDS 9500 Director-class SAN switches.

Background

A large financial organization has decided to deploy a new data center as part of a global consolidation project. A unified I/O design has been specified as the access architecture, with a pair of Nexus 2232 Fabric Extenders serving as the ToR switches for the chassis-based servers that are connected with converged network adapters (CNA). The ToR switches are dual-connected to a pair of Nexus 5020 EoR switches, which provide redundant connectivity to the upstream IP network and SAN fabric. A pair of Nexus 7010s forms a collapsed distribution/core layer serving the data center IP traffic, while a pair of MDS 9509s Director-class switches forms the collapsed distribution/core for the two SAN fabrics.

Figures 14-1 and 14-2 illustrate the physical and logical test topologies that are built to validate the respective IP and Fibre Channel over Ethernet (FCoE) designs. A representation of the WAN infrastructure is included in the test bed to validate branch connectivity to the data center.

This test plan is broken down into three separate parts, each focusing on separate elements of the unified design:

- Traditional IP testing

- FCoE and SAN testing

- Combined testing

Physical and Logical Test Topology

Figure 14-1 illustrates the IP topology to be tested.

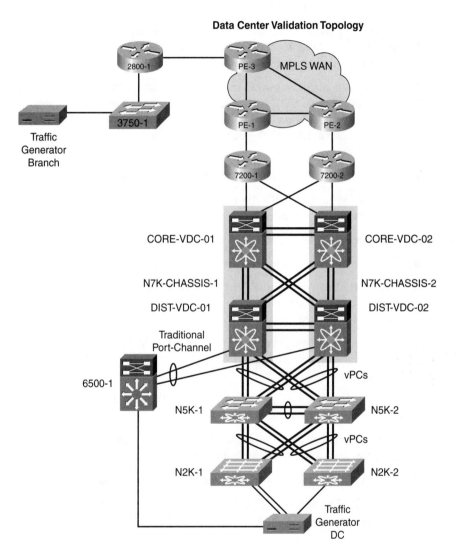

Figure 14-1 *Nexus Unified I/O IP Testing Topology*

Technical details of the IP topology test setup are as follows:

- The branch WAN router (2800-1) is using eBGP to advertise the local branch network to the MPLS WAN routers, which announce only the default route back.

- The MPLS WAN routers send only an aggregate route representing all of the branch IP networks to the 7200 WAN routers via eBGP. The 7200s send an aggregate route for all of the data center IP networks to the MPLS PE routers.

- The Nexus 7010s each have two virtual device contexts (VDC) configured. A core VDC and a distribution VDC are defined to delineate the interfaces and processes serving each function. These VDCs are interconnected via external 10GE connections aggregated into L3 port-channels.

- IP access layer VLANs defined on the Nexus 5020s are extended up to the Nexus 7010 distribution VDCs with L2 trunked virtual port channels (vPC).

- OSPF is enabled on the WAN 7200 as well as the core and distribution VDCs on the Nexus 7010s in the data center.

  - The core VDCs and the WAN 7200 routers are OSPF neighbors in Area 0.

  - The core and distribution VDCs are OSPF neighbors in Area 0.

  - The Nexus 7010 distribution VDCs function as OSPF ABRs for the VLANs that are defined and trunked across the connections to the Nexus 5020 L2 switches.

- The distribution VDCs have switch virtual interfaces (SVI), which are the default gateways for all of the data center VLANs. These SVIs are defined as HSRP pairs for redundancy purposes.

- All of the connections between the distribution VDCs and the Nexus 5020 EoR switches are trunked L2 vPCs.

- All of the connections between the Nexus 5020 EoR switches and the Nexus 2322PP FEX ToR switches are trunked L2 vPCs.

- The Cisco Catalyst 6500 is connected to the distribution VDCs using a vPC.

- All L3 interfaces are configured for PIM sparse mode and the static Anycast multicast RPs are running on the distribution VDCs.

Figure 14-2 illustrates the FCoE/SAN topology to be tested.

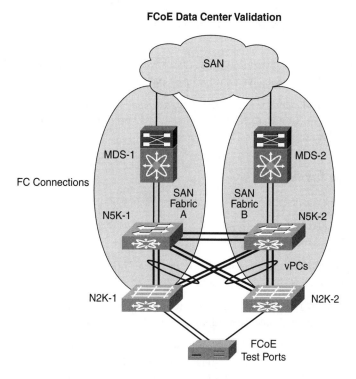

Figure 14-2 *Nexus Unified I/O FCoE/SAN Testing Topology*

Technical details of the FCoE/SAN topology test setup are as follows:

■ The FCoE test tool is connected to both ToR Nexus 2232 FEXs.

■ The Nexus 5020s are running in N-Port Virtualization (NPV) mode.

■ Each Nexus 5020 is connected to a different Cisco MDS 9509 Director running N-Port ID Virtualization (NPIV) over two separate Fibre Channel (FC) interfaces.

■ Each Cisco MDS 9509 is running as a separate virtual SAN (VSAN) fabric with its own zone set.

■ The MDS 9509s are both connected to a lab FC storage array with 50 LUNs created and masked specifically for this test. The masking maps the test LUNs so they can be reached via either MDS 9509 and by the World Wide Port Names (WWPN) configured on the IxSAN FCoE interfaces.

■ The VSANs are not allowed to pass between the two Nexus 5020s, to keep the fabrics separate.

Test Objectives

The primary objectives for this test include the following:

1. Validate that the proposed ToR unified I/O architecture will meet the enterprise's requirements.

2. Verify that the VDCs in the Nexus 7010s will allow the enterprise to collapse the core and distribution layers into a single pair of switches.

3. Ensure that the end-to-end design with a virtualized/collapsed core/distribution, vPCs, and FEX unified I/O ToR "switches" will provide the level of high availability required by the enterprise.

Traffic Flows for All Tests

The following traffic flows will be used during testing:

- 25 emulated TCP flows from FEX N2K-1 to the branch, each flow running at 100 pps. The frames should be random in size.

- 25 emulated TCP flows from the 6500 to FEX N2K-2, each flow running at 10,000 pps. The frames should be random in size.

- 25 emulated TCP flows from the branch to FEX N2K-1, each flow running at 100 pps. The frames should be random in size.

- Five emulated UDP multicast flows with groups sourcing from five different IP addresses should be set up originating from N2K-1. There should be four separate receivers, using IGMP to join all five groups; the receivers should be located at the branch, the 6500, N2K1 (separate port), and N2K-2. The flows should be running at 100 pps. All of the frames should be 64 bytes.

- Two IxSAN FCoE interfaces (or a server with a dual-port CNA running Iometer), each running IOPS tests against a unique LUN. The tests should run at five IOPS per interface.

Test Case Summary

Table 14-1 contains a brief summary of the tests to be conducted to certify the data center architecture previously described.

Table 14-1 *Test Cases Summary Table*

Test ID:	Brief Test Description
DC-BASE-1	Baseline Configuration Verification Test
DC-BASE-2	Network and SAN Traffic Test
DC-PERF-1	Nexus 2322PP Maximum Throughput Test
DC-PERF-2	Maximum FEX Architecture Throughput Test
DC-PERF-3	FEX Architecture Latency Test
DC-PERF-4	FCoE Throughput Test
DC-FEAT-1	Virtual Device Context (VDC) Feature Validation Test
DC-FEAT-2	Virtual Port Channel (vPC) Validation Test
DC-FEAT-3	Fabric Interconnect Feature Validation Test
DC-FEAT-4	SAN Feature Validation Test
DC-FEAT-5	In Service Software Upgrade (ISSU) Feature Validation Test
DC-DUTY-1	Chassis Failure and Recovery Test
DC-DUTY-2	Line Card Failure and Recovery Test
DC-DUTY-3	Interface Failure and Recovery Test
DC-DUTY-4	Software Forced Failover Test

Detailed Test Cases

The following tables contain detailed test cases to be conducted to certify the Data Center 3.0 topology described earlier. These cases provide you with guidance on testing data center switching and SAN technologies and should be modified to fit your specific needs.

Table 14-2 *Baseline Configuration Verification Test*

Test ID:	DC-BASE-1
Node List:	Routers: CORE-VDC-1, CORE-VDC-2, DIST-VDC-1, DIST-VDC-2, 7200-1, 7200-2, 2800-1, PE-1, PE-2, PE-3
	Switches: N5K-1, N5K-2, 6500-1
	Fabric Extenders: N2K-1, N2K-2
	SAN Directors: MDS-1, MDS-2
Test Phase:	Baseline
Test Description:	Baseline Configuration Verification Test

Table 14-2 *Baseline Configuration Verification Test*

Test Setup:	• Build the IP network, as shown in Figure 14-1. • Build the SAN, as shown in Figure 14-2. • Configure all services, such as VDCs, multicast, and QoS, that are required by the design. • Configure all the L2 features as per design requirements, including IP VLANs, SAN VLANs, and vPCs. • Bring up the FEX interfaces as unified I/O trunk ports between the Ixia tool's CNA adapters and the N2Ks. Both IP and SAN VLANs should be in forwarding state. • Configure all of the routing protocols between the routers in the Node List. • Configure the SAN and FCoE as per the design parameters.
Test Steps:	**Step 1.** Verify that BGP is up between 7200-1, 7200-2, 2800-1, and MPLS-WAN routers. Ensure the 2800-1 router is receiving the default route and the 7200-1 and 7200-2 routers are receiving the branch route.
	Step 2. Verify that OSPF is up between the 7200-1, 7200-2, CORE-VDC-1, CORE-VDC-2, DIST-VDC-1, and DIST-VDC-2 routers. Confirm that 7200-1 and 7200-2 routers are receiving the data center subnets.
	Step 3. Confirm that all the vPCs between the Nexus 5000s and Nexus 7000s, and between the Nexus 5000s and Nexus 2000s, are up and running.
	Step 4. Check to see that all L3 port-channels between the VDCs are up.
	Step 5. Check to see that the Ixia FCoE interfaces have been able to log into the SAN fabric, and see their masked and zoned LUNs.
	Step 6. Verify that the data center Ixia ports can reach their IP default gateways on the distribution VDCs. Check that the Ixia port connected to the branch can ping the IPs of the Ixia port connected to the FEX.
	Step 7. Confirm that all L3 interfaces have PIM neighbors as expected and that Multicast Source Discovery Protocol (MSDP) is running between the DIST-VDC-1 and DIST-VDC-2 routers.
	Step 8. Check the logs of all of the devices in the Node List to make sure there are no unexpected errors. Clear the logs.

Table 14-2   *Baseline Configuration Verification Test*

	Step 9. Verify the CPU and memory utilization on all of the devices in the Node List.
	All of the configurations, connections, and features will work as designed.
Observed Results:	
Pass/Fail:	

Table 14-3   *Network and SAN Traffic Test*

Test ID:	DC-BASE-2
Node List:	Routers: CORE-VDC-1, CORE-VDC-2, DIST-VDC-1, DIST-VDC-2, 7200-1, 7200-2, 2800-1, PE-1, PE-2, PE-3
	Switches: N5K-1, N5K-2, 6500-1
	Fabric Extenders: N2K-1, N2K-2
	SAN Directors: MDS-1, MDS-2
Test Phase:	Baseline
Test Description:	Network and SAN Traffic Test
Test Setup:	• Build the IP network, as shown in Figure 14-1.
	• Build the SAN, as shown in Figure 14-2.
	• Configure all services, such as VDCs, multicast, and QoS, that are required by the design.
	• Configure all the L2 features as per design requirements, including IP VLANs, SAN VLANs, and vPCs.
	• Bring up the FEX interfaces as unified I/O trunk ports between the Ixia tool's CNA adapters and the N2Ks. Both IP and SAN VLANs should be in forwarding state.
	• Configure all of the routing protocols between the routers in the Node List.
	• Configure the SAN and FCoE as per the design parameters.

Table 14-3   *Network and SAN Traffic Test*

Test Steps:	This test is run for 24 hours.
	Step 1. Verify that the routing protocols are up and running.
	Step 2. Start the traffic flows described in the "Traffic Flows for All Tests" section.
	Step 3. Verify that the IP traffic is reaching all of the destination test ports as expected.
	Step 4. Verify that the multicast traffic is reaching all of the subscriber ports.
	Step 5. Confirm that the FCoE IOPS traffic is running as expected.
	Step 6. Verify the logs of all of the devices in the Node List to make sure there are no unexpected errors in the beginning and end of this test.
	Step 7. Verify the CPU and memory utilization on all of the devices in the Node List every 30 minutes.
Expected Results:	All DUTs in the Node List will remain stable throughout the 24 hours. No unexpected traffic drops will occur.
Observed Results:	
Pass/Fail:	

Table 14-4   *Nexus 2322PP Maximum Throughput Test*

Test ID:	DC-PERF-1
Node List:	Switches: N5K-1, N5K-2
	Fabric Extenders: N2K-1, N2K-2
Test Phase:	Performance
Test Description:	Nexus 2322PP Maximum Throughput Test
Test Setup:	• Build the network, as shown in Figure 14-1.
	• Configure all the L2 features as per design requirements, including IP VLANs, SAN VLANs, and vPCs.
	• Bring up the FEX interfaces as unified I/O trunk ports between the Ixia tool's CNA adapters and the N2Ks. Both IP and SAN VLANs should be in forwarding state.

Table 14-4 *Nexus 2322PP Maximum Throughput Test*

Test ID:	DC-PERF-1
Test Steps:	**Step 1.** Run the Ixia RFC2544 Throughput test using the two Ixia interfaces connected to N2K-1 using the same VLAN. Verify the CPU and memory utilization on all of the devices in the Node List. Run this test to completion three times and record the results.
	Step 2. Run the Ixia RFC2544 Throughput test using one Ixia interface connected to N2K-1 and one connected to N2K-2 on the same VLAN. Verify the CPU and memory utilization on all of the devices in the Node List. Run this test to completion three times and record the results.
Expected Results:	This is a scalability test. The results of the test will be reported in the Observed Results section.
Observed Results:	
Pass/Fail:	

Table 14-5 *Maximum FEX Architecture Throughput Test*

Test ID:	DC-PERF-2
Node List:	Routers: DIST-VDC-1, DIST-VDC-2
	Switches: N5K-1, N5K-2
	Fabric Extenders: N2K-1, N2K-2
Test Phase:	Performance
Test Description:	Maximum FEX Architecture Throughput Test
Test Setup:	• Build the network, as shown in Figure 14-1.
	• Configure all services, such as VDCs, multicast, and QoS, that are required by the design.
	• Configure all the L2 features as per design requirements, including IP VLANs, SAN VLANs, and vPCs.
	• Bring up the FEX interfaces as unified I/O trunk ports between the Ixia tool's CNA adapters and the N2Ks. Both IP and SAN VLANs should be in forwarding state.
	• Configure all of the routing protocols between the routers in the Node List.
	• Configure HSRP for all the appropriate SVIs.

Table 14-5   *Maximum FEX Architecture Throughput Test*

Test Steps:	**Step 1.** Run the Ixia RFC2544 Throughput test using the two Ixia interfaces connected to N2K-1 using two different VLANs. This should send the traffic through the distribution VDCs for L3 switching. Verify the CPU and memory utilization on all of the devices in the Node List. Run this test to completion three times and record the results.
	Step 2. Run the Ixia RFC2544 Throughput test using one Ixia interface connected to N2K-1 and one connected to N2K-2 using two different VLANs. This should send the traffic through the distribution VDCs for L3 switching. Verify the CPU and memory utilization on all of the devices in the Node List. Run this test to completion three times and record the results.
Expected Results:	This is a scalability test for the entire FEX architecture (not for a single FEX). The results of the test will be reported in the Observed Results section.
Observed Results:	
Pass/Fail:	

Table 14-6   *FEX Architecture Latency Test*

Test ID:	DC-PERF-3
Node List:	Routers: DIST-VDC-1, DIST-VDC-2
	Switches: N5K-1, N5K-2
	Fabric Extenders: N2K-1, N2K-2
Test Phase:	Performance
Test Description:	FEX Architecture Latency Test

Table 14-6   *FEX Architecture Latency Test*

Test Setup:	• Build the network, as shown in Figure 14-1. • Configure all services, such as VDCs, multicast, and QoS, that are required by the design. • Configure all the L2 features as per design requirements, including IP VLANs, SAN VLANs, and vPCs. • Bring up the FEX interfaces as unified I/O trunk ports between the Ixia tool's CNA adapters and the N2Ks. Both IP and SAN VLANs should be in forwarding state. • Configure all of the routing protocols between the routers in the Node List. • Configure HSRP for all the appropriate SVIs.
Test Steps:	**Step 1.** Run the Ixia RFC2544 Latency test using the two Ixia interfaces connected to N2K-1 using the same VLAN. Verify the CPU and memory utilization on all of the devices in the Node List. Run this test to completion three times and record the results.
	Step 2. Run the Ixia RFC2544 Latency test using one Ixia interface connected to N2K-1 and one connected to N2K-2 on the same VLAN. Verify the CPU and memory utilization on all of the devices in the Node List. Run this test to completion three times and record the results.
	Step 3. Run the Ixia RFC2544 Latency test using the two Ixia interfaces connected to N2K-1 using two different VLANs. This should send the traffic through the distribution VDCs for L3 switching. Verify the CPU and memory utilization on all of the devices in the Node List. Run this test to completion three times and record the results.
	Step 4. Run the Ixia RFC2544 Latency test using one Ixia interface connected to N2K-1 and one connected to N2K-2 across two different VLANs. This will send the traffic through the distribution VDCs where L3 switching will occur. Verify the CPU and memory utilization on all of the devices in the Node List. Run this test to completion three times and record the results.
Expected Results:	This is a latency test for the entire FEX architecture. The results of the test will be reported in the Observed Results section.
Observed Results:	
Pass/Fail:	

Table 14-7   *FCoE Throughput Test*

Test ID:	DC-PERF-4
Node List:	Switches: N5K-1, N5K-2
	Fabric Extenders: N2K-1, N2K-2
	SAN Directors: MDS-1, MDS-2
	Other: Lab Storage Array
Test Phase:	Performance
Test Description:	FCoE Throughput Test
Test Setup:	• Build the network, as shown in Figure 14-2.
	• Configure all services, such as VDCs, multicast, and QoS, that are required by the design.
	• Configure all the L2 features as per design requirements, including IP VLANs, SAN VLANs, and vPCs.
	• Bring up the FEX interfaces as unified I/O ports for the Ixia tool's CNA adapters.
	• Configure all of the routing protocols between the routers in the Node List.
	• Configure the SAN and FCoE as per the design parameters.
Test Steps:	**Step 1.** On the Ixia FCoE-capable port connected to N2K-1, run the IxSAN FCoE Throughput test against the storage array. Verify the CPU and memory utilization on all of the devices in the Node List.
	Run this test to completion three times and record the results.
	Step 2. On the Ixia FCoE-capable ports connected to both N2K-1 and N2K-2, run the IxSAN FCoE Throughput test against the storage array. Verify the CPU and memory utilization on all of the devices in the Node List.
	Run this test to completion three times and record the results. Check the utilization of FC links, disks, etc. throughout this test because the gating factor may be the MDS 9509/FC Uplinks or the storage array itself.
Expected Results:	This is a scalability test for the entire FEX/SAN architecture. The results of the test will be reported in the Observed Results section.
Observed Results:	
Pass/Fail:	

Table 14-8 *Virtual Device Context (VDC) Feature Validation Test*

Test ID:	DC-FEAT-1
Node List:	Routers: CORE-VDC-1, CORE-VDC-2, DIST-VDC-1, DIST-VDC-2 Physical Switches: Nexus 7010s
Test Phase:	Feature
Test Description:	Virtual Device Context (VDC) Feature Validation Test
Test Setup:	• Configure two separate VDCs in each Nexus 7010, a distribution VDC and a core VDC. Both of these VDCs should not be the default VDC. • Allocate Ethernet ports to each of the created VDCs, as per the architecture and Figure 14-1. • Set up the configurations in each VDC as per the test diagram.
Test Steps:	**Step 1.** Validate that each VDC is up and running and sees the assigned ports, memory, and resources as expected.
	Step 2. Confirm that each VDC is running as a separate logical router with its own Routing Information Base (RIB) and Forwarding Information Base (FIB), and other processes.
	Step 3. From the default VDC, add an extra Gigabit Ethernet interface to VDC DIST-VDC-1. Verify that the new interface is visible in the VDC and configurable.
	Step 4. Remove the interface added in Step 3. Check to see if the interface and its associated configuration have been removed.
	Step 5. Create a SPAN session in VDC CORE-VDC-1. Check that it is working.
	Step 6. Disable the SPAN session.
	Step 7. In the default VDC, create a resource limit for the VDC CORE-VDC-1 setting the allowed number of SPAN sessions to 0. `switch# `**`config t`** `switch(config)# `**`vdc CORE-VDC-1`** `switch(config-vdc)# `**`limit-resource monitor-session minimum 0 maximum 0`**
	Step 8. Attempt to re-create the SPAN session in CORE-VDC-1.

Table 14-8   *Virtual Device Context (VDC) Feature Validation Test*

	Step 9. Connect to VDC CORE-VDC-2 and reload it. Verify that DIST-VDC-2 and the default VDC stay functional while the core VDC reloads. Check that the VDC comes back up correctly.
Expected Results:	Each VDC runs as a separate logical router. The changes made in the default VDC to the other VDC's resource limits and physical interfaces are reflected in the logical router.
Observed Results:	
Pass/Fail:	

Table 14-9   *Virtual Port Channel (vPC) Validation Test*

Test ID:	DC-FEAT-2
Node List:	Routers: DIST-VDC-1, DIST-VDC-2 Switches: N5K-1, N5K-2, 6500-1 Fabric Extenders: N2K-1, N2K-2
Test Phase:	Feature
Test Description:	Virtual Port Channel (vPC) Validation Test
Test Setup:	• Build the network, as shown in Figure 14-1. • Configure all the vPCs as per the architecture design. This includes setting up the vPC peer link port-channel and keepalive links. • Make DIST-VDC-1 and N5K-1 the primary switches for their VPC domains by setting their role priority to 2000. • Bring up a vPC between DIST-VDC-1, DIST-VDC-2, and 6500-1. • Bring up a vPC between N5K-1, N5K-2 and N2K-1 and N2K-2 to create a dual-homed FEX topology. • Bring up the vPC between DIST-VDC-1, DIST-VDC-2 and N5K-1, N5K-2.

Table 14-9 *Virtual Port Channel (vPC) Validation Test*

Test Steps:	**Step 1.** Verify all of the vPCs are up and running and that the correct switches are primary for their domains.
	Step 2. Check that the vPC between the 6500-1 and DIST-VDC-1, DIST-VDC-2 is seen as a "regular" port-channel from the 6500-1 perspective.
	Step 3. Start the traffic flows described in the "Traffic Flows for All Tests" section.
	Step 4. With the traffic running, disable the interface between DIST-VDC-1 and 6500-1, check the state of the vPC, and verify that the traffic is still being forwarded.
	Step 5. Reverse the change in Step 4. Check the state of the vPC and verify that the traffic is still being forwarded.
	Step 6. With the traffic running, disable the interface between DIST-VDC-2 and 6500-1, check the state of the vPC, and verify that the traffic is still being forwarded.
	Step 7. Reverse the change in Step 6. Check the state of the vPC and verify that the traffic is still being forwarded.
	Step 8. With the traffic running, disable the two interfaces between N5K-1 and N2K-1, check the state of the vPC, and verify that the traffic is still being forwarded.
	Step 9. Reverse the change in Step 8. Check the state of the vPC and verify that the traffic is still being forwarded.
	Step 10. With the traffic running, disable one of the interfaces between N5K-2 and N2K-1, check the state of the vPC, and verify that the traffic is still being forwarded. Disable the second interface between N5K-2 and N2K-1, check the state of the vPC, and verify that the traffic is still being forwarded.
	Step 11. Reverse the change in Step 10 one interface at a time. Each time, check the state of the vPC and verify that the traffic is still being forwarded.
	Step 12. With the traffic running, disable one of the interfaces between N5K-1 and N5K-1 (one of the vPC peer links), check the state of the vPC, and verify that the traffic is still being forwarded. Disable the second vPC peer link interface, check the state of the vPC, and verify that the traffic is still being forwarded.

Table 14-9   *Virtual Port Channel (vPC) Validation Test*

Step 13.	Reverse the change in Step 12 one interface at a time. Each time check the state of the vPC and verify that the traffic is still being forwarded.
Step 14.	With the traffic running disable one the interfaces between DIST-VDC-2 and DIST-VDC-2 (one of the vPC peer links), check the state of the vPC, and verify that the traffic is still being forwarded. Disable the second vPC peer link interface check the state of the vPC and verify that the traffic is still being forwarded.
Step 15.	Reverse the change in Step 14 one interface at a time. Each time, check the state of the vPC and verify that the traffic is still being forwarded.
Step 16.	Shut down the vPC peer keepalive link between N5K-1 and N5K-2, check the state of the vPC, and verify that the traffic is still being forwarded.
Step 17.	Reverse the change in Step 16. Verify the state of the vPC and that the traffic is still being forwarded.
Step 18.	Physically disconnect the two connections between N5K-1 and DIST-VDC-1. Check the state of the vPCs on both the N5Ks and DIST-VDCs, and verify that the traffic is still being forwarded. Disconnect one of the interfaces between N5K-1 and DIST-VDC-2. Check the state of the vPCs on both the N5Ks and DIST-VDCs, and verify that the traffic is still being forwarded. Disconnect the final interface between N5K-1 and DIST-VDC-2. Check the state of the vPCs on both the N5Ks and DIST-VDCs, and verify that the traffic is still being forwarded.
Step 19.	Reconnect all of the interfaces between N5K-1 and DIST-VDC-1 and DIST-VDC-2. Check the state of the vPCs on both the N5Ks and DIST-VDCs, and verify that the traffic is still being forwarded.
Step 20.	Physically disconnect the vPC peer keepalive link between DIST-VDC-1 and DIST-VDC-2, check the state of the vPC and verify that the traffic is still being forwarded.
Step 21.	Reconnect the vPC peer keepalive link disconnected in Step 20. Verify the state of the vPC and that the traffic is still being forwarded.

Table 14-9 *Virtual Port Channel (vPC) Validation Test*

Expected Results:	All of the traffic, unicast IP, multicast IP, and FCoE should fail over.
Observed Results:	
Pass/Fail:	

Table 14-10 *Fabric Interconnect Feature Validation Test*

Test ID:	DC-FEAT-3
Node List:	Switches: N5K-1, N5K-2 Fabric Extenders: N2K-1, N2K-2
Test Phase:	Feature
Test Description:	Fabric Interconnect Feature Validation Test
Test Setup:	• Build the IP network, as shown in Figure 14-1. • Build the SAN, as shown in Figure 14-2. • Associate N2K-1 as FEX 100 and N2K-2 as FEX 200. • Bring up the FEX interfaces as unified I/O trunk ports between the Ixia tool's CNA adapters and the N2Ks. Both IP and SAN VLANs should be in forwarding state. • Configure the SAN and FCoE as per the design parameters, and tie the virtual Fibre Channel (vFC) interfaces in N2K-1 to VSAN 100 and in N2K-2 to VSAN 200.
Test Steps:	**Step 1.** Start the traffic flows described in the "Traffic Flows for All Tests" section.
	Step 2. Shut down one of the test ports on N2K-1. Verify that the appropriate traffic stopped being forwarded.
	Step 3. Reverse the change in Step 2 and note how long it takes for traffic to resume being forwarded.
	Step 4. Configure one of the test ports on N2K-1 as a host interface by using the **switchport host** command. Shut down the interface and verify that the appropriate traffic stopped being forwarded.

Table 14-10   *Fabric Interconnect Feature Validation Test*

Step 5.	Reverse the change in Step 4 and note how long it takes for traffic to resume being forwarded.
Step 6.	Disconnect the Ixia test port from the interface configured as a host port and plug in a switch or any device that produces BPDUs. Check if the interface gets "error-disabled."
Step 7.	Reconnect the Ixia test port and bring the N2K-1 interface back up. Verify that traffic is being forwarded.
Step 8.	Connect a switch or router to a "non-host port" on N2K-2 and enable CDP and LLDP on both the router and the N2K-2. Verify that both CDP and LLDP work as expected.
Step 9.	Verify whether IGMP snooping is working on the FEX ports by checking the multicast tables in both N5K-1 and N5K-2. IGMP snooping will also be verified in Steps 10 and 11.
Step 10.	Set up a SPAN for all the traffic being forwarded to the second Ixia port in N2K-1 (this is the port that is *not* generating the multicast traffic). Set the SPAN destination to one of the ports on N5K-1 and attach a laptop running Wireshark. Check that the traffic is indeed being exported to the destination port. Verify IGMP is working and that multicast traffic is being forwarded to this port, because it is subscribed to all of the multicast groups.
Step 11.	Connect the laptop to a port on N2K-1 in the same IP VLAN as the Ixia port receiving the multicast traffic. Run Wireshark and verify that no multicast traffic is being received on this port.
Step 12.	Configure the Ixia port connected to N2K-2 to add another VLAN to its trunk. This VLAN should exist in N5K-1 and N5K-2 and have an SVI reachable in the distribution routers. This VLAN *should not be allowed* on the trunk configured for the FEX port. Verify that the SVI IP address for the newly added VLAN is not reachable via ping. Check the interface trunking and make sure this new VLAN is still in the not allowed list.
Step 13.	Allow the VLAN added to the Ixia port in Step 12 on the interface trunk. Check to make sure the VLAN is now forwarding on the port. Verify that the Ixia chassis can now ping the SVI address.

Table 14-10   *Fabric Interconnect Feature Validation Test*

	Step 14. Verify zoning configured on both VSANs is working correctly for the FEX by checking that the IxSAN test tool can reach its configured LUN over both FEXs. Check that the test tool cannot see any of the LUNs for which it is not zoned.
	Step 15. From the N5K-1 and N5K-2 switches, verify that all of the port, serial number, code version, pinning, and name information for both N2K-1 and N2K-2 can be displayed via the CLI.
	Step 16. Enable and disable the locator LEDs on both N2K-1 and N2K-2.
Expected Results:	Host port, BPDU Guard, CDP, LLDP, IGMP, SPAN, FCoE, FEX CLI information, and the locator LED features should all work as expected for the Nexus 2232PP Fabric Extenders under test.
Observed Results:	
Pass/Fail:	

Table 14-11   *SAN Feature Validation Test*

Test ID:	DC-FEAT-4
Node List:	Switches: N5K-1, N5K-2
	Fabric Extenders: N2K-1, N2K-2
	SAN Directors: MDS-1, MDS-2
	Other: Lab Storage Array
Test Phase:	Feature
Test Description:	SAN Feature Validation Test

Table 14-11   *SAN Feature Validation Test*

Test Setup:	• Build the SAN, as shown in Figure 14-2.
	• Configure the SAN and FCoE as per the design parameters, and tie the vFC interfaces in N2K-1 to VSAN 100 and in N2K-2 to VSAN 200.
	• Configure N-Port Virtualization (NPV) mode for both N5K-1 and N5K-2. Configure the MDS-1 and MDS-2 for N-Port ID Virtualization (NPIV).
	• Configure separate zone sets for each VSAN (100 and 200). MDS-1 should have VSAN 100 configured and MDS-2 should have VSAN 200 configured.
	• The lab storage array should provide failover for the SAN by having FC interfaces connected into both MDSs, and having the LUNs masked in a way that allows them to be reachable via interfaces and correct initiators in both VSANs.
	• Connect a host with a two-port CNA (or two separate CNAs) to both N2K-1 and N2K-2. Configure the two FEX ports for unified I/O. Mask and zone a LUN for this host that is reachable over both VSANs. Install an OS locally on the host that will be able to use and see the LUN, as well as fail over between its two host bus adapters (HBA) to reach the test LUN. Install Iometer on the host.
Test Steps:	**Step 1.** Check the Fibre Channel name server (FCNS) statistics in the MDS Directors to verify that the Nexus 5020 switches have logged into the fabric using the NPV feature.
	Step 2. Verify that "test" FCoE ports are logged into the SAN fabrics of both MDSs. Check to see whether they have been assigned a Fibre Channel ID (FCID).
	Step 3. Configure the lab storage array to present a new LUN to the WWPN of the FCoE test tool connected to N2K-1. Make sure this new LUN is using the same FC interfaces that are already zoned in the MDSs. Verify whether the test tool "sees" the new LUN (this may require a rescan on the test tool).
	Step 4. Remove the lab storage array from the zone configured for the FCoE test tool connected to N2K-1. Activate the modified zone set. Check if the test tool still can reach/see the LUN.
	Step 5. Add the lab storage array back to the zone configured for the FCoE test tool connected to N2K-1. Activate the modified zone set. Check if the test tool can reach/see the LUN.

Table 14-11   *SAN Feature Validation Test*

	Step 6. Verify that the dual-connected host can see its LUN via both HBA interfaces. Change the zoning in MDS-2 by removing the lab storage array from the zone configured for the dual-connected host. Activate the changed zone set. Rescan the SAN from the host and verify that it now can only see the LUN on the interface connected to N2K-1.
	Step 7. Change back the zone configured for the dual-connected host in MDS-2 by adding the lab storage array back to it. Activate the changed zone set. Rescan the SAN from the host and verify that it now can see the LUN on both CNA ports.
	Step 8. Set up the dual-connected host so that it will use the interface connected to N2K-1 to reach its test LUN. Verify that the interface connected to N2K-2 can also "see" the LUN. Start Iometer and run a 30-minute I/O read/write test at 2 IOps against the test LUN, and set the runtime statistics to the lowest possible number the system will support. Begin the Iometer test. Verify that the test is running successfully over N2K-1.
	Step 9. With the Iometer test running, change the zoning in MDS-1 by removing the lab storage array from the zone configured for the dual-connected host. Activate the changed zone set. Verify whether the Iometer test fails over to using the port on N2K-2.
Expected Results:	All of the SAN zoning will be controlled on the MDSs and work as expected. The dual-connected host will be able to reach its LUN over both fabrics and use the dual-fabric design for SAN failover/HA.
Observed Results:	
Pass/Fail:	

Table 14-12 *In Service Software Upgrade (ISSU) Feature Validation Test*

Test ID:	DC-FEAT-5
Node List:	Routers: N7K-1, N7K-2
	Switches: N5K-1, N5K-2
	Fabric Extenders: N2K-1, N2K-2
Test Phase:	Feature
Test Description:	In Service Software Upgrade (ISSU) Feature Validation Test
Test Setup:	• Build the IP network, as shown in Figure 14-1.
	• Build the SAN, as shown in Figure 14-2.
	• Configure all services, such as VDCs, multicast, and QoS, that are required by the design.
	• Configure all the L2 features as per design requirements, including IP VLANs, SAN VLANs, and vPCs.
	• Bring up the FEX interfaces as unified I/O trunk ports between the Ixia tool's CNA adapters and the N2Ks. Both IP and SAN VLANs should be in forwarding state.
	• Configure all of the routing protocols between the routers in the Node List.
	• Configure the SAN and FCoE as per the design parameters.
	• Connect a host with a two-port CNA (or two separate CNAs) to both N2K-1 and N2K-2. Configure the two FEX ports for unified I/O. Mask and zone a LUN for this host that is reachable over both VSANs. Install an OS locally on the host that will be able to use and see a test LUN, as well as fail over between its two HBAs to reach the LUN. Install or use the existing HA IP interface driver on the host. Set up the two 10-Gigabit Ethernet interfaces to run in an active/standby mode. Install Iometer on the host.
	• Set up the dual-connected host so that it will use the interface connected to N2K-1 to reach its test LUN. Verify that the interface connected to N2K-2 can also "see" the LUN. Start Iometer and run a 24-hour I/O read/write test at 2 IOps against the test LUN, and set the runtime statistics to the lowest possible number the system will support. Begin the Iometer test. Verify that the test is running successfully over N2K-1.
	• Set up the dual-connected host to run two continuous pings, one to its HSRP default gateway IP address and one to the 2800-1 router's branch LAN interface's IP address.
	• Start the traffic flows described in the "Traffic Flows for All Tests" section.

Table 14-12 *In Service Software Upgrade (ISSU) Feature Validation Test*

Test Steps:	Monitor the traffic flows described in the "Traffic Flows for All Tests" section, as well as the pings and Iometer statistics from the dual-connected host, to verify that no traffic is dropped during any of the steps of this test. Monitor all syslog messages generated by these tests.
	Step 1. Perform an ISSU for N7K-1.
	Step 2. Wait until the network is stable after Step 1 and perform an ISSU for N5K-1. Set up a rolling ISSU upgrade for N2K-1 and N2K-2 using N5K-1.
	Step 3. Wait until N5K-1 and both FEXs are upgraded using ISSU, and then run an ISSU for N5K-2.
Expected Results:	All of the In Service Software Upgrades should cause no impact to any traffic forwarding.
Observed Results:	
Pass/Fail:	

Table 14-13 *Chassis Failure and Recovery Test*

Test ID:	DC-DUTY-1
Node List:	Routers: CORE-VDC-1, CORE-VDC-2, DIST-VDC-1, DIST-VDC-2, 7200-1, 7200-2, 2800-1, PE-1, PE-2, PE-3
	Switches: N5K-1, N5K-2, 6500-1
	Fabric Extenders: N2K-1, N2K-2
	SAN Directors: MDS-1, MDS-2
Test Phase:	Duty Cycle
Test Description:	Chassis Failure and Recovery Test

Table 14-13 *Chassis Failure and Recovery Test*

Test Setup:	• Build the IP network, as shown in Figure 14-1. • Build the SAN, as shown in Figure 14-2. • Configure all services, such as VDCs, multicast, and QoS, that are required by the design. • Configure all the L2 features as per design requirements, including IP VLANs, SAN VLANs, and vPCs. • Bring up the FEX interfaces as unified I/O trunk ports between the Ixia tool's CNA adapters and the N2Ks. Both IP and SAN VLANs should be in forwarding state. • Configure all of the routing protocols between the routers in the Node List. • Configure the SAN and FCoE as per the design parameters. • Connect a host with a two-port CNA (or two separate CNAs) to both N2K-1 and N2K-2. Configure the two FEX ports for unified I/O. Mask and zone a LUN for this host that is reachable over both VSANs. Install an OS locally on the host that will be able to use and see a test LUN, as well as fail over between its two HBAs to reach the LUN. Install or use the existing HA IP interface driver on the host. Set up the two 10-Gigabit Ethernet interfaces to run in an active/standby mode. Install Iometer on the host. • Set up the dual-connected host so that it will use the interface connected to N2K-1 to reach its test LUN. Verify that the interface connected to N2K-2 can also "see" the LUN. Start Iometer and run a 24-hour I/O read/write test at 2 IOps against the test LUN, and set the runtime statistics to the lowest possible number the system will support. Begin the Iometer test. Verify that the test is running successfully over N2K-1. • Set up the dual-connected host to run two continuous pings, one to its HSRP default gateway IP address and one to the 2800-1 router's branch LAN interface's IP address. • Start the traffic flows described in the "Traffic Flows for All Tests" section.
Test Steps:	Monitor the traffic flows described in the "Traffic Flows for All Tests" section, as well as the pings and Iometer statistics from the dual-connected host, to verify failover times for all of the steps of this test. Monitor all syslog messages generated by these tests.
	Step 1. Power down/suspend CORE-VDC-1 (using the CLI).
	Step 2. Wait until the network is stable after Step 1 and power CORE-VDC-1 back up.
	Step 3. Power down/suspend DIST-VDC-1 (using the CLI).

Table 14-13 *Chassis Failure and Recovery Test*

	Step 4. Wait until the network is stable after Step 3 and power DIST-VDC-1 back up.
	Step 5. Power down N7K-2 (the entire chassis).
	Step 6. Wait until the network is stable after Step 5 and power N7K-2 back up.
	Step 7. Power down N5K-1.
	Step 8. Wait until the network is stable after Step 7 and power N5K-1 back up.
	Step 9. Power down MDS-1.
	Step 10. Wait until the SAN is stable after Step 9 and power MDS-1 back up.
	Step 11. Power down N2K-1.
	Step 12. Wait until the dual-connected host has failed over after Step 11, and power N2K-1 back up.
Expected Results:	All the traffic should fail over successfully, except during Step 11, where only the dual-connected host will be able to fail over.
Observed Results:	
Pass/Fail:	

Table 14-14 *Line Card Failure and Recovery Test*

Test ID:	DC-DUTY-2
Node List:	Routers: CORE-VDC-1, CORE-VDC-2, DIST-VDC-1, DIST-VDC-2, 7200-1, 7200-2, 2800-1, PE-1, PE-2, PE-3
	Switches: N5K-1, N5K-2, 6500-1
	Fabric Extenders: N2K-1, N2K-2
	SAN Directors: MDS-1, MDS-2
Test Phase:	Duty Cycle
Test Description:	Line Card Failure and Recovery Test

Table 14-14   *Line Card Failure and Recovery Test*

Test Setup:	• Build the IP network, as shown in Figure 14-1. • Build the SAN, as shown in Figure 14-2. • Configure all services, such as VDCs, multicast, and QoS, that are required by the design. • Configure all the L2 features as per design requirements, including IP VLANs, SAN VLANs, and vPCs. • Bring up the FEX interfaces as unified I/O trunk ports between the Ixia tool's CNA adapters and the N2Ks. Both IP and SAN VLANs should be in forwarding state. • Configure all of the routing protocols between the routers in the Node List. • Configure the SAN and FCoE as per the design parameters. • Connect a host with a two-port CNA (or two separate CNAs) to both N2K-1 and N2K-2. Configure the two FEX ports for unified I/O. Mask and zone a LUN for this host that is reachable over both VSANs. Install an OS locally on the host that will be able to use and see a test LUN, as well as fail over between its two HBAs to reach the LUN. Install or use the existing HA IP interface driver on the host. Set up the two 10-Gigabit Ethernet interfaces to run in an active/standby mode. Install Iometer on the host. • Set up the dual-connected host so that it will use the interface connected to N2K-1 to reach its test LUN. Verify that the interface connected to N2K-2 can also "see" the LUN. Start Iometer and run a 24-hour I/O read/write test at 2 IOps against the test LUN, and set the runtime statistics to the lowest possible number the system will support. Begin the Iometer test. Verify that the test is running successfully over N2K-1. • Set up the dual-connected host to run two continuous pings, one to its HSRP default gateway IP address and one to the 2800-1 router's branch LAN interface's IP address. • Start the traffic flows described in the "Traffic Flows for All Tests" section.
Test Steps:	Monitor the traffic flows described in the "Traffic Flows for All Tests" section, as well as the pings and Iometer statistics from the dual-connected host, to verify failover times for all of the steps of this test. Monitor all syslog messages generated by these tests.
	Step 1. Remove Linecard 5 (with shared ports between CORE-VDC-1 and DIST-VDC-1, and connections to 7200-1, CORE-VDC-2, DIST-VDC-2, and 6500-1) from N7K-1.

Table 14-14   *Line Card Failure and Recovery Test*

	Step 2. Wait until the network is stable after Step 1 and reinsert Linecard 5 into N7K-1.
	Step 3. Remove the active Supervisor from N7K-2.
	Step 4. Wait until the network is stable after Step 3 and reinsert the Supervisor into N7K-2
	Step 5. Make the secondary Supervisor in N7K-2 active.
	Step 6. Remove Linecard 1 (connected to N5K-1) from MDS-1.
	Step 7. Wait until the SAN is stable after Step 6 and reinsert Linecard 1.
	Step 8. Remove the active Supervisor from MDS-2.
	Step 9. Wait until the SAN is stable after Step 8 and reinsert the Supervisor into MDS-2.
	Step 10. Make the secondary Supervisor in MDS-2 active.
Expected Results:	All the traffic should fail over successfully.
Observed Results:	
Pass/Fail:	

Table 14-15   *Interface Failure and Recovery Test*

Test ID:	DC-DUTY-3
Node List:	Routers: CORE-VDC-1, CORE-VDC-2, DIST-VDC-1, DIST-VDC-2, 7200-1, 7200-2, 2800-1, PE-1, PE-2, PE-3
	Switches: N5K-1, N5K-2, 6500-1
	Fabric Extenders: N2K-1, N2K-2
	SAN Directors: MDS-1, MDS-2
Test Phase:	Duty Cycle
Test Description:	Interface Failure and Recovery Test

Table 14-15   *Interface Failure and Recovery Test*

Test Setup:	• Build the IP network, as shown in Figure 14-1. • Build the SAN, as shown in Figure 14-2. • Configure all services, such as VDCs, multicast, and QoS, that are required by the design. • Configure all the L2 features as per design requirements, including IP VLANs, SAN VLANs, and vPCs. • Bring up the FEX interfaces as unified I/O trunk ports between the Ixia tool's CNA adapters and the N2Ks. Both IP and SAN VLANs should be in forwarding state. • Configure all of the routing protocols between the routers in the Node List. • Configure the SAN and FCoE as per the design parameters. • Connect a host with a two-port CNA (or two separate CNAs) to both N2K-1 and N2K-2. Configure the two FEX ports for unified I/O. Mask and zone a LUN for this host that is reachable over both VSANs. Install an OS locally on the host that will be able to use and see a test LUN, as well as fail over between its two HBAs to reach the LUN. Install or use the existing HA IP interface driver on the host. Set up the two 10-Gigabit Ethernet interfaces to run in an active/standby mode. Install Iometer on the host. • Set up the dual-connected host so that it will use the interface connected to N2K-1 to reach its test LUN. Verify that the interface connected to N2K-2 can also "see" the LUN. Start Iometer and run a 24-hour I/O read/write test at 2 IOps against the test LUN, and set the runtime statistics to the lowest possible number the system will support. Begin the Iometer test. Verify that the test is running successfully over N2K-1. • Set up the dual-connected host to run two continuous pings, one to its HSRP default gateway IP address and one to the 2800-1 router's branch LAN interface's IP address. • Start the traffic flows described in the "Traffic Flows for All Tests" section.
Test Steps:	Monitor the traffic flows described in the "Traffic Flows for All Tests" section, as well as the pings and Iometer statistics from the dual-connected host, to verify failover times for all of the steps of this test. Monitor all syslog messages generated by these tests.
	Step 1. Remove the cable from the interface between CORE-VDC-1 and 7200-1.

Table 14-15 *Interface Failure and Recovery Test*

Step 2. Wait until the network is stable after Step 1 and reinsert the cable.
Step 3. Remove the cable from one of the interfaces between CORE-VDC-1 and CORE-VDC-2.
Step 4. Wait until the network is stable after Step 3 and reinsert the cable.
Step 5. Remove the cable from one of the interfaces between CORE-VDC-1 and DIST-VDC-1.
Step 6. Wait until the network is stable after Step 5 and reinsert the cable.
Step 7. Remove the cable from the interface between DIST-VDC-1 and 6500-1.
Step 8. Wait until the network is stable after Step 7 and reinsert the cable.
Step 9. Remove the cable from one of the interfaces between DIST-VDC-1 and DIST-VDC-2.
Step 10. Wait until the network is stable after Step 9 and reinsert the cable.
Step 11. Remove the cable from one of the interfaces between DIST-VDC-1 and N5K-2.
Step 12. Wait until the network is stable after Step 11 and reinsert the cable.
Step 13. Remove the cable from one of the interfaces between N5K-1 and N5K-2.
Step 14. Wait until the network is stable after Step 13 and reinsert the cable.
Step 15. Remove the cable from one of the interfaces between N5K1 and N2K-2.
Step 16. Wait until the network is stable after Step 15 and reinsert the cable.
Step 17. Remove the cable from one of the Fibre Channel interfaces between N5K-1 and MDS-1.

Table 14-15   *Interface Failure and Recovery Test*

	Step 18. Wait until the network is stable after Step 17 and reinsert the cable.
Expected Results:	All the traffic should fail over successfully for each test.
Observed Results:	
Pass/Fail:	

Table 14-16   *Software Forced Failover Test*

Test ID:	DC-DUTY-4
Node List:	Routers: CORE-VDC-1, CORE-VDC-2, DIST-VDC-1, DIST-VDC-2, 7200-1, 7200-2, 2800-1, PE-1, PE-2, PE-3
	Switches: N5K-1, N5K-2, 6500-1
	Fabric Extenders: N2K-1, N2K-2
	SAN Directors: MDS-1, MDS-2
Test Phase:	Duty Cycle
Test Description:	Software Forced Failover Test

Table 14-16 *Software Forced Failover Test*

Test Setup:	<ul><li>Build the IP network, as shown in Figure 14-1.</li><li>Build the SAN, as shown in Figure 14-2.</li><li>Configure all services, such as VDCs, multicast, and QoS, that are required by the design.</li><li>Configure all the L2 features as per design requirements, including IP VLANs, SAN VLANs, and vPCs.</li><li>Bring up the FEX interfaces as unified I/O trunk ports between the Ixia tool's CNA adapters and the N2Ks. Both IP and SAN VLANs should be in forwarding state.</li><li>Configure all of the routing protocols between the routers in the Node List.</li><li>Configure the SAN and FCoE as per the design parameters.</li><li>Connect a host with a two-port CNA (or two separate CNAs) to both N2K-1 and N2K-2. Configure the two FEX ports for unified I/O. Mask and zone a LUN for this host that is reachable over both VSANs. Install an OS locally on the host that will be able to use and see a test LUN, as well as fail over between its two HBAs to reach the LUN. Install or use the existing HA IP interface driver on the host. Set up the two 10-Gigabit Ethernet interfaces to run in an active/standby mode. Install Iometer on the host.</li><li>Set up the dual-connected host so that it will use the interface connected to N2K-1 to reach its test LUN. Verify that the interface connected to N2K-2 can also "see" the LUN. Start Iometer and run a 24-hour I/O read/write test at 2 IOps against the test LUN, and set the runtime statistics to the lowest possible number the system will support. Begin the Iometer test. Verify that the test is running successfully over N2K-1.</li><li>Set up the dual-connected host to run two continuous pings, one to its HSRP default gateway IP address and one to the 2800-1 router's branch LAN interface's IP address.</li><li>Start the traffic flows described in the "Traffic Flows for All Tests" section.</li></ul>
Test Steps:	Monitor the traffic flows described in the "Traffic Flows for All Tests" section, as well as the pings and Iometer statistics from the dual-connected host, to verify failover times for all of the steps of this test. Monitor all syslog messages generated by these tests.

Table 14-16 *Software Forced Failover Test*

Step 1.	Rerun all of the tests in DC-DUTY-1, DC-DUTY-2, and DC-DUTY-3 using NXOS commands to cause the "failures." Reload the N7Ks, N5K, N2Ks, and MDSs, reset or soft power down the line cards, and shut down the interfaces as appropriate.
Step 2.	Cause a failover by resetting the OSPF process in CORE-VDC-1.
Step 3.	Cause a failover by resetting the BGP process in CORE-VDC-1.
Step 4.	Cause a failover by shutting down an SVI where the HSRP is "active."
Expected Results:	All the traffic should fail over successfully for each test.
Observed Results:	
Pass/Fail:	

End Note

[1] Cisco.com. "Evolving Data Center Architectures: Meet the Challenge with Cisco Nexus 5000 Series Switches." www.cisco.com/en/US/solutions/collateral/ns340/ns517/ns224/ns783/white_paper_c11-473501.html.

Chapter 15

IPv6 Functionality Test Plan

It is a safe assumption that anyone reading this book is at least vaguely aware of Internet Protocol Version 6 (IPv6), the newer version of IP that was designed to overcome the shortcomings and limitations of the IPv4 standard. While up to this point it may have been possible for many network professionals to remain largely ignorant of IPv6 concepts and solutions, the current state of IPv4 address exhaustion is forcing enterprise adoption much faster than expected. By all accounts, it is apparent that IPv6 is being certified, piloted, and in some cases fully integrated into most enterprise networks across the globe. As IPv6 applications and products become more and more integrated into the network, it is imperative that your solutions testing include IPv6 test cases. Because of this ever-increasing necessity, this IPv6 functionality test plan chapter has been added to the book as a starting point and reference for engineers planning to validate IPv6 solutions in their networks.

To get you started on the road of IPv6 testing, we will first present a high-level overview of the technology, pointing out key differences between IPv4 and IPv6, and suggesting when and how testing should be done to certify important features. After taking you through this overview, we will lay out a high-level IPv6 functionality test plan. The chapter does not provide a detailed explanation of every aspect of IPv6 or its various new functions; rather, it lays out its basic functionality and gives guidance on how to develop test approaches.

The IPv6 Specification

IPv6 introduces in its base specification several new features to improve upon some of the shortcomings of IPv4. This high-level protocol overview will highlight some of the nuances you must consider when testing IPv6.

Note This chapter draws from several of the scenarios referenced in RFC 2460, "Internet Protocol, Version 6 (IPv6)."

The current implementation of IPv4 has proven to be robust, easily implemented, and interoperable, and has stood the test of scaling an internetwork to a global utility the size of today's Internet. However, the initial design did not anticipate the following:

■ The recent exponential growth of the Internet and the impending exhaustion of the IPv4 address space.

■ The capability of Internet backbone routers to maintain large routing tables.

■ The need for simpler configuration, better security, and better QoS.

To address these concerns, the Internet Engineering Task Force (IETF) developed a suite of protocols and standards known as IP Version 6 (IPv6). This new version, previously called IP The Next Generation (IPng), incorporates the concepts of many proposed methods for updating the IPv4 protocol.

The specific new features of the IPv6 protocol are

■ New header format

■ Larger address space

■ Stateless and stateful address configuration

■ Built-in security

■ Better support for QoS

■ New protocol for neighboring node interaction

Considerations for IPv6 Testing

The sections that follow highlight some of the new IPv6 features that are covered in this test plan.

IPv6 Header Format

The primary motivation for IPv6 is the need to meet the anticipated future demand for globally unique IP addresses. To meet this requirement, IPv6 has a vastly larger address space than IPv4. This results from the use of a 128-bit address, whereas IPv4 uses only 32 bits. Because of the 128-bit addressing, IPv6 can support 2^{128}, or about 3.4×10^{38}, total unique addresses. The new 40-byte IPv6 header consists of eight fields, as shown in Figure 15-1. The figure shows a comparison between the 20-byte IPv4 header and the IPv6 40-byte base header.

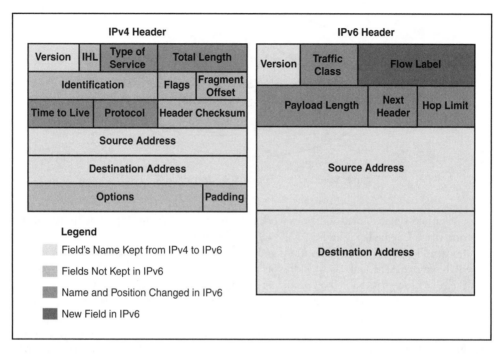

Figure 15-1 *Comparison Between the IPv4 and IPv6 Headers (Source: Cisco com; "IPv6 Extension Headers Review and Considerations" [White Paper], last updated Oct. 2006.)*

Note   The detailed IPv6 field definitions can be found in RFC 2460.

IPv6 Address Scopes

It is important to understand that, due to fundamental operations, multiple IPv6 addresses are expected to be found on a single router interface, whereas in an IPv4 deployment a single address is normally sufficient. In IPv6, specific interfaces may have multiple combinations of unicast addresses from different scopes. Figure 15-2 illustrates how IPv6 unicast address scopes are related to each other.

As Figure 15-2 shows, the IPv6 unicast address scopes are hierarchical. The Global scope, as its names implies, is reachable globally, whereas the Unique Local address space is typically confined within the administrator's domain. Consider the Unique Local space as private IPv6 address blocks similar to IPv4 RFC 1918 space. In turn, the Link Local scope refers to IPv6 addresses only accessible on that physical link.

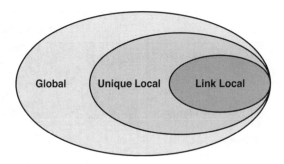

Figure 15-2 *IPv6 Unicast Address Scope*

Global and Unique Local addresses work the same way for the most part, with the exception that a Unique Local address will be filtered at the network boundaries. The Link Local address is extremely important and serves as one of the base foundations of the IPv6 protocol. The Link Local address is automatically assigned by the IPv6 node once the IPv6 process is enabled on particular interfaces. All Link Local unicast addresses are assigned from the prefix fe80::/10 in standard IPv6 notation. This concept holds true for both hosts and routers. Because the Link Local address is not tied to any global addressing scheme, and for the most part does not require to be changed, it is inherently used by most IPv6 routing protocols as a next hop. It is also used for nodes establishing communication on a particular segment. The "ICMPv6" and "IPv6 Neighbor Discovery" sections cover the importance of the Link Local address.

Note   Refer to RFC 4291 for more information on the IPv6 addressing architecture.

Table 15-1 presents a detailed breakdown of all IPv6 address scopes.

Table 15-1   *IPv6 Address Type Prefixes*

Address Type	Binary Prefix	IPv6 Notation
Unspecified	000...0 (128 bits)	::/128
Loopback	000...1 (128 bits)	::1/128
Multicast	11111111	FF00::/8
Link Local (unicast)	1111111010	FE80::/10
Site Local (unicast)	1111111111	FEC0::/10
Global (unicast)	All other addresses	
Anycast	Taken from the unicast address space	

Source: Cisco.com; Cisco ASA 5500 Series Configuration Guide Using the CLI, 8.3, *"Addresses, Protocols, and Ports"* *(in the "Reference" section).*

IPv6 Extension Headers

In additional to the base header, IPv6 uses the concept of IPv6 extension headers (EH). The base IPv6 header is equivalent to the basic IPv4 one, despite some field differences that are the result of lessons learned from operating IPv4 (see Figure 15-1 for more on this). The IPv4 Options field performs a very important role in the IP operation; therefore, the capability had to be preserved in IPv6. On the other hand, the impact of IPv4 Options on performance was taken into consideration in the development of IPv6. In IPv6 the functionality of Options is removed from the main header and implemented through the set of additional EHs. The main header remains fixed in size (40 bytes), while customized EHs are added as needed. Figure 15-3 shows where the extension sits within the header and the capability to stack multiple EHs.

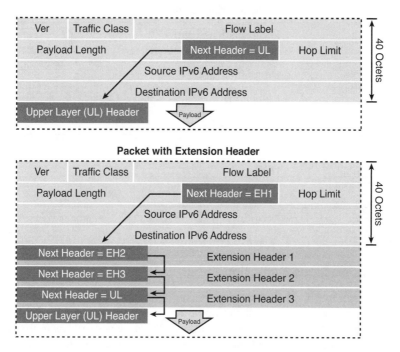

Figure 15-3 *Implementation of IPv6 Extension Headers (Source: Cisco.com; Cisco ASA 5500 Series Configuration Guide Using the CLI, 8.3, "Addresses, Protocols, and Ports" ["Reference" section].)*

RFC 2460 defines the extension headers as shown in Table 15-2, along with the Next Header values assigned to them.

It is important to understand the impact of the IPv6 EHs when testing IPv6. Not all EHs are processed in hardware, and hardware processing capabilities change between different platforms. Understanding the device under test (DUT) limitations in EH handling and making adjustments to your test plan accordingly is vital.

Table 15-2   *IPv6 Extension Headers and Their Recommended Order in a Packet*

Order	Header Type	Next Header Code
1	Basic IPv6 Header	—
2	Hop-by-Hop Options	0
3	Destination Options (with Routing Options)	60
4	Routing Header	43
5	Fragment Header	44
6	Authentication Header	51
7	Encapsulation Security Payload Header	50
8	Destination Options	60
9	Mobility Header	135
	No next header	59
Upper Layer	TCP	6
Upper Layer	UDP	17
Upper Layer	ICMPv6	58

Source: Cisco.com; Cisco ASA 5500 Series Configuration Guide Using the CLI, 8.3, *"Addresses, Protocols, and Ports"* *("Reference" section).*

IPv6 Source Address Selection

As we have discussed, an IPv6 interface is expected to have multiple IPv6 addresses, either statically assigned by an administrator or dynamically assigned by the protocol stack. As one would imagine, these could potentially cause network connectivity issues because an initiating host would need to understand which address to use for a particular function. To solve this, IPv6 implements two specific algorithms, defined in RFC 3484: one for source address selection (SAS) and one for destination address selection (DAS). It is important to understand that SAS will not override the addresses used in upper-layer protocols or a specific application. It simply uses information contained within the specific request and applies it through a list of rules specified within the SAS algorithm. The result generates the address to be used in its communications with an end host. Also, dual- or hybrid-stack implementations, which support both IPv6 and IPv4, very often need to choose between IPv6 and IPv4 when initiating communication. RFC 3484 uses the example of a dual-stack host requesting the IP address of a server from DNS. If the DNS name resolves to a Global IPv6 address and an IPv4 address, SAS will decide which address (IPv4 or IPv6) on the host interface will be used to communicate with the server.

Because of this complexity, SAS must be well understood and tested in any IPv6 implementation.

> **Note** Refer to RFC 3484 for detailed information on default address selection for IPv6.

ICMPv6

ICMPv6 is an integral part of the IPv6 architecture and must be completely supported by all IPv6 implementations. It combines functionalities supported in IPv4 under different protocols: Internet Control Message Protocol Version 4 (ICMPv4), Internet Group Membership Protocol (IGMP), and Address Resolution Protocol (ARP). ICMPv6 runs over IPv6 unicast and multicast; as such, it is nonreliable and cannot be used for features that require reliability.

Similar to ICMPv4, ICMPv6 enables IPv6 nodes to report errors and performs various control plane functions. Many of the existing ICMPv4 functionalities have been carried over to ICMPv6, while some were simplified and many more were added.[1]

ICMPv6 is used in IPv6 for a multitude of functions. ICMPv6 can be found in address resolution, error reporting, autoconfiguration, mobile IPv6, and Path Maximum Transmission Unit Discovery. Testing of ICMPv6 functionality is critical to the success of any IPv6 implementation. The next few sections describe IPv6 features that rely on ICMPv6 to function properly.

> **Note** ICMPv6 is described in RFC 2463.

IPv6 Neighbor Discovery

ICMPv6 is used by the IPv6 Neighbor Discovery Protocol (NDP), which provides IPv6 speakers with a vast variety of operational functionality. Some of the most commonly used features are address resolution, Duplicate Address Detection (DAD), Neighbor Unreachability Detection (NUD), Stateless Address Autoconfiguration, Prefix Request, Neighbor Solicitation (NS), and Router Solicitation (RS). NDP enables IPv6 nodes to build the necessary knowledge to send IPv6 packets to a neighbor automatically. IPv6 nodes will receive advertisements from all local link speakers and create a knowledge base of information required to effectively communicate on that link without causing disruption. The advertisements used to build the knowledge base can be solicited or unsolicited.

From a testing perspective, it is important to understand the following about IPv6 Neighbor Discovery Protocol:

- Neighbor Discovery allows a device to discover the link address of another node on the same subnet. It is a built-in function of IPv6 and replaces the concept of ARP in IPv4.

- Routers send out Router Advertisements (RA) on the local link with multiple fields including information about prefixes assigned to the local LAN. IPv6 hosts obtain interface configuration information, including their Global IPv6 address, from the RAs.

- An IPv6 router will send out RAs periodically, based on a configured timer. IPv6 hosts on the local segment may also send a Router Solicitation message at any time, to obtain a default router or other local router information.

- DAD is one of the initial phases as the IPv6 stack assigns an IPV6 address to an interface. DAD is performed on all IP address scopes, including the Link Local and Global addresses, and it is an integral part of NDP.

Note IPv6 NDP definitions can be found in RFC 2461.

Neighbor discovery details include the following:

- Uses ICMPv6 messages originated from the node's Link Local address with a hop limit of 255

- Consists of IPv6 header, ICMPv6 header, Neighbor Discovery header, and Neighbor Discovery options

- Five defined Neighbor Discovery messages:

  - Router Solicitation (ICMPv6 type 133)

  - Router Advertisement (ICMPv6 type 134)

  - Neighbor Solicitation (ICMPv6 type 135)

  - Neighbor Advertisement (ICMPv6 type 136)

  - Redirect (ICMPV6 type 137)

IPv6 Autoconfiguration

The IPv6 (stateless) autoconfiguration mechanism, commonly referred to as Stateless Address Autoconfiguration (SLAAC), requires no manual configuration of the hosts, minimal configuration of routers, and no additional requirements for address allocation servers. This built-in address allocation method allows a host to generate its own IPv6 addresses, using a combination of locally available information and information advertised by routers on the local segment. The routers advertise IPv6 prefixes that identify the subnet or subnets associated with a particular link, while the hosts generate an "interface identifier" that uniquely identifies an interface on a subnet. An IPv6 address is formed by combining the subnet advertised by the router and the interface identifier from the host. This feature can work independently, or it can be tied into a more comprehensive address allocation back-end system via an additional IPv6 feature referred to as Prefix Delegation. The main focus during test considerations, regardless of the features working independently or using a back-end system, is to understand the local behavior of these messages on the IPv6 nodes.

During the testing phase, the impact of hosts' and routers' behaviors when configuration information is provided requires careful consideration. If an operator chooses not to use SLAAC, the operator needs to understand the impact of turning off the feature, and to make sure that it is disabled on all IPv6 nodes.

Note Detailed information on IPV6 Autoconfiguration (SLAAC) can be found in RFC 4862.

IPv6 PMTUD

Another IPv6 feature that relies on ICMPv6 is IPv6 Path Maximum Transmission Unit Discovery (PMTUD). There are two new rules in IPv6 related to MTU handling:

- The MTU of a link should never be smaller than 1280 bytes.

- Intermediate devices in the communications path do not do packet fragmentation.

Whereas having PMTUD functioning correctly in IPv4 is useful, in IPv6 it is absolutely critical because intermediary devices in IPv6 cannot fragment oversized packets. Careful testing should be conducted to ensure that IPv6 PMTUD is working, particularly when dealing with designs that use overlay networks, which can add extra overhead to your traffic.

IPv6 Security

When integrating any new protocol such as IPv6 into your network, security is a primary concern. In essence, with IPv6, you are enabling for your network another transport that can be used to access your devices and services. This access can be used as designed such as with e-commerce and web services, or for malicious intentions such as a launch point for denial-of-service attack or theft of services.

The primary method for enforcing security on networking devices, such as routers and switches, is to use access control lists (ACL). IPv6 ACLs work similarly to IPv4 ACLs and should be tested the same way. The tests should ensure that IPv6 ACLs can be used to appropriately filter IPv6 traffic and log traffic as configured. Having a good understanding of IPv6 addressing, masking, and scopes is imperative in creating appropriate IPv6 ACLs, as is the understanding of new features such as Neighbor Discovery and extension headers.

When doing IPv6 ACL testing, note the handling of traffic when an ACL is applied, particularly the hit on the DUT's CPU and memory and the increase in packet delivery delay. Each hardware platform, or code level, may handle IPv6 ACLs differently, and understanding these differences is essential.

Tip　Each IPv6 ACL contains implicit permit rules to enable IPv6 Neighbor Discovery. These rules can be overridden by the user by placing a **deny ipv6 any any** statement within an ACL. The IPv6 Neighbor Discovery process uses the IPv6 network layer service; therefore, by default, IPv6 ACLs implicitly allow IPv6 Neighbor Discovery packets to be sent and received on an interface. In IPv4, the Address Resolution Protocol (ARP), which is equivalent to the IPv6 Neighbor Discovery process, uses a separate data link layer protocol; therefore, by default, IPv4 ACLs implicitly allow ARP packets to be sent and received on an interface.[2]

Physical and Logical Test Topology

The test cases in this chapter cover the base functionality required to run an IPv6 network. These basic feature tests should be run for each IPv6 test in conjunction with the solution that will be conducted for your enterprise. They can be conducted on a variety of test topologies. The topology illustrated in Figure 15-4 was used for the test cases in this chapter.

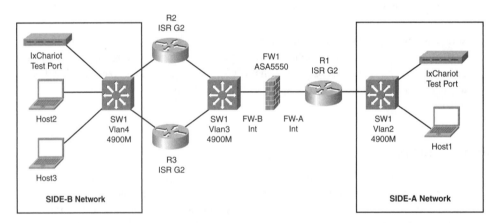

Figure 15-4　*Topology for Basic IPv6 Testing*

Technical details of the test setup are as follows:

- Cisco ISR G2 routers (Cisco 2911 and Cisco 3945) are used for IPv6 L3 testing.

- An ASA 5500 Series Adaptive Security Appliance is used as the IPv6 firewall.

- A Catalyst 4900M with a WS-X4920-GB-RJ45 (20-port wire-speed 10/100/1000 [RJ-45] half-card) expansion module is used as the IPv6 L2 switch.

- The 4900M switch is configured with three separate VLANs: two VLANs for host connectivity (Vlan2 and Vlan4) and one VLAN for connectivity between the firewall and R2 and R3 (Vlan3). This is done to test VLAN separation on the 4900M but is not considered a security best practice. Note that R1 is directly connected to FW1, bypassing the need for a switch connection.

■ SW1 has **spanning-tree portfast** enabled for all host, node, and firewall ports.

■ Microsoft Windows 7 x64 operating systems are running on the hosts.

■ All three hosts have the Wireshark sniffer software installed, which is capable of capturing and decoding IPv6 packets.

■ An IPv6 tester (in our case, Ixia's IxChariot Suite) is connected on both sides of the network.

■ All connections are 1 Gigabit.

■ R1 has a Global Unicast address in the 2001:0DB8:1000::/64 subnet for the SIDE-A Network, and a 2001:0DB8:2000::/64 subnet on the firewall FW-A Int side (understanding that this subnet is only for testing).

■ R2 and R3 have a Global Unicast address in the 2001:0DB8:3000::/64 subnet on the FW-B Int side and 2001:0DB8:4000::/64 on the SIDE-B Network side.

■ There is a static route in R1 for subnet 2001:0DB8:4000::/64 pointed at the FW-A Int interface of the ASA, and from R2 and R3 to 2001:0DB8:1000::/64 pointed at the FW-B Int address of the ASA. This will force all the communication between SIDE-A and SIDE-B to go through the ASA firewall.

■ FW1 has the appropriate static routing configured to connect SIDE-A to SIDE-B.

■ The Global IPv6 addressing is assigned as described in Table 15-3.

Table 15-3 *Global IPv6 Address Assignments for Testing*

Device/Interface	IPv6 Subnet	IPv6 Address
R1/SIDE-A	2001:0DB8:1000::/64	2001:0DB8:1000::1
R1/FW-A Int	2001:0DB8:2000::/64	2001:0DB8:2000::1
R2/FW-B Int	2001:0DB8:3000::/64	2001:0DB8:3000::2
R2/SIDE-B	2001:0DB8:4000::/64	2001:0DB8:4000::2
R3/FW-B Int	2001:0DB8:3000::/64	2001:0DB8:3000::3
R3/SIDE-B	2001:0DB8:4000::/64	2001:0DB8:4000::3
FW-1/FW-A Int	2001:0DB8:2000::/64	2001:0DB8:2000::10
FW-1/FW-B Int	2001:0DB8:3000::/64	2001:0DB8:3000::10
Host1 & Test Port	2001:0DB8:1000::/64	Auto Assigned
Host2 and Host3 & Test Port	2001:0DB8:4000::/64	Auto Assigned

Test Objectives

The primary objectives for this test are as follows:

1. To validate that the DUTs (ISR G2, ASA 5550, and 4900M) can support basic IPv6 functionality.

2. To ensure that the basic IPv6 configurations to be rolled out in the network will function as expected.

Test Case Summary

Table 15-4 contains a brief summary of the tests to be conducted to certify basic IPv6 functionality as previously described.

Table 15-4   *Test Case Summary Table*

Test ID:	Brief Test Description
IPv6-FEAT-1	IPv6 Neighbor Discovery (ND) Test
IPv6-FEAT-2	IPv6 Autoconfiguration (SLAAC) Test
IPv6-FEAT-3	IPv6 Router Advertisement (RA) Test
IPv6-FEAT-4	IPv6 Duplicate Address Detection (DAD) Test
IPv6-FEAT-5	ICMPv6 Ping, Unreachable, and Redirect Test
IPv6-FEAT-6	IPv6 Path MTU Discovery (PMTUD) Test
IPv6-FEAT-7	IPv6 Extension Header Test
IPv6-FEAT-8	IPv6 Basic Access Control List (ACL) Test

Detailed Test Cases

The following tables contain detailed test cases to be conducted to certify the topology described earlier. These cases provide you with guidance on testing basic IPv6 functionality and should be modified to fit your specific needs.

Table 15-5   *IPv6 Neighbor Discovery (ND) Test*

Test ID:	IPv6-FEAT-1
Node List:	R2, R3, SW1, Host3
Test Phase:	Feature
Test Description:	IPv6 Neighbor Discovery (ND) Test

Table 15-5 *IPv6 Neighbor Discovery (ND) Test*

Test Setup:	• Build the IPv6 network, as shown in Figure 15-4. • Enable IPv6 process on all nodes and routers. • Configure IPv6 addressing on all relevant interfaces using the Global IPv6 addresses in Table 15-3. • Allow Host3 to obtain an IPv6 address using Autoconfiguration (SLAAC). • Configure the R2 Link Local address as FE80::1 and the R3 Link Local address as FE80::2.
Test Steps:	**Step 1.** Configure a SPAN session on SW1. The source should be the SIDE-B port R2 is connected into (both Rx and Tx packets) and the destination should be the port where Host3 is connected. On Host3, enable the Wireshark software and capture all IPv6 spanned traffic.
	Step 2. Shut down the R3 SIDE-B interface. Wait 5 seconds and bring the interface back up.
	Step 3. Verify that R2 and R3 have established a "neighborship" on their SIDE-B interfaces. Check the captured traffic in Host3 and verify whether ICMP Neighbor Solicitation and ICMP Neighbor Advertisement messages were exchanged between the routers.
	Step 4. Check to ensure that both R2 and R3 have the correct link layer addresses for each other.
	Step 5. Verify the Wireshark captures and note whether 1. R2 is listening to the solicited-node multicast group (you will be able to tell by the fact that it replies to messages sent to the multicast address). 2. R2 responded to the solicitation from R3. 3. R2 learned the link address of R3 and vice versa.
Expected Results:	R2 and R3 will form a neighbor relationship using appropriate IPv6 ICMP messages. They will learn each other's link layer addresses automatically.
Observed Results:	
Pass/Fail:	

Table 15-6   *IPv6 Autoconfiguration (SLAAC) Test*

Test ID:	IPv6-FEAT-2
Node List:	R2, R3, SW1, Host2, Host3, Test Port
Test Phase:	Feature
Test Description:	IPv6 Autoconfiguration (SLAAC) Test
Test Setup:	• Build the IPv6 network, as shown in Figure 15-4. • Enable IPv6 process on all nodes and routers. • Configure IPv6 addressing on all relevant interfaces using the Global IPv6 addresses in Table 15-3. • Configure the R2 Link Local address as FE80::1 and the R3 Link Local address as FE80::2. • Leave Host2 powered down.
Test Steps:	**Step 1.** Configure a SPAN session on SW1. The source should be the SIDE-B ports R2 and R3 are connected into (both Rx and Tx packets) and the destination should be the port where Host3 is connected. On Host3, enable the Wireshark software and capture all IPv6 spanned traffic.
	Step 2. Boot up Host2. Verify that Host2 automatically configures its Link Local and Global IPv6 addresses and that the Global address matches the information on the R2 and R3 SIDE-B interfaces. Confirm that Host2 has a router address to leave its local segment.
	Step 3. Stop the capture and check it to verify that Host2 did indeed receive its IPv6 autoconfiguration from the R2 and R3 routers.
	Step 4. Enable the test port and verify that it gets the correct IPv6 autoconfiguration information.
Expected Results:	The hosts will be configured with their IPv6 information automatically, similar to the operation of DHCP for IPv4.
Observed Results:	
Pass/Fail:	

Table 15-7 *IPv6 Router Advertisement (RA) Test*

Test ID:	IPv6-FEAT-3
Node List:	R2, R3, SW1, Host2, Host3, Test Port
Test Phase:	Feature
Test Description:	IPv6 Router Advertisement (RA) Test
Test Setup:	• Build the IPv6 network, as shown in Figure 15-4. • Enable IPv6 process on all nodes and routers. • Configure IPv6 addressing on all relevant interfaces using the Global IPv6 addresses in Table 15-3. • Configure the R2 Link Local address as FE80::1 and the R3 Link Local address as FE80::2. • Allow Host3 and the test port to obtain IPv6 addresses using SLAAC. • Leave Host2 shut down for now.
Test Steps:	**Step 1.** Configure a SPAN session on SW1. The source should be the SIDE-B ports R2 and R3 are connected into (both Rx and Tx packets) and the destination should be the port where Host3 is connected. On Host3, enable the Wireshark software and capture all IPv6 spanned traffic.
	Step 2. Shut down the R3 SIDE-B interface.
	Step 3. Use the test port to send out a Router Solicitation message.
	Step 4. Check the Host3 capture and verify that the router received the solicitation sent by the test port (the solicitation should have the IPv6 address of the test port), and that R2 sent back an RA with the appropriate information. Restart the capture.
	Step 5. Boot up Host2. Once Host2 is up, check the Wireshark capture on Host3 and verify that Host2 sent out a Router Solicitation during its autoconfiguration (using the unspecified IPv6 address of 0:0:0:0:0:0:0:0) and that R2 replied back with a correct RA.
	Step 6. Bring up the R3 SIDE-B interface and wait until the neighbor relationship between R2 and R3 is established in their SIDE-B interfaces.
	Step 7. Restart the capture on Host3 and use the test port to send out a Router Solicitation message.
	Step 8. Check the Host3 capture and verify that the routers received the solicitation sent by the test port (the solicitation should have the IPv6 address of the test port), and that both R2 and R3 sent back an RA with the appropriate information.

Table 15-7   *IPv6 Router Advertisement (RA) Test*

	Step 9. Restart the capture, reboot Host2, and wait until it is autoconfigured. Check the router Host2 is going to be using for off-link destinations.
	Step 10. Stop the capture and verify that both routers sent RAs to Host2. Check to see which router sent its RA first (this should be the router Host2 will be using).
	Step 11. Configure the Default Router Preference (DRP) for R2 to **high** and R3 to **medium**.
	Step 12. Restart the capture, reboot Host2, and wait until it is autoconfigured. Check the router Host2 is going to be using for off-link destinations (it should be R2).
	Step 13. Stop the capture and verify that both routers sent RAs to Host2. Verify the ICMP flags in both RAs and make sure that R2's Router Preference flag is set to **high** and R3's is set to **medium**.
	Step 14. Restart the capture on Host3 and let it run for 5 minutes. Stop the capture and verify whether R2 and R3 are sending out RAs automatically every 200 seconds (this is the default in Cisco IOS Software).
	Step 15. Configure R2 and R3 to send RAs every 100 seconds on their SIDE-B interfaces.
	Step 16. Restart the capture on Host3 and let it run for 5 minutes. Stop the capture and verify whether R2 and R3 are now sending out RAs automatically every 100 seconds.
Expected Results:	The routers will send RAs as configured. They will respond to RSs as expected.
Observed Results:	
Pass/Fail:	

Table 15-8 *IPv6 Duplicate Address Detection (DAD) Test*

Test ID:	IPv6-FEAT-4
Node List:	R2, R3, SW1, Host2, Host3
Test Phase:	Feature
Test Description:	IPv6 Duplicate Address Detection (DAD) Test
Test Setup:	• Build the IPv6 network, as shown in Figure 15-4. • Enable IPv6 process on all nodes and routers. • Configure IPv6 addressing on all relevant interfaces using the Global IPv6 addresses in Table 15-3.
Test Steps:	**Step 1.** Configure a SPAN session on SW1. The source should be the SIDE-B ports R2 and R3 are connected into (both Rx and Tx packets) and the destination should be the port where Host3 is connected. On Host3, enable the Wireshark software and capture all IPv6 spanned traffic.
	Step 2. On routers R2 and R3, enable **debug** for IPv6 Neighbor Discovery (**debug ipv6 nd**) and enable terminal monitoring.
	Step 3. Configure the R2 and R3 Link Local address as FE80::1 (duplicate address).
	Step 4. Watch the debug messages in the router terminals for DAD and duplicate ICMPv6 messages.
	Step 5. Disable the debug and stop the capture. Note the ICMPv6 messages used for duplicate IPv6 address discovery in the capture.
	Step 6. Shut down the SIDE-B interface for R3. Restart the debugs and Wireshark capture.
	Step 7. Configure the R3 Link Local address as FE80::2, and bring the R3 SIDE-B interface back up.
	Step 8. Watch the debug messages in the router terminals for DAD and DAD unique ICMPv6 messages (on R3).
	Step 9. Disable the debug and stop the capture. Note the ICMPv6 messages used for duplicate IPv6 address discovery in the capture.

Table 15-8   *IPv6 Duplicate Address Detection (DAD) Test*

Step 10.	Shut down the SIDE-B interfaces in both R2 and R3. Configure them both with the same IPv6 Global Address (2001:3DB8:3000::2). The Link Local addresses should stay unique—the R2 Link Local address as FE80::1 and the R3 Link Local address as FE80::2.
Step 11.	Restart the debugs and Wireshark capture and enable the SIDE-B interfaces for both R2 and R3.
Step 12.	Watch the debug messages in the router terminals for DAD and DAD unique ICMPv6 messages for the Link Local addresses, and for DAD duplicate ICMPv6 messages for the Global addresses.
Step 13.	Stop the debugs and captures and verify the ICMPv6 DAD messages that were captured by Host3.
Step 14.	Fix the IPv6 addressing for R2 and R3 and repeat the duplicate address tests using Host2 by performing the following tests: 1. Manually configure the same Link Local address on Host2 as the one on R2. Allow the Global address to be autoconfigured. Verify if a Global address is received. 2. Allow the Host2 Link Local address to be autoconfigured and manually configure a duplicate Global address. Verify if Host2 gets a unique Link Local address. 3. Manually configure unique Link Local and Global addresses for Host2 and verify whether DOD ICMPv6 messages are used anyway.
Expected Results:	ICMPv6 will automatically be used to detect duplicate addressing. Link Local addresses should be checked before Global addresses in DAD.
Observed Results:	
Pass/Fail:	

Table 15-9 *ICMPv6 Ping, Unreachable, and Redirect Test*

Test ID:	IPv6-FEAT-5
Node List:	R1, R2, R3, SW1, FW1, Host1, Host2, Host3
Test Phase:	Feature
Test Description:	ICMPv6 Ping, Unreachable, and Redirect Test
Test Setup:	• Build the IPv6 network, as shown in Figure 15-4. • Enable IPv6 process on all nodes and routers. • Configure IPv6 static routing on the nodes and the firewall as described in the "Physical and Logical Test Topology" section. • Configure IPv6 addressing on all relevant interfaces using the Global IPv6 addresses in Table 15-3. • Allow the hosts and test ports to obtain IPv6 addresses using SLAAC. • Configure an IPv6 "permit any" ACL in FW1 allowing all traffic to go between SIDE-A and SIDE-B. (Tip: The address ::/0 means "any" in IPv6.)
Test Steps:	**Step 1.** Verify that all of the hosts have autoconfigured their IPv6 Link Local and Global addresses as expected.
	Step 2. Verify that R2 can ping R3's SIDE-B interface.
	Step 3. Verify that R2 can ping the R1 SIDE-A interface when sourcing the ping from its SIDE-B interface (no route for the FW-B Int exists in R1).
	Step 4. Verify that Host1 can ping R1.
	Step 5. Verify that Host2 can ping R2, R3, and Host3.
	Step 6. Verify that Host1 can ping Host2.
	Step 7. Configure a SPAN session on SW1. The source should be the port Host2 is connected into (both Rx and Tx packets) and the destination should be the port where Host3 is connected. On Host3, enable the Wireshark software and capture all IPv6 spanned traffic.
	Step 8. From Host2, ping R1's FW-A Int IP address; verify that ICMP Unreachables are being received (there should be no route for FW-A in R2 and R3). In Host3's sniffer capture, verify that Host2 is sending the ping packets and is receiving ICMPv6 Unreachables from either R2 or R3.

Table 15-9   *ICMPv6 Ping, Unreachable, and Redirect Test*

	Step 9. Change the SPAN configured in Step 7 to have the R2 SIDE-B port as the source (Rx and Tx) and Host3 as the destination. Enable Wireshark in Host3 and capture all the IPv6 spanned traffic.
	Step 10. With the SPAN running, shut down the R3 SIDE-B interface. This will ensure that only R2 will respond to autoconfiguration messages.
	Step 11. Change the SIDE-A static route in R2 to point at the R3 SIDE-B IPv6 address as the next hop (all traffic destined to SIDE-A coming to R2 will now be sent to R3 when the R3 interface is brought back up).
	Step 12. Reload Host2. Once it is back up, verify that it has received its IPv6 autoconfiguration from R2.
	Step 13. Bring the R3 SIDE-B interface back up, and wait until R2 and R3 form a "neighborship" on their SIDE-B interfaces.
	Step 14. From Host2, ping Host1. Verify that the ping is successful. Check whether Host2 has received an ICMP Redirect from R2 by checking the sniffer captures. Verify that R2 is redirecting Host2 to use R3 for SIDE-A destined traffic.
	Step 15. Restore the static route in R2 to its original next hop (FW1).
Expected Results:	ICMPv6 pings will work as anticipated. The routers will send ICMPv6 Unreachables and Redirects as expected.

Observed Results:

Pass/Fail:

Table 15-10   *IPv6 Path MTU Discovery (PMTUD) Test*

Test ID:	IPv6-FEAT-6
Node List:	R1, R2, R3, SW1, FW1, Host3, test ports
Test Phase:	Feature
Test Description:	IPv6 Path MTU Discovery (PMTUD) Test
Test Setup:	<ul><li>Build the IPv6 network, as shown in Figure 15-4.</li><li>Enable IPv6 process on all nodes and routers.</li><li>Configure IPv6 static routing on the routers and the firewall as described in the "Physical and Logical Test Topology" section.</li><li>Configure IPv6 addressing on all relevant interfaces using the Global IPv6 addresses in Table 15-3.</li><li>Allow the hosts and test ports to obtain IPv6 addresses using SLAAC.</li><li>Configure an IPv6 "permit any" ACL in FW1 allowing all traffic to go between SIDE-A and SIDE-B. (Tip: The address ::/0 means "any" in IPv6.)</li><li>Set the MTU of all router interfaces to 1500.</li></ul>
Test Steps:	**Step 1.** Verify that all of the hosts and test ports have autoconfigured their IPv6 Link Local and Global addresses as expected.
	Step 2. Configure a SPAN session on SW1. The source should be the interface the SIDE-B test port is connected into (both Rx and Tx packets) and the destination should be the port where Host3 is connected. On Host3, enable the Wireshark software and create an ICMPv6 capture filter (only ICMPv6 packets should be displayed and saved).
	Step 3. Create an IPv6 test flow sending traffic from the SIDE-B test port to the SIDE-A test port (using their autoconfigured Global addresses) at 500 Kbps. All the frames should be 1400 bytes. Verify that the traffic is being received without any drops.
	Step 4. Stop the capture in Host3 and verify whether the SIDE-B test port has received any ICMPv6 messages related to PMTUD.
	Step 5. Restart the capture on Host3.
	Step 6. Change the MTU on the R1 SIDE-A interface to 1280.

Table 15-10   *IPv6 Path MTU Discovery (PMTUD) Test*

	Step 7. Verify whether your test traffic is still being received without any drops. This can only happen if your IPv6 test equipment is capable of adjusting the test flow MTU automatically. Check the MTU of the packets arriving to the SIDE-A Test Port.
	Step 8. Stop the capture in Host3 and verify whether the SIDE-B test port has received any ICMPv6 messages related to PMTUD.
	Step 9. Stop the test traffic. The following tests should only be done if your test equipment was able to change the MTU of the transmitted traffic automatically in Step 7.
	Step 10. In FW-1, add a line to the "permit any" ACL being used that denies all ICMPv6 traffic (before the "permit any" line).
	Step 11. Restart the Wireshark capture in Host3. Restart the test traffic.
	Step 12. Verify whether your test traffic is being received.
	Step 13. Stop the capture in Host3 and verify whether the SIDE-B test port has received any ICMPv6 messages related to PMTUD.
	Step 14. Change the MTU on the R1 SIDE-A interface back to 1500 and verify whether the test traffic is being received.
Expected Results:	R1 will send a "Too Big" ICMP message to the SIDE-B test port when its MTU is set to 1280 and the traffic has an MTU of 1400. The test traffic should be adjusted automatically to use the new MTU (assuming the test tool is capable of doing this). With the ICMP messages blocked, frames that are too big will simply be dropped because the ICMP "Too Big" messages cannot make it from R1 to the test port.
Observed Results:	
Pass/Fail:	

Table 15-11   *IPv6 Extension Header Test*

Test ID:	IPv6-FEAT-7
Node List:	R1, R2, R3, SW1, FW1, test ports
Test Phase:	Feature/Performance
Test Description:	IPv6 Extension Header Test
Test Setup:	<ul><li>Build the IPv6 network, as shown in Figure 15-4.</li><li>Enable IPv6 process on all nodes and routers.</li><li>Configure IPv6 static routing on the routers and the firewall as described in the "Physical and Logical Test Topology" section.</li><li>Configure IPv6 addressing on all relevant interfaces using the Global IPv6 addresses in Table 15-3.</li><li>Allow the hosts and test ports to obtain IPv6 addresses using SLAAC.</li><li>Configure an IPv6 "permit any" ACL in FW1 allowing all traffic to go between SIDE-A and SIDE-B. (Tip: The address ::/0 means "any" in IPv6.)</li></ul>
Test Steps:	**Step 1.** Create a bidirectional IPv6 test flow sending traffic between the SIDE-A and SIDE-B test ports (using their autoconfigured Global addresses) at 50 Mbps. All the frames should be 1400 bytes.
	Step 2. Verify that the bidirectional traffic is being received without any drops. Check the latency and jitter of the flows. Record the CPU and memory utilization of R1, R2, R3, SW1, and FW1. Check whether the packets are hardware or process switched.
	Step 3. Change the traffic configured in Step 1 by configuring a Hop-by-Hop Options extension header (second option in Table 15-2) in all of the frames. (The Hop-by-Hop EH is the *only* EH that *must* be fully processed by all network devices.) Restart the test traffic and run it for at least 5 minutes.
	Step 4. Verify that the bidirectional traffic is being received without any drops. Check the latency and jitter of the flows. Record the CPU and memory utilization of R1, R2, R3, SW1, and FW1. Check whether the packets are hardware or process switched.
	Step 5. Change the traffic configured in Step 3 by adding a second EH from Table 15-2 to all of the frames. Restart the test traffic and run it for at least 5 minutes.

Table 15-11   *IPv6 Extension Header Test*

	Step 6. Verify that the bidirectional traffic is being received without any drops. Check the latency and jitter of the flows. Record the CPU and memory utilization of R1, R2, R3, SW1, and FW1. Check whether the packets are hardware or process switched.
	Step 7. Repeat Steps 5 and 6 until all of the headers in Table 15-2 have been tested or the network becomes unstable. Record the "configuration" of any headers or header combinations that cause unexpected behavior.
Expected Results:	This is a "performance" test for the entire IPv6 architecture. The results of the test will be reported in the Observed Results section.
Observed Results:	
Pass/Fail:	

Table 15-12   *IPv6 Basic Access Control List (ACL) Test*

Test ID:	IPv6-FEAT-8
Node List:	R1, R2, R3, SW1, FW1, test ports
Test Phase:	Feature/Performance
Test Description:	IPv6 Basic Access Control List (ACL) Test

Test Setup:	• Build the IPv6 network, as shown in Figure 15-4.
	• Enable IPv6 process on all nodes and routers.
	• Configure IPv6 static routing on the routers and the firewall as described in the "Physical and Logical Test Topology" section.
	• Configure IPv6 addressing on all relevant interfaces using the Global IPv6 addresses in Table 15-3.
	• Allow the hosts and test ports to obtain IPv6 addresses using SLAAC.
	• Configure an IPv6 "permit any" ACL in FW1 allowing all traffic to go between SIDE-A and SIDE-B. (Tip: The address ::/0 means "any" in IPv6.)
	• Configure four bidirectional traffic flows between the SIDE-A and SIDE-B test ports autoconfigured Global IPv6 addresses as follows:
	  • Flow 1: UDP traffic with source port of 6500 and destination port of 53. Running at 10 Mbps with IMIX frame sizes (max size of 1500).
	  • Flow 2: UDP traffic with source port of 7500 and destination Port of 153. Running at 10 Mbps with IMIX frame sizes (max size of 1500).
	  • Flow 3: TCP traffic with source port of 8500 and destination Port of 80. Running at 10 Mbps with IMIX frame sizes (max size of 1500).
	  • Flow 4: TCP traffic with source port of 9500 and destination Port of 180. Running at 10 Mbps with IMIX frame sizes (max size of 1500).

Table 15-12 *IPv6 Basic Access Control List (ACL) Test*

Test Steps:	**Step 1.** Start all of the test traffic described in the Test Setup section.
	Step 2. Verify that all of the bidirectional traffic is being received without any drops. Check the latency and jitter of the flows. Record the CPU and memory utilization of R1, R2, R3, SW1, and FW1. Check whether the packets are hardware or process switched.
	Step 3. Create an extended ACL in R1 that permits all IPv6 traffic. Apply the ACL to the SIDE-A interface in the incoming direction.
	Step 4. Verify that all of the bidirectional traffic is being received without any drops. Check the latency and jitter of the flows. Record the CPU and memory utilization of R1, R2, R3, SW1, and FW1. Check whether the packets are hardware or process switched.
	Step 5. Create an extended ACL in R1 that permits Flow 1 (use /64 IPv6 addressing and port numbers) and Flow 3 (use /128 IPv6 addressing and port numbers) from the Test Setup section, and denies all of the rest (use an actual **deny** statement). Apply the ACL to the SIDE-A interface in the incoming direction.
	Step 6. Verify that all of the traffic from SIDE-B to SIDE-A is being received without any drops. Verify that Flows 1 and 3 from SIDE-A to SIDE-B are being received and Flows 2 and 4 are in fact being dropped. Check the latency and jitter of the flows. Record the CPU and memory utilization of R1, R2, R3, SW1, and FW1. Check whether the packets are hardware or process switched.
	Step 7. Add a **log** statement to the "deny all" line of the ACL created in Step 5.
	Step 8. Verify that all of the traffic from SIDE-B to SIDE-A is being received without any drops. Verify that Flows 1 and 3 from SIDE-A to SIDE-B are being received and Flows 2 and 4 are in fact being dropped. Ensure that the dropped packets (Flows 2 and 4) in R1 are being logged. Check the latency and jitter of the flows. Record the CPU and memory utilization of R1, R2, R3, SW1, and FW1. Check whether the packets are hardware or process switched.
	Step 9. Add 50 lines to the beginning of the ACL created in Step 5 (the **permit** statements would be lines 51 and 52 of the ACL and the **deny** statement would be line 53). Leave the logging enabled for the **deny** statement. Apply the ACL to the SIDE-A interface in the incoming direction.

Table 15-12 *IPv6 Basic Access Control List (ACL) Test*

Step 10.	Verify that all of the traffic from SIDE-B to SIDE-A is being received without any drops. Verify that Flows 1 and 3 from SIDE-A to SIDE-B are being received and Flows 2 and 4 are in fact being dropped. Ensure that the dropped packets (Flows 2 and 4) in R1 are being logged. Check the latency and jitter of the flows. Record the CPU and memory utilization of R1, R2, R3, SW1, and FW1. Check whether the packets are hardware or process switched.
Step 11.	Repeat Steps 3 thorough 10, this time applying the ACL to R1's SIDE-A interface in the *outgoing* direction. Record the results.
Step 12.	Repeat Steps 3 thorough 11, this time applying the ACL to FW1's FW-A and FW-B interfaces at the same time. Record the results.
Expected Results:	Permitted traffic will be allowed through and denied traffic will be dropped. Logging will work as expected. This is also a "performance" test for the IPv6 architecture. The results of the test will be reported in the Observed Results section.
Observed Results:	
Pass/Fail:	

End Notes

1. Popoviciu, Ciprian, Eric Levy-Abegnoli, and Patrick Grossetete. *Deploying IPv6 Networks*. Indianapolis, IN: Cisco Press, 2006.

2. Cisco.com. *Cisco IOS IPv6 Configuration Guide, Release 12.4*, "Implementing Traffic Filters and Firewalls for IPv6 Security." www.cisco.com/en/US/docs/ios/ipv6/configuration/guide/12_4/ipv6_12_4_book.html.

Chapter 16

MPLS/VPN: Scalability and Convergence Test Plan

Over the past several years, enterprise organizations have been increasingly turning to Multiprotocol Label Switching (MPLS)-based VPN solutions as the mainstay of their next-generation WAN architectures. The advantages of an MPLS-based networking fabric as a secure alternative to traditional WAN solutions such as ATM or Frame Relay are undeniable. For years, service providers have touted ubiquitous circuit access, standard pricing regardless of distance, and reduced customer design complexity as the major benefits to attract consumers to their MPLS/VPN service offerings. Enterprise consumers initially approached these offerings with caution, slowly migrating legacy Frame Relay WANs, and often deploying overlay routing solutions based on GRE or IPsec tunnels, until a degree of confidence was obtained with the service provider's ability to offer a stable, secure service for the enterprise organization's converged application needs. As enterprise adoption and consumer confidence have dramatically increased in recent years, many large organizations are now deploying their own self-managed MPLS/VPN networks, taking a service provider approach to securely segment multiple organizations, services, and applications, while operating a single MPLS-based network infrastructure.

Enterprise architects are now faced with many of the same concerns that designers of service provider MPLS networks have faced for years:

■ How do we determine what is the right balance of fast convergence and scalability such that today's advanced applications such as VoIP and Cisco TelePresence will be able to meet stringent service-level agreements (SLA) in a world where hardware failures, software crashes, and human error are inevitable?

■ How do the various protocols of an MPLS/VPN fabric interact, and how large can each grow?

■ What factors will increase the network deployment size? For example, when is a dedicated P-router core justified, or how many CE routers can be provisioned on a single PE router when aggressive protocol timers are necessary to meet the convergence requirements of real-time applications?

Over the years, some of the world's most talented engineers have attempted to answer these questions with theoretical approaches that delve into mathematical calculations, protocol and feature optimizations, and deep analyses of platform-specific limitations. White papers, Internet drafts, and even complete books have been written on the subject of designing and scaling MPLS/VPN networks. New features for fast convergence and scalability are developed in virtually every version of Cisco router operating systems, providing more design options for network engineers, but also raising questions on how the various features will interact. Experience has shown that while there is no substitute for due diligence during the planning and design phase for new MPLS/VPN deployments, thorough testing is absolutely necessary to answer the questions as to "how fast" or "how far" these networks can be pushed before stability is compromised.

The following test plan assists you in developing an approach to assessing the convergence and scalability aspects of an MPLS/VPN network.

Background

A global financial organization is planning to deploy a new MPLS/VPN backbone as part of a global core upgrade and network virtualization strategy. The new network must support current and future application needs, many of which require stringent SLAs in terms of availability, performance, and security. A history of mergers and acquisitions over time has resulted in organic growth of the network in an unstructured manner, resulting in over- and underutilization of circuits, operational complexity, decreased performance, and network outages. Given the history, architects of the new MPLS network have decided to deploy a new hierarchical design centered on a global network "Tier 1" core, connecting the critical sites (data centers and trading locations), and various "Tier 2" regional cores that extend connectivity to the smaller "Tier 3" processing centers and retail bank locations. A high-level illustration of the new logical topology is shown in Figure 16-1.

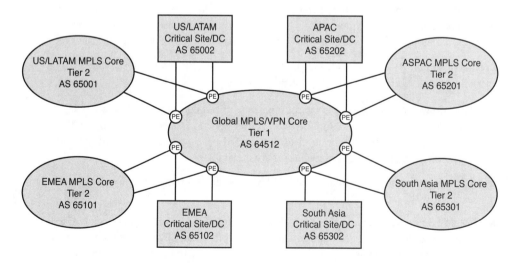

Figure 16-1 *Global MPLS/VPN High-Level Architecture*

Architects of the new network are faced with the challenges of designing a converged network platform capable of delivering "five nines" of availability for various voice, video, and data services. The high-level breakdown of critical services included the following unicast and multicast IP applications:

- General-purpose business data

- Business-class VoIP

- Streaming and real-time video

- Market data

- Trading flows

With the primary goals of scalability, low latency, fast convergence, and high availability, architects chose to deploy a hierarchical architecture with Cisco CRS-1 and ASR 1000 carrier-class platforms functioning as the P, PE, and route reflector (RR) roles. Details of the logical routing design include the following:

- Five separate MPLS/VPN domains, each delineated by its own BGP autonomous system (AS)

- Each of the four regional domains operating as a Tier 2 BGP AS to the global/Tier 1 BGP AS

- OSPF as the IGP for each domain

- Label Distribution Protocol (LDP) deployed in each domain for MPLS forwarding

- Dedicated, out-of-band, ASR 1002 BGP RRs deployed in pairs within each AS

- Multicast VPN (MVPN) solution based on the IETF Rosen-Draft to carry multicast traffic within each AS

- Inter-AS Option B for VPN connectivity (unicast and multicast) between domains

A highlight of the optimization features to be tested includes the following:

- Bidirectional Failure Detection (BFD) with aggressive timers for fast fault detection

- OSPF Optimizations (SPF/LSA tuning and prefix prioritization)

- MPLS Optimizations, including the controlled distribution of LDP labels and the IGP LDP synchronization feature to prevent traffic loss during link failures.

- BGP Next-Hop Tracking (NHT) for fast convergence during remote PE router failures.

- BGP Prefix Independent Convergence (PIC) feature enabled on the Core and Edge, for fast BGP convergence during link and node failures.

■ Platform-specific redundancy features such as Nonstop Routing (NSR) and Nonstop Forwarding (NSF)

Physical and Logical Test Topology

Figure 16-2 shows the high-level physical topology used for this test.

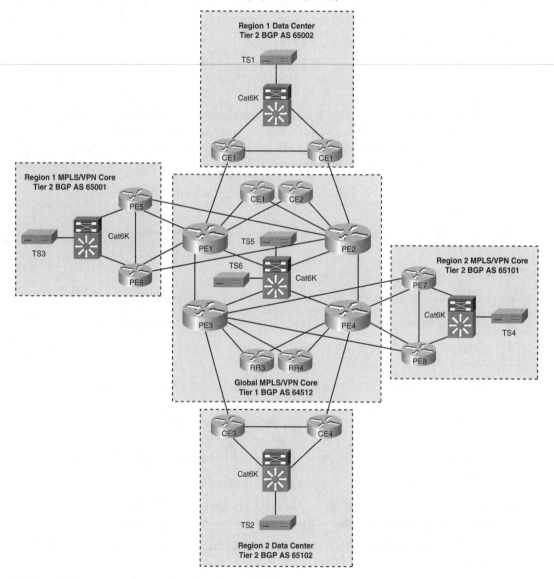

Figure 16-2 *Network Topology for MPLS/VPN Convergence and Scalability Testing*

Technical Details of the Test Topology

A prototype network topology representing the global core, two regional cores, and two data center/trading sites is assembled in the lab to validate the feature functionality, routing, and scalability characteristics of the design. Details of the system are as follows:

- Four CRS-1, 4-slot routers are functioning as PE/P routers in the global core (PE1–PE4).

- Four ASR 1002 routers are functioning as BGP RRs in the global core (RR1–RR4).

- PE1–PE4 are interconnected in a "ring" topology with OC48 SONET links forming the core. Connections to the BGP RRs (RR1–RR4) are made with direct Gigabit Ethernet (GE) connections from PE1–PE4, respectively.

- PE1–PE4 and RR1–RR4 all run OSPF as the core IGP, with core interfaces participating in OSPF Area 0. External connections are not configured with OSPF.

- PE1–PE4 are configured as BGP RR clients to RR1–RR4 in two unique clusters in AS 64512: PE1 and PE2 with redundant peer connections to RR1 and RR2, exchanging VPNv4 and IPv4 Multicast Distribution Tree (MDT) Subaddress Family Identifier Information (SAFI) reachability and PE3 and PE4 with redundant peer connections to RR3 and RR4 and exchanging the same address family reachability.

- RR1–RR4 is configured in a BGP full mesh, exchanging VPNv4 and MDT SAFI reachability.

- Ten RFC 2547 VPNs are provisioned on PE1–PE4, configured in a full mesh topology.

- All ten VPNs are configured as MVPNs on PE1–PE4. PIM-SSM is used to build multicast MDT state in the MPLS core.

- RP addresses for the first five mVRFs configured in the VRF contexts of PE1, and for the second five mVRFs in the VRF contexts of PE3.

- Four ASR 1002 routers are functioning as data center/trading site CE routers. Each router connects to a local PE router via OC12 POS connections, mapping into the first VRF.

- eBGP is configured as the CE-PE routing protocol between each CE to the directly connected PE router.

- OSPF is configured as the IGP within each data center, for the purposes of exchanging loopback addresses that will be used as BGP local addresses for iBGP purposes.

- iBGP is configured between each CE router within the data center.

- BGP PIC Core and Edge optimization features are configured on each CE and PE router in the topology.

- Multicast PIM-SM routing is enabled on each CE router, PE router, and the Ixia test set. Multicast RP for each group are manually configured using static RP assignments on each CE router.

- A Catalyst 6506 switch is connected with GE connections to each of the PE routers in the global core to provide VLAN connectivity from Ixia test ports facilitating router emulation and control plane loading.

- Two ASR 1006 routers are functioning as PE routers in each regional core (PE5–PE8).

- PE1, PE2, PE5, and PE6 are interconnected within a fully meshed 10-Gigabit Ethernet topology.

- PE3, PE4, PE7, and PE8 are interconnected in a fully meshed 10-Gigabit Ethernet topology.

- PE5 and PE6 are configured as OSPF neighbors and MP-iBGP peers in AS 65001.

- PE7 and PE8 configured as OSPF neighbors and MP-iBGP peers in AS 65101. Exchanging VPNv4 and IPv4 MDT SAFI address reachability.

- PE5-PE8 and six Ixia test ports are connected to a 10-Gigabit Ethernet Catalyst 6500 VLAN switch, to facilitate control plane load and any-to-any test traffic across the topology.

- Inter-AS Option B is configured between the regional PE router and its directly connected global PE router. (MP-eBGP exchange of VPNv4 routes and labels between PE routers that function as ASBRs.) Static routes configured for loopback/BGP peering reachability between each AS.

- mVPN Inter-AS Option B support is enabled between each regional PE router and its directly connected global PE router.

Emulated Control Plane Scale

Table 16-1 provides an example of the scale parameter specification that would be emulated in the lab environment before the test cases are executed. The actual figures would be derived from the anticipated scale of the MPLS/VPN deployment.

Table 16-1 *Baseline Control Plane Load/Scaling Parameters*

Scale Parameter	Requirement	Note
OSPF Routes	500 per PE	IGP includes only core circuit and loopback IP prefixes.
OSPF Adjacencies	10 per PE	Each with MD5 authentication and BFD.
LDP Neighbors	10 per PE	Each with MD5 authentication.
LDP Labels	100 per PE	Labels constrained to only /32 loopbacks of PE routers.
eBGP Peers	50 per PE	PE-CE links, each with MD5 authentication and BFD.

Table 16-1   *Baseline Control Plane Load/Scaling Parameters*

Scale Parameter	Requirement	Note
iBGP Peers	2 per PE	Each PE peers to a pair of redundant RRs in a single cluster.
iBGP Peers	25 per BGP router reflector	To simulate the load induced by the planned deployment of PE routers.
Total MP-BGP Paths	500,000 per PE	
Number of L3 interfaces	50 per PE	
Multicast routes	500 per PE	
mVPN PIM PE-CE neighbors	50 per PE	
mVPN MDT/PIM neighbors	25 per PE	
Global PIM Neighbors	10 per PE	Core multicast links.
BFD peers	50 per PE	BFD timers tuned to 150-ms interval with multiplier of 3 to support subsecond OSPF and eBGP neighbor failure detection.

Control Plane Scale Methodology

Ixia test ports are used to emulate MPLS P and PE routers in order to load the control plane to the desired number of interfaces, adjacencies, routes and labels. Figure 16-3 provides an example of how this emulation is achieved on a system under test including PE1, RR1, and RR2.

Test Objectives

The primary objectives for this test are as follows:

1. Validate functionality of the unicast and multicast VPN routing design.

2. Examine impact of optimizations and fast convergence features on DUT stability, during steady-state conditions and various failure scenarios.

3. Examine impact of optimizations and fast convergence features on test traffic emulating network applications during various failure scenarios.

4. Identify any scalability bottlenecks that exist that would require additional resources (devices, memory, CPU) prior to deployment.

5. Identify any critical hardware or software defects that require remediation prior to deployment.

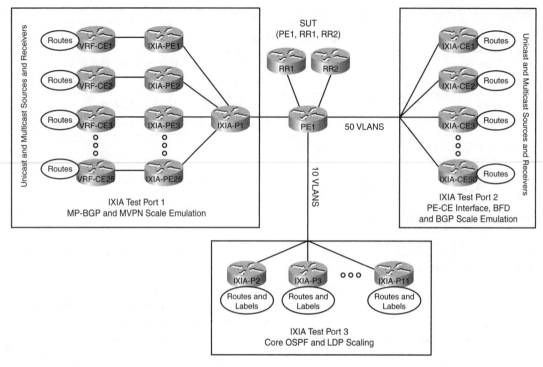

Figure 16-3   *Using Ixia IxNetwork for Control Plane Scaling*

Test Case Summary

Table 16-2 provides a brief description of each test case.

Table 16-2   *Test Cases Summary Table*

Test ID	Brief Test Description
OSPF-BASE-1	Global MPLS Core OSPF Baseline Configuration and Scale Test
OSPF-BASE-2	Regional MPLS Core OSPF Baseline Configuration and Scale Test
OSPF-BASE-3	Regional Data Center OSPF Baseline Configuration and Scale Test
LDP-BASE-4	Global Core LDP Baseline Configuration and Scale Test
LDP-BASE-5	Regional Core LDP Baseline Configuration and Scale Test
BGP-BASE-6	Global MPLS Core BGP Baseline Configuration and Scale Test
VPN-BASE-7	Global MPLS Core RFC 2547 Layer 3 VPN Baseline Configuration and Scale Test
MVPN-BASE-8	Global Core MVPN Baseline Configuration and Scale Test
BGP-BASE-9	Regional Data Center eBGP Baseline Configuration Test

Table 16-2   *Test Cases Summary Table*

Test ID	Brief Test Description
BGP-BASE-10	Regional MPLS Core BGP Baseline Configuration and Scale Test
VPN-BASE-11	Regional MPLS Core RFC 2547 Layer 3 VPN Baseline Configuration and Scale Test
MVPN-BASE-12	Regional MPLS Core MVPN Baseline Configuration and Scale Test
INTER-AS-BASE-13	INTER-AS Option B for Layer 3 VPN (Unicast) Configuration and Verification Test
INTER-AS-BASE-14	MVPN INTER-AS Option B Support Configuration and Verification Test
BFD-FEAT-1	BFD Feature and Scalability Test
OSPF-FEAT-2	OSPF High Availability Feature Test
LDP-FEAT-3	LDP High Availability Feature Test
BGPNHT-FEAT-4	BGP Next-Hop Tracking Feature Test
BGPPIC-FEAT-5	BGP PIC Feature Test
BGP-FEAT-6	BGP High Availability Feature Test
PE-PERF-1	PE Router Scalability and Duty Cycle Test
RR-PERF-2	BGP RR Router Scalability and Duty Cycle Test
BGP-DUTY-1	Device Failure and Recovery Test
BGP-DUTY-2	Circuit and Line Card Failure and Recovery Test

Detailed Test Cases

The following tables contain detailed test cases to be conducted to certify the MPLS/VPN topology described earlier. These cases provide you with guidance on testing MPLS/VPN technologies and should be modified to fit your specific needs.

Table 16-3 *Global MPLS Core OSPF Baseline Configuration and Scale Test*

Test ID:	OSPF-BASE-1
Node List:	Global Core Routers: PE1–PE4, RR1–RR4 Ixia Test Ports: TS5 and TS6 (ten VLANs each)
Test Phase:	Baseline
Test Description:	Global MPLS Core OSPF Baseline Configuration and Scale Test
Test Setup:	• Build the network, as described in Figure 16-2. • Configure PE1–PE4 and RR1–RR4 to participate in OSPF Area 0. Enable OSPF on core-facing interface and loopback interfaces only. • Configure VLANs 2–11 on PE1 and PE2 GE trunk connections to Catalyst 6500 and enable OSPF in Area 0. • Configure VLANs 2–11 on Ixia TS5 and enable OSPF in Area 0. • Configure VLANs 12–21 on PE3 and PE4 GE trunk connections to Catalyst 6500 and enable OSPF in Area 0. • Configure VLANs 12–21 on Ixia TS6 and enable OSPF in Area 0. • Enable OSPF MD5 authentication between all neighbors. • Enable NSR for OSPF. • Reference bandwidth for OSPF is set to 1 Tbps using the auto-cost reference command. • Enable BFD on each core interface and Ixia test set, with OSPF registered as client. • Set the default OSPF hello/dead timers on each interface. • Create ten emulated Ixia P routers on TS5 advertising 250 OSPF prefixes to PE1 and PE2. • Create ten emulated Ixia P routers on TS6 advertising 250 OSPF prefixes to PE3 and PE4. • Create 250 bidirectional test flows configured between TS5 and TS6, using emulated OSPF routes as source/destination. • Set MTU on all interfaces to 4470.
Test Steps:	**Step 1.** Verify that all OSPF neighbors are fully adjacent between routers and Ixia emulated routers as appropriate.
	Step 2. Verify that BFD neighbor sessions are established between routers and Ixia emulated routers as appropriate.
	Step 3. Ensure ping and traceroute reachability between all PE routers and RRs succeeds and follows the expected path.
	Step 4. Ensure OSPF database and routing tables on each PE router and RR are consistent.

Table 16-3 *Global MPLS Core OSPF Baseline Configuration and Scale Test*

	Step 5. Ensure OSPF syslog messages and SNMP traps are generated when neighbor state changes due to MD5 password mismatch, MTU mismatch, area mismatch, timer mismatch, or network type mismatch.
	Step 6. Disable BFD on one PE router interface and ensure that OSPF neighbor adjacency drops on remote router.
	Step 7. Generate test traffic as described in the Test Setup and let it run for at least 5 minutes. Examine Ixia traffic statistics for loss on any particular flow.
	Step 8. Verify that all of the devices in the Node List are running without issues by checking their logs and CPU and memory utilization.
Expected Results:	OSPF adjacencies are established on all connected links. The OSPF database is consistent with no traffic loss on test flows. DUTs are stable with no elevated CPU or memory consumption during full load. Syslog messages and SNMP traps are generated when OSPF neighbor state changes.
Observed Results:	
Pass/Fail:	

Table 16-4 *Regional MPLS Core OSPF Baseline Configuration and Scale Test*

Test ID:	OSPF-BASE-2
Node List:	Region 1 Core Routers: PE5, PE6 Region 2 Core Routers: PE7, PE8 Ixia Test Ports: TS3 and TS4 (ten VLANs each)
Test Phase:	Baseline
Test Description:	Regional MPLS Core OSPF Baseline Configuration and Scale Test

Table 16-4 *Regional MPLS Core OSPF Baseline Configuration and Scale Test*

Test Setup:	• Build the network, as described in Figure 16-2.
	• Configure PE5 and PE6 in Region 1 to participate in OSPF Area 0. Enable OSPF on regional core–facing interface and loopback interfaces only.
	• Configure VLANs 2–11 on PE5 and PE6 GE trunk connections to Catalyst 6500 and enable OSPF in Area 0.
	• Configure VLANs 2–11 on Ixia TS3 and enable OSPF in Area 0.
	• Configure PE7 and PE8 in Region 2 to participate in OSPF Area 0 (different domain than Region 1). Enable OSPF on regional core–facing interface and loopback interfaces only.
	• Configure VLANs 12–21 on PE7 and PE8 GE trunk connections to Catalyst 6500 and enable OSPF in Area 0.
	• Configure VLANs 12–21 on Ixia TS4 and enable OSPF in Area 0.
	• Enable OSPF MD5 authentication between all neighbors.
	• Enable NSF for OSPF.
	• Set OSPF auto-cost reference to 1 Tbps.
	• Enable BFD on each core interface and Ixia test set, with OSPF registered as client.
	• Set the default OSPF hello/dead timers on each interface.
	• Create ten emulated Ixia P routers on TS3 advertising 250 OSPF prefixes to PE5 and PE6.
	• Create ten emulated Ixia P routers on TS4 advertising 250 OSPF prefixes to PE7 and PE8.
	• Create 125 bidirectional test flows configured between different VLANs on TS3 using emulated OSPF routes as source/destination.
	• Create 125 bidirectional test flows configured between different VLANs on TS4 using emulated OSPF routes as source/destination.
	• Set MTU on all interfaces to 4470.
Test Steps:	**Step 1.** Verify that all OSPF neighbors are fully adjacent between routers and Ixia emulated routers as appropriate.
	Step 2. Verify that BFD neighbor sessions are established between routers and Ixia emulated routers as appropriate.
	Step 3. Ensure ping and traceroute reachability between all PE routers and RRs succeeds and follows the expected path.
	Step 4. Ensure OSPF database and routing tables on each PE router and RR are consistent.

Table 16-4 *Regional MPLS Core OSPF Baseline Configuration and Scale Test*

	Step 5. Ensure OSPF syslog messages and SNMP traps are generated when neighbor state changes due to MD5 password mismatch, MTU mismatch, area mismatch, timer mismatch, or network type mismatch.
	Step 6. Disable BFD on one PE router interface and ensure that OSPF neighbor adjacency drops on remote router.
	Step 7. Generate test traffic as described in the Test Setup and let it run for at least 5 minutes. Examine Ixia traffic statistics for loss on any particular flow.
	Step 8. Verify that all of the devices in the Node List are running without issues by checking their logs and CPU and memory utilization.
Expected Results:	OSPF adjacencies are established on all connected links. OSPF database is consistent with no traffic loss on test flows. DUTs are stable with no elevated CPU or memory consumption during full load. Syslog messages and SNMP traps are generated when OSPF neighbor state changes.
Observed Results:	
Pass/Fail:	

Table 16-5 *Regional Data Center OSPF Baseline Configuration and Scale Test*

Test ID:	OSPF-BASE-3
Node List:	Region 1 Data Center Routers: CE1, CE2 Region 2 Data Center Routers: CE3, CE4 Ixia Test Ports: TS1 and TS2 (ten VLANs each)
Test Phase:	Baseline
Test Description:	Regional Data Center OSPF Baseline Configuration and Scale Test

Table 16-5 *Regional Data Center OSPF Baseline Configuration and Scale Test*

Test Setup:	• Build the network, as described in Figure 16-2.
	• Configure CE1 and CE2 in Region 1 to participate in OSPF Area 0. Enable OSPF on Data Center LAN interface and loopback interfaces only.
	• Configure VLANs 2–11 on CE1 and CE2 GE trunk connections to Catalyst 6500 and enable OSPF in Area 0.
	• Configure VLANs 2–11 on Ixia TS1 and enable OSPF in Area 0.
	• Configure CE3 and CE4 in Region 2 to participate in OSPF Area 0 (different domain than Region 1). Enable OSPF on Data Center LAN interface and loopback interfaces only.
	• Configure VLANs 12–21 on CE3 and CE4 GE trunk connections to Catalyst 6500 and enable OSPF in Area 0.
	• Configure VLANs 12–21 on Ixia TS2 and enable OSPF in Area 0.
	• Enable OSPF MD5 authentication between all neighbors.
	• Enable NSF for OSPF.
	• Set OSPF auto-cost reference to 1 Tbps.
	• Enable BFD on each core interface and Ixia test set, with OSPF registered as client.
	• Set the default OSPF hello/dead timers on each interface.
	• Create ten emulated Ixia P routers on TS1 advertising 250 OSPF prefixes to CE1 and CE2.
	• Create ten emulated Ixia P routers on TS2 advertising 250 OSPF prefixes to CE3 and CE4.
	• Create 125 bidirectional test flows configured between different VLANs on TS1 using emulated OSPF routes as source/destination.
	• Create 125 bidirectional test flows configured between different VLANs on TS2 using emulated OSPF routes as source/destination.
	• Set MTU on all interfaces to 4470.
Test Steps:	**Step 1.** Verify that all OSPF neighbors are fully adjacent between routers and Ixia emulated routers as appropriate.
	Step 2. Verify that BFD neighbor sessions are established between routers and Ixia emulated routers as appropriate.

Table 16-5 *Regional Data Center OSPF Baseline Configuration and Scale Test*

	Step 3. Ensure ping and traceroute reachability between all PE routers and RRs succeeds and follows the expected path.
	Step 4. Ensure OSPF database and routing tables on each PE router and RR are consistent.
	Step 5. Ensure OSPF syslog messages and SNMP traps are generated when neighbor state changes due to MD5 password mismatch, MTU mismatch, area mismatch, timer mismatch, or network type mismatch.
	Step 6. Disable BFD on one PE router interface and ensure that OSPF neighbor adjacency drops on remote router.
	Step 7. Generate test traffic as described in the Test Setup and let it run for at least 5 minutes. Examine Ixia traffic statistics for loss on any particular flow.
	Step 8. Verify that all of the devices in the Node List are running without issues by checking their logs and CPU and memory utilization.
Expected Results:	OSPF adjacencies are established on all connected links. OSPF database is consistent with no traffic loss on test flows. DUTs are stable with no elevated CPU or memory consumption during full load. Syslog messages and SNMP traps are generated when OSPF neighbor state changes.
Observed Results:	
Pass/Fail:	

Table 16-6 *Global Core LDP Baseline Configuration and Scale Test*

Test ID:	LDP-BASE-4
Node List:	Global Core Routers: PE1–PE4 Ixia Test Ports: TS5 and TS6 (ten VLANs each)
Test Phase:	Baseline
Test Description:	Global Core LDP Baseline Configuration and Scale Test
Test Setup:	• Build the network, as described in Figure 16-2. • Configure PE1–PE4 with MPLS LDP forwarding on core-facing and Ixia-facing interfaces. Interfaces connected to RRs will *not* be configured for MPLS LDP. • Enable LDP forwarding on VLANs 2–11 of Ixia TS5 and on VLANs 12–21 of Ixia TS6. • Enable LDP MD5 authentication between all neighbors (DUT and emulated Ixia). • Configure Loopback 0 as MPLS router ID. • Enable NSR for LDP. • Configure an ACL that restricts LDP label distribution to only the routes associated with the PE router loopback addresses. • Enable the IGP LDP Synchronization feature (under OSPF). • Create ten emulated Ixia P routers on TS5 advertising unique LDP labels for the 250 OSPF prefixes previously advertised to PE1 and PE2. • Create ten emulated Ixia P routers on TS6 advertising unique LDP labels for the 250 OSPF prefixes previously advertised to PE3 and PE4. • Create 250 bidirectional test flows configured between TS5 and TS6, using emulated LDP routes as source/destination.
Test Steps:	**Step 1.** Verify that all LDP neighbors are established between the physical routers and the Ixia emulated routers as appropriate.
	Step 2. Verify that the Label Information Base (LIB) includes label bindings for all of the OSPF prefixes (Liberal Retention Mode).
	Step 3. Verify that the Label Forwarding Information Base (LFIB) includes label bindings associated with the preferred IGP interface.

Table 16-6   *Global Core LDP Baseline Configuration and Scale Test*

	Step 4. Modify the LDP Label allocation ACL such that only the DUT loopback addresses are permitted. Ensure that labels are not allocated or advertised to peers for the Ixia emulated prefixes. Once verified, restore to the previous configuration.
	Step 5. Enable the MPLS Operations and Management (OAM) feature and ensure LSP is available between all PE routers using the MPLS ping utility.
	Step 6. Ensure LDP syslog messages and SNMP traps are generated when neighbor state changes due to MD5 password mismatch or when LDP is disabled on one end of a circuit.
	Step 7. Flap one of the established LDP session between PE routers by shutting down and enabling a connected link. Verify that OSPF cost for the type-1 LSA associated with the link prefix is raised to the maximum metric of 65535 due to the MPLS LDP synchronization feature being enabled.
	Step 8. Generate test traffic as described in the Test Setup and let it run for at least 5 minutes. Examine Ixia traffic statistics for loss on any particular flow.
	Step 9. Verify that all of the devices in the Node List are running without issues by checking their logs and CPU and memory utilization.
Expected Results:	LDP Neighbors are established on all connected links as appropriate. No traffic loss on labeled test flows. DUTs are stable with no elevated CPU or memory consumption during full load. Syslog messages and SNMP traps are generated when LDP neighbor state changes.

Observed Results:

Pass/Fail:

Table 16-7 *Regional Core LDP Baseline Configuration and Scale Test*

Test ID:	LDP-BASE-5
Node List:	Region 1 Core Routers: PE5, PE6
	Region 2 Core Routers: PE7, PE8 Ixia Test Ports: TS3 and TS4 (ten VLANs each)
Test Phase:	Baseline
Test Description:	Regional Core LDP Baseline Configuration and Scale Test
Test Setup:	• Build the network, as described in Figure 16-2. • Configure PE5 and PE6 with MPLS LDP forwarding on core-facing and Ixia-facing interfaces. • Enable LDP forwarding on VLANs 2–11 of Ixia TS3 and on VLANs 12–21 of Ixia TS4. • Enable LDP MD5 authentication between all neighbors (DUT and emulated Ixia). • Configure Loopback 0 as MPLS router id. • Enable NSF for LDP. • Create an LDP Label Allocation ACL that permits only the IP address range associated with the PE router (DUT and emulated) loopback ranges. • Enable the IGP LDP Synchronization feature (under OSPF). • Create ten emulated Ixia P routers on TS3 advertising unique LDP labels for the 125 OSPF prefixes previously advertised to PE5 and PE6. • Create ten emulated Ixia P routers on TS4 advertising unique LDP labels for the 125 OSPF prefixes previously advertised to PE7 and PE8. • 125 bidirectional test flows configured between different VLANs on TS3 using emulated OSPF routes as source/destination. • 125 bidirectional test flows configured between different VLANs on TS4 using emulated OSPF routes as source/destination.
Test Steps:	**Step 1.** Verify that all LDP Neighbors are established between routers and Ixia emulated routers as appropriate.
	Step 2. Verify that the LIB includes label bindings for all of the OSPF prefixes (Liberal Retention Mode).
	Step 3. Verify that the LFIB includes label bindings associated with the preferred IGP interface.

Table 16-7   *Regional Core LDP Baseline Configuration and Scale Test*

Step 4.	Modify the LDP Label allocation ACL such that only the DUT loopback addresses are permitted. Ensure that labels are not allocated or advertised to peers for the Ixia emulated prefixes. Once verified, restore to the previous configuration.
Step 5.	Enable MPLS OAM and ensure LSP is available between all PE routers using the MPLS ping utility.
Step 6.	Ensure LDP syslog messages and SNMP traps are generated when neighbor state changes due to MD5 password mismatch or when LDP is disabled on one end of a circuit.
Step 7.	Flap one of the established LDP sessions between PE routers by shutting down and enabling a connected link. Verify that OSPF cost for the type-1 LSA associated with the link prefix is raised to the maximum metric of 65535 due to the MPLS LDP synchronization feature being enabled.
Step 8.	Generate test traffic as described in the Test Setup and let it run for at least 5 minutes. Examine Ixia traffic statistics for loss on any particular flow.
Step 9.	Verify that all of the devices in the Node List are running without issues by checking their logs and CPU and memory utilization.
Expected Results:	LDP Neighbors are established on all connected links as appropriate. No traffic loss on labeled test flows. DUTs are stable with no elevated CPU or memory consumption during full load. Syslog messages and SNMP traps are generated when LDP neighbor state changes.

Observed Results:

Pass/Fail:

Table 16-8   *Global MPLS Core BGP Baseline Configuration and Scale Test*

Test ID:	BGP-BASE-6
Node List:	Global Core Routers: PE1–PE4, RR1–RR4 Ixia Test Ports: TS5 and TS6 (25 emulated PE routers/BGP sessions each)
Test Phase:	Baseline
Test Description:	Global MPLS Core iBGP Baseline Configuration and Scale Test
Test Setup:	• Build the network, as described in Figure 16-2. • PE1–PE4 are configured as BGP RR clients to RR1–RR4 in two unique clusters in AS 64512. • PE1 and PE2 are configured with redundant peer connections to RR1 and RR2, exchanging VPNv4 and IPv4 MDT SAFI address family reachability. • PE3 and PE4 are configured with redundant peer connections to RR3 and RR4 and exchanging VPNv4 and IPv4 MDT SAFI address family reachability. • RR1–RR4 are configured in a BGP full mesh, exchanging VPNv4 and MDT SAFI reachability. • Configure 25 emulated PE routers on Ixia TS5 and TS6, respectively. Advertise BGP peering addresses through OSPF via an emulated P router. (Refer to Figure 16-3.) • Configure each emulated PE router with redundant peering sessions to RR1 and RR2 to bring the total number of MP-iBGP peers on each RR to 54 (50 emulated and 4 DUT). • Enable BGP MD5 authentication between all neighbors. • Enable NSR for BGP. • BGP keepalive/holddown timers 30/90 seconds, respectively, between all iBGP peers. • Enable IP TCP Path MTU Discovery increase the maximum segment sizes (MSS) of the BGP/TCP sessions. • Set MTU on all interfaces to 4470.
Test Steps:	**Step 1.** Verify that all BGP peers are established between RRs, PE routers, and Ixia emulated PE routers.
	Step 2. Verify that peer neighbor capabilities include VPNv4 and MDT SAFI for all peers.
	Step 3. Verify that MSS of BGP sessions is 4426, when the core MTU is configured as 4470 and TCP Path MTU Discovery is enabled.

Table 16-8 *Global MPLS Core BGP Baseline Configuration and Scale Test*

	Step 4. Ensure BGP syslog messages and SNMP traps are generated when neighbor state changes due to MD5 password mismatch or peer address mismatch.
	Step 5. Verify that all of the devices in the Node List are running without issues by checking their logs and CPU and memory utilization.
Expected Results:	All BGP configured peers are in established state on RR and PE routers. DUTs are stable with no elevated CPU or memory consumption during full load. Syslog messages and SNMP traps are generated when BGP peer state changes.
Observed Results:	
Pass/Fail:	

Table 16-9 *Global MPLS Core RFC 2547 Layer 3 VPN VRF Baseline Configuration and Scale Test*

Test ID:	VPN-BASE-7
Node List:	Global Core Routers: PE1–PE4 Ixia Test Ports: TS5 and TS6 (25 emulated PE routers, each provisioned with ten RFC 2547 VPNs, 50 emulated CE routers per test port)
Test Phase:	Baseline
Test Description:	Global MPLS Core RFC 2547 Layer 3 VPN VRF Baseline Configuration and Scale Test

Table 16-9 *Global MPLS Core RFC 2547 Layer 3 VPN VRF Baseline Configuration and Scale Test*

Test Setup:	• Build the network, as described in Figure 16-2. • Configure ten RFC 2547 VRFs on each DUT (actual PE router) and on each of the emulated Ixia PE routers. • Map the PE-CE interface on PE1 and PE2 toward Region 1 Data Center CE routers CE1 and CE2 into the first VRF. • Map the PE-CE interface on PE3 and PE4 toward Region 2 Data Center CE routers CE3 and CE4 into the first VRF. • Create 50 additional VLANs on PE1 and PE3 router ports connecting to the Catalyst 6500 connected to the Ixia test ports that will function as directly connected emulated CE routers. Map into the ten VRFs (contiguous groups of five) and assign unique /30 IPv4 addresses. Refer to Figure 16-3 for an illustration. • Create 50 corresponding VLAN interfaces on each of the Ixia test ports and assign appropriate /30 IPv4 addresses. • Add the address-family IPv4 unicast VRF <vrfname> for each of the configured VPNs under the BGP subconfiguration. • Enable eBGP as the CE-PE routing protocol on all PE routers. All eBGP sessions should be MD5 authenticated with BFD enabled, and AS override configured such that all CE routers can be in the same BGP AS (AS 65000). • Advertise 250 IPv4 unicast prefixes from each emulated CE router to the directly connected PE router. • Redistribute connected routes into the IPv4 unicast VRF address family and verify that they are reachable as iBGP prefixes to the remote PE routers. • Advertise 1000 VPNv4 unicast prefixes from each emulated PE router (RR clients) for each of the ten configured VRFs toward each of the redundant ASR 1002 RRs. • Create 100 bidirectional flows between TS5 and TS6, sourced/destined between advertised routes of the emulated Ixia PE routers. • Create 100 bidirectional flows between TS5 and TS6, sourced/destined between advertised routes of the emulated Ixia CE routers.
Test Steps:	**Step 1.** Verify that all BGP peers are established between RR, PE routers, and Ixia emulated PE routers.

Table 16-9 *Global MPLS Core RFC 2547 Layer 3 VPN VRF Baseline Configuration and Scale Test*

	Step 2. Verify that the total VPNv4 prefixes is approximately 250,000 on each RR (prefixes received from emulated PE routers and from redistributed PE-CE connected routes).
	Step 3. Verify that each of the connected routes is present in the appropriate VRF routing and forwarding tables on the PE routers.
	Step 4. Verify that 50,000 IPv4 prefixes are present in each of the ten VRF routing and forwarding tables on PE1–PE4 from the emulated PE and CE routers.
	Step 5. Issue an extended VRF ping sourced from the PE-CE interface connected to the data center CE routers to a remote PE-CE interface of another PE to verify PE-to-PE connectivity within a VRF.
	Step 6. Generate test traffic as described in the Test Setup and let it run for at least 5 minutes. Examine Ixia traffic statistics for loss on any particular flow.
Expected Results:	All VRFs are created on each PE router with consistent RIB and FIB tables populated with connected (PE-CE) prefixes and prefixes from emulated PE and CE routers. No loss on test flows. DUTs are stable with no elevated CPU or memory consumption during full load.
Observed Results:	
Pass/Fail:	

Table 16-10   *Global MPLS Core MVPN Baseline Configuration and Scale Test*

Test ID:	MVPN-BASE-8
Node List:	Global Core Routers: PE1–PE4 Ixia Test Ports: TS5 and TS6 (25 emulated PE routers, each provisioned with ten RFC 2547 VPNs, with MVRF capabilities)
Test Phase:	Baseline
Test Description:	Global MPLS Core MVPN Baseline Configuration and Scale Test
Test Setup:	• Build the network, as described in Figure 16-2. • Enable IP multicast routing in the global context and in each of the VRF contexts. • Enable multicast and PIM on each of the core interfaces in the global routing table. • Enable SSM as the protocol to build core multicast state. • Configure MVRF capabilities on each of the previous ten RFC 2547 VRFs defined on every DUT (actual PE router) and on each of the emulated Ixia PE routers. Configure a common MDT default group and MDT data range for all PE routers in the same VRF. • Designate PE1 to be the c-RP for each of the ten mVRFs by specifying the first IPv4 (PE-CE) address in each VRF as the PIM RP address. • Configure all CE routers (DUT and emulated Ixia) for PIM-SM with static RP assignments chosen above. • Create 100 emulated multicast sources in each of the ten VRFs behind each of the Ixia emulated PE routers. • Create 100 emulated multicast receivers in each of the ten VRFs behind each of the Ixia emulated CE routers. • Generate multicast test traffic within each VRF by sending traffic from sources to receivers.
Test Steps:	**Step 1.** Ensure MDT SAFI is received from each of the PE routers (DUT and emulated).

Table 16-10   *Global MPLS Core MVPN Baseline Configuration and Scale Test*

	Step 2. Verify all core PIM neighbors are formed between directly connected PE routers.
	Step 3. Verify all VRF PIM neighbors are formed between the PE routers and directly connected emulated CE routers.
	Step 4. Verify that all PE routers (emulated and DUT) are present as VRF PIM neighbors across the appropriate MDT Tunnel interface.
	Step 5. Generate test traffic as described in the Test Setup and let it run for at least 5 minutes. Examine Ixia traffic statistics for loss on any particular flow.
Expected Results:	PIM adjacencies and multicast routes and forwarding entries are present in global and VRF tables. DUTs are stable with no elevated CPU or memory consumption during full load. No loss on traffic flows.
Observed Results:	
Pass/Fail:	

Table 16-11   *Regional Data Center eBGP Baseline Configuration Test*

Test ID:	eBGP-BASE-9
Node List:	Region 1 Data Center Routers: CE1, CE2 Region 2 Data Center Routers: CE3, CE4 Ixia Test Ports: TS1 and TS2 (traffic testing only—no emulation required)
Test Phase:	Baseline
Test Description:	Regional Data Center eBGP Baseline Configuration Test

Table 16-11 *Regional Data Center eBGP Baseline Configuration Test*

Test Setup:	• Build the network, as described in Figure 16-2. • Configure CE1 and CE2 in Region 1 for BGP AS 65002, with eBGP peers of PE1 and PE2, respectively. • Configure CE1 and CE2 as iBGP peers, using the lo0 address as the BGP local address. • Configure CE3 and CE4 in Region 2 for BGP AS 65102, with eBGP peers of PE3 and PE4, respectively. • Configure CE3 and CE4 as iBGP peers, using the lo0 address as the BGP local address. • Redistribute connected routes into BGP from each CE router. • Configure an IP AS Path filter and BGP route map that permits the CE routers to announce only the site local routes to BGP neighbors (denies transit routes). • Enable BGP MD5 authentication between all neighbors. • Enable BFD on each eBGP session. • Configure BGP keepalive/holdown timers of 30/90. • Enable Path MTU Discovery on data center CE routers to enable BGP MSS of 4426. • Configure bidirectional flow between Ixia TS1 and TS2.
Test Steps:	**Step 1.** Verify that all eBGP and iBGP sessions are established with appropriate MSS, BGP timers, authentication, and capabilities exchange.
	Step 2. Verify that BFD neighbor sessions are established between CE and PE routers.
	Step 3. Ensure ping and traceroute reachability between CE routers and Ixia ports at remote sites.
	Step 4. Ensure BGP syslog messages and SNMP traps are generated when neighbor state changes due to MD5 password mismatch.
	Step 5. Disable BFD on one PE router interface and ensure that BGP peer session drops on the remote router.
	Step 6. Generate test traffic as described in the Test Setup and let it run for at least 5 minutes. Examine Ixia traffic statistics for loss on any particular flow.
	Step 7. Verify that all of the devices in the Node List are running without issues by checking their logs and CPU and memory utilization.

Table 16-11 *Regional Data Center eBGP Baseline Configuration Test*

Expected Results:	All configured BGP peering sessions are established. BGP routing table is consistent with no traffic loss on test flows. DUTs are stable with no elevated CPU or memory consumption during full load. Syslog messages and SNMP traps are generated when BGP peer state changes.
Observed Results:	
Pass/Fail:	

Table 16-12 *Regional MPLS Core iBGP Baseline Configuration and Scale Test*

Test ID:	iBGP-BASE-10
Node List:	Region 1 Core Routers: PE5, PE6 Region 2 Core Routers: PE7, PE8 Ixia Test Ports: TS3 and TS4 (emulated PE routers and BGP RR)
Test Phase:	Baseline
Test Description:	Regional MPLS Core iBGP Baseline Configuration and Scale Test
Test Setup:	• Build the network, as described in Figure 16-2. • Configure Region 1 PE5 and PE6 as iBGP peers to Ixia emulated RRs in AS 65001. • Configure Region 2 PE7 and PE8 as iBGP peers to Ixia emulated RRs in AS 65101 • Configure all PE routers and RR to use iBGP to announce both VPNv4 and IPv4 MDT address family reachability. • Configure 50 emulated PE routers on Ixia TS3 in Region 1 with MP-iBGP peers to emulated RR in AS 65001. • Configure 50 emulated PE routers on Ixia TS4 in Region 2 with MP-iBGP peers to emulated RR in AS 65101. • Enable BGP MD5 authentication between all neighbors. • Enable NSF for BGP on ASR 1006 DUT PE routers. • Configure BGP keepalive/holddown timers of 30/90 seconds, respectively, between all iBGP peers. • Enable IP TCP Path MTU Discovery to allow large MSS on BGP sessions.

Table 16-12   *Regional MPLS Core iBGP Baseline Configuration and Scale Test*

Test Steps:	**Step 1.** Verify that all BGP peers are established between RR, PE routers, and Ixia emulated PE routers.
	Step 2. Verify that peer neighbor capabilities include VPNv4 and MDT SAFI for all peers.
	Step 3. Verify that MSS of BGP sessions is 4426, when the core MTU is configured as 4470 and TCP Path MTU Discovery is enabled.
	Step 4. Ensure BGP syslog messages and SNMP traps are generated when neighbor state changes due to MD5 password mismatch or peer address mismatch.
	Step 5. Verify that all of the devices in the Node List are running without issues by checking their logs and CPU and memory utilization.
Expected Results:	All BGP configured peers are in established state on RR and PE routers. DUTs are stable with no elevated CPU or memory consumption during full load. Syslog messages and SNMP traps are generated when BGP peer state changes.
Observed Results:	
Pass/Fail:	

Table 16-13   *Regional MPLS Core RFC 2547 (VPN Unicast) Baseline Configuration and Scale Test*

Test ID:	VPN-BASE-11
Node List:	Region 1 Core Routers: PE5, PE6 Region 2 Core Routers: PE7, PE8 Ixia Test Ports: TS3 and TS4 (emulated CE, PE routers and BGP RR)
Test Phase:	Baseline
Test Description:	Regional MPLS Core RFC 2547 Layer 3 VPN Baseline Configuration and Scale Test

Table 16-13   *Regional MPLS Core RFC 2547 (VPN Unicast) Baseline Configuration and Scale Test*

Test Setup:	• Build the network, as described in Figure 16-2.
	• Configure ten RFC 2547 VRFs on each DUT (actual PE router) and on each of the emulated Ixia PE routers.
	• For both regions, create 50 VLAN interfaces on each PE DUT router port connecting to the Catalyst 6500 linked to the Ixia test ports. (Ixia test ports will be configured to emulate 50 CE routers.) Map each VLAN into one of the existing ten VRFs, so that there are contiguous groups of five VLANs per VRF. Assign unique /30 IPv4 addresses to the PE-CE connections. Refer to Figure 16-3 for an illustration.
	• Create 100 corresponding VLAN interfaces on each of the Ixia test ports and assign relevant /30 IPv4 addresses to the appropriate PE routers.
	• Add the address-family IPv4 unicast VRF <vrfname> for each of the configured VPNs under the BGP subconfiguration.
	• Enable eBGP as the CE-PE routing protocol on all PE routers and emulated CE routers. All eBGP sessions will be MD5 authenticated with BFD enabled, and AS override configured such that all CE routers can be in the same BGP AS (AS 65000).
	• Advertise 2500 IPv4 unicast prefixes from each emulated CE router to the directly connected PE router with eBGP.
	• Redistribute connected routes into the IPv4 unicast VRF address family and verify that they are reachable as iBGP prefixes to the remote PE routers.
	• Advertise 1000 VPNv4 unicast prefixes from each emulated PE router for each of the ten configured VRFs toward each of the redundant RRs.
	• Create 100 bidirectional flows sourced/destined between advertised routes of the emulated Ixia PE routers (test traffic in this scenario flows in/out of the same Ixia port in the regional core).
	• Create 100 bidirectional flows sourced/destined between advertised routes of the emulated Ixia CE routers (test traffic in this scenario flows in/out of the same Ixia port in the regional core).
Test Steps:	**Step 1.** Verify that all BGP peers are established between RR, PE routers, and Ixia emulated PE routers.
	Step 2. Verify that the total VPNv4 prefixes is approximately 250,000 on each RR (prefixes received from emulated PE routers and from redistributed PE-CE connected routes).
	Step 3. Verify that the PE-CE connected routes present in the VRF routing and forwarding tables of every PE routers.

Table 16-13 *Regional MPLS Core RFC 2547 (VPN Unicast) Baseline Configuration and Scale Test*

	Step 4. Verify that 50,000 IPv4 prefixes are present in each of the ten VRF routing and forwarding tables on PE1–PE4 from the emulated PE and CE routers.
	Step 5. Issue an extended VRF ping sourced from the PE-CE interface of one PE DUT connected to the emulated CE routers to a remote PE-CE interface of another PE DUT to verify PE-to-PE connectivity within a VRF.
	Step 6. Generate test traffic as described in the Test Setup and let run it for at least 5 minutes. Examine Ixia traffic statistics for loss on any particular flow.
Expected Results:	All VRFs are created on each PE router with consistent RIB and FIB tables populated with connected (PE-CE) prefixes and prefixes from emulated PE and CE routers. No loss on test flows. DUTs are stable with no elevated CPU or memory consumption during full load.
Observed Results:	
Pass/Fail:	

Table 16-14 *Regional MPLS Core MVPN Baseline Configuration and Scale Test*

Test ID:	MVPN-BASE-12
Node List:	Region 1 Core Routers: PE5, PE6 Region 2 Core Routers: PE7, PE8 Ixia Test Ports: TS3 and TS4 (emulated MVPN PE routers, CE routers, BGP RR, and emulated multicast sources and receivers)
Test Phase:	Baseline
Test Description:	Regional MPLS Core MVPN Baseline Configuration and Scale Test

Table 16-14 *Regional MPLS Core MVPN Baseline Configuration and Scale Test*

Test Setup:	• Build the network, as described in Figure 16-2. • Enable IP multicast routing in the global context and in each of the VRF contexts. • Enable multicast and PIM on each of the core interfaces in the global routing table. • Enable SSM as the protocol to build core multicast state. • Configure MVRF capabilities on each of the ten RFC 2547 VRFs previously defined on each DUT (actual PE router) and on each of the emulated Ixia PE routers. Configure a common MDT default group and MDT data range for all PE routers in the same VRF. • Designate PE5 to be the c-RP for each of the ten mVRFs in Region 1 by specifying the first IPv4 (PE-CE) address in each VRF as the PIM RP address. • Designate PE7 to be the c-RP for each of the ten mVRFs in Region 2 by specifying the first IPv4 (PE-CE) address in each VRF as the PIM RP address. • Configure all CE routers (DUT and emulated Ixia) for PIM-SM with static RP assignments chosen above. • Create 100 emulated multicast sources in each of the ten VRFs behind each of the Ixia emulated PE routers. • Create 100 emulated multicast receivers in each of the ten VRFs behind each of the Ixia emulated CE routers. • Generate multicast test traffic within each VRF by sending traffic from sources to receivers.
Test Steps:	**Step 1.** Ensure MDT SAFI is received from each of the PE routers (DUT and emulated).
	Step 2. Verify all core PIM neighbors are formed between directly connected PE routers.
	Step 3. Verify all VRF PIM neighbors are formed between the PE routers and directly connected emulated CE routers.
	Step 4. Verify that all PE routers (emulated and DUT) are present as VRF PIM neighbors across the appropriate MDT tunnel interface.
	Step 5. Generate test traffic as described in the Test Setup and let it run for at least 5 minutes. Examine Ixia traffic statistics for loss on any particular flow.
Expected Results:	PIM adjacencies and Mrib/Mfib routes are present in global and VRF tables. DUTs are stable with no elevated CPU or memory consumption during full load. No loss on traffic flows.

Table 16-14 *Regional MPLS Core MVPN Baseline Configuration and Scale Test*

Observed Results:

Pass/Fail:

Table 16-15 *Inter-AS Option B for Layer 3 VPN (Unicast) Configuration and Verification Test*

Test ID:	InterAS-BASE-13
Node List:	Global Core Routers: PE1–PE4
	Region 1 Core Routers: PE5, PE6
	Region 2 Core Routers: PE7, PE8
	Ixia Test Ports: TS3–TS6 (emulated CE routers for unicast sources and receivers for inter-AS traffic generation)
Test Phase:	Baseline
Test Description:	Inter-AS Option B for Layer 3 VPN (Unicast) Configuration and Verification Test
Test Setup:	• Build the network, as described in Figure 16-2.
	• Ensure that Inter-AS Option B uses eBGP between ASBRs in different autonomous systems to advertise VPNv4 prefixes with MPLS label.
	• Configure PE router inter-AS interfaces with /30 IPv4 addresses (in the global context).
	• Configure eBGP peering sessions between each of the PE routers at the Inter-AS boundaries, exchanging only VPNv4 address-family capabilities.
	• Ensure that eBGP peers are all MD5 authenticated with BFD configured for fast failover detection.
	• Configure BGP "next-hop-self" policy on PE router to local AS RR neighbor session, to prevent unnecessary redistribution of Inter-AS external OSPF routes.
	• Create 100 bidirectional flows sourced/destined between advertised routes of the emulated Ixia CE routers in Regions 1 and 2.

Table 16-15 *Inter-AS Option B for Layer 3 VPN (Unicast) Configuration and Verification Test*

Test Steps:	**Step 1.** Validate that eBGP peering sessions are established between all AS peering points on the PE routers in the core and all the regions.
	Step 2. Validate that BGP VPNv4 updates between ASBRs (inter-AS PE routers) change the BGP next hop, and include an MPLS label.
	Step 3. Validate that BGP VPNv4 updates that are advertised to local RRs change the BGP next hop to the ASBR loopback address, and include a double label stack including the IGP/LDP label and the eBGP-learned/VPN label.
	Step 4. Generate test traffic as described in the Test Setup and let it run for at least 5 minutes. Examine Ixia traffic statistics for loss on any particular flow.
Expected Results:	Control plane exchange of prefixes and labels will occur as described in the Test Setup. DUTs are stable with no elevated CPU or memory consumption during full load. No loss seen on traffic flows.
Observed Results:	
Pass/Fail:	

Table 16-16 *MVPN Inter-AS Support (Option B) Configuration and Verification Test*

Test ID:	InterAS-BASE-14
Node List:	Global Core Routers: PE1–PE4 Region 1 Core Routers: PE5, PE6 Region 2 Core Routers: PE7, PE8 Ixia Test Ports: TS3–TS6 (emulated CE routers for multicast sources and receivers for inter-AS traffic generation)
Test Phase:	Baseline
Test Description:	MVPN Inter-AS Support (Option B) Configuration and Verification Test

Table 16-16 *MVPN Inter-AS Support (Option B) Configuration and Verification Test*

Test Setup:	• Build the network, as described in Figure 16-2.
	• Configure MVPN Inter-AS Support (Option B) to use BGP extensions (BGP connector attribute, BGP MDT SAFI, and RPF Vector) to extend MDT across Inter-AS boundaries.
	• Configure PIM-SM across all Inter-AS boundaries.
	• Configure the RPF Vector for each VRF that is needed to cross AS boundaries, specifying the RD keyword.
	• Enable the address-family IPv4 MDT SAFI on the previously configured eBGP peering sessions between each of the PE routers at the Inter-AS boundaries.
	• Configure BGP "next-hop-self" on PE router to Inter-AS peer.
	• Create 100 bidirectional multicast flows sourced/destined between the emulated Ixia multicast sources and receivers behind routers in Region 1 and 2 (there should be 50 sources and 50 receivers in each of the regions).
Test Steps:	**Step 1.** Validate that eBGP peering sessions are established between all AS peering points on the PE routers in both the core and the regions, and that the address-family IPv4 MDT updates are being exchanged.
	Step 2. Validate that BGP IPv4 MDT updates between ASBRs (inter-AS PE routers) change the BGP next hop, and include an MPLS label.
	Step 3. Verify that the RPF interface for the mroute associated with the MDT for a source in a different AS is indeed the source PE router in the peer AS
	Step 4. Verify that the proxy-vector RPF interface for the same mroute examined in Step 3 is the ASBR in the peer AS.
	Step 5. Generate test traffic as described in the Test Setup and let it run for at least 5 minutes. Examine Ixia traffic statistics for loss on any particular flow.
Expected Results:	Control plane exchange of prefixes and labels will occur as described in the Test Setup. DUTs are stable with no elevated CPU or memory consumption during full load. No loss seen on traffic flows.
Observed Results:	
Pass/Fail:	

Table 16-17 *BFD Feature and Scalability Test*

Test ID:	BFD-FEAT-1
Node List:	Global Core Routers: PE1–PE4 Region 1 Core Routers: PE5, PE6 Region 2 Core Routers: PE7, PE8 Ixia Test Ports: TS3–TS6 (emulated CE routers running BFD for eBGP sessions)
Test Phase:	Feature
Test Description:	BFD Feature and Scalability Test
Test Setup:	• Build the network, as described in Figure 16-2. • Configure BFD fast failure detection on all eBGP links (PE-CE sessions and Inter-AS boundaries) in the global and regional cores with BFD minimum intervals of 150 ms and a multiplier of 3. • Configure BFD fast failure detection on all OSPF interfaces in the global and regional cores with BFD minimum intervals of 150 ms and a multiplier of 3. • Configure Interface Dampening to prevent excessive BFD/routing protocol churn during periods of interface instability.
Test Steps:	**Step 1.** Validate that BFD sessions are established for all BGP and OSPF neighbors, with the configured timers.
	Step 2. Remove BFD configuration from one side of an OSPF adjacency in the global core and verify that the remote neighbor OSPF state immediately changes from FULL to DOWN.
	Step 3. Remove BFD configuration from one side of an OSPF adjacency in the regional core and verify that the remote neighbor OSPF state immediately changes from FULL to DOWN.
	Step 4. Remove BFD configuration from one side of an eBGP peer in the global core and verify that the remote neighbor immediately drops the BGP connection.
	Step 5. Remove BFD configuration from one side of an eBGP peer in the regional core and verify that the remote neighbor immediately drops the BGP connection.
	Step 6. Measure the CPU impact (line card or RP as it applies) of enabling the 50 BFD/eBGP sessions on the DUT (ASR 1000 Series and CRS-1) routers.
	Step 7. Intentionally raise the CPU of a DUT (launch multiple SNMP Management Information Base (MIB) walks simultaneously using a script) and ensure the BFD peers do not flap.

Table 16-17   *BFD Feature and Scalability Test*

	Step 8. Ensure the BFD packets are marked with IP Precedence 6 on each DUT.
	Step 9. Perform an OIR of a nonrelated line card and ensure BFD sessions do not flap.
	Step 10. Perform an RP switchover and ensure the BFD sessions do not flap.
	Step 11. Intentionally flap an interface multiple consecutive times (pulling and replacing a fiber on a neighbor) to validate the Interface Dampening feature prevents excessive churn.
Expected Results:	All features will work as described in the Test Steps.
Observed Results:	
Pass/Fail:	

Table 16-18   *OSPF High Availability Feature Test*

Test ID:	OSPF-Feat-2
Node List:	Global Core Routers: PE1–PE4 Region 1 Core Routers: PE5, PE6 Ixia Test Ports: TS3–TS6 (emulated P routers running OSPF)
Test Phase:	Feature
Test Description:	OSPF High Availability Feature Test
Test Setup:	• Build the network, as described in Figure 16-2. • Configure OSPF SPF Prefix Prioritization on the CRS-1 PE routers in the global core so that convergence of the CRS-1 PE router loopback range is given priority over LSAs in the database. • Configure OSPF NSR on CRS-1 PE routers in the global core. • Configure OSPF NSF on ASR 1006 PE routers in regional cores. • Create 250 bidirectional test flows between TS5 and TS6, in the global core, using emulated OSPF routes as source/destination. • Create ten additional bidirectional test flows between TS5 and TS6 in the global core, sourced/destined from emulated OSPF routes addressed out of the same IP range as the PE router loopbacks (to validate SPF Prefix Prioritization). • Create 125 bidirectional test flows between different VLANs on TS3 in Region 1 Core using emulated OSPF routes as source/destination.

Table 16-18   *OSPF High Availability Feature Test*

Test Steps:	Step 1. Generate traffic streams as described in the Test Setup.
	Step 2. Apply OSPF costs to global core links such that all test traffic flows across a particular link (for example, the PE1-PE3 SONET link).
	Step 3. For the SPF Prefix Prioritization test in the global core, flap the global core link across which the traffic is flowing and note the traffic loss on the test flows (250 nonpriority prefixes and the ten additional priority prefixes).
	Step 4. Restore all global core links and allow OSPF to reconverge so that there is no loss on test flows. Repeat the test described in Step 3 for five iterations.
	Step 5. For the NSR test on the global core, remove the primary route processor (RP) on one of the global core CRS-1 routers in the forwarding path and check for loss on test flows. Reinsert the RP and let it come up as a "backup." Verify that no traffic is lost while the RP comes on line. Repeat the test for five iterations.
	Step 6. To verify NSR on the global core, crash the OSPF process on the CRS-1 used for the Step 5 test, and check for loss on test flows. Repeat the test for five iterations.
	Step 7. As an NSF test for the regional core, remove the primary RP on one of the regional core ASR 1006 PE routers in the forwarding path of the test traffic and check for loss on test flows. Repeat the test for five iterations.
	Step 8. For a final NSF test on the regional core, force an RP switchover, from the CLI, of the regional core ASR 1006 PE router in the forwarding path of the test traffic and check for loss on the test flows. Repeat the test for five iterations.
Expected Results:	The CRS-1 SPF Prefix Prioritization feature should result in faster reconvergence of the test flows associated with the "priority prefixes" over the others. Global core RP failovers should result in zero loss on test flows when the CRS-1 NSR feature is enabled. Regional core RP failovers should result in minimal loss (ms) on test flows when the ASR 1006 NSF feature is enabled.
Observed Results:	
Pass/Fail:	

Table 16-19 *LDP High Availability Feature Test*

Test ID:	LDP-Feat-3
Node List:	Global Core Routers: PE1–PE4 Region 1 Core Routers: PE5, PE6 Ixia Test Ports: TS3–TS6 (emulated P routers running OSPF)
Test Phase:	Feature
Test Description:	LDP High Availability Feature Test
Test Setup:	• Build the network, as described in Figure 16-2. • Enable MPLS LDP Synchronization on the CRS-1 and ASR 1006 routers (this feature is configured under OSPF). • Configure LDP NSR on the CRS-1 PE routers in the global core. • Configure LDP Graceful Restart on the ASR 1006 PE routers in the regional cores (testing on one regional core is sufficient because hardware and enabled features are identical). • Enable LDP label allocations for all of the emulated OSPF routes so that test flows are MPLS tagged. • Create 250 bidirectional test flows configured between TS5 and TS6 in the global core, using emulated OSPF/LDP routes as source/destination. • Create 125 bidirectional test flows configured between different VLANs on TS3 in Region 1 Core using emulated OSPF/LDP routes as source/destination.
Test Steps:	**Step 1.** Generate traffic streams as described in the Test Setup.
	Step 2. Apply OSPF costs to global core links such that all test traffic flows across a particular link (for example, the PE1-PE3 SONET link). Steps 3–5 are done to validate the MPLS IGP Synchronization feature:
	Step 3. Manually shut down all redundant links so that only one path is available between a pair of PE routers. Display the OSPF route metric for a prefix associated with a /32 loopback address of the remote PE router that is reachable over a directly connected link.
	Step 4. On the remote PE router, break the LDP neighbor by removing the LDP configuration on the link.
	Step 5. On the local PE router, verify that the OSPF route metric for the /32 prefix is raised to max-metric (65536). Restore all links and LDP configuration once complete. Steps 6 and 7 are done to validate the CRS-1 LDP NSR feature in the global core.

Table 16-19 *LDP High Availability Feature Test*

	Step 6. Remove the primary RP on one of the global core CRS-1 routers in the forwarding path and check for loss on labeled test flows. Repeat the test for several iterations.
	Step 7. Crash the LDP process on the same CRS-1 active RP and check for loss on labeled test flows. Repeat the test for several iterations. Steps 8 and 9 are done to validate the ASR 1000 LDP Graceful Restart feature in the regional core.
	Step 8. Remove the primary RP on one of the regional core ASR 1006 PE routers in the forwarding path and check for loss on labeled test flows. Repeat the test for several iterations.
	Step 9. Force an RP switchover from the CLI of the same regional core ASR 1006 PE routers in the forwarding path and check for loss on labeled test flows. Repeat the test for several iterations.
Expected Results:	The OSPF metric will be raised to 65535 for the connected routes between PE routers that have not fully formed an LDP peer relationship. Global core RP failovers should result in zero loss on labeled test flows when the CRS-1 LDP NSR feature is enabled. Regional core RP failovers should result in minimal loss (ms) on labeled test flows when the ASR 1006 LDP Graceful Restart feature is enabled.
Observed Results:	
Pass/Fail:	

Table 16-20 *BGP Next-Hop Tracking Feature Test*

Test ID:	BGPNHT-FEAT-4
Node List:	Global Core Routers: PE1–PE4 Region 1 Data Center Routers: CE1, CE2 Region 2 Data Center Routers: CE3, CE4 Ixia Test Ports: TS1 and TS2
Test Phase:	Feature
Test Description:	BGP Next-Hop Tracking Feature Test

Table 16-20   *BGP Next-Hop Tracking Feature Test*

Test Setup:	• Build the network, as described in Figure 16-2. • BGP Next-Hop Tracking (NHT) is enabled by default on both the CRS-1 and ASR 1006 platforms. This test will be run to validate that VPNv4 convergence events are "event driven" and not subjected to a BGP Scanner process timer. • Create one bidirectional flow sourced/destined between the Ixia ports TS1 and TS2 in different regional data centers.
Test Steps:	**Step 1.** Start the test traffic between the data centers.
	Step 2. On PE3, note the BGP next hop associated with the VPNv4 prefix in Data Center 1. The preferred (best path) BGP next hop should be either PE1 or PE2 depending on IGP cost preference.
	Step 3. Power cycle or crash the PE router that is the preferred next hop from the PE3 perspective and note flow loss.
	Step 4. Restore the powered-down router and wait until the network is stable. Repeat the test with BGP NHT disabled from the configuration.
Expected Results:	BGP reconvergence should be triggered immediately after the PE router loopback is removed from OSPF. Flow loss should be much greater when BGP NHT is disabled.
Observed Results:	
Pass/Fail:	

Table 16-21   *BGP PIC Feature Test*

Test ID:	BGPPIC-FEAT-5
Node List:	Global Core Routers: PE1–PE4 Region 1 Data Center Routers: CE1, CE2 Region 2 Data Center Routers: CE3, CE4 Ixia Test Ports: TS1 and TS2
Test Phase:	Feature
Test Description:	BGP PIC Feature Test

Table 16-21 *BGP PIC Feature Test*

Test Setup:	• Build the network, as described in Figure 16-2. • Enable BGP PIC Core and Edge on the CE and PE routers so that additional backup paths are installed in the BGP FIB for the VPNv4 and IPv4 prefixes, respectively. • Create 1000 bidirectional flows sourced/destined between Ixia ports TS1 and TS2 in different regional data centers. Ensure that the Ixia default gateways are set appropriately so that some flows exit out each CE router into the MPLS core.
Test Steps:	**Step 1.** Start the test traffic between the data centers. Steps 2–4 are done to validate the BGP PIC Core feature on the global core PE routers.
	Step 2. On PE3, note the BGP next hop associated with the VPNv4 prefix in Data Center 1. The preferred (best path) BGP next hop should be either PE1 or PE2 depending on IGP cost preference, with the other PE router next hop installed as "backup."
	Step 3. Power cycle or crash the PE router that is the preferred next hop from PE3 perspective and note flow loss.
	Step 4. Repeat Steps 2 and 3 with BGP PIC configuration disabled from the configuration. Restore BGP PIC configuration after this test is completed. Steps 5–7 are done to validate the BGP PIC Edge feature on the global core PE routers.
	Step 5. On PE1 and PE2, note the next hops associated with the VPNv4 prefix in the Region 1 Data Center. The best path will be the eBGP-learned route from the directly connected CE router, with the "backup" path being the iBGP-learned route from the other PE router.
	Step 6. Ensure that some flows are traversing the PE1-to-CE1 link and reboot the CE1 router. Note the loss on the flows. Upon restoration of the CE1 router, repeat the test by rebooting the CE2 router and noting loss.
	Step 7. Repeat Steps 5 and 6 with BGP PIC configuration disabled from the configuration. Restore BGP PIC configuration after this test is completed. Steps 8–10 are done to validate the BGP PIC Edge feature on the regional data center CE routers.

Table 16-21   *BGP PIC Feature Test*

Step 8.	On CE1 and CE2, note the next hops associated with the IPv4 prefixes in the Region 2 Data Center. The best path will be the eBGP-learned route from the directly connected PE router, with the "backup" path being the iBGP-learned route from the other CE router.
Step 9.	Ensure that some flows are traversing the CE1-to-PE1 link and reboot the PE1 router. Note the loss on the flows. Upon restoration of the PE1 router, repeat the test by rebooting the PE2 router and noting loss.
Step 10.	Repeat Steps 8 and 9 with BGP PIC configuration disabled from the configuration. Restore BGP PIC configuration after this test is completed.
Expected Results:	Flow loss should be considerably less when BGP PIC is enabled than when it is disabled in the various scenarios.
Observed Results:	
Pass/Fail:	

Table 16-22   *BGP High Availability Test*

Test ID:	BGP-HA-FEAT-6
Node List:	Global Core Routers: PE1–PE4 Region 1 Data Center Routers: CE1, CE2 Region 2 Data Center Routers: CE3, CE4 Region 1 Core Routers: PE5, PE6 Ixia Test Ports: TS1–TS4
Test Phase:	Feature
Test Description:	BGP High Availability Test
Test Setup:	• Build the network, as described in Figure 16-2. • Create 1000 bidirectional flows sourced/destined between Ixia ports TS1 and TS2 in different regional data centers. Ensure that the Ixia default gateways are set appropriately so that some flows exit out each CE router into the MPLS core. • Create 1000 bidirectional flows sourced/destined between different VLAN interfaces of TS3, so that traffic traverses PE5 and PE6.

Table 16-22   *BGP High Availability Test*

Test Steps:	**Step 1.** Start the test traffic between the data centers. Steps 2–4 are done to validate the BGP NSR feature on the global core PE (CRS-1) routers.
	Step 2. Ensure that some traffic between Data Centers 1 and 2 is passing through PE1.
	Step 3. Remove the active RP on the PE1 router (CRS-1) and check for flow loss. Reinsert the RP and wait for it to come back on line. Watch for any traffic loss while the RP is coming back up. Repeat for five iterations.
	Step 4. Crash the BGP process on the active RP on the PE1 router and check for flow loss. Repeat for five iterations. Steps 5 and 6 are done to validate the BGP NSF feature on the regional core (ASR 1006) PE routers.
	Step 5. Remove the active RP on the PE5 router (ASR 1006) and check for flow loss. Reinsert the RP and wait for it to come back on line. Watch for any traffic loss while the RP is coming back up. Repeat for five iterations.
	Step 6. Perform an RP switchover on the active RP on the PE5 router from the CLI and check for flow loss. Repeat for several iterations.
Expected Results:	No traffic loss in flows is expected when BGP NSR is enabled on the CRS-1 routers during the various failure scenarios. A minimal amount of loss (ms) is expected during the failure scenarios on the ASR 1006 with BGP NSF enabled.

Observed Results:

Pass/Fail:

Table 16-23 *PE Router Scalability and Duty Cycle Test*

Test ID:	PE-PERF-1
Node List:	Global Core Routers: PE1–PE4 Regional Core Routers: PE5, PE6 Ixia Test Ports: TS1–TS3, TS5, TS6
Test Phase:	Performance
Test Description:	PE Router Scalability and Duty Cycle Test
Test Setup:	• Build the network, as described in Figure 16-2. • Enable the full control plane load, as described in Table 16-1. • Enable a full mesh of bidirectional unicast and multicast traffic (at least 5000 flows) between various points in the network. Note the traffic paths and ensure there is no loss in steady-state conditions. • Enable all NMS Infrastructure/System features, such as SNMP polling, NetFlow Export, AAA, DNS, syslog, NTP, SSH, Telnet, and IPSLA as appropriate to emulate the expected production router template.

Test Steps:	**Step 1.** The following sanity/integrity checks should be taken before and after every one of the subsequent tests is executed. It is highly recommended that scripts be developed to automate these checks:
	  • No process crashes
	  • No unexpected tracebacks
	  • No configuration loss
	  • All CRS devices in IOS-XR ready state
	  • Redundancy is ready for all RPs
	  • All routing protocols converged
	  • No traffic loss on test streams
	  • No alarms or LEDs
	  • No BFD flaps
	  • No protocol flaps
	  • RIB and FIB consistent
	  • CPU and memory recorded

	Step 2. Poll the CPU and memory of all device routing processors and line card CPU (when applicable) from multiple SNMP engines.
	Step 3. Repeatedly telnet and ssh to the router for at least 6 hours.
	Step 4. Repeatedly provision and de-provision a VPN (add/delete VRF and BGP parameters).

Table 16-23   *PE Router Scalability and Duty Cycle Test*

	Step 5. Repeatedly provision and de-provision a QoS Service Policy onto an interface.
	Step 6. Modify OSPF costs, BGP policies, and authentication key chains. (A small amount of loss may be detected during these changes as adjacencies flap.)
	Step 7. Perform pings, traceroutes, debugs, and traces.
	Step 8. Repeatedly **shut** and **no shut** interfaces.
	Step 9. Perform Software Maintenance Upgrades (SMU).
	Step 10. Repeatedly execute CLI commands that require long completion times (such as **show bgp vpnv4 unicast**) with console logging enabled, and terminal length set to 0.
Expected Results:	Expected results are described in Step 1 of the Test Steps. CPU and memory utilization are recorded for each test as a baseline.
Observed Results:	
Pass/Fail:	

Table 16-24   *BGP RR Router Scalability and Duty Cycle Test*

Test ID:	RR-PERF-2
Node List:	RR1–RR4
Test Phase:	Performance
Test Description:	BGP RR Router Scalability and Duty Cycle Test
Test Setup:	• Build the network, as described in Figure 16-2. • Enable the full control plane load, as described in Table 16-1. • Enable a full mesh of bidirectional unicast and multicast traffic (at least 5000 flows) between various points in the network. Note the traffic paths and ensure there is no loss in steady-state conditions. • Enable all NMS Infrastructure/System features, such as SNMP polling, NetFlow Export, AAA, DNS, syslog, NTP, SSH, Telnet, and IPSLA as appropriate to emulate the expected production router template.

Table 16-24   *BGP RR Router Scalability and Duty Cycle Test*

Test Steps:	**Step 1.** The following sanity/integrity checks should be taken before and after every one of the subsequent tests is executed. It is highly recommended that scripts be developed to automate these checks: • No process crashes • No unexpected tracebacks • No configuration loss • Redundancy is ready for all RPs • All routing protocols converged • No traffic loss on test streams • No alarms or LEDs • No BGP flaps • RIB and FIB consistent
	Step 2. Poll the CPU and memory of all device routing processors and line card CPU (when applicable) from multiple SNMP engines.
	Step 3. Repeatedly telnet and ssh to the router for at least 6 hours.
	Step 4. Repeatedly provision and de-provision BGP peers.
	Step 5. Modify OSPF costs and BGP peer group parameters.
	Step 6. Perform pings, traceroutes, debugs, and traces.
	Step 7. Repeatedly **shut** and **no shut** interfaces.
	Step 8. Repeatedly execute CLI commands that require long completion times (such as **show bgp vpnv4 unicast**) with console logging enabled, and terminal length set to 0.
	Step 9. Increase the number of emulated peers to twice the number of the planned deployment and note the effect on CPU and memory.
Expected Results:	Expected results are described in Step 1 of the Test Steps. CPU and memory utilization are recorded for each test as a baseline.
Observed Results:	
Pass/Fail:	

Table 16-25 *Device Failure and Recovery Test*

Test ID:	BGP-DUTY-1
Node List:	All
Test Phase:	Duty Cycle
Test Description:	Device Failure and Recovery Test
Test Setup:	• Build the network, as described in Figure 16-2. • Enable the full control plane load, as described in Table 16-1. • Enable a full mesh of bidirectional unicast and multicast traffic (at least 5000 flows) between various points in the network. Note the traffic paths and ensure there is no loss in steady-state conditions. • Enable all NMS Infrastructure/System features, such as SNMP polling, NetFlow Export, AAA, DNS, syslog, NTP, SSH, Telnet, and IPSLA as appropriate to emulate the expected production router template.
Test Steps:	**Step 1.** The following sanity/integrity checks should be taken before and after every one of the subsequent tests is executed. It is highly recommended that scripts be developed to automate these checks: • No process crashes • No unexpected tracebacks • No configuration loss • Redundancy is ready for all RPs • All routing protocols converged • No traffic loss on test streams • No alarms or LEDs • No BGP flaps • RIB and FIB consistent
	Step 2. Reload the CE1 router and record traffic loss to/from the regional data center when the router goes down.
	Step 3. Check for additional traffic loss when the CE1 router recovers and is fully operational.
	Step 4. Reload RR1. No loss should occur when this router goes down or recovers.
	Step 5. Reload the PE3 router. Minimal loss should occur when BGP PIC is enabled.
	Step 6. Check for additional traffic loss when the PE3 router recovers and is fully operational.

Table 16-25   *Device Failure and Recovery Test*

Expected Results:	Expected results are described in Step 1 of the Test Steps. CPU and memory utilization are recorded for each test as a baseline.
Observed Results:	
Pass/Fail:	

Table 16-26   *Circuit and Line Card Failure and Recovery Test*

Test ID:	BGP-DUTY-2
Node List:	All
Test Phase:	Duty Cycle
Test Description:	Circuit and Line Card Failure and Recovery Test
Test Setup:	• Build the network, as described in Figure 16-2. • Enable the full control plane load, as described in Table 16-1. • Enable a full mesh of bidirectional unicast and multicast traffic (at least 5000 flows) between various points in the network. Note the traffic paths and ensure there is no loss in steady-state conditions. • Enable all NMS Infrastructure/System features, such as SNMP polling, NetFlow Export, AAA, DNS, syslog, NTP, SSH, Telnet, and IPSLA as appropriate to emulate the expected production router template.
Test Steps:	**Step 1.** The following sanity/integrity checks should be taken before and after every one of the subsequent tests is executed. It is highly recommended that scripts be developed to automate these checks: • No process crashes • No unexpected tracebacks • No configuration loss • All CRS devices in IOS-XR ready state • Redundancy is ready for all RPs • All routing protocols converged • No traffic loss on test streams • No alarms or LEDs • No BFD flaps • No protocol flaps • RIB and FIB consistent • CPU and memory recorded

Table 16-26   *Circuit and Line Card Failure and Recovery Test*

	Step 2. Pull a PE-to-PE link and record loss on unicast and multicast test flows.
	Step 3. Restore the PE-to-PE link and record loss on unicast and multicast test flows.
	Step 4. Pull a CE-to-PE link and record loss on unicast and multicast test flows.
	Step 5. Restore the CE-to-PE link and record loss on unicast and multicast test flows.
	Step 6. Pull a link at the Inter-AS boundary and record loss on unicast and multicast test flows.
	Step 7. Restore the link at the Inter-AS boundary and record loss on unicast and multicast test flows.
	Step 8. Reset line cards (one at a time) in CE1, PE1, PE5, and RR1 from the CLI and record loss on unicast and multicast test flows.
	Step 9. Check for loss when the line card recovers.
	Step 10. Perform an OIR of a line card on PE1 and record loss on unicast and multicast test flows.
	Step 11. Remove the power supply on PE1 and record loss on unicast and multicast test flows.
Expected Results:	Expected results are described in Step 1 of the Test Steps. CPU and memory utilization are recorded for each test as a baseline.
Observed Results:	
Pass/Fail:	

Chapter 17

WAN and Application Optimization: Performance Routing and Wide Area Application Services Test Plan

As rich content and multimedia applications are becoming a bigger part of everyday business processes, companies are looking at new technologies and solutions to optimize their performance over WANs. Lower bandwidth, higher latency, jitter, and packet dropping are considered common pitfalls of a WAN when it is contrasted to the more predicable and expedited packet delivery of a LAN. Degraded WAN performance inevitably leads to poor voice and video quality and considerable slowdowns in the delivery of data to remote users. To deliver these new services more efficiently, enterprises often look at the Cisco Borderless Network Architecture and its promise to allow people to connect to the resources they need, from any location.

Note A Borderless Network creates a collaborative environment for employees and partners located at different geographic locations by enabling rich media technologies such as interactive and on-demand video, voice, and web collaboration, video to mobile devices, and Cisco TelePresence.

As more companies adopt the Cisco Borderless Network Architecture, they will place even higher demands on their WAN infrastructure. To meet this set of higher demands, enterprises must deploy the right set of tools.

Cisco Wide Area Application Services (WAAS) and Performance Routing (PfR) are two prominent, complementary Cisco WAN Optimization tools that improve the reliability, performance, and delivery of applications. Where Cisco WAAS provides WAN optimization and application-level acceleration through advanced caching and compression techniques, Cisco PfR routes data packets through the best-performing IP path between remote network locations. This is accomplished by enhancing the best-path decision-making process of a routing protocol to include network latency, packet loss, jitter, link capacity, and traffic load on WAN circuits.

This test plan assists you in validating an optimization solution that includes both PfR and WAAS to improve application performance across a WAN.

Background

As part of a branch office refresh, an enterprise organization developed a new WAN design to improve existing application performance and to prepare for a rich media (VoIP and video) rollout. The legacy WAN was built exclusively with IPsec-VPN tunnels extending applications to the remote offices across the Internet. This infrastructure, which met the needs of the business for many years, began to buckle under the increased demands of the new applications being deployed. Chronic problems with point-of-sale (POS) timeouts and slow database replications began to impact the business, leading enterprise architects to believe that simply "throwing bandwidth at the problem" was not the right answer.

With new requirements for video and VoIP in mind, architects responsible for the redesign made several changes, including the following:

- Added an MPLS connection to each branch to supplement existing bandwidth provided by IPsec over the Internet

- Replaced equipment that was rapidly approaching end of life with new ISR-G2 routers with integrated Ethernet switches and WAAS/WAE modules

- Enabled the Performance Routing feature to "steer" high-priority traffic over the best path while using the "slower" path for noncritical traffic

- Used WAAS to accelerate applications over the WAN and preposition content

Physical and Logical Test Topology

Figure 17-1 shows the high-level physical topology used for this test.

Technical details of the test setup are as follows:

- The branch routers, CE1 and CE2, are Cisco 2921s with SM-ES2-16-P switch modules and SM-SRE-900-K9 (WAE-1 and WAE-2) application modules running WAAS with Enterprise licensing.

- The CE1 branch router is a PfR border router (BR), the PfR master controller (MC) for the branch and the HSRP standby router. CE1 has a 5-Mbps Ethernet connection to the test network named Internet. It reaches the data center via an IPsec-encrypted GRE tunnel over which it runs eBGP with CE3 to exchange routing. The IP MTU on the GRE tunnel is set to 1300 to accommodate GRE and IPsec header overhead. CE1 has a single /32 static route pointed at the Internet service provider (ISP) to establish the GRE/IPsec tunnel.

- The CE2 branch router is a PfR BR and the HSRP active router. It is connected to the data center over a "private MPLS network." CE2 is connected to the MPLS network over a 5-Mbps Ethernet "circuit" and is running eBGP with the ISP to get its data center routes.

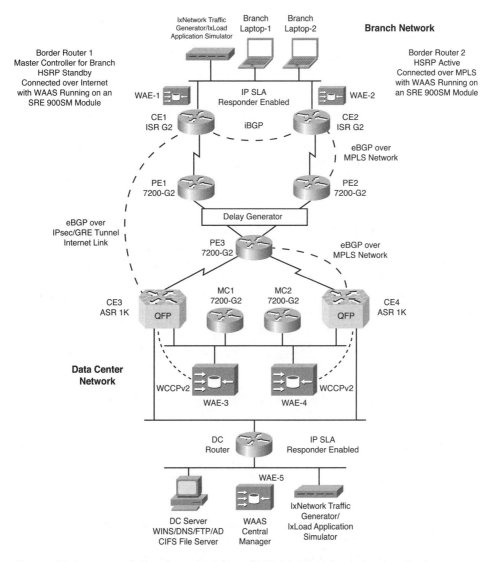

Figure 17-1 *Network Topology for PfR and WAAS WAN Optimization Testing*

- CE1 and CE2 are running iBGP with each other over their LAN.

- The data center aggregation routers, CE3 and CE4, are Cisco ASR 1006 using dual RP2 and ESP 20 forwarding engines, with embedded hardware encryption. They are both PfR BRs.

- CE3 is connected to the Internet over a 150-Mbps Ethernet circuit. It is connecting to the branches over an IPsec-encrypted multipoint GRE (mGRE) tunnel interface (a single GRE interface to support multiple GRE and IPsec tunnels to simplify the size and complexity of the configuration). CE3 is running eBGP with the branch routers over the IPsec-encrypted GRE tunnels. The MTU for the mGRE tunnel is set to 1300 to accommodate GRE and IPsec header overhead.

■ CE4 is connected to the private MPLS network over a 150-Mbps Ethernet circuit. It runs eBGP with the ISP to exchange routing information.

■ In this testing, we will be using dedicated PfR MCs at the Data Center site, MC1 and MC2 (both Cisco 7201 NPE-G2s with 2 GB of DRAM). The dedicated MC topology is typically recommended at data center or WAN hub locations terminating a large number of remote sites. Although the PfR MC feature does not support stateful redundancy at the time of this writing, customers often deploy it in pairs with a primary MC controlling both BRs and a secondary MC operating in a "warm standby" mode.

Note Stateless redundancy can be achieved with PfR by enabling HSRP, on a common Ethernet segment, between the MC1 and MC2 routers and defining the virtual IP address as the PfR MC address. When the primary MC fails, the BRs drop their TCP sessions upon loss of keepalives. This triggers an immediate withdrawal of controlled prefixes or applications such that routing reverts to its default state. As the standby MC assumes the HSRP active role for the virtual IP address, the BRs build new TCP sessions, and the entire process of learning, measuring, and enforcement begins again.

In this test, MC1 was defined with a higher priority to function as the active HSRP router, and as such the primary MC. MC1 and MC2 are each connected to an Ethernet segment outside of the normal application data path. The PfR "learn" feature is enabled to specify that all BRs enable NetFlow and export data to the MC with a periodic interval and monitor periods set to 1 minute.

■ The learned prefix lengths will be set to /32s and the number of max learned prefixes will be set to 2500.

Caution By default, the learned prefix lengths are aggregated into groups of /24. We are changing them to /32 for the purposes of this test to demonstrate PfR in a small topology with limited routes. It is recommended that this PfR parameter be left at the default /24 in most production deployments.

■ The WAE-3 and WAE-4 appliances at the data center site are Cisco WAE-7341s running Enterprise licenses. They sit on a separate subnet that is not in the data path (same subnet as MC1 and MC2 in this test).

■ The WAE-5 appliance is a Cisco WAE-674 configured as the WAAS Central Manager.

Note   You must deploy WAAS Central Manager on a dedicated appliance. Although the WAAS Central Manager device runs the WAAS software, its sole purpose is to provide management functions. The WAAS Central Manager communicates with the WAEs, which are registered with it, in the network. Through the WAAS Central Manager GUI, you can centrally manage the configuration of the WAEs individually or in groups. The WAAS Central Manager also gathers management statistics and logs for its registered WAEs.

- The data center and branch WAE appliances are added into DNS and registered with the Central Manager.

- CE1, CE2, CE3, and CE4, as well as WAE-1, WAE-2, WAE-3, and WAE-4, are running WCCP Version 2 and the TCP promiscuous mode service (WCCP Version 2 services 61 and 62) to redirect TCP traffic for acceleration services.

- WCCP service groups are configured in the branches and the data center to allow for site load balancing and high availability. CE1 and CE2 have WAE-1 and WAE-2 configured as a service group (WAE-1 has the lowest IP address, making it the lead branch WAE). CE3 and CE4 have WAE-3 and WAE-4 configured as a service group (WAE-3 has the lowest IP address, making it the lead DC WAE). Flow protection is enabled in all WAEs.

- Each PE router is connected to a WAN simulator capable of creating delay, jitter, and packet drops to all traffic or specific flows as required. This device is a critical component when attempting to demonstrate the benefits of WAAS and PfR in a WAN environment.

- CE1, CE2, and DC-Router have the IP SLA "responder" feature enabled to allow PfR active monitoring of traffic classes.

- A server in the data center is configured as DNS, WINS, FTP, and AD for the network. It also has Common Internet File System (CIFS) enabled to test WAN acceleration. There are two laptops connected to the branch network that will be used as clients for CIFS and FTP file transfers.

Because PfR path control is unidirectional, in the outbound direction only, the testing includes verification of dynamic PfR changes at both the branch and data center locations. To test several different scenarios, the following baseline state is defined in the test topology:

- All VoIP traffic (identified by its DSCP marking of EF and CS5) is forwarded over the MPLS network using the PfR link group traffic-steering feature, provided that the MPLS path is performing within an acceptable tolerance.

- VoIP will fail over to the Internet link if the mean opinion score (MOS) calculated by IP SLA drops below 4. The IP SLA MOS calculation measures the delay and loss of test packets to assign an estimated MOS between 1 and 5.

■ All HTTP traffic is forwarded over the IPsec/Internet network with a similar PfR link grouping policy.

HTTP traffic will be dynamically rerouted to the MPLS link if PfR detects that the primary Internet link is blackholing traffic or is significantly impaired in terms of jitter or loss.

■ The remaining "unclassified" UDP and stateful TCP traffic flows are load-balanced across both WAN links.

A QoS service policy is configured on the outgoing interfaces (Ethernet for MPLS and GRE for Internet) as an additional verification method for PfR traffic steering. This policy is configured to match each traffic type as follows:

1. Match DSCP EF and CS5 for VoIP.

2. Match destination port TCP 80 for HTTP.

3. Match TCP and UDP source port of 5000, for branch load-balanced traffic, and TCP and UDP source port of 6000 for data center load-balanced traffic.

Each of these matched traffic groups will be policed for 30 percent of the link; the conform-action, exceed-action, and violate-action flags will be set to transmit, thus allowing us to see the number of passed packets without any policing happening.

Test Traffic

As PfR leverages NetFlow data for dynamic application learning and passive monitoring of traffic flows, it is important to generate stateful traffic when creating TCP application flows. In contrast to other types of testing, where simple "bit blasting" of stateless traffic is sufficient, PfR will not control TCP flows if it detects that a stateful session (SYN, SYN-ACK, ACK exchange) has not been established. Because PfR rerouting happens only in an outbound direction, simulated application flows will be generated in both directions as described here:

Data Center Subnet: 10.1.1.0/24

Branch Subnet: 20.1.1.0/24

Flow 1: UDP traffic from ten separate DC IPs to ten branch IPs with DSCP set to EF, all the packets are 64 bytes in size.

Table 17-1 *Simulated VoIP Traffic Profile—Data Center Outbound*

Type	Source IP	Src Port	DestIP	Dest Port	DSCP	Packet Size/Rate	Description
UDP	10.1.1.10 to 10.1.1.20	65123	20.1.1.10 to 20.1.1.10	3000	EF	64 bytes @ 10 pps	DC to branch VoIP traffic

Flow 2: UDP traffic from ten separate branch IPs to ten DC IPs with DSCP set to EF; all the packets are 64 bytes in size.

Table 17-2 *Simulated VoIP Traffic Profile—Data Center Inbound*

Type	Source IP	Src Port	Dest IP	Dest Port	DSCP	Packet Size/Rate	Description
UDP	20.1.1.10 to 20.1.1.20	65123	10.1.1.10 to 10.1.1.10	3000	CS5	64 bytes @ 10 pps	Branch to DC VoIP traffic

Flow 3: Stateful HTTP traffic from 50 separate branch IPs to ten DC "server" IPs getting a web page closing the connection and repeating it.

Table 17-3 *Simulated Internet Web Server Traffic Profile—Data Center Inbound*

Type	Source IP	Src Port	Dest IP	Dest Port	DSCP	Packet Size/Rate	Description
TCP	20.1.1.21 to 20.1.1.70	Random	10.1.1.11 to 10.1.1.20	80	0	Total transfer rate of 1 Mbps	Branch to DC HTTP traffic

Flow 4: Stateful Telnet TCP traffic from 25 separate branch IPs to 25 DC IPs running at ~1 Mbps.

Table 17-4 *Simulated Telnet Traffic Profile—Data Center Inbound*

Type	Source IP	Src Port	Dest IP	Dest Port	DSCP	Packet Size/Rate	Description
TCP	20.1.1.71 to 20.1.1.95	5000	10.1.1.71 to 10.1.1.95	23	0	128 bytes @ 125 pps	Branch to DC TCP traffic

Flow 5: UDP traffic from 25 separate branch IPs to 25 DC IPs running at ~1 Mbps.

Table 17-5 *Simulated Bulk Data Traffic Profile—Data Center Inbound*

Type	Source IP	Src Port	Dest IP	Dest Port	DSCP	Packet Size/Rate	Description
UDP	20.1.1.96 to 20.1.1.125	5000	10.1.1.96 to 10.1.1.125	6001	0	128 bytes @ 125 pps	Branch to DC UDP traffic

Flow 6: Stateful TCP Telnet traffic from 25 separate DC IPs to 25 branch IPs running at ~1 Mbps.

Table 17-6   *Simulated Telnet Traffic Profile—Data Center Outbound*

Type	Source IP	Src Port	Dest IP	Dest Port	DSCP	Packet Size/Rate	Description
TCP	10.1.1.126 to 10.1.1.150	6000	20.1.1.126 to 20.1.1.150	23	0	128 bytes @ 125 pps	DC to branch TCP traffic

Flow 7: UDP traffic from 25 separate DC IPs to 25 branch IPs running at ~1 Mbps.

Table 17-7   *Simulated Bulk Data Traffic Profile—Data Center Outbound*

Type	Source IP	Src Port	Dest IP	Dest Port	DSCP	Packet Size/Rate	Reason
UDP	10.1.1.151 to 10.1.1.175	6000	20.1.1.151 to 20.1.1.175	8001	0	128 bytes @ 125 pps	DC to Branch UDP traffic

When all the preceding traffic flows are enabled, there will be about 3.5 Mbps of traffic flowing in each direction. This will allow for all of the traffic to run over a single "circuit" during failovers.

Test Objectives

The primary objectives for this test are as follows:

- Validate that the proposed PfR design will work as designed with the disparate WAN topologies.

- Verify that the WAAS WAN optimization will work as expected and quantify the gains of deploying the WAEs.

Test Case Summary

Table 17-8 contains a brief summary of the tests to be conducted to validate the WAN optimization solution.

Table 17-8 *Summary of Test Cases*

Test ID	Brief Test Description
PFR-BASE-1	PfR/WAAS Network Baseline Test
PFR-BASE-2	PfR Traffic-Class Route Enforcement Under Steady State Network Conditions Test
PFR-BASE-3	PfR/WAAS Network Extended Baseline Test to Determine PfR and WAAS Interoperability
PFR-FEAT-1	PfR Reroute Using Link Groups for Traffic Steering Test
PFR-FEAT-2	PfR Reroute Due to Delay Policy Violation Test
PFR-FEAT-3	PfR Reroute Due to Jitter Policy Violation Test
PFR-FEAT-4	PfR VoIP Optimization with IP SLA MOS Measurements Test
PFR-FEAT-5	PfR Reroute Due to Packet Loss Policy Violation Test
PFR-FEAT-6	PfR Black Hole Detection and Fast Reroute Test
PFR-FEAT-7	PfR Redundant Master Controller Test
WAAS-FEAT-1	WAAS Application Acceleration of FTP/CIFS Test
WAAS-FEAT-2	Prepositioning of Content with WAAS Test
WAAS-FEAT-3	Upgrading WAE Code with the Central Manager Test
PFR-SCALE-1	PfR Prefix Scalability Test
PFR-DUTY-1	Router/WAE Chassis Failure and Recovery Test
PFR-DUTY-2	Link Failure and Recovery Test

Detailed Test Cases

The following tables contain detailed test cases to be conducted to validate the PfR and WAAS features in the architecture described earlier. These cases provide you with guidance on testing PFR and WAAS and should be modified to fit your specific deployment.

Table 17-9   *PfR/WAAS Network Baseline Test*

Test ID:	PFR-BASE-1
Node List:	Routers: CE1, CE2, CE3, CE4, MC1, MC2, PE1, PE2, PE3, DC-Router WAEs: WAE-1, WAE-2, WAE-3, WAE-4, WAE-5
Test Phase:	Baseline
Test Description:	PfR/WAAS Network Baseline Test (configurations applied and test traffic measurements taken prior to PfR or WAAS optimization)
Test Setup:	• Build the network, as shown in Figure 17-1. • Configure CE1 and CE2 as PfR border routers (BR), with CE1 as the master controller (MC), define the internal and external interfaces, ensuring that the WAE network module's service interface is defined as internal. Enable PfR learning and logging. • Configure CE3 and CE4 as PfR BRs, with MC1 (Primary) and MC2 (Standby) as MCs, and define the internal and external interfaces, ensuring that the interface connected to the WAE subnet is defined as internal. Enable PfR learning and logging. • Build the baseline network topology as specified in the "Physical and Logical Topology" section. • Define BGP peers (both iBGP and eBGP) on all CE routers. • Configure IPsec-encrypted GRE tunnels between CE1 and CE3 with the specified interface MTU. • Connect CE2 and CE4 indirectly via the MPLS/VPN network. • Configure CE2 as HSRP Active for the branch network to ensure that by default (with no PfR rerouting) all traffic will use the MPLS link to reach the DC. • Configure the QoS policies on the external interfaces of CE1, CE2, CE3, and CE4 routers. • Configure a default static route on DC-Router pointing at CE4 to ensure that by default (with no PfR rerouting) all traffic will use the MPLS link to reach the branch. • Configure WAE-5 as a Central Manager and register WAE-1, WAE-2, WAE-3, and WAE-4 as managed assets. In the Central Manager, make sure that HTTP application acceleration is disabled for this test. • Configure WCCPv2 service groups and redirect. • Configure the external interfaces of CE1, CE2, CE3, and CE4 to be seen as 5 Mbps by using a bandwidth statement. Set the load interval of all interfaces to 30 seconds. • Configure the test traffic as described in the "Test Traffic" section.
Test Steps:	**Step 1.** Verify that the GRE tunnels, IPsec, routing, HSRP, and WCCPv2 are up and running as expected.

Table 17-9 *PfR/WAAS Network Baseline Test*

	Step 2. Confirm that the PfR MCs are seeing the BR as anticipated.
	Step 3. Run a traceroute from Branch Laptop-1 to the DC server and verify that the traffic is going over the MPLS network.
	Step 4. Run a traceroute from the DC Server to Branch Laptop-1 and verify that the traffic is going over the MPLS network.
	Step 5. Start all of the test traffic flows.
	Step 6. Wait 3 minutes and verify that all of the traffic from the branch to the DC is going over the MPLS network by checking the counters of the policy maps configured on the external interfaces of CE1 and CE2.
	Step 7. Verify that all of the traffic from the DC to the branch is going over the MPLS network by checking the counters of the policy maps configured on the external interfaces of CE3 and CE4.
	Step 8. Verify that WCCPv2 is working as expected by logging into the WAEs in the branch and DC and confirming that they are seeing redirected HTTP traffic as expected.
	Step 9. Validate that the MCs in the branch and the DC are seeing all traffic as In Policy, and learning /32 prefixes being used by test traffic.
	Step 10. Verify that all of the devices in the Node List are running without issues by checking their logs and CPU and memory utilization.
Expected Results:	All enabled features will be working as expected. All traffic will be running over the MPLS network. PfR will be "learning" prefixes according to the test traffic.
Observed Results:	
Pass/Fail:	

Table 17-10 *PfR Traffic-Class Route Enforcement Under Steady State Network Conditions Test*

Test ID:	PFR-BASE-2
Node List:	Routers: CE1, CE2, CE3, CE4, MC1, MC2, PE1, PE2, PE3, DC-Router WAEs: WAE-1, WAE-2, WAE-3, WAE-4, WAE-5
Test Phase:	Baseline
Test Description:	PfR Traffic-Class Route Enforcement Under Steady State Network Conditions Test
Test Setup:	• Build the network, as shown in Figure 17-1. • Configure CE1 and CE2 as PfR BRs, with CE1 as the MC, and set the internal and external interfaces. Make sure to configure the WAE network module's interface as internal. Enable PfR learning and logging. • Configure CE3 and CE4 as PfR BRs, with MC1 (Primary) and MC2 (Standby) as MCs, and set the internal and external interfaces. Make sure to configure the WAE network's interface as internal. Enable PfR learning and logging. • Configure iBGP and eBGP as described in the "Physical and Logical Test Topology" section. • Configure CE1 and CE3 to use GRE over IPsec as described in the "Physical and Logical Test Topology" section, including setting the interface MTU. • Configure CE2 and CE4 to use the MPLS network as described in the "Physical and Logical Test Topology" section. • Configure CE2 as HSRP Active for the branch network to ensure that by default (with no PfR rerouting) all traffic will use the MPLS link to reach the DC. • Configure a default static route on DC-Router pointing at CE4 to ensure that by default (with no PfR rerouting) all traffic will use the MPLS link to reach the branch. • Configure the QoS policies described in the "Physical and Logical Test Topology" section on the external interfaces of CE1, CE2, CE3, and CE4 routers. • Configure WAE-5 as a Central Manager and register WAE-1, WAE-2, WAE-3, and WAE-4 as managed assets. In the Central Manager, make sure that HTTP application acceleration is disabled for this test. • Configure WCCPv2 service groups and redirect as described in the "Physical and Logical Test Topology" section. • Configure the external interfaces of CE1, CE2, CE3, and CE4 to be seen as 5 Mbps by using a **bandwidth** statement. Set the load interval of all interfaces to 30 seconds. • Configure the test traffic as described in the "Test Traffic" section.

Table 17-10 *PfR Traffic-Class Route Enforcement Under Steady State Network Conditions Test*

Test Steps:	Step 1. Start the test traffic and verify that all traffic is running over the MPLS network by checking the counters of the policy maps configured on the external interfaces of CE1, CE2, CE3, and CE4.
	Step 2. Validate that the MCs in the branch and the DC are seeing all traffic as In Policy, and learning /32 prefixes being used by test traffic.
	Step 3. In all the MCs, create an extended ACL called **VoIP** that matches all traffic with a DSCP of EF or CS5. Create an ACL called *HTTP* that matches all traffic to TCP port 80 and all traffic from TCP port 80.
	Step 4. In all MCs, make the external interfaces connected to the MPLS network members of link-group *MPLS*. Make the interfaces connected to the GRE/IPsec/Internet network members of link-group *INTERNET*.
	Step 5. In all MCs, create a PfR policy with an OER learn list that matches the ACL *VoIP*. Set this policy to use link-group *MPLS* as its primary path and link-group *INTERNET* as its fallback path.
	Step 6. In all MCs, create a PfR policy with an OER learn list that matches the ACL *HTTP*. Set this policy to use link-group *INTERNET* as its primary path and link-group *MPLS* as its fallback path.
	Step 7. Verify that all of the VoIP traffic between the DC and the branch is going over the MPLS network by checking the counters of the policy maps configured on the external interfaces of CE1, CE2, CE3, and CE4. Check that all of the HTTP traffic is going over the Internet link.
	Step 8. Verify that PfR policy enforcement is responsible for the traffic steering of HTTP traffic by ensuring that dynamic PBR route maps and ACLs are created on CE1, CE2, CE3, and CE4.
	Step 9. Verify that all of the TCP and UDP (non VoIP or HTTP) traffic between the DC and the branch is going over the MPLS network by checking the counters of the policy maps configured on the external interfaces of CE1, CE2, CE3, and CE4.
	Step 10. Enable throughput learning in all MCs. Verify that the MCs are learning /32 prefixes as expected.

Table 17-10 *PfR Traffic-Class Route Enforcement Under Steady State Network Conditions Test*

	Step 11. In all MCs, create another PfR policy. This policy should match the learned throughput and set the *utilization* priority to 5 and the variance to *20%*.
	Step 12. After the learning phase is complete, check the BGP routing tables of all CE routers. Verify whether several /32 BGP routes have been injected into BGP to help load-balance the TCP/UDP traffic.
	Step 13. Verify whether all of the TCP and UDP (non VoIP or HTTP) traffic between the DC and the branch is being load-balanced by checking the counters of the policy maps configured on the external interfaces of CE1, CE2, CE3, and CE4.
	Step 14. Check that WCCPv2 is still working as expected by logging into the WAEs in the branch and DC and confirming that they are seeing redirected HTTP traffic as expected.
	Step 15. Verify that all of the devices in the Node List are running without issues by checking their logs and CPU and memory utilization.
Expected Results:	All enabled features will be working as expected. All traffic will be load-balanced over the MPLS and Internet networks as per the defined PfR policies.
Observed Results:	
Pass/Fail:	

Table 17-11 *PfR/WAAS Network Extended Baseline Test to Verify PfR and WAAS Interoperability*

Test ID:	PFR-BASE-3
Node List:	Routers: CE1, CE2, CE3, CE4, MC1, MC2, PE1, PE2, PE3, DC-Router WAEs: WAE-1, WAE-2, WAE-3, WAE-4, WAE-5
Test Phase:	Baseline
Test Description:	PfR/WAAS Network Extended Baseline Test to Verify PfR and WAAS Interoperability

Table 17-11   *PfR/WAAS Network Extended Baseline Test to Verify PfR and WAAS Interoperability*

Test Setup:	
	• Build the network, as shown in Figure 17-1.
	• Configure CE1 and CE2 as PfR BRs, with CE1 as the MC, and set the internal and external interfaces. Make sure to configure the WAE network module's interface as internal. Enable PfR learning and logging.
	• Configure CE3 and CE4 as PfR BRs, with MC1 (Primary) and MC2 (Standby) as MCs, and set the internal and external interfaces. Make sure to configure the WAE network's interface as internal. Enable PfR learning and logging.
	• Configure iBGP and eBGP as described in the "Physical and Logical Test Topology" section.
	• Configure CE1 and CE3 to use GRE over IPsec as described in the "Physical and Logical Test Topology" section, including setting the interface MTU.
	• Configure CE2 and CE4 to use the MPLS network as described in the "Physical and Logical Test Topology" section.
	• Configure CE2 as HSRP Active for the branch network to ensure that by default (with no PfR rerouting) all traffic will use the MPLS link to reach the DC.
	• Configure a default static route on DC-Router pointing at CE4 to ensure that by default (with no PfR rerouting) all traffic will use the MPLS link to reach the branch.
	• Configure the QoS policies described in the "Physical and Logical Test Topology" section on the external interfaces of CE1, CE2, CE3, and CE4 routers.
	• Configure WAE-5 as a Central Manager and register WAE-1, WAE-2, WAE-3, and WAE-4 as managed assets. In the Central Manager, make sure that HTTP application acceleration is disabled for this test.
	• Configure WCCPv2 service groups and redirect as described in the "Physical and Logical Test Topology" section.
	• Configure the external interfaces of CE1, CE2, CE3, and CE4 to be seen as 5 Mbps by using a **bandwidth** statement. Set the load interval of all interfaces to 30 seconds.
	• Set the PfR policy, in the DC and branch, so that all VoIP traffic will use the MPLS network, all the HTTP traffic will use the Internet network, and all the rest of the traffic will be load-balanced across both links.
	• Configure the test traffic as described in the "Test Traffic" section.
	• Create a traffic "flow" that will copy a 50-MB file, using FTP, from the DC to the branch at 1 Mbps. The FTP job should keep rerunning every 10 minutes. The file being copied using FTP should be the same for every time the job runs (this can be done using a script or advanced traffic generators).

Table 17-11 *PfR/WAAS Network Extended Baseline Test to Verify PfR and WAAS Interoperability* (*continued*)

Test Steps:	This test should be run for 24 hours.
	Step 1. Start all of the traffic, including the FTP.
	Step 2. Verify that the traffic is being load-balanced as expected (you may have to wait for the learning period to complete).
	Step 3. Check that the WAEs are seeing the HTTP and FTP redirected traffic as expected. Verify that the FTP transfer is being cached on the branch WAEs as anticipated.
	Step 4. Check the logs and CPU and memory of all the devices in the Node List every 30 minutes to make sure they remain stable. Record your results.
Expected Results:	All enabled features will be working as expected. All traffic will be load-balanced over the MPLS and Internet networks as per the defined PfR policies. The WAEs will "accelerate" the FTP transfer. There will be no unexpected memory leaks, errors, or CPU spikes.
Observed Results:	
Pass/Fail:	

Table 17-12 *PfR Reroute Using Link Groups for Traffic Steering Test*

Test ID:	PFR-FEAT-1
Node List:	Routers: CE1, CE2, CE3, CE4, MC1, MC2, PE1, PE2, PE3, DC-Router
Test Phase:	Feature
Test Description:	PfR Reroute Using Link Groups for Traffic Steering Test

Table 17-12 *PfR Reroute Using Link Groups for Traffic Steering Test*

Test Setup:	• Build the network, as shown in Figure 17-1.
	• Configure CE1 and CE2 as PfR BRs, with CE1 as the MC, and set the internal and external interfaces. Make sure to configure the WAE network module's interface as internal. Enable PfR learning and logging.
	• Configure CE3 and CE4 as PfR BRs, with MC1 (Primary) and MC2 (Standby) as MCs, and set the internal and external interfaces. Make sure to configure the WAE network's interface as internal. Enable PfR learning and logging.
	• Configure iBGP and eBGP as described in the "Physical and Logical Test Topology" section.
	• Configure CE1 and CE3 to use GRE over IPsec as described in the "Physical and Logical Test Topology" section, including setting the interface MTU.
	• Configure CE2 and CE4 to use the MPLS network as described in the "Physical and Logical Test Topology" section.
	• Configure CE2 as HSRP Active for the branch network to ensure that by default (with no PfR rerouting) all traffic will use the MPLS link to reach the DC.
	• Configure a default static route on the DC-Router pointing at CE4 to ensure that by default (with no PfR rerouting) all traffic will use the MPLS link to reach the branch.
	• Configure the QoS policies described in the "Physical and Logical Test Topology" section on the "external" interfaces of CE1, CE2, CE3, and CE4 routers.
	• Configure the external interfaces of CE1, CE2, CE3, and CE4 to be seen as 5 Mbps by using a **bandwidth** statement. Set the load interval of all interfaces to 30 seconds.
	• Configure the test traffic as described in the "Test Traffic" section.
Test Steps:	**Step 1.** Start all of the test traffic
	Step 2. As in the PFR-BASE-2 test, in all the MCs, create an extended ACL called *VoIP* that matches all traffic with a DSCP of EF or CS5. Create an ACL called *HTTP* that matches all traffic to TCP port 80 and all traffic from TCP port 80.

Table 17-12 *PfR Reroute Using Link Groups for Traffic Steering Test*

Step 3.	In all MCs, make the external interfaces connected to the MPLS network members of link-group *MPLS*. Make the interfaces connected to the GRE/IPsec/Internet network members of link-group *INTERNET*.
Step 4.	In all MCs, create a PfR policy with an OER learn list that matches the ACL *VoIP*. Set this policy to use link-group *MPLS* as its primary path and link-group *INTERNET* as its fallback path.
Step 5.	In all MCs, create a PfR policy with an OER learn list that matches the ACL *HTTP*. Set this policy to use link-group *INTERNET* as its primary path and link-group *MPLS* as its fallback path.
Step 6.	Verify that all of the VoIP traffic between the DC and the branch is going over the MPLS network by checking the counters of the policy maps configured on the external interfaces of CE1, CE2, CE3, and CE4. Check that all of the HTTP traffic is going over the Internet link.
Step 7.	Verify whether dynamic Policy Based Routing (PBR) entries and ACLs are created in CE1, CE2, CE3, and CE4 for rerouting the HTTP traffic.
Step 8.	Shut down the branch external interface on CE2 (the one connected to the MPLS network). Verify whether the VoIP traffic has failed over to the Internet link in both directions. Check the reason for the failover in all MCs and BRs. Bring the interface back up.
Step 9.	In all of the MCs, change the *VoIP* policy to use link-group *INTERNET* as its primary path and link-group *MPLS* as its fallback path. Verify that the VoIP traffic is using the Internet link by checking the counters of the policy maps configured on the external interfaces of CE1, CE2, CE3, and CE4.
Step 10.	Verify the dynamic PBRs that are created on CE2 and CE4 for the VoIP traffic.

Table 17-12   *PfR Reroute Using Link Groups for Traffic Steering Test*

	Step 11. In all of the MCs, change the *VoIP* policy back to using link-group *MPLS* as its primary path and link-group *INTERNET* as its fallback path. Verify that the VoIP traffic is using the MPLS link by checking the counters of the policy maps configured on the external interfaces of CE1, CE2, CE3, and CE4.
	Step 12. Check the logs and CPU and memory of all the devices in the Node List to make sure they remained stable during all of the changes.
Expected Results:	All VoIP traffic will use the configured link-group for its path, bypassing the "default" routing/HSRP configuration. The traffic will fail over if the primary link-group path is unavailable.
Observed Results:	
Pass/Fail:	

Table 17-13   *PfR Reroute Due to Delay Policy Violation Test*

Test ID:	PFR-FEAT-2
Node List:	Routers: CE1, CE2, CE3, CE4, MC1, MC2, PE1, PE2, PE3, DC-Router Delay Generator
Test Phase:	Feature
Test Description:	PfR Reroute Due to Delay Policy Violation Test

Table 17-13 *PfR Reroute Due to Delay Policy Violation Test*

Test Setup:	• Build the network, as shown in Figure 17-1.
	• Configure CE1 and CE2 as PfR BRs, with CE1 as the MC, and set the internal and external interfaces. Make sure to configure the WAE network module's interface as internal. Enable PfR learning and logging.
	• Configure CE3 and CE4 as PfR BRs, with MC1 (Primary) and MC2 (Standby) as MCs, and set the internal and external interfaces. Make sure to configure the WAE network's interface as internal. Enable PfR learning and logging.
	• Configure iBGP and eBGP as described in the "Physical and Logical Test Topology" section.
	• Configure CE1 and CE3 to use GRE over IPsec as described in the "Physical and Logical Test Topology" section, including setting the interface MTU.
	• Configure CE2 and CE4 to use the MPLS network as described in the "Physical and Logical Test Topology" section.
	• Configure CE2 as HSRP Active for the branch network to ensure that by default (with no PfR rerouting) all traffic will use the MPLS link to reach the DC.
	• Configure a default static route on the DC-Router pointing at CE4 to ensure that by default (with no PfR rerouting) all traffic will use the MPLS link to reach the branch.
	• Configure the QoS policies described in the "Physical and Logical Test Topology" section on the "external" interfaces of CE1, CE2, CE3, and CE4 routers.
	• Configure the external interfaces of CE1, CE2, CE3, and CE4 to be seen as 5 Mbps by using a **bandwidth** statement. Set the load interval of all interfaces to 30 seconds.
	• Configure the test traffic as described in the "Test Traffic" section.
Test Steps:	**Step 1.** Enable "delay" as the primary factor in each of the MC's learning configurations. Set the periodic interval and the monitor interval to 1 minute.
	Step 2. As in previous tests, in all the MCs, create an extended ACL called *HTTP* that matches all the traffic to TCP port 80 and all traffic from TCP port 80.
	Step 3. In all MCs, create a PfR policy with an OER learn list that matches the ACL *HTTP*. Set the delay threshold for this policy to 100 ms.
	Step 4. Start all the test traffic.

Table 17-13   *PfR Reroute Due to Delay Policy Violation Test*

Step 5.	Verify all test traffic initially follows the "default" HSRP/routing path over the MPLS network by checking the counters of the policy maps configured on the external interfaces of CE1, CE2, CE3, and CE4.
Step 6.	Make sure the MCs are learning prefixes from NetFlow by checking logs and CLI.
Step 7.	Check the delay statistics for all of the traffic flows in the traffic generator. Use the delay generator tool to add 150 ms of delay to the "MPLS link" between PE2 and PE3. Verify that the delay statistics on the traffic generator have increased as expected.
Step 8.	Watch the logs in the BRs and MCs for messages related to route changes for HTTP prefixes due to delay being Out of Policy (OOP).
Step 9.	Verify that the HTTP traffic is rerouted over the Internet link, while the remaining traffic is still taking the "default" HSRP/routing path over the MPLS network by checking the counters of the policy maps configured on the external interfaces of CE1, CE2, CE3, and CE4.
Step 10.	Verify the BGP routing information in the BRs and the OER master information in the MCs for the prefixes for the HTTP traffic (these are the IP addresses used for Flow 3 in the "Test Traffic" section). Compare these to the ones for VoIP traffic and record the results.
Step 11.	Remove the delay from the link between PE2 and PE3. Wait a few minutes until the holddown timer expires (5 minutes by default) and verify whether the HTTP traffic is back on the MPLS link by checking the logs, routing, and the policy map counters on the BR routers. Check the logs and detailed prefix information in the MCs as well.
Step 12.	Check the logs and CPU and memory of all the devices in the Node List to make sure they remained stable during all of the changes.

Table 17-13 *PfR Reroute Due to Delay Policy Violation Test*

Expected Results:	The HTTP traffic will reroute over the Internet link when the delay on the MPLS link makes it go OOP. The rest of the traffic will continue to use the default HSRP/routing path. By default, the HTTP traffic *should not* fail back to the MPLS link once its delay is back In Policy and the holddown timer is expired. When the periodic timer expires, the MC evaluates current exit links based on default or user-defined policies. If all exit links are In Policy, no changes are made. The HTTP traffic will fail back to the MPLS path once the Internet path is OOP.
Observed Results:	
Pass/Fail:	

Table 17-14 *PfR Reroute Due to Jitter Policy Violation Test*

Test ID:	PFR-FEAT-3
Node List:	Routers: CE1, CE2, CE3, CE4, MC1, MC2, PE1, PE2, PE3, DC-Router Delay Generator
Test Phase:	Feature
Test Description:	PfR Reroute Due to Jitter Policy Violation Test

Table 17-14 *PfR Reroute Due to Jitter Policy Violation Test*

Test Setup:	• Build the network, as shown in Figure 17-1.
	• Configure CE1 and CE2 as PfR BRs, with CE1 as the MC, and set the internal and external interfaces. Make sure to configure the WAE network module's interface as internal. Enable PfR learning and logging.
	• Configure CE3 and CE4 as PfR BRs, with MC1 (Primary) and MC2 (Standby) as MCs, and set the internal and external interfaces. Make sure to configure the WAE network's interface as internal. Enable PfR learning and logging.
	• Configure iBGP and eBGP as described in the "Physical and Logical Test Topology" section.
	• Configure CE1 and CE3 to use GRE over IPsec as described in the "Physical and Logical Test Topology" section, including setting the interface MTU.
	• Configure CE2 and CE4 to use the MPLS network as described in the "Physical and Logical Test Topology" section.
	• Configure CE2 as HSRP Active for the branch network to ensure that by default (with no PfR rerouting) all traffic will use the MPLS link to reach the DC.
	• Configure a default static route on the DC-Router pointing at CE4 to ensure that by default (with no PfR rerouting) all traffic will use the MPLS link to reach the branch.
	• Configure the QoS policies described in the "Physical and Logical Test Topology" section on the "external" interfaces of CE1, CE2, CE3, and CE4 routers.
	• Configure the external interfaces of CE1, CE2, CE3, and CE4 to be seen as 5 Mbps by using a **bandwidth** statement. Set the load interval of all interfaces to 30 seconds.
	• Configure the test traffic as described in the "Test Traffic" section.
Test Steps:	**Step 1.** As in previous tests, in all the MCs, create an extended ACL called *VoIP* that matches all traffic with a DSCP of EF or CS5. Create an ACL called *HTTP* that matches all traffic to TCP port 80 and all traffic from TCP port 80.
	Step 2. In all MCs, make the external interfaces connected to the MPLS network members of link-group *MPLS*. Make the interfaces connected to the GRE/IPsec/Internet network members of link-group *INTERNET*.
	Step 3. In the branch MC (CE1), create a PfR policy with an OER learn list that matches the ACL *VoIP*. Set this policy to use link-group *MPLS* as its primary path and link-group *INTERNET* as its fallback path. Set the policy's **jitter threshold** to a maximum of 30 ms. In this policy, create an IP SLA jitter probe with a destination IP of DC-Router. Set the probe frequency to 2 seconds.

Table 17-14 *PfR Reroute Due to Jitter Policy Violation Test*

Step 4.	In the DC MCs (MC1 and MC2), create a PfR policy with an OER learn list that matches the ACL *VoIP*. Set this policy to use link-group *MPLS* as its primary path and link-group *INTERNET* as its fallback path. Set the policy's **jitter threshold** to a maximum of 30 ms. In this policy, create an IP SLA jitter probe with a destination IP of CE1's LAN address. Set the probe frequency to 2 seconds.
Step 5.	In all MCs, create a PfR policy with an OER learn list that matches the ACL *HTTP*. Set this policy to use link-group *INTERNET* as its primary path and link-group *MPLS* as its fallback path.
Step 6.	Start the test traffic.
Step 7.	Verify that all of the VoIP traffic between the DC and the branch is going over the MPLS network by checking the counters of the policy maps configured on the external interfaces of CE1, CE2, CE3, and CE4. Check that all of the HTTP traffic is going over the Internet link. Finally, confirm that the stateful TCP and UDP traffic flows are running over the MPLS network.
Step 8.	Set the delay generator to increase the jitter for all traffic going between PE2 and PE3 to 40 ms.
Step 9.	Watch the logs in the BRs and MCs for messages related to route changes for VoIP prefixes due to jitter being OOP. Verify that all VoIP traffic is now traveling over the Internet link along with the HTTP traffic. Check that the stateful TCP and UDP traffic is still using the MPLS network.
Step 10.	Verify and record the routing, dynamic PBRs, dynamic ACLs, logs, PfR, and IP SLA information for the VoIP prefixes in all BRs and MCs.
Step 11.	Move the jitter from the PE2 link to the PE1 link.
Step 12.	Watch the logs in the BRs and MCs for messages related to route changes for VoIP prefixes due to jitter being OOP. Verify that all VoIP traffic is now traveling over the MPLS link along with the UDP and stateful TCP traffic. Check that the HTTP traffic is still using the Internet network.

Table 17-14 *PfR Reroute Due to Jitter Policy Violation Test*

	Step 13. Verify and record the routing, dynamic PBRs, dynamic ACLs, logs, PfR, and IP SLA information for the VoIP prefixes in all BRs and MCs again.
	Step 14. Check the logs and CPU and memory of all the devices in the Node List to make sure they remained stable during all of the changes.
Expected Results:	If a path is OOP due to jitter, only the VoIP traffic will move to a secondary link; all the other traffic will stay on the "high-jitter link" because the policy does not apply to it.
Observed Results:	
Pass/Fail:	

Table 17-15 *PfR VoIP Optimization with IP SLA MOS Measurements Test*

Test ID:	PFR-FEAT-4
Node List:	Routers: CE1, CE2, CE3, CE4, MC1, MC2, PE1, PE2, PE3, DC-Router Delay Generator
Test Phase:	Feature
Test Description:	PfR VoIP Optimization with IP SLA MOS Measurements Test

Table 17-15 *PfR VoIP Optimization with IP SLA MOS Measurements Test*

Test Setup:	• Build the network, as shown in Figure 17-1. • Configure CE1 and CE2 as PfR BRs, with CE1 as the MC, and set the internal and external interfaces. Make sure to configure the WAE network module's interface as internal. Enable PfR learning and logging. • Configure CE3 and CE4 as PfR BRs, with MC1 (Primary) and MC2 (Standby) as MCs, and set the internal and external interfaces. Make sure to configure the WAE network's interface as internal. Enable PfR learning and logging. • Configure iBGP and eBGP as described in the "Physical and Logical Test Topology" section. • Configure CE1 and CE3 to use GRE over IPsec as described in the "Physical and Logical Test Topology" section, including setting the interface MTU. • Configure CE2 and CE4 to use the MPLS network as described in the "Physical and Logical Test Topology" section. • Configure CE2 as HSRP Active for the branch network to ensure that by default (with no PfR rerouting) all traffic will use the MPLS link to reach the DC. • Configure a default static route on DC-Router pointing at CE4 to ensure that by default (with no PfR rerouting) all traffic will use the MPLS link to reach the branch. • Configure the QoS policies described in the "Physical and Logical Test Topology" section on the "external" interfaces of CE1, CE2, CE3, and CE4 routers. • Configure the external interfaces of CE1, CE2, CE3, and CE4 to be seen as 5 Mbps by using a **bandwidth** statement. Set the load interval of all interfaces to 30 seconds. • Configure the test traffic as described in the "Test Traffic" section.
Test Steps:	**Step 1.** As in previous tests, in all the MCs, create an extended ACL called *VoIP* that matches all traffic with a DSCP of EF or CS5. Create an ACL called *HTTP* that matches all traffic to TCP port 80 and all traffic from TCP port 80.
	Step 2. In all MCs, make the external interfaces connected to the MPLS network members of link-group *MPLS*. Make the interfaces connected to the GRE/IPsec/Internet network members of link-group *INTERNET*.

Table 17-15   *PfR VoIP Optimization with IP SLA MOS Measurements Test*

Step 3. In the branch MC (CE1), create a PfR policy with an OER learn list that matches the ACL *VoIP*. Set this policy to use link-group *MPLS* as its primary path and link-group *INTERNET* as its fallback path. Set the policy's **MOS threshold** to a minimum of 4.0 and the percentage below this threshold to 20. (The number of MOS samples over a period of time that are below the threshold MOS value are calculated. If the percentage of MOS samples below the threshold is greater than the configured percentage, PfR determines that the exit link is OOP and searches for an alternate exit link.) In this policy, create an IP SLA jitter probe with a destination IP of DC-Router using g729a as the codec (the codec is needed for the MOS). Set the probe frequency to 2 seconds.

Step 4. In the DC MCs (MC1 and MC2), create a PfR policy with an OER learn list that matches the ACL *VoIP*. Set this policy to use link-group *MPLS* as its primary path and link-group *INTERNET* as its fallback path. Set the policy's **MOS threshold** to a minimum of 4.0 and the percentage below this threshold to 20. In this policy, create an IP SLA jitter probe with a destination IP of CE1's LAN address, using g729a as the codec. Set the probe frequency to 2 seconds.

Step 5. In all MCs, create a PfR policy with an OER learn list that matches the ACL *HTTP*. Set this policy to use link-group *INTERNET* as its primary path and link-group *MPLS* as its fallback path.

Step 6. Start the test traffic.

Step 7. Verify that all of the VoIP traffic between the DC and the branch is going over the MPLS network by checking the counters of the policy maps configured on the external interfaces of CE1, CE2, CE3, and CE4. Check that all of the HTTP traffic is going over the Internet link. Finally, confirm that the stateful TCP and UDP traffic flows are running over the MPLS network.

Step 8. Set the delay generator to increase the delay for all traffic going between PE2 and PE3 to 40 ms and to drop 5% of all packets.

Step 9. Watch the logs in the BRs and MCs for messages related to route changes for VoIP prefixes due to MOS being OOP. Verify that all VoIP traffic is now traveling over the Internet link along with the HTTP traffic. Check that the UDP and stateful TCP traffic is still using the MPLS network.

Table 17-15   *PfR VoIP Optimization with IP SLA MOS Measurements Test*

	Step 10. Verc ACLs, logs, PfR, and IP SLA information for the VoIP prefixes in all BRs and MCs.
	Step 11. Move the delay and drops from the PE2 to the PE1 link.
	Step 12. Watch the logs in the BRs and MCs for messages related to route changes for VoIP prefixes due to MOS being OOP. Verify that all VoIP traffic is now traveling over the MPLS link along with the UDP and stateful TCP traffic. Check that the HTTP traffic is still using the Internet network.
	Step 13. Verc ACLs, logs, PfR, and IP SLA information for the VoIP prefixes in all BRs and MCs again.
	Step 14. Check the logs and CPU and memory of all the devices in the Node List to make sure they remained stable during all of the changes.
Expected Results:	Only the VoIP traffic will be initially rerouted to the secondary link due to OOP condition caused by MOS degradation. Remaining traffic will stay on the impaired (high delay/packet drop) link unless the impairment exceeds the default PfR relative policies.
Observed Results:	
Pass/Fail:	

Table 17-16   *PfR Reroute Due to Packet Loss Policy Violation Test*

Test ID:	PFR-FEAT-5
Node List:	Routers: CE1, CE2, CE3, CE4, MC1, MC2, PE1, PE2, PE3, DC-Router Delay Generator
Test Phase:	Feature
Test Description:	PfR Reroute Due to Packet Loss Policy Violation Test
Test Setup:	• Build the network, as shown in Figure 17-1. • Configure CE1 and CE2 as PfR BRs, with CE1 as the MC, and set the internal and external interfaces. Make sure to configure the WAE network module's interface as internal. Enable PfR learning and logging. • Configure CE3 and CE4 as PfR BRs, with MC1 (Primary) and MC2 (Standby) as MCs, and set the internal and external interfaces. Make sure to configure the WAE network's interface as internal. Enable PfR learning and logging. • Configure iBGP and eBGP as described in the "Physical and Logical Test Topology" section. • Configure CE1 and CE3 to use GRE over IPsec as described in the "Physical and Logical Test Topology" section, including setting the interface MTU. • Configure CE2 and CE4 to use the MPLS network as described in the "Physical and Logical Test Topology" section. • Configure CE2 as HSRP Active for the branch network to ensure that by default (with no PfR rerouting) all traffic will use the MPLS link to reach the DC. • Configure a default static route on DC-Router pointing at CE4 to ensure that by default (with no PfR rerouting) all traffic will use the MPLS link to reach the Branch. • Configure the QoS policies described in the "Physical and Logical Test Topology" section on the "external" interfaces of CE1, CE2, CE3, and CE4 routers. • Configure the external interfaces of CE1, CE2, CE3, and CE4 to be seen as 5 Mbps by using a **bandwidth** statement. Set the load interval of all interfaces to 30 seconds. • Configure the test traffic as described in the "Test Traffic" section.
Test Steps:	**Step 1.** As in previous tests, in all the MCs, create an extended ACL called *VoIP* that matches all traffic with a DSCP of EF or CS5. Create an ACL called *HTTP* that matches all traffic to TCP port 80 and all traffic from TCP port 80.

Table 17-16   *PfR Reroute Due to Packet Loss Policy Violation Test*

Step 2.	In all MCs, make the external interfaces connected to the MPLS network members of link-group *MPLS*. Make the interfaces connected to the GRE/IPsec/Internet network members of link-group *INTERNET*.
Step 3.	In the branch MC (CE1), create a PfR policy with an OER learn list that matches the ACL *VoIP*. Set this policy to use link-group *MPLS* as its primary path and link-group *INTERNET* as its fallback path. Set the policy's **loss threshold** to 100 packets per million (ppm). In this policy, create an IP SLA jitter probe with a destination IP of DC-Router using g729a as the codec (if the Fast Reroute feature is implemented to support voice or video over IP, and packet loss is one criteria desired to trigger the reroute, then an explicitly configured jitter probe is required). Set the probe frequency to 2 seconds.
Step 4.	In the DC MCs (MC1 and MC2), create a PfR policy with an OER learn list that matches the ACL *VoIP*. Set this policy to use link-group *MPLS* as its primary path and link-group *INTERNET* as its fallback path. Set the policy's **loss threshold** to 100 ppm. In this policy, create an IP SLA jitter probe with a destination IP of CE1's LAN address, using g729a as the codec. Set the probe frequency to 2 seconds.
Step 5.	In all MCs, create a PfR policy with an OER learn list that matches the ACL *HTTP*. Set this policy to use link-group *INTERNET* as its primary path and link-group *MPLS* as its fallback path.
Step 6.	Start the test traffic.
Step 7.	Verify that all of the VoIP traffic between the DC and the branch is going over the MPLS network by checking the counters of the policy maps configured on the external interfaces of CE1, CE2, CE3, and CE4. Check that all of the HTTP traffic is going over the Internet link. Finally, confirm that the stateful TCP and UDP traffic flows are running over the MPLS network.
Step 8.	Set the delay generator to drop 1% of all packets going between PE2 and PE3.
Step 9.	Watch the logs in the BRs and MCs for messages related to route changes for VoIP prefixes due to loss being OOP (this may take a couple of minutes). Verify that all VoIP traffic is now traveling over the Internet link along with the HTTP traffic. Check that the UDP and stateful TCP traffic is still using the MPLS network.

Table 17-16   *PfR Reroute Due to Packet Loss Policy Violation Test*

Step 10. Verc ACLs, logs, PfR, and IP SLA information for the VoIP pre-fixes in all BRs and MCs.	
Step 11. Move the packet drops from the PE2 to the PE1 link.	
Step 12. Watch the logs in the BRs and MCs for messages related to route changes for VoIP prefixes due to loss being OOP (this may take a couple of minutes). Verify that all VoIP traffic is now traveling over the MPLS link along with the UDP and stateful TCP traffic. Check that the HTTP traffic is still using the Internet network.	
Step 13. Verc ACLs, logs, PfR, and IP SLA information for the VoIP pre-fixes in all BRs and MCs again.	
Step 14. Check the logs and CPU and memory of all the devices in the Node List to make sure they remained stable during all of the changes.	
Expected Results: If a path is OOP due to packet loss, only the VoIP traffic will move to a secondary link; all the other traffic will stay on the "bad link" because the policy does not apply to it.	
Observed Results:	
Pass/Fail:	

Table 17-17 *PfR Black Hole Detection and Fast Reroute Test*

Test ID:	PFR-FEAT-6
Node List:	Routers: CE1, CE2, CE3, CE4, MC1, MC2, PE1, PE2, PE3, DC-Router
Test Phase:	Feature
Test Description:	PfR Black Hole Detection and Fast Reroute Test
Test Setup:	• Build the network, as shown in Figure 17-1. • Configure CE1 and CE2 as PfR BRs, with CE1 as the MC, and set the internal and external interfaces. Make sure to configure the WAE network module's interface as internal. Enable PfR learning and logging. • Configure CE3 and CE4 as PfR BRs, with MC1 (Primary) and MC2 (Standby) as MCs, and set the internal and external interfaces. Make sure to configure the WAE network's interface as internal. Enable PfR learning and logging. • Configure iBGP and eBGP as described in the "Physical and Logical Test Topology" section. • Configure CE1 and CE3 to use GRE over IPsec as described in the "Physical and Logical Test Topology" section, including setting the interface MTU. • Configure CE2 and CE4 to use the MPLS network as described in the "Physical and Logical Test Topology" section. • Configure CE2 as HSRP Active for the branch network to ensure that by default (with no PfR rerouting) all traffic will use the MPLS link to reach the DC. • Configure a default static route on DC-Router pointing at CE4 to ensure that by default (with no PfR rerouting) all traffic will use the MPLS link to reach the branch. • Configure the QoS policies described in the "Physical and Logical Test Topology" section on the "external" interfaces of CE1, CE2, CE3, and CE4 routers. • Configure the external interfaces of CE1, CE2, CE3, and CE4 to be seen as 5 Mbps by using a **bandwidth** statement. Set the load interval of all interfaces to 30 seconds. • Configure the test traffic as described in the "Test Traffic" section.
Test Steps:	**Step 1.** As in previous tests, in all the MCs, create an extended ACL called *VoIP* that matches all traffic with a DSCP of EF or CS5. Create an ACL called *HTTP* that matches all traffic to TCP port 80 and all traffic from TCP port 80.

Table 17-17 *PfR Black Hole Detection and Fast Reroute Test*

Step 2.	In all MCs, make the external interfaces connected to the MPLS network members of link-group *MPLS*. Make the interfaces connected to the GRE/IPsec/Internet network members of link-group *INTERNET*.
Step 3.	In all MCs, create a PfR policy with an OER learn list that matches the ACL *VoIP*. Set this policy to use link-group *MPLS* as its primary path and link-group *INTERNET* as its fallback path. Create a PfR policy with an OER learn list that matches the ACL *HTTP*. Set this policy to use link-group *INTERNET* as its primary path and link-group *MPLS* as its fallback path.
Step 4.	Start the test traffic.
Step 5.	Verify that all of the VoIP traffic between the DC and the branch is going over the MPLS network by checking the counters of the policy maps configured on the external interfaces of CE1, CE2, CE3, and CE4. Check that all of the HTTP traffic is going over the Internet link. Finally, confirm that the stateful TCP and UDP traffic flows are running over the MPLS network.
Step 6.	In CE2, create an extended ACL that permits BGP traffic and denies everything else. Apply the ACL to the PfR external interface inbound and outbound. This should keep the BGP session between CE2 and PE2 up but drop all other traffic, in essence creating a "black hole" condition.
Step 7.	Verify how long all the VoIP and stateful TCP and UDP traffic flows take to reroute. Record the time.
Step 8.	Remove the ACL from CE2 and let the traffic go back to normal, with the VoIP and stateful TCP and UDP traffic running over the MPLS network and the HTTP traffic running over the Internet.
Step 9.	In the branch MC (CE1), change the VoIP PfR policy by adding an IP SLA jitter probe with a destination target pointed at the IP of DC-Router, using g729a as the codec. Set the probe frequency to 2 seconds. Also, set the policy's route control monitor mode to **fast**.
Step 10.	In the DC MCs (MC1 and MC2), change the VoIP PfR policy by adding an IP SLA jitter probe with a destination IP of CE1's LAN address, using g729a as the codec. Set the probe frequency to 2 seconds. Set the VoIP policy's route control monitor mode to **fast**.

Table 17-17 *PfR Black Hole Detection and Fast Reroute Test*

	Step 11. Apply the "black hole" ACL back to the CE2 external interface (in both directions). Monitor the VoIP traffic in both directions to see how fast it reconverges this time. Check to see how fast the stateful TCP and UDP traffic reconverges. Record the results.
	Step 12. Check the logs and CPU and memory of all the devices in the Node List to make sure they remained stable during all of the changes.
Expected Results:	With **set mode monitor fast** configured under its policy, the VoIP traffic should reconverge much faster (approximately 5 seconds or less). This would lead to a rereoute that is fast enough to keep VoIP calls from dropping.
Observed Results:	
Pass/Fail:	

Table 17-18 *PfR Redundant Master Controller Test*

Test ID:	PFR-FEAT-7
Node List:	Routers: CE1, CE2, CE3, CE4, MC1, MC2, PE1, PE2, PE3, DC-Router
Test Phase:	Feature
Test Description:	PfR Redundant Master Controller Test

Table 17-18   *PfR Redundant Master Controller Test*

Test Setup:	<ul><li>Build the network, as shown in Figure 17-1.</li><li>Configure CE1 and CE2 as PfR BRs, with CE1 as the MC, and set the internal and external interfaces. Make sure to configure the WAE network module's interface as "\internal. Enable PfR learning and logging.</li><li>Configure CE3 and CE4 as PfR BRs, with MC1 (Primary) and MC2 (Standby) as MCs, and set the internal and external interfaces. Make sure to configure the WAE network's interface as internal. Enable PfR learning and logging.</li><li>Configure iBGP and eBGP as described in the "Physical and Logical Test Topology" section.</li><li>Configure CE1 and CE3 to use GRE over IPsec as described in the "Physical and Logical Test Topology" section, including setting the interface MTU.</li><li>Configure CE2 and CE4 to use the MPLS network as described in the "Physical and Logical Test Topology" section.</li><li>Configure CE2 as HSRP Active for the branch network to ensure that by default (with no PfR rerouting) all traffic will use the MPLS link to reach the DC.</li><li>Configure a default static route on DC-Router pointing at CE4 to ensure that by default (with no PfR rerouting) all traffic will use the MPLS link to reach the branch.</li><li>Configure the QoS policies described in the "Physical and Logical Test Topology" section on the "external" interfaces of CE1, CE2, CE3, and CE4 routers.</li><li>Configure the external interfaces of CE1, CE2, CE3, and CE4 to be seen as 5 Mbps by using a **bandwidth** statement. Set the load interval of all interfaces to 30 seconds.</li><li>Configure the test traffic as described in the "Test Traffic" section.</li></ul>
Test Steps:	**Step 1.** Start the test traffic.
	Step 2. Verify that all of the test traffic is running across the MPLS network because no PfR policies are applied.
	Step 3. As in previous tests, in all the DC MCs (MC1 and MC2), create an extended ACL called *VoIP* that matches all traffic with a DSCP of EF or CS5. Create an ACL called *HTTP* that matches all traffic to TCP port 80 and all traffic from TCP port 80.
	Step 4. In the DC MCs, make the external interfaces connected to the MPLS network members of link-group *MPLS*. Make the interfaces connected to the GRE/IPsec/Internet network members of link-group *INTERNET*.

Table 17-18   *PfR Redundant Master Controller Test*

Step 5.	In both DC MCs, create a PfR policy with an OER learn list that matches the ACL *VoIP*. Set this policy to use link-group *MPLS* as its primary path and link-group *INTERNET* as its fallback path. Create a PfR policy with an OER learn list that matches the ACL *HTTP*. Set this policy to use link-group *INTERNET* as its primary path and link-group *MPLS* as its fallback path.
Step 6.	Verify that all of the VoIP traffic from the DC to the branch is going over the MPLS network by checking the counters of the policy maps configured on the external interfaces of CE3 and CE4. Check that all of the HTTP traffic is going over the Internet link. Finally, confirm that the stateful TCP and UDP traffic flows are running over the MPLS network.
Step 7.	Check the BR to MC connectivity in CE3 and CE4 and MC1 and MC2. Note whether MC1 is the MC with the CE3 and CE4 BR connections (it should be, due to being HSRP Active).
Step 8.	Verify the dynamic PBR and ACLs created by the MC in both CE3 and CE4. Clear the logs in CE3 and CE4.
Step 9.	The next change may happen quickly, so setting the terminal on CE3 and CE4 to monitor may be required. Shut down MC1.
Step 10.	Check to see whether the HTTP traffic is still using the dynamic PBR to route via the Internet network by checking the counters of the policy maps configured on the external interfaces of CE3. Check the logs to see if CE3 and CE4 have lost connectivity to MC1. Verify that MC2 has taken over as the MC for CE3 and CE4. Make sure that once MC2 is done "learning," it applies the correct PfR policies to CE3 and CE4, and that the HTTP traffic is back to running over the Internet.
Step 11.	Check the logs and CPU and memory of all the devices in the Node List to make sure they remained stable during all of the changes.
Expected Results:	Once the active MC (MC1) is shut down, the standby MC will reset the BR connections and new ones will be established. MC2 will then reapply the PfR policies to the BRs.

Observed Results:

Pass/Fail:

Table 17-19 *WAAS Application Acceleration of FTP/CIFS Test*

Test ID:	WAAS-FEAT-1
Node List:	Routers: CE1, CE2, CE3, CE4, MC1, MC2, PE1, PE2, PE3, DC-Router WAEs: WAE-1, WAE-2, WAE-3, WAE-4, and WAE-5 Branch Laptop-1, Branch Laptop-2, DC-Server Delay Generator
Test Phase:	Feature
Test Description:	WAAS Application Acceleration of FTP/CIFS Test
Test Setup:	• Build the network, as shown in Figure 17-1. • Configure CE1 and CE2 as PfR BRs, with CE1 as the MC, and set the internal and external interfaces. Make sure to configure the WAE network module's interface as internal. Enable PfR learning and logging. • Configure CE3 and CE4 as PfR BRs, with MC1 (Primary) and MC2 (Standby) as MCs, and set the internal and external interfaces. Make sure to configure the WAE network's interface as internal. Enable PfR learning and logging. • Configure iBGP and eBGP as described in the "Physical and Logical Test Topology" section. • Configure CE1 and CE3 to use GRE over IPsec as described in the "Physical and Logical Test Topology" section, including setting the interface MTU. • Configure CE2 and CE4 to use the MPLS network as described in the "Physical and Logical Test Topology" section. • Configure CE2 as HSRP Active for the branch network to ensure that by default (with no PfR rerouting) all traffic will use the MPLS link to reach the DC. • Configure a default static route on the DC-Router pointing at CE4 to ensure that by default (with no PfR rerouting) all traffic will use the MPLS link to reach the branch. • Configure the QoS policies described in the "Physical and Logical Test Topology" section on the "external" interfaces of CE1, CE2, CE3, and CE4 routers. • Configure WAE-5 as a Central Manager and register WAE-1, WAE-2, WAE-3, and WAE-4 as managed assets. • Configure WCCPv2 service groups and redirect as described in the "Physical and Logical Test Topology" section. • Configure the external interfaces of CE1, CE2, CE3, and CE4 to be seen as 5 Mbps by using a **bandwidth** statement. Set the load interval of all interfaces to 30 seconds. • Load a 500-Mbps Microsoft Word or Text file in DC-Server's FTP folder. Share the FTP folder via CIFS (Microsoft sharing). • Enable the FTP server on DC-Server sharing the FTP folder.

Table 17-19 *WAAS Application Acceleration of FTP/CIFS Test*

Test Steps:	
	Step 1. In all of the MCs, make the external interfaces connected to the MPLS network members of link-group *MPLS*. Make the interfaces connected to the GRE/IPsec/Internet network members of link-group *INTERNET*.
	Step 2. Under the learn policy for the MCs, create a learn list named *FTP_TEST* that matches the "traffic-class application FTP."
	Step 3. In the MCs, create a PfR policy with an OER learn list that matches the list *FTP_TEST*. Set this policy to use link-group *INTERNET* as its primary path and link-group *MPLS* as its fallback path.
	Step 4. Disable WCCP in all CE routers (leave it on in the WAEs); this will allow us to do an FTP and a CIFS transfer while bypassing the WAE for control purposes.
	Step 5. Use the delay generator to create a 200-ms delay on both the MPLS and Internet links (PE1 to PE3 and PE2 to PE3 links).
	Step 6. Use a timer to record how long it takes to copy the 500-Mbps file, using FTP, from DC-Server to Branch Laptop-1 (begin the timer the moment you press Enter for the **GET** command).
	Step 7. Verify that the FTP traffic is running over the Internet link by checking the counters on the "external interfaces" of the CE routers (no other traffic should be running across the network).
	Step 8. Delete the file from Branch Laptop-1 and use a timer to record how long it takes to copy the 500-Mbps file, using FTP, from DC-Server to Branch Laptop-1 again (begin the timer the moment you press Enter for the **GET** command).
	Step 9. Use a timer to record how long it takes to copy the 500-Mbps file, using FTP, from DC-Server to Branch Laptop-2 (begin the timer the moment you press Enter for the **GET** command).
	Step 10. Delete the 500-Mbps file from both Branch Laptop-1 and Branch Laptop-2. Map the FTP folder from both branch laptops.
	Step 11. Use a timer to record how long it takes to copy the 500-Mbps file from DC-Server to Branch Laptop-1 using CIFS.

Table 17-19 *WAAS Application Acceleration of FTP/CIFS Test*

Step 12.	Delete the file from Branch Laptop-1 and use a timer to record how long it takes to copy the file over a second time.
Step 13.	Use a timer to record how long it takes to copy the 500-Mbps file from DC-Server to Branch Laptop-2 using CIFS. Delete the file from Laptop-2 after this measurement is taken.
Step 14.	"Unmap" the FTP folder from both branch laptops.
Step 15.	Enable WCCPv2 in all CE routers as described in the Test Setup. Verify that WCCPv2 communication is established with all the appropriate WAEs.
Step 16.	Use a timer to record how long it takes to move the 500-Mbps file, using FTP, from DC-Server to Branch Laptop-1 (begin the timer the moment you press Enter for the **GET** command), this time with the WAEs "inline."
Step 17.	Verify that the FTP traffic is running over the Internet link by checking the counters on the "external interfaces" of the CE routers (no other traffic should be running across the network). Check that the WAEs are seeing and "optimizing and caching" the FTP transfer as expected.
Step 18.	Delete the file from Branch Laptop-1 and use a timer to record how long it takes to copy the 500-Mbps file, usinf FTP, from DC-Server to Branch Laptop-1 again (begin the timer the moment you press Enter for the **GET** command). Check the branch WAEs and see if they see the traffic and file.
Step 19.	Use a timer to record how long it takes to copy the 500-Mbps file, using FTP, from DC-Server to Branch Laptop-2 (begin the timer the moment you press Enter for the **GET** command).
Step 20.	Delete the 500-Mbps file from both Branch Laptop-1 and Branch Laptop-2. Map the FTP folder from both branch laptops, this time with the WAEs inline. Check the WAEs to see if they recognize the CIFS connections.
Step 21.	Use a timer to record how long it takes to COPY the 500-Mbps file from DC-Server to Branch Laptop-1 using CIFS.
Step 22.	Delete the file from Branch Laptop-1 and use a timer to record how long it takes to COPY the file over a second time, this time with the WAEs inline.

Table 17-19 *WAAS Application Acceleration of FTP/CIFS Test*

	Step 23. Use a timer to record how long it takes to COPY the 500-Mbps file from DC-Server to Branch Laptop-2 using CIFS.
Expected Results:	The PfR and WAAS feature will work together as expected. With WCCPv2 enabled and the WAEs "inline," the file transfers should be much faster, especially after the file has already been transferred once.
Observed Results:	See Table 17-20 for an example of a format that can be used to capture and display results for this test. This table can be expanded per iteration of the test, or each iteration can have its own table.
Pass/Fail:	

Table 17-20 is an example format of how results can be recorded and displayed to quantify the optimization gains of WAAS.

Table 17-20 *Example of Results Table for WAAS Tests*

Test Type	FTP No Preposition	CIFS No Preposition
Size of File	500 Mbps	500 Mbps
Native Time (no WAAS)		
Cold Time (first time WAAS was used)		
Hot Time (after WAAS was used once)		
Total Reduction % Cold		
Total Reduction % Hot		

Table 17-21 *Prepositioning of Content with WAAS Test*

Test ID:	WAAS-FEAT-2
Node List:	Routers: CE1, CE2, CE3, CE4, MC1, MC2, PE1, PE2, PE3, DC-Router WAEs: WAE-1, WAE-2, WAE-3, WAE-4, and WAE-5 Branch Laptop-1, Branch Laptop-2, DC-Server Delay Generator
Test Phase:	Feature
Test Description:	Prepositioning of Content with WAAS Test

Table 17-21 *Prepositioning of Content with WAAS Test*

Test Setup:	• Build the network, as shown in Figure 17-1.
	• Configure CE1 and CE2 as PfR BRs, with CE1 as the MC, and set the internal and external interfaces. Make sure to configure the WAE network module's interface as internal. Enable PfR learning and logging.
	• Configure CE3 and CE4 as PfR BRs, with MC1 (Primary) and MC2 (Standby) as MCs, and set the internal and external interfaces. Make sure to configure the WAE network's interface as internal. Enable PfR learning and logging.
	• Configure iBGP and eBGP as described in the "Physical and Logical Test Topology" section.
	• Configure CE1 and CE3 to use GRE over IPsec as described in the "Physical and Logical Test Topology" section, including setting the interface MTU.
	• Configure CE2 and CE4 to use the MPLS network as described in the "Physical and Logical Test Topology" section.
	• Configure CE2 as HSRP Active for the branch network to ensure that by default (with no PfR rerouting) all traffic will use the MPLS link to reach the DC.
	• Configure a default static route on DC-Router pointing at CE4 to ensure that by default (with no PfR rerouting) all traffic will use the MPLS link to reach the branch.
	• Configure the QoS policies described in the "Physical and Logical Test Topology" section on the "external" interfaces of CE1, CE2, CE3, and CE4 routers.
	• Configure WAE-5 as a Central Manager and register WAE-1, WAE-2, WAE-3, and WAE-4 as managed assets.
	• Configure WCCPv2 service groups and redirect as described in the "Physical and Logical Test Topology" section.
	• Configure the external interfaces of CE1, CE2, CE3, and CE4 to be seen as 5 Mbps by using a **bandwidth** statement. Set the load interval of all interfaces to 30 seconds.
	• Load a 500-Mbps Microsoft Word or Text file in DC-Server's FTP folder. Share the FTP folder via CIFS (Microsoft sharing).
	• Enable the FTP server on DC-Server sharing the FTP folder.
Test Steps:	**Step 1.** In WAE-5 (the Central Manager), use **My WAN > Manage Locations** to create a Device Location called **Data_Center**. Add WAE-3 and WAE-4 to this location.

Table 17-21 *Prepositioning of Content with WAAS Test*

Step 2. In WAE-5, create a new preposition directive from the **Configure > File Services > Preposition** menu using the following information:

- Name: **WAAS_Test**
- CIFS – Use Legacy WAFS transport mode: Uncheck
- Status: **Enabled**
- Total File Size as % of Cache Volume, Max File Size, Min File Size, Duration, and Type: Leave at default values or blank
- File Server: The name of the DC-Server (this is where we shared the FTP folder)
- User name, Password, Confirm Password: Use the information to access the share on DC-Server
- Location: **Data_Center** (created in Step 1)
- Enable DSCP: Uncheck
- Root Share and Directories: Use the Browse button to find the "FTP" share or use server\share format to share the folder
- Include Sub Directories: Check
- File Name: **Any**

Step 3. Click **Submit**.

Step 4. Edit the **WAAS_Test** preposition directive to add Edge Device:

- From the WAAS Central Manager GUI, choose **Services > File > Preposition**. Click the edit icon next to WAAS_Test.
- Open the "Edge Device assignment for Preposition Directive" dialog by using the **Assign Edge Devices** link under **Contents**.
- Add **WAE-1 and WAE-2** by clicking the blue X icon next to each device name.

Step 5. Click **Submit**.

Step 6. Edit the **WAAS_Test** preposition directive to add Schedule:

- From the WAAS Central Manager GUI, choose **Services > File > Preposition**. Click the edit icon next to WAAS_Test.
- Open the Modifying Schedule dialog by using the **Schedule** link under **Contents**.
- Choose the **Now** option.

Table 17-21 *Prepositioning of Content with WAAS Test*

Step 7. Click **Submit**.
Step 8. Verify that the preposition directive completed successfully by checking the Preposition Status tab. Wait until the status shows Completed.
Step 9. In all of the MCs, make the external interfaces connected to the MPLS network members of link-group *MPLS*. Make the interfaces connected to the GRE/IPsec/Internet network members of link-group *INTERNET*.
Step 10. Under the learn policy for the MCs, create a learn list named *FTP_TEST* that matches the **traffic-class application FTP**.
Step 11. In the MCs, create a PfR policy with an OER learn list that matches the list *FTP_TEST*. Set this policy to use link-group *INTERNET* as its primary path and link-group *MPLS* as its fallback path.
Step 12. Use the delay generator to create a 200-ms delay on both the MPLS and Internet links (PE1 to PE3 and PE2 to PE3 links).
Step 13. Use a timer to record how long it takes to copy the 500-Mbps file, using FTP, from DC-Server to Branch Laptop-1 (begin the timer the moment you press Enter for the **GET** command).
Step 14. Verify whether the FTP traffic is running over the Internet link by checking the counters on the "external interfaces" of the CE routers (no other traffic should be running across the network).
Step 15. Use a timer to record how long it takes to copy the 500-Mbps file,using FTP, from DC-Server to Branch Laptop-2 (begin the timer the moment you press Enter for the **GET** command).
Step 16. Delete the 500-Mbps file from both Branch Laptop-1 and Branch Laptop-2. Map the FTP folder from both branch laptops.
Step 17. Use a timer to record how long it takes to COPY the 500-Mbps file from DC-Server to Branch Laptop-1 using CIFS.

Table 17-21 *Prepositioning of Content with WAAS Test*

	Step 18. Verify whether the CIFS traffic is running over the MPLS or Internet links by checking the counters on the "external interfaces" of the CE routers (no other traffic should be running across the network).
	Step 19. Use a timer to record how long it takes to COPY the 500-Mbps file from DC-Server to Branch Laptop-2 using CIFS.
Expected Results:	The file will be prepositioned as expected. Prepositioning the file will allow the "copy" traffic to stay local and off the WAN links.
Observed Results:	
Pass/Fail:	

Table 17-22 *Upgrading WAE Code with the Central Manager Test*

Test ID:	WAAS-FEAT-3
Node List:	Routers: CE1, CE2, CE3, CE4, MC1, MC2, PE1, PE2, PE3 WAEs: WAE-1, WAE-2, WAE-3, WAE-4, and WAE-5
Test Phase:	Feature
Test Description:	Upgrading WAE Code with the Central Manager Test
Test Setup:	• Build the network, as shown in Figure 17-1. • Configure iBGP and eBGP as described in the "Physical and Logical Test Topology" section to allow reachability between the DC and branch networks. • Configure WAE-5 as a Central Manager and register WAE-1, WAE-2, WAE-3, and WAE-4 as managed assets. • Configure WCCPv2 service groups and redirect as described in the "Physical and Logical Test Topology" section.

Table 17-22 *Upgrading WAE Code with the Central Manager Test*

Test Steps:	Step 1. Put the new software version for the WAEs in the FTP folder of DC-Server.
	Step 2. Check the software versions being run by all the WAEs on the **My WAN > Manage Devices** tab; this should be an older version than the "new" code in the FTP folder.
	Step 3. Specify the location of the new software to be used for the upgrades under the **Jobs > Software Update** tab by clicking the Create New Software File button and specifying the name and location of the file in the FTP folder used in Step 1. Make sure to check the "Auto Reload" check box.
	Step 4. Upgrade the WAAS Central Manager. Clear the browser cache after the WAE reboots.
	Step 5. Once the Central Manager reboots, verify that it is running the correct code.
	Step 6. Using the Central Manager GUI, upgrade WAE-1. Watch the status messages as the device is upgraded.
	Step 7. After WAE-1 is upgraded, using the Central Manager GUI, upgrade WAE-2, WAE-3, and WAE-4 together. Watch the status messages as the devices are upgraded.
	Step 8. After all the WAEs are upgraded, rerun the WAAS-FEAT-1 test (no need to run it with WCCPv2 disabled) to verify that the code upgrade worked as expected.
	Step 9. Check the logs and CPU and memory of all of CE1 and CE2 to make sure they remained stable during the upgrades.
Expected Results:	All devices will be upgraded successfully.
Observed Results:	
Pass/Fail:	

Table 17-23 *PfR Prefix Scalability Test*

Test ID:	PFR-SCALE-1
Node List:	Routers: CE1, CE2, CE3, CE4, MC1, MC2, PE1, PE2, PE3, DC-Router WAEs: WAE-1, WAE-2, WAE-3, WAE-4, WAE-5
Test Phase:	Scalability
Test Description:	PfR Prefix Scalability Test
Test Setup:	• Build the network, as shown in Figure 17-1. • Configure CE1 and CE2 as PfR BRs, with CE1 as the MC, and set the internal and external interfaces. Make sure to configure the WAE network module's interface as internal. Disable PfR learning and logging (this test is for scalability of the ASR and 7200 routers). • Configure CE3 and CE4 as PfR BRs, with MC1 (Primary) and MC2 (Standby) as MCs, and set the internal and external interfaces. Make sure to configure the WAE network's interface as internal. Enable PfR learning and logging. • Configure iBGP and eBGP as described in the "Physical and Logical Test Topology" section. • Configure CE1 and CE3 to use GRE over IPsec as described in the "Physical and Logical Test Topology" section, including setting the interface MTU. • Configure CE2 and CE4 to use the MPLS network as described in the "Physical and Logical Test Topology" section. • Configure CE2 as HSRP Active for the branch network to ensure that by default (with no PfR rerouting) all traffic will use the MPLS link to reach the DC. • Configure a default static route on DC-Router pointing at CE4 to ensure that by default (with no PfR rerouting) all traffic will use the MPLS link to reach the branch. • Configure the QoS policies described in the "Physical and Logical Test Topology" section on the "external" interfaces of CE1, CE2, CE3, and CE4 routers. • Configure WAE-5 as a Central Manager and register WAE-1, WAE-2, WAE-3, and WAE-4 as managed assets. In the Central Manager, make sure that HTTP application acceleration is disabled for this test. • Configure WCCPv2 service groups and redirect as described in the "Physical and Logical Test Topology" section. • Configure the external interfaces of CE1, CE2, CE3, and CE4 to be seen as 200 Mbps by using a **bandwidth** statement. Set the load interval of all interfaces to 30 seconds. • Configure the test traffic as described in the "Test Traffic" section.

Table 17-23   *PfR Prefix Scalability Test*

Test Steps:	
	Step 1. Configure the two DC MCs learning with aggregation prefix lengths set to /32 and periodic and monitor intervals set to 1 minute.
	Step 2. Start the test traffic and verify that all traffic is running over the MPLS network by checking the counters of the policy maps configured on the external interfaces of CE1, CE2, CE3, and CE4.
	Step 3. Validate that the MCs in the DC are seeing all traffic as In Policy, and learning /32 prefixes being used by test traffic.
	Step 4. Create 2000 unique HTTP flows between the data center and the branch network using your test tool. The flows should be between 20 HTTP servers in the DC and 100 HTTP clients in the branch office. Each of the 100 clients should connect to every HTTP server. Start the traffic flows.
	Step 5. In all the MCs, create an extended ACL called *VoIP* that matches all traffic with a DSCP of EF or CS5. Create an ACL called *HTTP* that matches all traffic to TCP port 80 and all traffic from TCP port 80.
	Step 6. In all MCs, make the external interfaces connected to the MPLS network members of link-group *MPLS*. Make the interfaces connected to the GRE/IPsec/Internet network members of link-group *INTERNET*.
	Step 7. In all MCs, create a PfR policy with an OER learn list that matches the ACL *VoIP*. Set this policy to use link-group *INTERNET* as its primary path and link-group *MPLS* as its fallback path.
	Step 8. Verify that all of the VoIP traffic between the DC and the branch is going over the Internet network by checking the counters of the policy maps configured on the external interfaces of CE1, CE2, CE3, and CE4.
	Step 9. Verify whether dynamic PBRs and ACLs are created in CE1, CE2, CE3, and CE4 for rerouting the VoIP traffic.
	Step 10. Verify that all of HTTP traffic between the DC and the branch is going over the MPLS network by checking the counters of the policy maps configured on the external interfaces of CE1, CE2, CE3, and CE4.

Table 17-23   *PfR Prefix Scalability Test*

Step 11.	Enable **throughput** learning in the DC MCs. Verify that the DC MCs are learning /32 prefixes as expected.
Step 12.	In the DC MCs, create another PfR policy. This policy should match the learned "throughput" and set the **utilization** priority to 5 and the variance to 20%.
Step 13.	After the learning phase is complete, check the BGP routing tables of all CE routers. Verify whether several /32 BGP routes have been injected into BGP to help load-balance the HTTP traffic from the DC to the branch.
Step 14.	Verify whether all of the HTTP traffic from the DC to the branch is being load-balanced by checking the counters of the policy maps configured on the external interfaces of CE1, CE2, CE3, and CE4.
Step 15.	Check that WCCPv2 is still working as expected by logging into the WAEs in the branch and DC and confirming that they are seeing redirected HTTP traffic as expected.
Step 16.	Verify whether MC1 and MC2 are seeing all 2000+ HTTP prefixes from CE3 and CE4. Verify that all of the devices in the Node List are running without issues by checking their logs and CPU and memory utilization.
Step 17.	Add another ten HTTP servers to the DC traffic profile (this should create a total of 3000 unique prefixes as each of the 100 clients in the branch connects to all 30 HTTP servers in the DC).
Step 18.	Verify whether MC1 and MC2 are seeing all 3000+ HTTP prefixes from CE3 and CE4. Verify that all of the devices in the Node List are running without issues by checking their logs and CPU and memory utilization.
Step 19.	Add another ten HTTP servers to the DC traffic profile (this should create a total of 4000 unique prefixes as each of the 100 clients in the branch connects to all 40 HTTP servers in the DC).
Step 20.	Verify whether MC1 and MC2 are seeing all 4000+ HTTP prefixes from CE3 and CE4. Verify that all of the devices in the Node List are running without issues by checking their logs and CPU and memory utilization.

Table 17-23 *PfR Prefix Scalability Test*

	Step 21. Add another ten HTTP servers to the DC traffic profile (this should create a total of 5000 unique prefixes).
	Step 22. Verify whether MC1 and MC2 are seeing all 5000+ HTTP prefixes from CE3 and CE4. Verify that all of the devices in the Node List are running without issues by checking their logs and CPU and memory utilization.
Expected Results:	This is a scalability test. The total number of supported prefixes will be reported. The test will be stopped at 5000 prefixes because, in the real world, the learn configuration would be set to /24, and 5000 flows between unique /24 source/destination pairs is more than would likely be encountered on a typical enterprise network.
Observed Results:	
Pass/Fail:	

Table 17-24 *Router/WAE Chassis Failure and Recovery Test*

Test ID:	PFR-DUTY-1
Node List:	Routers: CE1, CE2, CE3, CE4, MC1, MC2, PE1, PE2, PE3, DC-Router WAEs: WAE-1, WAE-2, WAE-3, WAE-4 and WAE-5
Test Phase:	Duty Cycle
Test Description:	Router/WAE Chassis Failure and Recovery Test

Table 17-24 *Router/WAE Chassis Failure and Recovery Test*

Test Setup:	• Build the network, as shown in Figure 17-1.
	• Configure CE1 and CE2 as PfR BRs, with CE1 as the MC, and set the internal and external interfaces. Make sure to configure the WAE network module's interface as internal. Enable PfR learning and logging.
	• Configure CE3 and CE4 as PfR BRs, with MC1 (Primary) and MC2 (Standby) as MCs, and set the internal and external interfaces. Make sure to configure the WAE network's interface as internal. Enable PfR learning and logging.
	• Configure iBGP and eBGP as described in the "Physical and Logical Test Topology" section.
	• Configure CE1 and CE3 to use GRE over IPsec as described in the "Physical and Logical Test Topology" section, including setting the interface MTU.
	• Configure CE2 and CE4 to use the MPLS network as described in the "Physical and Logical Test Topology" section.
	• Configure CE2 as HSRP Active for the branch network to ensure that by default (with no PfR rerouting) all traffic will use the MPLS link to reach the DC.
	• Configure a default static route on DC-Router pointing at CE4 to ensure that by default (with no PfR rerouting) all traffic will use the MPLS link to reach the branch.
	• Configure the QoS policies described in the "Physical and Logical Test Topology" section on the "external" interfaces of CE1, CE2, CE3, and CE4 routers.
	• Configure WAE-5 as a Central Manager and register WAE-1, WAE-2, WAE-3, and WAE-4 as managed assets. In the Central Manager, make sure that HTTP application acceleration is disabled for this test.
	• Configure WCCPv2 service groups and redirect as described in the "Physical and Logical Test Topology" section.
	• Configure the external interfaces of CE1, CE2, CE3, and CE4 to be seen as 5 Mbps by using a **bandwidth** statement. Set the load interval of all interfaces to 30 seconds.
	• In all the MCs, create an extended ACL called *VoIP* that matches all traffic with a DSCP of EF or CS5. Create an ACL called *HTTP* that matches all traffic to TCP port 80 and all traffic from TCP port 80.
	• In all MCs, make the external interfaces connected to the MPLS network members of link-group *MPLS*. Make the interfaces connected to the GRE/IPsec/Internet network members of link-group *INTERNET*.
	• In all MCs, create a PfR policy with an OER learn list that matches the ACL *VoIP*. Set this policy to use link-group *MPLS* as its primary path and link-group *INTERNET* as its fallback path.
	• In all MCs, create a PfR policy with an OER learn list that matches the ACL *HTTP*. Set this policy to use link-group *INTERNET* as its primary path and link-group *MPLS* as its fallback path.
	• Enable **throughput** learning in all MCs. Verify that the MCs are learning /32 prefixes as expected.
	• In all MCs, create another PfR policy. This policy should match the learned "throughput" and set the **utilization** priority to 5 and the variance to 20%.
	• Configure the test traffic as described in the "Test Traffic" section.
	• Load a 500-Mbps Microsoft Word or Text file in DC-Server's FTP folder. Share the FTP folder via CIFS (Microsoft sharing).
	• Enable the FTP server on DC-Server sharing the FTP folder.

Table 17-24 *Router/WAE Chassis Failure and Recovery Test*

Test Steps:	**Step 1.** Start all of the test traffic.
	Step 2. Verify that the traffic is running on the correct links as per the PfR policy, by checking the policy map counters of the CE routers.
	Step 3. Check that the WAEs are seeing traffic as expected.
	Step 4. Start an FTP transfer from DC-Server to Branch Laptop-1. Once the file transfer begins, verify which WAEs the traffic is going through by checking their statistics/load balancing. Verify which WAEs are used for the CIFS file copy between DC-Server and Branch Laptop-1.
	Step 5. Clear the cache in all WAEs and restart the FTP copy. Reset the "active" WAEs in the branch. Verify how long it takes for the FTP to re-establish. Check to see if any other traffic is affected. Ensure that there is no disruption of traffic when the WAE comes back online.
	Step 6. Clear the cache in all WAEs and restart the FTP copy. Reset the "active" WAE in the DC. Verify how long it takes for the FTP to re-establish. Check to see if any other traffic is affected. Ensure that there is no disruption of traffic when the WAE comes back online.
	Step 7. Clear the cache in all WAEs and restart the CIFS copy. Reset the "active" WAE in the branch. Verify how long it takes for the copy to re-establish. Check to see if any other traffic is affected. Ensure that there is no disruption of traffic when the WAE comes back online.
	Step 8. Clear the cache in all WAEs and restart the CIFS copy. Reset the "active" WAE in the DC. Verify how long it takes for the copy to re-establish. Check to see if any other traffic is affected. Ensure that there is no disruption of traffic when the WAE comes back online.
	Step 9. With the traffic running, power off CE1. Check to see how long it takes all the traffic to reconverge.
	Step 10. Power CE1 back on. Wait for the network to reconverge, and make sure that the PfR policies go back into effect.
	Step 11. Power down CE2. Check to see how long it takes all the traffic to reconverge.

Table 17-24 *Router/WAE Chassis Failure and Recovery Test*

	Step 12. Power CE2 back on. Wait for the network to reconverge, and make sure that the PfR policies go back into effect.
	Step 13. Power down CE3. Check to see how long it takes all the traffic to reconverge.
	Step 14. Power CE3 back on. Wait for the network to reconverge, and make sure that the PfR policies go back into effect.
	Step 15. Power down CE4. Check to see how long it takes all the traffic to reconverge.
	Step 16. Power CE4 back on. Wait for the network to reconverge, and make sure that the PfR policies go back into effect.
	Step 17. Check the logs and CPU and memory of all the devices in the Node List to make sure they remained stable during all of the failures.
Expected Results:	All traffic will recover as expected.
Observed Results:	
Pass/Fail:	

Table 17-25 *Link Failure and Recovery Test*

Test ID:	PFR-DUTY-2
Node List:	Routers: CE1, CE2, CE3, CE4, MC1, MC2, PE1, PE2, PE3, DC-Router WAEs: WAE-1, WAE-2, WAE-3, WAE-4 and WAE-5
Test Phase:	Duty Cycle
Test Description:	Link Failure and Recovery Test

Table 17-25 *Link Failure and Recovery Test*

Test Setup:	
	• Build the network, as shown in Figure 17-1.
	• Configure CE1 and CE2 as PfR BRs, with CE1 as the MC, and set the internal and external interfaces. Make sure to configure the WAE network module's interface as internal. Enable PfR learning and logging.
	• Configure CE3 and CE4 as PfR BRs, with MC1 (Primary) and MC2 (Standby) as MCs, and set the internal and external interfaces. Make sure to configure the WAE network's interface as internal. Enable PfR learning and logging.
	• Configure iBGP and eBGP as described in the "Physical and Logical Test Topology" section.
	• Configure CE1 and CE3 to use GRE over IPsec as described in the "Physical and Logical Test Topology" section, including setting the interface MTU.
	• Configure CE2 and CE4 to use the MPLS network as described in the "Physical and Logical Test Topology" section.
	• Configure CE2 as HSRP Active for the branch network to ensure that by default (with no PfR rerouting) all traffic will use the MPLS link to reach the DC.
	• Configure a default static route on DC-Router pointing at CE4 to ensure that by default (with no PfR rerouting) all traffic will use the MPLS link to reach the branch.
	• Configure the QoS policies described in the "Physical and Logical Test Topology" section on the "external" interfaces of CE1, CE2, CE3, and CE4 routers.
	• Configure WAE-5 as a Central Manager and register WAE-1, WAE-2, WAE-3, and WAE-4 as managed assets. In the Central Manager, make sure that HTTP application acceleration is disabled for this test.
	• Configure WCCPv2 service groups and redirect as described in the "Physical and Logical Test Topology" section.
	• Configure the external interfaces of CE1, CE2, CE3, and CE4 to be seen as 5 Mbps by using a **bandwidth** statement. Set the load interval of all interfaces to 30 seconds.
	• In all the MCs, create an extended ACL called *VoIP* that matches all traffic with a DSCP of EF or CS5. Create an ACL called *HTTP* that matches all traffic to TCP port 80 and all traffic from TCP port 80.
	• In all MCs, make the external interfaces connected to the MPLS network members of link-group *MPLS*. Make the interfaces connected to the GRE/IPsec/Internet network members of link-group *INTERNET*.
	• In all MCs, create a PfR policy with an OER learn list that matches the ACL *VoIP*. Set this policy to use link-group *MPLS* as its primary path and link-group *INTERNET* as its fallback path.
	• In all MCs, create a PfR policy with an OER learn list that matches the ACL *HTTP*. Set this policy to use link-group *INTERNET* as its primary path and link-group *MPLS* as its fallback path.
	• Enable **throughput** learning in all MCs. Verify that the MCs are learning /32 prefixes as expected.
	• In all MCs, create another PfR policy. This policy should match the learned "throughput" and set the **utilization** priority to 5 and the variance to 20%.
	• Configure the test traffic as described in the "Test Traffic" section.
	• Load a 500-Mbps Microsoft Word or Text file in DC-Server's FTP folder. Share the FTP folder via CIFS (Microsoft sharing).
	• Enable the FTP server on DC-Server sharing the FTP folder.

Table 17-25   *Link Failure and Recovery Test*

Test Steps:	**Step 1.** Start all of the test traffic.
	Step 2. Verify that the traffic is running on the correct links as per the PfR policy, by checking the policy map counters of the CE routers.
	Step 3. Check that the WAEs are seeing traffic as expected.
	Step 4. Start an FTP transfer from DC-Server to Branch Laptop-1. Once the file transfer begins, shut down the connection between PE2 and CE2. Check to see how long it takes all the traffic to reconverge.
	Step 5. Bring the link between PE2 and CE2 back up. Wait for the network to reconverge, and make sure that the PfR policies go back into effect.
	Step 6. Clear the cache of all WAEs. Start CIFS copy from DC-Server to Branch Laptop-1. Once the file copy begins, shut down the connection between PE1 and CE1. Check to see how long it takes all the traffic to reconverge.
	Step 7. Bring the link between PE1 and CE1 back up. Wait for the network to reconverge, and make sure that the PfR policies go back into effect.
Expected Results:	All traffic will recover as expected.
Observed Results:	
Pass/Fail:	

Chapter 18

Using the Lab for Hands-On Technology Training: Data Center 3.0 Configuration Lab Guide

Business travel and formal classroom training are two activities often eliminated by IT organizations working with reduced operating budgets. In an age where IT is relied upon almost as a *utility*, web collaboration and videoconferencing are making the argument for mandatory travel much more difficult, as they have proven to be a highly effective means of managing customer interactions. Completely eliminating formal classroom training, on the other hand, is a questionable decision in an industry where "knowledge is power" because a lack of learning opportunities affects employee morale and consequently their efficiency as they fall behind in their technical expertise. An analogy of drinking from a fire hose can be used to describe how technical members feel as they attempt to rapidly absorb the sheer volume of ever-changing technical concepts while fulfilling their everyday job responsibilities.

In most IT organizations, on-the-job training (OJT) has become the default training method, as a hectic workload and increased responsibilities do not permit the luxury of formal classroom training. Although OJT is undeniably cheap and flexible, its effectiveness can be questioned because it is normally taken on as an unstructured activity, with new or junior members shadowing senior team members designated as mentors by the management team. The reality is that many of these mentors are simply technical staff members who have been in the job the longest, and not always be the best-qualified people to teach or convey information to new team members. Because it does not produce consistent results, traditional OJT is unreliable and often inefficient.

Even without specific dollars set aside for training, there are many creative ways in which IT organizations can provide learning opportunities for their employees, one of which is to leverage the enterprise lab for hands-on training. The best training opportunities often present themselves during the Operate Phase of the enterprise network's lifecycle, when test activities are normally at their lowest, and during the Planning Phase, when demo gear may be available for evaluation. Hands-on training allows employees to work at their own pace to learn new concepts through the application of principles, a method that has consistently proven to work better than learning the concepts from books or presentations.

Creating an effective hands-on training lab begins with an organizational commitment to procuring and setting aside adequate equipment, dedicated to educational purposes for a certain amount of time. The training lab topology should be built to enterprise-specific design standards, including the appropriate hardware, software, and device configurations that would be deployed on the production network. A structured training guide as a supplement to the hands-on lab is extremely valuable, as it allows students to learn specific configuration or troubleshooting tasks by following a series of exercises, or steps, with each one building on the last. When appropriate, this guide would also incorporate a technology primer, including an explanation of the protocols and features in use, along with references to any enterprise architectural standards that may exist. It is important to include examples of the expected output for each exercise, so that students can follow along unattended and complete the training at their own pace. The training guide will also serve as an invaluable reference guide in the future, long after the lab equipment is redeployed for other purposes.

This chapter provides an example of a detailed, step-by-step lab training guide. While this particular example consists of lab exercises to build and provision a Data Center 3.0 topology, it can be customized and used as a template for your company's future hands-on training requirements.

Background

You need to consider several things before you start creating your hands-on lab guide:

- What is the skill set of your audience?
- What equipment do you have available?
- How long do you want the training to be?
- What technologies and topics do you want to cover?

If your audience is new to the technology, step-by-step instructions and screenshots are a must. For more experienced students with a higher level of proficiency, you can give instructions, such as "configure iBGP between Router A and Router B."

In this hands-on lab example, we assume almost no knowledge from our target audience; therefore, we try to supplement the lab exercises with technology briefs and tips. After training is completed, this lab manual can be used as reference material for the student.

The Data Center 3.0 configuration lab in our example is split up into the following exercises:

- **Lab 1:** Configuring UCS Ethernet Ports and Named VLANs Using Unified Computing System Manager
- **Lab 2:** Configuring UCS Network and Server-Related Pools
- **Lab 3:** Creating Virtual PortChannels on Nexus 7000 Series Switches
- **Lab 4:** Creating a VSAN Fabric and Enabling Fibre Channel Connectivity Between the UCS 6100 Fabric Interconnect and MDS 9506
- **Lab 5:** Configuring UCS Service Profiles

■ **Lab 6:** Configuring SAN Zoning and Core Switch Connectivity on the MDS 9506

■ **Lab 7:** Enabling IP and Routing Features on the Nexus 7000 Series Switches

■ **Lab 8:** Verifying the Blade Servers Boot VMware ESX 4.0

■ **Lab 9:** Adding the UCS Blade Servers into VMware vCenter

Physical and Logical Lab Topology

The Data Center 3.0 hands-on lab uses the equipment pod ("Pod") illustrated in Figure 18-1.

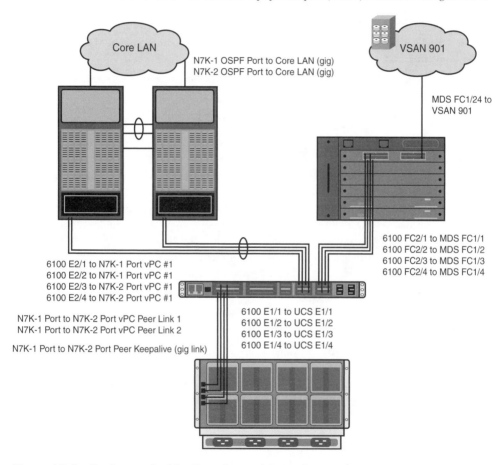

Figure 18-1   *Equipment Pod for Data Center 3.0 Hands on Lab*

The Pod contains the following:

■ One UCS blade enclosure chassis

■ Eight UCS half width blades

■ One Nexus 6120XP Switch with a 4-port Fibre Channel plus 4-port 10-Gigabit Ethernet expansion module

- One MDS 9506 Multilayer Storage Director
- Two Nexus 7000 VDCs
- Several LUNs on an EMC VMax SE system

Connectivity to this lab is provided via remote desktop to a lab PC. The lab PC has all the software and reachability required to complete the labs.

Lab Objectives

The primary objectives for this hands-on lab are as follows:

- Familiarize the students with the Cisco Unified Computing System Manager (UCSM) platform GUI
- Introduce the students to Nexus 7000 virtualization technologies such as VDCs and vPCs
- Give the students a basic understanding of SAN technologies

Detailed Hands-On Lab

The following step-by-step lab training guide is intended to be used as a training supplement for students having little or no expertise with a technical solution or subject matter. It provides detailed steps with screen shots and CLI captures to help students reinforce technical concepts through hands-on practice at their own pace. The guide is separated into several labs by technology, and each lab can be used separately to reinforce a concept. Many of the labs include a quick technology primer to familiarize the student with the new concepts they are learning. It begins with instructions on how to connect into the lab for the first time and ends with a newly built data center ready to deploy virtual machines.

Step 1: Log In to Your Assigned Pod

1. Launch a Remote Desktop Connection and connect to **10.1.1.1**, as shown in Figure 18-2.

2. As demonstrated in Figure 18-3, log into the lab PC using the following credentials:

    User Name: **administrator**

    Password: **LAB-Task**

3. A Remote Desktop Connection is launched to the lab PC in the enterprise lab. All of your configuration tasks are performed from this desktop.

Lab 1: Configuring Unified Computing System Ethernet Ports and Named VLANs Using Unified Computing System Manager

In this exercise, you will configure UCS 6100 Series Fabric Interconnect Ethernet ports and named VLANs using the UCSM GUI.

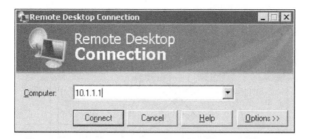

Figure 18-2 *Remote Desktop Connection Window*

Figure 18-3 *RDC Authentication Window*

Note Cisco UCSM creates a unified management domain and serves as the central nervous system of the Cisco Unified Computing System. Cisco UCSM is the embedded device-management software (residing on the UCS Fabric Interconnect hardware) that manages the system from end to end as a single logical entity through an intuitive GUI, a command-line interface (CLI), or an XML API.

All lab exercises will be conducted using the UCSM GUI/Java Web Start application.

Each UCS uses Ethernet ports to communicate between the blade servers' converged network adapters (or CNAs, which have capabilities to MUX both LAN and SAN traffic over Ethernet) and the UCS 2140 Fabric Extenders, also known as Input/Output Modules (IOM), which are line cards inside the 5100 Blade Server chassis. Each half-width blade server has a 10-Gigabit (10GE) connection into each fabric's (A and B) IOM. The IOMs in turn connect into the UCS 6100 Series Fabric Interconnect Switches, which have Ethernet ports on both the fixed and expansion port modules. The 6100 Fabric Interconnects (FI) can then connect to the LAN, using any free local Ethernet port, and to the SAN, using Fibre Channel ports or Ethernet ports for network-attached storage (NAS), as shown in Figure 18-4.

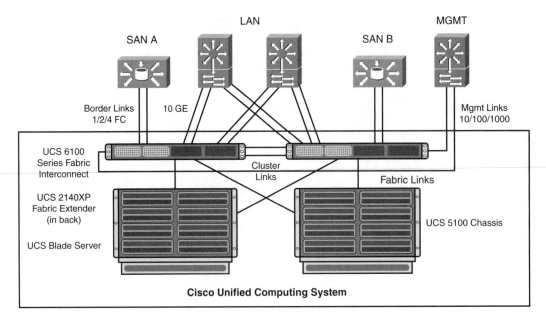

Figure 18-4 *UCS Reference Architecture*

UCS 6100 Ethernet ports on the fixed modules are not reserved for specific use, and must be configured as either Server Ports or Uplink Ports; Cisco UCS FIs provide the following port types:

- **Server Ports:** Handle data traffic between the UCS 6100 FI and the adapter cards on the servers. You can configure Server Ports only on the fixed port module. Expansion modules do not support Server Ports.

- **Uplink Ethernet Ports:** Connect to external LAN switches. Network-bound Ethernet traffic is pinned to one of these ports. You can configure Uplink Ethernet Ports on either the fixed module or an expansion module.

- **Uplink Fibre Channel Ports:** Connect to external SAN switches. Network-bound Fibre Channel traffic is pinned to one of these ports. You can configure Uplink Fibre Channel Ports only on an expansion module. The fixed module does not include Uplink Fibre Channel Ports.

A named VLAN creates a connection to a specific external LAN. For any VLAN to be supported on any blade, a VLAN object must be created in the global Cisco UCS configuration using the LAN tab on the navigation panel. The VLAN isolates traffic, including broadcast traffic, to that external LAN. The name that you assign to a VLAN ID adds a layer of abstraction that allows you to globally update all servers associated with service profiles that use the named VLAN. Service profiles are explained in detail in the section "Lab 5: Configuring UCS Service Profiles."

When dealing with VLANs in the UCS, it is important to understand

- You can create more than one named VLAN with the same VLAN ID. For example, if servers that host business services for HR and Finance need to access the same external LAN, you can create VLANs named HR and Finance with the same VLAN ID. Then, if the network is reconfigured and Finance is assigned to a different LAN, you have to change only the VLAN ID for the named VLAN for Finance.

- In a Cisco UCS instance with two FIs, you can create a named VLAN that is accessible to both FIs or to only one FI. (There is only a single FI in this lab.)

- You cannot create VLANs with IDs from 3968 to 4048. This range of VLAN IDs is reserved.

In this section, you will complete the following tasks:

1. Log in to the UCSM GUI.

2. Configure four of the 10GE ports on the fixed port module of the FI as Server Ports (connecting to the UCS Chassis).

3. Configure four of the 10GE ports on the expansion module as Uplink Ethernet Ports (connecting to the Nexus 7000 Switches).

4. Configure named VLANs on the UCS.

Step 1: Launch UCSM from a Web Browser

1. From your Remote Desktop, open Internet Explorer and connect to the management address of the UCS 6100 FI switch: **http://10.1.0.5**; you will see the site in Figure 18-5 displayed.

2. Click the **Launch** link and accept (click **Yes**) any security warnings. Click **Run** when Java Web Start asks if you want to run the application.

3. Log in to UCSM using the dialog box shown in Figure 18-6 with the following credentials:

   User Name: **admin**

   Password: **Cisco.123** (note the capital *C*)

4. Click the **Equipment** tab of the USCM application, as shown in Figure 18-7, and the Fabric Interconnect icon appears in the Main Topology View. You are now ready to proceed with the first configuration task.

Step 2: Enable the Server Ports Between the UCS 6100 Fabric Interconnect and the UCS Chassis

1. Click the **Equipment** tab, the **Policies** tab, and then the **Global Policies** tab, as shown in Figure 18-8.

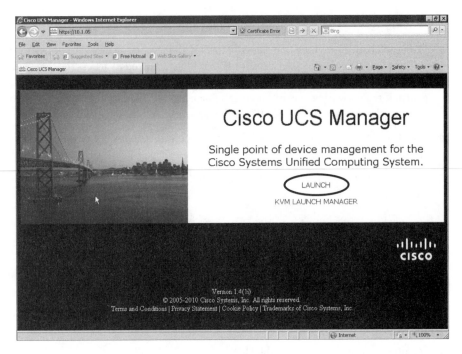

Figure 18-5   *UCSM Launch Screen*

Figure 18-6   *UCSM Login Dialog Box*

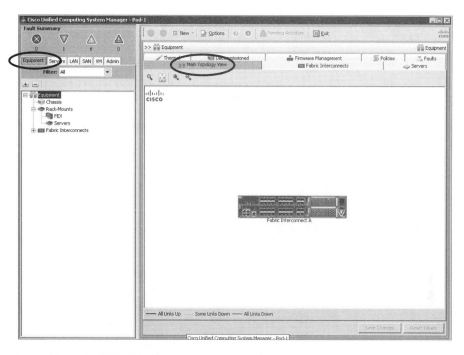

Figure 18-7 *UCSM Window—Equipment Tab*

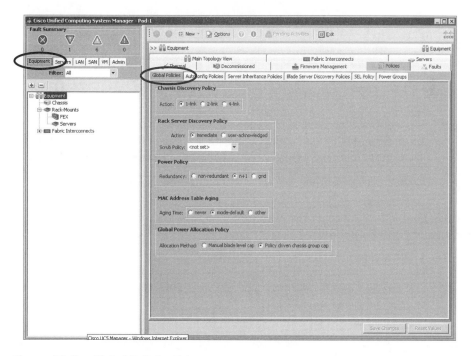

Figure 18-8 *Global Policies Tab*

2. In the Chassis Discovery Policy area, click the **4-Link** radio button, as shown in Figure 18-9, and click **Save Changes**. This automatically configures the UCS 6100 chassis to use all four of the 10GE ports connected between the UCS 2100 Series Fabric Extender module and the UCS 6100 Fabric Interconnect (for high availability; normally these would be redundantly connected via multiple 6100 fabrics). Physical connectivity options are 1-link (1×10GE), 2-link (2×10GE), or 4-link (4× 10GE) ports.

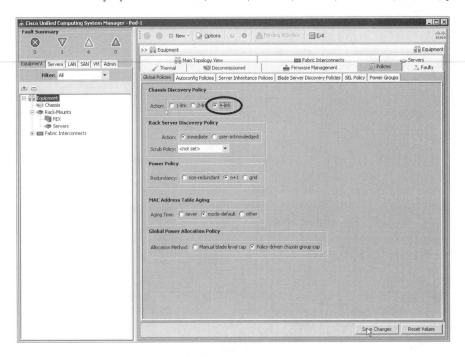

Figure 18-9   *Configuring a Global Discovery Policy*

3. Expand **Fabric Interconnects > Fabric Interconnect A > Fixed Module > Unconfigured Ethernet Ports** by clicking the **+** sign next to each. Right-click **Port 1** and choose **Configure as Server Port**, as shown in Figure 18-10. Click **Yes** to accept.

4. Configure Ports 2, 3, and 4 as Server Ports by repeating this process.

Step 3: Enable the Uplink Ports Between the UCS 6100 Fabric Interconnect and the Nexus 7000 Switches

1. Configure the four Ethernet Ports in Expansion Module 2 as Uplink Ports. A short-cut to do this all at once is to select all four ports (click **Port 1**, hold down the **Shift** key, and click **Port 4**), and then right-click **Port 1** and choose **Configure as Uplink Port**, as shown in Figure 18-11.

Note   Alternatively, you can select and configure ports individually by selecting **Action > Configure as Uplink Port**.

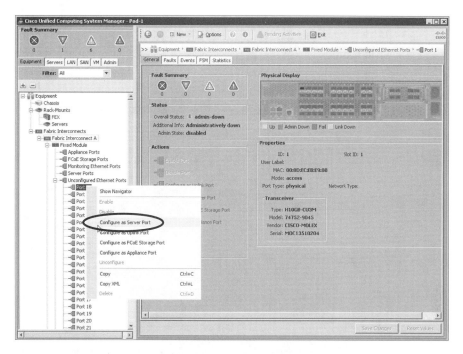

Figure 18-10   *Configuring a Server Port*

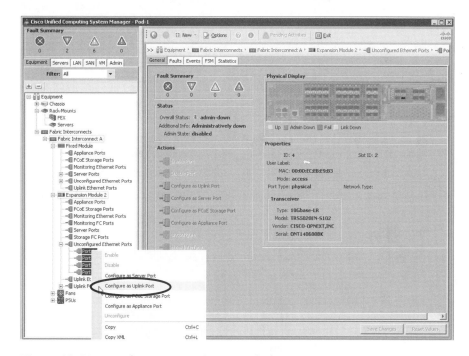

Figure 18-11   *Configuring an Ethernet Uplink Port*

2. In a few moments, the UCS Chassis is discovered and you can view the physical display by clicking the **Equipment** tab, expanding **Chassis**, and then clicking **Chassis 1**, as shown in Figure 18-12. While chassis discovery is happening, you may move on to the next step.

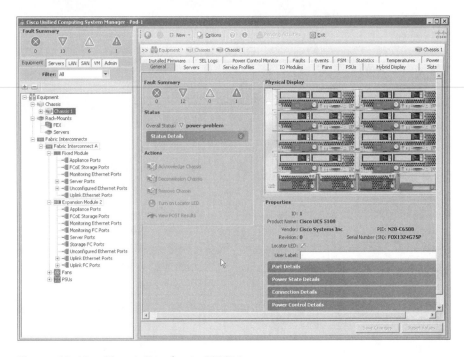

Figure 18-12 *Chassis Display in UCSM*

Step 4: Configure Named VLANs on the UCS

1. To configure new VLANs, click the **LAN** tab, expand **LAN Cloud > VLANs**, and either right-click the **VLANs** link and choose **Create VLANs**, as shown in Figure 18-13, or click the **+** button at the far-right side of the window.

2. In the Create VLANs dialog box, shown in Figure 18-14, add the VLAN with the following settings:

   VLAN Name/Prefix: **VLAN11**

   Click the **Common/Global** radio button (this makes the VLAN accessible to both FIs if a second fabric is installed at a later time).

   VLAN IDs: **11**

3. Click **OK**.

4. Repeat the preceding steps to create VLANs 12, 13, 14, and 15, which will be displayed as shown in Figure 18-15.

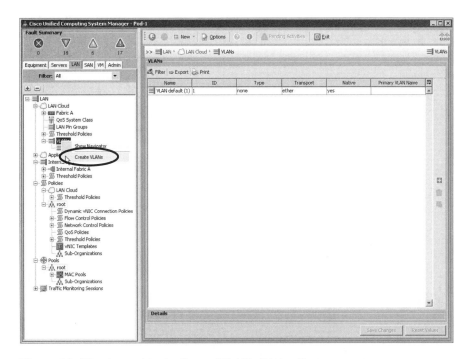

Figure 18-13   *Accessing the Create VLANs Dialog Box*

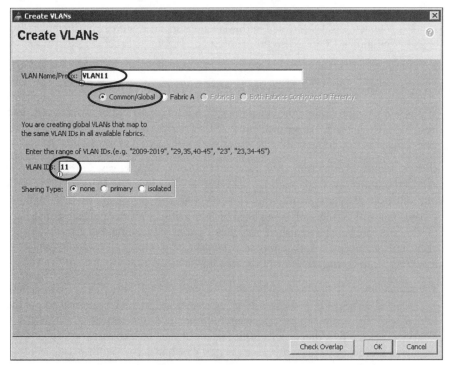

Figure 18-14   *Configuring the Create VLANs Dialog Box*

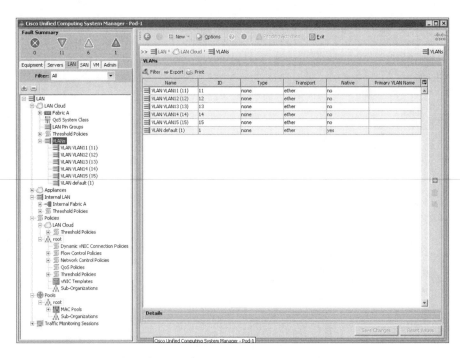

Figure 18-15 *The VLANs Display*

Lab 1 is complete. VLANs created in this lab are associated with a vNIC template later in "Lab 5 Configuring UCS Service Profiles."

Lab 2: Configuring UCS Network and Server-Related Pools

In this section, you explore the concept of UCS pools, by configuring a management IP pool for external blade management, and a MAC address pool that you will associate to a UCS service profile in the section "Lab 5: Configuring UCS Service Profiles."

UCS *pools* are collections of *identities*, or physical or logical resources, that are available in the system. All pools increase the flexibility of service profiles and allow you to centrally manage your system resources. You can use pools to segment unconfigured servers or available ranges of server identity information into groupings that make sense for the data center. For example, if you create a pool of unconfigured servers with similar characteristics and include that pool in a service profile, you can use a policy to associate that service profile with an available unconfigured server.

The *management IP pool* is a collection of external IP addresses. Cisco UCS Manager reserves each block of IP addresses in the management IP pool for external access that terminates in the baseboard management controller (BMC) on a server. Cisco UCS Manager uses the IP addresses in a management IP pool for external access to a server through a KVM Console, Serial over LAN (SoL), or Intelligent Platform Management Interface (IPMI).

A *MAC pool* is a collection of network identities, or MAC addresses, that are unique in their Layer 2 environments and are available to be assigned to vNICs (more on this later in the "Lab 5: Configuring UCS Service Profiles" section) on a server. If you use MAC pools in service profiles, you do not have to manually configure the MAC addresses to be used by the server associated with the service profile. In a system that implements multi-tenancy, you can use the organizational hierarchy to ensure that MAC pools can be used only by specific applications or business services. Cisco UCS Manager uses the name resolution policy to assign MAC addresses from the pool.

To assign a MAC address to a server, you must include the MAC pool in a vNIC policy. The vNIC policy is then included in the service profile assigned to that server (again, more on this later).

In this lab, you do the following:

1. Configure an IP pool for external blade management

2. Create a MAC address pool for the UCS

Step 1: Configure an IP Pool for External Blade Management

In this step, you create a pool of 50 IP addresses for out-of-band (OOB) management (only eight are needed because we have only eight blades). OOB connectivity is physically available via the management port of the 6100 FI in the Pod (the management port is connected to a 4948 switch in the lab, which is also the default gateway for the IP pool).

1. Click the **Admin** tab, expand **Communication Management**, and select **Management IP Pool**. Click the Create Block of IP Addresses link seen in the **General** tab in the middle of the screen, as illustrated in Figure 18-16, to access the Create a Block of IP Addresses dialog box.

2. Enter the following information, as shown in Figure 18-17:

   From: **10.1.0.200**

   Size: **50** (creates a scope of 50 IP addresses; 8 will be used by your blades)

   Subnet Mask: **255.255.255.0**

   Default Gateway: **10.1.0.1**

3. Click **OK**.

4. Verify by clicking the **IP Addresses** tab, as shown in Figure 18-18. Some of the addresses may already be allocated to the assigned server blades if the chassis discovery is complete.

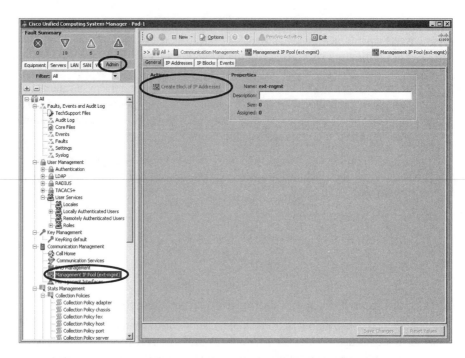

Figure 18-16   *Accessing the Create Block of IP Addresses Dialog Box*

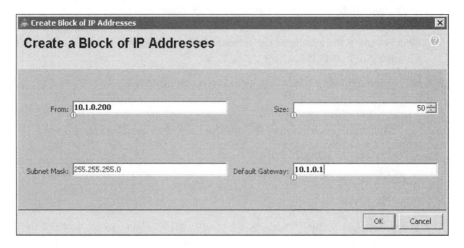

Figure 18-17   *Configuring the Create a Block of IP Addresses Dialog Box*

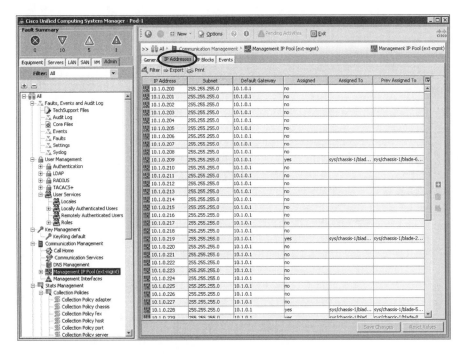

Figure 18-18   *Displaying the IP Pool*

Step 2: Create a MAC Address Pool for the UCS

1. To create a MAC address pool for your UCS, click the **LAN** tab, expand **Pools > root**, right-click **MAC Pools**, and choose **Create MAC Pool**, as shown in Figure 18-19.

2. Configure the MAC address pool name by entering **Pod-1-Mac-Pool** in the dialog box, as shown in Figure 18-20.

3. Click **Next**.

4. Click the **+ Add** button to add a pool, as shown in Figure 18-21.

5. Configure the MAC pool as shown in Figure 18-22:

   First MAC Address: **00:25:B5:01:00:00**

   Size: **256**

6. Click **OK**.

7. Click **Finish** to complete the MAC pool configuration.

Lab 2 is complete. In Lab 3, you configure features on the Nexus 7000 switches using the Putty terminal-emulation application installed on the lab PC. Minimize (but do not close) your UCSM browser window.

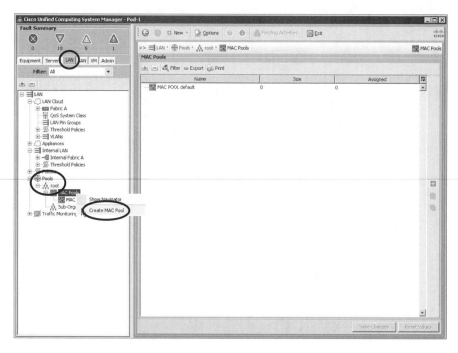

Figure 18-19   *Displaying the MAC Address Pool Dialog Box*

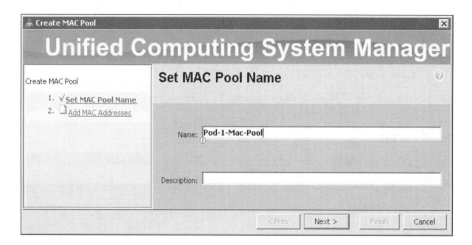

Figure 18-20   *The Create MAC Pool Name Dialog Box*

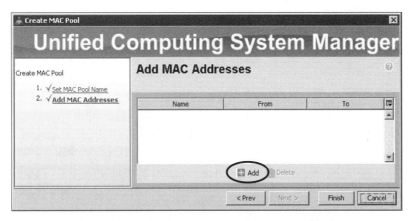

Figure 18-21 *Clicking the Add Button to Add a MAC Pool*

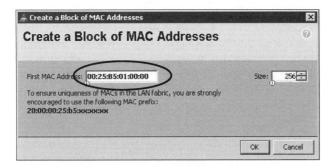

Figure 18-22 *Adding a MAC Pool in the Create a Block of MAC Addresses Dialog Box*

Lab 3: Creating Virtual PortChannels on the Nexus 7000 Series Switches

In this section, you explore the concepts of virtual device contexts (VDC) and virtual PortChannels (vPC) on the Nexus 7000 Series Switches.

Virtual Device Context Overview

A VDC runs as a separate logical entity within the Nexus 7000 physical device, maintains its own unique set of running software processes, has its own configuration, and can be managed by a separate administrator. VDCs virtualize the control plane, which includes all those software functions that are processed by the CPU on the active Cisco Supervisor Module. The control plane supports the software processes for the services on the physical device, such as the Routing Information Base (RIB) and the routing protocols.

The only physical resources that you can allocate to a VDC are the Ethernet interfaces. Each physical Ethernet interface can belong to only one VDC at any given time. Initially, all physical interfaces belong to the default VDC (VDC 1). When you create a new VDC, the NX-OS software creates the virtualized services for the VDC without allocating any physical interfaces to it. After you create a new VDC, you can allocate a set of physical interfaces from the default VDC to the new VDC. Once you allocate a physical interface to a VDC, you can configure it only in that VDC, and no other VDC has access to that interface, including the default VDC.

Note   VDCs have been pre-provisioned on the Nexus 7000s in the enterprise lab for the purposes of this course. A training VDC has been created and specific Ethernet interfaces have been allocated to it that connect to other lab equipment (UCS, MDS, 7600) in the Pod. Other VDCs are being used for proof-of-concept testing while this training is ongoing.

Students will not provision VDCs in this lab, but instead will work in the context of a VDC in the shared Nexus 7000s. Each VDC appears as a unique device to the student, and all configuration tasks are completed within the context of an assigned VDC.

Virtual PortChannel Overview

A virtual PortChannel (vPC) allows links that are physically connected to two different Cisco Nexus 7000 Series devices to appear as a single PortChannel to a third device. The third device can be a switch, server, or any other networking device that supports PortChannels, such as the UCS Fabric Interconnect switch you are working with in this lab. A vPC can provide Layer 2 multipathing, which allows you to create redundancy and increase bisectional bandwidth by enabling multiple parallel paths between nodes and allowing load balancing of traffic.

You can use only Layer 2 PortChannels in the vPC. (Layer 3 routing is possible across a vPC with the addition of switched virtual interfaces, or SVIs, on the Nexus 7000.) A vPC Domain is associated to a single VDC, so all vPC interfaces belonging to a given vPC Domain must be defined in the same VDC. You must have a separate vPC peer-link and peer-keepalive link infrastructure for each VDC deployed. Figure 18-23 depicts a vPC Reference Architecture.

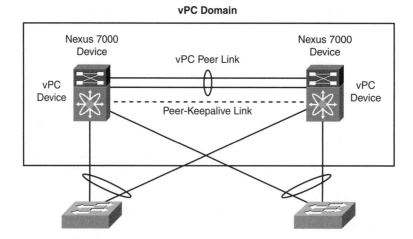

Figure 18-23   *vPC Reference Architecture*

vPC Terminology

When working with vPCs it is important to understand the language used to describe each part of the technology. The following terminology is most often used when configuring a vPC:

- **vPC:** The combined PortChannel between the vPC peer devices and the downstream device.

- **vPC peer device:** One of a pair of devices that are connected with the special PortChannel known as the vPC peer link.

- **vPC peer link:** The link used to synchronize states between the vPC peer devices. Both ends must be on 10-Gigabit Ethernet interfaces.

- **vPC Domain:** This domain includes both vPC peer devices, the vPC peer-keepalive link, and all of the PortChannels in the vPC connected to the downstream devices. It is also associated to the configuration mode that you must use to assign vPC global parameters.

- **vPC primary switch:** The switch with lower priority will be elected as the vPC primary switch. If the peer link fails, vPC peer will detect whether the peer switch is alive through the vPC peer-keepalive link. If the vPC primary switch is alive, the vPC secondary switch will suspend its vPC member ports to prevent potential looping while the vPC primary switch keeps all its vPC member ports active.

- **vPC peer-keepalive link:** Monitors the vitality of a vPC peer Cisco Nexus 7000 device. The peer-keepalive link sends configurable, periodic keepalive messages between vPC peer devices.

In this lab, you complete the following tasks:

1. Create VLANs on a pair of Nexus 7000 switches.

2. Create a vPC on a pair of Nexus 7000 switches (in the context of a VDC).

3. Create a 40-Gbps PortChannel on the UCS 6100 Fabric Interconnect for connectivity to the Nexus 7000 (vPC) pair.

4. Verify PortChannel and vPC on the Nexus 7000.

Step 1: Create VLANs on the Nexus 7000s

1. From the Remote Desktop, open two instances of the Putty application and ssh into the Nexus 7000 VDCs:

For Nexus 7000-A (N7K-A): **10.1.0.2**

For Nexus 7000-B (N7K-B): **10.1.0.3**

User Name: **admin**

Password: **Cisco.123**

2. Configure the VLANs you created in your UCS with UCSM—VLANs 11, 12, 13, 14, and 15.

The commands to create and verify the VLANs are highlighted below. In this example, we created VLANs 71, 72, 73, 74, and 75. Use the correct commands to create VLANs 11–15.

```
POD-7-N7K-A#
POD-7-N7K-A# conf t
Enter configuration commands, one per line.  End with CNTL/Z.
POD-7-N7K-A(config)# vlan 71,72,73,74,75
POD-7-N7K-A(config-vlan)# end
POD-7-N7K-A# sh vlan !This verifies that the VLANs were created


VLAN Name                             Status    Ports
---- -------------------------------- --------- --------------------------
1    default                          active
71   VLAN0071                         active
72   VLAN0072                         active
73   VLAN0073                         active
74   VLAN0074                         active
75   VLAN0075                         active


VLAN Type
---- -----
1    enet
71   enet
72   enet
73   enet
74   enet
75   enet


Remote SPAN VLANs
-------------------------------------------------------------------------


Primary  Secondary  Type          Ports
```

```
-------   ---------   ---------------   -----------------------------------------




POD-7-N7K-A#
```

3. Create these same VLANs on the second Nexus 7000 (N7K-B) by following the process just described.

Step 2: Create a vPC on the Nexus 7000s for Connectivity to Your UCS Chassis

1. Issue the **show interface brief** command on each Nexus 7000 switch to verify which physical interfaces have been mapped to the VDC that you are using in your Pod.

Note   Both 10-Gigabit and 1-Gigabit interface types are represented as Ethernet interfaces in a Nexus NX-OS platform.

```
POD-7-N7K-A# show interface brief


--------------------------------------------------------------------------------

Port   VRF           Status IP Address                        Speed    MTU
--------------------------------------------------------------------------------

mgmt0  --            up     --                                1000     1500


--------------------------------------------------------------------------------

Ethernet       VLAN   Type Mode   Status  Reason            Speed    Port
Interface                                                            Ch #
--------------------------------------------------------------------------------

Eth1/2         --     eth  routed up      none              10G(S) --
Eth1/4         --     eth  routed up      none              10G(S) --
Eth1/6         --     eth  routed up      none              10G(S) --
Eth1/8         --     eth  routed up      none              10G(S) --
Eth1/10        --     eth  routed down    SFP not inserted  auto(S) --
Eth1/12        --     eth  routed down    SFP not inserted  auto(S) --
Eth1/14        --     eth  routed down    SFP not inserted  auto(S) --
Eth1/16        --     eth  routed down    SFP not inserted  auto(S) --
```

```
Eth3/9        --    eth  routed up     none                     1000(D) --

Eth3/10       --    eth  routed up     none                     1000(D) --

Eth3/11       --    eth  routed down   Administratively down    auto(D) --

Eth3/12       --    eth  routed down   Administratively down    auto(D) --

POD-7-N7K-A#
```

Note Ethernet interfaces can be allocated to VDCs by ASIC port groups. In this example, we are configuring the interfaces on the Cisco Nexus 7000 Series 32-port 10-Gbps Ethernet module (N7K-M132XP-12), which has been installed for this lab. This module has eight port groups that consist of four interfaces each. You must assign all four interfaces in a port group to the same VDC. Table 18-1 shows the port numbers associated with each port group for this card.

Table 18-1 *ASIC/Port Group Distribution for the N7K-M132XP-12 Line Card*

Port Group	Port Numbers
Group 1	1, 3, 5, 7
Group 2	2, 4, 6, 8
Group 3	9, 11, 13, 15
Group 4	10, 12, 14, 16
Group 5	17, 19, 21, 23
Group 6	18, 20, 22, 24
Group 7	25, 27, 29, 31
Group 8	26, 28, 30, 32

  2. Enable the vPC feature on both Nexus 7000s (N7K-A and -B) by configuring **feature vpc** as shown in the following output. Verify that the feature has been enabled.

Note Many NX-OS features are not enabled by default, to save memory, enhance performance, and cut down on running processes. These features must be explicitly enabled prior to configuring.

3. Follow this example to enable vPC feature on both of the N7K switches:

```
POD-7-N7K-A# conf t

Enter configuration commands, one per line.  End with CNTL/Z.

POD-7-N7K-A(config)# feature vpc

POD-7-N7K-A(config)#

POD-7-N7K-A(config)# show feature

Feature Name         Instance  State

------------------   --------  --------



<snip>



udld                 1         disabled

vpc                  1         enabled

vrrp                 1         disabled
```

4. Configure a vPC peer-keepalive link on each switch. Copper connections between 1GE ports on card 3 of each Nexus 7000 switch are used as peer-keepalive links for each VDC. Hint: The correct port information can be obtained by entering **show cdp neighbors**.

Note   Cisco recommends that you associate peer-keepalive links to a separate VRF, mapped to a Layer 3 interface, in each vPC peer device. If you do not configure a separate VRF, the system uses the management VRF by default.

5. Create a VRF context called keepalive on both switches and associate the designated peer-keepalive link port on card 3 with it. Assign an address (.1 or .2) from subnet 1.1.1.0/30 to this link (the Pod can use the Any subnet for this link because it exists in a separate VRF).

Example on N7K-A:

```
POD-7-N7K-A# conf t
Enter configuration commands, one per line.  End with CNTL/Z.
POD-7-N7K-A(config)# vrf context keepalive !This creates a VRF called
  "Keepalive"
POD-7-N7K-A(config-vrf)# exit
POD-7-N7K-A(config)# int e3/9 ! REFER TO POD DIAGRAM HANDOUT FOR PORT
  ASSIGNMENTS
POD-7-N7K-A(config-if)# no switchport  !This makes this an L3 Interface
  type
POD-7-N7K-A(config-if)# vrf member keepalive !This makes this int part of
  the VRF
POD-7-N7K-A(config-if)# ip address 1.1.1.1 255.255.255.252 !IP and Subnet
  Mask
POD-7-N7K-A(config-if)# end
POD-7-N7K-A#
```

Example on N7K-B:

```
POD-7-N7K-B# conf t
Enter configuration commands, one per line.  End with CNTL/Z.
POD-7-N7K-B(config)# vrf context keepalive
POD-7-N7K-B(config-vrf)# exit
POD-7-N7K-B(config)# interface ethernet 3/9
POD-7-N7K-B(config-if)# no switchport
POD-7-N7K-B(config-if)# vrf member keepalive
POD-7-N7K-B(config-if)# ip add 1.1.1.2/30
POD-7-N7K-B(config-if)# end
POD-7-N7K-B#
```

6. Verify IP connectivity in the VRF across the links with **ping 1.1.1.X vrf keepalive** (**ping 1.1.1.2** from N7K-A and **1.1.1.1** from N7K-B).

7. Create the vPC Domain and add the keepalive information to the configuration. Make N7K-A the vPC primary switch by assigning priority 2000. Use 7 as the Domain number.

Example on N7K-A:

```
POD-7-N7K-A# conf t
Enter configuration commands, one per line.  End with CNTL/Z.
```

```
POD-7-N7K-A(config)# vpc domain 7   !Any domain ID will work
POD-7-N7K-A(config-vpc-domain)# peer-keepalive destination 1.1.1.2 source
  1.1.1.1 vrf keepalive
  !This is all ONE line. Note IPs and VRF


POD-7-N7K-A(config-vpc-domain)# role priority 2000 !Lower is better
  32667 is default
Warning:
  !!:: vPCs will be flapped on current primary vPC switch while attempting
  role change ::!!
Note:
  --------:: Change will take effect after user has re-initd the vPC
  peer-link  ::--------
POD-7-N7K-A(config-vpc-domain)# end
POD-7-N7K-A#
```

Example on N7K-B:

```
POD-7-N7K-B# conf t
Enter configuration commands, one per line.  End with CNTL/Z.
POD-7-N7K-B(config)# vpc domain 7
POD-7-N7K-B(config-vpc-domain)# peer-keepalive destination 1.1.1.1 source
  1.1.1.2 vrf keepalive
!Note the IP address change between N7K-A and N7K-B
POD-7-N7K-B(config-vpc-domain)# end
POD-7-N7K-B#
```

8. Verify that the peer is alive by issuing **show vpc peer-keepalive** on each switch.

9. Configure a vPC peer link between Nexus 7000 switches that is used to synchronize states between the vPC peer devices. Two 10-Gigabit interfaces allocated to the VDC in the Pod have been interconnected between the Nexus 7000s for this purpose (check the connectivity using the **show cdp neighbor** command). These interfaces are aggregated into a 20-Gbps PortChannel and trunked. Follow the example shown next to enable **feature lacp** and create a 20-Gbps PortChannel that is used as the vPC peer link between your Nexus 7000 switches.

Example on N7K-A:

```
POD-7-N7K-A# conf t
Enter configuration commands, one per line.  End with CNTL/Z.
POD-7-N7K-A(config)# feature lacp  !Enable PortChannel Capability
```

```
POD-7-N7K-A(config)#
POD-7-N7K-A(config)# interface port-channel 7 !Create a PortChannel
  interface for the vPC peer-link.
POD-7-N7K-A(config-if)# no shut
POD-7-N7K-A(config-if)# switchport !Make it a L2 interface
POD-7-N7K-A(config-if)# switchport mode trunk !Make it a trunk interface
POD-7-N7K-A(config-if)# vpc peer-link !Use it as the vPC peer link
Please note that spanning tree port type is changed to "network" port type
  on vPC peer-link.
This will enable spanning tree Bridge Assurance on vPC peer-link provided
  the STP Bridge Assurance
(which is enabled by default) is not disabled.
POD-7-N7K-A(config-if)#
POD-7-N7K-A(config-if)# interface e1/2  !Use "show cdp neighbor" for
  correct int
POD-7-N7K-A(config-if)# switchport
POD-7-N7K-A(config-if)# switchport mode trunk
POD-7-N7K-A(config-if)# channel-group 7 mode active  !Make it a part of Po7
POD-7-N7K-A(config-if)#
POD-7-N7K-A(config-if)# interface e1/4  !Use "show cdp neighbor" for
  correct int
POD-7-N7K-A(config-if)# switchport
POD-7-N7K-A(config-if)# switchport mode trunk
POD-7-N7K-A(config-if)# channel-group 7 mode active
POD-7-N7K-A(config-if)# end
```

Example on N7K-B:

```
POD-7-N7K-B# conf t
Enter configuration commands, one per line.  End with CNTL/Z.
POD-7-N7K-B(config)# feature lacp
POD-7-N7K-B(config)# interface port-channel 7
POD-7-N7K-B(config-if)# no shut
POD-7-N7K-B(config-if)# switchport
POD-7-N7K-B(config-if)# switchport mode trunk
POD-7-N7K-B(config-if)# vpc peer-link
Please note that spanning tree port type is changed to "network" port type
  on vPC peer-link.
This will enable spanning tree Bridge Assurance on vPC peer-link provided
  the STP Bridge Assurance
```

```
(which is enabled by default) is not disabled.
POD-7-N7K-B(config-if)#
POD-7-N7K-B(config-if)# int e1/2,e1/4  !Shortcut to configure 2 interfaces
  in one line
POD-7-N7K-B(config-if-range)# switchport
POD-7-N7K-B(config-if-range)# switchport mode trunk
POD-7-N7K-B(config-if-range)# channel-group 7 mode active
```

10. Verify vPC peer-link status:

```
POD-7-N7K-A# sh vpc
Legend:
                (*) - local vPC is down, forwarding via vPC peer-link


vPC domain id               : 7
Peer status                 : peer adjacency formed ok
vPC keep-alive status       : peer is alive
Configuration consistency status: success
Type-2 consistency status   : failed
Type-2 consistency reason   : Consistency Check Not Performed
vPC role                    : primary
Number of vPCs configured   : 0
Peer Gateway                : Disabled
Dual-active excluded VLANs  : -


vPC Peer-link status
---------------------------------------------------------------------
id   Port   Status Active vlans
--   ----   ------ -------------------------------------------------
1    Po7    up     1,71-75
POD-7-N7K-A#
POD-7-N7K-A#
POD-7-N7K-A# sh vpc role


vPC Role status
-------------------------------------------------
vPC role                    : primary
Dual Active Detection Status : 0
```

```
vPC system-mac              : 00:23:04:ee:be:07
vPC system-priority         : 32667
vPC local system-mac        : 00:24:98:6f:41:c2
vPC local role-priority     : 2000
POD-7-N7K-A


#
```

11. Configure a 20-Gbps vPC from each Nexus 7000 switch to the UCS 6100 FI. When completed, the vPC appears as a single 40-Gbps PortChannel interface from the perspective of the UCS 6100 FI. First, you configure the vPC member ports on the Nexus 7000 switches. Use the **show cdp neighbor** command and the lab diagram to determine the particular Ethernet port numbers that have been connected from your Nexus 7000s to the Nexus 6100.

On N7K-A:

```
POD-7-N7K-A# conf t
Enter configuration commands, one per line.  End with CNTL/Z.
POD7-N7K-A(config)# interface port-channel 1
POD-7-N7K-A(config-if)# switchport
POD-7-N7K-A(config-if)# switchport mode trunk
POD-7-N7K-A(config-if)# vpc 1   ! Command associates PortChannel 1 to vPC 1.
  Best practices
suggests matching vpc number with PortChannel number, but it is not a hard
  requirement.
POD-7-N7K-A(config-if)# no shut
POD-7-N7K-A(config-if)#
POD-7-N7K-A(config-if)# int e1/6,e1/8   !Range to configure multiple ints
  at once
POD-7-N7K-A(config-if-range)# switchport
POD-7-N7K-A(config-if-range)# switchport mode trunk
POD-7-N7K-A(config-if-range)# channel-group 1 mode active
POD-7-N7K-A(config-if-range)# no shut
POD-7-N7K-A(config-if-range)#
```

On N7K-B:

```
POD-7-N7K-B# conf t
Enter configuration commands, one per line.  End with CNTL/Z.
POD-7-N7K-B(config)# interface port-channel 1
POD-7-N7K-B(config-if)# switchport
```

```
POD-7-N7K-B(config-if)# switchport mode trunk

POD-7-N7K-B(config-if)# vpc 1

POD-7-N7K-B(config-if)# no shut

POD-7-N7K-B(config-if)#

POD-7-N7K-B(config-if)# int e1/6,e1/8

POD-7-N7K-B(config-if-range)# switchport

POD-7-N7K-B(config-if-range)# switchport mode trunk

POD-7-N7K-B(config-if-range)# channel-group 1 mode active

POD-7-N7K-B(config-if-range)# no shut

POD-7-N7K-B(config-if-range)#
```

The PortChannel status remains down until you configure the relevant links on the UCS 6100 FI as PortChannel links.

Step 3: Create a 40-Gbps PortChannel on the UCS 6100 Fabric Interconnect for Connectivity to the Nexus 7000 Pair

1. Return to the UCSM window (maximize the Java Web Start window), click the **LAN** tab, expand **LAN Cloud > Fabric A**, and click **Port Channels**, as shown in Figure 18-24. Click the **+** sign on the far-right side of the screen to add a Port Channel.

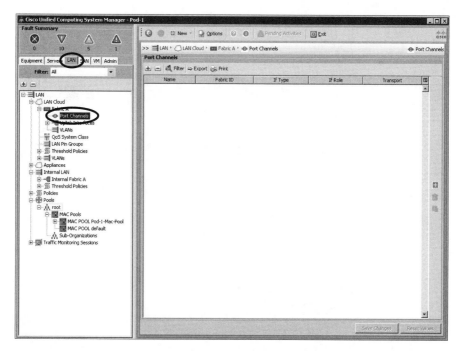

Figure 18-24 *Accessing the Create Port Channel Dialog Box*

2. In the Set Port Channel Name dialog box, shown in Figure 18-25, leave the ID as 1 and click **Next** to add ports.

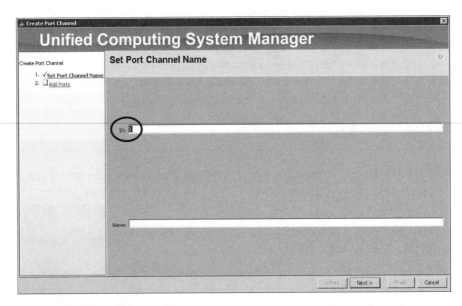

Figure 18-25   *Configuring the Port Channel Name Dialog Box*

3. Select ports 2/1, 2/2, 2/3, and 2/4, as shown in Figure 18-26, and click **>>** to move them into the Ports in the Port Channel box. Click **Finish**.

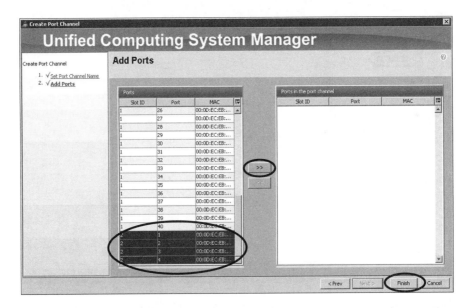

Figure 18-26   *Configuring the Add Ports Dialog Box*

4. Enable the Port Channel by clicking the newly created **Port-Channel 1** and then clicking **Enable Port Channel** in the middle panel, as shown in Figure 18-27.

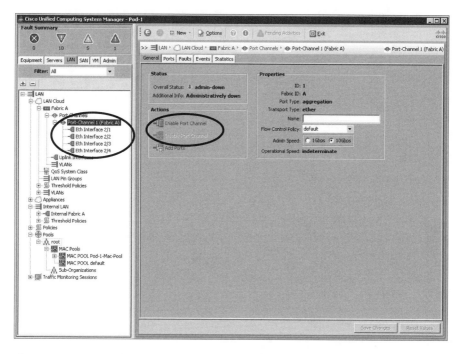

Figure 18-27 *Enabling the Port Channel*

After a few moments, the Overall Port Channel Status changes to Up. The Physical Port Membership also changes to Up.

Step 4: Verify PortChannel and vPC on the Nexus 7000

1. Return to the Putty application and verify the PortChannel status on N7K-A:

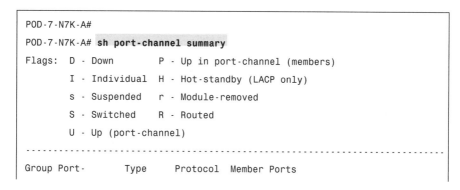

```
POD-7-N7K-A#
POD-7-N7K-A# sh port-channel summary
Flags:  D - Down        P - Up in port-channel (members)
        I - Individual  H - Hot-standby (LACP only)
        s - Suspended   r - Module-removed
        S - Switched    R - Routed
        U - Up (port-channel)
--------------------------------------------------------------------
Group Port-         Type     Protocol  Member Ports
```

```
      Channel

-------------------------------------------------------------------

1     Po1(SU)   Eth      LACP       Eth1/6(P)    Eth1/8(P)

7     Po7(SU)   Eth      LACP       Eth1/2(P)    Eth1/4(P)

POD-7-N7K-A# sh vpc

Legend:
                (*) - local vPC is down, forwarding via vPC peer-link


vPC domain id                 : 7

Peer status                   : peer adjacency formed ok

vPC keep-alive status         : peer is alive

Configuration consistency status: success

Type-2 consistency status     : failed

Type-2 consistency reason     : Consistency Check Not Performed

vPC role                      : primary

Number of vPCs configured     : 1

Peer Gateway                  : Disabled

Dual-active excluded VLANs    : -


vPC Peer-link status
--------------------------------------------------------------------

id   Port    Status Active vlans
--------------------------------------------------------------------

1    Po7     up     1,71-75


vPC status
--------------------------------------------------------------------

id   Port    Status Consistency Reason            Active vlans
--------------------------------------------------------------------

1    Po1     up     success    success            1,71-75


POD-7-N7K-A#
```

2. Save your Nexus 7000 configurations with the **copy running-config startup-config** command.

3. The configurations on the UCS 6100 Fabric Interconnect/UCS/UCSM are automatically saved as you apply/save the configurations.

Lab 3 is complete. LAN connectivity between UCS Fabric and Nexus 7000 is complete. In Lab 4, you begin to build a virtual SAN (VSAN) topology.

Lab 4: Creating a VSAN and Enabling Fibre Channel Connectivity Between the UCS 6100 Fabric Interconnect and MDS 9506

Over the course of the next three labs, you will create a VSAN in your Pod by configuring various parameters on the UCS 6100 Fabric Interconnect and MDS 9506 platforms. By the end of Lab 6, the UCS will be connected to a large storage array (EMC VMAX) in the lab via the 9506 in your Pod. The UCS blade servers can boot their OS from the EMC VMAX and use it for storage.

In Lab 4, you create the initial VSAN on the UCS and MDS 9506, as shown in Figure 18-28.

Terminology

When working with Storage Area Networks (SAN) it is important to understand the language used to describe each part of the technology. The following terminology is most often used when configuring a SAN on a Cisco MDS 9000 Series Multilayer Switch:

- **Fibre Channel (FC):** FC is a multigigabit-speed network technology primarily used for storage networking. FC is a serial data transfer architecture developed by a consortium of computer and mass storage device manufacturers and is the widely accepted protocol used for SAN.

- **Fibre Channel Protocol (FCP):** FCP is the transport protocol (similar to TCP used in IP networks), which transports SCSI commands over Fibre Channel networks.

- **Fibre Channel over Ethernet (FCoE):** FCoE is an encapsulation of Fibre Channel frames over Ethernet networks. This allows FC to use 10-Gigabit Ethernet networks while preserving FCP.

- **Fibre Channel host:** A computer system (typically a server) that accesses a FC network by means of an FC interface card known as a host bus adapter (HBA).

- **Storage-area network (SAN):** An architecture to attach remote computer storage devices to servers in such a way that the devices appear as locally attached to the operating system. Elements in the SAN include switches, fabric, connections, and storage devices (such as disk arrays, tape libraries, and optical jukeboxes).

- **SAN fabric:** The hardware that connects workstations and servers to storage devices in a SAN is referred to as a *fabric*. The SAN fabric enables any-server-to-any-storage device connectivity through the use of FC switching technology.

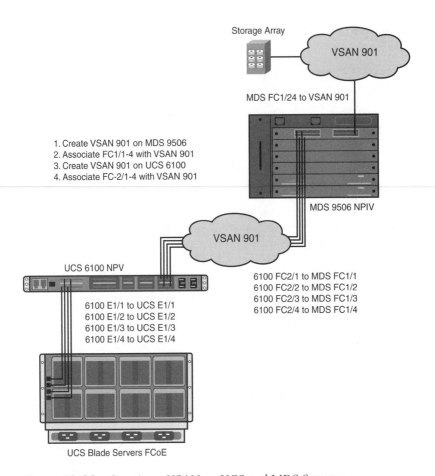

Figure 18-28   *Creating a VSAN on UCS and MDS Systems*

- **SAN switches:** Network switches compatible with FCP. SAN (or FC) switches allow the creation of a Fibre Channel fabric that is currently the core component of most SANs.

- **N_Port:** An end node port on the FC fabric. This could be an HBA in a server or a target port (storage processor) on a storage array.

- **F_Port:** A port on an FC switch that is connected to an N_Port. The port into which a server's HBA or a storage array's target port is connected is an F_Port.

- **E_Port:** A port on an FC switch that is connected to another FC switch. The connection between two E_Ports forms an Inter-Switch Link (ISL).

- **N_Port Virtualization (NPV):** An FC solution designed to reduce switch management and overhead in larger SAN deployments. Switches operating in the NPV mode do not join a fabric; rather, they pass traffic between NPV core switch links and end devices, which eliminates the domain IDs for these edge switches.

- **N_Port ID Virtualization (NPIV):** An FC solution that allows multiple N_Port IDs to share a single physical N_Port. This allows multiple FC initiators to occupy a single physical port, easing hardware requirements in SAN design, especially where VSANs are called for.

- **Virtual SAN (VSAN):** A collection of ports from a set of connected FC switches that forms a virtual fabric. Ports within a single switch can be partitioned into multiple VSANs, despite sharing hardware resources. Conversely, multiple switches can join a number of ports to form a single VSAN.

- **Fabric Login (FLOGI):** An FC process where FC hosts or disks are allocated a Fibre Channel ID (FC_ID) from a directly connected FC switch.

> **Note**   As of the writing of this book, the UCS 6100 FI switch operates in NPV mode and not as a FC switch in the fabric. The FI joins the fabric through a normal FLOGI and is issued N_Port IDs from the MDS.
>
> You must enable the MDS 9506 to support NPIV mode for all VSANs, giving it most of the intelligence required in the SAN. NPIV allows access control, zoning, and port security to be implemented at the application level.
>
> FLOGIs and zoning are also controlled by the MDS 9506 when it is in NPIV mode, as in this lab.

In this lab, you will complete the following tasks:

1. Enable NPIV mode, create a VSAN, and associate the Fibre Channel ports of the MDS to the new VSAN. Create a new VSAN in the UCS 6100 Fabric Interconnect.

2. Create a new VSAN on the UCS.

3. Associate FC interfaces with the UCS VSAN.

To log in to the Pod's MDS 9506, use Putty on your Remote Desktop to SSH into:

- IP: **10.1.0.4**

- User Name: **admin**

- Password: **Cisco.123**

Step 1: Enable NPIV Mode, Create a VSAN, and Associate the Fibre Channel Ports of the MDS to the New VSAN

1. Enable NPIV for all VSANs on the MDS by entering **feature npiv** at a config prompt. You can verify which features are enabled by entering **show feature**.

```
POD-7-MDS-A#

POD-7-MDS-A# conf t

Enter configuration commands, one per line.  End with CNTL/Z.
```

```
POD-7-MDS-A(config)# feature npiv

POD-7-MDS-A(config)# end

POD-7-MDS-A#

POD-7-MDS-A# sh feature

Feature Name           Instance  State

-------------------    --------  --------

ivr                    1         disabled

fcip                   1         disabled

fcsp                   1         disabled

...

scheduler              1         disabled

npiv                   1         enabled

...

cluster_test_app       1         disabled

POD-7-MDS-A#
```

2. Configure the VSAN. We are using VSAN 901 for this lab. Associate VSAN 901 with the four Fibre Channel interfaces connected to the UCS 6100 FI (interfaces fc1/1, fc1/2, fc1/3, and fc1/4).

```
POD-7-MDS-A# conf t

Enter configuration commands, one per line.  End with CNTL/Z.

POD-7-MDS-A(config)# vsan database !Enter VSAN Database

POD-7-MDS-A(config-vsan-db)# vsan 901 !Create VSAN 901

POD-7-MDS-A(config-vsan-db)# vsan 901 interface fc1/1 !Add FC1/1 to VSAN

Traffic on fc1/1 may be impacted. Do you want to continue? (y/n) y

POD-7-MDS-A(config-vsan-db)# vsan 901 interface fc1/2-4 !Add multiple ints

Traffic on fc1/2 may be impacted. Do you want to continue? (y/n) y

Traffic on fc1/3 may be impacted. Do you want to continue? (y/n) y

Traffic on fc1/4 may be impacted. Do you want to continue? (y/n) y

POD-7-MDS-A(config-vsan-db)# end

POD-7-MDS-A#
```

3. Save your MDS configuration by entering **copy running-config startup-config** into your MDS.

Step 2: Create a New VSAN on the UCS

1. Return to the UCSM window.

2. To configure the VSAN, click the **SAN** tab, expand **Storage Cloud**, and then either right-click **VSANs** and choose **Create Storage VSAN**, as shown in Figure 18-29, or click **+** at the far-right side of the window.

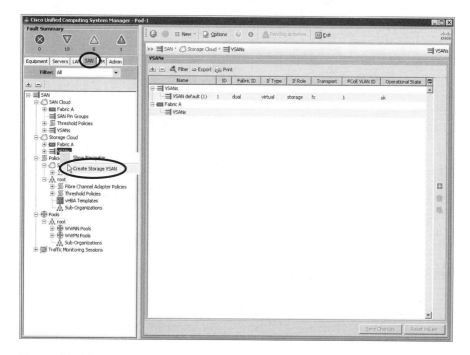

Figure 18-29   *Accessing the Create VSAN Dialog Box*

3. Complete the Create Storage VSAN dialog box as follows, as shown in Figure 18-30:

   Name: **VSAN901**

   Click the **Fabric A** radio button

   VSAN ID: **901**

   FCoE VLAN: **901**

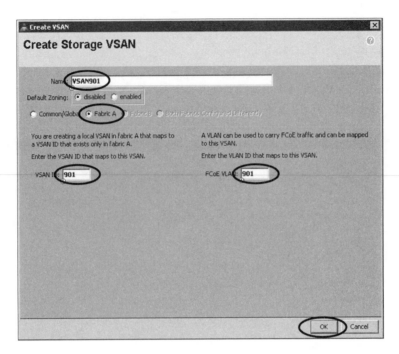

Figure 18-30   *Configuring the Create Storage VSAN Dialog Box*

Step 3: Associate Fibre Channel Interfaces with the UCS VSAN

1.   Go back to the **Equipment** tab, expand **Fabric Interconnects > Fabric Interconnect A > Expansion Module 2 > Uplink FC Ports**. Associate all four FC ports (FC Port 1, FC Port 2, FC Port 3, and FC Port 4) with VSAN 901 by using the VSAN drop-down menu in the middle of the page, as shown in Figure 18-31. Click **Save Changes**.

2.   The Overall Status on all four Fibre Channel ports should change to Up and the ports should turn green in the Physical Display area of the UCSM.

Lab 4 is complete. All of the physical and logical connectivity needed between the UCS, the LAN, and the SAN is now established. It is time to configure the blade servers. To do this, you define pools, service profile templates, and service profiles.

Lab 5: Configuring UCS Service Profiles

A *service profile* specifies every server attribute that is provisioned in Cisco UCS. The service profile represents a logical view of a single blade server, without the need to know exactly which blade you are referencing. The profile object contains the server's personality, such as its Universally Unique Identifier (UUID), as well as network and SAN information. The profile can then be associated with a physical blade, imparting to it all of its "personality." The concept of profiles was invented to support the notion of logical server mobility, or the transfer of identity transparently from one blade to another, as well as the pooling concept.

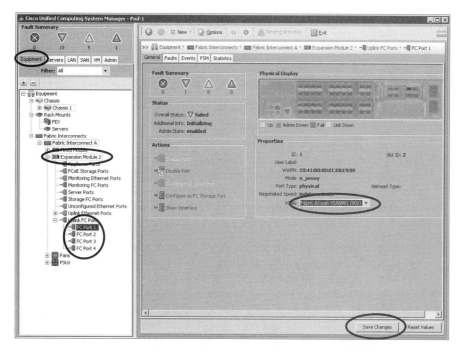

Figure 18-31   *Associating a Fibre Channel Interface to a VSAN in UCSM*

Service profiles are stored in the Cisco UCS 6100 Series Fabric Interconnects. When a service profile is deployed to a server, UCS Manager automatically configures the server, adapters, fabric extenders, and fabric interconnects to match the configuration specified in the service profile. This automation of device configuration reduces the number of manual steps required to configure servers, NICs, HBAs, and LAN and SAN switches.

Service profiles typically includes four types of information:

■ **Server definition:** Defines the resources (for example, a specific server or a blade inserted into a specific chassis) to which the profile is applied.

■ **Identity information:** Includes the UUID, MAC address for each virtual NIC (vNIC), and World Wide Name (WWN) specifications for each virtual HBA (vHBA).

■ **Firmware revision specifications:** Used when installation of a specific firmware revision is required.

■ **Connectivity definition:** Used to configure network adapters, fabric extenders, and parent interconnects; however, this information is abstract, as it does not include the details of how each network component is configured.

Server administrators can also create a *service profile template* that can be used later to create service profiles in an easier way. A service profile can be derived from a service profile template, with server and I/O interface identity information abstracted. Instead of specifying exact UUID, MAC address, and WWN values, a service profile template specifies where to get these values. For example, a service profile template might specify the standard network connectivity for a web server and the pool from which its interfaces' MAC addresses can be obtained. Service profile templates can be used to provision many servers with the same simplicity as creating a single one.

There are two types of service profiles in a UCS:

- **Service profiles that inherit server identity:** These service profiles are similar in concept to a rack-mounted server. They use the burned-in values (like MAC addresses, WWN addresses, BIOS version and settings, etc.) of the hardware. Due to the permanence of these values, these profiles are not easily portable and cannot be used when moving one server to another. In other words, these profiles exhibit a 1:1 mapping nature and thus require changes to be made to them when moving from one server to another.

- **Service profiles that override server identity:** These service profiles exhibit the nature of stateless computing in a UCS. These service profiles assume the resources (like MAC addresses, WWN addresses, BIOS version, etc.) from a resource pool already created in the UCS Manager. The settings or values from these resource pools override the burned-in values of the hardware. Hence, these profiles are very flexible and can be moved from one server to another easily, and this movement is transparent to the network. In other words, these profiles provide a 1-to-many mapping and require no change to be made to them when moving from one server to another.

See the white paper "Understanding Cisco Unified Computing System Service Profiles" at Cisco.com for more information.

Terminology for Service Profiles

When working with service profiles it is useful to understand the language used to describe each part of the technology. The following terminology is most often used when configuring a service profile:

- **Universally Unique Identifier (UUID):** A 128-bit number used to uniquely identify a component worldwide. Cisco UCS Manager generates a unique UUID for each server blade when a pool is defined in a service profile.

- **Virtual host bus adapter (vHBA):** A virtual interface providing FCoE from a server blade to a VSAN through a virtual interface on the 6100 Fabric Interconnect.

- **Virtual Network Interface Controller (vNIC):** A virtual interface providing Ethernet connectivity to a VLAN through a virtual interface on the 6100 FI.

- **WWN address:** A 64-bit address that is used within the FC specification for assigning a unique ID to each element within a FC fabric. WWNs are classified as WWPN and WWNN.

- **World Wide Port Name (WWPN):** A unique address assigned to a port (vHBA) in a FC fabric. The WWPN performs a function equivalent to the MAC address in the Ethernet protocol.

■ **World Wide Node Name (WWNN):** A unique address assigned to a node (UCS server blade) in a FC fabric. It is valid for the same WWNN to be seen on many different ports (different addresses) on the network, identifying the ports as multiple network interfaces of a single network node.

■ **Intelligent Platform Management Interface (IPMI):** An open standard technology that defines how administrators monitor system hardware and sensors, control system components, and retrieve logs of important system events to conduct remote management and recovery.

■ **Preboot eXecution Environment (PXE):** A protocol used to boot computers using a network interface independently of available data storage devices or installed operating systems. PXE is approximately a combination of TFTP and DHCP.

■ **Logical Unit (LUN):** An identification/addressing scheme for storage disks. Fibre Channel supports 32 addresses (0–31). A LUN may refer to a single disk, a subset of a single disk, or an array of disks.

In this lab, you complete the following tasks:

Step 1.   Create a vNIC template.

Step 2.   Create a SAN pool and vHBA template.

Step 3.   Configure server boot policies (SAN and LAN).

Step 4.   Create an IPMI profile.

Step 5.   Create a local disk configuration policy.

Step 6.   Create a Serial over LAN policy.

Step 7.   Create a UUID suffix pool.

Step 8.   Create a server pool.

Step 9.   Create a service profile template.

Step 10.   Create a service profile from a template.

Step 11.   Clone and manually associate a service profile.

Step 1: Create a vNIC Template

1. In Lab 2, you created a MAC address pool of 256 MAC addresses on the UCS. Verify that this pool was successfully created by clicking the **LAN** tab, expanding **Pools > root > MAC Pools**. If you do not find a named MAC pool (other than default), return to Lab 2 and follow the directions in "Step 2: Create a MAC Address Pool for the UCS."

2. Create a vNIC template. This will be applied to a service profile that you will create in a later step in this lab. Click the **LAN** tab and expand **Policies > root**. You can

right-click **vNIC Templates** and choose **Create a vNIC Template** or you can click **vNIC Templates** and click the add **+** button on the bottom of the screen. Complete the Create vNIC Template dialog box as follows, as shown in Figure 18-32:

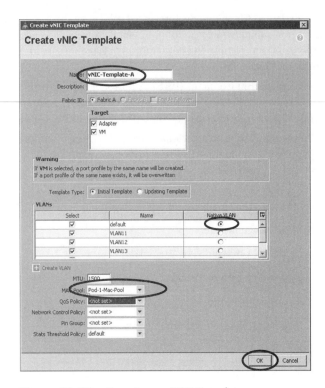

Figure 18-32 *Creating a vNIC Template*

Name: **vNIC-Template-A**

Fabric ID: **Fabric A**

Target: Check **Adapter** and **VM**

Template Type: **Initial Template**

VLANs: Select all of the VLANs (these should be all the VLANs you created plus default), and make default your Native VLAN by clicking its radio button

MTU: **1500**

MAC Pool: Choose the MAC pool you created earlier

QoS Policy, Network Control Policy, Pin Group, and Stats Threshold Policy: Leave the default settings, **<not set>** or **default**

3. Click **OK**. This creates a vNIC template that will be applied to a service profile in a later step.

Note The differences between initial templates and updating templates are as follows:

- **Initial template:** vNICs/vHBAs created from this template are not updated if the template changes. Service profiles created from an initial template initially inherit all the properties of the template, but after you create the profile, it is no longer connected to the template. If any changes are made to one or more profiles created from this template, you must change each profile individually.

- **Updating template:** vNICs/vHBAs created from this template are updated if the template changes. Service profiles created from an updating template inherit all the properties of the template and remain connected to the template. Any changes to the template automatically update the service profile created from the template.

There are reasons to use both types of templates. It is important to understand that certain service profile changes will reset the server. If you change an updating template, it may cause every server associated to a service profile with that template to reset. This may be what you want, because it allows you to make changes to several servers at once. However, it is important to understand what a change to an updating template will do to your infrastructure.

Step 2: Create a SAN Pool and vHBA Template

In this section, you create a WWNN pool, a WWPN pool, and a vHBA template, which will be applied to a service profile you will create in a later step of this lab.

1. To create a WWNN pool, click the **SAN** tab, expand **Pools > root**, right-click **WWNN Pools,** and choose **Create WWNN Pool.**

2. Name your WWNN pool: **Pod-1-WWNN-Pool**

3. Click **Next.**

4. Click **+ Add.**

5. Complete the Create WWN Block dialog box, shown in Figure 18-33, as follows:

   From: 50:00:00:25:B5:00:01:00 (be *very* careful to add this information correctly)

   Size: 8 (this would be much larger in the real world)

6. Click **OK.**

7. Click **Finish.**

8. To create a WWPN pool, click the **SAN** tab, expand **Pools > root**, right-click **WWPN Pools,** and choose **Create WWPN Pool.**

9. Name your WWPN pool: **Pod-1-WWPN-Pool**

10. Click **Next.**

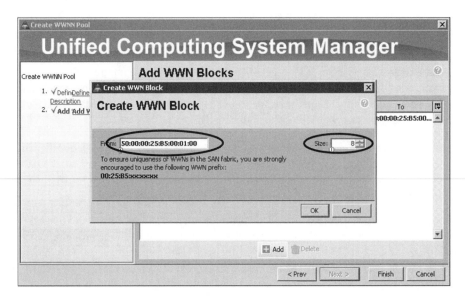

Figure 18-33   *Creating a WWNN Pool*

11. Click **+ Add**.

12. Complete the Create WWN Block dialog box, shown in Figure 18-34, as follows:

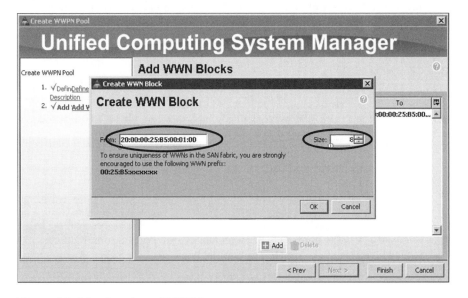

Figure 18-34   *Creating a WWPN*

From: **20:00:00:25:B5:00:01:00** (be *very* careful to add this information correctly)

Size: **8** (this would be much larger in the real world)

13. Click **OK**.

14. Click **Finish**.

15. To create a vHBA template, click the **SAN** tab, expand **SAN > Policies > root**, right-click **vHBA Templates**, and choose **Create vHBA Template**. Complete the Create vHBA Template dialog box as follows, as displayed in Figure 18-35:

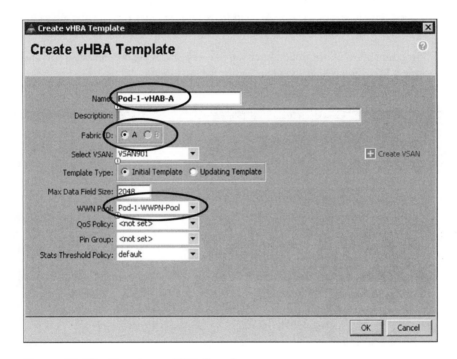

Figure 18-35   *Creating a vHBA Template*

Name: **Pod-1-vHBA-A**

Fabric ID: **A**

Select VSAN: **VSAN901**

Template Type: **Initial Template**

Max Data Field Size: **2048**

WWN Pool: **Pod-1-WWPN-Pool**

QoS Policy: **<not set>**

Pin Group: **<not set>**

Stats Threshold Policy: **default**

16. Click **OK**.

You are now done with all the SAN pools and templates and can move on to the next step.

Step 3: Configure Server Boot Policies (SAN and LAN)

In the next few steps, you create SAN and LAN boot policies that are applied to your server blades with a service profile you will create in a later portion of this lab.

1. To create a SAN boot policy, click the **Servers** tab, expand **Policies > root**, and select **Boot Policies**, as shown in Figure 18-36.

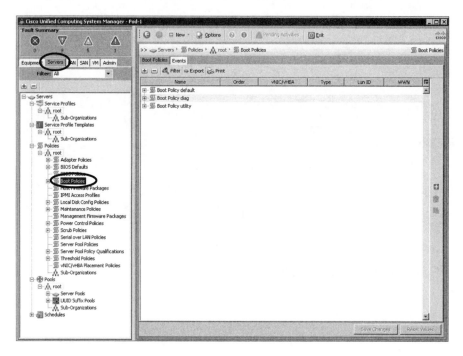

Figure 18-36 *Accessing the Create Boot Policy Dialog Box*

2. Right-click **Boot Policies**, choose **Create Boot Policy**, and complete the Name field of the Create Boot Policy dialog box as follows (shown in Figure 18-37):

Name: **Pod-1-SAN-Boot**

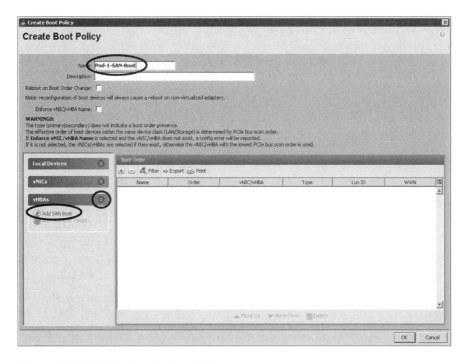

Figure 18-37 *Naming the Boot Policy*

3. Click the **down arrows** next to vHBAs to expose Add SAN Boot.

4. Click **Add SAN Boot** and complete the Add SAN Boot dialog box as follows, as shown in Figure 18-38:

    vHBA: **Pod-1-vHBA-A**

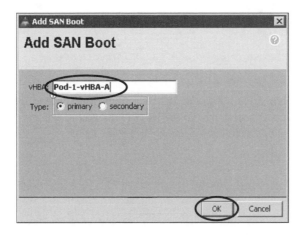

Figure 18-38 *Add SAN Boot Dialog Box*

Caution It is *very* important to enter this name correctly, as it has to match the vHBA name referenced in the service profile template you will create in a later step. Write this name down, as you will need it later. This name is case sensitive.

    Type: **Primary**

5.   Click **OK**.

6.   Select **SAN primary** and click **Add SAN Boot Target**, as shown in Figure 18-39.

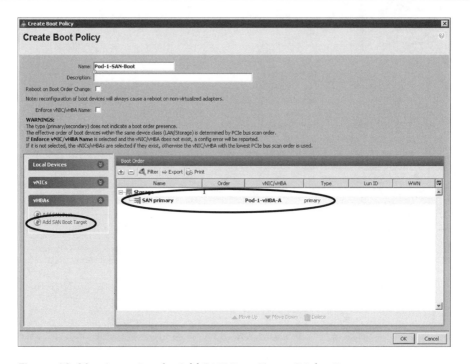

Figure 18-39 *Accessing the Add SAN Boot Target Dialog Box*

7.   The SAN boot target for this lab is a boot LUN that has been created on the EMC VMAX that is FC-connected to the MDS in the Pod. Complete the Add SAN Boot Target dialog box as follows, as shown in Figure 18-40:

    Boot Target LUN: **0**

    Boot Target WWPN: **50:00:09:72:C0:07:3D:99** (be sure to enter the correct information)

8.   To add a LAN (PXE) boot as a secondary option, click the **down arrows** next to vNICs and click **Add LAN Boot** to open the Add LAN Boot dialog box, shown in Figure 18-41.

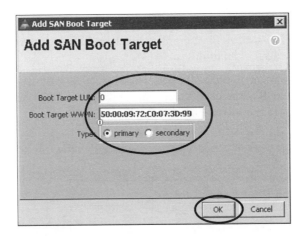

Figure 18-40 *Configuring the Add SAN Boot Target Dialog Box*

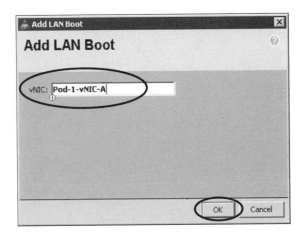

Figure 18-41 *Add LAN Boot Dialog Box*

In the dialog box, enter the following:

vNIC: **Pod-1-vNIC-A**

Caution It is *very* important to enter this name correctly, as it has to match the vNIC name referenced in the service profile template you will create in a later step. Write this name down, as you will need it later. This name is case sensitive.

9. Click **OK**.

10. Click **OK** in the Create Boot Policy dialog box. You should now be able to see the new boot policy you created, under the **Servers** tab, expand **Policies > root**, and select **Boot Policies**.

Step 4: Create an IPMI Profile

In this section, you create an IPMI profile that will be used in the service profile template you will create in a later step of this lab.

1. Click the **Servers** tab, expand **Policies > root**, right-click **IPMI Access Profiles**, and choose **Create IPMI Access Profile**. Fill out the Create IPMI Access Profile dialog box as follows, as displayed in Figure 18-42:

   Name: **Pod-1-IPMI**

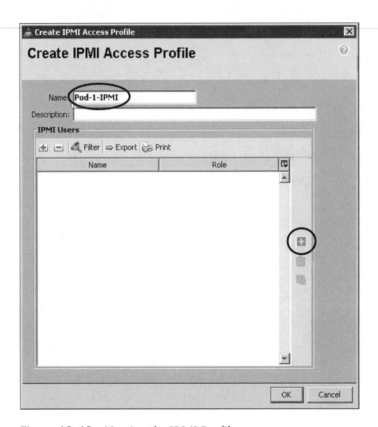

Figure 18-42   *Naming the IPMI Profile*

2. Click the **+** button.

3. Complete the Create IPMI User dialog box as follows, as shown in Figure 18-43:

   Name: **admin**

   Password: **Cisco.123**

   Confirm Password: **Cisco.123**

   Role: **admin**

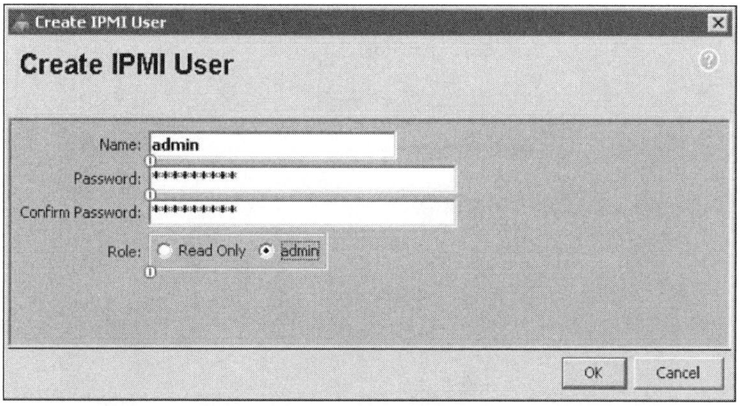

Figure 18-43   *Creating the IPMI User*

4. Click **OK**.

5. Click **OK** in the Create IPMI Access Profile dialog box. You should now be able to see the new profile you created under IPMI Access Profiles.

Note   IPMI runs on the baseboard management controller (BMC) of the server blade and thus operates independently of the operating system, enabling administrators to monitor, manage, diagnose, and recover systems, even if the operating system has hung or the server is powered down.

Step 5: Create a Local Disk Configuration Policy

The local disk configuration policy is used for the configuration of the local hard drives (if blades are purchased with local drives).

1. Click the **Servers** tab, expand **Policies > root**, right-click **Local Disk Config Policies**, and choose **Create Local Disk Configuration Policy**. Configure the local disk policy as follows, as shown in Figure 18-44:

Name: **Pod-1-HD**

Mode: **RAID Mirrored**

Protect Configuration: Check this box

2. Click **OK**.

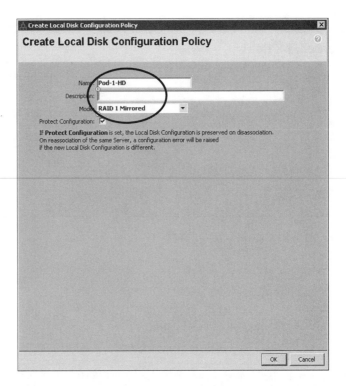

Figure 18-44   *Creating a Local Disk Configuration Policy*

Step 6: Create a Serial over LAN Policy

Serial over LAN (SoL) is a mechanism that enables the input and output of the serial port of a managed system to be redirected over IP.

1. Under Policies > root, right-click **Serial over LAN Policies** and choose **Create Serial over LAN Policy**. Configure the SoL Policy as follows, as shown in Figure 18-45:

    Name: **Pod-1-SOL**

    Serial over LAN State: **enable**

    Speed: **9600**

2. Click **OK**.

Step 7: Create a UUID Suffix Pool

A Universally Unique Identifier (UUID) is an identifier standard used in software construction, standardized by the Open Software Foundation (OSF) as part of the Distributed Computing Environment (DCE). The intent of UUIDs is to enable distributed systems to uniquely identify information without significant central coordination.

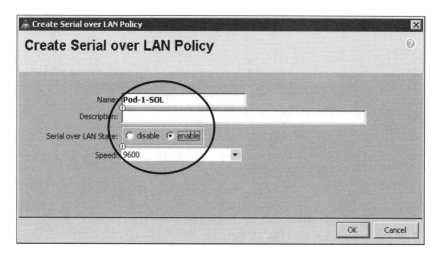

Figure 18-45 *Creating an SoL Policy*

1. To create a UUID suffix pool (the prefix is also changeable), click the **Servers** tab, expand **Pools > root**, right-click **UUID Suffix Pools**, and choose **Create a UUID Suffix Pool.** Use the following information to complete the Create UUID Suffix Pool dialog box, as shown in Figure 18-46:

   Name: **Pod-1-UUID-Pool**

   Prefix: **derived** (take a look at **other** to see how you can set this manually)

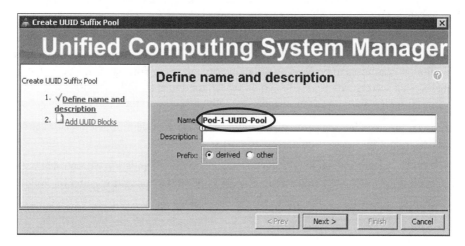

Figure 18-46 *Defining a Name for the UUID Policy*

2. Click **Next**.

3. Click the **+** button at the far-right side and configure the Create UUID Suffix Pool dialog box as follows, as shown in Figure 18-47:

From: **0700-000000000001**

Size: **64**

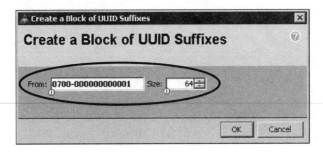

Figure 18-47   *Create UUID Suffix Pool Dialog Box*

4. Click **OK**.

5. Click **Finish** in the Create UUID Suffix Pool dialog box.

Step 8: Create a Server Pool

A server pool contains a set of servers. These servers typically share the same characteristics, which can be their location in the chassis, or an attribute such as server type, amount of memory, local storage, type of CPU, or local drive configuration. You can manually assign a server to a server pool, or use server pool policies and server pool policy qualifications to automate the assignment.

If your system implements multi-tenancy through organizations, you can designate one or more server pools to be used by a specific organization. For example, a pool that includes all servers with two CPUs could be assigned to the Marketing organization, while all servers with 64 GB of memory could be assigned to the Finance organization.

A server pool can include servers from any chassis in the system. A given server can belong to multiple server pools.

1. To create a server pool, click the **Servers** tab, expand **Pools > root**, right-click **Server Pools**, and choose **Create Server Pool**. In the dialog box, enter the following:

   Name: **Pod-1-Server-Pool-1**

2. Click **Next**.

3. In the Add Servers dialog box, choose servers **Chassis 1 Slot 3** through **Chassis 1 Slot 8** and move them into the **Pooled Servers** box by clicking the **>>** button.

   This creates a named pool of six blade servers from the eight available in the chassis, as shown in Figure 18-48.

4. Click **Finish**.

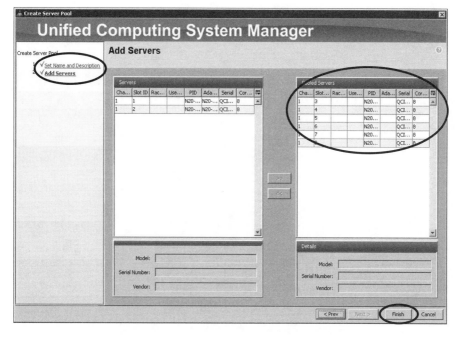

Figure 18-48   *Adding Servers to a Server Pool*

Step 9: Create a Service Profile Template

Service profile templates enable you to create a large number of similar service profiles. With a service profile template, you can quickly create several service profiles with the same basic parameters, such as the number of vNICs and vHBAs, and with identity information drawn from the same pools.

You create a service profile template by using the advanced wizard in UCSM.

1. Click the **Servers** tab and expand **Service Profile Templates > root**. There are several options in the middle of the screen. Choose **Create a Service Profile Template** as depicted in Figure 18-49. Be careful to choose the correct option, as many of them look similar.

2. The Create Service Profile Template wizard opens to the Identify Service Profile Template page, as shown in Figure 18-50. Use the following information to complete this page:

   Name: **Pod-1-Initial-Template-1**

   Type: **Initial Template**

   UUID Assignment: **Pod-1-UUID-Pool** (which you created earlier)

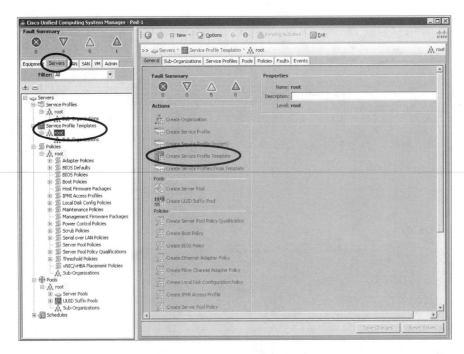

Figure 18-49   *Creating a Service Profile Template*

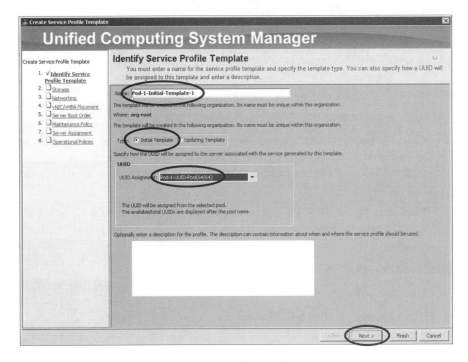

Figure 18-50   *Identifying a Service Profile Template*

3.   Click **Next**.

4.   On the Storage page, shown in Figure 18-51, use the following information:

Local Storage: **Pod-1-HD**

How would you like to configure SAN connectivity?: **Expert**

WWNN Assignment: **Pod-1-WWNN-Pool**

Scroll down to see the rest of the Storage page.

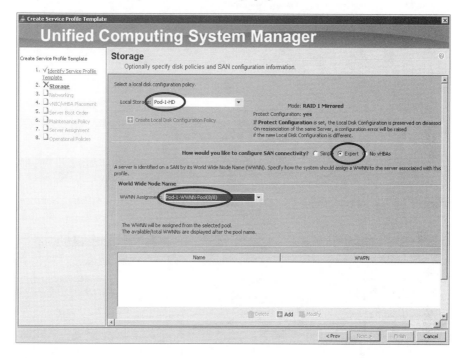

Figure 18-51   *Configuring the Storage Page While Creating a Service Profile Template*

5.   Click the **+** button under the Name/WWPN window, as shown in Figure 18-52, to open the Create vHBA dialog box.

6.   Complete the Create vHBA dialog box as follows:

Name: **Pod-1-vHBA-A** (this is the case-sensitive vHBA name you wrote down when you created the LAN boot policy)

Use SAN Connectivity Template: Check this box

7.   The dialog box changes once you check the Use SAN Connectivity Template check box. Use the following information to complete it, as shown in Figure 18-53:

vHBA Template: **Choose Pod-1-vHBA-A**

Adapter Policy: **<not set>**

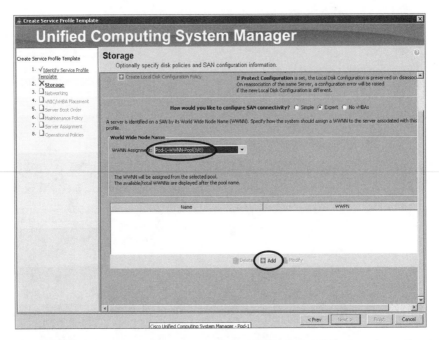

Figure 18-52 *Accessing the Create vHBA Dialog Box While Creating a Service Profile Template*

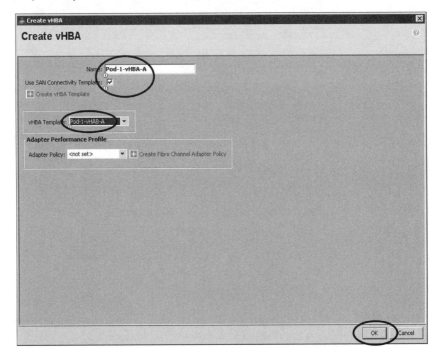

Figure 18-53 *Configuring the Create vHBA Dialog Box While Creating a Service Profile Template*

8. Click **OK**, and then click **Next** to move to the Networking page of the wizard.

9. On the Networking page, use the following information to complete this page:

   Dynamic vNIC Connection Policy: **no dynamic**

   How would you like to configure LAN connectivity?: **Expert**

10. Click the **Add +** button on the bottom of the page to open the Create vNIC dialog box. Use the following information:

    Name: **Pod-1-vNIC-A** (this is the case-sensitive vNIC name you wrote down when you created the SAN boot policy)

    Use LAN Connectivity Template: Check this box

11. The dialog box changes once you check the Use LAN Connectivity Template check box, as shown in Figure 18-54. Use the following information to complete it:

    vNIC Template: **vNIC-Template-A**

    Adapter Policy: **<not set>**

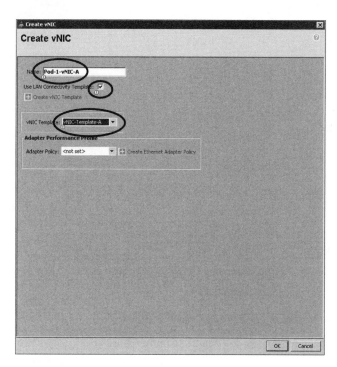

Figure 18-54 *Configuring the Create vNIC Dialog Box While Creating a Service Profile Template*

12. Click **OK**.

13. Click **Next** to move to the vNIC/vHBA Placement page of the wizard.

14. On the vNIC/vHBA Placement page, shown in Figure 18-55, use the following setting:

Select Placement: **Let System Perform Placement**

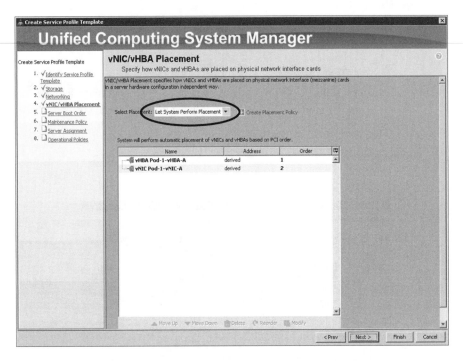

Figure 18-55   *Configuring the vNIC/vHBA Placement Page While Creating a Service Profile Template*

15. Click **Next** to move to the Server Boot Order page of the wizard.

16. On the Server Boot Order page, shown in Figure 18-56, use the following setting:

Boot Policy: **Pod-1-SAN-Boot**

17. Click **Next** to move to the Maintenance Policy page.

18. On the Maintenance Policy page, shown in Figure 18-57, use the following settings:

Maintenance Policy: **Select (Policy "default" used by default)**

19. Click **Next** to move to the Server Assignment page of the wizard.

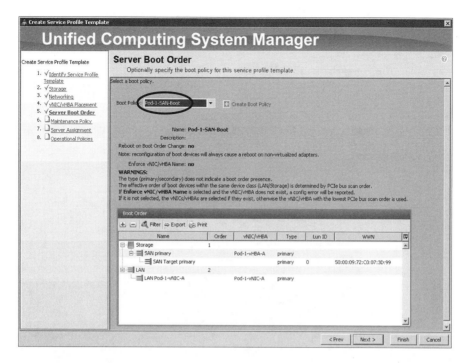

Figure 18-56   *Configuring the Server Boot Order Page While Creating a Service Profile Template*

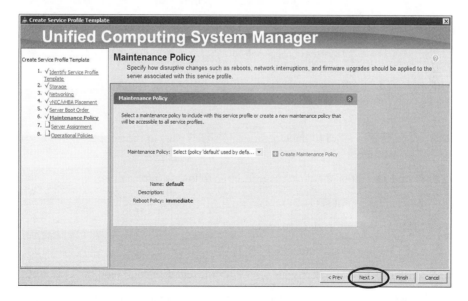

Figure 18-57   *Configuring Maintenance Policy Page While Creating a Service Profile Template*

20. On the Server Assignment page, shown in Figure 18-58, use the following settings:

Pool Assignment: **Pod-1-Server-Pool-1**

Select the Power State to Be Applied...: **up** (this powers up your blades by default)

Server Pool Qualification: **<not set>**

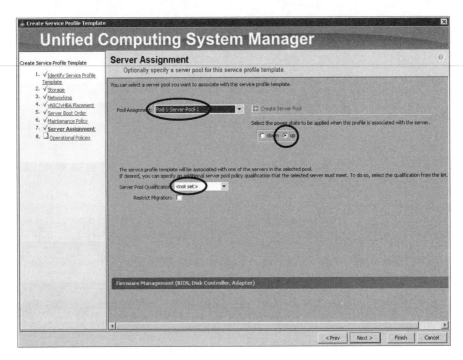

Figure 18-58 *Configuring the Server Assignment Page While Creating a Service Profile Template*

21. Click **Next** to move to the Operational Policies page of the wizard, shown in Figure 18-59.

22. On the Operational Policies page, use the following information:

BIOS Policy: **<not set>**

IPMI Access Profile: **Pod-1-IPMI**

SoL Configuration Profile: **Pod-1-SOL**

23. Click **Finish** to complete your service profile template configuration.

At this point, you can see the service profile template you created under **Service Profile Templates > root**, as shown in Figure 18-60. Take a bit of time to look at all the parameters that you have configured and all the different configuration tabs in the template.

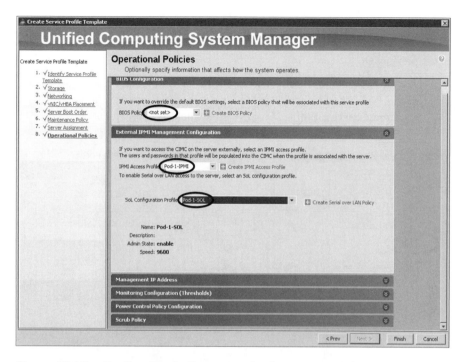

Figure 18-59 *Configuring the Operational Policies Page While Creating a Service Profile Template*

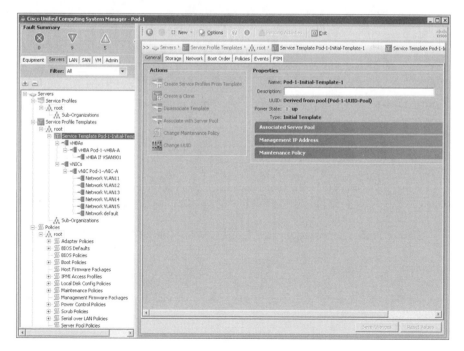

Figure 18-60 *Displaying the New Service Profile Template*

Step 10: Create Service Profiles from a Service Profile Template

Create six service profiles for your servers using the service profile template you created in the previous step.

1. Click the **Servers** tab, expand **Service Profiles > root** (make sure you are using root under Service Profiles and not under Service Profile Templates). In the middle pane, click **Create Service Profiles From Template** link, as shown in Figure 18-61.

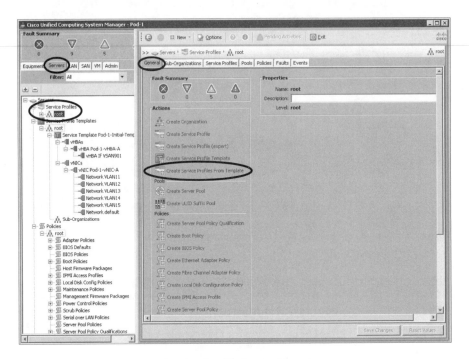

Figure 18-61 *Creating a Service Profile from a Template*

2. Complete the Create Service Profiles from Template dialog box as follows, as depicted in Figure 18-62:

   Naming Prefix: **Pod-1-SP1-** (note that the hyphen at the end of the name is needed)

   Number: **6**

   Service Profile Template: **Service Template Pod-1-Initial-Template-1** (it will be under root).

3. Click **OK**.

You should now see six new service profiles under **Service Profiles > root**, as shown in Figure 18-63.

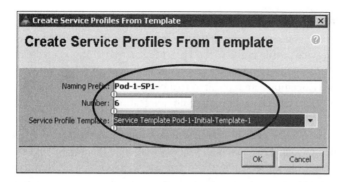

Figure 18-62 *Create Service Profiles From Template
Dialog Box*

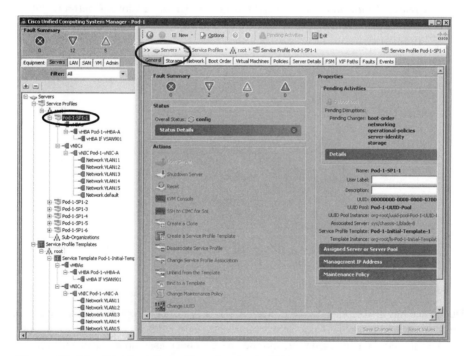

Figure 18-63 *Displaying the New Service Profiles*

The server blade associated with a particular service profile can be viewed on the General
tab. Under the Storage and Network tabs, you can retrieve the WWPN and MAC
addresses that have been associated with your vNIC and vHBA adapters of the server.
These were allocated from the pools you created earlier.

Step 11: Clone and Manually Associate a Service Profile

If you need only one service profile with values similar to an existing service profile, you can clone a service profile in the Cisco UCS Manager GUI. If you create a profile with pool associations—for example, server pool, MAC pool, WWNN pool, and so forth—then all pool associations are replicated to a cloned template. New values for MAC, WWNN, WWPN, UUID and any other unique features are assigned from the appropriate pools to the newly created profile because these values must be unique. Other values, such as VLANs, VSANs and Boot Policies, are copied exactly from the original service profile to the new one. Once created, you can associate the new service profile manually to existing server blades, or use it to pre-provision an empty slot. If there are any pools that have been exhausted because all of their values have already been associated to other service profiles, an error will be displayed.

1. To create a clone, either right-click one of your existing service profiles and choose **Create a Clone** or, on the General tab, choose **Create a Clone**. Configure the Create Clone From dialog box as depicted in Figure 18-64. Use the following information:

    Clone Name: **Pod-1-SP1-7**

    Org: **root**

2. Click **OK**.

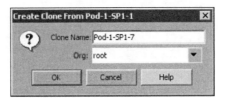

Figure 18-64 *Create Clone From Service Profile Dialog Box*

Tip Once this new service profile is created, you may notice an error on the General tab. This is because this profile is associated to the Pod-1-Server-Pool-1 pool. This server pool only had six servers associated to it, and they have all been used up in the previous six service profiles we created. To fix this issue, this service profile must be associated with an existing free server.

3. To assign this service profile to a particular server, click the profile **Pod-1-SP1-7** and, on the General tab, click **Change Service Profile Association**. The Associate Service Profile dialog box opens, as shown in Figure 18-65. Use the following information to complete the dialog box:

Server Assignment: **Select existing Server**

Click the **Available Servers** radio button

Click the **Chassis ID 1/Slot 1** radio button

4. Click **OK** to associate this server with the cloned service profile.

5. Create another clone and associate the service profile with a slot. Repeat step 4 to clone one of the existing service profiles and name it **Pod-1-SP1-8**.

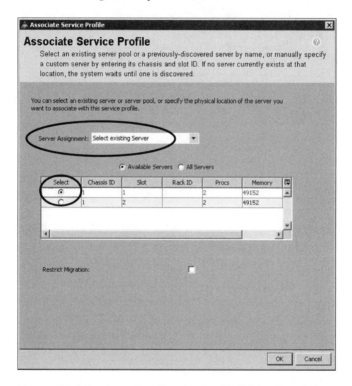

Figure 18-65 *Associate Service Profile Dialog Box Select Existing Server View*

6. Once the new service profile is created, associate it with a slot by clicking the new service profile (Pod-1-SP1-8) and then **Change Service Profile Association**. The dialog box in Figure 18-66 opens. This time use the following information:

Server Assignment: **Pre-provision a slot**

Chassis ID: **1**

Slot ID: **2**

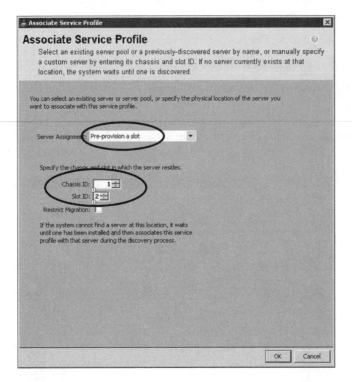

Figure 18-66   *Associate Service Profile Dialog Box Pre-Provision a Slot View*

7.   Click **OK** to associate the service profile to this slot. Even if you do not have a blade in this slot, the service profile reserves the MAC, WWNN, and other information for it, and a newly installed blade assumes this information as soon as it is inserted.

Lab 5 is complete. The server blades have been provisioned. The next step is to finish configuring the VSAN environment on the MDS 9506.

Lab 6: Configuring SAN Zoning and Core Switch Connectivity on the MDS 9506

SAN zoning is a method of arranging Fibre Channel devices into logical groups over the physical configuration of the fabric. Zoning is one of the most common tools for managing and securing a SAN. It provides an easy method to limit which groups of devices/users can connect with which storage volumes, as well as matching operating systems with their storage.

SAN zoning offers a number of benefits:

- **Security:** Zoning keeps users from accessing information they do not need, or need to know.

- **Manageability:** By splitting the SAN up into chunks, zoning makes it easier to keep track of devices, storage, and users.

- **Separation by purpose:** Setting up zones to reflect operational categories, such as Engineering or Human Resources, organizes storage logically. It also makes it easy to establish specialized networks for testing or other purposes.

- **Separation by operating system:** Putting different OSs in different zones reduces the possibility of data corruption.

- **Allowing temporary access:** Administrators can remove the zone restrictions temporarily to allow tasks such as nightly backup.

The two most common methods of zoning are name server, or "soft," zoning, and port, or "hard," zoning. Name server zoning partitions zones based on the WWN of devices on the SAN. It is the easiest to set up and the most flexible, but it is the least secure.

Port zoning allows devices attached to particular ports (specified by WWPN) on the switch to communicate only with devices attached to other ports in the same zone. The SAN switch keeps a table indicating which WWPNs are allowed to communicate with each other.

In this lab, you configure SAN port zoning on the MDS 9506.

Tasks in this lab include the following:

1. Record UCS service profile WWPN assignments.

2. Create a zone for each service profile on the MDS.

3. Place the zones in a zoneset for your POD/VSAN 901.

4. Activate the zoneset on the MDS.

5. Configure MDS connectivity to the core SAN.

Step 1: Record UCS Service Profile WWPN Assignments

To create SAN zoning rules on the MDS, you need to know the WWPNs that are assigned to the UCS service profiles. These were allocated from the pools you created after service profiles were created and applied to the server blades in Lab 5.

1. Log in to your MDS 9506 and issue a **show flogi database** command to see all of the WWPNs/WWNNs that are logged into the fabric.

Note that the logins should be seen across all four FC interfaces connected between the UCS 6100 FI and the MDS 9506 due to a default load-balancing algorithm based on a hash of src/dest FCID.

```
POD-7-MDS-A#
POD-7-MDS-A# sh flogi database
----------------------------------------------------------------------------
INTERFACE        VSAN    FCID        PORT NAME               NODE NAME
----------------------------------------------------------------------------
fc1/1            901     0x820000    20:41:00:0d:ec:da:ab:40 23:85:00:0d:ec:da:ab:41
fc1/1            901     0x820004    20:00:00:25:b5:00:01:07 50:00:00:25:b5:00:07:07
fc1/1            901     0x820006    20:00:00:25:b5:00:01:06 50:00:00:25:b5:00:07:06
fc1/2            901     0x820001    20:42:00:0d:ec:da:ab:40 23:85:00:0d:ec:da:ab:41
fc1/2            901     0x820005    20:00:00:25:b5:00:01:04 50:00:00:25:b5:00:07:04
fc1/2            901     0x820007    20:00:00:25:b5:00:01:02 50:00:00:25:b5:00:07:02
fc1/3            901     0x820002    20:43:00:0d:ec:da:ab:40 23:85:00:0d:ec:da:ab:41
fc1/3            901     0x820008    20:00:00:25:b5:00:01:03 50:00:00:25:b5:00:07:03
fc1/3            901     0x82000a    20:00:00:25:b5:00:01:01 50:00:00:25:b5:00:07:01
fc1/4            901     0x820003    20:44:00:0d:ec:da:ab:40 23:85:00:0d:ec:da:ab:41
fc1/4            901     0x820009    20:00:00:25:b5:00:01:05 50:00:00:25:b5:00:07:05
fc1/4            901     0x82000b    20:00:00:25:b5:00:01:00 50:00:00:25:b5:00:07:00


Total number of flogi = 12.

POD-7-MDS-A#
```

2. To retrieve the specific WWPN information you need to create the zoning, go to the **SAN** tab on the UCSM and look at the WWPN pool you created. This is Pod-1-WWPN-Pool on the Initiators tab, as shown in Figure 18-67.

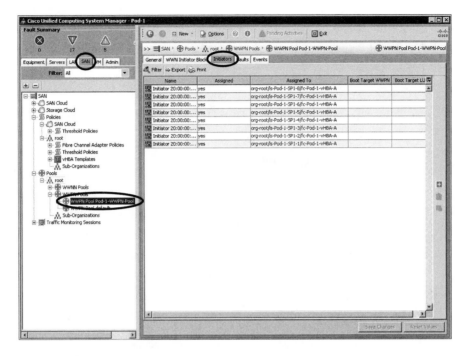

Figure 18-67 *WWPN Initiator Association*

Step 2: Create a Zone for each Service Profile on the MDS

Port zoning specifies the WWPNs of the devices that are allowed to communicate with each other on the SAN. For this lab, we allow the WWPNs associated with the service profile to speak with the WWPN mapped to the boot LUNs and the WWPN mapped to the datastores on the EMC VMAX.

1. To create your zones, you need the following information:

    ■ Zone naming convention (based on service profile)

    ■ WWPN associated with each UCS service profile

    ■ WWPN for the boot LUN on the EMC VMAX

    ■ WWPN for the datastores on the EMC VMAX

2. The zone naming convention to be used in this lab is as follows:

    POD-1-SP1-1

    POD-1-SP1-2

    POD-1-SP1-3

    POD-1-SP1-4

POD-1-SP1-5

POD-1-SP1-6

POD-1-SP1-7

POD-1-SP1-8

3. The WWPNs for the EMC VMAX boot LUN and datastore are as follows:

WWPN for Boot LUN: **50:00:09:72:C0:07:3D:99**

WWPN for datastore: **50:00:09:72:C0:07:3D:98**

4. WWPNs for UCS service profiles are obtained in step 1

5. The zone configuration syntax on the MDS is as follows (note that MDS syntax identifies WWPN as **pwwn**):

```
zone name POD-1-SP1-1 vsan 901 !Using Name As described above

member pwwn 50:00:09:72:C0:07:3D:99 !The WWPN for the Boot LUN

member pwwn 50:00:09:72:C0:07:3D:98 !The WWPN for the Data LUN
member pwwn 20:00:00:25:B5:00:01:07 !WWPN for Pod-1-SP1-1 from SAN Tab
```

Zone configuration on the MDS 9506 is most easily accomplished using a text file and a cut and paste method. Use the Notepad application on the lab PC to create a zone file. You can then paste the information to the MDS in the next steps.

6. Log in to your MDS, enter configuration mode, and configure the zone information for your Pod as shown in the following example:

```
POD-1-MDS-A#
POD-1-MDS-A# conf t
Enter configuration commands, one per line.  End with CNTL/Z.
POD-1-MDS-A(config)# zone name POD-1-SP1-1 vsan 901
POD-1-MDS-A(config-zone)# member pwwn 50:00:09:72:C0:07:3D:99
POD-1-MDS-A(config-zone)# member pwwn 50:00:09:72:C0:07:3D:98
POD-1-MDS-A(config-zone)# member pwwn 20:00:00:25:B5:00:01:07
POD-1-MDS-A(config-zone)#
POD-1-MDS-A(config-zone)# zone name POD-1-SP1-2 vsan 901
POD-1-MDS-A(config-zone)# member pwwn 50:00:09:72:C0:07:3D:99
POD-1-MDS-A(config-zone)# member pwwn 50:00:09:72:C0:07:3D:98
POD-1-MDS-A(config-zone)# member pwwn 20:00:00:25:B5:00:01:06
POD-1-MDS-A(config-zone)#
POD-1-MDS-A(config-zone)# zone name POD-1-SP1-3 vsan 901
POD-1-MDS-A(config-zone)# member pwwn 50:00:09:72:C0:07:3D:99
POD-1-MDS-A(config-zone)# member pwwn 50:00:09:72:C0:07:3D:98
POD-1-MDS-A(config-zone)# member pwwn 20:00:00:25:B5:00:01:05
POD-1-MDS-A(config-zone)#
```

```
POD-1-MDS-A(config-zone)# zone name POD-1-SP1-4 vsan 901
POD-1-MDS-A(config-zone)# member pwwn 50:00:09:72:C0:07:3D:99
POD-1-MDS-A(config-zone)# member pwwn 50:00:09:72:C0:07:3D:98
POD-1-MDS-A(config-zone)# member pwwn 20:00:00:25:B5:00:01:04
POD-1-MDS-A(config-zone)#
POD-1-MDS-A(config-zone)# zone name POD-1-SP1-5 vsan 901
POD-1-MDS-A(config-zone)# member pwwn 50:00:09:72:C0:07:3D:99
POD-1-MDS-A(config-zone)# member pwwn 50:00:09:72:C0:07:3D:98
POD-1-MDS-A(config-zone)# member pwwn 20:00:00:25:B5:00:01:03
POD-1-MDS-A(config-zone)#
POD-1-MDS-A(config-zone)# zone name POD-1-SP1-6 vsan 901
POD-1-MDS-A(config-zone)# member pwwn 50:00:09:72:C0:07:3D:99
POD-1-MDS-A(config-zone)# member pwwn 50:00:09:72:C0:07:3D:98
POD-1-MDS-A(config-zone)# member pwwn 20:00:00:25:B5:00:01:02
POD-1-MDS-A(config-zone)#
POD-1-MDS-A(config-zone)# zone name POD-1-SP1-7 vsan 901
POD-1-MDS-A(config-zone)# member pwwn 50:00:09:72:C0:07:3D:99
POD-1-MDS-A(config-zone)# member pwwn 50:00:09:72:C0:07:3D:98
POD-1-MDS-A(config-zone)# member pwwn 20:00:00:25:B5:00:01:01
POD-1-MDS-A(config-zone)#
POD-1-MDS-A(config-zone)# zone name POD-1-SP1-8 vsan 901
POD-1-MDS-A(config-zone)# member pwwn 50:00:09:72:C0:07:3D:99
POD-1-MDS-A(config-zone)# member pwwn 50:00:09:72:C0:07:3D:98
POD-1-MDS-A(config-zone)# member pwwn 20:00:00:25:B5:00:07:00
POD-1-MDS-A(config-zone)# end
POD-1-MDS-A#
```

Step 3: Place the Zones in a Zoneset for Your POD/VSAN 901

Once you have created the zones, you have to put them into a zoneset. The syntax is as follows:

```
zoneset name POD-1 vsan 901   ! This creates a zoneset named POD-1 in VSAN 901.
```

Then add the zones one at a time with the command:

```
member POD-1-SP1-1 ! This adds zone POD-1-SP-1 to zoneset POD-1
member POD-1-SP1-2
member POD-1-SP1-8
```

Log in to your MDS, enter configuration mode, and configure the zoneset information for your Pod as shown in the following example:

```
POD-7-MDS-A# conf t
Enter configuration commands, one per line.  End with CNTL/Z.
POD-7-MDS-A(config)#
POD-7-MDS-A(config)# zoneset name POD-1 vsan 901
```

```
POD-7-MDS-A(config-zoneset)# member POD-1-SP1-1
POD-7-MDS-A(config-zoneset)# member POD-1-SP1-2
POD-7-MDS-A(config-zoneset)# member POD-1-SP1-3
POD-7-MDS-A(config-zoneset)# member POD-1-SP1-4
POD-7-MDS-A(config-zoneset)# member POD-1-SP1-5
POD-7-MDS-A(config-zoneset)# member POD-1-SP1-6
POD-7-MDS-A(config-zoneset)# member POD-1-SP1-7
POD-7-MDS-A(config-zoneset)# member POD-1-SP1-8
POD-7-MDS-A(config-zoneset)#
POD-7-MDS-A(config-zoneset)# end
POD-7-MDS-A#
```

Step 4: Activate the Zoneset on the MDS

You should now activate the zoneset by using the command **zoneset activate name POD-1 vsan 901**:

```
POD-7-MDS-A# conf t
Enter configuration commands, one per line.  End with CNTL/Z.
POD-7-MDS-A(config)# zoneset activate name POD-1 vsan 901
Zoneset activation initiated. check zone status
POD-7-MDS-A(config)# end
POD-7-MDS-A#
```

Step 5: Configure MDS Connectivity to the Core SAN

To get your blades to see their LUNs, connect your MDS 9506 into the rest of the lab SAN.

To do this, you configure an ISL trunk between the Pod's MDS switch and the SAN core MDS switch. By default, when the ISL trunk between the two MDS switches comes up, they merge their active zonesets. It is considered a best practice to make MDS trunk ports "dedicated rate" interfaces. When the port rate mode is configured as dedicated, a port is allocated required fabric bandwidth and related resources to sustain line rate traffic at the maximum operating speed configured for the port. In this mode, ports do not use local buffering and all receive buffers are allocated from a global buffer pool. This means that, during times of heavy utilization, your trunk port does not have to share resources with any other ports using the same ASIC. To enable this mode, enter the **switchport rate-mode dedicated** command into your MDS switch, under the correct interface.

1. The MDS switch in this lab has interface fc1/18 connected to the SAN core switch. To configure the trunk, enter the following:

```
POD-7-MDS-A# conf t
Enter configuration commands, one per line.  End with CNTL/Z.
POD-7-MDS-A(config)# vsan database
```

```
POD-7-MDS-A(config-vsan-db)# vsan 901 interface fc1/18

POD-7-MDS-A(config-vsan-db)#

POD-7-MDS-A(config)# interface fc1/18

POD-7-MDS-A(config-if)# switchport rate-mode dedicated !Enable
  dedicated rate

POD-7-MDS-A(config-if)# switchport mode auto !Enable trunk negotiation

POD-7-MDS-A(config-if)# no shut

POD-7-MDS-A(config-if)# end

POD-7-MDS-A#
```

2. Verify that fc1/18 is up and in trunking mode:

```
POD-7-MDS-A# sh int fc1/18

fc1/18 is trunking

    Hardware is Fibre Channel, SFP is short wave laser w/o OFC (SN)

    Port WWN is 20:01:00:0d:ec:d5:34:00

    Peer port WWN is 20:01:00:0d:ec:b0:14:c0

    Admin port mode is auto, trunk mode is on

    snmp link state traps are enabled

    Port mode is TE

    Port vsan is 901

    Speed is 4 Gbps

    Rate mode is dedicated

    ...




    Trunk vsans (admin allowed and active) (1,901)

        Trunk vsans (up)                    (1,901)

        Trunk vsans (isolated)                  ()

        Trunk vsans (initializing)              ()

    ...


POD-9134-A#
```

3. Verify that the active zonesets have merged by entering **show zoneset active vsan 901**:

```
POD-7-MDS-A# sh zoneset active vsan 901

zoneset name POD-1 vsan 901

  zone name SP1-1 vsan 901
```

```
        pwwn 50:00:09:72:c0:07:3d:99

        pwwn 50:00:09:72:c0:07:3d:98

      * fcid 0x820004 [pwwn 20:00:00:25:b5:00:07:07]


    zone name SP1-2 vsan 901

      pwwn 50:00:09:72:c0:07:3d:99

      pwwn 50:00:09:72:c0:07:3d:98

    * fcid 0x820006 [pwwn 20:00:00:25:b5:00:07:06]

...

zone name Pod1-blade1-3 vsan 901

  * fcid 0x560007 [pwwn 50:00:09:72:c0:07:3d:99]

  * fcid 0x7a0004 [pwwn 20:00:00:25:b5:01:00:af]


    zone name Pod1-blade1-7 vsan 901

    * fcid 0x560007 [pwwn 50:00:09:72:c0:07:3d:99]

    * fcid 0x7a000f [pwwn 20:00:00:25:b5:01:00:3f]


POD-7-MDS-A#
```

If you see the active zoneset information from the core switch (e.g., Pod1-blade1-X in the preceding output), you have successfully completed this exercise. Your server blades should be able to access their LUNs on the SAN.

4. Save your MDS configuration by entering **copy running-config startup-config**.

Lab 6 is complete. The VSAN environment is configured. In the next lab, you configure IP and routing features on the Nexus 7000 switches.

Lab 7: Enabling IP and Routing Features on the Nexus 7000 Series Switches

In Lab 1, you configured named VLANs on the UCS (VLAN11–VLAN15) to logically segment and reduce the size of the broadcast domains associated with the server blades in the Pod. In Lab 3, you created these same VLANs on the Nexus 7000s in the Pod and enabled the vPCs to the UCS 6100 Fabric Interconnect as trunks. In this lab, you enable the network infrastructure to provide IP connectivity and network reachability to these VLANs. This requires the following configuration tasks on the Nexus 7000 switches:

Step 1. Configure Layer 3 VLAN interfaces with IPv4 addressing.

Step 2. Configure Hot Standby Router Protocol (HSRP).

Step 3. Configure OSPF routing on the core and VLAN interfaces.

Step 4. Enable OSPF routing on the VLAN interfaces.

Step 5. Add a redundant path to the core—add OSPF adjacency between Nexus 7000s across the PortChannel trunk.

Step 1: Configure Layer 3 VLAN Interfaces with IPv4 Addressing

A VLAN interface or switch virtual interface (SVI) is a virtual routed interface that connects a VLAN on the device to the Layer 3 router engine on the same device. You can route across VLAN interfaces to provide Layer 3 inter-VLAN routing by configuring a VLAN interface for each VLAN that you want to route traffic to and assigning an IP address on the VLAN interface.

You must enable the VLAN network interface feature before you can configure it.

1. Log in to both Nexus 7000s in your Pod and enable **feature interface-vlan.**

   Do this in both Switch-A and Switch-B:

   ```
   POD-7-N7K-A# conf t

   Enter configuration commands, one per line.  End with CNTL/Z.

   POD-7-N7K-A(config)# feature interface-vlan
   POD-7-N7K-A(config)# end
   ```

2. Verify the VLAN (numbers) that you created in Lab 3 and create the associated VLAN interfaces. Configure VLAN interfaces with IPv4 addresses using the following address convention:

   Switch-A: **10.1.V.2** (where V is the last digit of the VLAN ID)

   Switch-B: **10.1.V.3** (where V is the last digit of the VLAN ID)

   Example for addressing interface VLAN11:

   Switch-A: **ip address 10.7.1.2 255.255.255.0**

   Switch-B: **ip address 10.7.1.3 255.255.255.0**

3. Follow the example shown next to create and address VLAN interfaces on both of the Nexus 7000s.

   On N7K-A:

   ```
   POD-7-N7K-A# sh vlan !This verifies that the VLAN are created

   VLAN Name                            Status    Ports
   ---- -------------------------------- --------- ---------------------------
   1    default                          active
   ```

```
71   VLAN0071                         active
72   VLAN0072                         active
73   VLAN0073                         active
74   VLAN0074                         active
75   VLAN0075                         active


POD-7-N7K-A# conf t
POD-7-N7K-A(config-if)# interface vlan 11
POD-7-N7K-A(config-if)# ip address 10.1.1.2 255.255.255.
POD-7-N7K-A(config-if)# no shut
POD-7-N7K-A(config-if)# interface vlan 12
POD-7-N7K-A(config-if)# ip address 10.1.2.2 255.255.255.0
POD-7-N7K-A(config-if)# no shut
POD-7-N7K-A(config-if)# interface vlan 13
POD-7-N7K-A(config-if)# ip address 10.1.3.2 255.255.255.0
POD-7-N7K-A(config-if)# no shut
POD-7-N7K-A(config-if)# interface vlan 14
POD-7-N7K-A(config-if)# ip address 10.1.4.2 255.255.255.0
POD-7-N7K-A(config-if)# no shut
POD-7-N7K-A(config-if)# interface vlan 15
POD-7-N7K-A(config-if)# ip address 10.1.5.2 255.255.255.0
POD-7-N7K-A(config-if)# no shut
```

On N7K-B:

```
POD-7-N7K-B# sh vlan !This verifies that the VLAN are created


VLAN Name                             Status    Ports
---- -------------------------------- --------- -----------------------
1    default                          active
71   VLAN0071                         active
72   VLAN0072                         active
73   VLAN0073                         active
74   VLAN0074                         active
75   VLAN0075                         active
```

```
POD-7-N7K-B# conf t
POD-7-N7K-B(config-if)# interface vlan 11
POD-7-N7K-B(config-if)# ip address 10.1.1.3 255.255.255.0
POD-7-N7K-B(config-if)# no shut
...


POD-7-N7K-B(config-if)# interface vlan 15
POD-7-N7K-B(config-if)# ip address 10.1.5.3 255.255.255.0
POD-7-N7K-B(config-if)# no shut
```

Step 2: Configure Hot Standby Router Protocol

HSRP is a first-hop redundancy protocol (FHRP) that allows a transparent failover of the first-hop IP router. HSRP provides first-hop routing redundancy for IP hosts on Ethernet networks configured with a default gateway IP address. You use HSRP in a group of routers for selecting an active gateway and a standby gateway. In a group of gateways, the *active gateway* is the gateway that routes packets; the *standby gateway* is the gateway that takes over when the active gateway fails or when preset conditions are met. When you use HSRP, you configure the HSRP virtual IP address as the host's default router (instead of the IP address of the actual router). The virtual IP address is an IP address that is shared among a group of routers that run HSRP.

When you configure HSRP on a network segment, you provide a virtual MAC address and a virtual IP address for the HSRP group. You configure the same virtual address on each HSRP-enabled interface in the group. You also configure a unique IP address and MAC address on each interface that acts as the real address. HSRP selects one of these interfaces to be the active router. The active router receives and routes packets destined for the virtual MAC address of the group.

HSRP interoperates with vPCs by forwarding traffic through both the active HSRP router and the standby HSRP router. This enhancement provides, in effect, an active-active HSRP configuration with no changes to current HSRP configuration recommendations or best practices and no changes to HSRP. The HSRP control protocol still acts like an active-standby pair, so that only the active device responds to Address Resolution Protocol (ARP) requests, but a packet destined for the shared HSRP MAC address is accepted as local on either the active or standby HSRP device.

In this lab, you will enable HSRP on the VLAN interfaces that you created in Step 1, on both Nexus 7000s. Server traffic arriving on the vPC interface (of either Nexus 7000) is forwarded to the destination network.

1. You must enable the HSRP feature before you can configure it. Log into both Nexus 7000s in your Pod and enable **feature hsrp**.

Do this in both Switch-A and Switch-B:

```
POD-7-N7K-A# conf t
Enter configuration commands, one per line.  End with CNTL/Z.
```

```
POD-7-N7K-A(config)# feature hsrp
POD-7-N7K-A(config)# end
```

2. Enable HSRP on each of the VLAN interfaces you created in Step 1. Specify the first available address in the subnet as the virtual IP address. Configure N7K-A with an HSRP priority of 150 to make it the active router, and enable MD5 authentication with a password of **cisco** on all HSRP sessions following the example shown next.

On N7K-A:

```
POD-7-N7K-A# conf t
POD-7-N7K-A(config-if-hsrp)# interface vlan 11
POD-7-N7K-A(config-if)# hsrp 1
POD-7-N7K-A(config-if-hsrp)# ip 10.1.1.1 !IP address for the HSRP Group
POD-7-N7K-A(config-if-hsrp)# authentication md5 key-string cisco
POD-7-N7K-A(config-if-hsrp)# priority 150 !Set the Priority
POD-7-N7K-A(config-if-hsrp)# preempt !enable preemption
POD-7-N7K-A(config-if-hsrp)# interface vlan 12
POD-7-N7K-A(config-if)# hsrp 1
POD-7-N7K-A(config-if-hsrp)# ip 10.1.2.1
POD-7-N7K-A(config-if-hsrp)# authentication md5 key-string cisco
POD-7-N7K-A(config-if-hsrp)# priority 150
POD-7-N7K-A(config-if-hsrp)# preempt
POD-7-N7K-A(config-if-hsrp)# interface vlan 13
POD-7-N7K-A(config-if)# hsrp 1
POD-7-N7K-A(config-if-hsrp)# ip 10.1.3.1
POD-7-N7K-A(config-if-hsrp)# authentication md5 key-string cisco
POD-7-N7K-A(config-if-hsrp)# priority 150
POD-7-N7K-A(config-if-hsrp)# preempt
POD-7-N7K-A(config-if-hsrp)# interface vlan 14
POD-7-N7K-A(config-if)# hsrp 1
POD-7-N7K-A(config-if-hsrp)# ip 10.1.4.1
POD-7-N7K-A(config-if-hsrp)# authentication md5 key-string cisco
POD-7-N7K-A(config-if-hsrp)# priority 150
POD-7-N7K-A(config-if-hsrp)# preempt
POD-7-N7K-A(config-if-hsrp)# interface vlan 15
POD-7-N7K-A(config-if)# hsrp 1
POD-7-N7K-A(config-if-hsrp)# ip 10.1.5.1
```

```
POD-7-N7K-A(config-if-hsrp)# authentication md5 key-string cisco
POD-7-N7K-A(config-if-hsrp)# priority 150
POD-7-N7K-A(config-if-hsrp)# preempt
POD-7-N7K-A(config-if-hsrp)# end
POD-7-N7K-A#
```

On N7K-B:

```
POD-7-N7K-B# conf t
POD-7-N7K-B(config-if-hsrp)# interface vlan 11
POD-7-N7K-B(config-if)# hsrp 1
POD-7-N7K-B(config-if-hsrp)# ip 10.1.1.1 !Has to match the IP in N7K-A
POD-7-N7K-B(config-if-hsrp)# authentication md5 key-string cisco
POD-7-N7K-B(config-if-hsrp)#!Note no priority will use the default of 100
POD-7-N7K-B(config-if-hsrp)# interface vlan 12
POD-7-N7K-B(config-if)# hsrp 1
POD-7-N7K-B(config-if-hsrp)# ip 10.1.2.1
POD-7-N7K-B(config-if-hsrp)# authentication md5 key-string cisco
POD-7-N7K-B(config-if-hsrp)#
POD-7-N7K-B(config-if-hsrp)# interface vlan 13
POD-7-N7K-B(config-if)# hsrp 1
POD-7-N7K-B(config-if-hsrp)# ip 10.1.3.1
POD-7-N7K-B(config-if-hsrp)# authentication md5 key-string cisco
POD-7-N7K-B(config-if-hsrp)#
POD-7-N7K-B(config-if-hsrp)# interface vlan 14
POD-7-N7K-B(config-if)# hsrp 1
POD-7-N7K-B(config-if-hsrp)# ip 10.1.4.1
POD-7-N7K-B(config-if-hsrp)# authentication md5 key-string cisco
POD-7-N7K-B(config-if-hsrp)#
POD-7-N7K-B(config-if-hsrp)# interface vlan 15
POD-7-N7K-B(config-if)# hsrp 1
POD-7-N7K-B(config-if-hsrp)# ip 10.1.5.1
POD-7-N7K-B(config-if-hsrp)# authentication md5 key-string cisco
POD-7-N7K-B(config-if-hsrp)# end
```

3. Verify your work by issuing the following commands in both switches:

   b. `show run hsrp`

   c. `show hsrp brief`

   d. `show hsrp`

Step 3: Configure OSPF Routing on Core and VLAN Interfaces

Each Nexus 7000 VDC has been cabled to one of the core 7603 routers with fiber connections, as shown in Figure 18-1. The Gigabit Ethernet interfaces on each 7603 have been configured with IP addresses in point-to-point /30 subnets and enabled for OSPF routing in Area 0. In this step, you configure the associated core IP addressing on the Nexus 7000s, and place the interfaces into OSPF Area 0 so that they form adjacencies with the core 7603 routers. This will allow your Nexus 7000s to learn how to reach the rest of the networks being advertised in your lab core.

In each of your Nexus 7000 switches, interface e3/11 is connected to the core. You will need to use this interface for the next set of configuration steps.

1. Assign the appropriate IP address to the core interfaces on each of the Nexus 7000s in your Pod:

   IP 10.100.0.26/30 in N7K-A

   IP 10.200.0.26/30 in N7K-B

2. You must also enable OSPF as a feature with the **feature ospf** command, as shown in the following example:

   N7K-A:

```
POD-7-N7K-A# conf t
Enter configuration commands, one per line.  End with CNTL/Z.
POD-7-N7K-A(config)# feature ospf !enable the OSPF feature
POD-7-N7K-A(config)#
POD-7-N7K-A(config)# interface e3/11
POD-7-N7K-A(config-if)# no switchport
POD-7-N7K-A(config-if)# ip address 10.100.0.26 255.255.255.252
POD-7-N7K-A(config-if)# end
POD-7-N7K-A#
```

   N7K-B (example of how to use / notation to represent subnet mask in NX-OS):

```
POD-7-N7K-B# conf t
Enter configuration commands, one per line.  End with CNTL/Z.
POD-7-N7K-B(config)# feature ospf
POD-7-N7K-B(config)#
POD-7-N7K-B(config)# interface e3/11
POD-7-N7K-B(config-if)# no switchport
POD-7-N7K-B(config-if)# ip address 10.200.0.26/30 !Alt. method to
  assign mask
```

```
POD-7-N7K-B(config-if)# end
POD-7-N7K-B#
POD-7-N7K-B#
```

3. Enable OSPF process 1 on both routers and configure Area 0 authentication. This requires routers in Area 0 to use authentication before forming a neighbor relationship. Message digest authentication is used so that the passwords are not sent in clear text between neighbors.

On both N7Ks:

```
POD-7-N7K-A# conf t
Enter configuration commands, one per line.  End with CNTL/Z.
POD-7-N7K-A(config)# router ospf 1 !Enables OSPF Process for AS 1
POD-7-N7K-A(config-router)# area 0 authentication message-digest !Enables
  auth
POD-7-N7K-A(config-router)# end
POD-7-N7K-A#
```

4. Enable OSPF on the core interfaces of the Pod along with MD5 authentication. These are the interfaces to which you assigned IP addresses earlier.

On both N7Ks:

```
POD-7-N7K-A# conf t
Enter configuration commands, one per line.  End with CNTL/Z.
POD-7-N7K-A(config)# interface e3/11
POD-7-N7K-A(config-if)# ip router ospf 1 area 0 !Puts int in Area 0 for AS 1
POD-7-N7K-A(config-if)# ip ospf authentication message-digest !Enables
  Auth MD5
POD-7-N7K-A(config-if)# ip ospf authentication-key cisco !Sets auth key
POD-7-N7K-A(config-if)#
POD-7-N7K-A(config-if)# end
POD-7-N7K-A#
```

5. Verify your OSPF configuration and core connectivity with the following commands:

```
show running-config ospf
```

```
show ip ospf interface
```

```
show ip ospf neighbors
```

```
show ip route ospf
```

Example of outputs in N7K-A:

```
POD-7-N7K-A# sh ip ospf neighbors
OSPF Process ID 1 VRF default
Total number of neighbors: 1
Neighbor ID     Pri State          Up Time  Address          Interface
 10.100.0.253     1 FULL/DR         00:09:42 10.100.0.25      Eth3/11
POD-7-N7K-A#
POD-7-N7K-A# sh ip route ospf
IP Route Table for VRF "default"
'*' denotes best ucast next-hop
'**' denotes best mcast next-hop
'[x/y]' denotes [preference/metric]


10.1.0.0/24, ubest/mbest: 1/0
    *via 10.100.0.25, Eth3/11, [110/41], 00:09:58, ospf-1, intra

10.100.0.16/30, ubest/mbest: 1/0
    *via 10.100.0.25, Eth3/11, [110/41], 00:09:58, ospf-1, intra

10.100.0.20/30, ubest/mbest: 1/0
    *via 10.100.0.25, Eth3/11, [110/41], 00:09:58, ospf-1, intra

10.100.0.252/30, ubest/mbest: 1/0
    *via 10.100.0.25, Eth3/11, [110/41], 00:09:58, ospf-1, intra

10.200.0.16/30, ubest/mbest: 1/0
    *via 10.100.0.25, Eth3/11, [110/42], 00:09:58, ospf-1, intra

10.200.0.20/30, ubest/mbest: 1/0
    *via 10.100.0.25, Eth3/11, [110/42], 00:09:58, ospf-1, intra
POD-7-N7K-A#
```

Step 4: Enable OSPF Routing on the VLAN Interfaces

The next step is to enable OSPF on the VLAN interfaces of the Nexus 7000 switches so that the server VLAN subnets are announced to the rest of the network. The VLAN interfaces in each Pod are configured into regular (non-backbone) areas so that routes are announced as LSA type-3 (inter-area) by the Nexus 7000.

1. Enable OSPF on the VLAN interfaces in the Pod by placing them in OSPF Area 1.

2. Enable each VLAN interface as OSPF **passive-interface** to suppress hello packets from being sent on them. This is not necessary, because no other OSPF neighbors are present; however, it does save some CPU cycles, and is considered best practice.

On both N7Ks (see the example):

```
POD-7-N7K-A# conf t
POD-5-N7K-B(config)# interface vlan 11
POD-5-N7K-B(config-if)# ip router ospf 1 area 1
POD-5-N7K-B(config-if)# ip ospf passive-interface
POD-5-N7K-B(config-if)# interface vlan 12
POD-5-N7K-B(config-if)# ip router ospf 1 area 1
POD-5-N7K-B(config-if)# ip ospf passive-interface
POD-5-N7K-B(config-if)# interface vlan 13
POD-5-N7K-B(config-if)# ip router ospf 1 area 1
POD-5-N7K-B(config-if)# ip ospf passive-interface
POD-5-N7K-B(config-if)# interface vlan 14
POD-5-N7K-B(config-if)# ip router ospf 1 area 1
POD-5-N7K-B(config-if)# ip ospf passive-interface
POD-5-N7K-B(config-if)# interface vlan 15
POD-5-N7K-B(config-if)# ip router ospf 1 area 1
POD-5-N7K-B(config-if)# ip ospf passive-interface
OD-5-N7K-B(config-if)#
```

Step 5: Add a Redundant Path to the Core—Add OSPF Adjacency Between Nexus 7000s Across the PortChannel Trunk

In Lab 3, you created a 20-Gbps PortChannel (L2 trunk) interface between the pair of Nexus 7000s that was designated as a vPC peer-link. In this step, you will configure a new VLAN interface on each Nexus 7000, which serves as a Layer 3 routing interface across this link and provides a redundant OSPF path to the core.

1. Create a new VLAN 100 on each of the Nexus 7000s.

2. Create a new VLAN 100 interface (SVI) on each of the Nexus 7000s.

3. Assign an IP address to this VLAN interface:

IP 10.1.200.1/30 on N7K-A

IP 10.1.200.2/30 on N7K-B

4. Enable OSPF on these new VLAN interfaces by placing them into the regular OSPF Area 1

5. Enable each VLAN as OSPF network type point-to-point to avoid DR/BDR election and improve upon convergence.

Example on N7K-A:

```
POD-7-N7K-A# conf t
POD-5-N7K-A(config)# vlan 100
POD-5-N7K-A(config-vlan)# name interswitch_routing
POD-5-N7K-A(config-vlan)# interface vlan 100
POD-5-N7K-A(config-if)# no shut
POD-5-N7K-A(config-if)# ip address 10.1.200.1/30
POD-5-N7K-A(config-if)# ip ospf network point-to-point !makes the OSPF
  net P2P
POD-5-N7K-A(config-if)# ip router ospf 1 area 1
POD-5-N7K-A(config-if)#
```

Example on N7K-B:

```
POD-7-N7K-B# conf t
POD-5-N7K-B(config)# vlan 100
POD-5-N7K-B(config-vlan)# name interswitch_routing
POD-5-N7K-B(config-vlan)# interface vlan 100
POD-5-N7K-B(config-if)# no shut
POD-5-N7K-B(config-if)# ip address 10.1.200.2/30 !Note IP address
POD-5-N7K-B(config-if)# ip ospf network point-to-point
POD-5-N7K-B(config-if)# ip router ospf 1 area 1
POD-5-N7K-B(config-if)#
```

6. Verify that an OSPF adjacency forms across these interfaces and that summary LSAs are learned from the peer Nexus 7000.

Example on N7K-A:

```
POD-5-N7K-A# show ip ospf neighbors


OSPF Process ID 1 VRF default  Total number of neighbors: 2


Neighbor ID     Pri State           Up Time  Address         Interface


10.100.0.253     1 FULL/DR          04:37:50 10.100.0.17       Eth3/3

10.1.1.3         1 FULL/ -          03:16:00 10.1.200.2     Vlan100


POD-5-N7K-A# show ip ospf database summary area 1 adv-router 10.1.1.3
!Address from output above


OSPF Router with ID (10.5.2.2) (Process ID 1 VRF default)

Summary Network Link States (Area 0.0.0.1)


Link ID         ADV Router       Age      Seq#     Checksum
10.1.0.0         10.1.1.3         95       0x8000000b 0xc843

10.1.1.0         10.1.1.3         95       0x8000000b 0x5988

10.100.0.0       10.1.1.3         95       0x8000000b 0x1892

10.100.0.16      10.1.1.3         95       0x8000000b 0x7723

10.100.0.20      10.1.1.3         95       0x8000000b 0x4f47

10.100.0.24      10.1.1.3         95       0x8000000b 0x276b

10.100.0.252     10.1.1.3         95       0x8000000b 0x2c82

10.200.0.16      10.1.1.3         95       0x8000000b 0xae89

10.200.0.20      10.1.1.3         95       0x8000000b 0x90a2

10.200.0.24      10.1.1.3         95       0x8000000b 0x68c6
```

Lab 7 is complete. The Data Center 3.0 infrastructure is now fully built, with connectivity established to the core LAN and SAN. In the next sections, you will verify that the server blades in the Pod have booted a VMware ESX 4.0 hypervisor and then add them into a VMware vCenter "virtual data center."

Lab 8: Verifying the Blade Servers Boot VMware ESX 4.0

In this lab, you will verify the blade servers have booted VMware ESX 4.0, and that they have IP connectivity to a VMware vCenter Server connected to a core VLAN outside of the Pod.

> **Note** VMware ESX is a bare-metal hypervisor, meaning it installs directly on top of a physical server and partitions it into multiple virtual machines that can run simultaneously, sharing the physical resources of the underlying server. Each virtual machine represents a complete system, with processors, memory, networking, storage, and BIOS, and can run an unmodified operating system and applications.

Step 1: Connect to Server KVM Console and Verify Boot Status

VMware ESX 4.0 has been loaded on an EMC VMAX boot LUN reserved for each blade server during the initial installation process. In Lab 5, you configured a UCS service profile that included a server boot policy that specified **Boot from SAN**; this directed UCS servers to attempt a SAN boot by specifying the boot target LUN and WWPN of the EMC VMAX. In this lab, you connect to the blade server's software-based KVM Consoles and verify the server blades have booted successfully.

During this checkout process, you may find that your server blades have not successfully booted ESX. This does not necessarily suggest a problem in your configuration; rather, a possible "time out" condition occurred as a result of how the configuration tasks were ordered in the previous labs. In Lab 5, the service profile was created, and then in Lab 6, the SAN zoning was configured. If a blade server attempts to boot before the SAN zone is operational, it will fail to boot from the boot LUN and require a manual restart.

1. From the UCSM application, click the **Servers** tab and expand **Service Profiles > root**. Right-click one of the service profiles and choose **KVM Console**, as shown in Figure 18-68.

    A Java-based KVM Console opens. If a message indicating the server failed to boot appears on the screen (or the blade continuously attempts to PXE boot and fails), you will need to reset the server blade.

2. To reset the server blade, click the **Reset** key on your KVM Console, click the **Power Cycle** radio button, and then click **OK**, as depicted in Figure 18-69.

    The server blade has successfully booted from SAN if the VMware ESX 4.0 login appears on the screen as shown in Figure 18-70.

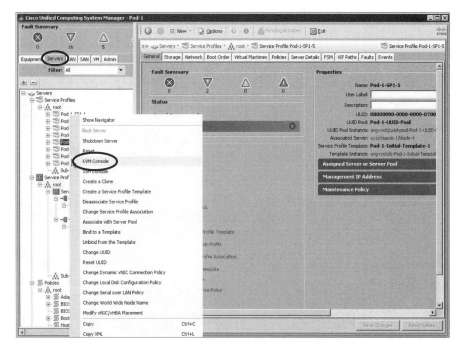

Figure 18-68   *Launching the KVM Console*

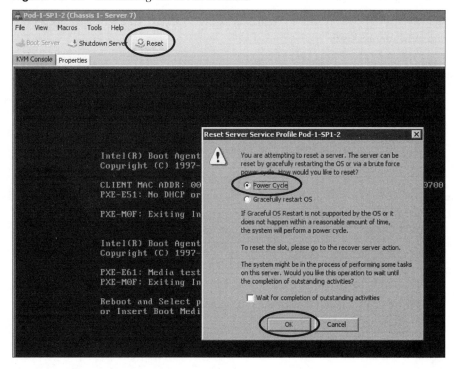

Figure 18-69   *Reset Server Service Profile Dialog Box*

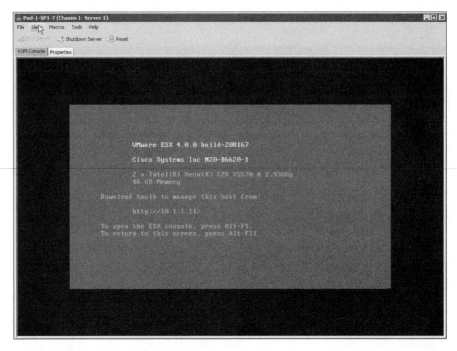

Figure 18-70 *VMware ESX Console Screen*

3. Repeat steps 1 and 2 for the remaining servers to make sure they have booted
VMware ESX 4.0.

Step 2: Verify ESX Service Console IP Connectivity

As part of the initial installation process, an ESX service console network interface was
configured for each server blade with an IP address in VLAN 11. In this step, you will
ensure that the service console has IP reachability outside the Pod, verifying that it has
been set up properly and that routing features configured in Lab 7 have been successfully
deployed.

> **Note** The service console in ESX is a general-purpose operating system used as the boot-
> strap for the VMware kernel, vmkernel, and as a management interface. These console OS
> functions are being deprecated as VMware migrates to exclusively the "embedded" ESX
> model (ESXi). The service console, for all intents and purposes, is the operating system
> used to interact with VMware ESX and the virtual machines that run on the server.

1. Press **Alt-F1** and log in with the following credentials:

Login: **root**

Password: **Cisco.123**

2. Verify the IP address that has been configured on the ESX service console of each server blade using **ifconfig -a.**

3. Ping the default gateway of the ESX service console (this is the HSRP virtual IP address allocated to the VLAN 11 interface that was configured on the Nexus 7000 pair):

   ping 10.1.1.1

   Successful replies are received from the default gateway, as shown in Figure 18-71, if the interfaces and vPC/PortChannel were configured correctly in the prior lab exercises.

Figure 18-71   *Success Echo Replies Shown in the ESX Console*

4. Press **Control-C** to stop the pings.

5. Ping the VMware vCenter Server that has been deployed on a UCS blade server in the network lab core:

   ping 10.10.1.103

   Successful replies are received if OSPF routing was configured correctly in the prior lab exercises.

6. Press **Control-C** to stop the pings.

Lab 8 is complete. Server blades have booted and IP connectivity to the vCenter Server has been verified.

Lab 9: Adding the UCS Blade Servers into VMware vCenter

In this lab, you will add the UCS blade servers into VMware vCenter for centralized management.

1. Double-click the **VMware vSphere Client** icon (shown in Figure 18-72 on the lab PC desktop) to connect to VMware vCenter.

2. Log in as shown in Figure 18-73, using the following credentials:

   IP Address/Name: **10.10.1.103**

   Check the **Use Windows Session Credentials** check box

Figure 18-72 *VMware vSphere Client Icon*

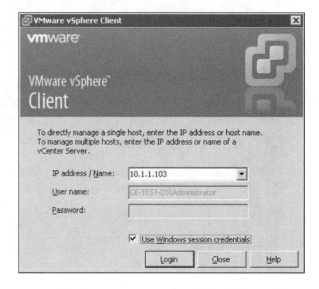

Figure 18-73 *VMware vSphere Client Login Screen*

3. Click **Login**.

4. Click **Ignore** for the security warning depicted in Figure 18-74.

   vCenter opens with a data center named Pod-1, as shown in Figure 18-75.

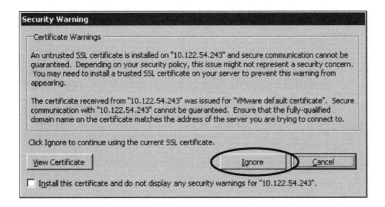

Figure 18-74 *VMware vSphere Client Certificate Warning*

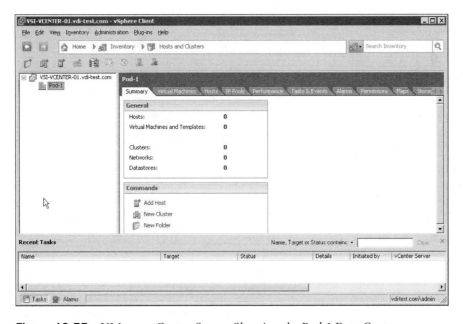

Figure 18-75 *VMware vCenter Screen Showing the Pod-1 Data Center*

5. Click the **Hosts and Clusters** tab to add the blade servers to the data center. Click **Pod-3**. Choose the **Summary** tab. Click **Add Host** Click Add Host (see Figure 18-76).

6. The Add Host Wizard opens (see Figure 18-77). Use the following credentials:

    Host: **10.1.1.11**. This is the IP address that was assigned to the service console of the first server blade (Pod-1-SP1-1 profile). Verify this address with **ifconfig –a** from the console, as described in Step 2.2 in Lab 8, before adding the host address.

    User Name: **root**

    Password: **Cisco.123**

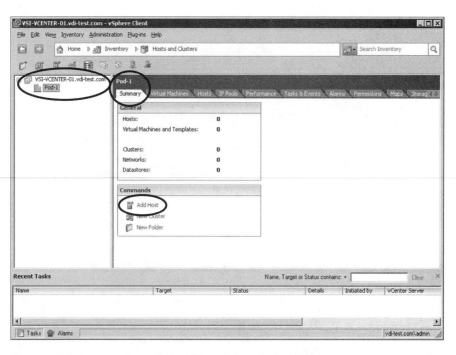

Figure 18-76   *Launching the Add Host Wizard in vCenter*

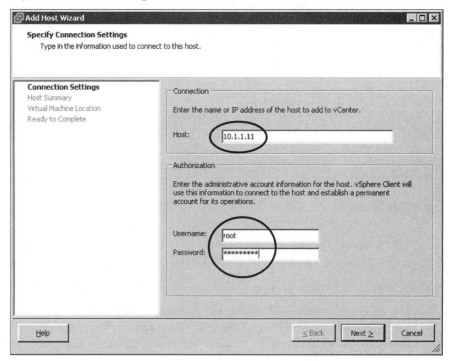

Figure 18-77   *Specify Connection Settings Page of the Add Host Wizard in vCenter*

7. Click **Next.** Accept the security alert, shown in Figure 18-78, by clicking **Yes.**

Figure 18-78   *Security Alert of the Add Host Wizard in vCenter*

8. The Host Summary wizard page appears, as displayed in Figure 18-79.

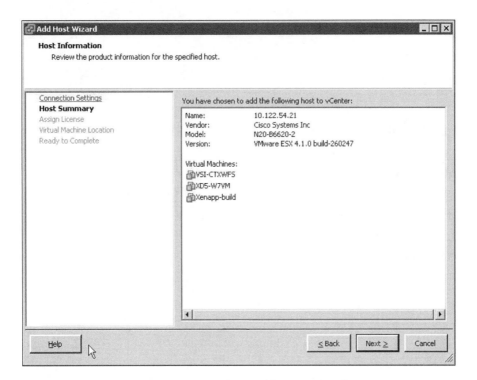

Figure 18-79   *Host Summary Page of the Add Host Wizard in vCenter*

9. Click **Next**. The Assign License wizard page appears, as depicted in Figure 18-80. Leave this blank for the lab (this is where an administrator would normally assign VMware licenses).

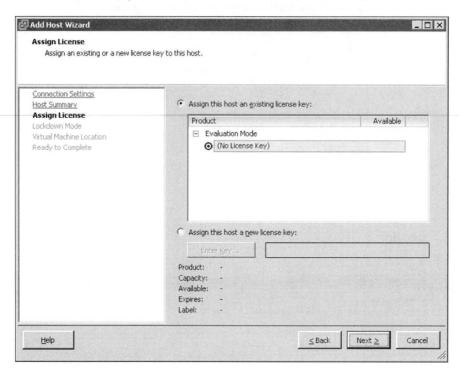

Figure 18-80 *Assign License Page of the Add Host Wizard in vCenter*

10. Click **Next**. The Virtual Machine Location wizard page is displayed, as shown in Figure 18-81. Only one data center is configured. Choose **Pod-1**.

11. Click **Next**. The Ready to Complete wizard page is displayed, as shown in Figure 18-82.

12. Click **Finish**.

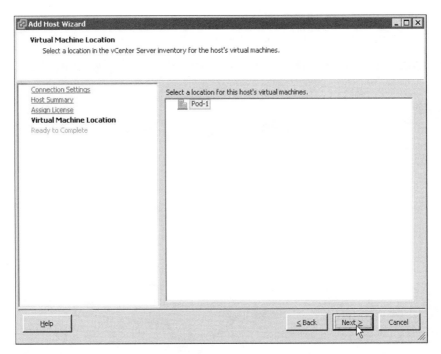

Figure 18-81   *Virtual Machine Location Page of the Add Host Wizard in vCenter*

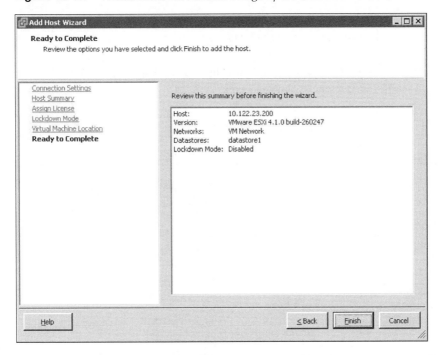

Figure 18-82   *Ready to Complete Page of the Add Host Wizard in vCenter*

13. After a few seconds, the host is added to the data center. Click it and check the **Summary** tab, shown in Figure 18-83, to see more information.

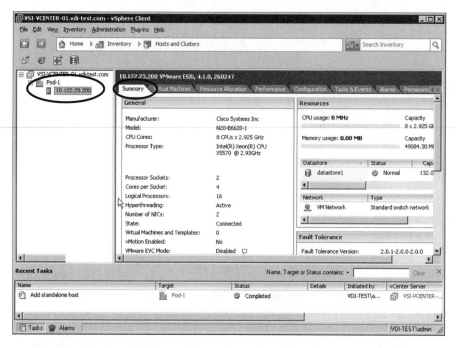

Figure 18-83   *Summary Tab of the VMware vCenter*

14. Repeat Steps 1 through 14 to add the other seven blade servers into the data center. Their IP addresses are as shown in Table 18-2.

Table 18-2   *IP Addressing of Remaining Hosts*

Name	IP Address
Pod-1-SP1-2	10.1.1.12
Pod-1-SP1-3	10.1.1.13
Pod-1-SP1-4	10.1.1.14
Pod-1-SP1-5	10.1.1.15
Pod-1-SP1-6	10.1.1.16
Pod-1-SP1-7	10.1.1.17
Pod-1-SP1-8	10.1.1.18

Lab 9 is complete. Your Data Center is now ready to deploy Virtual Machines.

Index

Numerics

A

B

C

D

E

F

Q-R

S

T

FREE Online Edition

Your purchase of **Enterprise Network Testing** includes access to a free online edition for 45 days through the Safari Books Online subscription service. Nearly every Cisco Press book is available online through Safari Books Online, along with more than 5,000 other technical books and videos from publishers such as Addison-Wesley Professional, Exam Cram, IBM Press, O'Reilly, Prentice Hall, Que, and Sams.

SAFARI BOOKS ONLINE allows you to search for a specific answer, cut and paste code, download chapters, and stay current with emerging technologies.

Activate your FREE Online Edition at www.informit.com/safarifree

> **STEP 1:** Enter the coupon code: BJVPGBI.

> **STEP 2:** New Safari users, complete the brief registration form.
> Safari subscribers, just log in.

If you have difficulty registering on Safari or accessing the online edition, please e-mail customer-service@safaribooksonline.com